RESEARCH HANDBOOK ON EXECUTIVE PAY

RESEARCH HANDBOOKS IN CORPORATE LAW AND GOVERNANCE

Elgar *Research Handbooks* are original reference works designed to provide a broad overview of research in a given field while at the same time creating a forum for more challenging, critical examination of complex and often under-explored issues within that field. Chapters by international teams of contributors are specially commissioned by editors who carefully balance breadth and depth. Often widely cited, individual chapters present expert scholarly analysis and offer a vital reference point for advanced research. Taken as a whole they achieve a wide-ranging picture of the state-of-the-art.

Making a major scholarly contribution to the field of corporate law and governance, the volumes in this series explore topics of current concern from a range of jurisdictions and perspectives, offering a comprehensive analysis that will inform researchers, practitioners and students alike. The *Research Handbooks* cover the fundamental aspects of corporate law, such as insolvency governance structures, as well as hot button areas such as executive compensation, insider trading, and directors' duties. The *Handbooks*, each edited by leading scholars in their respective fields, offer far-reaching examinations of current issues in corporate law and governance that are unrivalled in their blend of critical, substantive analysis, and in their synthesis of contemporary research.

Each *Handbook* stands alone as an invaluable source of reference for all scholars of corporate law, as well as for practicing lawyers who wish to engage with the discussion of ideas within the field. Whether used as an information resource on key topics or as a platform for advanced study, volumes in this series will become definitive scholarly reference works in the field.

Research Handbook on Executive Pay

Edited by

Randall S. Thomas

Vanderbilt Law School, USA

Jennifer G. Hill

Sydney Law School, Australia

RESEARCH HANDBOOKS IN CORPORATE LAW AND GOVERNANCE

Edward Elgar

Cheltenham, UK • Northampton, MA, USA

Published by
Edward Elgar Publishing Limited
The Lypiatts
15 Lansdown Road
Cheltenham
Glos GL50 2JA
UK

Edward Elgar Publishing, Inc.
William Pratt House
9 Dewey Court
Northampton
Massachusetts 01060
USA

A catalogue record for this book
is available from the British Library

Library of Congress Control Number: 2012930576

MIX
Paper from
responsible sources
FSC® C018575

ISBN 978 1 84980 396 0 (cased)

Typeset by Servis Filmsetting Ltd, Stockport, Cheshire
Printed and bound by MPG Books Group, UK

Contents

Contributors

Carlo Amatucci, University of Naples Federico II, Italy

Ruth Bender, Cranfield University School of Management, UK

Sanjai Bhagat, University of Colorado at Boulder, USA

William Bratton, University of Pennsylvania Law School, USA

Salim Chahine, American University in Beirut, Lebanon

Rajesh Chakrabarti, Indian School of Business, India

Martin J. Conyon, The Wharton School of Business, USA, and Lancaster University Management School, UK

Guido Ferrarini, University of Genoa, Italy

Michael Firth, Lingnan University, Hong Kong

Marc Goergen, Cardiff Business School, UK

Brigitte Haar, House of Finance at Goethe-University of Frankfurt, Germany

Lerong He, State University of New York at Brockport, USA

M. Todd Henderson, University of Chicago Law School, USA

Jennifer G. Hill, Sydney Law School, Australia

Katsuyuki Kubo, Waseda University, Japan

Tak Yan Leung, City University of Hong Kong

Glen Loutzenhiser, University of Oxford, UK

Manlio Lubrano di Scorpaniello, University of Sannio, Italy

Joseph A. McCahery, Tilburg University and DSF, Netherlands

Niamh Moloney, London School of Economics and Political Science (LSE), UK

Kevin J. Murphy, University of Southern California, USA

Lars Oxelheim, Lund University and Research Institute of Industrial Economics, Stockholm, Sweden

Luc Renneboog, Tilburg University, Netherlands

Roberta Romano, Yale Law School, USA

Oliver M. Rui, China Europe International Business School (CEIBS), China

Zacharias Sautner, University of Amsterdam and DSF, Netherlands

Kym Sheehan, Sydney Law School, Australia

Krishnamurthy Subramanian, Indian School of Business, India

Randall S. Thomas, Vanderbilt Law School, USA

Steve Thompson, Nottingham University, UK

Grzegorz Trojanowski, University of Exeter, UK

Harwell Wells, Temple University Beasley School of Law, USA

Clas Wihlborg, Chapman University, USA

Jaap Winter, Duisenberg School of Finance (DSF), Netherlands

Pradeep K. Yadav, University of Oklahoma Price College of Business, USA

Yesha Yadav, Vanderbilt Law School, USA

Jianhua Zhang, University of Göthenburg, Sweden

Introduction

Society has a perennial fascination with money. Horace, for example, counselled, "If possible, honestly, if not, somehow, make money."[1] Executive compensation became a key aspect of corporate governance debate during the 1990s, a period when the regulatory pendulum swung away from legislative intervention in favour of self-regulation. Pay for performance offered the prospect of a self-executing governance technique to align the interests of management with those of shareholders. Since that time, however, academic debate in the United States and elsewhere has raged on the question whether executive compensation is determined efficiently by disinterested corporate directors, reflecting the existing corporate governance system (the optimal contracting model) or skewed due to a power imbalance between managers and shareholders (the managerial power model).

Recent corporate scandals and crises, including the global financial crisis, have again brought executive compensation to center stage and onto the regulatory agenda. Indeed, according to the UK Turner Review, the global financial crisis challenged fundamental assumptions about the market's efficiency, rationality and ability to self-regulate, which had previously underpinned financial law.[2] These developments have focused public and academic attention on many facets of executive compensation. In this introduction, we highlight a few of the key debates in the field, and then discuss how the contributors to this Handbook have addressed them.

OPTIMAL CONTRACTING VS. MANAGERIAL POWER

There are two competing schools of thought that dominate academic discussions about US executive compensation practices today: managerial power and optimal contracting theory. Managerial power theorists argue that American CEOs dominate friendly boards of directors comprised of their loyal subordinates and largely passive outsiders. These compliant directors and their well-paid, amenable compensation consultants will, according to this model, make little attempt to negotiate the CEO's pay in a manner that forcefully protects the shareholders' interests. Rather, they will prefer to rely on industry surveys of pay levels which have the (un)intended consequence of continuously ratcheting up executive pay levels.

Optimal contracting theorists respond that executive compensation contracts are designed to maximize shareholder value net of contracting costs and transactions costs. Thus, according to this competing model, executive contracts minimize agency costs and the costs of any residual divergence of interests between a principal and agent. Contracts reflect the underlying US corporate governance system, which although imperfect may in

---

[1]   The Epistles.
[2]   Financial Services Authority (UK), *The Turner Review: A Regulatory Response to the Global Banking Crisis*, 39ff (2009).

fact be extremely good given the existence of information costs, transactions costs, and the existing legal and regulatory system. As will become apparent in reading the chapters of this Handbook, scholars tend to be divided between these two camps.

CONCENTRATED VS. DISPERSED OWNERSHIP

American corporations generally have more dispersed share ownership structures than most other jurisdictions. For US firms, the dispersed ownership structure means that the interests of managers and shareholders can diverge in important ways. Agency costs pose a crucial problem because there is no single shareholder, or group of shareholders, with sufficient equity ownership to monitor managers as closely and effectively as would be possible in many other jurisdictions. US shareholders will therefore seek alignment mechanisms which can ensure that managers behave as if their interests were identical with those of shareholders. Stock option and equity-based compensation is often regarded as fulfilling this function. Unsurprisingly, US CEOs' pay packages on average contain far more equity-based pay than those of the foreign CEOs.

In controlling shareholder-dominated companies, which are the dominant form of organization in most countries outside the US (excepting the UK and perhaps Australia), the owners have the practical ability to dismiss, or otherwise discipline, the managers that run the company on their behalf. Theoretically, at least, there is less need for stock options and other forms of equity-based pay in this scenario because the controlling shareholder can already effectively constrain self-serving managerial conduct, eliminating the agency costs rationale for incentive-based pay. Monitoring, in other words, can function as a substitute for performance-related compensation.

PAY FOR PERFORMANCE: PANACEA OR PROBLEM?

Stock options, and other forms of equity-based compensation, have become an increasingly important part of executive pay packages at companies all over the world. Reward-based and incentive-based rationales exist to explain their use. In the US and UK, this form of remuneration is frequently justified on the grounds that it represents pay for performance, by linking an executive's remuneration to an increase in corporate value. Options are said to stimulate managers to work harder to increase the corporation's value by providing them with a share of any gains that they helped to create. Viewed in this way, options may align the incentives of managers and shareholders to maximize firm value. As noted above, this is particularly important in widely held public companies.

Despite this apparent shift toward greater use of equity-based pay, some disadvantages of this trend have become apparent over time. As the global financial crisis highlighted, stock options have little downside risk. Executives holding large quantities of options potentially have incentives to take significant risks in order to drive up their companies' stock prices, thereby increasing the value of their options. However, executives will also tend to undervalue the downside risks of failure, as appeared to be the case at some financial institutions during the recent crisis.

Options may also create opportunities for corporate executives to exploit their informational advantages over shareholders. Corporate insiders with access to superior information about their companies than outside shareholders will have critical knowledge about the timing of important corporate disclosures or major industry changes. The ability of insiders to exercise options provides them with an excellent and relatively inexpensive means of capitalizing on this informational advantage.

GOVERNMENT INTERVENTIONS: MISGUIDED OR EFFECTIVE?

Its political salience, particularly in the light of populist backlash during the global financial crisis, has increasingly made executive compensation the subject of government regulation. Although these reforms are generally well-intentioned, there is fierce debate as to whether they are beneficial to shareholders and, more generally, society as a whole. Broadly speaking, managerial-power theorists support government regulation to address perceived excesses in this area, though admittedly, the devil is in the design of such regulatory efforts to reduce pay levels and improve pay structure.

Optimal-contracting theorists are less sanguine in this regard. They almost unanimously condemn such government regulation, on the basis that it is costly, ineffective, and cumbersome. These theorists argue that politicians are uniquely unsuited to intervene in labor markets, that courts are less knowledgeable than directors about appropriate pay levels, and that shareholders also lack the requisite information and skills to make these determinations.

AN OVERVIEW OF CHAPTERS IN THIS HANDBOOK

The Handbook addresses these and many other issues concerning executive compensation. It provides a contemporary analysis of executive compensation from a variety of perspectives, and against the backdrop of the global financial crisis. The chapters are written by leading scholars in the field of corporate governance across several continents.

In Part I, consistent with the view that it is impossible to understand the present without an appreciation of the past, the Handbook starts with an examination of the history and theory of executive compensation. Kevin J. Murphy leads off with an in-depth exploration of the history of legislative efforts in the United States to regulate executive pay beginning with the Depression-era regulations and ending with the 2010 Dodd-Frank Act. He documents the assorted ways in which this regulation has been attempted: tax policies, accounting rules, disclosure requirements, and direct limitations, among others. Overall, Murphy concludes that these regulations have frequently been reactions to reported isolated abuses, typically during recessions or economic downturns, and that they have generally been fruitless and ineffectual.

Harwell Wells follows with a historical analysis of executive pay in the United States, using as his starting point the 1930s, when pay issues first attracted national attention. His chapter recounts the rise of executive compensation over the last century, shedding light on the political, social and legal factors that influenced its path. Wells shows that changes in executive compensation are, and continue to be, inextricably tied to the evolution of the US industrial system as a whole.

Next, Steve Thompson looks back on twenty years of UK corporate governance reforms and their effect on executive remuneration in that country. Beginning with the establishment of the landmark Cadbury Committee, he traces the effort to tie executive remuneration practices more closely to shareholder interests and to tighten the connection between executive rewards and corporate performance. He then evaluates the empirical evidence about the efficacy of these efforts on the role of independent directors in setting pay; the sensitivity of pay to performance and company size; executive job tenure; and shareholders' role in the pay setting process, including the use of "say on pay."

Luc Renneboog and Grzegorz Trojanowski pursue a similar line of inquiry in their empirical study assessing whether UK reforms adopted in the 1990s were successful in curbing excessive executive compensation. They assess the effectiveness of these governance changes and find evidence of contractual alignment of manager and shareholder incentives, as well as some indication of potential managerial self-dealing. By analyzing both executive pay and the potential for termination of managers simultaneously, Renneboog and Trojanowski's work sheds light on the interaction of these two important aspects of the managerial labor market.

Bill Bratton looks at contemporary executive compensation practices through the prism of agency theory. He asks whether these practices support the view that unaccountable managers are grossly overpaid, or, rather, if they legitimately enhance and reward wealth creation on behalf of shareholders. Noting that executive pay is a highly politicized subject, he explores the differences between the "hierarchies" perspective of agency cost analysis, embedded in the managerial power critique of current pay practices, versus the "markets" strand of agency theory, which supports the optimal-contracting model of pay-setting practices. Bratton concludes that the various positions of participants in the classic executive compensation debate are best explained by adherence to particular strands of agency theory.

In Part II, we turn to the structure of executive pay, with particular emphasis on the relationship between pay and performance and potential flaws in executive compensation design. The global financial crisis highlighted the vital role of executive pay practices at financial institutions. The next two chapters, one by Guido Ferrarini, and the second by Sanjai Bhagat and Roberta Romano, distil some of the lessons of that experience by investigating executive compensation practices of banks and other financial institutions. Ferrarini questions the widespread assumption that, in the lead up to the financial crisis, the structure of executives' compensation at banks was predominantly short-term. Instead, he argues that existing empirical evidence is consistent with the view that bankers' pay was largely aligned with shareholders' long-term incentives. Ferrarini further claims that banking regulators should not, as a matter of policy, set executive pay, but rather assume a much more limited role in this area.

Bhagat and Romano recognize that the political fallout from the financial crisis has made regulatory reform to some extent inevitable. They offer a reform proposal (for financial institutions that receive government funding, or potentially pose a systemic risk to financial markets) which is, however, considerably less radical than those advanced by some other commentators. Bhagat and Romano seek to promote long-term shareholder value and reduce excessive risk by requiring that incentive compensation at these institutions should comprise only restricted stock or stock options, with a holding period of two to four years after the recipient leaves office. They defend the superiority of their proposal on the basis that it is straightforward, transparent and leads to the creation of long-term value for shareholders.

Lars Oxelheim, Clas Wihlborg and Jianhua Zhang highlight the difficulties of structuring executive pay to reflect skill and effort, as opposed to good (or bad) luck. In particular, they focus on controlling for macroeconomic fluctuations that affect firms and estimate these effects for Swedish companies during the period from 2001 to 2007. They find that macroeconomic conditions had a strong positive effect on executive pay at their sample companies.

Although most literature in the field relates to compensation packages at mature firms, Salim Chahine and Marc Goergen scrutinize CEO stock options at IPO (initial public offering) firms. They argue that two competing forces are at work with stock option awards in the IPO setting: options provide CEOs of IPO firms with incentives to take additional risks that may improve corporate performance, but they may also give the same executives a means of expropriating wealth from other pre-IPO shareholders. Chahine and Goergen conclude that the role played by stock options at IPO firms depends on the effectiveness of other monitoring mechanisms in place at firms.

In his contribution, Jaap Winter engages in a fundamental reassessment of the basic behavioural assumptions of modern performance-based pay. In a searching critique building upon current research in the field of cognitive science, he questions whether performance-based pay can ever be effective. Winter concludes that performance-based pay cannot work because people do not behave in the way that its proponents assume, and that it should accordingly be abandoned.

In Part III, the Handbook shifts its attention to the relationship between corporate governance structures, regulatory interventions and managerial compensation. Jennifer Hill explores the impact of recent financial shocks, such as the global financial crisis, on the regulation of executive pay across three common law jurisdictions – the United States, the United Kingdom and Australia. She asks whether executive pay is excessive in America, whether it contributed to the recent financial crisis, and whether subsequent regulatory developments will affect pay in the future. Hill concludes that it is too soon to tell if regulatory responses will result in long term shifts in pay practices.

Noting the growing role of institutional investors in corporate governance, Joseph McCahery and Zacharias Sautner evaluate institutional investor preferences regarding levels and structure of executive pay in the United States and the Netherlands. They discover that a majority of these investors prefer reductions in the level of severance payments for departing CEOs in both countries. By contrast, McCahery and Sautner determine that a majority of institutions do not support reductions in overall CEO pay levels in the Netherlands, although they do in America.

Shareholder advisory votes on executive compensation packages, so-called "say on pay" votes, are another relatively recent change in corporate governance practices. Kym Sheehan undertakes a qualitative analysis of changes in compensation practice and the impact of say on pay during its first three years of operation in the United Kingdom and Australia. She conducts an empirical study of say on pay's operation in those two countries and finds that the vote has had more of an effect on *ad hoc* payments to executives than on overall remuneration practices. Sheehan concludes that governments seeking to lower overall pay levels by granting this power to shareholders are likely to be disappointed.

Glen Loutzenhiser reflects on the extent to which tax law can be used as a "tool of social policy" by governments seeking to control the level and structure of executive pay. He argues that traditional principles of tax policy point toward treating all forms of executive compensation in the same manner, although implementation of such a strategy will be difficult. Loutzenhiser then examines recent tax measures enacted in the United States and United Kingdom and concludes that they were not consistent with good tax policy.

Some commentators have advocated tougher government regulation of insider trading and market manipulation to control a potential dark side of performance-based compensation. M. Todd Henderson's chapter examines the implications for insider trading policy of the major shift in the last thirty years from cash to equity-based compensation, the growth in trading by insiders, and the regulatory impact of Rule 10b5-1 of the Securities Exchange Act 1934 from this perspective. He claims that government efforts to regulate insider trading have failed. Instead, Henderson supports a laissez-faire approach to the perceived problem, arguing that significant benefits will flow from allowing insiders to trade.

Compensation consultants have become an increasingly important aspect of the executive compensation regulatory landscape in recent years. Ruth Bender's chapter investigates the various reasons why corporations use consultants, including the need for legitimation, and surveys the executive compensation consulting industry, which is dominated by a small number of large firms. She considers the forces that affect the consulting industry and their effect on its customers. Bender finishes with a review of research on the impact of consultants on executive compensation levels and structure, concluding that companies using consultants pay more and grant more stock options than companies which do not, although the reasons for these differences are unclear.

Finally, Part IV of this Handbook critically examines the executive pay systems of a number of other international jurisdictions. Even if one accepts that either the optimal-contracting, or the managerial-power model of executive compensation, has greater explanatory power in the United States, this will not necessarily be the case in other countries. Other jurisdictions can therefore reveal fascinating similarities and differences in the executive pay arena.

Focusing first on Australia, Randall Thomas's chapter provides an overview of the evolving regulatory environment for executive compensation there. Using data based on interviews with Australian remuneration consultants, directors and other corporate governance participants, he reveals interesting differences in the regulatory system for pay, and the role played by compensation consultants, in Australia and the United States. Thomas maintains that Australia's experience with regulatory reform should be carefully examined by other countries if they are considering implementing more regulation.

Turning next to Asia, Katsuyuki Kubo focuses on three topics: recent changes in the pay setting process at Japanese corporations, including the new disclosure rules; empirical evidence on presidents' salaries in Japanese corporations; and changes in the pay for performance sensitivities in Japanese executive pay. He finds that the new disclosure rules do not apply to most Japanese presidents because their pay levels are below the disclosure threshold. Kubo also demonstrates that there have been rapid increases in presidents' salaries since 2000 and that executive compensation has become more sensitive to performance in Japan over that same time period, although it is still far lower than in the United States.

The two following chapters take a close look at executive compensation in China, addressing the traditional dearth of empirical data in this regard. Michael Firth, Tak-Yan Leung and Oliver Rui describe senior executive pay in "the world's largest transitional economy," beginning with a review of Chinese economic reforms and performance. They then provide empirical evidence on pay levels, the effect of corporate governance on pay, and several other determinants of executive compensation. They observe that pay levels have increased rapidly in recent years, that the determinants are similar to those in the United States, and, finally, that there are also signs of an emerging labor market for executives in China.

Martin Conyon and Lerong He examine the influence of the Chinese state control ownership on patterns of executive compensation, the level of correlation between pay and performance in state controlled firms, and the impact of firm size on pay. They discover that stock options and equity-based pay are new developments in China, but that pay is positively correlated with performance. Firm size, they determine, is a driver of pay levels, in much the same way as in the western countries. Conyon and Lerong also show that state control has a negative effect on the pay for performance nexus at controlled firms.

In relation to India, another booming Asian economy, Rajesh Chakrabarti, Krishnamurthy Subramanian, Pradeep Yadav, and Yesha Yadav discuss recent executive salary trends in Indian listed companies. Their analysis highlights the effects that the presence of a private control shareholder may have on executive pay, a fact that distinguishes the Indian corporate governance scene from that in China (state control ownership) or the United States (dispersed ownership). They conclude that executive pay levels are much higher at larger firms and include a higher proportion of variable pay, but that overall pay levels have increased rapidly at all size levels. The presence of a private control shareholder is also correlated with higher pay levels.

Three chapters focus on executive pay in the European context. Niamh Moloney leads off with a regional approach, assessing the European Union's (EU) experience with executive pay and the efficacy of EU regulation in this regard. The EU, she claims, provides an interesting model because it contains both dispersed and concentrated ownership systems, and has had substantial experience with harmonization of executive pay regulations. Moloney concludes that the EU experience provides a dramatic illustration of the impact of different governance structures on executive pay, and the pitfalls of importing a system designed for dispersed-ownership countries into jurisdictions with concentrated ownership.

Brigitte Haar provides an overview of executive pay practices in Germany in the aftermath of the high profile *Mannesmann* case. She gives an in-depth summary of the existing empirical evidence on managerial compensation, the German corporate governance system, and its legal rules governing executive pay. Haar carefully explains how *Mannesmann* has led to significant changes in executive pay rules and practices in Germany.

In the final chapter, Carlo Amatucci and Manlio Lubrano di Scorpaniello discuss the complex web of regulation governing executive compensation in Italian public listed and unlisted corporations. Their comprehensive treatment of Italian law covers a wide variety of topics, including the effects of concentrated ownership on pay, the key regulatory principles established by the Italian market regulator, Consob, and the operation of the Italian Stock Exchange's corporate governance code.

We would like to thank all the authors for their fine contributions to this Handbook. Thanks also go to Alice Grey, Leonor Jardim, and especially Oliver Peglow, for their editorial assistance.

Jennifer Hill and Randall Thomas
August 2011

PART I

HISTORY AND THEORY

1 The politics of pay: a legislative history of executive compensation[1]

Kevin J. Murphy

1 INTRODUCTION

After a rare decline during the 2008–2009 Great Recession, CEO pay increased sharply in 2010. The median total realized compensation (including gains from exercising stock options) for chief executives in S&P (Standard and Poor's) 500 firms rose 35 percent from 2009 levels, the largest year-over-year change in realized pay in at least four decades. This dramatic increase in realized pay is likely a harbinger of even greater increases to come, given massive unrealized gains in unvested stock and non-exercisable options that were granted mid-recession at or near the bottom of the stock market. The revelations of these pay levels – coupled with relatively high rates of unemployment – has fueled calls for regulating executive compensation even beyond the reforms imposed by the 2010 Dodd-Frank Act.

Any debate over whether executive pay should be regulated must begin by recognizing that CEO pay is *already* heavily regulated, through tax policies, accounting rules, disclosure requirements, direct legislation, and myriad other rules stretching back nearly a century. In this chapter, I will explore the legislative history of executive compensation, starting with Depression-era regulations leading to the 1934 creation of the Securities and Exchange Commission (SEC), and ending with the ongoing implementation of the Dodd-Frank Act. I show that many common features and trends can be traced directly to government attempts to regulate both the level and structure of compensation for US executives.

While the specific regulations have varied widely over time, I show that they share several common themes. First, the regulations have often been imposed as reactions to relatively isolated perceived abuses in executive pay. Second, the controversies triggering these reactions have typically occurred in economic recessions or downturns that followed years of relative prosperity associated with large increases in executive compensation (and increases in US income inequality more generally). Third, with few exceptions, the regulations have generally been either ineffective or counterproductive, typically increasing (rather than reducing) CEO pay and leading to a host of unintended consequences.

The emerging conclusion is that attempts to regulate CEO pay have been mostly unblemished by success. Part of the problem is that regulation – even when well intended – inherently focuses on relatively narrow aspects of compensation, allowing plenty of scope for costly circumvention. An apt analogy is the Dutch boy using his fingers to plug

---

[1] This chapter draws from a variety of related papers, especially Jensen, Murphy and Wruck (2012) and Murphy (2012).

holes in a dike, only to see new leaks emerge. The only certainty with pay regulation is that new leaks will emerge in unsuspected places, and that the consequences will be both unintended and costly.

A larger part of the problem is that the regulation is often mis-intended. The regulations are inherently political and driven by political agendas, and politicians seldom embrace "creating shareholder value" as their governing objective. While the pay controversies fueling calls for regulation have touched on legitimate issues concerning executive compensation, the most vocal critics of CEO pay (such as members of labor unions, disgruntled workers and politicians) have been uninvited guests to the table who have had no real stake in the companies being managed and no real interest in creating wealth for company shareholders. Indeed, a substantial force motivating such uninvited critics is one of the least attractive aspects of human beings: jealousy and envy. Although these aspects are seldom part of the explicit discussion and debate surrounding pay, they are important and impact how and why governments intervene into pay decisions.

2   DISCLOSURE REQUIREMENTS

2.1   The New Deal and Pay Disclosures

We have become accustomed to the idea that shareholders – and the public in general – have a right to know the details of the compensation paid to top executives in publicly traded corporations. However, the push for pay disclosure was not driven by shareholders but rather by "New Deal" politicians outraged by perceived excesses in executive compensation.

In 1933 Franklin D. Roosevelt became president, ushering in the New Deal in a country recovering from the Great Depression. In the April prior to the 1932 election – in the face of proposed bailout loans from the government's Reconstruction Finance Corporation (RFC) – the Interstate Commerce Commission demanded that all railroads disclose executives making more than $10,000 per year.[2] The disclosed pay levels outraged the new Administration, and in May 1933 the RFC required railroad companies receiving government assistance to reduce executive pay by up to 60 percent.[3] Ultimately, the US Senate authorized the Federal Coordinator of Transportation to impose an informal (but uniformly complied with) cap of $60,000 per year for all railroad presidents.

The mandated pay disclosures for railroad executives sparked the interest of other US regulators. By mid-1933 the Federal Reserve began investigating executive pay in its member banks, the RFC conducted a similar investigation for non-member banks, and the Power Commission investigated pay practices at public utilities. In October 1933, the

---

[2]   "Railroad Salary Report: I.C.C. Asks Class 1 Roads About Jobs Paying More Than $10,000 a Year," *Wall Street Journal* (1932).

[3]   The required reductions ranged from 15 percent (for executives earning less than $15,000) to 60 percent (for executives earning more than $100,000). See "RFC Fixed Pay Limits: Cuts Required to Obtain Loans," *Los Angeles Times* (1933); "Cut High Salaries or Get No Loans, is RFC Warning," *New York Times* (1933).

Federal Trade Commission (FTC) requested disclosure of salaries and bonuses paid by all corporations with capital and assets over \$1 million (approximately 2,000 corporations).[4] Business leaders questioned whether the FTC had the legal authority to compel such disclosures, but were reminded that, "Congress in its present temper would readily authorize" whatever the FTC wanted.[5] Executives were particularly incensed that the FTC would demand such closely guarded information without any explanation of how the information would be used and without any confidentiality guarantees.

Following the Securities Act of 1934, the responsibility for enforcing pay disclosures for top executives in publicly traded corporations was consolidated into the newly created Securities and Exchange Commission (SEC). In December 1934, the SEC issued permanent rules demanding that companies disclose the name and all compensation (including salaries, bonuses, stock, and stock options) received by the three highest-paid executives. The securities of companies not complying with the new regulations by June 1935 would be removed from exchanges. Several companies, including United States Steel Corporation, pleaded unsuccessfully for the SEC to keep the data confidential, arguing that publication "would be conducive to disturbing the morale of the organization and detrimental to the best interests of the registrant and its stockholders."[6]

Under the Securities Act, details on executive pay are publicly disclosed in company 10-K or proxy statement issued in connection with the company's annual shareholders' meeting. Ultimately, these disclosures have provided the fodder for all subsequent pay controversies. Proxy statements for companies with December fiscal closings are typically issued in late March or early April, triggering a deluge of pay-related articles in the popular and business press each spring. This annual rite began in 1935, when the media pounced on the SEC's first pay disclosures. *Forbes* and *Business Week* began offering extensive lists of the highest-paid executives in 1970. *Fortune* and the *Wall Street Journal* quickly followed suit, and by now most major newspapers conduct their own CEO pay surveys for companies based in their local metropolitan areas.

While the SEC has no direct power to regulate the level and structure of CEO pay, the agency *does* determine what elements of pay are disclosed and how they are disclosed. The SEC has routinely expanded disclosure requirements from year to year, with major overhauls in 1978, 1993, 2006, and 2011. Under the theory that sunlight is the best disinfectant, the SEC's disclosure rules have long been a favorite method used by the SEC and Congress in attempts to curb perceived excesses in executive compensation. Indeed, most additions to disclosure requirements over time reflect policy responses to perceived abuses.

---

[4]   See Robbins, "Inquiry into High Salaries Pressed by the Government," *New York Times* (1933) and "President Studies High Salary Curb: Tax Power is Urged as Means of Controlling Stipends in Big Industries," *New York Times* (1933). In addition to investigating corporate executive pay, President Roosevelt personally called attention to lavish rewards in Hollywood, resulting in a provision added to the moving-picture code that imposed heavy fines on companies paying unreasonable salaries.

[5]   "Federal Bureau Asks Salaries of Big Companies' Executives," *Chicago Daily Tribune* (1933).

[6]   "U.S. Steel Guards Data on Salaries: Sends Details Confidentially to SEC Head with Request that they be Kept Secret," *New York Times* (1935).

2.2   Perquisites and the 1978 Disclosure Rules

During the stagnant stock market of the 1970s, the void in compensation created by worthless stock options was quickly filled by a plethora of new plans designed to provide more predictable payouts.[7] In addition, companies began relying to a greater extent on shareholder-subsidized perquisites or perks such as low-interest loans, yachts, limousines, corporate jets, club memberships, hunting lodges and corporate retreats at exotic locations. By the late 1970s, perceived abuses in perquisites attracted the ire of Congress and President Carter, who famously rallied against companies taking deductions for the "three-martini lunch" and other perks.[8] The SEC responded by issuing a series of rulings clarifying which perquisites should be included as compensation in corporate proxy statements. In 1978 – representing the first major overhaul of pay disclosures since 1934 – the SEC required tabular pay disclosures including a column devoted to the value of perquisites and insurance payments. In addition, individual pay disclosure was expanded from the three highest-paid executives to the five highest-paid (the SEC backed down on their initial proposal to require disclosures for the top 10 corporate officers).

2.3   Stock Options and the 1992 Disclosure Rules

Stock options had become increasingly popular by the late 1980s, and many options were issued or repriced following the October 1987 market crash (Hall and Liebman (1998); Saly (1994)). The early 1990s created a perfect storm for controversies over CEO pay: companies were laying off workers and unemployment was high, but the US stock market was robust as the US emerged from the 1990–1991 recession, leading to large gains to executives exercising options and increasing pay disparities between top executives and rank-and-file workers.

In response to growing outrage, legislation was introduced in the House of Representatives disallowing deductions for compensation exceeding 25 times the amount paid to the lowest-paid worker, and the Corporate Pay Responsibility Act was introduced in the Senate to force disclosure of total compensation (rather than descriptions of the various components) and to give shareholders more rights to propose compensation-related policies. The SEC preempted the pending Senate bill in February 1992 by requiring companies to include non-binding shareholder resolutions about CEO pay in company proxy statements,[9] and in October 1992 announced sweeping new pay disclosure rules. The new rules required a Summary Compensation Table summarizing the major components of compensation received by the CEO and other highly paid execu-

---

[7]   Ricklefs, "Sweetening the Pot: Stock Options Allure Fades, So Firms Seek Different Incentives," *Wall Street Journal* (1975); Hyatt, "No Strings: Firms Lure Executives By Promising Bonuses Not Linked To Profits," *Wall Street Journal* (1975); Ricklefs, "Firms Offer Packages of Long-Term Incentives as Stock Options Go Sour for Some Executives," *Wall Street Journal* (1977).

[8]   Rankin, "Incentives for Business Spending Proposed in Corporate Package," *New York Times* (1978); "Excerpts From Carter Message to Congress on Proposals to Change Tax System," *New York Times* (1978).

[9]   "Shareholder Groups Cheer SEC's Moves on Disclosure of Executive Compensation," *Wall Street Journal* (1992).

tives over the past three years, and additional tables describing option grants, option holdings, and option exercises in much greater detail than under previous rules.

The most widely debated issue surrounding the SEC's new disclosure rules was how stock options would be valued in the Summary Compensation Table. Congress and the SEC had wanted a total dollar value of option grants so that the components could be added together to yield a value for total compensation, and lobbied for calculating option values using a Black–Scholes (1973) or related approach. The SEC's proposal was vehemently opposed by high option-granting firms (especially from the Silicon Valley and Boston's 128 corridor) and by compensation consulting and accounting firms. Ultimately, a compromise was struck: the Summary Compensation Table would include the *number*, but not the value, of options granted, thus defeating the SEC's objective of reporting a single number for total compensation.[10] In Section 6.1, I will argue that this compromise helped facilitate the explosion in stock option grants between 1993 and 2000.

2.4   Accounting Scandals and the 2006 Disclosure Rules

The disclosure of executive compensation was expanded significantly in 2006 in response to a variety of scandals involving accounting fraud, backdating options, severance pay, and pensions. For example:

- In September 2004, General Electric settled charges with the SEC after divorce papers revealed that General Electric's former CEO Jack Welch had received perquisites and benefits (including a luxury Manhattan apartment, a chauffeured limousine and access to GE aircraft) far in excess of those disclosed to GE's shareholders (or perhaps GE's board).[11] In April 2005, the SEC charged that Tyson Foods failed to disclose over $1 million in perquisites to its CEO, and also sued Tyco's CEO L. Dennis Kozlowski over excessive perquisites (including a $6,000 shower curtain).[12] In response to these and other high-profile cases, the SEC significantly expanded perquisite disclosure by lowering the threshold triggering disclosure from $50,000 to $10,000 and demanding a new table to identify and quantify any perquisite exceeding $10,000.
- In September 2003, Richard Grasso was forced to resign as CEO of the New York Stock Exchange after revelations that he was to receive total pension benefits of nearly $140 million. The outrage over Grasso's pension benefits (based on formulas approved by the NYSE board years earlier) led the SEC to require companies to

---

[10]   In addition, companies would have a choice in the Option Grant Table to report either the Black–Scholes grant-date value or the *potential* value of options granted (under the assumption that stock prices grow at 5 percent or 10 percent annually during the term of the option. Based on a sample of approximately 600 large companies granting options to their CEOs during fiscal 1992, Murphy (1996) shows that about one-third of the companies reported grant-date values, while the remaining two-thirds reported potential values. Companies with higher dividend yields and lower volatilities (both factors that decrease Black–Scholes values) were significantly more likely to report Black–Scholes rather than potential values.

[11]   Kranhold, "GE Settles Charges Over Failure To Spell Out Pact With Ex-CEO," *Wall Street Journal* (2004).

[12]   Solomon, "In SEC Complaint, Tale of Chicken Mogul Feathering His Nest – Don Tyson Took In Millions In Poorly Disclosed Perks; $84,000 in Lawn Care," *Wall Street Journal* (2005).

disclose the actuarial value of pension benefits (and year-to-year changes in that value) for all proxy-named executives.

- In 2005 and early 2006, several high-profile but poorly performing CEOs were ousted from their firms, but only after receiving large severance and retirement packages from their former employers. The media was particularly harsh on Pfizer's Henry McKinnell (who left in July 2006 with a $190 million exit package), Sovereign Bank's Jay Sidhu (October 2006, $44 million), Viacom's Tom Freston (September 2005, $85 million), and Hewlett-Packard's Carly Fiorina (February 2005, $21 million). In most cases, the exit packages included vested pension benefits as well as contractual obligations associated with "terminations without cause." As a response to the seemingly excessive payments, the SEC demanded that companies disclose tabularly all contractual severance payments in the event of terminations (including for-cause, without cause, resignations, or change in control).
- In 2005, academic research by University of Iowa professor Erik Lie and subsequent investigations by the *Wall Street Journal* unearthed a practice that became known as option backdating.[13] Under this practice, companies deliberately falsified stock option agreements so that options granted on one date were reported as if granted on an earlier date when the stock price was unusually low – commonly the lowest price in the quarter or in the year. Thus, options that were reported as granted at the money (that is, with an exercise price equal to the market price on the reported grant date) were in reality granted in the money (that is, with an exercise price well below the market price on the actual grant date). As a response to these scandals – which violated existing accounting, tax, and disclosure policies – the SEC required disclosure of not only option grant dates but also the date when the grant was formally approved by the board.
- By 2006, compensation consultants increasingly came under attack as being complicit in perceived excesses in compensation, culminating in Congressional hearings in 2007. As part of the 2006 disclosure rules, the SEC required companies to identify and describe the role of all consultants who provided advice on executive compensation, and to disclose whether the consultants were engaged directly by the compensation committee rather than by management. In December 2009, the SEC expanded its disclosure rules by requiring firms that purchase more than $120,000 in other services from their executive-pay consultants to disclose fees paid for both compensation consulting and other services. Under the new regulations, firms could avoid such disclosures if the board retained its own compensation consultant and if that consultant provided no other services (see Murphy and Sandino (2010)).

The 2006 rules included a plethora of additional disclosures, resulting in a significant increase in the size of the typical proxy statement. Indeed, the first proxy statements

---

[13]   Key references include Lie (2005), Heron and Lie (2006b), Heron and Lie (2006a), Maremont, "Authorities Probe Improper Backdating of Options: Practice Allows Executives to Bolster their Stock Gains; a Highly Beneficial Pattern," *Wall Street Journal* (2005), Forelle and Bandler, "Backdating Probe Widens as Two Quit Silicon Valley Firm; Power Integrations Officials Leave Amid Options Scandal; 10 Companies Involved So Far," *Wall Street Journal* (2006), Forelle, "How Journal Found Options Pattern," *Wall Street Journal* (2006).

issued in the 1930s after the formation of the SEC were typically about three to five pages long, with less than one page devoted to executive compensation. In 2006 – before the 2006 disclosure rules – the average length for the 100 largest firms (ranked by revenues) had grown to 45 pages. One year later – after the new rules – the average length exceeded 70 pages, nearly all focused on compensation.

2.5   Dodd-Frank and the 2011 Disclosure Rules

In July 2010, President Obama signed into law the Dodd-Frank Wall Street Reform and Consumer Protection Act or Dodd-Frank Act, which was the culmination of the President's and Congress's controversial and wide-ranging efforts to regulate the financial services industry. While ostensibly focused on regulating Wall Street, the authors of the Dodd-Frank Act seized the opportunity to pass a sweeping reform of executive compensation and corporate governance imposed on all large publicly traded US firms across all industries.

Among other reforms, the Act instructed the SEC to promulgate a large number of new disclosure rules. For example, under the Act companies must disclose:

- the independence of compensation consultants, attorneys, accountants, and other advisors to the compensation committees;
- the relation between realized compensation and the firm's financial performance, including stock-price performance;
- company policies regarding hedging by employees to protect against reductions in company stock prices;
- company policies and practices on why the company chooses either to separate the Chairman and CEO positions, or combine both roles;
- the ratio of CEO compensation to the median pay for all other company employees.

Perhaps the most mischievous new disclosure rule is the ratio of CEO pay to the median pay of all employees. The calculation costs alone can be immense for large multinational or multi-segment corporations where payroll is decentralized: to compute the median the company needs an often non-existent single compensation database with all employees worldwide. More importantly, however, is what shareholders are supposed to do with this new information, or how they should determine whether a ratio is too high or too low. Ultimately, the provision reflects a belief in Congress that CEO pay is excessive and that disclosing the ratio will shame boards into lowering CEO pay.

Final SEC rules on the disclosure provisions are not expected until late 2011 or 2012. Therefore, the final rules on most provisions are not yet known, and it will be a few years before the consequences of the Dodd-Frank Act are fully analyzed.

2.6   Executive Pay Disclosure: Is It Worth It?

For nearly sixty years following the 1934 Securities Act, detailed disclosure of executive compensation was a uniquely American experience. Canada adopted US-style disclosure rules in 1993, followed by the United Kingdom in 1997, Ireland and South Africa in 2000 and Australia in 2004. In May 2003, the European Union (EU) Commission issued an "Action Plan" recommending that all listed companies in the EU report details on individual compensation packages by 2006; most EU countries have passed rules requiring such disclosure by 2011.

Disclosure policy has evolved over time in response to perceived excesses in compensation. However, there is little evidence that enhanced disclosure has led to reductions in objectionable practices: for example, perquisites increased after 1978 as executives learned what was common at other firms, options exploded following the 1993 rules, and executive compensation in Canada increased significantly after disclosure was introduced. Similarly, the use of compensation consultants increased following the 2006 disclosure rules, as boards hired their own "independent" consultants to supplement those hired by management.

The demand for disclosure reflects both legitimate shareholder concerns and public curiosity. It is generally accepted that shareholders – and the public, for that matter – have a right to know how much the CEO and other top officers are paid, and that more disclosure is always preferred to less. Although shareholders do not presume similar rights to know what the company pays other factors of production, the determination of top-management pay seems different because of the perception that CEOs set their own pay levels by pushing generous pay packages past acquiescent corporate boards. Thus, the logic of disclosure – from the standpoint of legitimate shareholder concerns – is not so shareholders can decide whether particular executives are overpaid or underpaid, but rather to give shareholders information relevant in monitoring the performance of the potentially acquiescent board of directors.

Although disclosure facilitates better monitoring of outside directors, the public curiosity aspect of disclosure imposes large costs on organizations. The recurring populist revolts against CEO pay, for example, could not have been waged without public pay disclosure. Public disclosure effectively ensures that executive contracts in publicly held corporations are not a private matter between employers and employees but are rather influenced by the media, labor unions, and by political forces operating inside and outside companies. Compensation committees – elected by but not perfect agents for shareholders – will naturally respond to these political pressures through less-efficient but politically more acceptable pay packages. These important but often ignored costs of disclosure must be weighed against the benefits (better monitoring of directors) in determining the optimal amount of pay disclosure for top managers.

3   TAX POLICIES

3.1   The Rise (and Fall) of Restricted Stock Options

Since the creation of the US income tax, Congress has used the tax code to influence the level and structure of executive compensation. In the 1920s, the income tax was new, the use of stock options was new, and no one had figured out how options would be taxed: (1) as compensation when options are exercised (and hence taxed as ordinary income for the individual, and representing a deductible business expense for the company); or (2) as capital gains when the stock purchased upon exercise was ultimately sold (and hence taxed at a lower capital gains rate for the individual, with the company forgoing deductibility). After a series of court cases starting in 1928, the Supreme Court ultimately ruled in 1946 that the gain upon exercise is compensation, thereby taxable as ordinary income. To circumvent the unpopular Court ruling, a business-friendly Congress created a new type of stock options called "restricted stock options" that would be taxable not upon exercise but only when the shares were ultimately sold (and then taxed as capital gains). At the time, the highest marginal tax rate on ordinary income had swelled to 91 percent compared to a capital gains rate of 25 percent, making restricted stock options extremely advantageous from a tax standpoint.[14]

The use of restricted stock options exploded following the Revenue Act of 1950, and options became a material part of compensation for senior executives (Lewellen (1968); Frydman and Saks (2008)). When many of the options granted in the early 1950s fell underwater in the 1953 post-Korean War recession, Congress made two additional changes to restricted stock options as part of the Revenue Act of 1954. First, Congress officially sanctioned option repricing, allowing the exercise price of a previously granted option to be lowered if it turned out that the market price of the optioned stock declined subsequent to the granting of the option. Second, the 1954 Act limited exercise terms to 10 years (which continues to be the most common term for options granted through current times).

The increasingly popular practice of repricing options became highly controversial in the early years of the Kennedy Administration, leading to a series of Congressional hearings aimed at repealing the favorable tax treatment for restricted stock options.[15] In 1961, the President demanded that Congress repeal the tax treatment, instead taxing options as ordinary income upon exercise (most of which would be subject to the 91 percent top marginal tax rate). The issue was debated in Congress for the next two years, and the controversy intensified in late 1963 and early 1964 when it was revealed that executives at Chrysler had realized $4.2 million in gains from exercising stock options in 1963, and had sold nearly 200,000 shares acquired through earlier exercises.[16] Ultimately, as part of the Revenue Act of 1964, Congress stopped short of removing the favorable tax status of restricted stock options, but took several steps that substantially reduced their attractiveness. In particular, under the new law:

---

[14] For example, at a 91 percent tax rate on ordinary income and 50.75 percent corporate tax rate, it cost shareholders $5.47 in after-tax profit to give the executive $1 in after-tax income. In contrast (and for simplicity ignoring the timing issues), when the pay is taxed at the 25 percent capital gain rate rather than ordinary income, it cost shareholders only $1.33 to convey $1 in after-tax income to the executive (even though shareholders forfeit the deduction).

[15] "Options on the Wane: Fewer Firms Plan Sale of Stock to Executives at Fixed Exercise Prices," *Wall Street Journal* (1960); "Congress and Taxes: Specialists Mull Ways to Close 'Loopholes' in Present Tax Laws," *Wall Street Journal* (1959); "House Group Hears Conflicting Views on Stock Option Taxes," *Wall Street Journal* (1959).

[16] "Chrysler Chairman Defends Option Plan, Offers to Discuss It With Federal Officials," *Wall Street Journal* (1963); "Chrysler Officers Got Profit of $4.2 Million On Option Stock in '63," *Wall Street Journal* (1964); "Chrysler Officers' Sale of Option Stock Could Stir Tax Bill Debate," *Wall Street Journal* (1963); "House Unit Seen Favoring Curbs on Stock Options," *Wall Street Journal* (1963); "Senate Unit Votes to Tighten Rules on Stock Options" (1964).

- Executives were required to hold stock acquired through option exercises for three years (rather than six months) in order to be taxed at the lower capital gains rate.
- Exercise prices were to be set at no less than 100 percent of the grant-date market prices.
- The maximum option term was reduced from ten years to five years.
- The option price could not be reduced during the term of the option, nor could an option be exercised while there was an outstanding option issued to the executive at an earlier time. (This provision was designed to halt the practice of repricing options or canceling out-of-the-money options and replacing them with options with lower exercise prices.)

To distinguish options meeting these new requirements from restricted options granted under the Revenue Act of 1950 provisions, the 1964 Act referred to new grants as "qualified stock options" rather than restricted stock options.

Finally (but perhaps most importantly), the 1964 law reduced the top marginal tax rate on ordinary income from 91 percent to 70 percent, which significantly reduced the attractiveness of restricted options over cash compensation. The popularity of qualified stock options fell as a result of the 1964 tax law[17] and collapsed following the Tax Reform Act of 1969, which gradually reduced the top marginal tax rate on earned income from 77 percent in 1969 to 50 percent by 1972, reduced the corporate tax rate from 52.8 percent to 48 percent, and raised the top capital gains tax rate from 25 percent in 1969 to 36.5 percent. Once the new rates were fully implemented, qualified stock options became tax disadvantageous compared to non-qualified stock options for executives and companies in the highest tax brackets, and have remained so throughout the early 2000s. Indeed, Hite and Long (1982) provide evidence that the 1969 Act explains the dramatic shift from qualified stock options to non-qualified stock options that took place during the early 1970s. Restricted or qualified stock options – which had been the dominant form of long-term incentives for two decades – virtually disappeared from existence.

Congress resurrected a new form of qualified options (now called Incentive Stock Options or ISOs) as a last-minute addition to the Economic Recovery Tax Act of 1981.[18] ISOs carried many of the restrictions common for qualified stock options (holding periods after exercise, minimum exercise prices, etc.), and in addition were limited to $100,000 per executive per year (calculated as the stock price multiplied by the number of options on the date of grant). While ISOs have continued to be popular in the 2000s for middle-level managers (where the $100,000 limitation is not binding) and for companies without taxable profits (where loss of deductibility for ISOs is not costly), virtually all options granted to CEOs and other top executives since 1972 have been non-qualified stock options.

---

[17]   See Stanton, "Cash Comeback: Stock Options Begin to Lose Favor in Wake of Tax Law Revision," *Wall Street Journal* (1964). Stock options briefly resurged in 1966, following at 25 percent increase in the Dow Jones average from 1964 to early 1966 (Elia, "Opting for Options: Stock Plans Continue in Widespread Favor Despite Tax Changes," *Wall Street Journal* (1967)).

[18]   Bettner, "Incentive Stock Options Get Mixed Reviews, Despite the Tax Break They Offer Executives," *Wall Street Journal* (1981).

3.2   Golden Parachutes and Section 280(G)

An important pay-related development in the takeover market of the 1980s was the evolution of golden parachute agreements that awarded payments to incumbent executives following a change in control – generally when CEOs lost their jobs but in many cases even when they remained employed with their firm. Although often introduced as a takeover defense (since these agreements make it more costly to acquire a firm), these agreements arguably facilitated transactions by lessening incumbent management resistance to takeovers.

Change-in-control arrangements became controversial following a $4.1 million payment to William Agee, the CEO of Bendix. In 1982, Bendix launched a hostile takeover bid for Martin Marietta, which in turn made a hostile takeover bid for Bendix. Bendix ultimately found a "white knight" and was acquired by Allied Corp., but only after paying CEO Agee the golden parachute. The payment sparked outrage in Washington, but Congress could not ban golden parachute payments outright because such a ban would pre-empt state corporation laws. Congress does, however, control the tax laws, which allow corporations to deduct compensation from income only if the payments represent reasonable compensation for services rendered. By defining particular types or dollar amounts of compensation as unreasonable, Congress can directly determine whether compensation is deductible for corporate tax purposes.

Congress attempted to discourage golden parachutes by adding Sections 280(G) and 4999 to the tax code as part of the Deficit Reduction Act of 1984. Section 280(G) of the Code provides that, if change-in-control payments exceed three times the individual's base amount, then *all* payments in excess of the base amount are nondeductible to the employer. Also, Section 4999 imposes a 20 percent excise tax on the recipient of a parachute payment on the amount of payment above the base amount. The base amount is typically calculated as the individual's average total taxable compensation (i.e., W-2 compensation, which includes gains from exercising stock options) paid by the company over the prior five years).

Because of the complexity of what appears to be a simple rule, modest increases in parachute payments can trigger substantial tax payments by both the company and executive. For example, suppose an executive with five-year average taxable compensation of $1 million receives a golden parachute payment of $2.9 million, which is less than three times the $1 million base amount.[19] In this case, the entire $2.9 million parachute payment would be deductible by the company, and would be taxable as ordinary income to the executive. In contrast, suppose that the golden parachute payment was $3.1 million, which is more than three times the $1 million base amount. Under Section 280(G), the company would not be able to deduct $2.1 million (of the $3.1 million parachute payment) as a compensation expense, and (under Section 4999) the executive would owe $420,000 in excise taxes (i.e., 20 percent of $2.1 million) in addition to ordinary income taxes on the full $3.1 million parachute payment.

---

[19]   The golden parachute payment includes not only cash payments but also the value of accelerated vesting of stock and options, as long as the payment is contingent on a change of control or ownership of the company.

The new Section 280(G) impacted executive compensation in several ways. First, the new law led to a proliferation in change-in-control agreements, which had previously been fairly rare. The Deficit Reduction Act was signed into law on July 18, 1984. By 1987, 41 percent of the largest 1,000 corporations had golden parachute agreements for their top executives, and the prevalence of golden parachutes increased to 57 percent in 1995 and to 70 percent by 1999.[20] In addition, the standard golden parachute payment quickly became the government prescribed amount of three times the base compensation. By 1991, 47.5 percent of CEO golden parachute arrangements specified a multiple of three times base pay; and by 1999 71 percent specified three times base pay. Thus, the rule designed to limit the generosity of parachute payments led to both a proliferation and a standardization of golden parachute payments in most large corporations. Apparently compensation committees and executives took the regulation as effectively endorsing such change-in-control agreements as well as the payments of three times the average compensation (which quickly became the standard).

Second, Section 280(G) (and the corresponding Section 4999) gave rise to the "excise tax gross up," in which the company would offset the tax burden of the 20 percent excise tax by paying an additional amount for the tax (and the tax on the additional amount).[21] The percentage of agreements that included gross-up provisions increased from 38 percent in 1991 to over 82 percent by 1999. This gross-up concept was subsequently applied to a variety of executive benefits with imputed income taxable to the executive, such as company cars, club memberships, and personal use of corporate aircraft.

Third, Section 280(G) also provided incentives for companies to shorten vesting periods in stock option plans, and incentives for executives to exercise stock options even earlier than they would normally be exercised. Consider two otherwise identical executives with golden parachutes paying three times base compensation and holding identical options. Suppose that one of the executives exercises a year prior to the change in control, while the other holds up until the change in control. Since base compensation under Section 280(G) includes gains from exercising options, the first executive can receive a higher parachute payment before triggering the excise tax, thus increasing the benefits from early exercise. Moreover, unexercisable stock options routinely become vested (or exercisable) upon a change in control, and the value of these options is defined by the Internal Revenue Service (IRS) as part of the parachute payment subject to the excise taxes. Therefore, companies and executives can reduce change-in-control related tax liabilities by shortening the time until options become exercisable, and by exercising early and therefore reducing the incentive effects of those plans.

Similarly, unvested restricted stock routinely become vested upon a change in control, and the value of these shares upon vesting is defined by the IRS as part of the parachute

---

[20]   Alpern and McGowan (2001), p. 6.

[21]   For example, continuing with the example above, suppose the CEO owed $420,000 in excise taxes (i.e., 20 percent of the $2.1 million excess benefit). If the CEO had a gross-up clause (and assuming a marginal tax on ordinary income of 50 percent on top of the 20 percent excise tax), he would receive a gross-up payment of $1.4 million and a total change-in-control payment of $4.5 million, leaving him with after-tax income of $1.55 million (which is what he would have received without an excise tax).

payment subject to the excise taxes. Thus, companies can also reduce change-in-control related tax liabilities by shortening the vesting period for restricted stock.

Finally, but perhaps most importantly, the 1984 tax laws regarding golden parachutes appear to have triggered the proliferation of Employment Agreements for CEOs and other top-level executives in most large firms since the mid-1980s. Section 280(G) applies only to severance payments contractually tied to changes of control. Individual CEO employment agreements typically provide for severance payments for *all* forms of terminations without cause, including (but not limited to) terminations following control changes. Therefore, companies can circumvent the Section 280(G) three-times-base-compensation limitations (at a potentially huge cost to shareholders) by making payments available to all terminated executives, and not only those terminated following a change in control.

In summary, although Section 280(G) was meant to reduce the generosity of parachute payments, the government action appears to have increased the prevalence of: (i) change-in-control plans; (ii) tax gross-ups; (iii) early exercise of stock options; (iv) short vesting periods for restricted stock and stock options; and (v) employment agreements. Each of these outcomes both reduces the incentive effects of incentive compensation for CEOs and other executives and increases the costs of these plans to their firms.

3.3   The Clinton $1 Million Deductibility Cap

The controversy over CEO pay became a major political issue during the 1992 US presidential campaign.[22] Bill Clinton promised to end the practice of allowing companies to take unlimited tax deductions for excessive executive pay; Dan Quayle warned that corporate boards should curtail some of these exorbitant salaries paid to corporate executives that were unrelated to productivity; Bob Kerry called it unacceptable for corporate executives to make millions of dollars while their companies were posting losses; Paul Tsongas argued that excessive pay was hurting America's ability to compete in the international market; and Pat Buchanan argued that you could not have executives running around making $4 million while their workers were being laid off.

After the 1992 election, president-elect Clinton reiterated his promise to define compensation above $1 million as unreasonable, thereby disallowing deductions for all compensation above this level for all employees. Concerns about the loss of deductibility contributed to an unprecedented rush to exercise options before the end of the 1992 calendar year, as companies urged their employees to exercise their options while the company could still deduct the gain from the exercise as a compensation expense.[23] In anticipation of the loss of deductibility, large investment banks accelerated their 1992 bonuses so that they would be paid in 1992 rather in 1993. In addition, several publicly traded Wall Street firms, including Merrill Lynch, Morgan Stanley, and Bear Stearns,

[22]   "Politics and Policy – Campaign '92: From Quayle to Clinton, Politicians are Pouncing on the Hot Issue of Top Executives' Hefty Salaries," *Wall Street Journal* (1992).

[23]   Chronicle Staff and Wire Reports, "Big Earners Cashing in Now: Fearful of Clinton's Tax Plans, They Rush to Exercise their Options," *San Francisco Chronicle* (1992).

announced that they were considering returning to a private partnership structure if Clinton's plan was implemented.[24]

By February 1993, President Clinton backtracked on the idea of making *all* compensation above $1 million unreasonable and therefore non-deductible, deciding that only pay unrelated to the productivity of the enterprise was unreasonable.[25] In April, details of the considerably softened plan began to emerge.[26] As proposed by the Treasury Department and eventually approved by Congress as part of the Omnibus Budget Reconciliation Act of 1993, Section 162(m) of the tax code applies only to public firms and not to privately held firms, and applies only to compensation paid to the CEO and the four highest-paid executive officers as disclosed in annual proxy statements (compensation for all others in the firm is fully deductible, even if in excess of the million-dollar limit). More importantly, Section 162(m) does not apply to compensation considered performance-based for the CEO and the four highest-paid people in the firm.[27]

Performance-based compensation, as defined under Section 162(m), includes commissions and pay based on the attainment of one or more performance goals, but only if (1) the goals are determined by an independent compensation committee consisting of two or more outside directors, and (2) the terms of the contract (including goals) are disclosed to shareholders and approved by shareholders before payment. Stock options generally qualify as performance based, but only if the exercise price is no lower than the market price on the date of grant. Base salaries, restricted stock, and options issued with an exercise price below the grant-date market price do not qualify as performance based.

Under the IRS definition, a bonus based on formula-driven objective performance measures is considered performance based (so long as the bonus plan has been approved by shareholders), while a discretionary bonus based on *ex post* subjective assessments is not considered performance based (because there are no predetermined performance goals). In addition, the tax law has been interpreted as allowing negative but not positive discretionary payments: the board can use its discretion to pay less but not more than the amount indicated by a shareholder-approved objective plan.

In enacting Section 162(m), Congress used (or abused) the tax system to target a small group of individuals (the five highest-paid executives in publicly traded firms) and to punish shareholders of companies who pay high salaries. Indeed, the explicit objective of the proposal that evolved into Section 162(m) was not to increase tax revenues or improve incentives but rather to reduce the level of CEO pay. For example, the House Ways and Means Committee described the congressional intention behind the legislation:

---

[24]   Siconolfi, "Wall Street is Upset by Clinton's Support on Ending Tax Break for 'Excessive' Pay," *Wall Street Journal* (1992).

[25]   Freudenheim, "Experts See Tax Curbs on Executives' Pay as More Political than Fiscal," *New York Times* (1993).

[26]   Greenhouse, "Deduction Proposal is Softened," *New York Times* (1993).

[27]   In 2006, the disclosure rules were changed to require disclosure of the CEO, the Chief Financial Officer (CFO), and the three-highest paid executives (other than the CEO and CsFO). Since disclosure of CFO compensation was not required prior to 2006 (unless the CFO happened to be among the four highest-paid), the IRS ruled in 2007 that CFO compensation was exempt from Section 162(m) deductibility limits.

Recently, the amount of compensation received by corporate executives has been the subject of scrutiny and criticism. The committee believes that excessive compensation will be reduced if the deduction for compensation (other than performance-based compensation) paid to the top executives of publicly held corporations is limited to $1 million per year.[28]

Ironically, although the objective of the new IRS Section 162(m) was to reduce excessive CEO pay levels by limiting deductibility, the ultimate result (similar to what happened in response to the golden parachute restrictions) was a significant *increase* in CEO pay. First, since compensation associated with stock options is generally considered performance-based and therefore deductible (as long as the exercise price is at or above the grant-date market price), Section 162(m) encouraged companies to grant more traditional stock options. Second, while there is some evidence that companies paying base salaries in excess of $1 million lowered salaries to $1 million following the enactment of Section 162(m) (Perry and Zenner (2001)), many others raised salaries that were below $1 million to exactly $1 million (Rose and Wolfram (2002)). Finally, companies subject to Section 162(m) typically modified bonus plans by replacing sensible discretionary plans with overly generous formulas (Murphy and Oyer (2004)).

It is difficult to argue with the principle that companies should only be able to deduct reasonable compensation expenses for services rendered. However, the $1 million reasonableness standard is inherently arbitrary and has not been indexed for either inflation (50 percent from 1993–2010) or changes in the market for executive talent: compensation plans that seemed excessive in 1993 are considered modest by current standards. More importantly, Section 162(m) disallows deductions for many value-increasing plan designs. For example, Section 162(m) disallows deductions for restricted stock or for options issued in the money, even when such grants are accompanied by an explicit reduction in base salaries. In addition, Section 162(m) disallows deductions for discretionary bonuses based on boards' subjective assessment of value creation. Many compensation committees have welcomed the tax-related justification for not incorporating subjective assessments in executive reward systems. After all, no one likes receiving unfavorable performance evaluations, and few directors enjoy giving them. But, by failing to make the inherently subjective appraisals, directors are breaching one of their most important duties to the firm.

Moreover, Section 162(m) has distorted the information that companies give to shareholders. In particular, in order to circumvent restrictions on discretionary bonuses, companies have created a formal shareholder-approved plan that qualifies under the IRS Section 162(m) while actually awarding bonuses under a different shadow plan (often called the "plan-within-a-plan") that pays less than the maximum allowed under the shareholder-approved plan. Quite often, these shadow plans have little or nothing to do with the performance criteria specified in the shareholder-approved plans, rendering meaningless the discussions of bonus plans in corporate proxy statements.

Finally, it is worth noting that Section 162(m) is highly discriminatory, applying only to the compensation received by the top five executive officers, and applying only to publicly traded companies and not to private firms or partnerships. Ultimately, arbitrary and

---

[28] 1993 U.S. Code Congressional and Administrative News 877, as cited in Perry and Zenner (2001).

discriminatory tax rules such as Section 162(m) have increased the cost imposed on publicly traded corporations and have made going-private conversions more attractive.

3.4   Enron and Section 409(A)

Enron, like many other large companies, allowed mid-level and senior executives to defer portions of their salaries and bonuses through the company's non-qualified deferred-compensation program. When Enron filed for Chapter 11 bankruptcy protection in December 2002, about 400 senior and former executives became unsecured creditors of the corporation, eventually losing most (if not all) of the money in their accounts.[29] However, just before the bankruptcy filing, Enron allowed a small number of executives to withdraw millions of dollars from their deferred-compensation accounts. The disclosure of these payments generated significant outrage (and lawsuits) from Enron employees who lost their money, and attracted the ire of Congress.

As a direct response (some would say knee-jerk reaction) to the Enron situation, Section 409(A) was added to the Internal Revenue Code as part of the American Jobs Creation Act of 2004. In essence, the objectives of Section 409(A) were to limit the flexibility in the timing of elections to defer compensation in nonqualified deferred-compensation programs, to restrict withdrawals from the deferred accounts to pre-determined dates (and to prohibit the acceleration of withdrawals), and to prevent executives from receiving severance-related deferred compensation until six months after severance. Section 409(A) imposes taxes on individuals with deferred compensation as soon as the amounts payable under the plan are no longer subject to a substantial risk of forfeiture. Individuals failing to pay taxes in the year the amounts are deemed to no longer be subject to the substantial forfeiture risk owe a 20 percent excise tax and interest penalties on the amount payable (even if the individual has not received or may never receive any of the income).

One of the notable features of Section 409(A) is that it significantly broadens the definition of deferred compensation. For example, annual bonuses or reimbursement of expenses paid more than two and a half months after the close of the fiscal year are considered deferred compensation subject to Section 409(A). Similarly, supplemental executive retirement plans (SERPs), phantom stock awards, stock appreciation rights, split-dollar life insurance arrangements, and individual employment agreements allowing deferral of compensation or severance awards are also (under many circumstances) considered deferred compensation subject to Section 409(A).

While developed as a response to the Enron situation, Section 409(A) was still being drafted when the option-backdating scandals came to light. As a result, Congress defined discount options (i.e., options with an exercise price below the market price on the date of grant) as deferred compensation subject to Section 409(A). In particular, Section 409(A) requires discount options to have a fixed exercise date (that is, a date in the future when the option must be exercised). Unless the option holder pre-commits to the future date when the option will be exercised, the holder is subject to a 20 percent penalty tax, in addition to regular income tax, plus possible interest and other penalties, regardless of

---

[29]   Barboza, "Enron's Many Strands: Executive Compensation. Enron Paid Some, Not All, Deferred Compensation," *New York Times* (2002).

whether the option is ever exercised. The new section applies retroactively to options granted before 2005 but not vested as of December 31, 2004, and is explicitly designed to penalize options granted to senior executives through backdating schemes.

4   RULES AND LEGISLATION

4.1   Stock Options and the Short-Swing Profit Rule (May 1991)

Under Section 16(b) of the Securities Act of 1934, executives had to return any profits realized from buying and selling (or selling and buying) shares of their company's stock within any period of less than six months. This constraint was not problematic for executives exercising restricted or qualified stock options, since the provisions of the 1951 and 1964 Revenue Acts already required executives to hold shares for six months (for restricted options) or three years (for qualified options) before trading. However, the six-month holding period was particularly troublesome for non-qualified options, since executives were required to pay ordinary income tax when the option was exercised and not when the underlying shares were sold. Given the depressed stock market and high tax rates in the 1970s, the taxes paid upon exercise were often greater than the value of the shares when they became tradable.

In December 1976, the SEC formally exempted stock appreciation rights (SARs) from the Section 16(b) short-swing profit prohibition.[30] Executives holding a SAR were entitled to receive the appreciation on one share of stock. Like stock options, SARs had a pre-determined term but executives were generally free to exercise their SARs at any time prior to this term (after some minimum time had elapsed). As a result of the ruling, many companies replaced their option grants with SAR grants, or issued tandem SARs and options, allowing the executive to decide which to exercise. For the next fifteen years, SARs became a ubiquitous component of long-term compensation for most executives.

In May 1991 the SEC declared that the six-month holding period begins when options are granted, and not when executives acquire shares upon exercise. Therefore, as long as the executive has held the option for at least six months, he is allowed to sell immediately shares acquired when options are exercised. This new ruling eliminated the primary advantage of SARs over non-qualified options and, as a result, SARs largely disappeared from existence.[31] In addition, the SEC rule effectively encouraged the practice – commonplace today – of selling shares immediately upon exercise.[32]

In Section 6 below, I argue that the 1991 SEC rule was a contributing factor leading to the explosion in option grants in the 1990s. In addition, the rise and ultimate fall of SARs is a tribute to the cleverness of companies in finding ways around rules that disadvantage

---

[30]   "SEC Exempts Rights To Stock Appreciation From 'Insider' Curbs," *Wall Street Journal* (1976).

[31]   There was one major disadvantage of SARs over non-qualified options: companies granting SARs were required to record an accounting charge for the evolving value of the SARs, while (as discussed below) there was typically no accounting charge for options.

[32]   Peers, "Executives Take Advantage of New Rules on Selling Shares Bought With Options," *Wall Street Journal* (1991).

executives (in this case, the six-month holding requirement). Moreover, the experience shows how seemingly innocuous government interventions (in this case, the 1976 and 1991 SEC rulings) can have a major impact on the composition of executive compensation.

4.2   Accounting Scandals and Sarbanes-Oxley

Accounting scandals erupted across corporate America during the early 2000s, destroying the reputations of once-proud firms such as Enron, WorldCom, Qwest, Global Crossing, HealthSouth, Cendant, Rite-Aid, Lucent, Xerox, Tyco International, Adelphia, Fannie Mae, Freddie Mac, and Arthur Andersen. In the midst of these scandals, Congress quickly passed the sweeping Sarbanes-Oxley Act in July 2002, setting or expanding standards for accounting firms, auditors, and boards of directors of publicly traded companies. The Act was primarily focused on accounting irregularities and not on compensation. However, Congress could not resist the temptation to use the new law to further regulate executive pay.

First, in direct response to the forgiveness of certain corporate loans given to executives at Tyco International, Section 402 of Sarbanes-Oxley prohibited all personal loans to executives and directors, regardless of whether such loans served a useful and legitimate business purpose. For example, prior to Sarbanes-Oxley, companies would routinely offer loans to executives to buy company stock, often on a non-recourse basis so that the executive could fulfill the loan obligations by returning the purchased shares.[33] Similarly, companies attracting executives would routinely offer housing subsidies in the form of forgivable loans, a practice made unlawful under the new regulations.[34] Finally, Sarbanes-Oxley is viewed as prohibiting company-maintained cashless exercise programs for stock options, where an executive exercising options can use some of the shares acquired to finance both the exercise price and income taxes due upon exercise.[35]

Second, Section 304 of Sarbanes-Oxley required CEOs and CFOs to reimburse the company for any bonus or equity-based compensation received, and any profits realized from selling shares, in the twelve months commencing with the filing of financial state-

---

[33]   Indeed, it is easy to show that a traditional at-the-money stock option is equivalent to a non-recourse loan to purchase company stock at a zero interest rate. Loans to purchase stock that carry a positive interest rate or require an executive down payment are less costly to grant than traditional options, and deliver better incentives by both forcing executives to invest some of their own money in the venture and only providing payouts when the stock price appreciates by at least the interest charged on the loan. It is unfortunate that Congress prohibited these types of plans.

[34]   Offering housing subsidies in the form of loans that are forgiven with the passage of time is preferable to a lump-sum subsidy, since the company can avoid paying the full subsidy if the executive leaves the firm before the loan is repaid or fully forgiven.

[35]   Technically, cashless exercise programs are implemented by offering the executive a short-term bridge loan to finance the purchase of the shares (including taxes), followed by open-market transactions to sell some of the shares to repay the loan. Subsequent to Sarbanes-Oxley, executives exercising options have turned to conventional banks for bridge-loan financing, significantly increasing the transaction costs and further diluting the shares outstanding (since under company-maintained programs, the company need only issue the net number of shares and not the full number of shares under option).

ments that are subsequently restated as a result of corporate misconduct. This "claw-back" provision of Sarbanes-Oxley – which was subsequently extended in the Dodd-Frank Act discussed below – was notable mostly for its ineffectiveness. Indeed, in spite of the wave of accounting restatements that led to the initial passage of Sarbanes-Oxley, the first individual claw-back settlement under Section 304 did not occur until more than five years later, when UnitedHealth Group's former CEO William McGuire was forced to return $600 million in compensation.[36] The SEC became more aggressive in 2009, launching two claw-back cases (CSK Auto and Diebold, Inc.) where the targeted executives were not accused of personal wrongdoing.[37]

Finally, Section 403 of Sarbanes-Oxley required that executives disclose new grants of stock options within two business days of the grant; before the Act options were not disclosed until 45 days after the company's fiscal closing. This provision had the unintended but ultimately beneficial effect of curbing option backdating for top executives more than two years before the unsavory practice was uncovered (Heron and Lie (2006a)).

4.3 The Dodd-Frank Executive Compensation Reform Act

In addition to the new disclosure requirements discussed above in Section 2.5, the 2010 Dodd-Frank Act instructed the SEC to promulgate and enforce a variety of other regulations related to executive pay, including:

1. *Say on pay* Shareholders will be asked to approve the company's executive compensation practices in a non-binding vote occurring at least every three years (with an additional vote the first year and every six years thereafter to determine whether the say on pay votes will occur every one, two, or three years). In addition, companies are required to disclose, and shareholders are asked to approve (again, in a non-binding vote), any golden parachute payments in connection with mergers, tender offers, or going-private transactions.

   In January 2011 – and effective for the 2011 proxy season – the SEC adopted rules concerning shareholder approval of executive compensation and golden parachute compensation arrangements. Shareholders of 98.5 percent of the 2532 companies reporting by July 2011 approved the pay plans; over 70 percent of the companies received more than 90 percent favorable support.[38]

2. *Claw-backs* Companies must implement and report policies for recouping payments to executives based on financial statements that are subsequently restated. The rule applies to any current or former executive officer (an expansion of Sarbanes-Oxley, where only the CEO and CFO were subject to claw-backs), and applies to any payments made in the three-year period preceding the restatement (Sarbanes-Oxley only applied for the twelve months following the filing of the inaccurate statement).

---

[36] Plitch, "Paydirt: Sarbanes-Oxley A Pussycat On 'Clawbacks'," *Dow Jones Newswires* (2006); Bowe and White, "Record Payback over Options," *Financial Times* (2007).

[37] Berman, "The Game: New Frontier For the SEC: The Clawback," *Wall Street Journal* (2010); Korn, "Diebold to Pay $25 Million Penalty," *Wall Street Journal* (2010).

[38] Holzer, "A 'Yes' In Say On Pay," *Wall Street Journal* (2011a).

The SEC intends to propose and adopt rules regarding the recovery of executive compensation in late 2011.

3. *Compensation committee independence*   Following Sarbanes-Oxley (2002) requirements for Audit Committees, publicly traded companies are required to have compensation committees comprised solely of outside independent directors (where independence takes into account any financial ties the outside directors might have with the firm).

In March 2011, the SEC proposed listing standards relating to the independence of the members on a compensation committee, the committee's authority to retain compensation advisers, and the committee's responsibility for the appointment, compensation and work of any compensation adviser. Once an exchange's new listing standards are in effect, a listed company must meet these standards in order for its shares to continue trading on that exchange for compensation committees. Final rules were expected in late 2011.

4. *Proxy access*   The Dodd-Frank Act authorized the SEC to issue rules allowing certain shareholders to nominate their own director candidates in the company's annual proxy statements.

The SEC issued its rules on Proxy Access in August 2010, but delayed implementation after lawsuits by the Business Roundtable and the US Chamber of Commerce claimed that the rules would distract management and advance special-interest agendas. In July 2011, the US Circuit Court of Appeals (Washington, DC) ruled in favor of the business groups and issued a sharp rebuke to the SEC, saying that the SEC failed in analyzing the cost the rule imposes on companies and in supporting its claim that the rule would improve shareholder value and board performance.[39]

It is too early to assess the ultimate effect of Dodd-Frank on executive compensation, since many of the rules have just been implemented or are still being written. In spite of its enormous length – the bill itself spans 848 pages – the full Act leaves most of the details to be promulgated by a variety of government entities, including the SEC, Federal Reserve System, the Department of Treasury, the Commodity Futures Trading Commission, the Financial Stability Oversight Council, the Federal Deposit Insurance Corporation, the Federal Trade Commission, the Government Accounting Office, and the Office of the Comptroller of the Currency. Indeed, attorneys at DavisPolk (2010) calculate that the Act requires regulators to create 243 new rules, conduct 67 studies, and issue 22 periodic reports. Without question, the Dodd-Frank Act as ultimately implemented will provide financial economists with research fodder for years to come.

5   ACCOUNTING POLICIES

No legislative history of executive compensation is complete without an analysis of the accounting rules affecting stock options and equity-based compensation. Indeed, while

---

[39]   Holzer, "Corporate News: Court Deals Blow to SEC, Activists," *Wall Street Journal* (2011b).

the rise (and fall) of restricted stock options in the 1950s was driven by tax policies, there is ample evidence that the popularity of non-qualified stock options in the 1990s – and their demise in popularity in the 2000s – in large part reflects accounting considerations.

5.1 There's No Accounting for Options (APB 25 and FAS 123)

The restricted and qualified stock options created by the 1950 and 1964 Revenue Acts were not formally considered compensation and therefore companies did not record an expense for such options for either tax or accounting purposes. The switch to non-qualified options in the 1970s – which were considered compensation for tax purposes – raised a new question: how should options be accounted for in company income statements? One possibility was to follow the tax code by recognizing an accounting expense at the time an option is exercised. But, in spite of its simplicity, this method is inconsistent with the basic tenet of accounting that expenses should be matched to the time period when the services associated with those expenses were rendered. Rather, the tenet suggested that options should be expensed over their term based on the grant-date value of the option. At the time, however (and for a long time to come) there was no accepted way of placing a value on an employee stock option.

In October 1972, the Accounting Principles Board (APB) – the predecessor to the current Financial Accounting Standards Board (FASB) – issued APB Opinion No. 25, Accounting for Stock Issued to Employees. Under APB Opinion No. 25, the compensation expense associated with stock option was defined as the (positive) difference between the stock price and the exercise price as of the first date when both the number of options granted and the exercise price become known or fixed. The expense for this spread between the price and exercise price – called the intrinsic value – was amortized over the period in which the employee was prohibited from exercising the option.[40] Under this rule, there was no charge for options granted with an exercise price equal to (or exceeding) the grant-date market price, because the spread is zero on the grant date.

The accounting treatment of options cemented the dominance of the traditional stock option (an option granted with a five- or ten-year term with an exercise price equal to the grant-date market price) and prevented companies from offering more novel option plans. For example, APB Opinion 25 imposes a higher accounting charge for options with an exercise price indexed to the stock-price performance of the market or industry, because the exercise price is not immediately fixed. Similarly, it imposes a higher accounting charge for options that only become exercisable if certain performance triggers are achieved, because the number of options is not immediately fixed. Finally, it imposes an accounting charge for options that are issued in the money but not for options issued at the money – a feature that became especially significant in the scandals three decades later involving backdating.

---

[40]   This period is often called the vesting period but this terminology is misleading since vesting implies that the executive is free to sell the option or keep it if he leaves the firm, as opposed to being able only to exercise the option.

The 1972 APB Opinion 25 defining the accounting treatment for stock options as the spread between the market and exercise price on the grant date pre-dated Black–Scholes (1973), which offered the first formula for computing the value of a traded call option. Academic research in option valuation exploded over the next decade, and financial economists and accountants became increasingly intrigued with using these new methodologies to value, and account for, options issued to corporate executives and employees.

In 1984, the Financial Accounting Standards Board (FASB) floated the idea that companies account for employee stock options using the so-called minimum value approach.[41] By June 1986, the FASB idea had evolved into a proposal with the important change that the accounting charge would be based on the fair market value (e.g., the Black–Scholes value) and not a minimum value. The proposal was vehemently opposed by all of the Big Eight accounting firms, the American Electronics Association (including more than 2,800 corporate members), the Financial Executives Institute, the Pharmaceutical Manufacturers Association, and the National Venture Capital Association.[42] In the face of this opposition, and without fanfare, the FASB tabled its 1986 proposal before submitting an exposure draft.

In April 1992, the FASB voted 7–0 to endorse an accounting charge for options, and issued a formal proposal in 1993. The proposal created a storm of criticism among business executives, high-tech companies, accountants, compensation consultants, the Secretary of the Treasury, and shareholder groups.[43] Even President Clinton, usually a critic of high executive pay, waded into the debate, expressing that it would be unfortunate if the FASB's proposal inadvertently undermined the competitiveness of some of America's most promising high-tech companies.[44] In March 1994, the FASB held public hearings on the issue. In the aftermath of the overwhelmingly negative response, the Board announced it was delaying the proposed accounting change by at least a year, and in December it dropped the proposal.

In 1995, the FASB issued a compromise rule, FAS 123, which *recommended* but did *not require* that companies expense the fair market value of options granted (using Black–

---

[41]   The minimum value approach is identical to the value of a forward contract to purchase a share of stock at some date in the future at a pre-determined price (that is, an option without the option to refrain from buying when the price falls below the exercise price). For example, the minimum value of an option on a non-dividend-paying stock is calculated as the current stock price minus the grant-date present value of the exercise price. Thus, the value of a ten-year option granted with an exercise price of $30 when the grant-date market price was $25 would be $V = \$25 - \$30/(1+r)^{10}$, where r is the risk-free rate.

[42]   See, for example, Rudnitsky and Green, "Options Are Free, Aren't They?," *Forbes* (August 26, 1985); Gupta and Berton, "Start-up Firms Fear Change in Accounting," *Wall Street Journal* (1986); Fisher, "Option Proposal Criticized," *New York Times* (1986); Eckhouse, "Tech Firms' Study: Accounting Rule Attacked," *San Francisco Chronicle* (1987).

[43]   See, for example, Berton, "Business Chiefs Try to Derail Proposal on Stock Options," *Wall Street Journal* (1992); Harlan and Berton, "Accounting Firms, Investors Criticize Proposal on Executives' Stock Options," "*Wall Street Journal* (1992); "Bentsen Opposes FASB On Reporting Stock Options," *Wall Street Journal* (1993); Berton, "Accounting Rule-Making Board's Proposal Draws Fire," *Wall Street Journal* (1994); Harlan, "High Anxiety: Accounting Proposal Stirs Unusual Uproar In Executive Suites," *Wall Street Journal* (1994).

[44]   "Clinton Enters Debate Over How Companies Reckon Stock Options," *Wall Street Journal* (1993).

Scholes or a similar valuation methodology). However, while the FASB allowed firms to continue reporting under APB Opinion 25, it imposed the additional requirement that the value of the option grant would be disclosed in a footnote to the financial statements. Predictably, only a handful of companies adopted the FASB's recommended approach; it was not until the accounting scandals in the early 2000s that firms voluntarily began to expense their option grants.

The accounting treatment of options promulgated the mistaken belief that options could be granted without any cost to the company. This view was wrong, of course, because the opportunity or economic cost of granting an option is the amount the company could have received if it sold the option in an open market instead of giving it to employees. Nonetheless, the idea that options were free (or at least cheap) was erroneously accepted in too many boardrooms. Options were particularly attractive in cash-poor start-ups (such as in the emerging new economy firms in the early 1990s) which could compensate employees through options without spending any cash. Indeed, providing compensation through options allowed the companies to generate cash, since when options were exercised the company received the exercise price and could also deduct the difference between the market price and exercise price from its corporate taxes. The difference between the accounting and tax treatment gave option-granting companies the best of both worlds: no accounting expense on the companies' books, but a large deduction for tax purposes.

5.2　FIN 44 and the End of Option Repricing

One of the most-common but more-controversial practices in executive compensation is "repricing" options by canceling higher-priced options and replacing them with options with lower exercise prices. On December 4, 1998, the FASB announced that repriced options issued on or after December 15, 1998 would be treated under "variable accounting," meaning that the company would take an accounting charge each year for the repriced option based on the actual appreciation in the value of the option. The FASB issued its final rule in March 2000 as FASB Interpretation No. 44, or FIN 44, indicating that the Board did not consider this a new rule but rather a re-interpretation of an old rule. In particular, the FASB reasoned that the "fixed accounting" under APB Opinion 25 (in which the option expense was equal to the spread between the market and exercise price on the first date when both the number of options granted and the exercise price become known or fixed) did not apply to companies that had a policy of revising the exercise price.

Companies with underwater options rushed to reprice those options in the 12-day window between December 4 and 15, 1998.[45] Indeed, Carter and Lynch (2003) document a dramatic increase in repricing activities during the short window, followed by dramatic declines; Murphy (2003) shows that repricings virtually disappeared after the accounting charge. Many companies with declining stock prices circumvented the accounting charge on repriced options by canceling existing options and re-issuing an equal number of

---

[45]　Johnston, "Fast Deadline On Options Repricing: As of Next Tuesday, It's Ruled an Expense," *New York Times* (1998).

options after waiting six months or more. But this replacement is not neutral. It imposes substantial risk on risk-averse employees since the exercise price is not known for six months and can conceivably be *above* the original exercise price. In addition, canceling and reissuing stock options in this way provides perverse incentives to keep the stock-price down for six months so that the new options will have a low exercise price. All of this scrambling to avoid an accounting charge!

5.3   FAS 123R and the Rise in Restricted Stock

The scandals that erupted across corporate America during the early 2000s focused attention on the quality of accounting disclosures, which in turn renewed pressures for companies to report the expense associated with stock options on their accounting state-ments. Before 2002, only a handful of companies had elected to expense options under FAS 123; the remainder elected to account for options under the old rules (where there was typically no expense). In the summer of 2002, several dozen firms announced their intention to expense options voluntarily; more than 150 firms had elected to expense options by early 2003 (Aboody, Barth and Kasznik (2004)). Moreover, shareholder groups (most often representing union pension funds) began demanding shareholder votes on whether options should be expensed; more than 150 shareholder proposals on option expensing were submitted during the 2003 and 2004 proxy season (Ferri and Sandino (2009)). By late 2004, about 750 companies had voluntarily adopted or announced their intention to expense options. In December 2004, the FASB announced FAS 123R which revised FAS 123 by *requiring* all US firms to recognize an accounting expense when granting stock options, effective for fiscal years beginning after June 15, 2005.

Under the accounting rules in place since 1972 (and continuing under FAS 123R), companies granting restricted stock recognize an accounting expense equal to the grant-date value of the shares amortized over the vesting period. Under FAS 123R, the expense for stock options is similar to that of shares of stock: companies must recognize an accounting expense equal to the grant-date value of the options amortized over the period when the option is not exercisable. Option expensing (whether voluntarily under FAS 123, or by law under FAS 123R) significantly leveled the playing field between stock and options from an accounting perspective. As a result, companies reduced the number of options granted to top executives (and other employees), and greatly expanded the use of restricted shares.

Financial economists generally dismiss the idea that executives would react to account-ing changes that have no effect on current or future cash flows. But there is ample evidence that options were granted in such great quantities, and to so many employees, precisely because executives and boards of directors viewed options as essentially free (or at least cheap) to grant. Advocates in Congress of broad-based option programs, fearing that fair market-value accounting for options would end option grants to low-level employees, introduced several (ultimately shelved) bills to protect such programs. Ultimately, and predictably, the expensing of options indeed curtailed the practice of broad-based option plans: firms that already had such plans granted fewer options, and virtually no firms without plans introduced one.

6 SUMMARY: HOW REGULATION HAS SHAPED PAY

6.1 The 1990s Option Explosion

The unparalleled rise in CEO pay from the mid-1980s through 2001, propelled primarily by increases in the grant-date value of option awards, has generated a great deal of academic attention. The academic literature focused on explaining the increase in CEO pay (beyond that accounted for by risk premia) is roughly divided into two camps: the "managerial power" camp and the "efficient contracting" camp; see Frydman and Jenter (2010) for a useful and thorough review. Briefly, the "managerial power" camp – most closely associated with Bebchuk, Fried and Walker (2002) – argues that both the level and composition of pay are determined not by competitive market forces but rather by captive board members catering to rent-seeking entrenched CEOs. The "efficient contracting" camp (e.g., Murphy and Zábojník (2007); Gabaix and Landier (2008)) maintains that the observed level and composition of compensation reflects a competitive equilibrium in the market for managerial talent, and that incentives are structured to optimize firm value.

The legislative history supports a third, non-mutually exclusive hypothesis: the explosion in stock options that led to the escalation in pay was in large part the (arguably unintended) consequence of government policy. In particular, government policy in the early 1990s created a perfect storm that virtually guaranteed the explosion in option grants:

- In 1991, the SEC determined that shares acquired by exercising options could be sold immediately upon exercise (effectively eliminating the six-month holding requirement).
- In 1992, the SEC required disclosure of only the number of options granted, and not the value of options granted.
- In 1993, Section 162(m) (which ironically was imposed to reduce levels of executive pay) provided a safe harbor for stock options, by exempting options from the $1 million deductibility limit.
- In 1995, after pushing for expensing, the FASB backed down and allowed options to be granted without an accounting expense to the company (thus preserving the illusion that options were nearly costless to grant).

And, explode they did. As documented by Murphy (2012), CEO incentive compensation in the early 1990s was split about evenly between options and accounting-based bonuses. By 1996, options had become the largest single component of CEO compensation in S&P 500 firms, and the use of options was even greater in smaller firms (and especially high-tech start-ups). By 2000, stock options accounted for more than half of total compensation for a typical S&P 500 CEO.

6.2 The Rise of Restricted Stock

The most pronounced change in executive compensation in the early 2000s has been the shift from stock options to restricted stock as the primary form of equity-based compensation. In 2001, the value of stock options at the award date accounted for 53 percent of the pay for the typical S&P 500 CEO, while restricted stock accounted for less than 8 percent.[46] By 2010, options accounted for only 20 percent of total pay, while restricted stock had ballooned to 34 percent.

One obvious explanation for the drop in stock options and the rise in restricted stock since the early 2000s is the stock market crash associated with the burst of the Internet Bubble in 2000 and exacerbated by the terrorist attacks on the World Trade Center in 2001. Indeed, stock options have always become more popular when stock markets are trending upward (i.e., bull markets) and less popular when markets trend down (i.e., bear markets). However, the fact that options continued to decline (and restricted stock continued to grow) in the robust stock market from 2005 to 2008 suggests that the changes reflect more than market trends.

The rise in restricted stock cannot be easily explained by either "managerial power" or "efficient contracting," but can be explained by changes in government policy. In particular, and as discussed in Section 5.3, option expensing leveled the playing field between stock and options from an accounting perspective, resulting in an expansion in the use of restricted stock.

6.3   The "Plain Vanilla" Stock Option

Conceptually, the parameters of an option contract suggest a multitude of design possibilities: for example, exercise prices could be "indexed" to the industry or market, options could be forfeited unless a performance "trigger" is reached, option terms could match the expected executive horizons, etc. In practice, however, there is little cross-sectional variation in granting practices: most options expire in ten years and are granted with exercise prices equal to the "fair market value" on date of grant. Bebchuk, et al. (2002) cite this "one-size-fits-all" approach to option granting as evidence for their "managerial power" hypothesis. However, the standard features of option contracts can also be traced to the legislative history:

- Although the 1950 Revenue Act placed no restrictions on expiration terms for restricted stock options, the 1954 and 1964 Acts imposed maximum terms of ten and five years, respectively. Incentive Stock Options (the modern-day equivalent to restricted or qualified options) have a maximum term of ten years. While there are no government-imposed restrictions for non-qualified stock options, it is not a coincidence that most options have ten-year terms (with five-year terms also common).
- A variety of government policies have discouraged options with exercise prices set at less than the market price on the date of grant:
    - In order to qualify for capital-gains tax treatment, modern-day ISOs (like the old qualified options) must have exercise prices that equal or exceed the grant-date market price.

---

[46]   The typical pay components are derived by computing the ratio of options and restricted stock to total compensation for each executive, and then averaging across executives. See Murphy (2012) for details.

- Under APB 25 and FAS 123, companies granting options with an exercise price less than the grant-date market price would incur an accounting charge.
- Under IRS Section 162(m), options with an exercise price less than the grant-date market price are considered "non-performance-based" and are subject to the $1 million deductibility limit.
- Under IRS Section 409(A) options with an exercise price less than the grant-date market price are subject to immediate taxation and excise taxes (unless the exercise date is set in advance).
- While there are no obvious restrictions to issuing indexed or performance-triggered options in a post-FAS 123R environment (in which the options are expensed when granted), companies granting such options under APB 25 and FAS 123 were subject to an accounting charge.

6.4 Other Effects of Legislation

Beyond the growth and structure of equity-pay arrangements, the "Legislative Hypothesis" helps explain:

- The proliferation of golden parachute agreements, employment contracts, and contractual income tax gross-ups (as consequences of IRS Section 280(G)).
- The obfuscation of information about bonus plans and performance measures for firms offering "plans-within-plans" qualified under IRS Section 162(m).
- The common practice of immediately selling stock acquired by exercising options (allowed by the 1991 SEC rule and encouraged under IRS Section 280(G)).
- The decreased used of subjective performance assessments leading to discretionary bonuses (which are non-qualified under IRS Section 162(m) and subject to separate reporting under the 2006 disclosure rules).
- The increased used of multiple compensation consultants (including consultants working exclusively for the compensation committee), without any evidence that such structures lead to either lower or more efficient pay.

7 SHOULD EXECUTIVE PAY BE (FURTHER) REGULATED?

As documented in this chapter, the reality is that executive pay *is* already heavily regulated. There are disclosure rules, tax policies, and accounting standards designed explicitly to address perceived abuses in executive compensation. Common to all existing and past attempts to regulate pay are important (and usually undesirable) unintended consequences. For example, the 1984 laws introduced to reduce golden parachute payments led to a proliferation of change-in-control arrangements, employment contracts, and tax gross-ups. Similarly, a variety of rules implemented in the early 1990s is largely responsible for fueling the escalation in pay levels and option grants in the 1990s, and the enhanced disclosure of perquisites in the 1970s is generally credited with fueling an explosion in the breadth of benefits offered to executives.

The unintended consequences from regulation are not always negative. For example, reporting requirements in the 2002 Sarbanes-Oxley bill (in which executives receiving options had to report those options within 48 hours) are generally credited for stopping the unsavory practice of "option backdating," even though the authors of the bill had no idea the practice existed. As another example, the draconian regulations imposed on banks accepting government bailouts had the positive effect of getting investors paid back much more quickly than anyone expected, in order to escape the regulations. Even the 1993 deductibility cap – which backfired in its attempt to slow the growth in CEO pay – had the positive effect of greatly increasing the alignment between CEOs and their shareholders. But, these positive effects are accidents and cannot be relied upon. Thus, the emerging conclusion is to resist calls for further government regulation, and indeed re-examine the efficacy of policies already in place.

REFERENCES

Aboody, David, Mary E. Barth, and Ron Kasznik, 2004, Firms' Voluntary Recognition of Stock-Based Compensation Expense, *Journal of Accounting Research* 42, 123–50.

Alpern, Richard L. and Gail McGowan, 2001, *Guide to Change of Control: Protecting Companies and Their Executives* (Executive Compensation Advisory Services).

Barboza, David, 2002, "Enron's Many Strands: Executive Compensation. Enron Paid Some, Not All, Deferred Compensation," *New York Times* (February 13).

Bebchuk, Lucian A., Jesse M. Fried, and David I. Walker, 2002, Managerial Power and Rent Extraction in the Design of Executive Compensation, *University of Chicago Law Review* 69, 751–846.

"Bentsen Opposes FASB On Reporting Stock Options," 1993, *Wall Street Journal* (April 7).

Berman, Dennis K., 2010, "The Game: New Frontier For the SEC: The Clawback," *Wall Street Journal* (June 22).

Berton, Lee, 1992, "Business Chiefs Try to Derail Proposal on Stock Options," *Wall Street Journal* (February 5).

Berton, Lee, 1994, "Accounting Rule-Making Board's Proposal Draws Fire," *Wall Street Journal* (January 5).

Bettner, Jill, 1981, "Incentive Stock Options Get Mixed Reviews, Despite the Tax Break They Offer Executives," *Wall Street Journal* (August 24).

Black, Fischer and Myron S. Scholes, 1973, The Pricing of Options and Corporate Liabilities, *Journal of Political Economy* 81, 637–54.

Bowe, Christopher and Ben White, 2007, "Record Payback over Options," *Financial Times* (December 7).

Carter, Mary Ellen and Luann J. Lynch, 2003, The Consequences of the FASB's 1998 Proposal on Accounting for Stock Option Repricing, *Journal of Accounting & Economics* 35, 51–72.

Chronicle Staff and Wire Reports, 1992, "Big Earners Cashing in Now: Fearful of Clinton's Tax Plans, They Rush to Exercise their Options," *San Francisco Chronicle* (December 29).

"Chrysler Chairman Defends Option Plan, Offers to Discuss It With Federal Officials," 1963, *Wall Street Journal* (December 23).

"Chrysler Officers Got Profit of $4.2 Million On Option Stock in '63," 1964, *Wall Street Journal* (January 15).

"Chrysler Officers' Sale of Option Stock Could Stir Tax Bill Debate," 1963, *Wall Street Journal* (December 18).

"Clinton Enters Debate Over How Companies Reckon Stock Options," 1993, *Wall Street Journal* (December 23).

"Congress and Taxes: Specialists Mull Ways to Close 'Loopholes' in Present Tax Laws," 1959, *Wall Street Journal* (January 7).

"Cut High Salaries or Get No Loans, is RFC Warning," 1933, *New York Times* (May 29).

Davis Polk, 2010, *Summary of the Dodd-Frank Wall Street Reform and Consumer Protection Act, Enacted into Law on July 21, 2010* (July 21).

Eckhouse, John, 1987, "Tech Firms' Study: Accounting Rule Attacked," *San Francisco Chronicle* (April 10).

Elia, Charles J., 1967, "Opting for Options: Stock Plans Continue in Widespread Favor Despite Tax Changes," *Wall Street Journal* (July 15).

"Excerpts From Carter Message to Congress on Proposals to Change Tax System," 1978, *New York Times* (January 22).

"Federal Bureau Asks Salaries of Big Companies' Executives," 1933, *Chicago Daily Tribune* (October 18).

Ferri, Fabrizio and Tatiana Sandino, 2009, The Impact of Shareholder Activism on Financial Reporting and Compensation: The Case of Employee Stock Options Expensing, *The Accounting Review* 84, 433–66.

Fisher, Lawrence M., 1986, "Option Proposal Criticized," *New York Times* (December 27).

Forelle, Charles, 2006, "How Journal Found Options Pattern," *Wall Street Journal* (May 22).

Forelle, Charles and James Bandler, 2006, "Backdating Probe Widens as Two Quit Silicon Valley Firm; Power Integrations Officials Leave Amid Options Scandal; 10 Companies Involved so far," *Wall Street Journal* (May 6).

Freudenheim, Milt, 1993, "Experts See Tax Curbs on Executives' Pay as More Political than Fiscal," *New York Times* (February 12).

Frydman, Carola and Dirk Jenter, 2010, CEO Compensation, *Annual Review of Financial Economics* 2, 75–102.

Frydman, Carola and Raven E. Saks, 2008, Executive Compensation: A New View from a Long-Term Perspective, 1936–2005, FEDS Working Paper No. 2007-35.

Gabaix, Xavier and Augustin Landier, 2008, Why has CEO Pay Increased So Much?, *Quarterly Journal of Ecoonomics* 123, 49–100.

Greenhouse, Steven, 1993, "Deduction Proposal is Softened," *New York Times* (April 9).

Gupta, Udayan and Lee Berton, 1986, "Start-up Firms Fear Change in Accounting," *Wall Street Journal* (June 23).

Hall, Brian J. and Jeffrey B. Liebman, 1998, Are CEOs Really Paid Like Bureaucrats?, *Quarterly Journal of Economics* 113, 653–91.

Harlan, Christi, 1994, "High Anxiety: Accounting Proposal Stirs Unusual Uproar In Executive Suites," *Wall Street Journal* (March 7).

Harlan, Christi and Lee Berton, 1992, "Accounting Firms, Investors Criticize Proposal on Executives' Stock Options," *Wall Street Journal* (February 19).

Heron, Randall A. and Erik Lie, 2006a, Does Backdating Explain the Stock Price Pattern Around Executive Stock Option Grants?, *Journal of Financial Economics* 83, 271–95.

Heron, Randall A. and Erik Lie, 2006b, What Fraction of Stock Option Grants To Top Executives Have Been Backdated or Manipulated, Unpublished Working Paper.

Hite, Gailen L. and Michael S. Long, 1982, Taxes and Executive Stock Options, *Journal of Accounting and Economics* 4, 3–14.

Holzer, Jessica, 2011a, "A 'Yes' In Say On Pay," *Wall Street Journal* (July 8).

Holzer, Jessica, 2011b, "Corporate News: Court Deals Blow to SEC, Activists," *Wall Street Journal* (July 23).

"House Group Hears Conflicting Views on Stock Option Taxes," 1959, *Wall Street Journal* (December 8).

"House Unit Seen Favoring Curbs on Stock Options," 1963, *Wall Street Journal* (February 25).

Hyatt, James C., 1975, "No Strings: Firms Lure Executives By Promising Bonuses Not Linked To Profits," *Wall Street Journal* (December 24).

Jensen, Michael C., Kevin J. Murphy, and Eric Wruck, 2012, *CEO Pay and What To Do About It: Restoring Integrity to Both Executive Compensation and Capital-Market Relations* (Harvard Business School Press, Cambridge, MA).

Johnston, David Cay, 1998, "Fast Deadline On Options Repricing: As of Next Tuesday, It's Ruled an Expense," *New York Times* (December 8).

Korn, Melissa, 2010, "Diebold to Pay $25 Million Penalty," *Wall Street Journal* (June 3).

Kranhold, Kathryn, 2004, "GE Settles Charges Over Failure To Spell Out Pact With Ex-CEO," *Wall Street Journal* (September 24).

Lewellen, Wilbur G., 1968, *Executive Compensation in Large Industrial Companies* (National Bureau of Economic Research, New York).

Lie, Erik, 2005, On the Timing of CEO Stock Options Awards, *Management Science* 51, 802–12.

Maremont, Mark, 2005, "Authorities Probe Improper Backdating of Options: Practice Allows Executives to Bolster their Stock Gains; a Highly Beneficial Pattern," *Wall Street Journal* (November 11).

Murphy, Kevin J., 1996, Reporting Choice and the 1992 Proxy Disclosure Rules, *Journal of Accounting, Auditing, and Finance* 11, 497–515.

Murphy, Kevin J., 2003, Stock-Based Pay in New Economy Firms, *Journal of Accounting & Economics* 34, 129–47.

Murphy, Kevin J., 2012, Executive Compensation: Where We Are, and How We Got There, in George Constantinides, Milton Harris, and René Stulz, eds, *Handbook of the Economics of Finance* (forthcoming).

Murphy, Kevin J. and Paul Oyer, 2004, Discretion in Executive Incentive Contracts, USC Working Paper.

Murphy, Kevin J. and Tatiana Sandino, 2010, Executive Pay and "Independent" Compensation Consultants, *Journal of Accounting and Economics* 49, 247–62.

Murphy, Kevin J. and Jan Zábojník, 2007, Managerial Capital and the Market for CEOs, USC Working paper.

"Options on the Wane: Fewer Firms Plan Sale of Stock to Executives at Fixed Exercise Prices," 1960, *Wall Street Journal* (December 6).

Peers, Alexandra, 1991, "Executives Take Advantage of New Rules on Selling Shares Bought With Options," *Wall Street Journal* (June 19).

Perry, Tod and Marc Zenner, 2001, Pay for Performance? Government Regulation and the Structure of Compensation Contracts, *Journal of Financial Economics* 62, 453–88.

Plitch, Phyllis, 2006, "Paydirt: Sarbanes-Oxley A Pussycat On 'Clawbacks'," *Dow Jones Newswires* (June 9).

"Politics and Policy – Campaign '92: From Quayle to Clinton, Politicians are Pouncing on the Hot Issue of Top Executives' Hefty Salaries," 1992, *Wall Street Journal* (January 15).

"President Studies High Salary Curb: Tax Power is Urged as Means of Controlling Stipends in Big Industries," 1933, *New York Times* (October 23).

"Railroad Salary Report: I.C.C. Asks Class 1 Roads About Jobs Paying More Than $10,000 a Year," 1932, *Wall Street Journal* (April 28).

Rankin, Deborah, 1978, "Incentives for Business Spending Proposed in Corporate Package," *New York Times* (January 22).

"RFC Fixed Pay Limits: Cuts Required to Obtain Loans," 1933, *Los Angeles Times* (May 29).

Ricklefs, Roger, 1975, "Sweetening the Pot: Stock Options Allure Fades, So Firms Seek Different Incentives," *Wall Street Journal* (May 27).

Ricklefs, Roger, 1977, "Firms Offer Packages of Long-Term Incentives as Stock Options Go Sour for Some Executives," *Wall Street Journal* (May 9).

Robbins, L. H., 1933, "Inquiry into High Salaries Pressed by the Government," *New York Times* (October 29).

Rose, Nancy L. and Catherine D. Wolfram, 2002, Regulating Executive Pay: Using the Tax Code to Influence Chief Executive Officer Compensation, *Journal of Labor Economics* 20, S138–S175.

Rudnitsky, Howard and Richard Green, 1985, "Options Are Free, Aren't They?," *Forbes* (August 26).

Saly, P. Jane, 1994, Repricing Executive Stock Options in a Down Market, *Journal of Accounting and Economics* 18, 325–56.

"SEC Exempts Rights To Stock Appreciation From 'Insider' Curbs," 1976, *Wall Street Journal* (December 29).

"Senate Unit Votes to Tighten Rules on Stock Options," 1964 (January 15).

"Shareholder Groups Cheer SEC's Moves on Disclosure of Executive Compensation," 1992, *Wall Street Journal* (February 14).

Siconolfi, Michael, 1992, "Wall Street is Upset by Clinton's Support on Ending Tax Break for 'Excessive' Pay," *Wall Street Journal* (October 21).

Solomon, Deborah, 2005, "In SEC Complaint, Tale of Chicken Mogul Feathering His Nest – Don Tyson Took In Millions In Poorly Disclosed Perks; $84,000 in Lawn Care," *Wall Street Journal* (April 29).

Stanton, Ted, 1964, "Cash Comeback: Stock Options Begin to Lose Favor in Wake of Tax Law Revision," *Wall Street Journal* (August 10).

"U.S. Steel Guards Data on Salaries: Sends Details Confidentially to SEC Head with Request that they be Kept Secret," 1935, *New York Times* (June 2).

2 U.S. executive compensation in historical perspective
*Harwell Wells**

1 INTRODUCTION

To understand executive compensation we must understand its history. That history is surprisingly long; for almost a century Americans have fought over how much, and how, those who run giant corporations should be paid. It sweeps broadly, for questions of executive compensation are tied not only to issues of internal corporate governance but to the evolution of the U.S. industrial system, corporate disclosure and privacy, the tax system, the balance of power in the national political economy, international economic competitiveness, and Americans' basic intuitions of fairness and justice. And it is illuminating. The history of executive compensation does not merely provide colorful anecdotes or a backdrop to current debates; it is essential to understanding today's executive compensation.

The history breaks into three parts: (1) the origins of modern executive compensation in the decades before World War II, during which executive compensation developed and, in the 1930s, first attracted national attention; (2) the postwar period from the 1940s to the 1970s, when executive compensation's growth slowed and it receded as a major public issue; and (3) the current phase, beginning in the mid-1970s, when it began to grow at a faster clip even as average workers' wages stagnated, and so again became a focus for public outrage and new debates over how the giant corporation is to be governed. This chapter cannot hope to address all issues raised by the development of executive compensation. It instead recounts the growth of executive compensation over the past century, highlighting political, social, and legal contexts sometimes underplayed in accounts more tightly focused on pay level and composition, and concludes by identifying several puzzles raised by executive compensation's history that have yet to be solved.

2 ORIGINS

Before the twentieth century, there was no debate over executive compensation, for there were no executives, at least as we understand the term. The great majority of business enterprises were comparatively small, run by managers who had significant ownership stakes and whose economic rewards came chiefly through that ownership rather than a fixed salary or similar compensation. If a firm needed to recruit new managers from outside its circle of ownership, they were typically promised or given ownership interests

*   My thanks to William Bratton, Lyman Johnson, and Wyatt Wells for helpful comments on earlier versions.

upon recruitment or when ascending the ranks (H. Wells 2010, Landry 1994). While railroads, the largest corporate enterprises, developed a professional, salaried *middle* management in the nineteenth century, decisions at the top were most often made not by autonomous senior officers but by active boards of directors, whose members were, or represented, major owners (McCraw 1997, Cochran 1953).

Executives – top managers whose compensation was not chiefly derived from an ownership stake – appeared with rapid economic changes that occurred at the beginning of the twentieth century. A "great merger movement" swept the industrial sector as almost 2000 small manufacturing firms combined into approximately 150 large corporations (Lamoreaux 1988). Owners who had run the small manufacturers often wanted to cash out, and their successors were frequently experienced managers who neither owned a large part of the new firm, nor whose wealth was concentrated in it. These new managers were compensated by salaries. Proprietary management began to give way to executive management (Landry 1994).

Few gave much thought to whether these new executives should be paid differently than any other employee. Before World War I, according to the only useful survey, senior executives at large industrial firms were compensated almost completely through fixed salaries (Taussig and Barker 1925). The authors of the survey contrasted this with European management systems where top executives' pay was incentive-based, often linked to company profits. They also noted that the average executive's annual salary at a large firm (defined as having capital above $1,500,000) was $9,958 (approximately $220,000 in 2010 dollars), a sum the study's authors deemed "modest." While a fair number of surveyed executives did have significant ownership in their firms, attesting to the slow transition from proprietary to executive management, some senior managers, even at the largest firms surveyed, owned no stock at all, meaning they were compensated solely through salary[1] (Id.).

Even before World War I, however, a few prescient business leaders concluded that a fixed salary could never replicate the incentives provided by ownership (Landry 1994). As American Tobacco's James B. Duke put it, these new managers, no longer having a major ownership stake, still needed to believe that "they are part owners of the business and that their personal success and prosperity are measured by the success and prosperity they achieve for the company" (Houston 1933). To link the executive's "personal success and prosperity" to that of his firm, a number of large corporations, beginning in the 1910s with American Tobacco and U.S. Steel, adopted bonus systems for senior executives. These bonus plans typically paid the senior-most managers a percentage of annual firm profits as well as a base salary (Landry 1994, Baker 1938). The new plans, the first modern executive compensation systems, looked both backwards to older traditions of a "moral economy" that saw salaried work as servile and valorized the man who owned his own business, and forward to the twentieth century's concern with the separation of ownership and control in the modern corporation and search for ways to align managers' incentives with shareholders' interests.

---

[1]   The studies cited in this chapter employed different samples and methodologies, so comparison between them is often difficult. How much the "average CEO," "average executive," or "average worker" made in a given year depends, after all, on what sample they are drawn from.

Bonus systems gained popularity in the 1920s. By 1928, one survey of 100 large industrial companies found that 64 percent paid executives some form of bonus, most often cash linked to the firm's yearly profits, and that in 1929, at firms paying them, the bonuses constituted 42 percent of an average executive's compensation (Baker 1938). The same survey found that executive compensation appeared to have risen since the war; in 1928, at the surveyed firms, the median president's annual compensation was $69,728, equivalent to approximately $892,000 in 2010 dollars (Id.).

The available evidence gives us only a rough sense of executive compensation during the 1920s because, before the mid-1930s, data on executive compensation was not gathered or publicly available. Compensation reporting was not mandated, and firms treated executives' compensation as proprietary information, unavailable even to shareholders. Isolated reports did surface of compensation in a few industries, notably federally regulated railroads, but these were sporadic at best (H. Wells 2010).

Legal checks on executive compensation at public corporations were also minimal; while directors were prohibited from setting their own compensation, they were free to fix officers' compensation, and so long as proper procedures were followed compensation agreements were generally upheld (Ballantine 1927). The Internal Revenue Bureau (forerunner to the Internal Revenue Service) did occasionally investigate compensation practices at close corporations, to ensure that (non-deductible) dividends were not being improperly characterized as (deductible) compensation, and disallowed deductions on compensation that was not "reasonable" (Payne 1934). But its scrutiny did not extend to public corporations, and before the 1930s no other mechanism allowed shareholders to guess at, much less second guess, compensation at public firms.

3 PROTEST AND REFORM IN THE 1930s

In the 1930s a series of government investigations and shareholder lawsuits thrust executives' pay into the spotlight and generated a wave of protest and reforms that would transform executive compensation. For the first time, executive compensation became a public issue.

The conflicts can be dated to 1930, when a fairly mundane lawsuit against Bethlehem Steel, challenging not pay levels but a proposed acquisition, revealed that Bethlehem president W. R. Grace had received over $1,600,000 as compensation in 1929, and that the steel firm had paid senior managers millions in bonuses during the late 1920s, even in years when it did not pay shareholders a dividend (H. Wells 2010). Reports of Grace's "million dollar a year" income were front page news, astonishing observers and infuriating Bethlehem shareholders. It soon turned out that his pay was not unique. Later that year a lawsuit against American Tobacco revealed that the firm's president, G. W. Hill, was scheduled to receive nearly $2 million compensation that year, mostly from stock and bonus plans, compensation again not disclosed to shareholders. The next few years saw similar disclosures at other firms, culminating in Congress's 1932–33 Pecora hearings into the securities industry, where it was revealed that National City Bank's Charles Mitchell, a man blamed for much of Wall Street's frenzy leading up to the crash of 1929, had taken home more than a million dollars a year in the late 1920s (Seligman 2003). These sums were not typical – most executives made far less – but they were taken by the public as representative. A million dollars a year soon became a byword for greed.

These disclosures might have angered shareholders at any time, but coming in the midst of the Great Depression, with millions unemployed and even those with jobs facing wage cuts, they called forth widespread public outrage. Courts and the Federal government were soon compelled to deal with executive pay.

Executive compensation came before the courts when shareholders of several firms sued their boards of directors, alleging that the huge compensation packages awarded lacked a rational business purpose and so constituted "waste" under well-established corporate law doctrine forbidding, in essence, giving away corporate assets. Initially, the suits enjoyed some success. In 1933, the U.S. Supreme Court held, in *Rogers v. Hill* (a challenge to the American Tobacco payments), that compensation having "no relation to the value of services for which it is given" constituted waste. The Court did not, however, reach the question of whether Hill's pay package met this standard, instead remanding the case to the district court for that determination. While some at the time believed *Rogers* augured more vigorous judicial oversight of compensation, that promise proved false. *Rogers* settled before the district court could rehear it, and over the rest of the decade courts retreated from the case's activist implications back to their traditional deference to business judgments made by boards of directors (H. Wells 2010). Indeed, despite *Rogers* and several other cases challenging executive compensation, no court ever found an executive pay package waste on account of its size (Washington 1942).

With greater long-term effect, executive compensation also became an issue for Congress. Politicians had various motives for seizing on executive compensation, motives that shaped their understanding of just what the executive compensation "problem" was. For some, the problem was chiefly that firms receiving government assistance were paying their executives too much, notably air- and ocean-mail carriers, which were effectively subsidized through generous government contracts, and firms receiving emergency loans from the new Reconstruction Finance Corporation (RFC). The legislative fix for this was simply to limit salaries at recipients of government aid (at airlines receiving mail contracts, for instance, Congress capped executives' salaries at $17,500). Others in Congress were apparently outraged by the mere size of executives' pay packages, regardless of how earned, leading to unsuccessful proposals to cap pay through confiscatory marginal tax rates (Leff 1984, Patch 1935).

The most popular and effective response, however, turned on disclosure. Well before the New Deal, reformers had advocated greater disclosure of corporate affairs in order to rein in the power of large corporations and, in particular, to give small shareholders greater leverage over increasingly powerful corporate managers (Ripley 1926, Berle and Means 1932). The collapse of securities markets following the 1929 Crash, and the perception that the Crash occurred in part because of widespread deception in securities offerings and trading, created further support for disclosure-based reforms. Compensation reform was swept up into the national push for greater disclosure, and found its way into the new Securities Act of 1933 and the Securities Exchange Act of 1934 (H. Wells 2010, Seligman 2003). Both Acts mandated disclosure of senior officers' pay, the 1934 Act's requirements being most consequential. Beginning in 1935, the new Form 10-K, promulgated under the 1934 Act, required that public corporations disclose the compensation of the top three officers making more than $20,000 a year, including bonus payments.

While 10-Ks were not provided directly to shareholders, they were available for public review at Securities and Exchange Commission (SEC) offices in Washington. More direct disclosure soon followed; in 1938, the SEC required that annual shareholder proxies disclose compensation received by a corporation's top three income earners, and further changes in 1942 required that the proxy disclosure appear in tabular form (Dew-Becker 2009). Although the Securities Acts did the most to bring compensation figures to light, other mandates also made compensation data available. The Revenue Act of 1934, for instance, required corporations to disclose to Congress the compensation of all employees earning more than $15,000 a year, a provision not rescinded until the late 1940s (Kornhauser 2009).

Compensation disclosure made once-private pay decisions the stuff of public debate. Beginning in 1935, the *New York Times* used this information to assemble annual lists of high-paid corporate executives, in some years devoting an entire page to the data. *The New Republic* did it one better, annually publishing lists of highly compensated executives paired with pay figures of average workers in the executives' industry. In 1936, for instance, a reader could compare the annual salary of Jones & Laughlin Steel's president – $250,000 – to the average weekly wage of a steelworker – $17. The message was clear: the compensation of senior executives was closely tied to broader questions of wealth and justice, as well as economic recovery, and was a matter of legitimate concern not only for shareholders and directors, but for workers and the general public.

The 1930s outcry over executive compensation welled up from several sources. Some outrage certainly came from the spectacle of executives receiving large paychecks while deceiving shareholders or, worse, helping drive the economy into the ditch. Some, too, can be traced to anger at high pay at firms receiving government subsidies. Yet underlying much of the anger was a belief, not always articulated, that there were limits to the salary anyone should earn. In 1936, when *Fortune* magazine polled respondents to determine if they believed executives of large corporations were paid "too much or too little for the work they do," 54.5 percent answered "too much," with only 5.8 percent answering "too little." Some respondents told the pollsters that "no man can be worth $100,000 a year" (Fortune 1936).

Surprisingly, it is not clear that the public outrage, and new disclosure requirements, fundamentally changed executive compensation practices in the 1930s. Pay was, to be sure, more widely publicized, and executive compensation did drop sharply from 1929 to 1932, as profit-linked bonuses disappeared. In 1929, for instance, a survey of 100 large industrial companies found 19 executives receiving compensation above $175,000, a number that dropped to 7 in 1932, and total executive compensation at those firms in 1932 had declined by 40 percent from 1929 levels. (Interestingly, while compensation decreased, the total number of executives remained stable, suggesting that many executives took pay cuts but few lost their jobs (Baker 1938).) But by the mid-1930s, a period when the economy was still sluggish, compensation began to recover and even rise. The most thorough study of executive compensation levels and structure across the twentieth century, that of Carola Frydman and Raven Saks, which draws on SEC data beginning in 1936 (the first year of comprehensive reporting), shows that executive compensation actually rose between 1936 and 1940, with top executives in their sample of large publicly traded companies being paid compensation at levels not reached again (adjusted for inflation) until the 1970s (Frydman and Saks 2010). It should be noted, though, that the state and Federal tax burden on salaries rose sharply through the decade. In 1930, an executive working in New York City being paid $300,000 a year would have taken home approximately $241,000 after taxes; in 1940, the same pretax income would have yielded only $111,000 (Washington 1941).

4   WARTIME AND EXECUTIVE COMPENSATION'S GREAT MODERATION

World War II marked the beginning of a new era of executive compensation, one that would stretch into the 1970s. This pay regime was characterized by slower growth in compensation packages and even intermittent declines in executive compensation. During much of this period, executives' compensation would grow at a slower pace than that of the average worker.

Soon after the U.S. entered the war, it imposed wage and price controls in an attempt to stem inflationary pressures created by mass mobilization (Rockoff 1984). While some leeway existed for raising wages in particular situations, in practice these measures chiefly allowed for raising the wages of less-skilled workers (Levy and Temin 2007). Even as the controls held down compensation overall, they also began to change its composition. Wage caps often did not take into account "fringe benefits" such as health care and retirement, leading employers aiming to increase wages to offer such benefits to many workers, including executives, a trend that would continue in the postwar era (Washington and Rothschild 1962).

The war's effect on corporations, and corporate executives, was mixed. It allowed many firms to rehabilitate their tattered public images, as they dived into the war effort and rapidly retooled to produce war materiel while also funding advertising campaigns emphasizing their patriotic *bona fides* (Marchand 1998). By war's end, the anti-corporate animus generated by the Great Depression was muted, if not erased, and corporations were able reclaim political terrain lost during the 1930s (Lichtenstein 2002).

Corporations' greater power and improved profiles did not, however, translate into radically increased compensation for their leaders. From 1945 to 1950 executive pay actually decreased, and from 1950 to 1975 it increased at an anemic 0.8 percent a year (Frydman and Saks 2010). This pattern in the growth of executive compensation appears to be merely one aspect of a broader shift in the nation's income structure during these decades. During the 1940s income inequality in the United States rapidly narrowed, producing what Claudia Goldin and Robert Margo have dubbed the "Great Compression," as unskilled labor's share of national income rose while the share of income going to the top wage-earners dropped, a wage structure that persisted into the 1970s (Goldin and Margo 1990). Explanations for the moderation in executive compensation, then, likely lie not with developments particular to the corporation, such as changes in corporate governance, but rather with broader developments that altered the income structure as a whole (This development is discussed further in the Conclusion.)

As the growth of executive pay slackened, and the economy enjoyed a prolonged boom, executive compensation faded as a major public issue. This is not to say it was static. The composition of executive compensation changed from the 1940s to the 1970s, often in response to changes in tax policy. Marginal tax rates had risen as the war drew near, and remained high afterwards. From war's end to the late 1950s, the marginal tax rate for incomes over $100,000 hovered around 90 percent, and into the 1970s the marginal rate for incomes over $200,000 was 70 percent, developments that encouraged forms of compensation that would not be characterized as ordinary income (Tax Foundation 2011). The postwar period, for example, saw the continued popularity of health and life insurance and retirement plans, benefits not generally counted as taxable income (Washington and Rothschild 1962).

High marginal tax rates made popular a new kind of compensation, stock options. While stock options were occasionally offered at firms in the 1930s, they were uncommon (Baker 1938). In 1950, though, Congress amended the Internal Revenue Code to add a new section, 130A, giving favorable tax treatment to firms issuing "restricted" stock options as compensation. So long as options were issued at at least 95 percent of the stock's fair market price, were held by the recipient for two years before exercise, and the resulting stock was held for at least six months, gain from the sale of the stock would be taxed not as ordinary income but at the much lower long-term capital gains rate (in 1954, 45.5 percent, against a top marginal rate of 91 percent imposed on income above $200,000) (Clark 1986, Dean 1953). Though cash bonuses had fallen out of favor in the 1930s, firms were still looking for tools to tie executives' economic fates to the company's. Stock options did this, and the tax benefits they offered recipients made them hugely popular (even though the options were not deductible from corporate income, as was regular compensation) (Dean 1953). By 1960, a majority of firms listed on the New York Stock Exchange offered stock options plans (Washington and Rothschild 1962). While stock options were popular, however, they were not exorbitant, and appeared more as a supplement to traditional salaries than a substitute for them. One survey has found that, during the 1950s, 16 percent of executives received an options grant in a given year, with the median value of the grant 20 percent to 30 percent of total pay (Frydman and Saks 2010). The availability of stock options also suggests that lowered executive compensation in the postwar era was not merely the product of high marginal tax rates. Had firms wished to funnel more income to senior managers, they could have given them large stock options grants. That they chose not to do so suggests other mechanisms must have been operating to restrict executive pay.

Executive compensation was not in this period the hot-button issue it had been in the 1930s (and would be again starting in the 1980s), but it did attract a steady drumbeat of legal and popular criticism. Legal challenges during this period focused on stock options, as shareholder litigants claimed that such options were essentially gifts to the recipients and so a new way to violate the waste doctrine. Taking an unexpectedly activist stance, Delaware courts initially sympathized with these claims; in the "stock options cases" of 1952 (*Gottlieb v. Heyden Chemical Co.* and *Kerbs v. California Eastern Airways*), Delaware's Supreme Court imposed stricter requirements on options than on other forms of compensation, applying a "reasonableness test" to them rather than deferring to board decisions, as was otherwise typical. The court backed away from this after 1960, displaying both growing comfort with the popular compensation tool and courts' ongoing reluctance to become too involved in compensation decisions (Vagts 1983, Thomas and Wells 2011).

The most visible protests against compensation were those mounted by shareholder "gadflies," notably the Gilbert brothers and Wilma Soss (of the Federation of Woman Shareholders in American Business, Inc.), somewhat marginal figures who gained attention by protesting executive compensation at firms' annual meetings (Livingston 1958).

Perquisites were a perennial issue, attracting shareholder complaints and even becoming the focus of a Hollywood comedy about shareholders and executive compensation, 1956's *The Solid Gold Cadillac*. Stock options also drew some criticism, as observers found various flaws in their administration, alleging that they represented a gift to executives, that the incentive effect was diluted by boards' habit of repricing options when the stock price declined, and that they were treated as "costless" compensation, but in fact diluted existing shareholders' stakes (Griswold 1960). None of these protests, though, appears to have significantly affected executive compensation.

Paralleling these popular critiques were new scholarly attempts to understand executive compensation. Traditional accounts of corporate governance began by depicting the CEO and other senior executives as working under, and controlled by, the corporation's board of directors. From this came the conventional wisdom about executive pay – that it was set through arm's-length bargaining between executives and a firm's board, and approximated the value the executive provided the firm (Simon 1957, Roberts 1956). But many had their doubts; critics of the corporation repeatedly challenged this model of corporate governance, arguing that the reality was just the opposite – that directors served at the pleasure and under the thumb of the CEO (Smith 1958, Livingston 1958). This led them to dissent from the conventional wisdom about executive pay setting. Corporation law required that an executive's pay be set by the Board in a process not involving the CEO, due to restrictions on self-dealing. Despite the formal distance between the Board and the CEO, these critics doubted that meaningful negotiations took place over the CEO's compensation; it was far more accurate, they believed, to describe the CEO as setting his own salary (Washington and Rothschild 1962, Livingston 1958). Some empirical studies seemed to back this up, finding little correlation between a firm's profits and a president's pay, as would be expected were the pay set in a competitive market and linked to corporate value. Instead, there appeared to be a link between a corporation's size, as measured by sales, and the pay of its executives (Murphy 1999). This finding was taken by some to indicate that a wily executive could increase his own compensation not by making a firm more profitable, but simply by increasing sales (Baumol 1967, Williamson 1963, McGuire et al. 1962).

Executive compensation remained a minor issue through the 1960s and early 1970s, perhaps because social changes of the time overshadowed it, or because of its slow growth. This lag in growth was not a secret; while the general public seemed to believe that executives' pay was rapidly growing, and a few scholars agreed (Lewellen and Huntsman 1970), more-careful observers recognized that it had stagnated for decades, with a few even concluding, wrongly, that average executives' compensation had shrunk since the end of the war (Drucker 1977, Patton 1965, Dean 1953). The composition of pay did change in the 1960s and early 1970s, due in part to legislative changes. The Revenue Act of 1964, for instance, imposed a longer holding requirement on restricted stock options, leading to a decline in their use, while the Act's new, lower marginal rates produced higher after-tax pay for executives (Frydman and Saks 2010, Clark 1986). But this did not change the fundamental pattern of executive compensation, whose growth lagged into the 1970s.[2]

---

[2] Pension benefits and perquisites were not reported and not always taxed during this period, though executives frequently received both. It is possible, then, that compensation grew at a faster

The great puzzle of executive compensation during this time – why did it grow so slowly? – is addressed further in the Conclusion. Pay patterns would change quickly, however, in the 1970s, making executive compensation again a national issue.

5 THE MODERN ERA

Executive compensation began growing at a faster rate in the mid-1970s, starting in roughly 1973 (Frydman and Saks 2010). The general trend is well known. The average CEO was paid approximately 24 times more than an average worker in 1965, 35 times the more in 1979, 71 times more in 1989, and 299 times more than an average worker's pay at the end of the century (Mishel et al. 2009). While executive compensation dipped somewhat after the bursting of the Internet bubble in 2000 and the financial crisis of 2008–09, the trend of accelerating growth of executive compensation does not appear to have stopped. And even as executive pay rose, the income of the average American worker began to stagnate, another development which often lay behind popular discontent with executive compensation (Piketty and Saez 2007).

Rising executive compensation drew new scrutiny by the early 1980s. This scrutiny had a different tone than in the past, for the new growth in executive compensation coincided with broader economic problems. After nearly thirty relatively flush years, a series of shocks that commenced with the appearance of "stagflation" (high inflation and low growth) in the early 1970s, followed by the Arab oil embargo of 1973–74, an ongoing decline in industrial productivity, and foreign challenges to American industry, led many to conclude that the American economy, and American industry, were in serious trouble (W. Wells 2003, Galambos and Pratt 1988). Well-publicized corporate scandals, especially the collapse of the Penn Central Railroad and the discovery of widespread illegal corporate donations in the wake of Watergate, further emphasized shortcomings in corporate governance and created doubts about the competence and integrity of CEOs and Boards of Directors (Murphy 1999). Issues of executive compensation were often folded into these larger developments. Thus, attacking executives' pay became shorthand for attacking corporate governance, and reforming pay practices became seen as a way to reform the corporate economy (Shorten 1992).

As executive pay rose, so did public criticism. Some hostility surely stemmed from executive pay's new visibility, which may have begun when CEO pay packages crossed the million-dollar-a-year threshold in the late 1970s, an important psychological barrier for several decades (Vagts 1983, Loomis 1982). The main source of discontent, though, was a growing impression that executives were taking home large compensation packages while their workers suffered. In the early 1980s, media reports focused on executives at struggling smokestack industries, notably the "Big Three" automakers, who received

---

rate than discussed here, with the additional growth coming through more pensions and perks. The disparity between pre- and post-1970s growth is so great, however, that as Frydman and Saks note, "the combined value of pensions, perquisites, and other untaxed benefits would need to have been implausibly large to explain the low growth rate in pay" before the 1970s (Frydman and Saks 2010).

performance bonuses while demanding salary "give-backs" from unionized workers, and who trooped to Congress to demand protection from foreign competitors – competitors who, some noted, paid their executives far less (Witteman et al. 1984, Drucker 1984, Patton 1985). Compensation connected to corporate takeovers drew similar fire. The 1980s saw a wave of hostile takeovers of poorly performing firms. For these firms' shareholders, these takeovers frequently paid off, as they received premia for their shares, but for workers a takeover often meant lost jobs. Yet former executives of these same firms did not similarly suffer, but walked away with a new kind of compensation payment, the "golden parachute" (Johnson 1985). Why, observers asked, were executives who had run their companies into the ground receiving outsized payments to leave?

Academic attention also returned to executive compensation in the 1980s, for obvious reasons: the desire to explain the rise in compensation, and the apparent disconnect between high compensation and poor corporate performance. Much of the new work took as its starting-point the modern theory of agency costs developed in the 1970s by Michael Jensen and William Meckling, which revived and gave new rigor to the insights of Berle and Means about the divergence of managers' and shareholders' interests (Jensen and Meckling 1976). Tied to this was a renewed emphasis on shareholder value as a, or even the, main focus for corporate managers' efforts. Unlike popular criticism, which often targeted the high level of compensation, the new academic work focused on the structure of compensation, and argued that compensation's problem (to the extent there was one) was that it was poorly designed. Compensation should be structured, economists and legal scholars claimed, to incentivize senior executives to pursue strategies that would most benefit shareholders (Murphy 1999). A significant portion of the new work also doubted whether executive compensation was, in fact, poorly designed or too high (Jensen and Murphy 1984). The main thrust of new academic work was summed up by the title of a *Harvard Business Review* article by Jensen and Murphy: "CEO Incentives – It's Not How Much You Pay, but How" (Jensen and Murphy 1990).

Executive compensation both grew and changed during the 1980s. It was, clearly, higher than it had been a decade before. During the 1970s, median CEO compensation, in a sample of large publicly traded firms, was approximately $1.17 million; during the 1980s, $1.81 million; during the 1990s, $4.09 million (all in 2000 dollars) (Frydman and Saks 2010). By 1990, CEO pay had returned to (inflation-adjusted) levels not seen since the 1930s (Jensen and Murphy 1990). The composition of pay packages was also evolving, as a larger share of compensation was linked to short- and long-term shareholder value. Since the 1950s, stock options, stock grants, and other forms of incentive pay had ensured there was some performance-based component to executive pay, but the amount of both compensation and overall executive wealth linked to performance rose during the 1980s and 1990s (Frydman and Saks 2010). By the early 1990s options grants had replaced a base salary as the largest single component of executive compensation (Useem 2011, Murphy 1999).

In the early 1990s popular discontent with executive pay boiled over. Publication of executive compensation consultant-turned-critic Graef Crystal's *In Search of Excess* was followed by a raft of popular articles attacking executive compensation, many claiming that CEOs essentially set their own compensation (Crystal 1991). In 1992, President George H. W. Bush took the heads of the still-struggling "Big Three" auto companies with him on a trip to Japan, providing a hook for another round of news stories that, as they had a decade before, contrasted the U.S. CEOs' high compensation with their firms' poor performance and the comparatively low pay of Japanese CEOs (Murphy 1995). In the 1992 presidential campaign, Bill Clinton targeted executive compensation in his stump speeches, and *Time* magazine called executive pay "the populist issue no politician can resist" (Murphy 1999).

In response to populist pressures, in 1993 both Congress and the SEC adopted new measures to rein in and refocus executive compensation. Congress altered the tax rules concerning compensation, adding Section 162(m) to the Tax Code to prevent public corporations from deducting compensation in excess of $1,000,000 paid to the firms' top executives unless the compensation was both "performance-based," defined as linked to performance goals determined by a compensation committee composed solely of independent directors, and part of a plan approved in a separate shareholder vote. The SEC adopted new disclosure requirements mandating more detailed disclosure of policies used in setting compensation as well as tabular reporting of senior executive compensation (disclosure requirements having been weakened in 1983 as part of the Reagan administration's anti-regulatory campaign) (Dew-Becker 2009). The SEC also modified rules concerning shareholder proposals, allowing shareholders to include nonbinding proposals criticizing pay practices in corporate proxies (Martin and Thomas 1999). These measures did not aim directly to reduce executive pay; rather, they embraced a "pay-for-performance" approach that accepted high compensation so long as it was both incentive-based and disclosed to shareholders. In effect, the shareholder value vision of executive compensation had won out; high compensation was fine, the new measures implied, so long as it was disclosed to shareholders and designed to increase shareholder wealth. While popular discontent surely reflected a lingering belief that no-one deserved to earn as much as some executives did, proposals aimed simply at pushing high pay down by, for instance, imposing punitive taxation on firms that paid CEOs above some multiple of the average worker's wage were rejected in Congress.

Whether these reforms can be said to have succeeded depends on what their goal was. They did little to stall overall growth of executive compensation. While exact measures varied, executive compensation, as discussed above, continued its growth during the 1990s, in both absolute terms and relative to ordinary workers' wages (Mishel et al. 2009). The reforms did, however, together with ongoing public criticism, and increasingly active institutional shareholders, appear to push firms towards still greater use of performance-linked compensation. While details varied across industries, stock options and other performance-linked rewards became a larger and larger component of senior executives' pay through the 1990s and into the twenty-first century (Useem 2011, Murphy 1999).

Despite their popularity, it is not clear whether the new pay-for-performance arrangements actually tied executive pay more closely to firm performance. Options grants in particular were promoted as a way to link executive compensation to shareholder value. Several features of the new options grants, however, led critics to claim they were not as sensitive to firm performance as promised, and were open to manipulation. For example, options grants were almost never "indexed" to net out the effect of a rising stock market; without indexing, though, an executive could reap rewards from options simply because of rising stock prices in her industry or the market as a whole, not because of value created by her efforts, an effect particularly pronounced in the stock run-up of the late 1990s. Likewise, boards' willingness to reprice options after stock prices had fallen led some to conclude the grants were a heads-I-win, tails-you-lose exercise (Bebchuk and Fried 2004). Other studies, though, focused on executives' long-term accumulation of stock and options, and concluded that executives' wealth became increasingly sensitive to firm performance after 1980 (Frydman and Saks 2010, Murphy 1999).

Even after these developments public criticism of executive compensation continued unabated, again often generated by the spectacle of CEOs earning bonuses while "downsizing" firms and firing workers – this time, white-collar workers. In 1996, for instance, *Newsweek* published a cover story entitled "The Hit Men," suggesting that layoffs followed when CEOs "messed up big time," but that workers and not CEOs were the ones who suffered (Sloan et al. 1996). Union agitation over high executive pay also increased and became more media-savvy, with the AFL-CIO setting up its "paywatch" website tracking CEO compensation in 1997 (Murphy 1999).

Academic commentary was more mixed. Most economists and legal scholars who examined executive compensation during the 1990s concluded it was pretty good, meaning that executive compensation agreements "maximized the net expected economic value to shareholders after transaction costs" (Core et al. 2003, Bebchuk et al. 2002). This came to be known as the "optimal contracting" approach. A smaller, but active, group of scholars strongly disagreed, contending that executives still retained power over their Boards sufficient to systemically extract rents from their corporations – the "managerial power" view (Bebchuk and Fried 2004). Whatever the merits of these academic camps, the managerial power view more closely fitted public perceptions of executive pay.

While changes in the tax code, and the new SEC disclosure requirements, may have had a marginal effect on executive compensation, other legal attempts to curb executive pay largely failed. Shareholder litigation proved of little use in changing broader pay trends. For the most part, courts asked to second-guess a Board's compensation decision continued to adhere to the business judgment rule, declining to become entangled in compensation disputes so long as proper procedures were followed and blatant self-dealing avoided. At the end of the 1990s, it briefly appeared that this might change through the *Disney* litigation. Disney had paid Michael Ovitz $140 million when he left the firm after serving as president for less than a year, and shareholders sued the board, arguing that in both his hiring and firing Disney board members had violated their fiduciary duties and committed waste. Early on in the protracted litigation, plaintiffs received some encouragement from Delaware courts hearing the case; the Delaware Supreme Court, for instance, warned that the "sheer size" of the payment to Ovitz "pushes the envelope of judicial respect for the business judgment of directors in making compensation decisions." In 2005, however, the Delaware courts declined to find Disney's board liable for Ovitz's payments, holding that, while procedures may have been sloppy, the board did not violate its fiduciary duties or commit waste. *Disney* seemed the death-knell to hopes that courts would impose substantive limits on executive compensation, no matter how high it rose.

6   THE TWENTY-FIRST CENTURY: A BRIEF LOOK FORWARD

The Internet bubble burst in 2000, leading to a sharp drop in CEO pay in 2001–03, as stock prices plunged far below many options' strike price. The bubble's bursting, followed a year later by the collapse of Enron and other major American corporations, led to speculation that this marked a change in America's regulation of corporations and thus executive compensation. But it was not to be. Executive pay resumed its rise in 2003, and continued on an upward slope until the financial crisis of 2008–09 (whose effects are beyond the scope of this chapter). The Sarbanes-Oxley Act of 2002, passed in Enron's wake, made significant changes in aspects of corporate governance but only tweaked executive compensation practices (for instance, banning certain loans to executives and allowing for "claw-backs" of compensation after an accounting restatement). Public anger and disgust with executive pay remained, but was ineffectual. New proposals to curb executive pay arose, particularly campaigns by academics and activist institutional investors to implement "Say-on-Pay" advisory shareholder votes, but they did not enjoy significant success before the 2008–09 crisis. The options backdating scandals of 2006, during which journalists revealed that a large number of companies had backdated options grants to executives and other senior employees, created a momentary firestorm but did not result in broad-gauged compensation reform (Fried 2008). Only two developments held out any promise for real change: the adoption by the Securities and Exchange Commission, in 2006, of new and expanded compensation reporting requirements, including a mandatory "Compensation Disclosure and Analysis" (CD&A), and the change to accounting rules in 2004 that required firms to expense stock options grants to employees. This last development led some firms to move from options to restricted stock (Frydman and Jenter 2010). Whether more fundamental reforms will follow the financial crisis of 2008–09 and the Dodd-Frank "Wall Street Reform and Consumer Protection Act" remains to be seen.

7 CONCLUSION: THE LONG VIEW OF EXECUTIVE COMPENSATION

As yet, no fully satisfactory explanation for the long-term evolution of executive compensation, and especially for what appears the crucial transition from a low-growth to a high-growth pay regime in the early 1970s, has appeared. This chapter cannot essay all the implications of the history, but two are readily apparent and can be briefly addressed. First, as others have noted, the existence of such different pay regimes casts doubt on several explanations offered for rising executive compensation in the present era. Second, the historical view also points to under-explored avenues deserving further study.

To begin, the long view of executive compensation raises issues for one popular explanation for rising executive compensation, the managerial power hypothesis. In this account, rising pay is a product of bad corporate governance that allows senior corporate managers, especially CEOs, to "capture" their boards of directors, gain disproportionate power in the pay process, and set their own pay with only minimal constraints (Bebchuk et al. 2002, Crystal 1991).[3] CEOs also dominated their boards in the decades before the 1970s, however; if anything, there were fewer checks on managerial power (e.g., independent directors) during that period (Gordon 2007, Mace 1971, Livingston 1958). Yet

---

[3] The next two paragraphs draw heavily on Frydman and Saks 2010.

executive compensation stagnated during mid-century, with top compensation packages remaining below the heights reached in the early 1930s (Jensen and Murphy 1990). This appears inconsistent with the claim that managers with disproportionate power will invariably use it to raise their own pay. To be clear, the historical record does not simply refute the managerial power hypothesis. It is quite possible that as-yet-unidentified factor(s) prevented managerial power from boosting executive pay in the decades before the 1970s, and changes during that decade removed this impediment, or that new developments opened the door to more aggressive rent-seeking. Looking at the stagnation of average workers' wages beginning in the 1970s, Thomas Piketty and Emmanuel Saez have suggested, for instance, that social norms concerning pay may have changed in the 1970s, and so led to a drop in the growth of average workers' wages (Piketty and Saez 2007). Or perhaps the development of theories that justified high executive pay, so long as it was linked to shareholder value creation, removed constraints on managerial rent-seeking. These are only tentative suggestions, and may well be wrong; but advocates of the managerial power approach will need to integrate their account into the larger historical narrative – to explain why managerial power did not, apparently, lead to higher CEO pay before the mid-1970s – to validate their thesis.

The historical record also raises difficulties for theories that explain rising executive compensation by pointing to changes in the economy or markets for talent. Scholars have, at various times, explained rising compensation by attributing it to growth in firm size (Gabais and Landier 2008), to a technologically driven "market for superstars" allowing the most talented to demand more for their talents (Rosen 1981), to increased use of performance-linked pay which leads risk-averse executives to demand higher overall pay packages (Murphy 1999), or to increased return to general managerial skills (Frydman 2005). These are all plausible explanations, and some, or all, may partially explain rising executive compensation. But the historical record again raises questions (Frydman and Saks 2010). If, for instance, firm size is linked to higher compensation, why didn't pay rise in line with firm growth in the 1950s? If rising pay is linked to technological innovation enabling a market for superstars, what innovation burst upon the scene in the early 1970s to jump-start this? If increased demand for general managerial talent helps explain the growth of pay, why did pay patterns change so abruptly in the 1970s, rather than more slowly as broadly applicable managerial skills slowly became more valuable? None of these objections are conclusive, but each should be addressed.

In the long view, the break between the two pay regimes in the early 1970s appears as *the* central event in the evolution of modern executive compensation. Renewed attention to this period may identify new avenues of research. As others have noted, the change in executive compensation patterns coincided almost exactly with a broader shift in American income distribution (the two events may well be two sides of the same coin). The "Great Compression" ended in the 1970s, and income distribution began widening as increasing shares of overall income went to the top wage earners (Piketty and Saez 2007). Certainly, many scholars have recognized links between the two developments, and attempted to determine whether and to what extent rising executive compensation caused growing income inequality, though no consensus has yet been reached (Bakija et al. 2010, Kaplan and Rauh 2009).

This has led a few scholars to ask what else changed in the early 1970s that may have changed pay and income patterns. Thomas Piketty and Emmanuel Saez, and David Levy and Peter Temin, have suggested that changes in overall income distribution should be attributed not solely to economic or technological changes but to alteration in "labor market institutions and more generally social norms regarding pay inequality" (Piketty and Saez 2007; Levy and Temin 2007). The years during which executive pay was restrained were, after all, also the years during which much of the American political economy operated within an informal concordat between labor unions, big business, and the Federal government, an era in which average workers' wages rose relatively rapidly, as political and economic institutions (notably unions) encouraged wide distribution of the fruits of economic growth, and where high tax rates signaled a broader social consensus that high wages should be moderated (Levy and Temin 2007, Piketty and Saez 2007). This concordat, which some have dubbed the "Treaty of Detroit" or the "New Deal Order," began eroding in the early 1970s, undermined both by economic changes such as stagflation and slowing productivity, and by political developments, notably the erosion of union membership, that shifted political power away from the middle class and may well have further eroded the social norms that also functioned to keep high-end wages down (Hacker and Pierson 2010, Fraser and Gerstle 1990). While the exact link between the social, political, and institutional changes of the 1970s and the rise in executive compensation (and more general increase in income inequality) remains unclear, the issue is certainly worthy of further investigation. There is much yet to be learned about the history of executive compensation.

BIBLIOGRAPHY

Baker, John Calhoun. 1938. Executive Salaries and Bonus Plans. New York: McGraw-Hill.
Baker, John Calhoun and W. S. Crum. 1935. Compensation of Corporate Executives: The 1928–1932 Record. 13 *Harv. Bus. Rev.* 321.
Bakija, John, Adam Cole, and Bradley Heim. 2010. Jobs and Income Growth of Top Earners and the Causes of Changing Income Inequality. Working Paper, Williams College.
Ballantine, Henry Winthrop. 1927. Ballantine on Corporations. Chicago: Callaghan and Co.
Baumol, William J. 1967. Business Behavior, Value, and Growth. New York: Macmillan.
Bebchuk, Lucien and Jesse Fried. 2004. Pay Without Performance: The Unfulfilled Promise of Executive Compensation. Cambridge, MA: Harvard University Press.
Bebchuk, Lucien, Jesse Fried, and David Walker. 2002. Managerial Power and Rent Extraction in the Design of Executive Compensation. 66 *U. Chi. L. Rev.* 751.
Berle, Adolf A. Jr. and Gardiner C. Means. 1932. The Modern Corporation and Private Property. New York: Macmillan.
Blumstein, Michael. 1984. Executives Being Challenged on Salaries and Self-Interest. *N.Y. Times* May 8.
Chandler, Alfred A. 1977. The Visible Hand: The Managerial Revolution in American Business. Cambridge, MA: Belknap Press.
Clark, Robert Charles. 1986. Corporate Law. Boston: Little, Brown and Co.
Cochran, Thomas C. 1953. Railroad Leaders 1845–1890: The Business Mind in Action. Cambridge, MA: Harvard University Press.
Core, John E., Wayne R. Guay, and David F. Larcker. 2003. Executive Equity Compensation and Incentives: A Survey. 9 *FRBNY Policy Research* 27.
Crystal, Graef. 1991. In Search of Excess. New York: W. W. Norton.
Dean, Arthur H. 1953. Employee Stock Options. 66 *Harv. L. Rev.* 1403.
Dew-Becker, Ian. 2009. How Much Sunlight Does it Take to Disinfect a Boardroom? A Short History of Executive Compensation Regulation in America. 55 *CESInfo Econ. Stud.* 434.
Drucker, Peter F. 1977. Is Executive Pay Excessive? *Wall St. J.* May 23.
Drucker, Peter F. 1984. Reform Executive Pay or Congress Will. *Wall St. J.* April 24
Fischel, Daniel R. 1982. The Corporate Governance Movement. 35 *Vand. L. Rev.* 1259.
Fortune. 1936. Big Salaries. April 215.

Fraser, Steve and Gary Gerstle. 1990. The Rise and Fall of the New Deal Order 1930–1980. Princeton, NJ: Princeton University Press.

Fried, Jesse M. 2008. Option Backdating and Its Implications. 65 *Wash. & Lee. L. Rev.* 853.

Frydman, Carola. 2005. Rising through the Ranks: The Evolution of the Market for Corporate Executives, 1936–2003. MIT Working Paper.

Frydman, Carola. 2009. Learning from the Past: Trends in Executive Compensation over the 20th Century. 55 *CESInfo Econ. Stud.* 458.

Frydman, Carola and Dirk Jenter. 2010. CEO Compensation. Working Paper.

Frydman, Carola and Raven Saks. 2010. Executive Compensation: A New View from a Long-Run Perspective, 1936–2005. 23 *Rev. Fin. Stat.* 2100.

Gabais, Olivier and Augustin Landier. 2008. Why Has CEO Pay Increased So Much? 123 *Q. J. Econ.* 1.

Galambos, Louis and Joseph Pratt. 1988. The Rise of the Corporate Commonwealth: United States Business and Public Policy in the 20th Century. New York: Basic Books.

Goldin, Claudia and Robert Margo. 1992. The Great Compression: The Wage Structure in the United States at Mid-Century. 107 *Q. J. Econ.* 1.

Gordon, Jeffrey. 2007. The Rise of Independent Directors in the United States 1950–2005. 59 *Stan. L. Rev.* 1465.

Gordon, Robert A. 1940. Ownership and Compensation as Incentives to Corporate Executives. 54 *Q. J. Econ.* 455.

Gordon, Robert A. 1945. Business Leadership in the Large Corporation. Washington, DC: Brookings Institute.

Gordon, Robert A. 1961. Business Leadership in the Large Corporation. Berkeley: University of California Press.

Griswold, Erwin N. 1960. Are Stock Options Getting Out of Hand? *Harv. Bus. Rev.* 49 (Nov./Dec.).

Hacker, Jacob S. and Paul Pierson. 2010. Winner-Take-All Politics: How Washington Made the Rich Richer – and Turned Its Back on the Middle Class. New York: Simon & Schuster.

Houston, R.E. 1933. The American Tobacco Company Case: A Study in Profit-Sharing. Yale Law School thesis.

Jensen, Michael C. and William H. Meckling. 1976. Theory of the Firm: Managerial Behavior, Agency Costs, and Ownership Structure. 3 *J. Fin. Ec.* 305.

Jensen, Michael and Kevin Murphy. 1984. The Flap over Executive Pay. *N. Y. Times* May 20.

Jensen, Michael and Kevin Murphy. 1990. CEO Incentives – It's Not How Much You Pay, But How. 68 *Harv. Bus. Rev.* 138.

Johnson, Kenneth C. 1985. Golden Parachutes and the Business Judgment Rule: Toward the Proper Standard of Review. 94 *Yale L.J.* 909.

Kaplan, Steven N. and Joshua Rauh. 2009. Wall Street and Main Street: What Contributes to the Rise in the Highest Incomes? 23 *Rev. Fin. Stat.* 1004.

Khurana, Rakesh. 2002. Searching for a Corporate Savior: The Irrational Quest for Charismatic CEOs. Princeton, NJ: Princeton University Press.

Kornhauser, Marjorie. 2009. Shaping Public Opinion and the Law: How a "Common Man" Campaign Ended a Rich Man's Law. 73 *Law & Contemp Prob.* 123.

Lamoreaux, Naomi. 1988. The Great Merger Movement in American Business 1895–1904. New York: Cambridge University Press.

Landry, John A. 1994. Corporate Incentives for Managers in American Industry, 1900–1940. Providence, RI: Brown University PhD dissertation.

Leff, Mark A. 1984. The Limits of Symbolic Reform: The New Deal and Taxation, 1933–1939. New York: Cambridge University Press.

Levy, Frank and Peter Temin. 2007. Inequality and Institutions in 20th Century America. MIT Department of Economics Working Paper 07-17.

Lewellen, Wilbur and Blaine Huntsman. 1970. Managerial Pay and Corporate Performance. 60 *Am. Ec. Rev.* 710.

Lichtenstein, Nelson. 2002. The State of the Union: A Century of American Labor. Princeton, NJ: Princeton University Press.

Livingston, James. 1958. The American Stockholder. New York: Lippincott.

Loomis, Carol. 1982. The Madness of Executive Compensation. *Fortune* July 12 4252.

Mace, Myles L. 1971. Directors: Myth and Reality. Boston: Harvard Business School Press.

Marchand, Roland. 1998. Creating the Corporate Soul. Berkeley, CA: University of California Press.

Martin, Kenneth and Randall Thomas. 1999. The Effect of Shareholder Proposals on Executive Compensation. 67 *U. Cin. L. Rev.* 1021.

McCraw, Thomas K. 1997. American Capitalism, in Creating Modern Capitalism, Thomas K. McCraw, ed. Cambridge, MA: Harvard University Press.

McGuire, Joseph W., John S.Y. Chiu, and Alvar Ebling. 1962. Executive Income, Sales, and Profits. 52 *Am. Ec. Rev.* 753.

Mishel, Lawrence, Jared Bernstein, and Heidi Shierholz. 2009. The State of Working America 2008/2009. Ithaca, NY: Cornell University Press.

Murphy, Kevin J. 1995. Politics, Economics, and Executive Compensation. 63 *U. Cin. L. Rev.* 713.

Murphy, Kevin J. 1999. Executive Compensation, in 3b Handbook of Labor Economics, Orley Ashenfelter and David Card, eds. Elsevier.

Patch, Buel W. 1935. Control of Corporate Salaries, 2 *Editorial Research Reports* 235.

Patton, Arch. 1961. Men, Money, and Motivation. New York: McGraw-Hill.

Patton, Arch. 1965. Deterioration in Top Executive Pay. 32 *Harv. Bus. Rev.* 106.

Patton, Arch. 1985. Those Million-Dollar-a-Year Executives. 63 *Harv. Bus. Rev.* 56.

Payne, Philip M. 1934. Corporate Salaries and Bonuses and the Federal Income Tax. 12 *Tax. Mag.* 301.

Piketty, Thomas and Emmanuel Saez. 2007. Income and Wage Inequality in the United States, 1913–2002, in Top Incomes Over the Twentieth Century, A. B. Atkinson and T. Piketty, eds. New York: Oxford University Press.

Ripley, William Z. 1926. Main Street and Wall Street. New York: Atlantic.

Roberts, David R. 1956. A General Theory of Executive Compensation Based on Statistically Tested Propositions. 70 *Q. J. Econ.* 270.

Roberts, David R. 1959. Executive Compensation. Glencoe, IL: Free Press.

Rockoff, Hugh. 1984. Drastic Measures: A History of Wage and Price Controls in the United States. New York: Cambridge University Press.

Rosen, Sherwin. 1981. The Economics of Superstars. 71 *Am. Ec. Rev.* 845.

Seligman, Joel. 2003. The Transformation of Wall Street: A History of the Securities and Exchange Commission and Modern Corporate Finance. New York: Aspen.

Shorten, Richard L. Jr. 1992. An Overview of the Revolt Against Executive Compensation. 45 *Rutgers L. Rev.* 121.

Simon, Herbert. 1957. The Compensation of Executives. 20 *Sociometry* 32.

Sloan, Allan, Anne Underwood, John McCormick, and Deborah Branscombe. 1996. The Hit Men. *Newsweek* February 26.

Smith, Everett. 1958. Put the Board of Directors to Work! 36 *Harv, Bus. Rev.* 41.

Taussig, F.W. and W. S. Barker. 1925. American Corporations and their Executives: A Statistical Inquiry. 40 *Q. J. Econ.* 1.

Tax Foundation. 2011. Federal Income Tax Rates History 1913–2011. http://www.taxfoundation.org/files/fed_individual_rate_history_nominal&adjusted-20110909.pdf.

Thomas, Randall and Harwell Wells. 2011. Executive Compensation in the Courts. 95 *Minn. L. Rev.* 846.

Useem, Michael. 2011. The Ascent of Shareholder Monitoring and Strategic Partnering: The Dual Function of the Corporate Board, in Sage Handbook on Corporate Governance, Thomas Clarke and Douglas Branson, eds.

Vagts, Detlev. 1983. Challenges to Executive Compensation: For the Markets or the Courts? 8 *J. Corp. L.* 231.

Washington, George T. 1941. Corporate Executives' Compensation. New York: Ronald Press.

Washington, George T. 1942. The Corporate Executive's Living Wage. 54 *Harv. L. Rev.* 733.

Washington, George T. and Henry Rothschild. 1952. Compensating the Corporate Executive. 2d ed. New York: Ronald Press.

Washington, George T. and Henry Rothschild. 1962. Compensating the Corporate Executive. 3d ed. New York: Ronald Press.

Wells, Harwell. 2010. "No Man Can be Worth $1,000,000 a Year": The Fight over Executive Compensation in 1930s America. 44 *U. Rich. L. Rev.* 669.

Wells, Wyatt. 2003. American Capitalism 1945–2000. Chicago: Ivan R. Dee.

Williamson, Oliver E. 1963. Managerial Discretion and Business Behavior. 53 *Am. Ec. Rev.* 1032.

Witteman, Paul A., Adam Zagorin, and Stephen Koepp. 1984. Those Million-Dollar Salaries. *Time* May 7.

3 Executive pay and corporate governance reform in the UK: what has been achieved?

Steve Thompson

1 INTRODUCTION

The purpose of this chapter is to evaluate the consequences of corporate governance reform on the remuneration and tenure of executives in the UK. The country has now experienced 20 years of corporate governance reforms since the establishment of the Cadbury committee in 1991. A consistent theme over this time has been the need to make the employment contracts of senior executives, and particularly their remuneration practices, more reflective of the interests of the shareholders they serve and to link executive rewards more closely to performance outcomes. This is explicitly formulated as a principle of the *UK Corporate Governance Code*, which currently requires:

> Levels of remuneration should be sufficient to attract, retain and motivate directors of the quality required to run the company successfully, but a company should avoid paying more than is necessary for this purpose. A significant proportion of executive directors' remuneration should be structured so as to link rewards to corporate and individual performance. (Financial Reporting Council, June 2010)

A battery of direct and indirect measures has been deployed to further these ends. These include the progressive strengthening of the importance, independence and responsibilities of non-executive directors, both absolutely and relative to the position of executives. Successive versions of the *Code* have become increasingly more prescriptive about the appropriate processes for determining executive rewards, structuring incentives, specifying tenure and minimizing executives' influence on the setting of their own remuneration. Supporting legislation and regulation has strengthened shareholder voice, most especially by the introduction of a mandatory 'say on pay' vote on the remuneration committee reports at the shareholders' annual general meeting (AGM). Indeed, taken together, the corporate governance reforms on pay represent an attempt to modify the internal behaviour of UK companies that is quite unprecedented in areas without an explicit social or environmental welfare aspect.

The thoroughgoing intention of the reforms is not in question. Nor, as will be seen, is their success in altering the observable institutional governance arrangements of UK companies. What is less clear, however, is what the underlying consequences of these changes have been, particularly in securing fundamental alterations to the way the executive labour market operates. Academics from very different perspectives have expressed scepticism about the prospects for effective change. Proponents of the 'rents capture' view of corporate governance, such as Bebchuk and Fried (2004), have emphasized that change is ultimately implemented by senior executives who typically possess a powerful influence over their boards and a strong incentive to preserve the status quo. From the contrasting ('Chicago') perspective it is argued that where governance changes enhance shareholder value they will tend to be implemented without the need for external intervention. Indeed, after Jensen and Meckling (1976), the introduction of value-maximizing corporate governance arrangements is predicted to coincide with the initial public offering of outside equity by the original owner. Thus, externalities apart, this view leaves little scope for beneficial changes except in the event of unforeseen circumstances (Hart, 1995). On such a view the shareholder-principals might be expected to be unenthusiastic about reforms which they have not identified as being worthy of implantation.

This chapter sets out to evaluate the empirical evidence of the effects of 20 years' changes in the UK. In doing so it will seek to explore the effects of reforms on:

- The role of independent non-executive directors in determining executive rewards.
- The sensitivity of executive remuneration to company performance and company size.
- Executive job tenure, including contract length, ease of dismissal and compensation for loss of position.
- The role shareholders in the executive pay determination process, including the introduction of 'say on pay'.

Many of the corporate governance changes discussed have been adopted elsewhere and the chapter will conclude with a review of empirical evidence of the effectiveness of these developments.

2   REFORMS AND PROCESS

2.1   The Rationale and Chronology of Reforms

'Managers write their contracts with one hand then sign with the other' – Oliver Williamson (1985).

It is now almost 20 years since the publication of the Cadbury report (1992) began the process of strengthening the independence and responsibilities of non-executive directors and building the structures intended to enable them to operate effectively. Much of this effort has been explicitly or implicitly concerned with the arrangements determining executive compensation and it has been overwhelmingly directed at trying to dismantle the kind of cosy arrangement Williamson described. Before Cadbury, executive rewards in the UK were largely treated as a private matter, with companies revealing very little beyond their statutory obligation to report total board remuneration and the pay of the (unnamed) 'highest paid director'. In the decades that have followed, increased disclosure, covering all elements of the compensation package, publication of a formal remuneration committee report and intense scrutiny of these by media, governance consultancies and pressure groups have ensured that senior executive rewards are very much in the public domain.

Cadbury also set the precedent for future governance change by seeking to incorporate 'best practice' guidelines in the form of a code which, though technically voluntary, was expected to form the default position for companies with a listing on the London Stock

Exchange. Subsequent governance reform has largely involved a progressive tightening of this code with its 'comply or explain' expectation. The 'say on pay' changes, described below, were given legal force and represent a rare exception to this generalization. The chronology of the *Code*'s development and its principal features relevant to executive remuneration may be briefly outlined.

Following a series of high-profile corporate scandals at the end of the 1980s, the Financial Reporting Council established a committee under Sir Adrian Cadbury, formerly chair of the eponymous confectionery firm, to review the 'financial aspects of corporate governance . . .' The ensuing report recommended the establishment of a code of good practice for quoted companies. It stopped short of calling for statutory force for its recommendations; instead it put the onus on the companies' managements with a 'comply or explain' requirement. The resulting Cadbury *Code* required compliant firms to establish a remuneration committee 'made up wholly or mainly of non-executive directors', which individuals were to be independent of management and appointed via a formal process for fixed terms. Furthermore, the *Code* (para. 3.2) specified 'full and clear disclosure of total emoluments . . . including pension contributions and stock options' for the chairman and highest paid director. However, events overtook the *Code* and increasing public dissatisfaction at rapidly growing executive rewards, especially options gains during the 1990s bull market and particularly in the newly privatized public utilities, led directly to the establishment of a second committee under Sir Richard Greenbury, ex-chairman of retailer Marks and Spencer, and a revision of the *Code*.

Among other things, the post-Greenbury *Code* required the publication of remuneration committee membership, now exclusively drawn from non-executives without financial involvement other than as shareholders, which was to be separately identified when they stood for re-election. The remuneration committee was to have access to professional advice and be required to consult the chairman and/or the CEO. Furthermore, the committee chair was to be accountable to the shareholders' annual general meeting (AGM). Greenbury also sought to end the windfall gains that option holders were enjoying as the stock market grew in the mid-1990s by replacing executive stock options with long-term incentive plans (LTIPs), in which rewards were linked to performance comparators. A review of the working of the Cadbury–Greenbury reforms by Hampel (1998) largely reiterated the earlier principles on director remuneration. It was unsympathetic to the idea of subjecting remuneration committee reports to shareholder approval, an innovation which occurred in 2002 after growing evidence of obfuscation of remuneration issues by many companies.[1]

The Higgs report (2003) set out good practice for the recruitment of non-executive directors (NEDs) and the performance of their duties, including detailed guidelines for the operation of the remuneration committee. These provisions were incorporated into the 2003 version of the *Combined Code*. Thereafter it required that non-executive directors (NEDs) serving on the remuneration committee meet a test of independence, based

---

[1]   Pensions and Investment Research Consultants (PIRC), a shareholder pressure group, reported that by 1998 only 2 percent of companies surveyed put critical remuneration committee reports to a shareholder vote. The same survey suggested lower standards of independence for remuneration committee members than Greenbury intended – see Chambers (2003) pp. 124–5.

on a lack of material or business association with management and, more controversially, no more than nine years' service to avoid 'capture.' Moreover, companies were required to publish details of non-executives' independence, noting departures, if any, from the best-practice guidelines.

2.2 The Evidence

Empirical testing of the role of governance factors in the pay determination process has generally taken the form of running an executive pay equation of the form:

Payit = f(Governance, Size, Performance, Controls)

where *Payit* represents CEO rewards (variously measured) at firm *i* in year *t*, *Governance* is a vector of variables describing such features as the number or relative strength of outsiders to insiders on the board and/or the remuneration committee; and *Size*, *Performance* and firm and individual characteristic *Controls* are added as appropriate. Such has been the compliance with the requirements of successive versions of the Code that cross-sectional variation in *measurable* governance arrangements declines over time.

Cadbury's suggestions did not, of course, arise in a vacuum and some UK companies had adopted comparable arrangements prior to the *Code*. A study by Main and Johnston (1993), using a cross-section of 220 UK companies in 1990, suggested that NEDs already comprised about 37 percent of board members and that 45 percent of boards with three or more such NEDs had a formally constituted remuneration committee. Furthermore, Main (1993) found that where remuneration committees existed they were (numerically) dominated by NEDs. However, even then it was unclear that such arrangements acted to curb executive pay in the interests of shareholders, or even to influence its composition. Main and Johnston (1993) reported that pay *rose* with both possession of a remuneration committee and the NED-to-total board membership ratio.[2] Furthermore, they found no tendency for the use of options to rise with the presence of a remuneration committee.

Analyses of the effects of *Governance* variables during the period of initial diffusion of the governance reforms present a mixed picture, with the results seemingly sensitive to sampling and the choice of estimator. Benito and Conyon (1999), using fixed effects (FE) estimation for a panel of 211 UK firms, 1985–1994, found no effect from the introduction of a remuneration committee, while Conyon and Peck (1998), with a fixed effects estimator for an overlapping sample of 94 firms 1991–94, reported that CEO pay *fell* with the proportion of insiders on the remuneration committee. By contrast, Conyon (1997a), using a generalized method of moments (GMM) estimator with a panel of 213 UK firms 1988–93 reports a small, but statistically significant, negative impact of remuneration committee introduction on CEO cash rewards. A follow-up study by the same author (Bonet and Conyon (2005)), using 505 firms 1999–2002, reports a significant positive effect for the numbers of insiders on the remuneration committee.

---

[2]   At the date of their sample, both the governance arrangements and the use of performance-related rewards might be considered organizational innovations; so that a positive correlation between good governance practice and executive remuneration may not be too surprising.

Gregory-Smith (2010) analyses the impact of director independence on CEO rewards for the FTSE 350[3] over the years 1996–2008, a period that spans the progressive tightening of the *Combined Code*. He further contrasts the self-reported incidence of independence with a more rigorous definition provided by Manifest, a corporate governance consultancy. Approximately 75 percent of over 40,000 NED-years in his sample met their companies' independence test compared to 55 percent on Manifest's criteria.

Gregory-Smith reports that the proportion of insiders on the remuneration committee has no effect on total CEO rewards, *whichever* definition of independence is employed: a result that is totally robust to the choice of estimator. A generally similar picture emerges with the proportion of insiders on the board. Here a simple pooled OLS estimation does yield a negative effect; but this disappears when the panel characteristics are recognized with the choice of a FE or GMM estimator. In short, Gregory-Smith finds no satisfactory evidence that increasing the independence of non-executive directors has reduced executive pay.

3   REFORMS AND OUTCOME 1: REWARDING SUCCESS

In evaluating the impact of UK corporate governance reforms on executive rewards it is important to recognize that these have been motivated less by the objective of limiting the growth of executive pay than by a desire to alter the process of pay determination. In general the aim has been to increase the importance and effectiveness of performance-related elements in the remuneration package, whilst limiting the potential for such instruments to generate 'undeserved' windfall gains. As noted above, reformers have further sought to make executive pay and its determination more transparent, whilst increasing professional involvement in setting rewards and generally trying to eliminate the influence of executives over their own pay awards. There have been no explicit restrictions on the overall level of pay; although, as indicated, one of the *Code*'s principles states that companies should only pay what is necessary 'to attract, retain and motivate' executives of sufficient quality to run them successfully.

There is a substantial literature, going back to Cosh (1975), which establishes very clearly that the most reliable predictor of executive rewards in the UK, as elsewhere, has been firm size. Indeed Sherwin Rosen (1992) considered this to be one of the most persistent empirical regularities in economics. By contrast, the pay–performance relationship has traditionally turned out to be weak and unstable. To the extent that the underlying intention of corporate governance changes has been to strengthen the alignment of interests of shareholders and executives, it seems appropriate to judge the effectiveness of the resulting institutional changes by assessing their impact in substituting performance for size in executive pay determination.

In assessing the reforms, it is immediately apparent that UK firms have proved highly compliant with the institutional requirements of successive versions of the *Code*. Conyon (1997b) documented the rapid adoption of the initial Cadbury recommendations, most

---

[3]   Since the 2003 Code provided rather weaker provisions for smaller companies outside the FTSE 350, this seems the appropriate population for analysis.

especially those relating to the establishment and operation of a remuneration committee dominated by non-executive directors. There was a similar response to the amended *Code* after Greenbury's (1995) call for the replacement of executive stock options by long-term incentive plans (LTIPs), in which vesting depended on some comparative indicators, usually involving the performance of industry rivals. Notwithstanding the importance of stock options in the UK executives' reward package by the mid-1990s (Main et al. (1996)), these were overwhelmingly replaced by LTIPs within two or three years (Conyon and Murphy (2000), Buck et al. (2003)).

If the effect of the reforms has been to encourage boards to reward performance, it would be expected that we should observe a strengthening of the pay–performance relationship and a weakening of the pay–size relationship over the two decades since Cadbury. Before reviewing the evidence, four measurement issues should be noted.

First, in valuing non-cash rewards many studies use a Black–Scholes-based approach to convert performance-contingent awards into an *ex ante* cash equivalent. However, even a straightforward executive stock option violates several of the Black and Scholes (1973) assumptions for European call option valuation. Most obviously, executives cannot short-sell their own stock and they typically hold asset portfolios in which investments (both financial and human capital) in their own firm dominate. This, as Murphy (1999) shows, implies that the option's subjective valuation by its recipient depends upon her individual coefficient of risk aversion, suggesting that the value to recipients will vary considerably (usually downwards) from the cost to the shareholders. Moreover, the more LTIPs diverge from pure stock options the more complex the valuation process required.

Second, since income is a flow concept, remuneration studies normally include new option grants at an appropriate valuation. However, Main et al. (1996) argue that the income definition should be extended to cover each year's *changes* in the stock options held, that is adjusted to accommodate realized value changes on options exercised or lapsed over the period. They argue that without such an adjustment researchers cannot expect to find a meaningful pay–performance sensitivity. Their own work (including Buck et al. (2003)) augments the pay variable accordingly. However, this approach raises several methodological difficulties, not least by causing rewards received to deviate further in value and time from their sanctioning by the remuneration committee.[4] Gregg et al. (2005) point out that it also introduces a purely mechanical relationship between share performance and executive compensation.

Third, ignoring the option element of remuneration, as some studies have done, may not matter until 2001 since until then the maximum yearly option grant was a set multiplier of base pay.[5]

Fourth, studies vary in their choice of firm performance measure: some using a stock-market-based approach and others an accounting ratio. A market-based measure is most obviously relevant, since the stock price is presumably the item of greatest interest to the shareholders. However, the use of shareholder return measures does raise timing issues:

---

[4]   It also arguably involves double counting if the option value at t reflects the possibility of gains on vesting at $t+1$.

[5]   Strictly the ABI guidelines required that the total value of shares covered was not to exceed four times base salary, excluding bonuses – see Girma et al. (2007) p. 70.

if favourable outcomes are anticipated prior to delivery, any stock price appreciation may predate the year of deliberation of the board's remuneration committee.

While due allowance must be given for the above measurement issues, estimates of the pay–performance sensitivity suggested it was at best weak before corporate governance reform started in 1992. Conyon and Gregg (1994) and Conyon and Leech (1994) each found a very small significant effect while Gregg et al. (1993) suggested that it had weakened after 1983 and had effectively disappeared by the eve of the Cadbury report in 1991. Main et al. (1996) reported a much larger effect in the 1980s, but as noted above, their compensation variable includes exercised option gains which necessarily reflect share price performance. Benito and Conyon (1999), by contrast, report a strengthening over the overlapping period 1985–95. Conyon and Sadler (2001) found evidence of considerable inter-firm heterogeneity.

More-recent studies that have explicitly looked at the effect of the governance reforms report little evidence of any strengthening in the pay–performance sensitivity. Girma et al. (2007), using an unbalanced panel of 992 firms between 1981 and 1996, find that the rate of growth of cash compensation slowed after 1992 (from 7.9 percent to 5.5 percent) but with considerable variation across the sample. However, using a fixed-effects estimator they report a weak pay growth–profit growth relationship for CEOs with no evidence of a 'Cadbury effect' at the mean. When they split their sample by size and re-estimate using quantile regression, to accommodate sample heterogeneity, Girma et al. report a small but statistically significant pay–performance relationship for CEOs whose cash pay exceeds the 50th percentile. They also find weak evidence of a post-Cadbury increase in pay–performance sensitivity for larger company CEOs lower down the pay distribution. Gregg et al. (2005) using a broadly similar approach across 415 firms estimate yearly CEO pay–shareholder return elasticity by year between 1995 and 2002. They report a sharp rise to 0.18 in 1997, but thereafter a steep fall such that it averages under 0.05 between 2000 and 2002.

Buck et al. (2003) do report much higher pay–performance sensitivities using a cross-sectional study of 287 companies in 1997–98, a year chosen to coincide with the replacement of stock options by LTIPs, and their option-gain adjusted dependent variable. However, as the same methodology led these authors to report a high pay–performance sensitivity across 59 UK firms 1981–89 (Main et al. (1996)) and since their results suggested that the presence of an LTIP *lowered* pay–performance sensitivity in 1997–98, they also conclude that corporate governance reform had not aligned manager and owner interest more effectively than before.

The general failure to find evidence of an enhanced performance effect is matched by a stubborn persistence in the pay–size elasticity. Gregg et al. (2005) find this was still averaging 0.2 in 2000–02, a similar figure to Buck et al. (2003) in 1997–98. Girma et al. (2007), whose sample includes smaller companies, report a similar 0.17 with no significant post-Cadbury effect at the mean but an *increase* for larger companies. A companion paper (Girma et al. (2006)) distinguishes growth via merger from organic growth and suggests that the former is separately rewarded in CEO pay rounds, arguably reinforcing the empire-building incentive implicit in high pay–size elasticities. Girma et al. (2007, p. 80) conclude: ". . .[I]f the underlying intention of Cadbury in altering the pay-setting machinery was to increase incentives to boost firm performance and reduce incentives to engage in managerial empire-building then it was unsuccessful."

The contrast between the reformers' success in achieving corporate compliance with the *Code* and their apparent failure to alter the outcome of the pay determination process is disappointing. It is tempting to think that the professionalization of pay determination may itself have contributed. Consultants looking for objective and easily measurable comparators are likely to stress size. If, as some researchers have suggested, there is an additional 'Lake Wobegon' effect[6] whereby consultants and boards agree that executive remuneration should be above the mean for the company's size class, a mechanism for inefficient pay determination is complete.

4   REFORMS AND OUTCOME 2: PENALIZING FAILURE

An enduring concern over two decades of UK corporate governance reforms has been the desire to reduce severance packages for departing executives. Where these are sufficiently generous they would appear to undermine the incentive effects of performance-related executive pay, both directly by rewarding apparent failure and indirectly by raising the costs of termination and so increasing the reluctance of boards to dismiss errant CEOs. At the same time, it has been recognized that compensation for loss of office does serve several important functions.

First, it facilitates the rapid replacement of underperforming managers without legal complication. Providing a legally robust definition of failure is inevitably problematic, not least because corporate performance is typically attributable to the efforts of many and not merely those of the CEO. Amongst other things this helps to explain why outgoing CEOs are rarely 'dismissed' but leave accompanied by euphemisms such as 'resigned with immediate effect to explore other opportunities.'

Second, a 'golden parachute' compensation for loss of office reduces the incentive for incumbent management to oppose any takeover approach, thus increasing the probability of the target's shareholders enjoying a bid premium and reducing the value destruction that might otherwise accompany a hostile bid (Jensen (1988)).

Third, the availability of compensation for loss of office acts as an inducement to risk-averse executives who might otherwise be reluctant to take positions in companies with volatile performance.

In the early 1990s, CEOs were frequently employed on contracts of three or even five years' duration (Department of Trade and Industry (2003)) and since contract length outstanding was the obvious determinant of compensation for loss of office, many outgoing CEOs were seen to be departing with multiples of their annual remuneration.[7] Furthermore, since liquidated damages – i.e. a payment unaffected by the recipient's future earnings – overwhelmingly dominated awards reduced by mitigation, it was not unusual for ousted executives to pocket their compensation and secure almost immediate reemployment elsewhere.

Unusually for UK governance reforms, the attack on generous severance was initiated

---

[6]   Reviewed in Schaefer and Hayes (2009).
[7]   In 1993 an IDS survey reported that the typical compensation for the loss of a three-year rolling contract was two years' salary plus the expected level of any bonus payments.

by shareholders. Hermes Asset Management, a pension fund, wrote to the FTSE 100 companies threatening to vote against three-year deals. The Greenbury report (1995) reiterated these concerns, suggesting that contracts should not exceed one year rolling; a recommendation that was soon incorporated into the *Combined Code* of best practice. After some initial reluctance,[8] this secured a high degree of compliance, with the average contract length falling to 12 months by 2003 (see Thompson (2005)).

Other aspects of compensation for loss of office have proved more durable. Hampel considered the case for mitigation but concluded that a preference on all sides for a clean break in the event of termination favoured a liquidated damages settlement. The House of Commons Select Committee (see Department of Trade and Industry (2003)) revisited this and expressed the hope that mitigation should occur; although submissions to the contemporaneous Green Paper argued that mitigation would be inefficient if its provisions discouraged ousted executives from seeking work until its provisions were exhausted. Similarly, the inclusion of forgone bonus payments is controversial. The Select Committee suggested that the use of suitably rigorous targets would obviate the problem since unsuccessful bosses who were then ousted would be unlikely to have earned such bonus payments.

The combination of lower compensation costs in the event of dismissal and greater powers and independence for non-executive directors on company boards, perhaps together with increasing shareholder activism, suggests that executive tenure *should* have become less secure as a result of corporate governance reforms. Two recent studies tend to confirm this. Dahya et al. (2002) use a sample of 460 UK firms, 1989–96, divided into those whose attributes are always Cadbury-compliant (150 cases) for their years of inclusion, those which never achieved compliance (22) and those which changed their arrangements to achieve compliance (288). The observations are further split into pre- (1989–92) and post-Cadbury (1993–96) sub-periods. To the expressed surprise of the authors, they find that not merely did management turnover increase in the post-Cadbury era, but that it rose following the adoption of Cadbury recommendations among the adopting sub-sample and performance sensitivity increased among these firms. Moreover, board composition was a significant driver of management turnover, which rose with the proportion of outsiders on the board. This stands in contrast to an earlier study by Franks et al. (2001) which failed to find an explanatory role for board composition in an analysis of turnover rates among poorly performing UK firms between 1988 and 1993, i.e. largely prior to the start of the reforms.

A difficulty with equating executive turnover rates with punishment levels is that managers leave for many reasons other than dismissal, some of which – such as being headhunted by another firm – seem likely to be positively related to their firm's performance. Gregory-Smith et al. (2009) use company and secondary sources to classify the causes of CEO departure for 1179 individuals working for 590 companies between 1996 and 2005. They then aggregate these into three categories – 'dismissal', 'retirement' and 'other'. They find, as expected, that completed CEO tenure falls significantly between 1996–2001 and 2001–05. Furthermore, tenure increases sharply with firm performance across quar-

---

[8]   A PIRC survey in 1998 found that almost one half of companies questioned were still to impose one-year contracts – see Chambers (2003) p. 125.

tiles: the hazard for those CEOs in the top quartile is only 20 percent of that experienced by those in the bottom quartile. Indeed, the latter now face a substantial risk: those remaining in the bottom quartile for two consecutive years face a greater than 50 percent chance of loss of office within a year. The authors then run a competing risk analysis which allows for multiple exit states with separate covariate effects. This confirms that the risk of a forced departure falls sharply with performance, a relationship not found for retirements or other departures. The authors also find that governance institutions matter, with variables representing the proportions of insiders and current CEO appointees *negatively* impacting dismissal risk and average NED tenure having a *positive* effect. Finally, Gregory-Smith et al. also find that the performance impact on the dismissal hazard falls with job tenure, consistent with an entrenchment effect among CEOs. If such an interpretation is correct, this would hint at systemic benefits from corporate governance reforms that reduce the power of CEOs relative to their boards.

In short, therefore, the empirical evidence suggests that whilst CEO remuneration has continued to grow during two decades of governance reforms, in other ways life has become tougher at the top. The reforms have cut back contract length and with it the entitlement to compensation on job termination; although mitigated damages remain the exception not the rule. Furthermore, this lowering of the relative costs of dismissal has been accompanied by an overall reduction of job tenure and an increase in the likelihood of termination for poor performance. Perhaps surprisingly, board composition does appear to have a significant influence in the direction the reformers would anticipate, with CEO tenure apparently falling with indicators of board independence.

5   EVALUATING 'SAY ON PAY'

Most projected corporate governance reforms are intended to alter the balance of power within the board of directors by increasing either the independence or the functions of the NEDs or they aim to extend the information available to NEDs and shareholders. Hence any strengthening of the voice of the shareholder-principals is strictly an indirect affair. By contrast, the 'say on pay' movement aims to make executive pay arrangements subject to the direct approval of a shareholders' vote. The movement has gathered considerable momentum across western economies, most recently because of the global financial crisis. There have been ongoing concerns that incentive pay arrangements were implicated in the excesses of risk-taking that preceded the financial crisis of 2008–09.[9] Since that crisis precipitated a wave of bail-outs of troubled financial institutions, there has been a further concern that banks in receipt of public funds should not revert to their former pay practices. In the USA, for example, those institutions covered by the Troubled Assets Relief Program (TARP) have been subject to mandatory pay votes since 2008 and the Restoring American Financial Stability Act of 2010 extends this.

A number of countries, including Australia, the Netherlands, the UK, Germany,

---

[9]   This proposition does not appear to be supported by empirical studies of bank behaviour (e.g. Fahlenbrach and Stulz (2009)); although there may, of course, be wider systemic influences on risk-taking.

Norway and Sweden now have variants of 'say on pay' covering non-financial corporations as well as the financial firms. In the UK the Directors' Remuneration Regulations (DRR), introduced in 2002 and given statutory force, require companies to subject the report of their remuneration committee to a shareholder resolution at the shareholders' AGM. The DRR also require companies to furnish the AGM with details of professional assistance given to the committee, together with information on individual directors' reward packages including performance criteria. The resolution is not binding but, on the very few occasions it has been rejected, the firm's compensation scheme has been revised and re-presented.[10]

A number of empirical studies have now been completed on the effects of 'say on pay' in the UK and some tentative conclusions may be drawn. First, the average level of dissent – i.e. votes against or abstentions – is small, averaging between 6 percent and 9 percent of the votes cast in resolutions since 2002. Furthermore, notwithstanding the high and generally increasing (proxy and remote) rates of shareholder participation, dissent has fallen since its peak 2002–03 levels (Gregory-Smith et al (2010),[11] Conyon and Sadler (2010)).

Second, the level of dissent on remuneration committee reports is considerably greater than the average (2 percent) level expressed for all other resolutions at the shareholders' AGM (Conyon and Sadler (2010)).

Third, a series of recent papers suggest CEO remuneration is a small but significant determinant of shareholder dissent. Conyon and Sadler (2010) (3300 remuneration resolutions, 2002–07), Carter and Zamora (2009), (830 resolutions, 2002–06) and Gregory-Smith et al. (2010) (the population of 2200 FTSE350 pay resolutions, 1998–mid-2008) report very similar results with respect to CEO pay. However, in each case the authors find the pay elasticity is dominated by a performance effect: shareholder returns (Gregory-Smith et al., Carter–Zamora) or return on assets (Conyon–Sadler) appear a more important determinant of voting behaviour than pay. Conyon–Sadler also find the performance effect substantially greater for pay resolutions than other types of resolution; suggesting that at least some shareholders 'punish' those seen as responsible for poor performance.

Conyon–Sadler and Carter–Zamora also report that dissent rises with the announcement of bonus/option/LTIP awards, suggesting some shareholders, at least, view these with suspicion. Gregory-Smith et al. (2010) examine 10 defeated remuneration resolutions and find that some extreme example of egregious behavior is usually to the fore.[12]

The evidence on the impact of voting on remuneration is less satisfactory. Some initial tabulations presented by Sheehan (2007a, b) display no evidence of lower remuneration in higher dissent cases. Ferri and Maber (2012) treat the introduction of compulsory

---

[10]   Most infamously, the GlaxoSmithKline remuneration committee report of 2003, detailing the highly generous rewards to be received by CEO Jean-Pierre Garnier in the event of his contract being terminated, was initially rejected and subsequently amended (Thompson (2006), Conyon and Sadler (2010)).

[11]   Gregory-Smith et al. (2010) report that this exceeded 60 percent representation by 2008, a proportion that compares with voter turnout in national elections in many countries.

[12]   These include several flagrant breaches of the *Code* and, in one case, a £500,000 *ex gratia* payment to a departing non-executive.

voting as an exogenous event and compare executive pay determination in the sub-periods 2000–02 and 2003–05. They find no immediate effect on either the level or growth of CEO pay. However, they do find some evidence of an increased sensitivity to performance, especially poor performance. Recognizing that this could reflect other environmental changes, most obviously increased shareholder activism, they introduce US corporations and UK firms listed on the smaller AIM market, where no 'say on pay' requirement applies, and find these have lower pay–performance sensitivities.[13]

The shareholder dissent studies cited above also assess the impact of dissent on subsequent executive remuneration. Conyon–Sadler, Carter–Zamora and Gregory-Smith et al. each fail to find any significant general effect of lagged dissent on either total remuneration or its component parts. Gregory-Smith et al. also explore Bebchuk and Fried (2004)'s contention that there should be an 'outrage constraint' restricting CEO rewards. Reasoning that this will become operative merely at higher levels of pay and dissent they use a quintile regression approach with piecewise variables up to and above a 5 percent dissent threshold. They find some modest support for the Bebchuk–Fried hypothesis, with a weakly significant effect at higher levels of dissent. Any substantial restraint seems to be limited to the top pay quintile.

In summary, the introduction of compulsory voting on the remuneration committee's recommendation does not appear to have a strong measurable impact on executive pay determination. Executive remuneration does have a small but significant impact in raising dissent, but in the context of ballots in which, on average, well over 90 percent of votes are cast in favour of the resolution. Not entirely surprisingly, firm performance appears to have a generally larger impact on shareholders' voting behaviour. It is clearly the case that extreme cases of egregious behavior do sometimes motivate a wider shareholder revolt, perhaps if they generate sufficiently large pre-vote adverse comment in the media.

The impact of dissent on subsequent executive rewards appears even less discernible. Most studies have failed to find any significant moderating effect at all; although, as noted, Gregory-Smith et al. (2010) do suggest there may be a weak influence among the most highly paid CEOs and at dissent levels above a five percent threshold.

This is not necessarily to conclude that shareholders are a toothless watchdog in guarding their own interests. Given a relatively high degree of vote concentration among city institutions, it could be that unofficial contacts highlight potential hotspots of dissent and induce remedial action before the formal presentation and vote. Certainly, recent research on shareholder activism suggests that some pension funds, such as Hermes, are effective interventionists in under-performing firms, often initiating changes of CEO (Becht et al. (2009)). Similarly, it seems reasonable to assume that boards wishing to avoid shareholder 'outrage' in the Bebchuk and Fried (2004) sense – and the occasional GlaxoSmithKline-style revolt is presumably highly embarrassing – use compensation consultants to alert them to potentially unacceptable excesses. However, in the end the

---

[13]   These comparator groups are not entirely convincing: AIM companies, for example, are much smaller than UK firms with a full listing and are typically young entrepreneurial firms where the founding family ownership remains substantial and the conventional agency problem is presumably weak.

cost to shareholders of overpaying their managers is perhaps simply insufficient to motivate taking actions that might destabilize the management. Contrast the low levels of dissent for pay resolutions with the not infrequent overturning of management resolutions on proposed acquisitions. Some modest overpayment of the senior executives might cost shareholders of a medium-to-large firm one percent of its annual earnings. A bungled takeover will dwarf this many times over.

6　CONCLUSION: THE UNFULFILLED PROMISE OF CORPORATE GOVERNANCE REFORM

An old saying runs that you can take a horse to water, but you can't make it drink. Applying such an analogy to UK corporate governance reforms, it seems the horses have been re-located poolside, but equine thirst-quenching has proceeded very slowly indeed! The most thoroughgoing effects in the UK seem to be with respect to job tenure. The move from three- or more year security to a one-year or less rolling contract has substantially reduced the payoffs for failure. Furthermore, it has clearly encouraged boards to be tougher: not only has average job tenure fallen among senior executives, but the sensitivity of dismissal to under-performance has increased such that the least successful now face a very substantial risk of termination. However, it is perhaps no coincidence here that contractual change was first initiated by shareholder action and pressure on executives has been maintained by activist intervention to oust under-performers.

It is not clear that increasing the independence, number and importance of non-executive directors has made any material difference to executive reward determination. It is perhaps unsurprising for there to be no robust empirical relationship between, for example, the ratio of non-executive to executive directors on the board and the level of executive pay; such measures may capture power relations poorly, while independence criteria for non-executives may be difficult to operationalize.

More surprising is the apparent failure of governance reforms to change the incentive structure for executives in large UK firms. Since the reformers from Cadbury onwards have acknowledged the need to link shareholder rewards more closely to firm performance it might be expected that pay–performance sensitivity would have risen and pay–size sensitivity fallen. Most researchers report pay–performance sensitivities that are little changed since the 1980s, before the era of governance reforms. Similarly, the pay–size elasticity appears to remain high, providing an ongoing encouragement to empire-building managements. It seems plausible that an unintended consequence of the professionalization of pay-setting, involving the use of consultants and explicit comparisons, has been to reinforce the place of size as an unambiguous comparator.

Governance changes have been more successful in altering the forms of payment enjoyed by executives. As seen, the LTIP, in which the vesting of share options is contingent upon some relative performance criteria, has completely superseded unrestricted options since the incorporation of Greenbury's proposals into the *Combined Code* in 1995. This has probably helped the UK to avoid some of the excesses associated with the use of executive stock options in the USA, but it was not found that LTIP adopters showed any noticeable differences in pay processes than non-adopters.

The early adoption of 'say on pay' in the UK does provide an opportunity to assess the effectiveness of this widely promoted policy. As seen, its measurable impact since 2002 has been strictly limited. Lagged remuneration does exert a significant – but small – effect on dissent, but almost invariably the overall level of dissent is insufficient to overturn the remuneration resolution. That said, the possibility of such an outcome – normally associated with some gross breach of the *Code* – must be expected to constitute some constraint. There is very little evidence that past dissent limits current pay increases. At best, such a constraint appears only to operate for the more highly paid CEOs and at higher levels of dissent; but even here the effects are quite small.

REFERENCES

Bebchuk, L. and Fried, J. (2004) *Pay without Performance: The Unfulfilled Promise of Executive Compensation*, Cambridge MA: Harvard University Press.

Becht, M., Franks, J., Mayer, C. and Rossi, S. (2009) Returns to Shareholder Activism: Evidence from a Clinical Study of the Hermes UK Focus Fund, *Review of Financial Studies*, 22, 3039–129.

Benito, A. and Conyon, M. (1999) The Governance of Directors' Pay for UK Companies, *Journal of Management and Governance*, 3, 117–36.

Black, F. and Scholes, M.S. (1973) The Pricing of Options and Corporate Liabilities, *Journal of Political Economy*, 81(3), 637–54.

Bonet, R. and Conyon, M. (2005) Compensation Committees and Executive Compensation, in Keasey et al. (2005).

Buck, T., Bruce, A., Main, B.G.M. and Udueni, H. (2003) Long Term Incentive Plans, Executive Pay and UK Company Performance, *Journal of Management Studies*, 40, 1709–27.

Cadbury, A. (1992) *The Financial Aspects of Corporate Governance*, London: Gee.

Carter, M.E. and Zamora, V. (2009) Shareholder Remuneration Votes and CEO Compensation Design, Boston College Working Paper.

Chambers, A. (2003) *Tolley's Corporate Governance Handbook*, Croydon: LexisNexis.

Combined Code (1999) *The Combined Code on Corporate Governance*, London: Financial Reporting Council.

Conyon, M. (1997a) Corporate Governance and Executive Compensation, *International Journal of Industrial Organization*, 15, 493–509.

Conyon, M. (1997b) Institutional Arrangements for Setting Directors' Compensation in UK Companies, in K. Keasey, S. Thompson and M. Wright (eds) *Corporate Governance: Economic and Financial Issues*, Oxford: Oxford University Press.

Conyon, M. and Gregg, P. (1994) Pay at the Top: A Study of the Sensitivity of Chief Executive Remuneration to Company Specific Shocks, *National Institute Economic Review*, 3, 88–92.

Conyon, M. and Leech, D. (1994) Top Pay, Company Performance and Corporate Governance, *Oxford Bulletin of Economics and Statistics*, 56, 229–47.

Conyon, M. and Murphy, K. (2000) The Prince and the Pauper? CEO Pay in the US and UK, *Economic Journal*, 110, 640–71.

Conyon, M. and Peck, S. (1998) Board Control, Remuneration Committees and Top Management Compensation, *Academy of Management Journal*, 41, 146–57.

Conyon, M. and Sadler, G. (2001) Executive Pay, Tournaments and Corporate Performance in UK Firms, *International Journal of Management Reviews*, 3, 141–68.

Conyon, M. and Sadler, G. (2010) Shareholder Voting and Directors' Remuneration Report Legislation: Say on Pay in the United Kingdom, *Corporate Governance: An International Review*, 18, 296–312.

Cosh, A. (1975) The Remuneration of Chief Executives in the UK, *Economic Journal*, 85, 75–94.

Dahya, J., McConnell, J.J. and Travlos, N.G. (2002) The Cadbury Committee, Corporate Performance and Top Management Turnover, *Journal of Finance*, LVII, 461–83.

Department of Trade and Industry (2003) *Rewards for Failure: Directors' Remuneration – Contracts, Performance and Severance*.

Fahlenbrach, R. and Stulz, R.M. (2009) Bank CEO Incentives and the Credit Crisis, NBER Working Paper 15212, Cambridge, MA.

Ferri, F. and Maber, D.F. (2012) Say on Pay Votes and CEO Compensation: Evidence from the UK, *Review of Finance* (forthcoming).

Franks, J., Mayer, C. and Renneboog, L. (2001) Who Disciplines Managers in Poorly Performing Companies, *Journal of Financial Intermediation*, 10, 209–48.
Girma, S., Thompson, S. and Wright, P. (2006) The Impact of Merger Activity on Executive Pay in the United Kingdom, *Economica*, 73, 321–39.
Girma, S., Thompson, S. and Wright, P. (2007) Corporate Governance Reforms and Executive Compensation Determination, *Manchester School*, 75, 65–81.
Greenbury, R. (1995) *Directors' Remuneration: Report of a Study Group Chaired by Sir Richard Greenbury*, London: Confederation of British Industry.
Gregg, P., Machin, S. and Szymanski, S. (1993) The Disappearing Relationship Between Directors' Pay and Corporate Performance, *British Journal of Industrial Relations*, 31, 1–9.
Gregg, P., Jewell, S. and Tonks, I. (2005) Executive Pay and Performance in the UK, Centre for Market and Public Organisation, University of Bristol, Working Paper 05/122.
Gregory-Smith, I. (2010) Chief Executive Pay and Remuneration Committee Independence, *Oxford Bulletin of Economics and Statistics* (forthcoming).
Gregory-Smith, I., Thompson, S. and Wright, P.W. (2009) Fired or Retired: A Competing Risks Analysis of Chief Executive Turnover, *Economic Journal*, 119, 463–81.
Gregory-Smith, I., Thompson, S. and Wright, P. (2010) Outrage or Mild Irritation. Don't Shareholders Care about CEO Pay? University of Nottingham mimeo.
Hampel, S.R. (1998) *Committee on Corporate Governance*, London: Gee.
Hart, O.D. (1995) Corporate Governance: Some Theory and Implications, *Economic Journal*, 105(430), 678–89.
Higgs, D. (2003) *Review of the Role and Effectiveness of Non-executive Directors*, London: Department of Trade and Industry.
Jensen, M. (1988) Takeovers: Their Causes and Consequences, *Journal of Economic Perspectives*, 2, 21–48.
Jensen, M.C. and Meckling, W. (1976) Theory of the Firm, Managerial Behavior, Agency Costs and Ownership Structure, *Journal of Financial Economics*, 3(4), 305–60.
Keasey, K., Thompson, S. and Wright, M. (eds) (2005) *Corporate Governance: Accountability, Enterprise and International Comparisons*, Chichester: John Wiley.
Main, B.G.M. (1993) Pay in the Boardroom: Practices and Procedures, *Personnel Review*, 3–14.
Main, B.G.M. and Johnston, J. (1993) Remuneration Committees and Corporate Performance, *Accounting and Business Research*, 23, 321–62.
Main, B.G.M., Bruce, A. and Buck, T. (1996) Total Board Remuneration and Company Performance, *Economic Journal*, 106, 1627–44.
Murphy, K. (1999) Executive Compensation, in O.C. Ashenfelter and D. Card (eds) *Handbook of Labor Economics*, vol. 3. Amsterdam: Elsevier, 2485–563.
Rosen, S. (1992) Contract and the Market for Executives, in L. Werin and H. Wijkander, *Contract Economics*, Oxford: Blackwell.
Schaefer, S. and Hayes, R. (2009) CEO Pay and the Lake Wobegon Effect, *Journal of Financial Economics*, 94, 280–90.
Sheehan, K.M. (2007a) A Model of the Outrage Constraint, Working Paper, University of Sydney Law School.
Sheehan, K.M. (2007b) Is the Outrage Constraint an Effective Constraint on Executive Remuneration: Evidence from the UK and Preliminary Results from Australia, Working Paper, University of Sydney, http://papers.ssrn.com/sol3/papers.cfm?abstract_id=974965.
Thompson, S. (2005) The Impact of Corporate Governance Reforms on the Remuneration of Executives in the UK, *Corporate Governance: An International Review*, 13, 19–25.
Williamson, O.E. (1985) *The Economic Institutions of Capitalism*, New York: Free Press.

4 Governance codes, managerial remuneration and disciplining in the UK: a history of governance reform failure?

Luc Renneboog and Grzegorz Trojanowski

1 INTRODUCTION

Over the 1990s, the UK corporate governance regime experienced a series of sweeping governance reforms initiated by the Code of Best Practice (so-called Cadbury report) in 1992 (and incorporated in the listing rules of the London Stock Exchange in July 1993) and then followed by the Greenbury report in 1995, the Hampel report in 1998, and, finally enshrined in the Combined Code of Corporate Governance in 1998. While some evidence exists of the effects of the earlier reforms, in particular of the Cadbury report (see e.g. Dahya et al., 2002, and Girma et al., 2007 for the effects of the Code introduction on CEO dismissal and executive compensation, respectively), this chapter provides a comprehensive examination of managerial remuneration and disciplining in the UK in both the pre-reform period (i.e. before 1993) and in the post-reform period (i.e. as of 1999). It allows us to assess the efficiency of the governance changes and relate to the critics claiming that the recommendations of the British governance committees did not have sufficient clout to curb the excesses in managerial compensation. Numerous calls for further improvements of practice in the area and for stronger shareholder involvement in the pay-setting process followed the dispute over the pay of GlaxoSmithKline's CEO Jean-Paul Garnier in 2003 and the ensuing shareholder revolt against corporate 'fat cats'. Needless to say, the recent financial crisis put the issue into the spotlight again and resulted in yet another set of governance recommendations (Walker, 2009).

However, governance problems pertaining to managerial compensation do not appear to be confined to the UK. One of the main deficiencies of widely held public corporations – 'strong managers, weak owners', in the words of Roe (2002) – may actually have led to a situation where the mechanisms meant to improve the governance standards like performance-related pay are misused by powerful directors to extract substantial rents from the companies they work for (Bebchuk and Fried, 2004). The early agency literature stipulates that shareholders' interests can be protected because managerial incentives can be (re)structured. As such, managers attempt to avoid poor performance due to the threat of dismissal and are stimulated to reach strong corporate performance as a result of the reward and incentive effects of compensation contracts (Holmström, 1982; Murphy, 1986). However, more recent US empirical literature casts doubt on the hypothesis of alignment of interests which may be brought about by pay-for-(stock price)-performance contracts and performance-related dismissals. For instance, Bebchuk and Fried's (2003) 'managerial-power model' points out that executive compensation should be seen as a manifestation of agency problems rather than a solution if remuneration contracting is not embedded in a proper governance system. Likewise, Bertrand and Mullainathan

(2000, 2001) give evidence that the performance-related contracts in the US do not correct for windfall profits which are not related to managerial efforts or skill, and that CEOs are hence paid for luck. Furthermore, they propose a model whereby 'agents without principals' (managers without proper governance mechanisms like a monitoring blockholder) are skimming corporate profits. Our results give a nuanced picture for the UK. We show evidence of contractual alignment, but we also detect circumstances which point at the danger of managerial self-dealing (in particular, in the pre-reform period). Self-dealing may particularly arise in firms where CEOs have a lot of discretion in decision making, which may result from a lack of monitoring by outside shareholders or the board of directors. Some of our results show indeed that powerful CEOs are shielded from forced departures and seem able to choose their preferred remuneration-related performance benchmark. This study thus contributes to the recent literature on the alignment versus skimming hypotheses.

Although a large body of academic literature exists (especially for the US) on both managerial disciplining and managerial compensation, these two aspects of the managerial labor market are usually – with the notable exception of Coughlan and Schmidt (1985) – treated separately. However, the two governance mechanisms in question are likely to be intertwined such that the results of studies of executive turnover and of managerial remuneration in isolation are likely to be biased. Furthermore, each of these governance mechanisms only addresses the agency problems at specific ranges of corporate performance. For instance, performance-sensitive managerial compensation contracts are designed only for average or high levels of performance because management may not be induced to exert further effort when they realize that the minimal performance thresholds triggering bonuses are out of reach (Geiler and Renneboog, 2011). Likewise, Jensen and Murphy (1990) argue that the probability of CEO dismissal is too low to align effectively the interests of managers and owners. Consequently, in order to cover a more complete spectrum of incentives, the carrot (performance-related compensation) and the stick (dismissal) need to be studied simultaneously. A simultaneous treatment of both governance mechanisms econometrically translates into a Heckman sample selection model (type-2 Tobit). This technique mitigates the sample selection biases induced by sample endogeneity affecting many of the studies analyzing managerial compensation. Thus, this chapter contributes to the literature by correcting the findings of earlier UK research which fell short of finding a relation between managerial remuneration and corporate performance (or documented a very weak relation). The lack of performance sensitivity in earlier UK studies may result from the biases induced by inappropriate estimation methodologies or may be due to benchmarking problems.

We analyze listed UK firms and find the CEO compensation to be performance-sensitive: remuneration rewards either past good accounting or stock price performance. Nevertheless, we cannot unambiguously show that remuneration contracts align the interests of managers and shareholders, nor can we demonstrate that the skimming/managerial-power model is valid in all cases. The fact that the levels of CEO compensation are lower when executive directors are powerful (in terms of voting rights) supports the alignment-of-interest hypothesis. However, for the pre-reform period, we find that when firms incur negative abnormal returns and their CEOs derive substantial wealth from the equity investment in their firms, CEOs compensate for the disappointing stock performance by augmenting their monetary compensation. This suggests self-dealing and therefore provides some support for the skimming or managerial-power theory. CEOs who also exercise the function of chairmen (and hence dominate the board) earn more when accounting performance is high (but not when share price performance has increased). Thus, powerful managers seem to prefer accounting standards as an evaluation criterion, presumably because they have more discretion over this benchmark and hence over their monetary compensation. In contrast, in firms with strong outsider (monitoring) shareholders, management cannot pick its preferred performance benchmark as it is required to focus on the creation of shareholder value (Crespi and Renneboog, 2010). The aforementioned relation between CEO power and the intricacies of pay–performance sensitivity persists in the post-reform years. In both periods analyzed, the CEOs of monitored firms (in particular of firms where non-executive directors and outside shareholders control large share blocks) enjoy lower remuneration, irrespective of performance.

In the pre-reform period, there are few characteristics of the board structure (apart from the separation of CEO and chairman) which have an impact on the pay-for-performance sensitivity. The proportion of non-executive directors on the board does not seem to have an impact on the remuneration policy of the firm. Furthermore, the presence of a remuneration committee has no significant impact either. In this respect, our results appear consistent with the widely perceived failure of this mechanism in tackling governance problems. Interestingly, in the post-reform period, a larger proportion of non-executive directors on the board weakens the link between CEO compensation and the accounting performance measure.

We also analyze the termination of a CEO employment contract. First, we find that CEO replacement rates are comparable in pre- and post-reform periods. Second, involuntary or forced turnover is performance-sensitive in both periods. Third, outside shareholders (institutions, families or individuals, other corporations) do not seem to be involved in general in disciplining the CEO even in the wake of poor performance (in either of the periods). In line with earlier research, we find that prior to the governance reforms of the 1990s, non-executive directors owning share blocks seem to protect the incumbent CEO in poorly performing companies, while in the post-reform period this effect is no longer significant (in line with the codes' spirit of fostering non-executive directors' governance role). Fourth, CEOs also holding the positions of chairmen of the board successfully impede replacement irrespective of corporate performance in the pre-reform period. Finally, until 1993, large boards and boards with a high proportion of non-executive directors replace the CEO more frequently. However, these boards are not more apt to replace underperforming management in either the pre-reform or the post-reform period.

2 DETERMINANTS OF CEO COMPENSATION AND OF MANAGERIAL TURNOVER

2.1 Background Agency Literature

Coughlan and Schmidt (1985) were the first to document that the likelihood of forced turnover is a decreasing function of corporate performance; a finding further corroborated by an extensive literature (*inter alia* Denis and Denis, 1995, for the US and Franks et al., 2001, and Dahya et al., 2002, for the UK).[1] The theoretical blueprint of pay-for-performance remuneration was laid by the principal–agent models of Jensen and Meckling (1976), and Grossman and Hart (1983). The performance-sensitivity of managerial compensation is empirically well documented for US firms (e.g. Jensen and Murphy, 1990): executive pay depends on both past stock returns and past accounting measures (Sloan, 1993) as well as on relative measures of performance (Gibbons and Murphy, 1990). Still, the level of executive compensation depends not only on past performance; also important are company size (Murphy, 1985; Girma et al., 2007) and CEO age and tenure (Conyon and Murphy, 2000).[2] The optimal balance of stock-based and monetary compensation solves a trade-off between short- and long-term incentives (Narayanan, 1996).

The recent literature criticizes the agency approach that considers managerial compensation as the optimal outcome of the contracting problem (Bertrand and Mullainathan, 2000; Bebchuk and Fried, 2003). According to the 'skimming model' of executive remuneration, directors are able to set their own (excessive) pay in firms with inferior governance standards (Bertrand and Mullainathan, 2001). Apart from the availability of funds, the only constraint deemed to curb such a managerial discretion is the fear of causing 'outrage' among shareholders potentially angered by excessive pay of the company's executives (Bebchuk et al., 2002).

2.2   Motivation of Hypotheses

The impact of the various corporate mechanisms (internal devices such as board composition, pay-for-performance, and external mechanisms such as ownership concentration by type of shareholder) will vary over time and their effectiveness will depend on the regulatory framework. Over the past 20 years, several important regulations were introduced. The Combined Code of Corporate Governance was launched in 1998 and united three earlier corporate governance codes: (i) the Cadbury report on good governance which was introduced in December 1992 (and included in the listing rules of the London Stock Exchange in July 1993), (ii) the Greenbury report of 1995 on remuneration transparency, and (iii) the Hampel report of 1998 which emphasized principles of good governance, rather than 'box-ticking' explicit rules.

The period prior to 1993 precedes the implementation of the first of the corporate governance reports adopted in the UK. This period is characterized by lower corporate

---

[1]   The disciplinary character of managerial turnover is influenced by board size (Yermack, 1996), board composition (Weisbach, 1988), ownership structure (Denis et al., 1997), and is industry-dependent (Parrino, 1997). Forced executive resignations in the US are usually accompanied by positive and statistically significant abnormal stock performance, provided that an outsider is appointed as the CEO (Rosenstein and Wyatt, 1997).

[2]   Furthermore, the following characteristics also explain part of the changes in remuneration: ownership structure (Core et al., 1999), board composition (Hallock, 1997), the threat of a takeover (Agrawal and Knoeber, 1998), merger and acquisition policy (Girma et al., 2006), company risk, growth opportunities, dividend policy (Lewellen et al., 1987), and the country where the company is operating (Conyon and Murphy, 2000).

governance standards than more recent years, and is therefore particularly interesting from an agency-theory point of view. Our second six-year sample period, labeled the post-reform period, covers the years following the adoption of the Combined Code (1999–2004). Using two time periods enables us to better assess the efficiency of improved governance standards as recommended by the codes. In the remainder of this subsection, we formulate our main hypotheses on the governance effects on turnover and on remuneration. We also indicate in which time period – the pre-reform or post-reform period – we expect the hypotheses to hold (more strongly).

The importance of the disciplining role of managerial dismissals is widely accepted. Still, setting a correct performance yardstick is problematic as both accounting and stock price performance have some deficiencies. Accounting information records only past corporate performance and can be manipulated over a period of several years by top management (see e.g. Chan et al., 2004). Stock price performance captures the firm's ability to generate value in the future and may hence already include the effects of an expected change in CEO. Therefore, we argue that both stock- and accounting-based measures of performance provide incremental information about executives' productivity.

Decisions about hiring and firing top management are ultimately taken by the board of directors.[3] The higher the degree of independence of the board from top management, the higher the level of performance-induced turnover is likely to be. Still, the empirical US literature comes up with conflicting results.[4] For the UK, Franks et al. (2001) find that a high proportion of independent directors does not lead to stronger managerial disciplining in poorly performing firms, while this conclusion is challenged by Dahya et al. (2002). According to Franks et al. (2001) what does seem to matter is separating the functions of the CEO and the chairman of the board. Also, Yermack (1996) reports that smaller boards operate more efficiently as they are more prone to replace underperforming CEOs of the US companies.

Hypothesis 1a (Governance effects on turnover): *Board independence positively affects the likelihood of managerial turnover in poorly performing firms. An inverse relation is expected for board size.*

As there are hardly any requirements in corporate law on board structure in the pre-reform period, we expect a stronger impact of board structure on turnover in the post-reform period (following the arguments by Dahya et al., 2002). An alternative hypothesis is that in the post-reform period, the board structures (degree of independence, number of non-executive directors, separation of the positions of CEO and chairman etc.) do not

---

[3]   Throughout the chapter, we use the UK definition of a director. A UK board of directors consists of executive directors (frequently called officers in the US) and non-executive directors (called directors in the US).

[4]   Weisbach (1988) shows that board structure affects the likelihood of disciplinary turnover: poorly performing CEOs are more frequently fired provided that the board is outsider-dominated. This conclusion is challenged by Mikkelson and Partch (1997), and Agrawal and Knoeber (1996) who show that managerial turnover is unrelated to board composition. Instead, turnover seems to result mainly from the pressure of the takeover market (Martin and McConnell, 1991).

vary to a large degree due to the implementation of the governance recommendations. Therefore the impact of board structure on turnover is marginal. If it were the case, superior internal board mechanisms (such as board independence, which can be expected to stimulate good governance) may only make a difference in the pre-reform period.

The essence of the agency literature is that, in order to induce agents to exert (costly) effort, the principal has to provide them with appropriate incentives. Jensen and Meckling (1976) suggest (partial) equity ownership by managers as a way of mitigating this problem, but Murphy (1986) finds only little empirical support for this mechanism. Fama (1980) discounts the idea of pay-for-performance contracts for managers with short track records because, if managers believe that subsequent wage offers will depend on current levels of performance, they will work hard today to build up reputational value independent of incentive compensation. Holmström (1982) challenges this idea and shows that although the effects of labor-market discipline can be substantial, it is not a perfect substitute for contracts. Gibbons and Murphy (1992) extend the Holmström model by introducing Fama's reputation concept and show that the best compensation contract optimizes total incentives (the combination of the implicit incentives from career concerns and the explicit incentives from the compensation contract).

Managerial compensation schemes may be an appropriate device complementing performance-related turnover for the following reasons. First, many managers can be subject to this incentive mechanism, while performance-induced disciplinary turnover only affects a few top managers. Second, for industries where industry-specific skills are required, performance-based compensation is likely to be a more effective solution to agency problems than the threat of dismissal. Third, as disciplinary turnover penalizes underperformance, the mere fact of being able to avoid poor performance (and hence dismissal) does not constitute the right incentive for well-performing managers to pursue a value-maximizing strategy. If higher managerial effort induces better corporate performance, then there is an important rewarding role for performance-dependent bonus and option schemes. However, imperfect observability of top management's actions creates opportunities for moral hazard that adversely affect the contracting with a manager (Holmström, 1979). The efficiency of contracting can be improved by using informative signals about executives' effort. Following this argument, Bushman and Indjejikian (1993), and Kim and Suh (1993) develop models in which the CEO's compensation depends on both accounting- and stock-based performance measures. Both indicators are considered noisy signals of managerial effort, but as long as they are incrementally informative about managerial actions, they enter a performance-dependent wage formula with non-zero weight.[5]

Corporate governance standards influence the terms of CEO remuneration contracts (Bertrand and Mullainathan, 2001): the degree of independence of the board of directors may have a direct impact on managerial compensation as it is the non-executive directors (or their representatives in the remuneration committee) who set the remuneration

---

[5]   This argument of using both types of performance measures (stock- and accounting-based) as determinants of CEO compensation is also invoked in some of the empirical literature for US firms (e.g. Core et al., 1999).

contracts. In a firm whose board of directors is dominated by a powerful CEO (for instance, when he or she also serves as the chairperson), the terms of the top management's remuneration contracts are more likely to be influenced by the CEO (Bebchuk and Fried, 2004). Yermack (1996) also argues that smaller boards appear to act more frequently in the shareholders' interest than larger boards. In particular, he documents an inverse relationship between board size and the performance sensitivity of managerial compensation.

Hypothesis 1b (Governance effects on compensation): *Board independence positively affects performance sensitivity of the CEO's compensation. An inverse relation is expected for board size.*

We expect the above hypothesis to be supported more strongly in the post-reform period as it may take a strong non-executive board/remuneration committee to impose an effective pay-for-performance mechanism.[6]

For the US, there is ample evidence that forced turnover follows from monitoring by large (activist) blockholders and by the external market for corporate control (e.g. Denis and Kruse, 2000). For UK firms, Franks et al. (2001) confirm that these mechanisms also play a leading role in the replacement of management. The intensity of monitoring may depend not only on mere ownership concentration, but also on the type of blockholders. In particular, substantial insider ownership may lead to managerial entrenchment, which decreases the performance-sensitivity of managerial turnover and reduces the likelihood of CEO dismissal (Crespi et al., 2002). In contrast, outside blockholders may hold management responsible for poor performance and attempt to remove them.

Hypothesis 2a (Blockholder identity effect on turnover): *The type of controlling shareholders affects the likelihood of managerial turnover: monitoring by outside blockholders (institutions, families and individuals, industrial firms) leads to increased performance-related CEO removal, whereas insider blockholders impede top executive changes in underperforming firms.*

We expect a stronger relation between the presence of share blocks and forced turnover of top management for the post-reform period. The reason is that shareholders have become better informed as a consequence of the increased corporate transparency requested in the various codes constituting the Combined Code. Furthermore, shareholders have become more vocal and activist at annual meetings and behind the scenes (see e.g. Becht et al., 2009).

Shareholders monitor the firm when their share stakes are sufficiently large and the benefits from monitoring exceed the costs (Kahn and Winton, 1998). Such powerful shareholders may also set the terms of CEO employment contracts. Clay (2000) argues

---

[6] However, following the reforms, there may be less cross-firm variability in board independence such that it may be more difficult to discern the effect of board independence on pay–performance sensitivity.

that monitoring activities are delegated to some classes of owners and that the presence of activist shareholders leads to higher levels of CEO compensation and increasing performance-sensitivity. In contrast, in firms where managers control large equity stakes and/or where the ownership is diffuse, managers are likely to enjoy a high level of decision discretion such that they can promote compensation schemes with only a limited relation to share price performance.[7]

Hypothesis 2b (Blockholder identity effect on compensation): *The presence of strong outside blockholders positively affects the performance sensitivity of the CEO's compensation, whereas the presence of large executive directors' holdings induces the opposite effect.*

We expect that Hypothesis 2b is more strongly supported in the post-reform period. The reason is that subsequent to 1995, firms ought to introduce pay-for-performance in their remuneration contracts and were expected to disclose the contract details of all the executive and non-executive directors. While stopping short of mandating shareholders' vote-on-pay at annual general meetings (AGMs), the Greenbury Report actively encourages shareholders to voice their concerns in the form of resolutions at the AGMs and recommends that executive long-term incentive schemes be approved by shareholders.

   The discussion above leaves out one potentially important group of shareholders, namely non-executive directors. The relationship between the size of their equity stakes and CEO compensation or turnover is an open empirical issue. On the one hand, if non-executive directors assume their fiduciary duties appropriately and act in the interest of all shareholders, the impact of non-executives' voting power on CEO compensation and turnover will be similar to that of the outside blockholders (postulated by Hypotheses 2a and 2b). On the other hand, if non-executive directors believe that their careers are closely tied to the fate of the incumbent CEO, they may opt to support the incumbent management and shield them from disciplinary actions. This would be in line with the findings of Franks et al. (2001) who argue that non-executive directors frequently support the incumbent management even in the wake of poor performance. Thus, while testing for Hypotheses 2a and 2b, we control for the size of equity holdings controlled by non-executive directors, but *a priori* we do not hypothesize about the direction of the effect.

3   SAMPLE DESCRIPTION AND METHODOLOGICAL APPROACH

3.1   Sample Description and Data Sources

We analyze and compare the determinants of managerial compensation and turnover between two six-year periods: the pre-reform period (1988–1993) and the post-reform

---

   [7]   Managers would then prefer remuneration packages related to accounting benchmarks as these can to some extent be manipulated by management (Jensen et al., 2004).

period (1999–2004). The pre-reform period precedes the implementation of the first of the corporate governance report adopted in the UK.[8] The post-reform period covers the years following the adoption of the Combined Code in 1998.[9]

The pre-reform period sample consists of 250 UK firms and is randomly drawn from the population of UK companies listed on the London Stock Exchange, excluding financial institutions, real estate companies, and insurance companies. For a company to be included in the sample, we require that data be available for at least three consecutive years within the six-year time window. Hence, the sample also includes those firms that were taken over or went bankrupt. Seven of the 250 companies were dropped because accounting data were not available from Datastream. All data on managerial compensation, turnover and board composition for the pre-reform sample were hand-collected and retrieved from the Directors' Report and the Notes in the annual reports. The same source is used to collect ownership data for each year of the period 1988–1993. All the directors' holdings greater than 0.1 percent are recorded as well as other shareholders' stakes of 5 percent and more (3 percent and above from 1990 when the statutory disclosure threshold was reduced). The status of the directors (executive/non-executive) and the dates of joining and leaving the board were also obtained from the annual reports and from contacting the firms directly by phone or fax. Non-beneficial share stakes held by the directors on behalf of their families or charitable trusts were added to the directors' beneficial holdings. Although directors do not obtain cash flow benefits from these non-beneficial stakes, they can usually exercise the voting rights. For equity stakes in nominee accounts, the identity of the shareholders was found by contacting the listed firms directly. In 97 percent of these cases, the shareholders of nominee accounts were institutional investors.

The post-reform sample is much more comprehensive and it is the intersection of the three databases: BoardEx (for managerial compensation, turnover, and board composition data), Worldscope (for accounting and other financial data) and the PricewaterhouseCoopers ownership database. This procedure yields a sample of 1,407 UK companies quoted on the London Stock Exchange (which corresponds to a sample of 6,424 CEO-years).[10] The ownership database provides information on all the holdings of the company directors and all the holdings of 3 percent or above for the other shareholders. The procedures for classifying non-beneficial stakes and nominee accounts in the post-reform sample are the same as the ones outlined above for the pre-reform sample.

---

[8]   It is possible that some firms may have adopted some of the Cadbury recommendations in the final year of our first sample. Excluding year 1993 from our data does not materially influence the results presented in this chapter.

[9]   The Combined Code was amended in 2003 (when the Higgs report on a more active and independent role of non-executive directors was published) and in 2007 (FRC, 2009). We only study the impact of the main regulatory changes (which took place between 1993 and 1998).

[10]   Whereas in the majority of UK firms, the identity of the CEO is undisputable, it is sometimes difficult to find out who is the (acting) CEO. If none of the executive directors carries the title of CEO, but there is a managing director, we consider the latter as CEO. If none of the board members holds a title of CEO or managing director while the board has an executive chairman, we consider this person as the CEO. Renneboog and Trojanowski (2010) find this procedure to be robust and to yield classification very similar to that obtained from alternative approaches (e.g. Girma et al., 2007).

3.2   Variable definitions and data description

In our pre-reform sample, approximately 11 percent of CEOs lost their position in a given year (Table 4.1), while the number for the post-reform period is slightly lower at 9.9 percent. This result is different from the one obtained by Dahya et al. (2002) who document the increase in turnover rates following the implementation of the Cadbury code. The turnover data are corrected for natural turnover.[11] As expected, most of the CEO turnover occurs in the lowest quintile of corporate performance. The median and mean logarithm of the monetary compensation (salary and bonus) in the pre-reform period was 11.88 and 11.91, respectively (which corresponds to £144,000 and £149,000). Expectedly, the corresponding numbers for the 1999–2004 sample are higher at 12.65 and 12.69, respectively (equivalent to £312,000 and £326,000). The improved disclosure requirements following the implementation of the Greenbury report (of 1995) enable us to undertake a more detailed analysis of the equity-based components of the compensation package.[12] These components (stocks, options, and Long-Term Incentive Plans or LTIPs) constitute a substantial part of the total CEO compensation in the post-reform period: the mean and median logarithms of total compensation are equal to 12.93 and 13.01, respectively (which correspond to £413,000 and £448,000).

The median age of a CEO is 52 years (with a mean of 52.6) for the pre-reform sample. The numbers for the post-reform sample (51 and 50.5, respectively) are slightly lower. While in the 1988–1993 period the median tenure equaled 4 years (with a mean of 5.2), it was considerably shorter in the period 1999–2004 with a median (mean) tenure of merely 2.9 (4.9) years. In the pre-reform period, every third CEO also held the position of the chairman of the board of directors, but this proportion has decreased substantially following the corporate governance codes (as in the Combined Code) to about 15 percent.

We observe a decrease in board size over time: while in the pre-reform period the median board consists of 9 directors, the corresponding board size in the post-reform period is 7. Finally, in approximately 26 percent of the sample firm-years from the pre-reform period, CEO compensation is determined by a remuneration committee. In our post-reform sample, virtually all firms have such a committee.

As is typical for Anglo-American firms, the ownership concentration is relatively low (Table 4.1). Most CEOs do not hold very substantial share stakes, but the corresponding numbers increase in recent years: the average CEO in the pre-reform period owns 2.8 percent, whereas the corresponding number for the post-reform period amounts to 4.5

---

[11]   We distinguish between natural and forced turnover, classifying a resignation as 'natural' if the director was described as having left the board for reasons of retirement, death or illness. Otherwise the resignation was classified as being forced. The normal retirement age is between 62 and 65 but we took 62 as the minimum retirement age and viewed any earlier retirement as forced unless the databases employed provided details of the stipulated retirement age for a particular CEO (this information was only available for the post-reform sample).

[12]   For the pre-reform period, only rudimentary information about equity-based CEO remuneration is disclosed. The annual reports usually only mention that management options had been granted during the financial year and/or were outstanding, without consistently revealing the number of options involved, the exercise price, and the number of options exercised in the preceding year. Renneboog and Trojanowski (2010) discuss an alternative approach of estimating equity-based compensation elements for that period and detail its shortcomings.

Table 4.1   Descriptive statistics

	Pre-reform sample: 1988–1993			Post-reform sample: 1999–2004		
	Median	Mean	Std. dev.	Median	Mean	Std. dev.
CEO turnover						
CEO dismissal (%)	0.0	11.0	31.3	0.0	9.9	29.9
CEO compensation						
Ind.-adj. logarithm of cash compensation	0.0	0.0	0.6	0.0	0.0	0.8
Logarithm of cash compensation	11.9	11.9	0.7	12.7	12.7	0.8
Ind.-adj. logarithm of total compensation	na	na	na	0.0	0.1	0.9
Logarithm of total compensation	na	na	na	12.9	13.0	1.0
CEO characteristics						
CEO age (years)	52.0	52.6	6.3	51.0	50.5	7.5
CEO tenure (years)	4.0	5.2	5.3	2.9	4.9	5.4
CEO is the board chairman (%)	0.0	33.5	47.2	0.0	15.4	36.1
Board composition						
Proportion of non-executive directors (%)	61.5	61.4	15.0	50.0	50.1	14.6
Board size	9.0	9.4	3.5	7.0	7.7	2.8
Remuneration committee presence (dummy)	0.0	25.9	43.8	100	100	na
Ownership variables (all in %)						
CEO stake (%)	0.0	3.0	8.1	0.0	4.5	11.7
Executives' stake (%)	0.1	4.6	10.8	1.3	6.0	11.4
Non-executives' stake (%)	0.0	3.9	9.6	0.0	3.0	8.7
Institutions' stake (%)	13.0	16.6	16.1	22.5	24.6	17.7
Families/indivs' and corporations' stake (%)	0.0	8.2	14.1	0.0	5.2	11.0
Firm-specific control variables						
Logarithm of firm size	11.3	11.3	1.8	11.9	12.0	2.3
Capital gearing (%)	29.7	32.7	24.8	16.5	21.4	46.2
Risk (%)	34.4	37.4	13.1	30.4	33.0	13.2

percent. In the pre-reform period, the median of the combined shareholdings of all executive directors (excluding the CEO) is 0.1 percent, with an average of about 4.6 percent. After 1999, the numbers increase to 1.3 percent and 6.0 percent, respectively. The average combined stakes of the non-executives do not exceed 4 percent in either period. The most important class of blockholders is the financial institutions: they hold a (cumulative) median stake of 13.0 percent (with a mean of 16.6 percent) over the 1988–1993 period. The importance of this class of blockholders increased further in the post-reform period: their median (average) blockholding amounted then to 22.5 percent (24.6 percent). Finally, other outsiders – individuals, families and industrial firms – control on average 8.2 percent of equity in the pre-reform period and 5.2 percent in the post-reform period.

In order to control for (potential) size effects, we include the logarithm of total assets (in £ thousands) at the end of a given year in our models. For the median (mean) company in our pre-reform sample, this the total assets equal approximately £85 million (£78 million). For the 1999–2004 sample, the corresponding number is £142 million (£166 million). The median and mean ratios of capital gearing (defined as long-term debt on total assets) equal 29.7 percent and 32.7 percent, respectively, for the pre-reform sample, and 16.5 percent and 21.4 percent, respectively for the post-reform sample. We measure risk by the annual volatility of stock returns: the median (mean) values in the pre-reform and post-reform periods amount to 34.4 percent (37.4 percent) and 30.3 percent (33.0 percent), respectively. Finally, we employ annual abnormal stock returns to capture corporate stock performance and return on assets (ROA) as an accounting performance measure.

3.3   Methodology

We simultaneously explain managerial turnover and compensation within a sample selection model framework. The model, often referred to as a type-2 Tobit model, is specified as follows:

$$\begin{cases} \textit{Turnover}^*_{it} = X'_{1it}\beta_2 + \varepsilon_{1it} & \text{(4.1a)} \\ \textit{Compensation}^*_{it} = X'_{2it}\beta_2 + \varepsilon_{2it} & \text{(4.1b)} \end{cases}$$

$$CEO\_stayed_{it} = \begin{cases} 1 & \text{if } \textit{Turnover}^*_{it} > 0 \\ 0 & \text{if } \textit{Turnover}^*_{it} \leq 0 \end{cases} \quad \text{(4.2)}$$

$$Observed\_compensation_{it} = \begin{cases} \textit{Compensation}^*_{it} & \text{if } \textit{Turnover}^*_{it} > 0 \\ \text{not observed} & \text{if } \textit{Turnover}^*_{it} \leq 0 \end{cases} \quad \text{(4.3)}$$

where $\{\varepsilon_{1it}, \varepsilon_{2it}\}$ are drawn from a bivariate normal distribution with mean 0, variances σ_1^2 and σ_2^2, and covariance σ_{12} (Amemiya, 1984).[13] β_1 and β_2 are vectors of the model coefficients. In our models, i corresponds to a firm and t to a year. $\textit{Turnover}^*_{it}$ and $\textit{Compensation}^*_{it}$ are underlying latent variables that are not observable. However, the sign of the $\textit{Turnover}^*_{it}$ variable can be observed and coded as a binary variable CEO_stayed_{it}: if a CEO lost his or her job (i.e., $\textit{Turnover}^*_{it} \leq 0$) it is coded as 0, otherwise it is coded as 1. Obviously, compensation is only observed for CEOs who were not dismissed (see Equation 4.3).

X_{1it} and X_{2it} are the sets of explanatory variables explaining CEO turnover and compensation, respectively. They include the measures of stock and accounting performance, board characteristics, ownership structure variables, and other control variables (e.g.,

---

[13]   In a standard setting, error terms are assumed to be i.i.d. drawings from a bivariate normal distribution. We relax the assumption of independence of ε's across t and allow clustering of observations corresponding to a given firm, i.e. we assume error terms to be i.i.d. across firms, but not necessarily for different observations within the same firm.

leverage, firm risk, time, or industry dummies). The two sets of explanatory variables, i.e. X_{1it} and X_{2it}, are not disjoint (they can differ, however).

Throughout the chapter we call Equation 4.1a the selection equation, while Equation 4.1b is the regression equation. The selection equation explains CEO turnover, i.e. $CEO\_stayed_{it} = 1$ corresponds to those firm-years when the CEO keeps his or her position. The regression equation explains the compensation of these CEOs in the subsequent year. As the notion of compensation sensitivity to previous year performance is not meaningful for new CEOs, we restrict the remuneration analysis to CEOs with tenure of more than one year. Estimating the parameters of the regression Equation 4.1b on the basis of the non-turnover sample only, would not be a valid alternative to the proposed method because the OLS estimator of β_2 is biased when the selection of the regression sample is endogenous (i.e. $\sigma_{12} \neq 0$). Instead, our sample selection model deals with the endogeneity of selection, and therefore renders reliable parameter estimates for the regression equation (Greene, 2000).

Our hypotheses are tested within Tobit-2 models with interaction terms. To estimate the models, we employ a two-step procedure developed by Heckman (1979), which yields consistent parameter estimates. We allow the explanatory variables to be time-varying, which results in multiple observations for each of the analyzed firms. In order to assure the robustness of the results and to take the panel data structure of our sample explicitly into account, we allow for a possible dependence between different observations corresponding to the same firm. We account for clustering and implement the procedure which assumes the observations to be independent across firms, but does not require different observations on the same firm to be independent (StataCorp, 2001).

4 RESULTS

4.1 The Impact of Performance on Managerial Disciplining and Remuneration

In Table 4.2, we examine whether performance influences CEO turnover (the selection equations of Panel A) and industry-adjusted CEO remuneration (the regression equations of Panel B). The results of Panel A support the disciplinary role of managerial turnover because performance is negatively correlated to future turnover (Model 1A).[14] In the pre-reform period, this effect is statistically significant for abnormal stock returns (but also for the industry-adjusted accounting-based performance measure reported in models presented in subsequent tables; see below). Unsurprisingly, managers generating strong corporate performance are more likely to keep their positions during the subsequent year. A more detailed analysis of the parameter estimates highlights the economic significance: for instance, Model 1A implies that in the pre-reform period the probability that a CEO of a well-performing company loses his or her job is almost half of the corresponding probability for the median performing company. In contrast, CEOs of poorly

---

[14] The performance coefficients in the regression equations are positive but this signifies that the relation between turnover and performance is negative because the dependent variable equals 1 if the CEO keeps his position and 0 when he departs (for reasons other than retirement).

Table 4.2 Sample selection models explaining CEO turnover and industry-adjusted compensation

Panel A: Selection equations

	Model 1A: Pre-reform		Model 1B: Post-reform		Model 1C: Post-reform	
	Dependent variable equals 0 if the CEO is replaced and 1 otherwise					
	Estimate	p-value	Estimate	p-value	Estimate	p-value
Intercept	3.27605	0.000	2.22414	0.000	1.94549	0.000
Performance indicators						
Abnormal stock returns in year t–1	0.00332	0.076	0.04218	0.477	0.05188	0.371
Industry-adjusted ROA in year t–1	0.00425	0.211	0.00711	0.004	0.00589	0.017
Firm size, leverage, and risk						
Firm size	−0.09618	0.027	−0.08378	0.000	−0.06409	0.001
Capital gearing	−0.00256	0.229	0.00055	0.792	0.00111	0.600
Risk	−0.00603	0.286	0.00297	0.457	0.00472	0.224
Year and industry control variables						
Year dummies	Yes		Yes		Yes	
Industry dummies	Yes		Yes		Yes	
Wald χ^2	$\chi^2(20) = 104.29$		$\chi^2(20) = 102.41$		$\chi^2(20) = 103.62$	
P-value for χ^2	< 0.001		< 0.001		< 0.001	

Panel B: Regression equations

Dependent variable:	Industry-adjusted CEO monetary remuneration		Industry-adjusted CEO monetary remuneration		Industry-adjusted CEO total remuneration	
	Estimate	p-value	Estimate	p-value	Estimate	p-value
Intercept	−3.06839	0.000	−3.02736	0.000	−3.93953	0.000
Performance indicators						
Abnormal stock returns in year t–1	0.00116	0.009	0.05319	0.006	0.06694	0.015
Industry-adjusted ROA in year t–1	0.00420	0.008	0.00296	0.015	0.00277	0.074

Firm size, leverage, and risk					
Firm size	0.24891	0.000	0.22409	0.000	0.28719	0.000
Capital gearing	0.00086	0.356	−0.00205	0.075	−0.00165	0.250
Risk	0.00535	0.038	0.00966	0.000	0.01341	0.000
Year control variables						
Year dummies	Yes		Yes		Yes	
Wald χ^2	$\chi^2(9) = 307.05$		$\chi^2(9) = 449.80$		$\chi^2(9) = 424.28$	
P-value for χ^2	< 0.001		< 0.001		< 0.001	

Panel C: Model statistics and tests

Total no. of observations	868	2282	2277
No. of censored observations	102	314	314
No. of uncensored observations	766	1968	1963
Log-likelihood	−658.71	−2255.21	−2728.93
Wald χ^2 statistics for testing joint significance of two equations	$\chi^2(29) = 676.33$	$\chi^2(29) = 822.22$	$\chi^2(29) = 780.08$
P-value for χ^2	< 0.001	< 0.001	< 0.001
Estimate of ρ	0.881	0.774	0.839
Wald χ^2 statistics for testing $\rho = 0$ (tests of equations independence)	$\chi^2(1) = 69.32$	$\chi^2(1) = 22.62$	$\chi^2(1) = 37.68$
P-value for χ^2	< 0.001	< 0.001	< 0.001

performing firms are almost twice as likely to lose their jobs as their counterparts of the median performing firm.[15] In the post-reform period (Models 1B and 1C), we find a stronger correlation with our accounting-based performance measure (return on assets), whereas the relation between turnover and stock performance is no longer statistically significant. Consequently, in the post-reform period, the probability of a CEO losing his or her job (as implied by Model 1C) are equal to 8.3 percent, 7.2 percent, and 9.5 percent in a median, a well-performing, and a poorly performing company, respectively. These findings do not unequivocally show that the performance sensitivity of CEO turnover increased following the implementation of the Cadbury code (which is the conclusion of Dahya et al., 2002).

The regression equations in Panel B of Table 4.2 show a positive relation between, respectively, the monetary remuneration (fixed salary and bonus) and total remuneration (which also includes equity-based compensation such as option plans and LTIPs), and abnormal returns and accounting performance (Models 1A–C). We do find that, both for the pre- and post-reform periods, the relation between CEO remuneration and the accounting and stock price performance measure is positive and statistically significant. As frequently documented in previous research, remuneration is strongly dependent on firm size both in the pre- and post-reform period (see e.g. Girma et al., 2007). We also show that risky firms also reward higher salaries to their top management.

We now perform a more detailed analysis and expand the above remuneration and turnover models with internal corporate governance characteristics (Section 4.2) and external governance devices (Section 4.3), while controlling for firm size, risk, leverage and industry.

4.2   Determinants of CEO Turnover

4.2.1   Internal governance
Panel A of Table 4.3 shows that board structure has an important impact on CEO turnover in the pre-reform period (Model 2A). We find that: (i) The presence of larger boards facilitates the replacement of the CEO. It may indeed be that larger boards represent a larger internal pool of managerial talent. (ii) Boards with a larger percentage of outside, independent directors replace CEOs more frequently. (iii) When a person fulfills the tasks of CEO and chairman of the board simultaneously (which is still the case in one third of the firms in the pre-reform period), the likelihood of his or her replacement significantly decreases. This implies that more powerful CEOs can successfully impede their replacement. This danger of conflicts of interest provides further support for the need to separate the positions of CEO and chairman (as stipulated in the Cadbury report). One would expect all of the above characteristics of the internal corporate governance mechanism to be much stronger related to turnover in the wake of poor corporate performance. We find however that this is not the case: the interaction terms of the proportion of non-executive

---

[15]   The median firm is characterized by median values of firm-specific characteristics (performance, board composition, control variables). We define a well-performing company as a company where both performance indicators are at the top quartile of performance while control variables take median values. Finally, in a poorly performing firm both performance indicators are at the bottom quartile of performance while control variables again take median values.

Table 4.3 Sample selection models explaining CEO turnover and industry-adjusted compensation

Panel A: Selection equations

	Model 2A: Pre-reform		Model 2B: Post-reform		Model 2C: Post-reform	
	Dependent variable equals 0 if the CEO is replaced and 1 otherwise					
	Estimate	p-value	Estimate	p-value	Estimate	p-value
Intercept	4.03002	0.003	1.47579	0.000	1.17269	0.003
Performance indicators						
Abnormal stock returns in year $t-1$	0.00654	0.019	0.68673	0.187	0.60951	0.174
Industry-adjusted ROA in year $t-1$	0.00907	0.315	0.01338	0.523	0.00695	0.751
Board composition						
Board size	−0.95282	0.008	0.11349	0.484	0.14205	0.358
Stock price perform. * Board size	0.00395	0.517	−0.25591	0.229	−0.20581	0.305
Accounting perform. * Board size	0.01521	0.223	−0.01108	0.282	−0.00893	0.398
Proportion of non-executives directors	−0.01339	0.024	0.00314	0.321	0.00435	0.173
Stock price perform. * Prop. of non-executives	−0.00008	0.574	−0.00201	0.658	−0.00225	0.604
Accounting perform. * Prop. of non-executives	−0.00013	0.679	0.00028	0.194	0.00032	0.168
CEO is also the chairman	0.30943	0.049	−0.27086	0.038	−0.34720	0.005
Stock price perf. * CEO is also the chairman	−0.00278	0.632	0.01375	0.935	−0.05373	0.720
Accounting perf. * CEO is also the chairman	−0.00367	0.721	0.00835	0.325	0.01030	0.175
Ownership concentration						
Executives' stakes	0.05166	0.178	0.00506	0.166	0.00487	0.181
Stock price perform. * Executives' stakes	0.00037	0.188	−0.00038	0.952	−0.00060	0.921
Accounting perform. * Executives' stakes	−0.00047	0.512	−0.00002	0.924	−0.00004	0.864
Outside block holdings	−0.00476	0.283	−0.00212	0.364	−0.00246	0.297
Stock price perform. * Outside block holdings	−0.00006	0.611	0.00187	0.665	−0.00025	0.952
Accounting perform. * Outside block holdings	0.00003	0.907	−0.00017	0.073	−0.00016	0.095

Table 4.3 (continued)

Panel A: Selection equations	Model 2A: Pre-reform		Model 2B: Post-reform		Model 2C: Post-reform	
	Dependent variable equals 0 if the CEO is replaced and 1 otherwise					
	Estimate	p-value	Estimate	p-value	Estimate	p-value
Ownership concentration						
Non-executives' stakes	0.00375	0.614	−0.00523	0.277	−0.00405	0.408
Stock price perform. * Non-executives' stakes	−0.00045	0.004	−0.00533	0.533	−0.00453	0.597
Accounting perform. * Non-executives' stakes	−0.00016	0.805	−0.00010	0.789	−0.00034	0.444
Firm size, leverage, and risk						
Firm size	0.10879	0.105	−0.09294	0.001	−0.07260	0.010
Capital gearing	0.00010	0.977	0.00048	0.826	0.00015	0.940
Risk	−0.00633	0.416	0.00713	0.043	0.00842	0.015
Year and industry control variables						
Year dummies	Yes		Yes		Yes	
Industry dummies	Yes		Yes		Yes	
Wald χ^2	$\chi^2(38) = 153.55$		$\chi^2(38) = 156.85$		$\chi^2(38) = 143.55$	
P-value for χ^2	< 0.001		< 0.001		< 0.001	

Panel B: Regression equations						
Dependent variable:	Industry-adjusted CEO monetary remuneration		Industry-adjusted CEO monetary remuneration		Industry-adjusted CEO total remuneration	
	Estimate	p-value	Estimate	p-value	Estimate	p-value
Intercept	−3.20470	0.000	−3.09582	0.000	−3.94607	0.000
Performance indicators						
Abnormal stock returns in year $t-1$	0.00287	0.001	−0.10655	0.186	−0.03572	0.751
Industry-adjusted ROA in year $t-1$	0.00310	0.194	0.01833	0.052	0.01008	0.503

Board composition

Board size	0.20572	0.009	0.27508	0.001	0.31036	0.002
Stock price perform. * Board size	−0.00087	0.486	0.05426	0.041	0.06881	0.054
Accounting perform. * Board size	0.00116	0.760	−0.00131	0.742	0.00274	0.655
Proportion of non-executives directors	0.00214	0.264	0.00609	0.000	0.00802	0.000
Stock price perform. * Prop. of non-executives	0.00005	0.234	0.00149	0.290	0.00004	0.983
Accounting perform. * Prop. of non-executives	−0.00001	0.924	−0.00021	0.048	−0.00020	0.213
CEO is also the chairman	0.02154	0.680	0.12420	0.092	0.00794	0.926
Stock price perf. * CEO is also the chairman	−0.00074	0.471	−0.03780	0.480	−0.10197	0.113
Accounting perf. * CEO is also the chairman	0.00699	0.041	0.00129	0.743	0.00331	0.487
Remuneration committee presence	0.00151	0.973	Dropped	Dropped	Dropped	
Stock price perform. * Remuneration committee presence	−0.00135	0.359	Dropped	Dropped	Dropped	
Accounting perform. * Remuneration committee presence	0.00049	0.866	Dropped	Dropped	Dropped	

Ownership concentration

Executives' stakes	−0.00468	0.031	−0.00517	0.001	−0.00694	0.000
Stock price perform. * Executives' stakes	−0.00010	0.025	−0.00090	0.522	−0.00163	0.409
Accounting perform. * Executives' stakes	0.00010	0.460	−0.00006	0.579	−0.00007	0.610
Outside block holdings	−0.00332	0.049	−0.00178	0.100	−0.00272	0.057
Stock price perform. * Outside block holdings	−0.00001	0.829	−0.00079	0.526	−0.00182	0.263
Accounting perform. * Outside block holdings	−0.00003	0.694	−0.00007	0.080	−0.00004	0.499
Non-executives' stakes	−0.00506	0.023	−0.00471	0.048	−0.00414	0.245
Stock price perform. * Non-executives' stakes	−0.00003	0.501	−0.00255	0.282	−0.00249	0.490
Accounting perform. * Non-executives' stakes	−0.00005	0.701	−0.00014	0.368	−0.00025	0.439

Table 4.3   (continued)

Panel B: Regression equations

Dependent variable:	Model 2A: Pre-reform Industry-adjusted CEO monetary remuneration		Model 2B: Post-reform Industry-adjusted CEO monetary remuneration		Model 2C: Post-reform Industry-adjusted CEO total remuneration	
	Estimate	p-value	Estimate	p-value	Estimate	p-value
Firm size, leverage, and risk						
Firm size	0.20799	0.000	0.17260	0.000	0.22374	0.000
Capital gearing	0.00034	0.699	−0.00277	0.014	−0.00294	0.030
Risk	0.00862	0.003	0.00744	0.000	0.01041	0.000
Year control variables						
Year dummies	Yes		Yes		Yes	
Wald χ^2	$\chi^2(30) = 481.57$		$\chi^2(27) = 591.29$		$\chi^2(27) = 546.76$	
P-value for χ^2	< 0.001		< 0.001		< 0.001	

Panel C: Model statistics and tests

Total no. of observations	847		1909		1905	
No. of censored observations	101		300		300	
No. of uncensored observations	746		1609		1605	
Log-likelihood	−550.00		−1746.53		−2149.73	
Wald χ^2 statistics for testing joint significance of two equations	$\chi^2(68) = 964.06$		$\chi^2(65) = 1322.83$		$\chi^2(65) = 1096.07$	
P-value for χ^2	< 0.001		< 0.001		< 0.001	
Estimate of ρ	−0.660		0.936		0.942	
Wald χ^2 statistics for testing $\rho = 0$ (tests of equations independence)	$\chi^2(1) = 1.10$		$\chi^2(1) = 185.38$		$\chi^2(1) = 166.45$	
P-value for χ^2	0.2953		< 0.001		< 0.001	

directors and either of the performance measures are not statistically significant in the pre-reform period. Also, the degree of entrenchment (the positions of CEO and chairman are combined) does not affect the performance sensitivity of turnover, as the corresponding interaction terms are insignificant.

In the post-reform period, we find no correlation between any of the board characteristics (and their interactions with performance) to the likelihood of forced managerial turnover with the exception of CEO–chairman duality (see below). This suggests that boards with a high proportion of non-executive directors do not appear significantly more apt to replace underperforming management. Hence, our results do not confirm Weisbach's (1988) findings that outsider-dominated boards, supposedly more independent from management, are more able to enforce disciplinary turnover. Our findings indicate that the main prescription of the 'Recommendations for Good Corporate Governance' (the 1992 Cadbury report and its successors), i.e. strengthening the role of non-executive directors, may not be as effective as it is assumed to be.

Interestingly, the effect of CEO–chairman duality gets reversed in the post-reform period: CEOs who are also chairmen are more likely to lose the CEO position. As the governance codes recommend the separation of the two positions, it may be the case that in the post-reform period, the cases where CEOs also act as chairmen reflect temporary solutions to the succession planning, e.g. the CEO holds on to both jobs until a suitable replacement can be found for one of the positions (frequently that of the CEO whereby the person in question subsequently only retains the position of non-executive chairman). As before, the interactions of the CEO–chairman duality variables with performance do not significantly affect the likelihood of CEO turnover. Thus, we conclude that our analysis fails to support Hypothesis 1a.

4.2.2 External governance

For the pre-reform period, Model 2A does not yield much support for Hypothesis 2a. Ownership concentration does not seem to affect the performance sensitivity of CEO turnover. In particular, neither an analysis with outsider ownership concentration (Model 2A), nor a more detailed analysis (not shown) with ownership concentration held by institutions (banks, pensions funds, mutual and investment funds, insurance companies), families and individuals not related to a director, other corporations, and the government provides evidence of outside shareholder monitoring. In some models which do not include the internal governance mechanisms, strong insider control implies a higher probability that the CEO will not be removed. Executive directors with large ownership stakes appear able to successfully ward off any attempts to replace the CEO regardless of corporate performance. As these results are not robust in larger models, they are not reported. Model 2A of Table 4.3 shows that the size of the shareholdings controlled by non-executive directors does not have a direct impact on the likelihood of CEO turnover. Interestingly, however, the significance of the interaction term between the non-executives' stake and past stock performance indicates that non-executive directors tend to protect the CEOs of firms whose stock underperformed (which is in line with the findings by Franks et al., 2001). This result further illustrates the lack of monitoring by non-executive directors. Thus, poor performance may be the result not only of poor management, but perhaps also of poor external corporate governance.

The situation for the post-reform period is similar: contrary to what Hypothesis 2a postulates, there is no strong link between ownership structures and the likelihood of managerial turnover in the post-reform period. Virtually all the coefficients corresponding to ownership variables or their interactions in selection equations of Models 2B and 2C are not statistically significant.

Finally, our control variables reveal that, over the pre-reform period, CEOs of larger firms were more able to maintain their position, whereas in the post-reform period, CEOs seem to be more easily disciplined in larger firms. Capital gearing does not affect the likelihood of CEO turnover, while CEOs of risky firms are less likely to lose their jobs in the post-reform period.

4.3   Determinants of CEO Compensation

4.3.1   Internal governance

We study the relation between top management remuneration, and performance and governance variables in both periods in Panel B of Table 4.3 (Models 2A–C). The impact of board size is consistently significant: CEOs of firms with large boards receive a larger compensation in both the pre-reform and post-reform periods. This effect is not performance-dependent in the pre-reform sample, while in the more recent period, the presence of larger boards strengthens the link between compensation and stock performance. Stronger abnormal returns are followed by higher monetary and total compensation (which distinguishes our results from those obtained for the US by Yermack, 1996).

In the pre-reform period (Model 2A), a high proportion of non-executive directors, the presence of a remuneration committee, and the separation of the functions of the CEO and the chairman do not seem related to the way managerial remuneration contracts were drawn up. The only statistically significant effect in this part of the analysis is the interaction of the CEO–chairman indicator with accounting performance. Apparently, in the pre-reform period, the remuneration of those CEOs who also acted as chairmen of the board was more sensitive to the return on assets. A possible interpretation may be that powerful executives were able to have accounting performance adopted as the performance yardstick on which their remuneration would be partially based. Due to the large degree of discretion that powerful CEOs could enjoy, they could have been able to manipulate this benchmark in the pre-reform period by means of specific accounting choices for a number of years. Finally, the presence of a remuneration committee (consisting of non-executive directors) did not have a significant impact on CEO compensation in the pre-reform period.

In the post-reform period, Models 2B and 2C (see Panel B) demonstrate that CEOs who are members of boards with a larger proportion of non-executive directors enjoy higher levels of both monetary and total compensation. Board independence hardly matters for the performance sensitivity of CEO remuneration in the post-reform period. The only exception is the statistically significant coefficient for the corresponding to one of the interaction terms in Model 2B: it suggests that the presence of a substantial number of non-executive directors on the board weakens the link between monetary compensation and accounting performance. While the focus of the governance reforms implemented in the UK in the 1990s was, among other things, on strengthening the role of non-executive directors, our results do not confirm any notable improvement in the governance efficiency of this mechanism. CEO–Chairman duality does not appear to affect either the level of managerial pay or its performance-sensitivity in the post-reform period.[16] Overall, we find little relation between board structure and compensation in either of the periods analyzed and therefore, we reject Hypothesis 1b.

4.3.2 External governance

We show for both the pre-reform and post-reform periods that, when executive directors hold large share stakes, the CEO's monetary remuneration is lower (Panel B of Table 4.3). It may be that when executive directors derive substantial wealth from their equity investments in their corporation, they care less about their monetary income. Still, for the pre-reform period, we find that when stock prices decrease, CEOs seem to compensate for disappointing stock returns by augmenting their monetary compensation. Thus, Model 2A illustrates a pernicious remuneration incentive scheme by which CEOs receive a higher monetary compensation in the wake of poor stock performance of firms in which they can exert considerable voting power. Notably, this effect has disappeared in the post-reform sample. Still, given that the levels of compensation are lower in firms with powerful executive directors, we cannot fully support the managerial-power (or the skimming) model for executive compensation as formulated by Bebchuk and Fried (2003).

When outside shareholders hold share blocks, CEO compensation appears to be lower (see Models 2A–C). However, outside shareholders do not seem to impose an *effective* pay-for-performance remuneration scheme, as the interaction of the size of the outside block holdings with corporate performance is not statistically significant. It may well be that pay-for-performance schemes and shareholder control are supplementary monitoring mechanisms. Consequently, we find only partial evidence supporting Hypothesis 2b: there is no evidence that CEO remuneration is more performance-related in outsider-dominated firms, but strong director control concentration led to a lower performance sensitivity of CEO remuneration in the pre-reform years.

Finally, the size of the equity stakes controlled by non-executive directors is negatively related to the level of monetary CEO pay for both the pre-reform and post-reform periods (see Models 2A and 2B, Panel B of Table 4.3). Apparently, in companies where non-executive directors are less powerful (in terms of voting power), the CEO is more likely to enjoy higher levels of compensation. Still, powerful non-executive directors do not impose a performance-related remuneration scheme on the management as the interaction terms are not statistically significant.

Table 4.3 (Panel B) also provides some interesting insights concerning the impact of firm-specific control variables (size, gearing, and risk) on CEO remuneration. In line with the UK remuneration literature (see e.g. Girma et al., 2007), CEOs of larger firms enjoy significantly higher industry-adjusted monetary compensation and higher total compensation. Top management usually tries to justify – rightly so or not – size-related compensation by the fact that special managerial skills (which are in short supply) are needed to

---

[16]   Only Model 2B suggests that CEOs who are also chairmen enjoy higher levels of cash-based compensation, but this effect is only marginally significant. We do not analyze the impact of the presence of a remuneration committee on compensation in the post-reform period. Following the recommendations of the governance codes, virtually all the firms have established such a committee by 1999 (i.e. the year when the post-reform sample starts).

manage larger firms. We also document that firm leverage has no impact on compensation in the pre-reform period. In more recent years, highly levered firms tend to pay their CEOs less. Finally, CEO remuneration increases with corporate risk.

4.4   Sample Selection Bias

Panels C of Tables 4.2 and 4.3 report the estimates of the correlation coefficients of the error terms in the selection and regression equations. The fact that those estimates are highly significant in most specifications confirms that an analysis of compensation performance-sensitivity based on a simple regression framework (OLS or fixed-effects estimations on a censored sample) is likely to suffer from a severe selection bias. Renneboog and Trojanowski (2010) illustrate that statistical inference based on the model ignoring the selectivity resulting from disciplinary CEO turnover can substantially underestimate the remuneration rewarding effect (and the impact of other covariates) and may lead to spurious conclusions. It may explain the differences in conclusions between our analysis (based on a sample selection model) and earlier UK compensation studies based on simple OLS or fixed effects (e.g. Conyon et al., 1995). This also suggests caution in interpreting the evidence of past studies on remuneration.

5   CONCLUSION AND DISCUSSION

We simultaneously analyze two mechanisms of the managerial labor market: CEO turnover and remuneration schemes. Sample selection models are applied to firms listed on the London Stock Exchange over two periods of six years: 1988–93 representing the period prior to the main changes in corporate governance regulation (the Cadbury, Greenbury, and Hampel reports which were bundled in the Combined Code) and the post-reform period of 1999–2004. Our approach yields some novel results compared to earlier UK research: the managerial remuneration and the termination of labor contracts play an important role in mitigating agency problems between managers and shareholders. We find that both the CEO's industry-adjusted compensation and CEO replacement are performance-sensitive. Top executive turnover is shown to serve as a disciplinary mechanism in case of corporate underperformance, whereas the level of CEO compensation rewards good past performance although the performance criterion chosen depends to some extent on the ownership concentration and board structure. Especially, our results on remuneration go against most past UK findings which had unveiled little pay-for-performance sensitivity, possibly due to biases introduced by inappropriate estimation techniques and an incorrect choice of remuneration measures and performance benchmarks.

Our analysis of CEO compensation reveals that CEOs are rewarded for corporate size and risk, but also for good accounting and stock price performance. The fact that the levels of remuneration are lower when executive directors are more powerful (in terms of voting rights) supports the alignment-of-interest hypothesis which states that managerial ownership aligns the objectives of management and of other shareholders. However, for the pre-reform period we also find that, when CEOs derived substantial wealth from the equity investment in their firms and when stock prices decreased and negative abnormal returns were incurred, CEOs seemed to compensate for the disappointing stock perform-ance by augmenting their monetary compensation package (salary and bonus). This suggests self-dealing and hence provides some support for an alternative theory, namely the skimming or managerial-power hypothesis (Bertrand and Mullainathan, 2000; Bebchuk and Fried, 2003). In the pre-reform period, CEOs who also exercise the function of chairman of the board had more discretion over this benchmark and hence over their monetary compensation. In contrast, in firms with strong outsider (monitoring) share-holders, the management could not pick its preferred performance benchmark as they were required to focus on the creation of shareholder value. The aforementioned prob-lems of self-dealing in firms with powerful executives do not persist in the post-reform years, which implies some improvement in corporate governance standards in the more recent regulatory regime.

In both periods, the CEOs of monitored firms (in particular in firms where non-executive directors and outside shareholders control large share blocks) enjoy lower remuneration, irrespective of performance. Moreover, in the pre-reform period, there were few characteristics of the board structure (apart from the separation of CEO and chairman) which had an impact on the pay-for-performance sensitivity. Neither the pro-portion of non-executive directors on the board nor the presence of a remuneration com-mittee seems to have had any impact on the remuneration policy of the firm. Interestingly, in the post-reform period, a larger board size is associated with a higher sensitivity of remuneration to stock performance, whereas a larger proportion of non-executive direc-tors on the board weakens the link between CEO compensation and the accounting performance measure. Overall, our results in this respect appear consistent with the widely perceived failure of internal governance mechanisms in tackling the agency problems associated with managerial pay:

> Ten years ago company boards set up remuneration committees to restrain greedy chief execu-tives and make the salary setting process more transparent. Yet the excesses seem to have increased as a result. The committees create a veneer of respectability that protects chief execu-tives from direct accountability. They rely on salary surveys and often use absurd overseas comparisons to justify huge salaries for UK-based executives. The committees generally want their chief executives to be paid an above-average wage, thereby creating an inflationary spiral. (*Financial Times*, May 20, 2003)

The implementation of the governance codes' guidelines has not resulted in increased CEO turnover rates: the dismissal probabilities appear comparable in the pre- and post-reform periods. We also document CEO dismissal to be performance-sensitive in both pre- and post-reform periods. There is little evidence of disciplinary monitoring by pow-erful outsider shareholders: institutions, families, or individuals, and other corporations do not seem to be more apt to remove CEOs even in the wake of poor performance in either period. This finding is consistent with the sentiment recently expressed in the press:

> The sad fact is that although reforms over the last few years have improved the transparency and accountability of firms to their shareholders, there hasn't been a corresponding increase in incentives or requirements for investors to act on the information provided. Asking questions about risks and long-term prospects of the companies they invested in makes good business sense for pension funds, insurers and savers. Some major investors and fund managers are taking on this challenge, but it is only through being consistently challenged and questioned by

pension fund trustees that kind of responsible ownership will become the norm. (*Financial Times*, February 23, 2009)

In line with earlier research, we find that in the pre-reform period non-executive directors owning share blocks seemed to protect the incumbent CEO in poorly performing companies, while in the post-reform period this effect is no longer significant (suggesting some improvement in governance standards following the implementation of codes' guidelines). In the pre-reform period, the lack of CEO–chairman duality in many firms fostered managerial entrenchment: prior to 1993 CEOs also holding the positions of chairmen of the board successfully impeded their replacement regardless of corporate performance. This confirms that the intention of the codes' governance guidelines to eliminate such types of entrenchment was entirely justified. Unfortunately, not all the codes' recommendations have yielded such beneficial effects. For instance, while prior to 1993 boards with a high proportion of non-executive directors replaced CEOs more frequently, this aspect of board independence does not appear to have had any effect on CEO dismissal in the post-reform period. Hence, we conclude that all the regulatory effort undertaken in the UK over the 1990s has had at best a moderate effect on increasing executives' accountability and the performance sensitivity of their forced turnover.

REFERENCES

Agrawal, Anup and Charles R. Knoeber. 1996. Firm performance and mechanisms to control agency problems between managers and shareholders, *Journal of Financial and Quantitative Analysis*, 31, 377–97.
Agrawal, Anup and Charles R. Knoeber. 1998. Managerial compensation and the threat of takeover, *Journal of Financial Economics*, 47, 219–39.
Amemiya, Takeshi. 1984. Tobit models: A survey, *Journal of Econometrics*, 24, 3–63.
Bebchuk, Lucian Arye and Jesse M. Fried. 2003. Executive compensation as an agency problem, *Journal of Economic Perspectives*, 17(3), 71–92.
Bebchuk, Lucian Arye and Jesse M. Fried. 2004. *Pay without Performance: The Unfulfilled Promise of Executive Compensation*, Cambridge, Harvard University Press.
Bebchuk, Lucian Arye, Jesse M. Fried, and David I. Walker. 2002. Managerial power and rent extraction in the design of executive compensation, *University of Chicago Law Review*, 69, 751–846.
Becht, Marco, Julian Franks, Colin Mayer, and Stefano Rossi. 2009. Returns to shareholder activism: evidence from a clinical study of the Hermes UK Focus Fund, *Review of Financial Studies*, 22, 3093–129.
Bertrand, Marianne and Sendhil Mullainathan. 2000. Agents with and without principals, *American Economic Review*, 90, 203–8.
Bertrand, Marianne and Sendhil Mullainathan. 2001. Are CEOs rewarded for luck? The ones without principals are, *Quarterly Journal of Economics*, 116, 901–32.
Bushman, Robert M. and Raffi J. Indjejikian. 1993. Accounting income, stock price, and managerial compensation, *Journal of Accounting and Economics*, 16, 3–23.
Chan, Konan, Narasimhan Jegadeesh, and Theodore Sougiannis. 2004. The accrual effect on future earning, *Review of Quantitative Finance and Accounting*, 22, 97–129.
Clay, Darin. 2000. The effects of institutional investment on CEO compensation, Working paper, University of Chicago, Chicago.
Conyon, Martin and Kevin J. Murphy. 2000. The prince and the pauper? CEO pay in the United States and the United Kingdom, *Economic Journal*, 110, 640–71.
Conyon, Martin, Paul Gregg, and Stephen Machin. 1995. Taking care of business: Executive compensation in the United Kingdom, *Economic Journal*, 105, 704–14.
Core, John E., Robert W. Holthausen, and David F. Larcker. 1999. Corporate governance, chief executive officer compensation and firm performance, *Journal of Financial Economics*, 51, 371–406.
Coughlan, Anne T. and Ronald M. Schmidt. 1985. Executive compensation, management turnover, and firm performance: An empirical investigation, *Journal of Accounting and Economics*, 7, 43–66.

Crespi, Rafel and Luc Renneboog. 2010. Is (institutional) shareholder activism new? Evidence from UK share-holder coalitions in the pre-Cadbury era, *Corporate Governance: An International Review,* 18, 274–95.

Crespi, Rafel, Carles Gispert, and Luc Renneboog. 2002. Cash-based executive compensation in Spain and UK, in Joseph McCahery, Piet Moerland, Theo Raaijmakers, and Luc Renneboog (eds), *Corporate Governance Regimes: Convergence and Diversity,* pp. 647–67. Oxford: Oxford University Press.

Dahya, Jay, John J. McConnell, and Nickolaos G. Travlos. 2002. The Cadbury committee, corporate perform-ance, and top management turnover, *Journal of Finance,* 57, 461–84.

Denis, David J. and Diane K. Denis. 1995. Performance changes following top management dismissals, *Journal of Finance,* 50, 1029–57.

Denis, David J. and Timothy A. Kruse. 2000. Managerial discipline and corporate restructuring following performance declines, *Journal of Financial Economics,* 55, 391–424.

Denis, David J., Diane K. Denis, and Atulya Sarin. 1997. Ownership structure and top executive turnover, *Journal of Financial Economics,* 45, 193–221.

Fama, Eugene F. 1980. Agency problems and the theory of the firm, *Journal of Political Economy,* 88, 288–307.

Franks, Julian, Colin Mayer, and Luc Renneboog. 2001. Who disciplines the management of poorly perform-ing companies?, *Journal of Financial Intermediation,* 10, 209–48.

FRC. 2009. *The Combined Code and associated guidance,* http://www.frc.org.uk/CORPORATE/COMBINEDCODE.CFM.

Geiler, Philipp and Luc Renneboog. 2011. Managerial compensation: Agency solution or problem?, *Journal of Corporate Law Studies,* forthcoming.

Gibbons, Robert and Kevin J. Murphy. 1990. Relative performance evaluation for chief executive officers, *Industrial and Labor Relations Review,* 43, 30-S–51-S.

Gibbons, Robert and Kevin J. Murphy. 1992. Optimal incentive contracts in the presence of career concerns: Theory and evidence, *Journal of Political Economy,* 100, 468–505.

Girma, Sourafel, Steve Thompson, and Peter Wright. 2006. Merger activity and executive pay, *Economica,* 73, 321–39.

Girma, Sourafel, Steve Thompson, and Peter Wright. 2007. Corporate governance reforms and executive com-pensation determination: Evidence from the UK, *Manchester School,* 75, 65–81.

Greene, William H. 2000. *Econometric Analysis.* Upper Saddle River, Prentice Hall.

Grossman, Sanford J. and Oliver Hart. 1983. An analysis of the principal–agent problem, *Econometrica,* 51, 7–45.

Hallock, Kevin F. 1997. Reciprocally interlocking boards of directors and executive compensation, *Journal of Financial and Quantitative Analysis,* 32, 331–44.

Heckman, James J. 1979. Sample selection bias as a specification error, *Econometrica,* 47, 153–61.

Holmström, Bengt. 1979. Moral hazard and observability, *Bell Journal of Economics,* 10, 74–91.

Holmström, Bengt. 1982. Managerial incentive schemes – a dynamic perspective, in *Essays in Economics and Management in Honour of Lars Wahlbeck,* Helsinki.

Jensen, Michael C. and William H. Meckling. 1976. Theory of the firm: Managerial behavior, agency costs, and ownership structure, *Journal of Financial Economics,* 3, 305–60.

Jensen, Michael C. and Kevin J. Murphy. 1990. Performance pay and top-management incentives, *Journal of Political Economy,* 98, 225–64.

Jensen, Michael C., Kevin J. Murphy, and Eric G. Wruck. 2004. Where we have been, how we got there, what are the problems and how to fix them, Working paper, Harvard NOM, http://ssrn.com/abstract=561305.

Kahn, Charles M. and Andrew Winton. 1998. Ownership structure, speculation, and shareholder intervention, *Journal of Finance,* 53, 99–129.

Kim, Oliver and Yoon Suh. 1993. Incentive efficiency of compensation based on accounting and market per-formance, *Journal of Accounting and Economics,* 16, 25–53.

Lewellen, Wilbur, Claudio Loderer, and Kenneth J. Martin. 1987. Executive compensation and executive incen-tive problems: An empirical analysis, *Journal of Accounting and Economics,* 9, 287–310.

Martin, Kenneth J. and John J. McConnell. 1991. Corporate performance, corporate takeovers, and manage-ment turnover, *Journal of Finance,* 46, 671–87.

Mikkelson, Wayne H. and M. Megan Partch. 1997. The decline of takeovers and disciplinary managerial turnover, *Journal of Financial Economics,* 44, 205–28.

Murphy, Kevin J. 1985. Corporate performance and managerial remuneration: An empirical analysis, *Journal of Accounting and Economics,* 7, 11–42.

Murphy, Kevin J. 1986. Incentives, learning, and compensation: A theoretical and empirical investigation of managerial labor contracts, *RAND Journal of Economics,* 17, 59–76.

Narayanan, M. P. 1996. Form of compensation and managerial decision horizon, *Journal of Financial and Quantitative Analysis,* 31, 467–91.

Parrino, Robert. 1997. CEO turnover and outside succession: A cross-sectional analysis, *Journal of Financial Economics,* 46, 165–97.

Renneboog, Luc and Grzegorz Trojanowski. 2010. *Managerial remuneration and disciplining in the UK: A tale of two governance regimes*. Tilburg University and University of Exeter, mimeo.

Roe, Mark J. 2002. *Political Determinants of Corporate Governance*. Oxford, Oxford University Press.

Rosenstein, Stuart and Jeffrey G. Wyatt. 1997. Inside directors, board effectiveness, and shareholder wealth, *Journal of Financial Economics*, 44, 229–50.

Sloan, Richard G. 1993. Accounting earnings and top executive compensation, *Journal of Accounting and Economics*, 16, 55–100.

StataCorp. 2001. *Stata Statistical Software: Release 7.0*. College Station, Stata Corporation.

Walker, David. 2009. *A Review of Corporate Governance in UK Banks and Other Financial Industry Entities*. Financial Reporting Council, http://www.frc.org.uk/corporate/reviewCombined.cfm.

Weisbach, Michael Steven. 1988. Outside directors and CEO turnover, *Journal of Financial Economics*, 20, 431–60.

Yermack, David. 1996. High market valuation of companies with a small board of directors, *Journal of Financial Economics*, 40, 185–211.

5 Agency theory and incentive compensation

William Bratton

1 INTRODUCTION

Oliver Hart shows that in an ideal (and taxless) world, first-best results can easily be achieved with an all-common-stock capital structure and a simple incentive compensation system. Hart describes a simple two-period situation where the firm is founded at $t = 0$ and liquidated at $t = 2$, with an intermediate decision respecting liquidation or continuance to be made at $t = 1$, along with a dividend payment. Hart would make the compensation of the manager depend entirely on the dividend d. That is, incentive compensation I should equal $B(d1 + d2)$, where B is a proportion of the firm's total returns. If the payment also covers liquidation proceeds, where $I = B[d1 + (d2, L)]$, the manager can be expected to make an optimal decision respecting liquidation at $t = 1$. If the expected value of L at $t = 1$ is greater than the total returns expected at $t = 2$, the firm is liquidated at $t = 1$ and no costly contracting designed to align the manager's incentives with those of outside investors is necessary (Hart 1995: 146–48). The problem, in Hart's conception, is that the bribe B required to align management incentives with those of outside security holders is unfeasibly large. Accordingly, a complex capital structure must be devised in order to align incentives in the direction of optimal investment and ensure that an actor with the appropriate incentives controls the assets.

Unfortunately, economic theorists have not yet managed to design that incentive-compatible capital structure, leaving us without a theoretical template to provide guidance respecting the terms of optimal executive pay arrangements. Certain broad outlines do follow from Hart's model and are well understood – the arrangement should align the incentives of managers and capital providers, reward effort and merit, and penalize failure. Beyond that there is little known for certain. Compensation design accordingly proceeds on a trial-and-error basis, looking to contracting practice and experience to learn further particulars. With patience, we will know more over time.

Unfortunately, executive pay is a politicized subject matter and patience is in short supply. Policy needs to be set today, whether as regards the design of a compensation package at a particular company, the design of governance procedures that channel pay determinations, or the regulation of the executive compensation under our regimes of corporate, securities, banking, and tax law.

Debates result over a range of policy questions concerning design, governance, and regulation. Within the academic community, discussion proceeds from a common set of assumptions grounded in agency theory, long the lens through which economists and legal academics view corporate relationships. Everyone agrees on four points: (1) shareholder wealth maximization proxies for social welfare maximization, (2) agency costs decrease shareholder wealth; (3) compensation arrangements should minimize agency costs by incenting managers to maximize shareholder value; and (4) given the appropriate incentive effect, the amount of compensation paid need not matter.

Positions in the debates project outward from these points of agreement to diverge in a familiar pattern. An anti-management offense takes shape on one side to face off against those who defend prevailing boardroom practice on the other. The anti-management side favors keener incentives and stricter controls, following up with a law reform agenda. The defensive side favors boardroom discretion and an unregulated status quo.

Both positions come weighted with political baggage. Anti-managerialism means reform and reform disempowers managers. It accordingly echoes the views of the progressive political camp that sees managers as empowered but unaccountable actors in society and the economy and seeks to bring them to account with regulatory controls. Managerialism echoes conservative politics. It accepts private authority as a legitimate means to the end of wealth creation and views new regulation of business as either the tool of rent-seeking interests or misplaced wealth redistribution.

A question arises concerning the contrasting positions' agency-theoretic roots: Which position follows from dispassionate agency cost analysis and which from bald political assertion? Proponents within the camps harbor no doubt as to the answer – their own camp hews to the agency theoretic ideal from which their politically motivated opponents defect. But this is not a question that camp insiders credibly can address.

This chapter takes up the question, showing that both sides retain close ties to agency theory and that neither emerges with the better of the agency case. The reason as much concerns agency theory as it does executive compensation – just as views on compensation diverge widely, so does agency hold out a framework capacious enough to accommodate them. Indeed, this chapter will show that the divergent views on compensation follow from divergent approaches to agency theory.

The chapter describes two contrasting approaches to agency analysis. One such perspective, here termed the "hierarchies" perspective, proactively inspects corporate governance arrangements for reducible agency costs. When a reducible cost is identified, reform is signaled so long as the cost reduction is projected as positive net of the costs of reform. The contrasting perspective, here called the "markets" perspective, hews more closely to the original agency text, Jensen and Meckling's Theory of the Firm: Managerial Behavior, Agency Costs and Ownership Structure (1976). It looks at corporate governance arrangements across time and assumes that competitive pressures bear materially on their development. From this point of view, given a reducible agency cost, actors in the market will devise a way to reduce it. In the literature on executive pay, the hierarchies perspective is manifested in criticism of prevailing practices and suggestions for reform, while the markets perspective signals policy passivity even given pay practices of questionable incentive compatibility.

The chapter begins with a more particular description of the two perspectives. It goes on to employ them to explain the leading positions in the compensation debate. On one side stand law professors like Lucian Bebchuk and Jessie Fried, who use the hierarchies perspective as the framework for an aggressive critique of pay practices and as the basis for a regulatory reform agenda. On the other side stand economists like Kevin Murphy who bring the market perspective to bear in making the defensive case. The comparison shows that in the pay debate particular compensation practices matter less than does the discussant's adherence to one or another perspective.

2   AGENCY THEORY DISAGGREGATED: HIERARCHIES AND MARKETS

We begin our discussion of variations on the agency theme by touching base with Jensen and Meckling's (1976: 308) basic text:

> . . . If both parties to [an agency] relationship are utility maximizers, there is good reason to believe that the agent will not always act in the best interests of the principal. The *principal* can limit divergences from his interest by establishing appropriate incentives for the agent and by incurring monitoring costs designed to limit the aberrant activities of the agent. In addition in some situations it will pay the *agent* to expend resources (bonding costs) to guarantee that he will not take certain actions which would harm the principal or to ensure that the principal will be compensated if he does take such actions.
>
> However, it is generally impossible for the principal or the agent at zero cost to ensure that the agent will make optimal decisions from the principal's viewpoint. In most agency relationships the principal and the agent will incur positive monitoring and bonding costs (non-pecuniary as well as pecuniary), and in addition there will be some divergence between the agent's decisions and those decisions which would maximize the welfare of the principal. The dollar equivalent of the reduction in welfare experienced by the principal as a result of this divergence is also a cost of the agency relationship, and we refer to this latter cost as the "residual loss."
>
> We define *agency costs* as the sum of: 1. the monitoring expenditures by the principal, 2. the bonding expenditures by the agent, 3. the residual loss.

All readers of this text agree that agency costs, thus defined, should be minimized. The question concerns the means to the end. The hierarchies perspective reflects the view that imperfect institutional arrangements can be expected to inhibit the cost-reductive operation of free market forces. It follows that excess agency costs will persist over time, absent reform of prevailing institutional arrangements. The markets perspective reflects the view that actors in corporations can be expected to minimize agency costs over time within their inherited institutional contexts, a view that suffuses Jensen and Meckling's text. But, as we shall see below, today's agency theory is a much larger enterprise than was the original, startup text.

2.1   The Hierarchies Perspective

The hierarchies perspective coalesced in legal theory as the result of the legal academy's reception and assimilation of the Jensen and Meckling agency model, a process that had a transformative effect on the source material.

2.1.1   The takeover era and thereafter

Jensen and Meckling gave legal theory a jolt, but not due to their identification and description of agency costs. Although both the definition and terminology were new, the operative concept was not – generations of lawyers, legislators and judges already had been addressing corporate agency costs otherwise denominated. The dislocation of settled assumptions lay in the new theory's direct application of microeconomic analysis to internal corporate relationships, the implications of which were bound up in a pair of assertions – the famous points that "most organizations are simply legal fictions which serve as a nexus for a set of contracting relationships among individuals," that bring their conflicting objectives into equilibrium, and that "the 'behavior' of the firm is like the behavior of a market, that is, the outcome of a complex equilibrium process" (Jensen and Meckling 1976: 310, 311).

Agency theory, thus introduced to legal theory as "contractarianism," provided a deregulatory counterweight to the Berle and Means (1933) separation of ownership and control, an analysis that had held sway in legal theory for a half century. The separation of ownership and control offered a diagnosis of chronic institutional failure. More particularly, the corporate mode of organization bestowed illegitimate power on managers, countervailing power was needed, and only regulation could effect the adjustment. Agency theory, with its models of governance as contracting among rational economic actors and the corporation as a series of contracts joining inputs to outputs, held out a contrary diagnosis. The problems subsumed under the "separation" rubric reemerged as agency costs, costs which firms competing in free markets would be forced to minimize. In the agency picture, managers were not empowered actors because competitive failure meant immediate removal, whether through the operation of the product market (where lack of success meant insolvency), the operation of the management labor market (where lack of success meant employment termination), or the operation of the market for corporate control (where lack of success meant a hostile takeover). The combined market constraints focused management incentives on long-run productive success for the firm (Bratton 1989a: 417–18). It followed that no new regulation was needed. Thus did agency theory take a market perspective in its first legal iteration.

But the assertion that free market forces by themselves minimize agency costs proved problematic. The corporate law community gave the assertion due consideration and emerged unpersuaded. The model's labor and product market correctives were pronounced to be more theoretical than real. The market for corporate control, in contrast, very well might have played the corrective role ascribed by the model. But events had gotten in the way. Agency theory came to legal theory in the early 1980s just as hostile takeovers burst onto the front pages of the financial section in unprecedented numbers. The control market's sudden vigor imported plausibility to the agency model – for a while it looked like markets really were controlling managers for the first time since the emergence of the large mass-producing corporation (Bratton 1989b: 1517–19). But then the takeover juggernaut lost impetus. State lawmakers, in particular the Delaware courts, responded to the outbreak of hostile activity by restating and reinforcing the corporate law's historical allocation of authority to management (Gilson and Schwartz 2001: 788). When takeover volume dropped off, lawmakers acting under the influence of the management interest were seen to have played a primary causal role.

It followed that agency theory needed to be modified. It was not at all clear that optimal management–shareholder contracts and governance arrangements were attainable within the large corporation's inherited legal framework. Collective action problems substantially impaired contractual self-protection by the dispersed equity interest and agency costs remained suboptimally high (Coffee 1989: 1675–76; Gordon 1989: 1577). It followed that the separation of ownership from control, consigned to the dustbin of history by contractarianism, returned to the top of the legal policy agendas as the problem corporate law needed to solve (Roe 1994: 6–17). That the problem for solution now was conceived in terms of excess agency costs mattered little. Even as agency theory came to enjoy paradigmatic supremacy in legal theory, it lost its initial focus on market controls. In legal context, hierarchies still mattered.

If hierarchies mattered, then they needed to be broken down so that market controls finally could get a chance to work. Attention accordingly turned to the legal model of the firm and its role in embedding barriers to productive inputs. Where agency theory posits that shareholders and managers occupy a natural principal–agent relationship, the legal model of the corporation makes the legal entity the principal and the directors and officers agents of the entity. The shareholders get an important input as electors of the board of directors, but are not accorded status as principals.

It followed that the legal model should be adjusted to assure that ultimate control of the business really did lie with the natural principals, the shareholders (Hansmann and Kraakman 2001: 440–41). Not that dispersed shareholders somehow could formulate the business plan. It was just that channels needed to be opened for shareholder inputs because agency cost reduction enhances value and enhanced principal control conceivably can lower agency costs. Shareholders, in turn, neatly fit the role of correctly incented principals. Their capital investment in the firm's residual interest lends them an undiluted, pure financial incentive to maximize the firm's value (ibid. 449; Holmström and Kaplan 2001: 138). From an incentive point of view, shareholders contrast favorably as against managers and independent directors, whose incentives are comprised by interests in compensation and job retention. Finally, the stock price was deemed to hold out an objective and accurate measure of the purely motivated shareholder maximand – "the principal measure" of the shareholder interest and the best source of instructions for governance and business policy (Hansmann and Kraakman 2001: 440–41).

The emphasis on shareholder incentives and market prices followed from the same set of observations that brought back Berle and Means. Shareholders were seen as having been on the right side of the valuation questions that arose during the takeover era. The capital markets similarly had emerged with an enhanced reputation as drivers of productivity. The era's corporate restructurings were deemed a productive success. It followed that capital markets had a comparative advantage over appointed managers in effecting structural reforms necessitated by deregulation and technological change. Firms tend to be expert in existing technologies, products, and processes. Markets, it is argued, have the advantage when it comes to recognizing the implications of new technologies, products, and processes – the markets move the capital to higher-valuing users who then put the capital into more productive projects (Holmström and Kaplan 2001: 122, 139).

If the shareholders could not surmount collective action problems themselves and force managers to follow market price signals, then law reform directed to lowering the costs and expanding the payoffs of shareholder intervention made sense. Today's shareholder law reform agenda serves these dual purposes. Proposals on the agenda fall into two categories. The first, narrower category accepts the legal model in its broad outline and focuses on process reforms designed to expand the range of shareholder choices in the election process and facilitate shareholder contests. The second type would give the shareholders the option to legislate their way out of the prevailing model to an agency model holding out direct control of business policy. Cost concerns are pervasive in both categories. Some reforms are designed to enhance the impact of existing low cost activist strategies like "just vote no" campaigns. All of the rest include outright subsidies to intervening shareholders.

2.1.2   Theoretical associations

The hierarchies perspective, while very much a product of legal theory, was not without support in economic theory, which underwent developments of its own in the years following the publication of the Jensen and Meckling model in 1976. The contracts that made up the nexus-of-contracts firm were reconceived under the rubric of "completeness" (Salanie 1998: 175–88; Holmström and Roberts 1998: 75–79). This posits that transacting actors can create producing institutions that assuredly evolve to first-best status only to the extent that they deal with "contractible" subject matter. Contractibility is not a safe assumption, particularly with respect to corporate governance (Grossman and Hart 1986; Holmström and Milgrom 1992). Indeed, the contracts that create and govern corporate capital structures are seen in this context as archetypical examples of second-best solutions to noncontractible governance problems. They are empty at the core, omitting important future variables due the difficulty or impossibility of *ex ante* description or *ex post* observation and verification. Shareholders, for example, contribute capital in the absence of terms governing such fundamental matters as investment policy, dividend payout rate, and management remuneration and tenure.

Where Jensen and Meckling had expunged power from the description of the corporation, incomplete-contracts theory restored it to the center of the picture. To the extent that advance contractual specification is not feasible, power allocations play a larger governance role and bear importantly on the firm's productivity (Rajan and Zingales 1998). More particularly, the contracts governing the rights of the firm's security holders deal with critical noncontractible future contingencies by providing open-ended processes that facilitate control's allocation and reallocation (Aghion and Bolton 1992: 479). Reallocations follow from the exercise of contingent powers to control the firm's assets, powers in some cases vested by the basic terms of corporate law and in other cases vested by contract. Control transfer mechanisms are particularly important when a firm performs badly – they determine whether the shareholders vote out the managers; whether a block holder emerges to put the managers under effective control; whether a tender offer occurs so as to effect needed change; and whether the bondholders take control of the assets in distress situations (Rajan and Zingales 1998). Exercises in incomplete-contracts theory proceed on the assumption that some power allocation mechanisms work better than others and try to identify the properties of superior arrangements. Toward this end, they model the impact of particular provisions for control transfer on *ex ante* incentives to make firm-specific investments of human and financial capital.

2.2   The Markets Perspective

We have seen that the hierarchies perspective holds that shareholder and market inputs cause agency costs to decline and capital to flow to the best use, and that agency costs will persist, absent law reform that clears obstacles in the inputs' way. Agency cost reduction and reformist intervention move in lockstep in this picture – you don't get one without the other. This *sine qua non* posits constant, highly salient agency costs and claims that fundamental law reform is the only way to reduce them.

If one takes a step back, a troubling implication arises: that the corporate governance system leaves big money on the table in the ordinary course. Such a proposition is counterintuitive to many observers.

A look back at Jensen and Meckling explains the intuition. Jensen and Meckling (1976: 306) began their famous paper with a list of questions their model would help answer. Here is the pair at the top of the list: first, "why an entrepreneur or manager in a firm which has a mixed financial structure . . . will choose a set of activities for the firm such that the total value of the firm is *less* than it would be if he were the sole owner . . ." and, second, "why his failure to maximize the value of the firm is perfectly consistent with efficiency." The answers to the questions lay in Jensen and Meckling's description of agency cost dynamics. Managers and shareholders address agency costs as they arise over time, in the managers' case by bonding their fidelity, and in the shareholders' case by monitoring their investments. Agency costs should not, however, be expected to be reduced to zero, and, to the extent they remain unaddressed, it is because the costs of removal incurred by the parties exceed the benefits.

Agency cost reduction, then, is as much an endogenous incident of the system's operation as are agency costs themselves. A prediction results for corporate governance: as new agency costs appear, we can expect the system to find ways to reduce them, even as a residual component of agency costs will persist in the wake of the system's adjustments.

The hierarchies perspective, in contrast, poses a static picture of agency costs and corporate governance institutions. It holds that managers will fail systematically to maximize value in predictable ways: they will favor conservative, low-leverage capital structures, misinvest excess cash in suboptimal projects, fail to reduce excess operating costs, and resist premium sales of control. These missed opportunities amount to agency costs that could be reduced if the law provided for greater shareholder input.

This fixed picture of systemic shortcomings derives more from a particular time and governance context than it does from anything in economic theory. The time, as we have seen, was the 1980s and the context was the debate over hostile takeovers. At the time, the management predilection for institutional stability had significant negative implications for productivity, with an open playing field for hostile bids as the agency cost corrective of choice (Kraakman 1988: 897–901). Takeover proponents dismissed the prevailing legal model out of hand because it had been deployed to block the takeover corrective. From that time forward, the hierarchies account would freeze the frame at the end of the 1980s, making a case for law reform by depicting the governance system as static and unresponsive.

Jensen and Meckling's picture offers a different lens through which to view the subsequent history, a lens showing the corporate governance system as dynamic rather than static in addressing agency costs. It is an agency cost story that starts out at the same place and time as the hierarchies account, with the external shocks of the 1980s. The shocks – deregulation, globalization, and new technology – were exogenous to the corporate governance system, but stemmed in turn from endogenous adjustments elsewhere in the economy. As time moves frame forward, the corporate governance system can be seen making a series of endogenous adjustments addressed to agency cost control both in the boardroom and in the financial markets.

Most importantly, managers emerged from the 1980s sensitized to the benefits of shareholder value maximization. Shareholder-oriented economic assumptions took hold within corporate boardrooms. Incentive realignment was essential in bringing this about, and the move to equity-based management compensation encouraged managers to see things the shareholders' way. Restructuring, something managers defended against during the 1980s, began to find its way into business strategic planning in the ordinary course. Corporate governance practices changed too, with the emergence of the independent, monitoring board. The move to board independence and more vigorous monitoring continues unabated (Kahan and Rock 2010).

Hostile takeovers decreased in policy salience as the market context changed. Merger volume reached new records, and the transactions were overwhelmingly friendly (Kahan and Rock 2002: 878–80). Managers proved willing to sell. Stock options and exit compensation provided a carrot, and majority-independent boards held out a stick in the form of a rising rate of CEO dismissals (ibid. 878–80, 896–97). Hostility became less a fundamental transactional distinction, and more a secondary strategy choice determined by cost–benefit calculations at the acquiring firm (Schwert 2000: 2600). The hostile offer's diminishing importance is further confirmed by the diminishing incidence of defensive devices in corporate contracts. Staggered boards (which together with poison pills afford the maximum available protection) among S&P 100 companies declined from 44 percent to 16 percent between 2003 and 2008; the decline among S&P 500 companies was from 57 percent in 2003 to 36 percent in 2007 (Kahan and Rock 2010).

But what of the "discipline" imported by the hostile takeover? It by no means disappeared. The private equity buyout, which experienced a remarkable revival beginning in the mid-1990s, continues to entail the post-closing governance discipline sought by the hierarchies camp. Buyout firms act as aggressive block holders, closely monitoring management performance and imposing performance targets (Cheffins and Armour 2007). The private equity business model includes and depends on an active threat of manager removal even as it also includes and depends on the participation of management incumbents and incentivises them with a share of the equity. Leverage enhances the threat by interpolating the possibility of downside disaster and magnifying the financial payoff for success. Discipline accordingly is wrought into these companies' governance structures. Pre-closing hostility, however, is avoided. When the recent buyout boom peaked in 2006, buyouts comprised 42 percent of total merger activity, by numbers of transactions (Bratton 2008: 513).

All of this shows the corporate governance system acting out the predictions of the Jensen and Meckling model in the post-takeover era. Managers bonded themselves by playing ball with the independent board, aligning their personal wealth with that of the shareholders, and in a growing number of cases, giving up their takeover defenses. Investors simultaneously stepped up their monitoring. Agency cost reduction was the end in view on both ends. The market power that first registered in the conflicts of the 1980s continued to register, but in a more cooperative framework. Shareholder value creation became embedded in corporate practice under the prevailing legal model. No fundamental, facilitative legal change was needed.

Add to all of this the appearance of hedge fund activists in recent years. This shows that the shareholder collective action problem is not as preclusive as generally assumed and that the prevailing legal model of the shareholder franchise can be well-suited to shareholder intervention. Activist hedge funds showed up in large numbers to take significant equity stakes in target companies – 5 to 15 percent of the stock is the range. They mount hostile challenges to managers and business plans at publicly traded firms worldwide. They are impatient shareholders, who look for value and want it realized in the near or intermediate term. They tell managers how to realize the value and challenge publicly those who resist the advice, using the proxy contest as a threat. The strategy proved successful during the bull market run up to 2008 (Brav et al. 2008: 1739–45).

The activist funds draw heavily on the financial agenda in the agency cost playbook. This sets out four main means to the end of agency cost reduction and value creation – increasing leverage, returning excess cash to shareholders, realizing premiums through the sale of going-concern assets, and cutting operating costs. The activists for the most part drew on the first three plays, using their newly discovered power to prompt borrowing, force the disgorgement of large cash accounts and the sale of operating divisions, and, in some cases, the target company itself. In contrast, the record on cost-cutting initiatives, which tend to require expertise and knowledge respecting internal operations, is more sketchy (Bratton 2007: 1390–401, 1413–15).

Meanwhile, the activists' record of success further testifies to the capital markets' ability to adapt within the prevailing legal framework. The strategy, while hostile, only rarely looks toward the market for corporate control (ibid. 1426–27). Instead, the players act out a game of threat and resistance in which victory lies in either the target's diffusion of the threat with a governance concession, or, in the larger number of cases, with the insurgent's entry to the boardroom as a minority block holder. Payoff through board membership means taking the benefit of the richer informational base available inside the company and in many cases, movement toward a cooperative outcome (ibid. 112–13).

Significantly, the appearance of these new block holders can be explained by reference to the alignment of incentives bound up in their shareholding. Hedge funds are independent actors where other institutional investors are not. They do not sell services to the class of companies they target, and so, unlike conventional mutual fund advisors, are unconflicted. They lock up investor money for longer periods than do mutual funds and so have time horizons better suited to governance activism. Finally, the funds in question concentrate on fundamental analysis, and so pick their targets on a fuller informational basis than customarily is the case with institutional equity investors.

It follows that the barriers to shareholder intervention embedded in the prevailing legal model are less salient than previously assumed. The problem lies less with the legal model and more with incentive constraints bound up in institutional shareholding. But the landscape is dynamic. Not that hedge fund activism by itself reduces agency costs to zero. Indeed, activist shareholder intervention, whether from a hedge fund block holder or in the course of a private equity buyout, confirms the continued presence of the agency costs that proponents of the hierarchies perspective seek to control. The point instead is that, given agency costs and the right incentive alignment, the system will address them aggressively, just as Jensen and Meckling predicted. With managers, the critical incentive change involved incentive compensation. With shareholders, the incentive barrier stemmed from the shareholders' own institutional frameworks. Once a framework conducive to governance intervention finally appeared, the capital markets provided ready support and the inherited model proved facilitative.

Cumulated, these developments provide a basis for a case that the governance system works dynamically within the prevailing legal model to remove money on the table stemming from excess agency costs. Significantly, the prevailing legal model is a constant factor in the account. The constancy follows from the legal model's capaciousness. It sets out a minimal list of mandates – management by the board, annual election by the share-holders, and the managers' duty of loyalty. Within this framework, parties may conduct governance as they deem appropriate. Thus can the model accommodate management domination and shareholder passivity on the one hand, and shareholder activism and management disempowerment on the other. Particular results follow from incentives, which in turn originate in contracts, contracts between the corporation and its managers and contracts between investing entities and their investors.

Jensen and Meckling predicted not only dynamic adaptation toward the end of remov-ing money from the table, but an agency cost residuum too costly for removal through private ordering. An important point follows: persistent residual agency costs do not by themselves justify regulatory intervention. The cost–benefit case for reducing residual agency costs by regulation must be made independently, and may lead to the conclusion that the participants are better off bearing the costs.

2.3   Summary

The hierarchies and markets perspectives posit conflicting interpretations of the same bundle of contracts and institutions. Hierarchies assumes defective institutional arrange-ments and actively inspects for means to reduce marginal real world agency costs. Markets leaves the marginal cost analysis to theoretical models and takes a more relaxed view of real world developments. Where hierarchies wants agency costs reduced now, markets is prepared to wait until real world actors with stakes in the game find a way to address them. Hierarchies assumes that legal intervention holds out no significant per-verse effects, at least so long as it follows from an agency cost analysis. Markets is more skeptical about law reform. Hierarchies emanates from legal theory, while markets has its center of gravity in business schools.

Neither perspective holds out a move with which to checkmate the opponent. When markets says that visible agency costs must be minimal because the actors themselves would eradicate anything salient, hierarchies comes back and points out institutional frictions that interfere with the cost reduction process. When hierarchies suggests a law reform targeting a given agency cost, markets can always minimize the cost's salience and thereby enhance that of its own list of perverse effects stemming from regulation.

Nor does either side enjoy a normative monopoly. On the one hand, hierarchies bears the imprimatur of history: the separation of ownership and control has been corporate law's unsolved problem for almost a century. Today's agency cost technicians have a valid claim as the first to have put together a plausible law reform agenda that might do something about it. The agenda, moreover, follows from economic analysis and bears no imprint of hands of progressive ideologues. On the other hand, corporate law is above all cautious about change, and the markets perspective is the voice of caution. Moreover, its description of endogenous agency cost reduction relies on contractual solutions to governance problems, and such solutions enjoy a favorable normative pre-sumption. But normative questions about the contractual status quo are by no means foreclosed. Indeed, the story of systemic responsiveness told above would, if extended to the extreme, imply that law is irrelevant, an extension few would be prepared to make.

3 AGENCY THEORY AND THE DEBATE OVER EXECUTIVE COMPENSATION

Where is the issue joined in the back and forth between the hierarchies and markets perspectives? We have seen that the legal framework for corporate governance is capacious and admits a range of results in actual practice. The results in turn follow from voluntary arrangements, and so carry the presumptive validity of contracts. Adherents of the markets perspective thus come to the debate with an advantage. The challenger must sustain the burden of showing that a given result is substantively unsound. But, absent a theoretical yardstick that measures sound results, the burden will be difficult to sustain. The challenge accordingly is redirected to the process context that generated the governance result, with the challenger positing that the context distorts the framework for contracting. The separation of ownership and control diagnosis comes to bear at this point.

Debates over executive compensation follow this template exactly. Results in practice, here compensation contracts, are protected by a presumption of validity, and so the burden falls on the challengers. Their substantive challenge goes to the tradeoff between compensation value and incentive compatibility. Consider a simple stock option grant. The option's exercise price can be set at the market price, below the market price, or above the market price. Arguably, the higher the exercise price, the more incentive-compatible the option, because the higher price means the executive must create more shareholder value in order to be in the money. At the same time, a higher exercise price makes the option less valuable to the executive. Alternatively, the compensation plan could impose alienation restraints on the stock for a period after the exercise of the option. Such a lock-down ties the executive's fortunes to those of the company for an extended period and thus arguably makes the compensation scheme more incentive-compatible, albeit with the same value-reductive impact on the executive. Strict incentive-compatibility, then, decreases the compensation value of equity grants. A question accordingly arises concerning the governance system's mediation of this conflict between compensation value and incentive effects. Economic theory holds out no calculative solution. There is no general theory of optimal incentive contracting with respect to corporate managers – if we had such a theory, there would be nothing to dispute except the level of pay (Bolton et al. 2005).

The challengers question the tradeoff between compensation and incentives made in real world contracts without the benefit of a falsifying metric. They bring to bear the hierarchies perspective in so doing, focusing on power allocations that impair the quality of the bargaining space in which corporate boards and top team members effect the tradeoffs. The leading critics, Lucian Bebchuk and Jesse Fried (2004: 4–5, 10–12, 61–117, 189–216), charge that compensation practices fail to satisfy the validation standard of an arm's-length contract. Managers, they say, possess and effectively wield power, assuring that compensation prevails over incentives and that performance rewards come on easy terms. Bebchuk and Fried make a short, direct prescription in the hierarchies mold: given that (a) the victims of the imbalanced arrangement are the shareholders and (b) the injury is due to management empowerment, it follows that (c) the only plausible cure lies in empowering the shareholders.

Their opponents deploy the markets perspective to offer three defenses of pay practices. First, the tradeoffs can be explicated in economic terms. The phenomena the critics ascribe to executive empowerment can be better explained in terms of the economic relationship between risk and return, as higher risks attending equity-based pay must be compensated with higher upside payouts. Second, to the extent the result falls short of the arm's-length ideal, responsibility lies not with institutional structures but with easily remedied informational shortcomings. Third, whatever the shortcomings of the practice, the system has been evolving in the right direction and is fundamentally sound. Managers have on the whole done well for the shareholders since shifting to performance pay in the early 1990s. Loud attacks only enhance the political credibility of the outsider social critics, whose calls for social justice will only crimp the incentive system.

This part of the chapter surveys the main points in the debate, showing how the hierarchies and markets perspectives inform and even determine the positions taken. As more and more details come into view, the ground separating the discussants narrows. In the end they are separated less by opposing views of best practices respecting compensation than by perspectival priors.

3.1   Hierarchies on the Attack: Power and Rents

Bebchuk and Fried's normative base point is a model of arm's-length bargaining – compensation arrangements pass or fail inspection depending on the deal that hypothetical parties at arm's-length would make. Under their model, executive pay packages should reward an executive with a sum in excess of his or her reservation price; should contain terms that encourage the executive to increase the value of the company; and should avoid terms that reduce the value of the company. More particularly, "arm's length" means modifying existing arrangements to add more upside pull.

Thus framed, Bebchuk and Fried's governing norm is more sensitive to power allocations than to market contexts. Indeed, given the hierarchies diagnosis of a chronic corporate power imbalance, negative normative findings are hard wired.

3.1.1   Equity incentives

Bebchuk and Fried contend that stock-option plans fail to motivate performance, singling out exercise prices, numbers of options granted, and vesting rules. Their main complaint goes to price. Most companies fix the option's exercise price at the stock price at the time they grant the option. A low-powered incentive results because the executive will be in the money so long as the stock price does not go down and stay down during the grant's ten-year life. A stronger incentive would follow if companies priced options out of the money, that is, above the stock's market price, but only a few do so (Bebchuk and Fried 2004: 160). The common practice of leaving the price fixed for the life of the option also reduces the incentive effect. A fixed price rewards the executive for market-wide and sector-wide upward price movement in addition to upward movement due to the company's own performance. Because the market tends to rise over time, a payoff is virtually guaranteed.

Bebchuk and Fried propose two ways to increase options' incentives. First, indexing would reset the exercise price upward and downward over time to filter out changes attributable to the market or sector. Alternatively, companies could condition vesting on meeting a fixed performance target (ibid. 139–42).

Bebchuk and Fried further argue that fewer stock options would be better. According to the empirical evidence they cite, the positive marginal effect of stock options on a manager's incentives declines as the number of stock options granted increases, and the benefits of the last option granted may be less than the cost (ibid. 138). "Reloading," or the automatic grant of a new option each time the holder exercises an existing option, is also a problem, because it enables the executive to lock in protection against a subsequent decline in the stock price, perversely turning stock price volatility into a source of personal profit (ibid. 169–70).

From all of this it follows that compensation contracts make suboptimal tradeoffs. Bebchuk and Fried offer a ready remedy. Whichever incentive-based improvement is effected, setting the exercise below the market price at grant or indexing the price over time, the bargaining result is the same, a decrease in the compensation value of each option granted. A reciprocal adjustment is proposed: the number of options granted can be increased to adjust for the price increase so that the present value of the grant (and thus the compensation) remains unchanged (ibid. 140–43). The idea is that incentives and compensation synchronize so that the firm's value can be increased due to intensified management effort without management having to give up even a single dollar of compensation value. Although the managers may end up working harder in exchange for the same overall compensation value, the harder work is rewarded with a bigger upside payoff.

3.1.2   The arm's-length bargain

Compensation packages, say Bebchuk and Fried, do not conform to the arm's-length model because managers influence independent directors. Restating the point, managers use power to extract rents, defined as benefits better than those available under an arm's-length bargain. A prediction follows: the more power a manager possesses, the greater the rents in the pay package (Bebchuk and Fried 2004: 63). Power, of course, cannot be observed and quantified directly, forcing Bebchuk and Fried to back their positive assertion with inferences drawn from institutional arrangements.

They cite four factors, all well known to students of corporate governance. First, the board itself is weak because process infirmities bind outside directors to the CEO, by virtue of either fear or unflagging loyalty. Large board sizes, CEO chairmanship, interlocks, and financial dependence on CEOs all decrease directors' abilities to bargain effectively. Second, most firms lack a substantial outside shareholder, whose financial interest would otherwise influence bargaining over pay. Third, oversight by large institutional shareholders tends to lead to more sensitive pay arrangements, and some firms have fewer large institutional shareholders than do others. Fourth, even for firms with large institutional shareholders, anti-takeover arrangements insulate most managers from the discipline the market for corporate control otherwise would impose.

In Bebchuk and Fried's view, the system's built-in checks do not suffice to correct the power imbalance and ensure that shareholder interests dominate. Consider, for example, the shareholder vote. Reelection to the board remains a practical certainty for most independent directors, at least so long as they remain on the CEO's good side (ibid. 25–26). The annual election accordingly does not amount to a significant threat. Nor do other shareholder votes much matter. Meanwhile back-scratching prevails inside the boardroom (ibid. 27–28, 31–33). Finally, the stock market checks only bigger, higher-profile wealth transfers (ibid. 53–58). The executive employment market similarly falls short. Contrary to casual appearances, the rate of executive firing increased only slightly in the 1990s (ibid. 41–42).

Bebchuk and Fried's assertions about power, rents, and the boardroom bargaining context all follow from a basic assumption concerning the appropriate tradeoff between incentives and compensation: an arm's-length deal, they assert, would tightly tie pay to performance. Thus does their entire critique rest on an intuitive association of hurdle height and value creation. One somehow expects more. But it becomes clear on reflection that there is no more – there is no robust positive theory of optimal incentive compensation. When Bebchuk and Fried assert that more discipline in the form of a tight performance tie is always better than less, they draw less on theory than on the historical story that animates the hierarchies perspective. Antitakeover regulation cuts off "discipline"; corporate contracts have lacked disciplinary bite ever since; more discipline is always better than less, and tighter performance ties import more discipline.

Bebchuk and Fried's substantive base is thin accordingly. But they make the most of the material on offer. Their account of process infirmities completes the case: if managers possess a bargaining advantage and intrinsically prefer more compensation and looser incentive constraints, then the resulting contracts will reflect their preference. Given the normative preference for discipline and its implications for the appropriate tradeoff, existing incentive contracts are *ipso facto* substantively infirm.

3.1.3   Shareholder empowerment

Bebchuk and Fried set out a menu of governance improvements that would ameliorate the infirmity. Some of the items on the list would tweak the present system so as to make it more likely that the shareholder voice registers inside boardrooms. For example, transparency could be enhanced and shareholders could be accorded more say on pay. The Dodd-Frank Act of 2010 completes the job of effecting these reforms. But Bebchuk and Fried would do more than tweak the system, going beyond nonbinding to binding shareholder initiatives on compensation. More than that, they would divest the board of its legally vested control of the agenda over important corporate legislation so that shareholders could remove entrenching provisions. Finally, they would extend to shareholders subsidized access to the ballot on terms broader than those promulgated by the Securities and Exchange Commission in 2010 (Bebchuk and Fried 2004: 192–94, 197–98, 210–12).

As the proposals become more radical, more questions arise about the effectiveness of shareholder inputs as solutions to problems respecting compensation, and, indeed, governance generally. To see the difficulty, consider the counterfactual possibility of a decade in all respects like the 1990s, except that Bebchuk and Fried's shareholder access reforms are in place. The question is whether the shareholder voice rises up to insist on reforms assuring that compensation packages effect a tight tie to performance and otherwise hold out no perverse effects respecting investments, financial reports, and payout policy. The scenario is highly unlikely. Shareholders at the time, including the institutional investors on which access schemes rely, were happy to ride market momentum. It took a bear market and scandals to trigger shareholder demands about bad mergers and the quality of financial reports. Even on compensation issues, it is not so clear that empowered shareholders would have opted for discipline, imposing out-of-the-money pricing and indexing. Inputs on pay may turn out to be more reactive than proactive. The shareholders, rather than pushing contract terms in a more productive direction, will punish managers in the wake of stock price reverses but otherwise avoid asking questions.

3.2 The Market Defense

Defenders of the practice respond to the critics at three levels. The first level presents a full-dress defense of prevailing practice based on economic fundamentals. The second level steps back to admit process infirmities, but to reject the unequal bargaining power description and focus on imperfections recognized in mainstream financial economics. The third level steps farther back still to admit management empowerment but to argue that the system is robust nonetheless.

3.2.1 The fair deal

The full-dress defense, put forward by Professor Murphy and others, draws on the economic relationship between risk and return to describe prevailing compensation practice as a fair trade (Hall and Murphy 2001). This analysis turns on comparison of outside and insider option valuation. From the firm's point of view, the cost of an executive stock option is the cash consideration the firm would receive from a third party investor for the same contingent interest in the stock. But third-party investors and firm employees differ in a critical respect as option buyers. Third-party investors are fully diversified and positioned to hedge the risk attending the option position (Murphy 2002: 859–60). They accordingly are risk-neutral, where employees are under-diversified and risk-averse. It follows that the option's value to the employee is less than its value to the third party (Jensen and Murphy 2004: 38). It further follows that an option makes no sense when considered as pure compensation in comparison to cash: in order to constitute $1 of pay in the eyes of the employee, option compensation must be increased to make up for the employee's valuation discount. The option thereby costs the firm more than the $1 in value the employee receives. An option nevertheless might make sense as incentive compensation. But the overall terms of an arm's-length option package should be expected to reflect the employee's risk aversion. This explains terms that otherwise could be seen as giveaways, such as exercise prices set at-the-money rather than at a discount, the failure to index the exercise price, and the allowance of both early exercise and stock sales after exercise (Hall and Murphy 2003: 3, 13).

  This fair deal emerges only on a critical assumption – that the employee's compensation objective and the firm's incentive objective may be traded off without any further scrutiny of the resulting contract's incentive properties. This contrasts sharply with Bebchuk and Fried's assumption that an arm's-length deal tightly ties pay to performance and avoids harm to the firm. Indeed, from a hierarchies perspective, the fair deal defense elides the central question. The tradeoffs that make the deal fair follow from the assumption that stock options, viewed solely as compensation, amount to an intrinsically inefficient form of compensation. It follows that option compensation can only be justified based on the incentives it creates. A justification that fails to evaluate these very incentive properties inevitably falls short.

3.2.2 The free-lunch fallacy

Now we turn to a process defense mooted to counter the charge of executive empowerment. The defense turns to orthodox financial economics, which does not incorporate the concept of power but does admit of imperfections in contracts, particularly in the presence of informational shortcomings. More particularly, the process defense begins with the same assertion as the fair deal defense: stock options, viewed as compensation, fail to pass the cost–benefit test. The follow-up assertion is that board members fail to appreciate the costs. They incorrectly believe stock options to be a bargain mode of compensation and overvalue options in comparison to cash payments by underestimating the options' economic cost to the shareholders whose stakes they dilute (Jensen and Murphy 2004: 37–39).

Jensen and Murphy use this point to account for a number of practices. For example, during the 1990s, firms continued to grant the same number of stock options year after year even as their stock prices doubled, causing the value of incentive grants to balloon. Had pay plans been tightly focused on performance sensitivity, the number of options would have been cut back as the market rose. In contrast, when the market fell after 2000, option value decreased in lockstep with it. Had the value of the grants been the center of attention, rather than the absolute number of shares granted, further adjustments would have been required (ibid. 37). (Indeed, if management were all-powerful, the market decline by itself should have caused a gross-up in the numbers.) For Jensen and Murphy, this "free lunch" fallacy does a better job of accounting for real-world practice than executive empowerment. They also look to lack of sophistication to explain the absence of indexing: prior to 2005, firms were required under GAAP (the Generally Accepted Accounting Principles) to expense the value of indexed options from their earnings, while no deduction was required for fixed-price, unindexed options. It follows that boards gave up performance sensitivity not because they were dominated but because they were naively fixated on earnings per share (EPS), and the applicable GAAP was badly articulated.

Murphy takes this a step farther, folding the free-lunch fallacy into the fair-deal story. The firm grants options not to incentivize, but because it mistakenly believes them to be cheap compensation (Murphy 2002: 865–66). It follows that concessions keyed to the managers' risk aversion – the fixed price set at market and the absence of restraints on alienation – bother the firm little because it does not view them as costly. The manager would prefer an exercise price set below market; the firm would prefer an exercise price above market; and they split the difference when they set the price at the market (ibid. 864–64).

From a hierarchies perspective, this analysis suffers from the same infirmity as the substantive defense in chief. The mistaken perception of low cost starts out as a positive observation that counters the power description, casting board decision-making in the positive light of good faith. But the observation ends up as a statement of purpose, and the purpose is compensation taken alone. The transformation creates a normative problem. Given that stock options are intrinsically inefficient when viewed only as compensation, a board that proceeds on this basis and trades away incentive properties may be making a bad deal. The hierarchies critique of the free-lunch defense thus reaches the same end point as does its critique of the fair-deal defense: option compensation can only be justified based on the incentives it creates, and a defense that fails to evaluate the incentive properties of the contractual end product ultimately itself fails.

The argument keyed to lack of sophistication resonates better as pure description. Of course, one can only go so far in depicting board members as dumb money. But the characterization still carries due to the agency context: board members are not trading for their own accounts when approving compensation packages, and they operate in a cooperative environment. Given these qualifications, it is plausible to model businesspeople reacting differently to cash and scrip. At the same time, EPS matters in the boardroom because it matters to noise traders in the markets. A boardroom seminar on basic financial economics accordingly would fall short as a cure. For whatever reason – and the fact that someone else's money is being spent provides a good reason – the economic costs of equity kickers are not perceived as equivalent to those of cash payments.

Here also the hierarchies perspective suggests a response. Admitting lack of sophistication into the picture detracts from the power explanation only if we define power narrowly as the authority to direct the actions of others, the power possessed by a sovereign or a military superior. If we relax the definition and describe power in terms of a position to exploit others economically, lack of sophistication fits neatly into the power description. The unequal bargaining power described in contract law is power in this lesser mode. It is also the mode of empowerment referenced by the critics.

It also can be noted that the lack-of-sophistication argument synchronizes badly with the market perspective's basic assumption of systemic responsiveness – the point that money gets taken off the table in the long run. Given the long run of practical experience with stock options prior to when the compensation debate heated up in the mid-2000s, it appears that a minor informational shortcoming caused a lot of money to be left on the table for a very long time. Evolutionary robustness arguments ring a bit hollow in so thick-headed a system.

3.2.3   Substantial performance

The third defense makes still more concessions. Just as management power is hard to prove, so is its presence hard to deny. Many defenders accordingly concede it a place in the institutional description (Hall and Murphy 2003: 27–28; Holmström and Kaplan 2003: 13; Jensen and Murphy 2004: 54; Core et al. 2005: 1160–61). Some even concede that some managers take excessive rewards, that equity compensation is more liquid than shareholders would want, and that perverse incentives have cropped up in the form of accounting manipulation (Holmström and Kaplan 2003).

The makers of these concessions do not see themselves as surrendering to the other side. Even as they admit the systemic imperfections, they stoutly dispute admission's normative implications. From a markets perspective, recognition of an imperfection does not by itself require a follow-on normative prescription. Instead, the observer takes a step back and takes a long view. As regards compensation, the question that then arises is whether the system succeeds or fails in cost-effectively channeling the energy of empowered managers to productive ends that serve the shareholder interest. Answering the question calls for a review of history followed by a judgment call.

Defenders of the practice make a three-part case for relative success. The first part of the defensive case takes a broad view and looks at the bright side. Shareholders, it is said, should be pleased with the way things have gone since the close of the takeover era. Returns, measured net of the cost of executive compensation, have been generally higher since the switch to option-based compensation. And the shift did succeed in aligning management interests with those of the shareholders to a greater extent than in the past (Holmström and Kaplan 2003: 3–4).

Defenders also point to governance improvements initiated in the 1990s. Boards became smaller and more independent, shareholders became more vigilant, compensation committees became the norm, and federal disclosure regulations required greater transparency than ever before (Hall and Murphy 2003: 27–28). Shareholders apparently welcomed the shift to option compensation as they enjoyed the bull market of the 1990s. In contrast, a much smaller net-pay increase to management during the 1980s triggered a populist backlash, due to the association of high salaries with layoffs, plant closings, and downsizing (Murphy 1998: 1).

Finally, the defenders argue that problems with executive compensation after the year 2000 mainly concern a few cases of abuse, and that any breakdowns due to the strain of the 1990s boom market have been addressed quickly (Jensen and Murphy 2004: 3–4). Cases where high pay and poor performance coincide can be identified statistically and dealt with accordingly. The existence of bad apples does not compel the conclusion that the whole economy suffers from governance problems (Core et al. 2005: 1166).

No one on either side of the debate questions any of these points. The core of the defense thus lies in its statement of the market perspective's normative preference for market adjustments. The defense thus parallels the attack, which at critical junctures relies on the hierachies perspective's basic normative assumptions.

4   CONCLUSION

The executive compensation debate is less about the terms of an optimal stock option plan than the variant of agency theory the participant brings to the table. Those who stick close to Jensen and Meckling's original model will condone the system on the theory that any money left on the table gets removed in due course and will cite history to support the position. Those who see the governance system as misshapen by legal barriers to shareholder empowerment will see agency costs that can be reduced by reshaping the system to empower shareholders and will cite history to support the position. So far as regards the particulars of incentive pay arrangements, disagreements will be minimal. The trade-offs are there for all to see. The question concerns the context in which they are made.

REFERENCES

Aghion, Phillippe and Patrick Bolton (1992), An Incomplete Contracts Approach to Financial Contracting, 59 *Review of Economic Studies* 473–94.

Bebchuk, Lucian and Jesse Fried (2004), *Pay Without Performance: The Unfulfilled Promise of Executive Compensation* (Cambridge: Harvard University Press).

Berle, Adolf A. and Gardiner C. Means (1933), *The Modern Corporation and Private Property* (New York: Macmillan).

Bolton, Patrick, José Scheinkman, and Wei Xiong (2005), Pay for Short-Term Performance: Executive Compensation in Speculative Markets (ECGI Finance Working Paper No. 79/2005), available at http://ssrn.com/abstract=691142.

Bratton, William W. (1989a), The "Nexus of Contracts" Corporation: A Critical Appraisal, 74 *Cornell Law Review* 407–65.

Bratton, William W. (1989b), The New Economic Theory of the Firm: Critical Perspectives from History, 41 *Stanford Law Review* 1471–527.

Bratton, William W. (2007), Hedge Funds and Governance Targets, 95 *Georgetown Law Journal* 1375–434.

Bratton, William W. (2008), Private Equity's Three Lessons for Agency Theory, 9 *European Business Organization Law Review* 509–33.

Brav, Alon, Wei Jiang, Frank Partnoy and Randall Thomas (2008), Hedge Fund Activism, Corporate Governance, and Firm Performance, 63 *Journal of Finance* 1729–75.

Cheffins, Brian R. and John Armour (2007), The Eclipse of Private Equity (Eur. Corp. Governance Inst., Law Working Paper No. 082), available at http://ssrn.com/abstract=982114.

Coffee, John C., Jr. (1989), The Mandatory/Enabling Balance in Corporate Law: An Essay in the Judicial Role, 89 *Columbia Law Review* 1618–91.

Core, John E., Wayne R. Guay, and Randall S. Thomas (2005), Is U.S. CEO Compensation Inefficient Pay without Performance? 103 *Michigan Law Review* 1142–85.

Gilson, Ronald J. and Alan Schwartz (2001), Sales and Elections as Methods for Transferring Corporate Control, 2 *Theoretical Inquiries in Law* 783–814.

Gordon, Jeffrey N. (1989), The Mandatory Structure of Corporate Law, 89 *Columbia Law Review* 1549–98.

Grossman, Sanford and Oliver Hart (1986), The Costs and Benefits of Ownership: A Theory of Vertical and Lateral Integration, 94 *Journal of Political Economy* 691–719.

Hall, Brian J. and Kevin J. Murphy (2001), Stock Options for Undiversified Executives (Harvard NOM Research Paper No. 00-05), available at http://ssrn.com/abstract=252805.

Hall, Brian J. and Kevin J. Murphy (2003), The Trouble with Stock Options (Harvard NOM Working Paper No. 03-33, available at http://ssrn.com/abstract=415040.

Hansmann, Henry and Reinier Kraakman (2001), The End of History for Corporate Law, 89 *Georgetown Law Journal* 439–68.

Hart, Oliver (1995), *Firms, Contracts, and Financial Structure* (Oxford: Clarendon Press).

Holmström, Bengt and Steven N. Kaplan (2001), Corporate Governance and Merger Activity in the United States: Making Sense of the 1980s and 1990s, 15 *Journal of Economic Perspectives* 121–44.

Holmström, Bengt and Steven N. Kaplan (2003), The State of U.S. Corporate Governance: What's Right and What's Wrong? (ECGI Finance Working Paper No. 23/2003), available at http://ssrn.com/abstract=441100.

Holmström, Bengt and Paul R. Milgrom (1992), Multitask Principal–Agent Analyses: Incentive Contracts, Asset Ownership, and Job Design, 7 *Journal of Law Economics and Organization* 24–52.

Holmström, Bengt and John Roberts (1998), The Boundaries of the Firm Revisited, 12 *Journal of Economic Perspectives* 73–94.

Jensen Michael C. and William H. Meckling (1976), Theory of the Firm: Managerial Behavior, Agency Costs and Ownership Structure, 3 *Journal of Financial Economics* 305–60.

Jensen, Michael C. and Kevin J. Murphy (2004), Remuneration: Where We've Been, How We Got to Here, What are the Problems, and How to Fix Them 24–25 (Harv. NOM Working Paper No. 04-28), available at http://ssrn.com/abstract=561305.

Kahan, Marcel and Edward B. Rock (2002), How I Learned to Stop Worrying and Love the Pill: Adaptive Responses to Takeover Law, 69 *University of Chicago Law Review* 871–915.

Kahan, Marcel and Edward Rock (2010), Embattled CEOs, 88 *Texas Law Review* 987–1051.

Kraakman, Reinier (1988), Taking Discounts Seriously: The Implications of "Discounted" Share Prices as an Acquisition Motive, *88 Columbia Law Review* 891–941.

Murphy, Kevin J. (1998), Executive Compensation, available at http://ssrn.com/abstract=163914.

Murphy, Kevin J. (2002), Explaining Executive Compensation: Managerial Power Versus the Perceived Cost of Stock Options, 69 *University of Chicago Law Review* 847–69.

Rajan, Raughuram U. and Luigi Zingales (1998), Power in a Theory of the Firm, 113 *Quarterly Journal of Economics* 387–432.

Roe, Mark J. (1994), *Strong Managers, Weak Owners: The Political Roots of American Corporate Finance* (Princeton: Princeton University Press).

Salanie, Bernard (1998), *The Economics of Contracts: A Primer* (Cambridge: MIT Press).

Schwert, G. William (2000), Hostility in Takeover: In the Eyes of the Beholder?, 55 *Journal of Finance* 2599–650.

PART II

THE STRUCTURE OF EXECUTIVE PAY

6   Bankers' compensation and prudential supervision: the international principles
Guido Ferrarini

1   INTRODUCTION

In the quest for possible causes of the recent financial crisis, commentators often argue that bank executives had poor incentives.[1] Critics claim, in particular, that executive compensation was not properly aligned with long-term performance (Bebchuk and Fried 2010; Posner 2009), while regulators seek ways to change practices in order to restore this alignment. At least two questions arise with respect to incentives practices. The first is whether executive compensation at banks before the crisis was predominantly short-term oriented. Academics and politicians answer this question differently. The latter argue, with the support of the media, that widespread short-term incentives to bank managers were at the root of the recent crisis. On the academic side of the current debate, recent empirical studies reveal no proof that short-term incentives led to excessive risks. In particular, an empirical study examined in section 2 of this chapter shows that, in the United States at least, pay was generally aligned with the long-term interest of shareholders (Fahlenbrach and Stulz 2010). Similar studies are not available for Europe because data needed to calculate the value of stock options and long-term incentives is generally not publicly available.[2] The second question, which is further analyzed in section 2, is whether banking regulation should cover compensation arrangements, either by mandating pay structures or by requiring their adjustment in order to avoid excessive risk taking. I submit that regulators should not replace boards in setting pay structures and that regulatory intervention concerning executive pay at banks should be limited in scope, so as to maintain the flexibility of executive pay arrangements. In section 3, I examine the Principles for Sound Compensation Practices and their Implementation Standards issued in 2009 by the Financial Stability Forum (which later became the Financial Stability Board), and critically assess the same in light of the preceding discussion (FSF 2009; FSB 2009). This chapter concludes with some remarks on the case for regulating bankers' pay.

---

[1]   This chapter draws on Guido Ferrarini and Maria Cristina Ungureanu, *Economics, Politics and the International Principles for Sound Compensation Practices. An Analysis of Executive Pay at European Banks*, ECGI Law Working Paper (2010); Vanderbilt Law Review (forthcoming, 2011).

[2]   However, before the crisis most banks declared that their remuneration policies were fairly balanced between fixed and variable pay and included long-term incentives. This was true for both ailing and non-ailing banks, making it unlikely that, before the crisis, bank managers followed a short-term approach induced by the structure of their incentives (Ferrarini and Ungureanu 2011).

2   THEORIES AND POLICIES

This section explores possible grounds for the regulation of bankers' pay by analyzing the empirical and theoretical literature recently developed in this area.

2.1   Bank Governance and the Financial Crisis

Banks are different from other firms for several reasons that matter from a corporate governance perspective. First, they are more leveraged, with the consequence that the conflict between shareholders and fixed claimants, present in all corporations, is more acute for banks (Macey and O'Hara 2003). Second, their liabilities are largely issued as demand deposits, while their assets (e.g. loans) often have longer maturities. The mismatch between liquid liabilities and illiquid assets may become a problem in a crisis situation, as we vividly saw in the recent financial turmoil, when bank runs took place at large institutions, threatening the stability of the whole financial system. Third, despite contributing to bank runs' prevention, deposit insurance generates moral hazard by incentivizing shareholders and managers of insured institutions to engage in excessive risk taking. Fourth, asset substitution is relatively easier in banks than in non-financial firms (Levine 2004). This allows for more flexible and rapid risk shifting, which further increases agency costs between shareholders and stakeholders (in particular bondholders and depositors) and moral hazard of managers. In addition, banks are more opaque, i.e. it is difficult to assess their risk profile and stability. Information asymmetries, in particular for depositors, hamper market discipline and, in turn, increase moral hazard of managers.

For all these reasons, "good" corporate governance (i.e. aligning the interests of managers and shareholders) may lead bank managers to engage in more risky activities (Laeven and Levine 2009). This is due to the fact that a major part of the losses are externalized to stakeholders, while gains are fully internalized by shareholders and managers (if properly aligned by the right incentives). Prudential regulation and supervision aim to reduce the excessive risk propensity of shareholders and managers in order to guarantee the "safety and soundness" of banks.

Some recent empirical studies confirm that good governance may not be enough for bank soundness. An example is the paper by Andrea Beltratti and René Stulz which investigates possible determinants of bank performance measured by stock returns, for a sample of ninety-eight large banks across the world, during the crisis (Beltratti and Stulz 2009). The authors find no evidence that failures and weaknesses in corporate governance arrangements were a primary cause of the financial crisis. In particular, they find no evidence that banks with better governance performed better during the crisis. On the contrary, banks with more pro-shareholder boards performed worse. In their opinion, bank balance sheets and bank profitability in 2006 explain the performance of banks in the following two years better than governance and regulation. Indeed, banks with the highest returns in 2006 had the worst returns during the crisis. In addition, banks that had a higher Tier 1 capital ratio in 2006 and more deposits generally performed better during the crisis.

The criteria for examining corporate governance employed by similar studies are debatable (Adams 2009). For instance, independent directors are used as a proxy for good monitoring by the board, but this monitoring depends on professional qualities and levels of engagement in board activities that are not necessarily captured by current definitions of independence. Moreover, international corporate governance indexes make reference to aspects such as internal controls, which do not necessarily reflect the detailed requirements for proper monitoring of complex risk management processes by a bank board (Bhagat et al. 2010). Thus, while establishing a *prima facie* case for excluding corporate governance as a main determinant of the crisis, these studies cannot be used for asserting that what appeared to be good governance at banks that failed was satisfactory in practice and in no need of reform.

2.2 Empirical Studies and the Regulation of Bankers' Pay

Empirical research focusing on executive pay and its role in the banking crisis offers results that are on the whole consistent with the Beltratti and Stulz study.

A paper by Rüdiger Fahlenbrach and René Stulz analyzes a sample of ninety-eight large banks across the world and finds "no evidence that banks with a better alignment of CEOs' interests with those of their shareholders had higher returns during the crisis" (Fahlenbrach and Stulz, 2010). The authors rather identify "some evidence that banks led by CEOs whose interests were better aligned with those of their shareholders had worse stock returns and a worse return on equity." According to their study, CEOs had substantial wealth invested in their banks, with the median CEO portfolio including stocks and options in the relevant bank worth more than eight times the value of the CEO's total compensation in 2006. Similar equity holdings should have led CEOs to focus on the long term, avoiding too much risk and excessive leverage for their banks. Instead, the study shows that a bank's stock return performance in 2007–08 was negatively related to the dollar value of its CEO's holdings of shares in 2006, and that a bank's return on equity in 2008 was negatively related to its CEO's holdings in shares in 2006.

A different view is offered by Bebchuk et al. (2010) in a paper on executive compensation at Bear Stearns and Lehman Brothers, focusing on the link between short-term incentives and risk taking. The authors argue that the large losses on shares that the top financiers suffered when their firms melted down do not offer a full picture of their payoffs, which should include what the same executives cashed out in the 2000–08 period and what they owned initially. In the observed timeframe, the relevant executives received large amounts of cash bonus compensation and "regularly took large amounts of money off the table by unloading shares and options." Indeed, performance-based compensation paid to top executives at Bear Stearns and Lehman Brothers substantially exceeded the value of their holdings at the beginning of the period. Bebchuk et al. argue that this provides a basis for concern about the incentives of the two banks' executives. Rather than producing a "tight alignment" of their interests with long-term shareholder value, the design of performance-based compensation provided executives of the relevant firms with substantial opportunities "to take large amounts of compensation based on short-term gains off the table and retain it even after the drastic reversal of the two companies' fortunes."

While the first study reviewed in this subsection shows that the interests of executives of troubled banks were substantially aligned with those of shareholders, the second highlights the potential of short-term incentives in inducing executives to take excessive risks even in the presence of large equity investments in their firms. It does not claim, however, that incentives in troubled banks before the crisis were mainly short-term, or that short-term incentives led banks' executives to undertake excessive risks. Rather, the paper recommends looking at the issue of short-term incentives and their impact on risk taking seriously from a reform perspective, in line with the international trends that will be analyzed in section 3.

2.3   Recent Proposals on the Optimal Structure of Bankers' Pay

Calls for regulating bankers' pay have been advanced post-crisis by financial economists and lawyers exploring, on theoretical grounds, the incentives to excessive risk taking created by remuneration structures and possible remedies from a regulatory perspective. A paper by Bolton et al. (2010) models a similar claim for regulation, starting from the proposition that the traditional theory of executive compensation does not directly apply to levered firms. In the presence of risky debt, shareholders have an incentive to shift risks to creditors: "Not surprisingly, structuring CEO incentives to maximize shareholder value in a levered firm tends to encourage excess risk taking." Bolton et al. suggest, therefore, that the CEO's compensation at similar firms, including financial institutions, "ought to be structured to maximize the whole value of the firm – equity and debt value – and not just the value of equity." In particular, they propose tying CEO compensation, at least in part, to a measure of default riskiness of the firm, such as a bank's credit default swap (CDS) spread over the performance evaluation period. An increase in the CDS spread would result in lower compensation, thus limiting risk shifting by the managers. Bolton et al. also recognize that it is not obvious that a bank's shareholders will make use of similar incentive contracts to reduce risk taking by executives. Indeed, the lower riskiness of the bank should translate into a lower cost of debt and induce shareholders to tie compensation to CDS spreads. However, deposit insurance and investors' misperception of risk would work against a similar compensation structure, by reducing shareholders' incentives to limit risk taking by the bank. In the authors' opinion, therefore, regulation should mandate the suggested structure, at least for large financial institutions.

Lucian Bebchuk and Holger Spamann (2010) recommend regulating executive pay at banks and designing a pay structure intended to avoid excessive risk taking. In their opinion, "regulation of executive pay would be warranted even if banks had no governance problems," for the same reasons that traditionally underlie bank regulation, i.e. that shareholders do not internalize losses that risk taking could impose on bondholders, depositors, and taxpayers. Moreover, mandating pay structures could usefully supplement the traditional regulation of banking activities: "Indeed, if pay arrangements are designed to discourage excessive risk taking, direct regulation of activities could be less tight than it should otherwise be." They argue that, at a minimum, bank supervisors should closely monitor compensation structures and take the same into account when assessing the risks posed by a bank and exercising their supervisory powers. Bebchuk and Spamann propose, in particular, that executive pay should be tied to the aggregate value of a basket of securities (including common shares, preferred shares and bonds) issued by either a bank holding company or a bank, rather than to the value of common shares only.

Other scholars recommend a mandatory structure for executive pay at banks, similarly designed to control risk taking, but making reference to instruments different from those considered so far. Frederick Tung suggests that subordinated debt should be included as part of managers' pay arrangements, to align their interests more closely with those of risk-averse debt holders and ultimately with those of regulators in assuring banks' safety and soundness (Tung, 2010). Jeffrey Gordon refers to subordinated debt from a different perspective, suggesting that senior executives should receive a significant portion of stock-related compensation in the form of "convertible equity-based pay," i.e. "equity that will convert into subordinated debt upon certain external triggering events, such as a downgrade by the regulators to a 'high risk category' or a stock price drop of a specified percentage over a limited time period" (Gordon 2010).

Both Gordon and Tung criticize Bebchuk and Spamann's proposal from various angles, focusing on its technical details, however sharing the core idea that executives' incentives at banks should take into account the interests of creditors, so as to avoid excessive risk taking. All papers considered in this subsection also agree that adoption of similar pay structures would be fraught, in practice, with serious collective-action problems and suggest regulatory intervention. The nature of this intervention is still unclear, with references being made either to regulators' promoting or to mandating similar structures (Bolton et al. 2010; Bebchuk and Spamann 2010), or to regulators' encouraging "appropriate amounts of subordinated debt in bankers' pay arrangements, while at the same time preserving the discretion of boards of directors to set pay" (Tung 2010).

2.4   Assessment

However, the case for regulating bankers' pay appears to be rather weak, especially since it is far from proven that pay structures generally contributed to excessive risk taking before the recent crisis. According to some of the above studies, corporate governance and compensation structures at banks that failed were not necessarily flawed. Even assuming that compensation structures were flawed, the need for regulation would not be automatically established. On the contrary, mandating pay structures would hamper the flexibility of compensation arrangements, which need tailoring to individual firms – according to their circumstances – and managers – also in light of their personal portfolios of their banks' securities.

In theory, regulators could devise different pay structures for different firms and situations, offering a menu of choices to supervised entities. However, this menu could hardly cover all situations that may exist in practice, while a broad set of choices would practically dilute the impact of regulation. In addition, regulators may not be professionally qualified for designing pay structures and monitoring their implementation in practice. Moreover, banks' boards would partially lose setting executive pay as one of their key governance functions, finding it more difficult to align executives' incentives to corporate strategy and risk profile. This would also create problems in keeping and attracting managerial talent, particularly from countries that adopt a more liberal stance or from firms that are not subject to regulatory constraints (such as hedge funds or private equities).

No doubt, regulators should take managerial incentives into account when setting the standards for banking activities and organization, and supervise their implementation in practice from the perspective of bank safety and soundness. Nonetheless, this should be done in ways that are appropriate for prudential regulation, which typically establishes conditions and limits to risk taking, rather than by fixing the incentive structures directly.

Indeed, prudential regulation establishes the conditions for the performance of banking activities, such as capital adequacy requirements and limits to risk concentration, without mandating the structure and contents of the individual transactions.[3] Bankers' remuneration should be treated no differently. Rather than designing compensation structures, which is a matter for boards, regulators should analyze the impact of existing structures on risk taking and conduct their supervisory action accordingly, for instance by imposing higher capital requirements on institutions adopting "aggressive" remuneration mechanisms.

In addition, regulators could establish requirements for the corporate governance of banks, including compensation governance, and for the disclosure of remuneration policies to investors and supervisors. Rather than interfering with pay structures, this type of regulation aims to ensure that organizational structures and procedures are in place for the setting of pay in compliance with safety and soundness requirements. More generally, regulators should acknowledge that even good corporate governance may not be enough to avoid excessive risk taking and therefore strengthen the traditional tools of prudential supervision, which have a direct impact on risk taking by banks (such as capital requirements and risk measurement criteria). Some of these guidelines have already been adopted by the Basel Committee on Banking Supervision (BCBS 2009, BCBS 2010).

Given the political pressure to regulate executive pay arrangements at banks, which is further illustrated in section 3, regulators – in addition to enforcing and strengthening the prudential regulation requirements along the above lines – should follow a soft approach to compensation standards by suggesting which structures, in their view, would hamper excessive risk taking by banks. From this perspective, the studies analyzed above offer useful insights to bank boards and supervisors, showing the pros and cons of different arrangements linking pay to the interests of depositors and other stakeholders. It is also clear that similar recommendations from supervisors would help solve the collective-action problems relative to the adoption of pay mechanisms that are not directly tied to wealth maximization purposes and actually could run against the short-term expectations of shareholders. However, the ultimate choice of pay structures should be left to the boards, which have better knowledge both of the business and of the situation of the individual bank, and of their managers' portfolio of their respective bank securities.

3   POLITICS AND REFORMS

The emergence of the FSB Principles and Standards and their rise was influenced by the national measures adopted during the crisis, when governments had to rescue banks and restructure the same in order to assure the survival of the international financial system (Ferrarini and Ungureanu 2010).

---

[3]   Regulation of structure and/or contents of transactions may be introduced for reasons other than prudential concerns, such as consumer protection. See, on the concept and scope of prudential regulation, the introductory chapter in Ferrarini (ed.), 1995.

3.1 The Rise of the FSB Principles

Indeed, the financial crisis has put the banking industry's compensation policies and incentive models under severe scrutiny from investors, regulators, politicians and the wider public, on both sides of the Atlantic. Two main problems have been discussed in the political arena. One is the level of remuneration at large banks, which appeared to be excessive in the United States, but also in Europe. The other is the remuneration structure, which, according to widespread opinion, may induce excessive risk taking and encourage short-termism. Social resentment focused on the former. Lavish compensation packages paid by banks, which governments subsequently had to rescue, amplified the social debate, often provoking a populist response by politicians. Regulatory concerns concentrated on the latter, regarding remuneration design as main contributor to excessive risk taking by rewarding bankers for superior performance, whilst not penalizing failure.

The FSB adopted the Principles following coordinated action by the G-20 governments, which rapidly responded to heavy political pressure deriving, both domestically and internationally, from the financial crisis and repeated bank failures. Through swift adoption of the Principles, authorities intended to show that reforms of the international financial system were timely put in place with respect to executive compensation. Moreover, international coordination was needed to solve collective-action problems amongst states, given that few governments would have been willing to regulate executive pay in the absence of similar interventions by other jurisdictions, for fear of competition from foreign financial institutions, both in the financial markets and in the market for managers.

The Principles and Standards address the areas of governance, remuneration structure and supervision and disclosure. Some principles are not new to the extent that they require a balanced pay structure and long-term approach, alignment of pay with performance, independence of the pay-setting process and disclosure of remuneration policies. Relatively new is the emphasis on effective alignment of compensation with prudent risk taking and compensation practices that reduce employees' incentives to take excessive risk.

3.2 Compensation Governance

The Principles call for the board of directors to actively oversee the compensation system's design and operation, requiring that relevant board members are independent and have expertise in risk management and compensation. They also require the board of directors to monitor and review the compensation system, so as to ensure that it operates as intended. The compensation system should engage control functions (including human resources, finance and risk management) in its decisions, while its practical operation should be reviewed regularly for compliance with design policies and procedures by the compliance and internal audit functions (Principle 1, FSF).

The Standards specify that significant financial institutions should have a board remuneration committee to oversee the compensation system's design and operation on behalf of the board of directors (Standard 1, FSB). The remuneration committee should be constituted in a way that enables it to exercise competent and independent judgment on compensation policies and practices and the incentives created for managing risk, capital, and liquidity. In addition, it should carefully evaluate practices by which compensation is paid for potential future revenues whose timing and likelihood remain uncertain. The remuneration committee should work closely with the firm's risk committee in the evaluation of the incentives created by the compensation system and ensure that the firm's compensation policy is in compliance with the relevant principles and standards.

3.3   Compensation Structure

As to the alignment with prudent risk taking, the Principles state that compensation must be adjusted for all types of risks, including those difficult to measure, such as liquidity risk, reputation risk, and capital cost (Principle 4, FSF; Standard 6, FSB). The Standards require "significant financial institutions" to ensure that total variable compensation does not limit their ability to strengthen their capital base. Compensation outcomes should be symmetric with risk outcomes. In particular, compensation systems should link the size of the bonus pool to the overall performance of the firm; employees' incentive payments should be tied to the contribution of the individual and business to such performance; and bonuses should diminish or disappear in the event of poor firm, divisional or business unit performance (Principle 5, FSF). Furthermore, subdued or negative financial performance of the firm should generally lead to a considerable contraction of the firm's total variable compensation, taking into account both current compensation and reductions in payouts of amounts previously earned, including through malus or claw-back arrangements (Standard 5, FSB).

Malus and claw-back clauses are rather new in compensation contracts, although adjustments of incentives according to performance criteria were also made pre-crisis. These clauses are applicable to both cash incentives and share-based payments. They enable boards to reduce or reclaim bonuses paid based on results that are unrepresentative of the company's performance over the long term or later prove to have been misstated. Where cash incentives are deferred, unvested portions should be clawed back in the event of negative business performance. However, not all regulations clearly differentiate between 'malus' and 'claw-back' clauses, which are still relatively rare in practice (Ferrarini and Ungureanu 2011).

Deferment of compensation was traditionally used as a retention mechanism on the basis that a "bad leaver" will generally lose unpaid deferrals. Post-crisis reforms give deferral a greater role, providing that compensation payout schedules should be sensitive to the time horizon of risks. Therefore as profits and losses of different activities of a financial firm are realized over different periods of time, variable compensation payments should be deferred accordingly (Principle 6, FSF). Payments should not be finalized over short periods where risks are realized over long periods. As specified by the relative standard, a substantial portion of variable compensation (i.e. forty to sixty percent) should be payable under deferral arrangements over a period of years. These proportions should increase significantly with the level of seniority and/or responsibility (for most senior management staff and the highest paid employees, the percentage of deferred variable compensation should be substantially higher, i.e. over sixty percent) (Standard 6, FSB). The deferral period should not be less than three years, provided that this period is correctly aligned with the nature of the business, its risks, and the activities of the employee in question (Standard 7, FSB). Moreover, compensation payable under deferral arrangements should generally vest no faster than on a pro rata basis (Standard 8, FSB).

"Guaranteed bonuses" caused much outrage following banks' bailouts (Ferrarini and Ungureanu 2010). Short-term guarantees are common at banks and are regarded as relatively harmless and often necessary when hiring staff mid-year. Contracts guaranteeing variable pay for several years are, however, problematic, as they violate principles of pay-for-performance. The guarantee insulates variable pay from poor performance, which may encourage more risk taking than would otherwise be the case. Pre-crisis rules and standards did not touch upon this issue. Under the FSB Standards guaranteed bonuses are not consistent with sound risk management or the pay-for-performance principle and should not be a part of prospective compensation plans. Exceptional minimum bonuses should only occur in the context of hiring new staff and be limited to the first year (Standard 11, FSB).

Severance packages of senior executives fired as a result of their firms' crisis also triggered public outrage for the excessive costs they imposed on shareholders. Consequently, the future of severance pay is changed by the new standards. Existing contractual arrangements related to employment termination should be re-examined and maintained only if there is a clear basis for concluding that the relevant payments are aligned with long-term value creation and prudent risk taking. In perspective, termination payments should be related to performance achieved over time and designed in a way that does not reward failure (Standard 12, FSB).

The Principles further expand on remuneration structures by requiring the mix of cash, equity and other forms of compensation to be consistent with risk alignment and adjusted according to the employee's position and role. Moreover, a substantial proportion (i.e. more than fifty percent) of variable compensation should be awarded in shares or share-linked instruments, as long as the same create incentives aligned with long-term value creation and the time horizons of risk. In any event, awards in shares or share-linked instruments should be subject to an appropriate share retention policy (Standard 8, FSB).

3.4   Disclosure and Supervision

Pre-crisis compensation regimes largely focused on disclosure; however, their enforcement did not always meet the relevant standards (Ferrarini et al. 2010). Appropriate disclosure of remuneration in the firm's annual report should benefit not only shareholders, but also other stakeholders (e.g. creditors and employees). Disclosure should identify the relevant risk management and control systems and facilitate the work of supervisors in this area. The FSB Principles recommend increased transparency by adding new items of disclosure. In line with the detailed requirements on pay design, new disclosure requirements include deferral, share-based incentives, and criteria for risk adjustment (Standard 5, FSB).

The Principles also require effective supervisory oversight (Principle 8, FSF). In the case of a failure by a firm to implement "sound" compensation policies and practices, "prompt remedial action" should be taken and "if necessary, appropriate corrective measures to offset any additional risk that may result from non-compliance or partial compliance [with the Standards]" (Standard 18, FSB). The FSB's Commentary on the Principles explains what these measures might be by stating: "Particularly when the totality of a firm's compensation practices are less than sound, supervisors should first exercise suasion on the affected firm, and in the absence of necessary improvement should consider escalation to firmer intervention, which may include increased capital requirements." This approach is consistent with this chapter's view on a softer role for regulating bankers' pay, in contrast to the approach implied by scholars who propose that regulators mandate a given structure of compensation in order to reduce risk taking by the managers.

3.5   A Critical Appraisal

The Principles represent a political compromise between the various interests at stake and the different views concerning executive compensation's role in the crisis. Those claiming that pre-crisis pay structures were too focused on short-term gains and led to excessive risk taking by financial institutions should be satisfied with the Principles' recognition of the need for long-term orientation and alignment of incentives with prudent risk taking. Financial institutions should not be disconcerted with the Principles' ratifying what was known as sound compensation practice already before the financial turmoil (Ferrarini and Ungureanu 2010b). They should also approve of the Principles' rejecting a "one size fits all" approach to executive compensation issues, leaving room for differences in compensation structures based on individual circumstances. Financial regulators are no doubt amongst the winners in the political contest that led to the adoption of the Principles, which require incentives to be aligned with prudent risk taking and extend the remit of prudential supervision to compensation practices at financial institutions.

The FSB Principles incorporate some traditional corporate governance standards, like those concerning the strategic and supervisory role of the board, which also apply to the setting and monitoring of executive pay arrangements. Additionally, the Principles reflect the post-crisis emphasis on bank risk management and its monitoring by the board of directors, who should determine the risk appetite of the firm. The Standards reiterate the role of the remuneration committee in the setting and overseeing of executive pay, requiring them to liaise with the firm's risk committee to ensure compliance with the relevant requirements. On the whole, the focus placed by the Principles and Standards on "effective governance of compensation" deserves approval and reflects a consolidated trend in bank regulation in acknowledging the role of corporate governance for financial stability purposes.

Compensation structures are considered by the Principles along lines that reflect, to a large extent, best practices already adopted before the crisis. Indeed, the role and limits of equity-based compensation, as well as the perverse effects of short-term incentives, have attracted increased attention in the last twenty years, particularly after Enron and other accounting scandals occurred at the beginning of this century (Bhagat and Romano 2010). However, the alignment of managers' incentives with shareholder wealth maximization has constantly been the main focus of the discussions. The FSB Principles break new grounds by emphasizing the alignment of compensation with prudent risk taking, as a result of the recent crisis and the problems of ailing banks.

Aligning bank managers' interests with stakeholders' interests was also pursued to some extent before the crisis, through compensation structures that included long-term incentives and stock-based compensation. In particular, the requirement that compensation include a mix of cash, equity and other forms of compensation consistent with risk alignment, to some degree reflects pre-crisis best practices, as shown by the remuneration policies for 2007 of the European large banks (Ferrarini and Ungureanu 2011).

As clarified in their Introduction, the Principles should not be seen as too prescriptive (FSF 2009). They are flexible enough to accommodate differences between firms and amongst managers within the same firm. Even the requirement to treat differently "two employees who generate the same short-run profit but take different amount of risk on behalf of their firm" (Principle 4, FSF) should not be construed too literally. While compensation structures and amounts should reflect differences in risk taking, other factors that justify similarities in pay, such as the need to promote new businesses within the firm or to attract new talent, could be valued.

The FSB's ultimate goal is to prevent excessive risk taking by reducing incentives to do so created by remuneration arrangements. It is implicit in the Principles that a bank's board should pursue a similar objective when setting and monitoring executive pay. Directors should ascertain that compensation arrangements do not lead the bank's managers to take excessive risks. This could become, under applicable law, a discrete duty of directors, who will be accountable to supervisors for compliance with this duty. However, the difficulties in defining "excessive risk-taking incentives" should not be underestimated (Core and Guay 2010). Moreover, one should consider that "taking on the right amount of investment and operating risk is essential to successfully compete within any industry, and that even creditors want firms to prudently take on some risk."

As discussed above, the Standards attempt to provide some guidance with regard to the equity portion of variable compensation. However, this can also be problematic. In fact, the incentives deriving from equity-based compensation depend on the individual executives' portfolio of securities of their respective banks. In the case of executives holding substantial equity stakes in their companies, as observed for US banks, stock-based compensation could "exacerbate" the incentive alignment problems. As a result, the standard in question should be applied taking into account the managers' equity holdings in their firms (which are in any case lower for European banks). Interestingly, neither the Principles nor the Standards attach detailed requirements to the vesting conditions of stock options and stock grants. Moreover, banks are asked to establish a share retention policy, whilst they are free to set the terms of this policy which must be disclosed in the annual report on compensation.

Deferment of variable compensation is key to controlling risk-taking incentives. Bolton et al. conducted empirical research on the link between deferred compensation at banks and credit quality and found that disclosure of deferred compensation is priced in credit markets through a reduction in CDS spreads at proxy announcements (Bolton et al. 2010). They explain this reduction by arguing that "banks are likely to be more conservative in terms of the riskiness of their investment choices," as a result of larger investments in CEO deferred compensation. Deferment is one of the aspects of variable remuneration more frequently found in 2007 and on the rise after the crisis (Ferrarini and Ungureanu 2010b). However, the detailed requirements for deferment, such as the percentage (forty to sixty) of variable remuneration that it should cover and the time of deferral (minimum three years) may appear too rigid, as this is an area which should be left to bank boards to decide upon.

However, the success or failure of the Principles in practice will largely depend on the ways in which they are implemented and enforced at national level. Domestic regulation could either enhance or limit their flexibility. Supervisors might exert more or less pressure on financial institutions to achieve compliance. Banks could experiment with new structures, provided that sufficient discretion is left to their boards. Also in light of the recent economic literature on the role of executive pay in the financial turmoil (Roubini and Mihm 2010; Acharya and Richardson 2009), regulation should be flexible and principle-based, allowing for innovation and diversity in executive pay structures, while preventing excessive risk taking. At the same time, the role of boards and disclosure of compensation practices through harmonization of remuneration reports should be enhanced (Ferrarini et al. 2010).

4   CONCLUSIONS

In this chapter I argue that there is no strong support for regulating bankers' compensation design at banks. According to some recent empirical studies, corporate governance and compensation structures at banks that failed in the recent crisis were not necessarily flawed. Other studies analyzing the optimal remuneration structures for financial institutions suggest that regulation should promote incentives enhancing enterprise value rather than shareholder value. However, bank prudential regulation is undergoing reforms in areas like capital adequacy and prompt corrective action, which tackle excessive risk taking by financial institutions directly. Regulation of executives' incentives, in contrast, would only have an indirect impact on these institutions' safety and soundness. Therefore, while the case for regulating bankers' compensation cannot be totally rejected, I suggest that any reform in this area should carefully consider the overall regulatory framework and the different tools that can be deployed to control risk taking. In addition, regulation of bankers' pay should mainly be principle-based and flexible enough to allow for experimentation and innovation in pay structures.

This chapter also notes that political support for regulating bankers' pay has been significant as a result of the recent crisis, and pressures to adopt reforms in this area are difficult to resist. Indeed, public opinion and mass media regard flawed compensation structures and short-term incentives as main determinants of the crisis, leading to claims for legal reforms, as well as for moderation in pay measures. As a result, post-crisis reforms focus on requiring long-term incentives, albeit this was already the practice for most financial institutions before the crisis, including those that later failed. The FSB Principles follow a similar pattern without meeting much resistance from the main financial circles, precisely because they reflect pre-crisis best practices. However, the Principles also widen the powers of supervisors by explicitly acknowledging that executive pay is an area for prudential regulation.

The Principles represent a political compromise between the various interest groups, incorporating traditional criteria and adapting the same to new circumstances. I suggest that a similar degree of flexibility should be kept when implementing the Principles in national jurisdictions. Domestic regulations of bankers' pay should be general in character and delegate to boards of directors and financial supervisors the respective tasks of defining the incentive structures applicable to individual institutions and prudentially monitoring the same.

REFERENCES

Acharya, Viral and Mathew Richardson (eds.), "Restoring Financial Stability: How to Repair a Failed System", NYU Stern (2009).

Adams, Renée, *Governance and the Financial Crisis*, ECGI Finance Working Paper N. 248 (2009), available at http://papers.ssrn.com/sol3/papers.cfm?abstract_id=1398583.

Bebchuk, Lucian and Jesse Fried, *Paying for Long-Term Performance*, 158 University of Pennsylvania Law Review, 1915–60 (2010).

Bebchuk, Lucian and Holger Spamann, *Regulating Bankers' Pay*, 98 Georgetown Law Journal 2, 247–87 (2010).

Bebchuk, Lucian, Alma Cohen and Holger Spamann, *The Wages of Failure: Executive Compensation at Bear Stearns and Lehman 2000–2008*, 10 Yale Journal on Regulation 27, 257–82 (2010).

Beltratti, Andrea and René Stulz, *Why Did Some Banks Perform Better during the Credit Crisis? A Cross-country Study of the Impact of Governance and Regulation*, ECGI Finance Working Paper N. 254 (2009), available at http://ssrn.com/abstract_id=1433502, at 2.

Bhagat, Sanjai and Roberta Romano, *Reforming Executive Compensation: Simplicity, Transparency and Committing to the Long-Term*, 7 European Company and Financial Law Review 2, 273 (2010).

Bhagat, Sanjai, Brian Bolton and Roberta Romano, *The Promise and Perils of Corporate Governance Indices*, 108 Columbia Law Review 8, 1803–82 (2010).

Bolton, Patrick, Hamid Mehran and Joel Shapiro, *Executive Compensation and Risk Taking*, Federal Reserve Bank of New York, Staff Report 456 (2010).

Core, John and Wayne Guay, *Is There a Case for Regulating Executive Pay in the Financial Services Industry?* Wharton University of Pennsylvania Working Paper (2010).

Fahlenbrach, Rüdiger and René M. Stulz, *Bank CEO Incentives and the Credit Crisis*, Journal of Financial Economics (2010), doi:10.1016/j.jfineco.2010.08.010.

Ferrarini, Guido (ed.), "Prudential Regulation of Banks and Securities Firms. European and International Aspects", 3–25 (Kluwer Law International, 1995).

Ferrarini, Guido and Maria Cristina Ungureanu, *Executive Pay at Ailing Banks and Beyond: a European Perspective*, 5 Capital Markets Law Journal 2, 197–217 (2010).

Ferrarini, Guido and Maria Cristina Ungureanu, *Economics, Politics and the International Principles for Sound Compensation Practices. An Analysis of Executive Pay at European Banks*, 64 Vanderbilt Law Review 431 (2011).

Ferrarini, Guido, Niamh Moloney and Maria Cristina Ungureanu, *Executive Remuneration in Crisis. A Critical Assessment of Reforms in Europe*, 10 Journal of Corporate Law Studies 1, 73–118 (2010).

Gordon, Jeffrey, *Executive Compensation and Corporate Governance in Financial Firms: The Case for Convertible Equity-Based Pay*, Columbia Law and Economics Working Paper 373 (2010); available at http://papers.ssrn.com/sol3/papers.cfm?abstract_id=1633906.

Laeven, Luc and Ross Levine, *Bank Governance, Regulation and Risk Taking*, 93 Journal of Financial Economics 2, 259–75 (2009).

Levine, Ross, *The Corporate Governance of Banks: A Concise Discussion of Concepts and Evidence*, World Bank Policy Research Working Paper 3404 (2004), available at http://www-wds.worldbank.org/external/default/WDSContentServer/IW3P/IB/2004/10/08/000012009_20041008124126/Rendered/PDF/WPS3404.pdf.

Macey, Jonathan and Maureen O'Hara, *The Corporate Governance of Banks*, 9 Economic Policy Review 1, 91–107 (2003).

Posner, Richard A., "A Failure of Capitalism. The Crisis of '08 and the Descent into Depression", Harvard University Press (2009).

Roubini, Nouriel and Stephen Mihm, "Crisis Economics: A Crash Course in the Future of Finance" (2010).

Tung, Frederick, *Pay for Banker Performance: Structuring Executive Compensation for Risk Regulation*, 105 Northwestern University Law Review (2010).

Basel Committee on Banking Supervision (BCBS), *Enhancements to the Basel II Framework* (July 2009).

Basel Committee on Banking Supervision (BCBS), *Principles for Enhancing Corporate Governance* (October 2010).

Financial Stability Board, *FSB Implementation Standards* (September 2009).

Financial Stability Forum, *FSF Principles for Sound Compensation Practices* (April 2009).

7 Reforming financial executives' compensation for the long term

*Sanjai Bhagat and Roberta Romano**

1 INTRODUCTION

A myriad of factors have been identified as contributing to the ongoing global financial crisis, running the gamut from misguided government policies to an absence of market discipline of financial institutions that had inadequate or flawed risk-monitoring and incentive systems.[1] Such government policies include low interest rates by the Federal Reserve and promotion of subprime risk-taking by government-sponsored entities dominating the residential mortgage market so as to increase home ownership by those who could not otherwise afford it, which fueled a housing bubble, and bank capital and institutional investor holding requirements dependent on credit ratings by entities which were either conflicted or incompetent (or both), providing triple-A ratings to securitized packages of subprime mortgages. Identified sources of inadequate market discipline include ownership restrictions, deposit insurance inducing moral hazard, ineffective prudential regulation including capital requirements that favored securitized subprime loans over more conventional assets, while internal organizational factors contributing to the crisis include business strategies dependent on high leverage and short-term financing of long-term assets, reliance on risk and valuation models with grossly unrealistic assumptions, and poorly designed incentive compensation. This myriad of factors, taken as a whole, encouraged what was, as can readily be observed with the benefit of hindsight, excessive risk-taking.

Yet only one of the items on the long laundry list of factors contributing to the crisis has consistently been a focal point of the reform agenda across nations: executive compensation. In the United States, for example, multiple legislative and regulatory initiatives have regulated the compensation of executives of financial institutions receiving

* For helpful suggestions on our proposal, we would like to thank Ian Ayres, Lucian Bebchuk, Victor Fleischer, Ronald Gilson, Steven Kaplan, Edward Rock, Karin Thorburn, and participants at programs at the New York University, Northwestern University, University of Pennsylvania and Yale law schools and the 4th ECFR Symposium. This chapter draws on essays published in the *Yale Journal on Regulation*, vol. 26, no. 2, pp. 359–72 (Summer 2009), and in the *European Company and Financial Law Review*, vol. 7, no. 2, pp. 273–96 (July 2010), with permission of the respective copyright holders, © Copyright 2009 by the Yale Journal on Regulation, P.O. Box 208215, New Haven CT 06520-8215, and Copyright © 2010 byWalter de DeGruyter GmbH & Co.

[1] For analyses of the government policies, market failure and internal organizational factors contributing to the crisis outlined in the text, see, for example, Calomiris (2008); Caprio, et al. (2008); and Herring (2008). Economists have further analyzed how the spike in subprime mortgage defaults led to the paralysis of the commercial paper and credit markets due to the opacity of securitized assets, creating a modern bank panic in the repo market that financed major financial institutions (Gorton and Metrick 2009; Gorton 2010).

government assistance. The governments of many European nations have followed a similar regulatory strategy, while the European Union's Competition Commissioner announced that it would be examining banks' compensation in light of government support received during the crisis (see, e.g., BNA 2009a; Ebrahimi 2009; Treanor 2009).[2] This turn of events might have seemed at first blush peculiar to an informed observer, however, given the manifold and more pressing regulatory issues that had been identified as having contributed to the crisis. Moreover, the best available evidence suggests that the more questioned form of incentive compensation, stock options, does not appear to have significantly adversely affected financial institutions' performance during the financial crisis and, consequently, it is improbable that they were the key contributing factor underlying the global credit crisis.[3] That being said, executive compensation is a perennial media flashpoint in democratic politics that lends itself easily to political grandstanding, and the current financial crisis is no exception, as it is self-evident that there were egregious instances where financial institutions' executives and traders did extremely well for themselves while taxpayers have picked up or will be picking up the check.

Given an environment in which political unease over financial executives' compensation is widespread and regulatory constraints have been imposed, we advance in this chapter what we consider to be a superior regulatory approach to that adopted by Congress and to debt-based proposals recently advanced by academics. In brief, we advocate providing all incentive compensation in the form of restricted stock and options—restricted in the sense that shares cannot be sold nor options exercised until two to four years after an individual's last day in office—albeit we would permit a modest amount to be paid out over time to address tax, liquidity and premature turnover concerns. The proposal meets three criteria that we think common-sense and economics suggest compensation packages should meet, not only to provide appropriate incentives, but also to be understandable by investors and the public: it should be simple, transparent and focused on creating and sustaining long-term shareholder value. Although our proposal is specifically addressed to what should be required of financial institutions, given

---

[2]   In addition, regulating bank executives' compensation took a prominent place on the agenda of the recent G-20 summit, which produced a set of principles as a guideline for nations' regulation of financial executives' pay (Weisman 2009; Treanor 2009).

[3]   See Cornett, et al. (2009) (comparing performance of publicly traded U.S. banks in 2003–06 and 2007–08, and finding banks whose CEOs had a higher proportion of pay in options performed better during the 2008 crisis); Erkens, et al. (2009) (assessing the performance of 306 financial firms in 31 countries over January 2007–December 2008, and finding firms awarding compensation in cash bonuses rather than equity incentives, which includes stock options, restricted shares and long-term incentive plans, experience higher losses); Fahlenbrach and Stulz (2011) (assessing the performance of 98 U.S. banks over July 2007–December 2008, and finding no evidence that banks with higher CEO option pay performed poorly and no evidence that those with higher CEO equity ownership performed better); Suntheim (2010) (examining CEO compensation at 77 banks in 18 countries, and finding form of compensation, equity incentive, cash bonus or otherwise, has no impact on equity returns during the financial crisis, 2007–08, but accounting performance was higher for banks whose CEOs held more equity and lower for banks whose CEOs had greater incentive pay, either short-term bonuses or option-based compensation). It should be noted that the large increases in executive compensation that have been the source of media attention and public outcry, as reviewed in section 2, were a function of increased use of stock option incentive compensation.

prudential concerns related to protecting the fisc, we are of the view that all firms ought to consider its adoption as well.

The chapter proceeds as follows. We first briefly review the rationale for equity-based incentive compensation, such as our proposal, and why executive compensation, particularly equity-based incentive compensation, has been the principal regulatory target. We then briefly describe the extensive regulation of financial executives' compensation that has been enacted by the United States in response to the credit crisis. Thereafter we explain the mechanics of our proposal, including how it would improve on the approach of Congress, and how it is crafted to respond to potential criticisms related to its incentive structure. We conclude with a brief critique of an alternative approach, shared by several recent reform proposals, that would compensate managers of financial institutions with debt securities, either as a substitute or as a complement to equity incentive compensation.

2   EQUITY-BASED INCENTIVE COMPENSATION AND THE FINANCIAL CRISIS

2.1   The Rationale for Equity-based Incentive Compensation

There is a well-developed and widely accepted economics literature on the fashioning of incentives to achieve consonance between managers' actions and shareholders' interests through the use of stock and stock-option compensation (Holmström 1979; Holmström 1999). Until the set of accounting scandals that began with Enron in late 2001, compensation in the form of stock and stock options was often emphasized as a key to improved corporate performance, and such compensation has been the most substantial component of executive pay for well over a decade. Even Congress implicitly acknowledged the incentive function of executive compensation when in 1993 it eliminated the corporate income tax deduction for executive salaries in excess of $1 million, since the limitation was applicable only to non-incentive-based compensation.[4]

In an influential study published in 1990, Michael Jensen and Kevin Murphy (1990a) lent support to the use of equity compensation by documenting what they considered to be trivial responsiveness of executive compensation to stock performance, calculating that CEO compensation changed by only $3.25 for a $1,000 change in stock value. Jensen and Murphy (1990b) viewed this disconnect to be a matter of considerable policy concern and advocated increasing equity incentive compensation. Brian Hall and Josh Liebman (1998) subsequently documented a significant increase in incentive compensation following the publication of Jensen and Murphy's study. The pay-for-performance

---

[4]   I.R.C. section 162(m) (2006). The provision was enacted in 1993 as part of the Omnibus Budget Reconciliation Act, at a time of public criticism of executive compensation (Rose and Wolfram 2002). Some commentators have attributed the Enron and related corporate scandals to that legislation. The contention is that, because managers could only receive substantial compensation in the form of stock and stock options, they had an incentive to engage in accounting manipulation to maintain high stock prices (Bartlett 2002).

sensitivity of CEO compensation increased over ten-fold from 1980 to 1999, and Bengt Holmström and Steven Kaplan (2003) contend that this shift to greater equity-based compensation produced a change in the mindset of corporate executives: they became more receptive to undertaking value-increasing transactions, such as acquisitions, and to improving productivity and profitability through internal restructuring, activities previously resisted, as they embraced more firmly shareholder value as the firm's objective.

2.2   Why was Executive Compensation the Initial Legislative Target?

The tide of popular opinion turned against equity- and option-based compensation after the Enron and other corporate accounting scandals of 2001–02 came to light, fueled by repeated assertions in the media by journalists, political officeholders, commentators, and public and union pension funds that executive compensation was unreasonably high. The heated rhetoric intensified with the political backlash to the financial panic and credit crisis, which began in 2007, and the government bailout of financial institutions commencing in 2008. This turn of events is not an altogether surprising development, as executive compensation has a long history in the United States of being targeted by populist attacks following market declines and scandals.[5] In the search for a scapegoat following a financial crisis that caught government regulators, financial institutions and investors alike by surprise, large bonuses paid to individuals at financial firms bailed out by the government had the salutary effect for public officials of providing a focal point that deflected attention from misguided or poorly executed government policies that contributed significantly to the crisis.

2.3   U.S. Financial Institutions' Executive Compensation Regulation

The regulatory architecture of executive compensation of U.S. financial institutions has gone through several permutations since the onset of the financial crisis. The first iteration was the financial-services industry rescue legislation, the Emergency Economic Stabilization Act of 2008 (EESA), which authorized funds with which the Treasury Department could acquire banks' poorly performing assets, the "troubled asset relief program" (TARP).[6] The EESA included provisions directed at limiting executive compensation in companies from which such assets were acquired. But as the rescue program transmuted into using TARP funds to purchase equity interests in financial institutions

---

[5]   For example, Seligman (1995: 25–26) notes that compensation of bank executives was a critical focus of the Pecora hearings that provided the basis for federal securities regulation in the 1930s, and Jensen and Murphy (1990b) list newspaper headlines attacking high executive compensation from the 1980s.

[6]   Pub. L. No. 110-343, section 111, 122 Stat. 3765 (2008). Incentive compensation for the top five senior executives that induced "unnecessary and excessive risk taking" was prohibited, bonuses were to be recouped ("claw-backs") if based on inaccurate performance metrics and golden parachute payments were limited to three times annual compensation. In addition, the tax deduction for executive compensation was limited to $500,000 in total, in contrast to the existing $1 million limit of deductibility for non-performance-based compensation.

instead of assets, the EESA compensation provisions appeared to be inapplicable and too timid, leading to increasing calls for greater regulation. The "rhetorical assault" by President Obama on Wall Street executives' bonuses as "shameful" echoed those sentiments (Lucchetti and Karnitschnig 2009).[7]

Congress responded to the ongoing criticism of executive pay in the February 2009 stimulus package, which allocated several hundred billion dollars in expenditures to revive the faltering economy, by including amendments to the EESA provisions that imposed further restrictions on the compensation of executives of firms receiving financial assistance from TARP funds. Under this legislation, incentive compensation and bonuses are prohibited for executives of those firms unless paid in restricted stock that does not vest until the firm has no outstanding TARP obligation, and that incentive compensation is limited to one-third of the total annual compensation the executive receives.[8] In addition, Congress expanded the EESA's claw-back of bonuses based on "materially inaccurate" financial statements or other performance metrics to reach more employees (top twenty-five instead of five most highly compensated employees). Not surprisingly, following this legislation, financial institutions sought to pay off their TARP obligations quickly and, of the largest entities receiving funds in 2008, by 2010, only a few, principally non-bank recipients, had not done so (Dash and Martin 2009; Ydstie 2010).

The regulatory impulse was not sated with the stimulus bill provisions, however. In June 2009, the Obama Administration issued rules implementing the compensation requirements in the stimulus bill, further tweaking the legislation's restrictions by, for example, mandating that firms exercise claw-backs and tightening restrictions on golden parachutes by prohibiting payment of individuals' taxes due on compensation. At the same time, and more significantly, it appointed a Special Master tasked with reviewing and approving the compensation arrangements of the top twenty-five executives of firms receiving exceptional assistance under TARP, as well as to review the "structure" of the compensation of all executive officers and the one hundred highest paid employees of those firms (Dept. of the Treasury 2009).[9] The Special Master was further required to review any prior bonuses and compensation paid to the top twenty-five executives and to

---

[7]   Shortly thereafter, the Administration issued rules limiting CEO pay to $500,000 for financial institutions receiving government assistance (Weisman and Lublin 2009).

[8]   American Recovery and Reinvestment Act of 2009, Pub. L. No. 111-5, section 7001, 123 Stat. 115 (2009). The number of executives to which the restriction applies depends on the amount of support received: it applies to the top twenty-five executives of firms receiving the highest amount of $500 million or more. The statute excludes from the period of an outstanding TARP obligation a situation in which the federal government's only holding in the TARP recipient is warrants to purchase common stock. Id., amending EESA section 111(a)(5). Other compensation provisions required annual shareholder advisory votes on executive compensation packages, prohibited expenditure policies that could be considered "excessive" or "luxury" items, and required the CEO and CFO to certify personally the need for any such expenditures.

[9]   The seven firms receiving exceptional assistance were the insurance company AIG, the Bank of America and Citigroup, and four auto-related firms, General Motors, GMAC, Chrysler and Chrysler Financial. The same seven firms' senior executives' non-restricted stock pay was further limited to $500,000.

negotiate their reimbursement if he determined that the payments were "contrary to the public interest."[10]

Lastly, in October 2009, the Federal Reserve proposed new supervisory guidance regarding banking organizations' compensation practices and launched two supervisory initiatives and an on-going review of banks' compensation practices for compliance with what the regulating agencies consider best practices, thereby aiming to expand the special master approach beyond a small number of large institutions receiving exceptional governmental financial assistance, to all banks.[11] The guidance specified the compensation "policies, procedures and systems" banks were expected to have, in conjunction with three general principles banks were expected to follow ("balanced risk-taking incentives, compatibility with effective controls and risk management, and strong corporate governance") not only for top executives (the Special Master's focus at TARP-recipients), but also for lower-level employees, including traders and loan officers (Federal Reserve System 2009; Andrews and Story 2009). The final guidance was issued in June 2010, essentially paralleling the proposed guidance, with some minor modifications, particularly for smaller banks that do not use incentive compensation, and clarifications of terminology, along with a statement of the banking regulators' expressed intention to "continue to regularly review incentive compensation practices of large banking organizations" (Dept. of the Treasury 2010).[12] With compensation now a formal part of the supervisory review process, regulators will continue to exert influence over financial firms' compensation practices long after TARP, or firms with unpaid TARP obligations, shut down.

---

[10] The Special Master issued the report in July 2010, in which he criticized bonus payouts made by most of the large TARP recipient firms in 2008 as "ill-advised," noted that he had "no enforcement authority" and that most had already repaid their TARP funds, and he did not require refunds from the six firms that had not paid back TARP as he did not find that any of the bonus payments were "contrary to the public interest" (Ydstie 2010).

[11] The Dodd-Frank Wall Street Reform and Consumer Protection Act extended to all public companies some of the provisions applicable to financial institutions: it requires public companies to adopt and disclose claw-back policies for incentive compensation upon restatements (broadening the claw-back provision of the Sarbanes-Oxley Act of 2002 to apply to more executives and to not require the restatement to be a result of misconduct) and to hold periodic shareholder advisory votes on executive compensation. Pub. L. No. 111-203 (2010). In addition, it requires all public firms to have independent compensation committees (a New York Stock Exchange and NASDAQ listing requirement since 2003), and that the advisors to those committees (lawyers and compensation consultants) be independent, and requires greater compensation disclosure, including the ratio of the median employee's compensation to that of the CEO.

[12] The final guidance was issued by all of the federal banking regulators (the Federal Reserve, Federal Deposit Insurance Corporation and the Office of the Comptroller of the Currency and Office of Thrift Supervision in the Treasury Department), so that it applies to all banks and not just those supervised by the Federal Reserve. Features in plans that commentators expect examiners to look for, in order to merit approval, include deferred bonus payments, claw-backs, and performance bonuses linked to risk, paralleling Congress's compensation requirements for TARP fund recipients (Andrews and Story 2009). But in contrast to Congress's strictures on TARP-recipients, the guidance neither mandates nor prohibits any specific form or level of compensation, incentive or otherwise.

3   OUR PROPOSAL: INCENTIVE COMPENSATION IN THE FORM OF RESTRICTED STOCK

3.1   Our Proposal In Brief

Rather than follow Congress's approach to financial executives' compensation, limiting the dollar amount and prohibiting bonus payments, an approach that the academic literature suggests could be both imprudent and counterproductive,[13] we recommend instead altering only the *form* in which equity-based incentive compensation is provided, to restricted stock, that is, equity interests that an executive could not sell until a specified number of years—we would suggest two to four—after he or she leaves a firm. In our judgment, this form of compensation will provide managers of publicly traded financial institutions with the proper incentives to operate the business in investors' and society's interest. We think it would be desirable public policy to require that a compensation package along the lines that we advance be adopted by all financial institutions, not solely entities still participating in TARP or any of the various bailout programs created by the Federal Reserve and Treasury Department to combat the financial crisis, because financial institutions are subsidized by the federal banking regime: not only do they participate in federal deposit insurance but they also can borrow at favorable rates from the federal funds window. As a consequence, their failure puts the fisc at risk.[14] As we will elaborate, our proposal is similar only in name to the restricted stock proposal that Congress included in the stimulus bill, which we consider to have taken a perverse form.[15]

Consistent with the academic literature, we think that incentive compensation in the form of stock and stock options is, in general, a highly effective mechanism for aligning manager and shareholder interests. However, in light of justifiable public concern over potentially perverse incentives from such compensation for banking organizations and the enactment of what we consider to be misguided government regulation, we suggest that instead of stock and stock options, incentive compensation plans for financial institutions' executives should consist only of *restricted stock* and *restricted stock options*, restricted in the sense that the shares cannot be sold (or the option cannot be exercised)

---

[13]   See the discussion *infra* related to research by Perry and Zenner (2001); Burns and Kedia (2006); Cohen, et al. (2007). Consistent with that literature, the Obama Administration has expressed concern that the compensation restrictions in the stimulus bill could be "counterproductive" and lead to a "brain drain" from U.S. institutions, suggesting that it would seek to rewrite the provisions (Lengell 2009).

[14]   In the 2007–08 financial crisis, as well as the earlier Savings & Loan crisis, the federal deposit insurance fund was inadequte to bail out the banking sector. There is every reason to expect that to be the case in the future (see, e.g., Reinhardt and Rogoff 2009). The subsidy is considered necessary given financial institutions' critical role in the payment and credit system, and their relation to systemic risk or contagion (the externality that the failure of one financial institution can lead to a banking panic, in which investors rush to withdraw their assets from other banks, which then also fail) (see, e.g., Gorton 2010).

[15]   We would, however, leave the decision to implement such a compensation policy for non-financial firms to their directors and investors, along with the specific duration of the selling restriction, so that the particulars can be tailored to specific firms' and individuals' needs. For a discussion of the need to tailor corporate governance mechanisms to individual firms' requirements, see Bhagat, et al. (2008: 1858–59, 1862–63).

for a period of at least two to four years after the executive's resignation or last day in office. Why do we advocate a two- to four-year waiting period? We think two years should be the short end of the waiting period because managers' discretionary authority, under current accounting conventions in the United States, to manage earnings unravels within a one- to two-year period. On the other side, four years is a reasonable time for at least the intermediate-term results of the executives' decisions to come to realization.[16]

Executives who have a significant part of their incentive compensation in the form of restricted stock and restricted options as we have outlined have diminished incentives to make public statements, manage earnings, or accept undue levels of risk, for the sake of short-term price appreciation. Accordingly, the proposal will diminish the unintended perverse incentives to manipulate or emphasize short-term stock prices over long-term value, yet retain the intended benefits to align manager and shareholder interests, of equity-based incentive compensation plans. Managers with longer horizons will, we think, be less likely to engage in imprudent business or financial strategies or short-term earnings manipulations when the ability to exit before problems come to light is greatly diminished. There are, in fact, data that are consistent with our contention. Natasha Burns and Simi Kedia (2006) find, for example, that as a CEO's ownership of restricted stock increases, a company is less likely to be involved in financial misreporting.[17]

3.2   Our Restricted Stock Proposal in Greater Detail

The idea of using restricted stock for executive incentive compensation is not original to us. For instance, many companies have restricted-stock plans, the use of which began to increase after stock options were required to be expensed in firms' financial statements, thereby equalizing the accounting treatment of the two forms of compensation (Personick 2005).[18] That change gave an edge to using restricted stock over options: with restricted

---

[16]   Two recent papers present theoretical models of optimal manager incentive compensation (Edmans, et al. 2009: 3–4, 33; Peng and Roell 2008: 20, 24–25). Both papers' models suggest that a significant component of incentive compensation should consist of stock and stock options with long vesting periods.

[17]   In addition, firms whose managers have large amounts in deferred compensation and defined benefit pension plans appear to follow less risky investment policies. For example Wei and Yermack (2010) find the initial disclosure of deferred compensation and defined benefit pensions of non-financial firms was accompanied by increases in bond prices and decreases in stock prices, and a decline in both security types' volatility; and Bolton, et al. (2010), examining 27 banks' compensation disclosures, find banks whose CEOs have a higher ratio of deferred compensation and pensions to equity holdings have significant reductions in credit-default swap spreads, which provide a measure of default risk as these instruments insure swap holders against default on the banks' debt. That may be desirable to reduce the moral hazard problem, discussed *infra* in section 3.4. It must be noted, however, that deferred compensation and pensions are not equivalent to restricted stock, because there is no upside: the future return (amount paid) is fixed at the time of deferment (Wei and Yermack (2010)) and this data may therefore be more relevant to the debt-focused compensation proposals discussed in section 3.4 of this chapter.

[18]   Personick (2005) predicted a trend to increased use of restricted stock because of the change in accounting treatment, and Cremers and Romano (2007: 16) report a significant increase in the use of restricted stock before and after the 2003 announcement that options would have to be

stock, an employee still receives something of value if the stock price declines post-grant, compared to what would be a worthless under-water option (Personick 2005: 8).

However, most restricted-stock plans differ from our proposal in an important respect: the vesting requirement is typically three years and the executive must still be employed at the end of the vesting period to receive the award.[19] The stimulus bill, in line with a plan initially advanced by the Obama Administration, went beyond existing plans and was closer to our proposal. As already mentioned, it both prohibited financial institutions receiving government assistance from TARP from paying any incentive compensation other than restricted stock that could not be sold until the government is repaid, and capped the amount of such incentive pay at one-third of the executive's annual compensation. But our proposal differs from Congress's mandate in three important—and we think critical—respects.

First, our proposal's term of the restricted stock is tied to the executives' term of employment (lasting two to four years after employment ends), and not the institution's indebtedness to TARP. We think this holding period better matches individual incentives with taxpayers' and other equity holders' interests. Permitting the sale of the restricted shares upon repayment of TARP funds encouraged executives to repay the funds quickly, which may have been premature and at the expense of the financial institution's long-term value. Because all of the TARP recipients who repaid the obligation are Federal Deposit Insurance Corporation-insured institutions, that long-term value should be of concern to taxpayers, and not just to equity investors. Moreover, to the extent that exiting TARP quickly was in the equity's long-term interest, our proposal furthers that objective because the longer horizon in which the stock is held post-repayment continues to align executives' incentives with equity's long-term interest.

Second, our proposal does not cap the amount of restricted stock that can be awarded executives to a small fraction of total compensation, as did Congress. As noted earlier, incentive compensation is a more desirable form of executive pay than fixed compensation. Incentive compensation should therefore not be the smaller component. The problems thought to have been generated from equity incentive compensation in the past decade—earnings manipulation or the taking on of unwarranted risk—are a function of the *structure*, not the level, of the incentive payments. Congress's restriction will, in fact, make pay even less sensitive to performance than it was before the credit crisis; that is the precise opposite of what is desirable of an executive compensation plan.

---

expensed in 2005. All other things being equal, companies preferred compensation that was not expensed under accounting rules because that increased reported earnings.

[19]   Some companies have restricted-stock plans that require that a specified percentage of shares be held until retirement. For example, since 2002, Exxon Mobil Corp. has had a restricted-stock plan in which 50 percent of equity compensation of senior executives is restricted for 10 years or until retirement, whichever is later (Exxon Mobil Corp. 2003–2010); and prior to coming under the Special Master's scrutiny, Citigroup, Inc. required senior executives to hold 75 percent of equity awarded or owned until they ceased to be members of senior management, albeit before 2006 the policy, adopted in 1999 upon the merger of Citicorp and Travelers Group, was described as a "commitment" (presumably contractual) and exempted restricted-stock plan transactions (Citigroup, Inc. 1999–2007). But, in contrast to our proposal, these companies provide executives additional types of incentive compensation, such as cash bonuses, subject to a shorter vesting period, along with the long-vesting restricted stock.

Moreover, empirical research indicates that companies find a way to circumvent Congressional limitations on compensation. The result is invariably higher and more opaque compensation, as adjustments are made to pre-regulation optimal compensation contracts; those adjustments can and have created perverse incentives for executives. For example, after Congress restricted the income tax deductibility of non-equity-incentive-based cash compensation to $1 million, firms altered the mix of compensation to reduce cash salaries and increase incentive compensation (Perry and Zenner 2001). One cannot help but appreciate the irony that Congressional action to reduce executive pay appears to have precipitated the mushrooming of equity incentive compensation, the bulk of which accounts for the very large amounts paid to executives that are the present object of attack, and that may have provided some executives with an incentive to engage in accounting improprieties (to bolster the value of their unrestricted stock options).[20]

A similar reorientation of pay packages with perverse consequences occurred after the Sarbanes-Oxley Act required claw-backs of incentive-based compensation when a firm's financials were restated: companies increased non-forfeitable, fixed-salary compensation and decreased incentive compensation, thereby providing insurance to managers for increased risk (Cohen, et al. 2007). As critics of executive compensation, including President Obama, object to large pay packages that are independent of performance, firms' adaptation to the claw-back provisions had precisely the opposite effect of what they would wish to see of a pay package. Our proposal, which does not place artificial and counterproductive limits on the amount of incentive compensation, as does the stimulus bill, would avoid such perverse adaptive behavior by firms.[21]

Third, our proposal applies to all executives and any individual whose decisions may substantially impact a firm (such as proprietary traders or structured product sales personnel), and not, as does the stimulus bill, only to the "most highly compensated"

---

[20]　For example Burns and Kedia (2006: 63) find CEO compensation in stock options is significantly related to accounting restatements, although in contrast, using a different statistical technique, Armstrong, et al. (2010) find no relation between any form of CEO equity incentive compensation and accounting improprieties. However, to the best of our knowledge, no publicly held company has an executive compensation plan mirroring the one we are recommending, so the studies' findings cannot truly inform us of what would be the effect of executive compensation policies that allow only restricted stock and restricted stock options as incentive compensation. Some financial firms do not permit executives to sell stock (or a substantial amount of their accrued incentive stock compensation) prior to their retirement or specified departures, similar to our proposal, e.g., Citigroup, Inc.'s (1999–2007) senior management stock ownership policy. Of particular interest is the following suggestive anecdote. Until Hank Greenberg retired as CEO in 2005, AIG had a long-term deferred equity compensation plan that did not pay out the shares to executives until retirement under an arrangement with Starr International Company (a company controlled by Greenberg and that owned approximately twelve percent of AIG) (American International Group, Inc. 2004: 7–10). But that was not the exclusive form of incentive compensation, as AIG also had stock-option grant programs with more conventional vesting terms (American International Group, Inc. 2004: 11). Nevertheless, if, as Greenberg states, AIG did not write credit-default swaps in huge volumes until after he retired and the incentive compensation post-retirement vesting period changed (Hu 2009), then that behavior would be consistent with our contention that our proposal would more properly align executive incentives with shareholders' interest than would existing shorter-horizon plans.

[21]　We also take account of the need to make adjustments to pay in order to compensate for the restricted form of incentive pay of our proposal; see, e.g., *infra* text accompanying note 26.

employees. We believe the broader coverage is necessary because decisions of individuals such as proprietary traders, who may not be among a financial institution's highest compensated individuals, can adversely affect, indeed implode, a firm.[22] Attention must thereby be directed at supplementing management oversight, by creating incentives for individuals in critical positions throughout an organization that are aligned with long-term performance, rather than transactions' short-term impact. For instance, at Merrill Lynch, top executives' incentive compensation was restructured in 2006 to require their holding stock that could not be liquidated for four years, yet that requirement did not avoid massive losses from a highly leveraged business model and a portfolio of securitized assets (Story 2009).

As earlier noted, the largest banking institutions have repaid their TARP obligations, no doubt largely to avoid the compensation restrictions. Quite apart from concerns over such firms potentially posing a systemic risk, we do not think that it would be overreaching for the government to impose our restricted-stock proposal on firms after they have repaid TARP funds, to the extent that those firms are still obtaining other benefits of government financial assistance (through, for example, access to the Federal Reserve Bank's discount window or participation in guaranteed short-term debt or deposit insurance programs). Indeed, we are of the view that the use of restricted-stock plans as the sole form of incentive compensation should be mandated for managers of financial institutions whose liabilities are guaranteed by the government through other forms of government guarantees or assistance, to align managerial incentives against unwarranted risk-taking and thereby protect the fisc.[23]

There are two further benefits of our proposal. First there is its natural "claw-back" feature that renders unnecessary intricate mechanisms requiring executives to pay back bonuses received on income from transactions whose value proved illusory. Because executives are compensated in equity that is not received until years after it is earned—two to four years after they leave the firm—they cannot capture short-lived income from transactions whose value is not long-lasting: the "compensation" will be dissipated as the value of the firm's shares decline. In other words, executives will receive less in value than the originally granted bonus if the stock price drops thereafter. This automatic "claw-back" is simpler to administer than the claw-backs mandated in legislation such as the stimulus bill and the Sarbanes-Oxley Act, which require specific triggers, such as an accounting restatement, and can be subject to litigation to resolve a host of thorny issues, such as whether an item in a financial statement was material or whether scienter is required for forfeiture of the incentive compensation.[24]

---

[22]   Traders who engage in small-scale transactions that could not threaten the firm's financial stability would, of course, not come under our proposal.

[23]   Value-based deferred-credit-type incentive plans, similar to restricted stock plans, could be designed for executives of non-stock (mutual) institutions. Small institutions, for which the systemic risk to the federal deposit insurance fund is trivial, could be exempt from the restricted stock requirement in exchange for paying a higher fee to the insurance fund to account for the higher risk of loss from having less desirable incentive pay structures.

[24]   American Recovery and Reinvestment Act of 2009, Pub. L. No. 111-5, 7001, 123 Stat. 115 (2009); Sarbanes-Oxley Act of 2002, Pub. L. No. 107-204, section 304, 15 U.S.C. section 7243 (2006). The Securities and Exchange Commission has brought claw-back charges for restatements against executives who were not involved in any wrongdoing, action that is the subject of ongoing

Second, because a CEO would be exposed to the impact of decisions made by his or her successor, the proposal will have the additional salutary influence of focusing the executive more attentively on succession planning. Exposure to successors' decisions could also have a perverse effect of increasing an executive's incentive to sell the company at a low price in order to cash out upon retirement. But a strategy of accepting a low sale price would be constrained by the need for shareholder approval (whether by tendering their shares or voting for the merger or asset sale) and by the probability that a low price would attract a competing bidder.[25] To the extent that those constraints are not perfect, this is a tradeoff in which, in our judgment, the cost of our proposal (a potential increase in sales at "too low" a price) is outweighed by the benefit (a reduction in mismatched incentives to engage in "too risky" transactions whose short-term profit may result in imploding the firm in the long term).

3.3 Concerns Raised by our Proposal

We note three important concerns raised by the proposal. First, if executives are required to hold restricted shares and options, then they would most likely be under-diversified. This would lower an executive's risk-adjusted expected return. One way of bringing an executive's risk-adjusted expected return back up to the former level (that before the executive was required to hold the shares and options) would be to increase the expected return by granting additional restricted shares and options to the executive.

To ensure that the incentive effects of restricted stock and options are not undone by self-help efforts at diversification, executives participating in such compensation plans should be prohibited from engaging in transactions, such as equity swaps, or borrowing arrangements, that hedge the firm-specific risk from their having to hold restricted stock and options (where not already restricted by law).[26] Of course, derivative transactions based on other securities, such as a financial industry stock index, could be used to undo the executive's interest in the restricted shares, subjecting the executive to the lower level of basis risk (the risk that co-movements in the firm's stock and the security or securities underlying the hedge are not perfect). To address this possibility, we would recommend that approval of the compensation committee or board of directors be required for other

---

litigation, *SEC v. Jenkins*, No. 2:09-cv-1510-GMS (D. Ariz. 2010), but some of the litigious issues will be eliminated in the future as the Dodd-Frank Act's claw-back provisions do not have the Sarbanes-Oxley Act's requirement that the restatement be a result of misconduct.

[25] The concern that restricted stock will encourage low-priced sales only involves cash offers, which are less likely to produce low valuations compared to stock offers, given the higher premiums paid in cash transactions; see Andrade, et al. (2001: 111) (abnormal stock returns for large cash acquisitions 50 percent higher than those for stock deals). This is because, if the consideration for the sale is stock or securities, then the post-retirement two- to four-year holding period for the executive's restricted stock would attach to those instruments, reducing any incentive to accept a low-priced bid.

[26] For a discussion of constraints on executives' hedging options and stock from contract, securities and tax laws, see Schizer (2000). It should be noted that these rules make it more difficult or costly to hedge options than stock (or at least stock that is not the subject of a compensation plan grant).

(non-firm-specific) derivative transactions, such as a put on a broader basket of securities.

In addition, to ensure that under-diversification does not result in managers taking a suboptimally low level of risk, compared to the risk preferences of shareholders (behavior that may be of particular concern as an aging executive nears retirement and may wish to protect the value of accrued shares), the incentive plan can be fine-tuned to provide a higher proportion in restricted options than shares to increase the firm's leadership's incentive to take risk (see, e.g., Holmström 1979). Of course there is a tradeoff with respect to using restricted options rather than stock in an effort to reduce managerial risk aversion: from the perspective of protecting the fisc, when the assistance takes the form of deposit insurance rather than government equity ownership, a more risk-averse executive may be precisely what is desired.[27]

Second, if executives are required to hold restricted shares and options past retirement, it would raise concerns regarding a lack of liquidity. To offset the loss of liquidity, we propose first that there be a higher limit on cash compensation for tax deductibility purposes, up to, say, $2 million for executives who receive equity compensation in the form of restricted stock, and a restoration of the unlimited deductibility for such incentive compensation, compared to the existing $500,000 limit on all compensation paid to executives of financial institutions receiving TARP funds (and the $1 million limit for cash compensation for all other employees and firms).[28] In addition, we propose that 85 to 90 percent, and not all, of the incentive compensation received in a given year be in the form of restricted stock or options whose receipt is postponed until two to four years beyond the term of employment. The executive would thereby be able to access a modest proportion (the remaining 10 to 15 percent in a given year) in the shorter time frame prevalent in existing restricted-stock plans or in the year of receipt, the choice of which we would leave to the decision of a firm's compensation committee.

---

[27]   For a model suggesting when stock option compensation results in managers taking less or more risk (which depends on how much "in the money"—exercise price below the stock price—the options are), see Lambert, et al. (1991).

[28]   I.R.C. section 162(m) (2006). We would therefore undo the decrease in the deduction contained in the EESA, and counsel against the idea, suggested by Senator Levin at Treasury Secretary Geithner's confirmation hearing, to expand the reduction in deductibility to all firms (BNA 2009b). David Walker (2009) suggests that firms might respond to this piece of our proposal by increasing fixed cash compensation and reducing the amount of incentive compensation, attenuating the link between pay and performance. Indeed, firms may respond with higher fixed pay regardless of the level of the tax deduction, as some firms have continued to pay executives over $1 million in cash despite the loss of the deduction, and the impact on net income from the loss of the tax shield from the deductibility of compensation over the lower $1 million level would appear to be trivial for many firms (Perry and Zenner 2001). Accordingly, executives who could not access incentive compensation until several years after retirement or termination, as we propose, would be likely to seek to obtain higher fixed cash payments to offset the reduction in available funds. But our proposal would have less of an effect in that regard than Congress's plan, which limits incentive pay to one-third of fixed compensation, thereby exacerbating the incentive for firms to increase fixed pay (as incentive pay depends upon that base). Moreover, two features of our proposal—the increase in the tax deduction and the allowance of an annual payout of a modest percentage of the restricted shares and options—should decrease the probability that compensation committees would perceive a need to provide a higher proportion of fixed compensation.

Whether our proposal adequately addresses well-founded concerns regarding liquidity can be better appreciated when informed by real-world comparisons. First, our proposed 10 to15 percent liquidity allowance is greater than the average annual percentage of personal equity holdings sold by CEOs of large financial institutions during the decade before the financial crisis.[29] Second, our proposal requires executives to not sell their shares or exercise their options for a period of at least two to four years after their last day in office. The median tenure of CEOs in larger U.S. corporations is five and one-half years (Bhagat, Bolton and Subramanian 2011: table 5).[30] Hence, on average, a CEO can expect to wait between seven and ten years before being allowed to sell shares or exercise options from assuming office.[31] In this regard, we would note a parallelism between our proposal and compensation in the non-public corporation setting, which buttresses the feasibility of our proposal: it is quite common for those firms' top executives to wait for seven to ten years before receiving a substantial portion of their compensation for work done earlier. For instance, the general partners of private equity partnerships commonly receive their compensation in two parts. The first part is a management fee which is typically two percent annually of the committed capital they are managing. The second part of the compensation is carried interest, which is a fraction (usually 20 percent) of the lifetime profits generated by the private equity partnership. Most of these profits are realized towards the end of the life of such partnerships, usually seven to ten years (Metrick 2007; Litvak 2009). The widespread use of such a deferred compensation structure in a real world setting where principal–agent problems are thought to be better managed, suggests that our proposal not only is plausible but also could improve substantially corporate managers' incentives, despite well-known differences between private equity and public company operating environments.

Third, to the extent an executive incurs tax liability from receiving restricted shares and options that is greater than the amount permitted to be received in the current year, then that individual should be allowed to sell enough additional shares (and/or exercise enough options) to pay the additional taxes.

In addition to the above concerns, there are three important questions about the efficacy of our proposal that need to be addressed. First, should not managers be rewarded on the basis of relative performance, that is, performance relative to an industry or targeted market benchmark? The suggestion has obvious merit in that controlling for industry or market performance would provide an arguably superior measure of a

---

[29]   Sanjai Bhagat and Brian Bolton (2010) examined the stock sales over 2000–07 of the CEOs of 14 large financial firms, including the major TARP recipients. The CEOs sold over $3 billion of stock during that interval, averaging an annual sale of 8 percent of their equity holdings.

[30]   Bhagat, et al.'s (2011) sample consists of all firms with available data in standard compensation and financial data sources from 1993–2007. The median tenure of CEOs of large banks is longer: in a sample of 134 large banks run by 200 different CEOS from 1994–2006, DeYoung, et al. (2010: 27 n.24) find that 84 percent of the CEOs ran their banks for seven years or fewer, with seven years the median tenure. The mean CEO tenure of the two studies is somewhat closer, at eight and nine years respectively.

[31]   Of course, many CEOs are employed at lower executive levels before reaching the top, and therefore the time frame in which they would not have access to their accrued incentive compensation would be longer. This is an ancillary reason for our advocacy of release of 10–15 percent of the incentive compensation of a given year from the long-term restriction.

manager's contribution to share price performance.[32] However, it should be noted that several recent papers suggest that relative performance pay is not optimal.[33] Moreover, as noted at the outset, we think it is critical for executive compensation reform to lead to policies that are simple and transparent. Relative performance measures are at odds with this aim, given the ambiguities in, and correlative ability to game, the selection of the appropriate industry or market benchmark.[34] Additionally, with relative perform-ance measures it is possible for managers to receive significant compensation even when their shareholders incur significant losses; this result would again undermine the credi-bility of manager compensation in the eyes of the investing and general public.[35] Our proposal does not pose such a perceptual problem. Finally, such options may increase managerial risk-taking beyond the impact of conventional options (a phenomenon Saul Levmore (2001) refers to as "super-risk alternation"), for with the ability to exert greater influence on firm-specific outcomes, executives might undertake high risk projects or otherwise seek inefficiently to differentiate themselves from other firms, to increase the chance of outperforming the benchmark (Levmore 2001: 1923, 1930). In the case of financial firms where the taxpayer bears the ultimate loss, exacerbating the risk-taking induced by stock options would be undesirable from the viewpoint of protecting the fisc.

Second, would our proposal lead to early management departures, as executives seek to convert (after the two to four year waiting period) illiquid shares and options into more liquid assets as soon as possible? We tend to think this scenario is improbable and over-blown, but perhaps that would be so. Permitting a fraction (10 to 15 percent as we have proposed) of each year's incentive compensation to vest and be sold should mitigate somewhat such a concern, particularly for lower-level managers, whose bonuses may not be as large as, and whose employment horizons under normal circumstances would be

---

[32] Some have criticized the stimulus bill mandate of restricted stock for covering executives who are lower level managers with limited responsibilities, on the ground that it is preferable to tie those individuals' pay to the unit rather than the company as a whole (Bebchuk 2009). That may be true but it misses the mark because it moves incentive compensation away from benchmarks that are simple, transparent, and not easily manipulable. The market currency of stock prices is a far better benchmark for performance than the accounting-based measures used to assess units' performance, which are themselves manipulable. In any event, the criticism can be accommodated within our proposal by combining a unit performance benchmark with a restricted-stock approach: lower-level managers could be allocated restricted shares in proportion to their unit's accounting perform-ance compared to that of the rest of the company.

[33] For a collection of references, see Frydman and Jenter (2010).

[34] As discussed in the next section, a recent executive compensation proposal by Lucian Bebchuk and Holger Spamann (2010) suffers from similar difficulties.

[35] Saul Levmore (2001) advances a parallel explanation for the nonuse of indexed options, that they would violate what he terms a norm of "nonconflicting fortunes": in a downturn, when the firm and economy have experienced poor absolute returns, if the firm did better than the bench-mark, employees with indexed options would fare well when others did not. It would not, he con-tends, be efficient to provide all employees with indexed options because they can exacerbate organizational risk-taking and consequently, the disparate outcomes they can produce would be inconsistent with what he views as a quite common preference or norm that everyone in a group should rise or fall together, to the extent necessary to prevent intragroup conflicts (Levmore 2001: 1932).

longer than, those of the CEO.[36] Further, informing our skepticism regarding this objection is our expectation that managers who develop a reputation for early departures from firm to firm are likely to negatively impact their future career opportunities. There is, for example, evidence of reputational effects in the managerial market as executives of public firms that file for bankruptcy do not appear to get a second chance at managing a public company (Gilson 1989). Finally, concern for managers' need for liquidity and consequent early departures needs a bit of perspective. Our proposal allows tax-deductible cash compensation up to $2 million for executives receiving incentive pay in the form of restricted stock. The adjusted gross income (AGI) of the top 0.5 percent in 2004 had a threshold of $0.48 million, and the AGI of the top 0.1 percent in 2004 had a threshold of $1.4 million (Kaplan and Rauh 2010). In addition, our proposed $2 million limit could be indexed to inflation, further mitigating liquidity concerns.

Third, the variety of existing compensation systems across firms suggests that mandating standardized pay packages may be inefficient, in that compensation may substitute or complement other governance mechanisms, which vary across firms, and undoubtedly getting incentives exactly right is quite complicated (Walker 2009; Yermack 2009: W2). This is, indeed, a concern. But we think that the need for variety or customization in incentive compensation arrangements is most pronounced across industry, rather than within an industry, which is the focus of our proposal. The variability in the nature of assets and business risk across industry sectors calls for different governance structures and, correspondingly, could prompt a need for different approaches to incentives.[37]

Our proposal's focus on financial institutions renders the need for such tailoring less of concern, although, of course, there are obvious and substantial differences between the operations of large complex banking organizations and small community banks. But our proposal provides room for some customization across financial institutions: for large institutions, we would permit variation in terms of the combination of restricted stock versus restricted options provided, and the amount and timing of distributable funds (within the suggested 10 to 15 percent range). For small institutions, whose threat to the fisc is limited, as earlier noted, we would not constrain them to use restricted stock for incentive compensation in exchange for charging a higher deposit insurance fee, or imposing higher capital requirements, in accordance with the increased risk from using shorter-vesting incentives.[38]

---

[36]   For instance, CEOs typically receive over one-third of total compensation paid to the top five executives in a firm (Bebchuk, et al. 2008).

[37]   For a study indicating that governance mechanisms are related to firm characteristics related to assets and investment strategies, see Gillan, et al. (2007).

[38]   Robert DeYoung and colleagues (2010) provide data suggesting that bank boards adjusted CEO compensation (increased options over stock) to incentivize managers, in the wake of regulatory changes, to undertake the now permissible more profitable albeit riskier activities, and conversely, they shifted CEO compensation to increased stock over options when they wished to reduce the bank's engaging in such risky activities. As they conclude, these data indicate that bank CEOs respond to compensation incentives directed at affecting their institution's risk-taking, which suggests a role for government regulation, but that government intervention to limit such risk-taking could as well "interfere" with bank boards' "compensation-based risk mitigation behaviors," as strengthen them, and that the data are consistent with a need for tailoring bank compensation and indicate that regulation, at best, should be focused on banks that pose systemic risk (DeYoung, et

A final consideration influences our judgment to eschew a more tailored approach. We think that it is desirable to have simple and transparent incentive compensation packages, particularly when a firm's failure implicates the fisc, as these characteristics will mitigate public skepticism toward high levels of executive pay in conjunction with poor performance. Using only restricted stock for incentive compensation meets those criteria.

3.4   Comparison to an Alternative Approach: Compensation in Debt Securities

A number of reform proposals have advocated compensating bank managers with a share of the bank's debt securities, rather than (or in addition to) equity-based incentive pay.[39] Although specifics of the proposed debt or debt-like compensation differ, the rationale is the same: to address the moral hazard, or agency problem of debt, using an idea suggested by Michael Jensen and William Meckling (1976: 352) in a classic article published over thirty years ago, to compensate managers with debt as well as stock to mitigate equity's incentive, in a levered firm, to take on increasingly risky projects because equity obtains the entire upside but does not have to pay creditors in full on the downside, given limited liability.[40] Deposit insurance, of course, only exacerbates the moral-hazard problem because the government stands behind the depositors, so they have no incentive to monitor the equity holders' risk-taking.

All of the debt-focused compensation proposals are, in our judgment, less desirable than our restricted-stock proposal, particularly from the desiderata that compensation plans be simple and transparent, as well as aligned with long-term firm value. First, reform proposals advocating a package of equity and debt or debt-like securities are more complex and opaque than restricted-stock compensation. For example, most senior securities of financial institutions are either not publicly traded or trade infrequently; the absence of market prices renders it difficult to value debt-based compensation packages with precision. In addition, given that firms' capital structures are dynamic, changing over time, executives' portfolios would require frequent rebalancing to maintain proportionate holdings, which would, in turn, require a complicated, and therefore costly,

---

al. 2010: 37). Our proposal is in the spirit of their conclusions, as it provides limited room for tailoring compensation at large institutions likely to pose systemic risk, and it is more likely to strengthen, than worsen, boards' efforts to influence executives' risk-taking, in contrast to Congress's approach of caps and minimal incentive pay for TARP recipients.

[39]   E.g., Bebchuk and Spamann (2010) (recommending compensation package of a proportionate mix of financial institutions' senior securities—debt and preferred stock—and equity); Bolton, et al. (2010) (recommending tying compensation to changes in the spread on credit default swaps, which are contracts written on debt securities that insure the holder against the debt's default); Gordon (2010) (advocating conversion of financial institutions' senior management's equity-based compensation into subordinated debt at a discount to the equity value, when a firm experiences financial difficulty); Tung (2010) (recommending compensation in the form of subordinated debt of the bank subsidiary). A detailed discussion of what are, in our judgment, feasibility and transparency problems with the Bebchuk and Spamann (2010) proposal is provided in Bhagat and Romano (2010). We discuss here the shared shortcomings of debt-focused compensation reform proposals.

[40]   Gordon (2010) further advocates the use of contingent debt compensation on the rationale that management with a large block of equity will not raise needed additional equity capital at a time of financial distress in order to avoid dilution of their ownership.

administrative process. Proposals that advocate pegging compensation to a specific debt security, such as credit-default swaps or subordinated debt, rather than a proportionate package of the capital structure, while seemingly avoiding complexity, do not satisfactorily avoid the problem, as those securities are also typically not publicly traded,[41] and it appears that, particularly in times of crisis, credit-default swap spreads understate the risk of loss, with volatility manifested in equity prices instead (Singh and Youssef 2010).[42] Finally, determining the appropriate formula with which to relate changes in default spreads to executive compensation bonuses or claw-backs would undoubtedly be a challenging task, for the calculation of swap prices is complex, as values do not change linearly with changes in other economic variables.[43] Furthermore, managers will have an incentive to misrepresent financial/accounting numbers (which may be partially under their control) that analysts use to compute the default spreads or other variables on which their compensation is contingent.

Second, although in theory a manager holding a mix of debt and equity securities might not take on inappropriate risk, we think that in practice it might well be otherwise. The gain on an equity position from following a high risk strategy might well exceed the loss on the position attributable to senior securities in the executive's portfolio. Moreover, if the value of the equity position is quite low compared to the senior securities in a compensation package, a manager would still have an incentive to take on risky projects,

---

[41]   As Bolton, et al. (2010: 28) state, their proposal would be feasible for only the largest financial institutions that have "highly liquid" credit default swap markets. In fact, credit default swaps are issued only on the larger financial institutions' securities. Hence, a proposal using such instruments as the benchmark for compensation is not suitable for the majority of financial institutions. Besides the lack of transparency from the absence of market pricing, because credit default swap spreads are computed using accounting figures which are partially under managers' control, they may also be subject to manipulation, as managers will have increased incentives to misrepresent figures used in swap pricing when it immediately would impact their compensation. Although credit default swaps have historically traded in private over-the-counter markets, the Dodd-Frank financial reform legislation requires regulators to implement rules to establish the use of centralized clearing exchanges to trade those products, which could increase the transparency of prices, but will not eliminate the need for accounting data to calculate spreads, as the underlying debt is infrequently traded.

[42]   An explanation for the understated spreads is that bondholders viewed the institutions as too big to fail, and therefore did not expect to bear losses (Milne 2010). Singh and Youssef (2010) suggest alternative complicated methodologies to better price risk than straightforward use of credit default swap spreads. The convertible security that Gordon (2010) proposes has further valuation difficulties: because management's stock differs significantly from that of other stockholders (i.e., management's shares will become debt securities, which are senior to the outstanding shares of stockholders, when the firm experiences financial difficulty), their stock will not be equivalent in value, nor will its value move in tandem with the value of the outstanding common stock. Moreover, determining the value of management's equity will be complicated because it depends on the likelihood of conversion, and the rate that will be applicable (which under the proposal requires a further calculation, the value of the common stock at an unknown point in time that is prior to the moment at which conversion occurs).

[43]   In discussing the formal model informing their proposal to tie bank executives' compensation to credit default swap spreads, Bolton, et al. (2010: 13) note that the optimal compensation contract consists of debt and equity in a ratio equal to the "rate of return promised to bondholders at the optimal risk level," which "may be difficult to calculate." In our judgment, this acknowledgment is too gentle.

given the option value of the position each year.[44] Additionally, the incentive to undertake riskier projects would be greater than the incentive to take on such projects created by our restricted stock proposal because with restricted-stock, the option value cannot be realized until years after the manager is no longer with the firm. Indeed, as we discussed earlier, incentive compensation paid in the form of restricted stock is likely to decrease managers' risk-taking, as it increases the under-diversification of executive portfolios, in addition to the long-term holding period for the stock.

Third, and importantly, government bailouts of banks, particularly in the recent 2008 crisis, have been by and large one of bailing out creditors, not shareholders. Given that experience, providing a portion of bank executives' compensation in debt would not necessarily lead the executives to take a socially optimal level of lower risk, as they would plausibly expect not to lose the value of debt securities on the downside while they would still expect to obtain the upside on the equity portion. If, however, the executives' debt is constructed so as not to be able to participate in a government bailout, then their securities would be of lesser value than those sold to investors, whose prices and terms would incorporate the rational expectation of a bailout should the institution fail, rendering debt market prices, such as they exist, inapposite for valuing precisely an executive's compensation. Yet a key component of debt-focused proposals is that market price signals of the riskiness of the debt, such as a bank's credit-default swap spread, or proportionate values of debt and equity securities, should determine an executive's compensation.

The concern over moral hazard induced by deposit insurance which motivates proposals to use debt, rather than equity, for bank executives' incentive compensation is, of course, well recognized, and we do not wish to minimize its seriousness; that is the principal rationale for regulating financial executives' compensation rather than leaving arrangements to the market. But we think it is daunting to determine, no less effectively implement, an optimal incentive compensation structure combining debt and equity. All-debt incentive compensation would certainly reduce the moral-hazard problem, but it would not necessarily be best from society's point of view to run banks in the interest of debtholders rather than shareholders: banks that take on nominal risk do not lend, a business strategy that is not conducive to economic growth. We think instead that the moral-hazard problem is better addressed directly by strengthened, possibly time-varying (countercyclical) capital requirements, and by encouraging changes in the form of debt in banks' capital structures, through those requirements, such as greater use of subordinated debt or creation of hybrid debt instruments, which convert to equity in situations of financial distress.[45]

---

[44]   As earlier noted, stock in a levered firm, from a finance perspective, is equivalent to an option on the firm, in which the equity holder obtains the upside of future risky projects but can walk away from the firm, without repaying creditors, if the firm's downside value is less than its liabilities. The model of executive compensation in Lambert, et al. (1991) indicates that managers are more likely to take on risk when the probability of the option finishing in the money is low, the scenario in the text, and of greatest concern to the fisc. With restricted stock, the longer horizon increases the probability that an option will finish in the money, which, in the Lambert, et al. (1991) model, *increases* the manager's aversion to risk, the exact opposite effect of that predicted by proponents of debt- rather than equity-based incentive compensation for banking executives.

[45]   Such recommendations are discussed in the Squam Lake Report (French, et al. 2010), a roadmap for financial reform offered by fifteen prominent economists; and Kashyap, et al. (2008).

4   CONCLUSION

The financial institutions' rescue legislation, stimulus bill, and Administration regulations may quench the public's ire over perceived excesses in executive compensation, but they are not an appropriate solution to the problem of compensation providing poor incentives. Our proposal would have incentive compensation take the form of only restricted stock and restricted stock options (restricted in the sense that the securities may not be sold or exercised until two to four years after the executive has left the firm), with a modest amount accessible by the executive to address tax, liquidity and premature turnover concerns. Our proposal protects the fisc, while providing superior incentives for executives to manage financial firms in investors' longer-term interest and avoiding the perverse incentives of both an artificial cap on incentive compensation and of unrestricted or short-vesting stock and option compensation plans prevalent at many firms, and the complexities and conflicting incentive effects of debt-based compensation proposals. While our restricted-stock proposal is directed at financial institutions, in light of the increased attention that will be paid to the work of compensation committees given the compensation-related provisions of the Dodd-Frank Act,[46] we think that public companies more generally should give serious consideration to adapting a version of it that best fits their circumstances as well.

Of course, changes in banks' executive compensation alone will not prevent another financial crisis because, as we have noted, compensation would not appear to have been the sole or even principal cause of the crisis. There is, accordingly, a pressing need to

---

The Squam Lake Report also advocates withholding a fixed amount of cash compensation of systemically important financial institutions' executives for several years. Those funds would be forfeited if the firm goes bankrupt or receives "extraordinary assistance" from the government (French, et al. 2010: 81–82). Conceptually the Squam Lake proposal has merit since the claw-back will discourage managers from undertaking high-risk negative net present value investments and trading strategies, and while cash with a fixed return is debt-like in its incentive effect regarding moral hazard, it is not subject to the valuation problems entailed by debt-based incentive compensation. However, the proposal's implementation would be problematic, because it is more complex and less transparent than our restricted-stock proposal. Consequently, the conceptual benefits might be difficult to realize. For example, how much is held back and for how long? What constitutes "bankruptcy" and "extraordinary government assistance"? If the withheld amount is not a substantial component of compensation, it is not likely to have much of an impact on managers' incentives. Nor will the time frame of a few years be as effective as our proposed long-term horizon through retirement (the cash will be withheld post-retirement only coincidentally, i.e., only for managers close to retirement age), and so it may prompt the taking of long-tail risk gambles, whose near-term gains could be undone by adverse consequences occurring after the withholding period ends. While our restricted-stock proposal is not insulated from gaming, we think its more straightforward, mechanical operation is likely to minimize the potential for such behavior. In addition, restricted-stock and option holdings provide for an automatic, ongoing, direct and proportionate impact of the change in a company's equity value on a manager's net worth, compared to the vagaries of a reduction in compensation only upon the extreme events of bankruptcy or extraordinary government assistance, which would lead to litigation and adjudication by a court, as managers or shareholders would seek a legal interpretation of whether a triggering event had occurred.

[46]   As mentioned in note 11, *supra*, the Act requires independent compensation committees and consultants, periodic say-on-pay votes, increased disclosure on compensation and includes expanded regulation of claw-back policies.

consider other institutional reforms, as many banking and financial economists have stressed, such as revising the regulatory approach to capital requirements to be less pro-cyclical and more sensitive to risk, and in determining how to revive the repo and securitization markets, which were regrettably not addressed in the Dodd-Frank Act.[47] Nevertheless, we believe that our proposal that financial institutions' incentive compensation take the form of restricted stock and options would contribute to getting the incentives of those firms' decision-makers right, and accordingly, not work at cross-purposes with other regulatory efforts to mitigate the likelihood of future financial crises.

REFERENCES

American International Group, Inc. 2004. Definitive 14A Proxy Statement (Apr. 5).
Andrade, Gregor, Mark Mitchell and Erik Stafford. 2001. New Evidence and Perspectives on Mergers, *Journal of Economic Perspectives*, 15: 103–20.
Andrews, Edmund L. and Louise Story. 2009. New Rules Seek to Force Banks to Restrict Pay, *New York Times*, A1 (Sept. 19).
Armstrong, Christopher S., Alan D. Jagolinzer and David F. Larcker. 2010. Chief Executive Officer Equity Incentives and Accounting Irregularities, *Journal of Accounting Research*, 14: 225–71.
Bartlett, Bruce. 2002. Not So Suite: Clinton Tax Law Is the Problem, Not Greedy Execs, *National Review Online* (Sept. 25), available at http://www.nationalreview.com/nrof_bartlett/bartlett092502.asp.
Bebchuk, Lucian A. 2009. Congress Gets Punitive on Executive Pay, *Wall Street Journal*, A15 (Feb. 17).
Bebchuk, Lucian A. and Holger Spamann. 2010. Regulating Bankers' Pay, *Georgetown Law Journal*, 98: 247–87.
Bebchuk, Lucian A., Martijn Cremers and Urs Peyer. 2008. CEO Centrality. Harvard Law School John M. Olin Center for Law, Economics, and Business Discussion Paper No. 601.
Bhagat, Sanjai and Brian Bolton. 2010. Investment Bankers' Culture of Ownership, Manuscript.
Bhagat, Sanjai and Roberta Romano. 2010. Reforming Executive Compensation: Simplicity, Transparency and Committing to the Long Term, *European Company and Financial Law Review*, 7: 273–96.
Bhagat, Sanjai, Brian Bolton and Roberta Romano. 2008. The Promise and Peril of Corporate Governance Indices, *Columbia Law Review*, 108: 1803–82.
Bhagat, Sanjai, Brian Bolton and Ajay Subramanian. 2011. Manager Characteristics and Capital Structure: Theory and Evidence, *Journal of Financial and Quantitative Analysis*, 46: 1581–627.
BNA. 2009a. EU Will Examine Bonus Structure of Banks Seeking State Aid, *Corporate Governance Report*, 12: 111 (Oct. 5).
BNA. 2009b. Executive Compensation: Geithner Gives Glimpse of Policy on Executive Compensation Under TARP, *Corporate Accountability Report*, 7: 125 (Jan. 30).
Bolton, Patrick, Hamid Mehran and Joel D. Shapiro. 2010. Executive Compensation and Risk-Taking, Federal Reserve Bank of New York Staff Report no. 456.
Burns, Natasha and Simi Kedia. 2006. The Impact of Performance-Based Compensation on Misreporting, *Journal of Financial Economics*, 79: 35–67.
Calomiris, Charles W. 2008. The Subprime Turmoil: What's Old, What's New, and What's Next, Columbia Business School Working Paper, available at http://www1.gsb.columbia.edu/mygsb/faculty/research/pub-files/3182/What%sOldNewNext.pdf.
Caprio, Jr., Gerard, Asli Demirgüç-Kunt and Edward J. Kane. 2008. The 2007 Meltdown in Structured Securitization: Searching for Lessons, Not Scapegoats, manuscript, available at http://www2.bc.edu/~kaneeb/.
Citigroup, Inc. 1999–2007. Definitive 14A Proxy Statements.
Cohen, Daniel A., Alyesha Dey and Thomas Z. Lys. 2007. The Sarbanes Oxley Act of 2002: Implications for Compensation Contracts and Managerial Risk-Taking, manuscript, available at http//ssrn.com/abstract=1027448.
Cornett, Marcia Millon, Jamie John McNutt and Hassan Tehranian. 2009. The Financial Crisis: Did Corporate

---

[47] See, for example, Kashyap, et al. (2008) on the need to revise capital requirements; and Gorton (2010) on the importance of reviving securitization.

Governance Affect the Performance of Publicly-Traded U.S. Bank Holding Companies?, manuscript, available at http://ssrn.com/abstract=1476969.

Cremers, Martijn and Roberta Romano. 2007. Institutional Investors and Proxy Voting: The Impact of the 2003 Mutual Fund Voting Disclosure Regulation, Yale Law & Economics Research Paper No. 349.

Dash, Eric and Andrew Martin. 2009. Wells Fargo to Repay U.S., a Coda to the Bailout Era, *New York Times*, B1 (Dec. 15).

Department of the Treasury. 2009. Interim Final Rule for TARP Standards for Compensation and Corporate Governance, Code of Federal Regulations 31: Part 30 (June 15), available at http://www/treas.gov/press/releases/reports/ec%20irf%20fr%20web%206.9.09tg164.pdf.

Department of the Treasury, Office of the Comptroller of the Currency, Federal Reserve System, Federal Deposit Insurance Corporation and Department of the Treasury, Office of Thrift Supervision. 2010. Final Guidance on Sound Incentive Compensation Policies, *Federal Register*, 75: 36, 395–6, 414 (June 25).

DeYoung, Robert, Emma Y. Peng and Meng Yan. 2010. Executive Compensation and Business Policy Choices at U.S. Commercial Banks, Federal Reserve Bank of Kansas City Research Working Paper 10-02.

Ebrahimi, Helia. 2009. Sarkozy Draws Up Plans for Global Bonus Clampdown, *Daily Telegram* 2 (Aug. 26).

Edmans, Alex, Xavier Gabaix, Tomasz Sadzik and Yuliy Sannikov. 2009. Dynamic Incentive Accounts, manuscript, available at http://ssrn.com/abstract=1361797.

Erkens, David, Mingyi Hung and Pedro Matos. 2009. Corporate Governance in the Recent Financial Crisis: Evidence from Financial Institutions Worldwide, ECGI—Finance Working Paper No. 249/2009, available at http://ssrn.com/abstract=1397685.

Exxon Mobile Corp. 2003–2010. Definitive 14A Proxy Statements.

Fahlenbrach, Rüdiger and René Stulz. 2011. Bank CEO Incentives and the Credit Crisis, *Journal of Financial Economics*, 99: 11–26.

Federal Reserve System. 2009. Proposed Guidance on Sound Incentive Compensation Policies, *Federal Register*, 74: 55, 227–55, 238 (Oct. 27).

French, Kenneth R., et al. 2010. *The Squam Lake Report*. Princeton NJ: Princeton University Press.

Frydman, Carol and Dirk Jenter. 2010. CEO Compensation, manuscript, available at http://ssrn.com/abstract=1582232.

Gillan, Stuart L., Jay A. Hartzell and Laura T. Starks. 2007. Tradeoffs in Corporate Governance: Evidence from Board Structures and Charter Provisions, manuscript, available at http://www.law.yale.edu/documents/pdf/cbl/starks_paper.pdf.

Gilson, Stuart C. 1989. Management Turnover and Financial Distress, *Journal of Financial Economics*, 25: 241–62.

Gordon, Jeffrey N. 2010. Executive Compensation and Corporate Governance in Financial Firms: The Case for Convertible Equity-Based Pay, Columbia University School of Law Center for Law and Economics Working Paper No. 373.

Gorton, Gary B. 2010. *Slapped in the Face by the Invisible Hand: Banking and the Panic of 2007*. New York: Oxford University Press.

Gorton, Gary B. and Andrew Metrick. 2009. Securitized Banking and the Run on Repo, Yale ICF Working Paper No. 09-14, available at http://ssrn.com/abstract-1440752.

Hall, Brian J. and Jeffrey B. Liebman. 1998. Are CEOs Really Paid Like Bureaucrats?, *Quarterly Journal of Economics*, 113: 653–91.

Herring, Richard J. 2008. Risk Management and Its Implications for Systemic Risk, Testimony before the Senate Banking Committee, Subcommittee on Securities, Insurance and Investment (June 19), available at http://www.law.yale.edu/documents/pdf/cbl/Herring_Senate_Testimony.pdf.

Holmström, Bengt. 1979. Moral Hazard and Observability, *Bell Journal of Economics*, 10: 74–91.

Holmström, Bengt. 1999. Managerial Incentive Problems—A Dynamic Perspective, *Review of Economic Studies*, 66: 169–82.

Holmström, Bengt and Steven N. Kaplan. 2003. The State of U.S. Corporate Governance: What's Right and What's Wrong?, *Journal of Applied Corporate Finance*, 15: 8–20.

Hu, Bei. 2009. AIG Shouldn't Have Paid Unit Bonuses, Greenberg Says, *Bloomberg* (Mar. 26), available at http://www.bloomberg.com/apps/news?pid=20601087&sid=aM1tb.djytxs&refer=home.

Jensen, Michael C. and William H. Meckling. 1976. Theory of the Firm: Managerial Behavior, Agency Costs and Ownership Structures, *Journal of Financial Economics*, 3: 305–60.

Jensen, Michael C. and Kevin J. Murphy. 1990a. Performance Pay and Top-Management Incentives, *Journal of Political Economy*, 98: 225–64.

Jensen, Michael C. and Kevin J. Murphy. 1990b. CEO Incentives—It's Not How Much You Pay But How, *Journal of Applied Corporate Finance*, 3: 36–49.

Kaplan, Steven and Joshua Rauh. 2010. Wall Street and Main Street: What Contributes to the Rise in the Highest Incomes?, *Review of Economic Studies*, 23: 1004–50.

Kashyap, Anil, Raghuram G. Rajan and Jeremy Stein. 2008. Rethinking Capital Requirements, in Federal Reserve Bank of Kansas City Symposium on Maintaining Stability in a Changing Financial System.

Lambert, Richard A., David F. Larcker and Robert E. Verrechia. 1991. Portfolio Considerations in Valuing Executive Compensation, *Journal of Accounting Research*, 29: 129–49.

Lengell, Sean. 2009. Obama Seeking to Ease Limits on Executive Pay, *Washington Times*, A09 (Feb. 16).

Levmore, Saul. 2001. Puzzling Stock Options and Compensation Norms, *University of Pennsylvania Law Review*, 149: 1901–40.

Litvak, Kate. 2009. Venture Capital Limited Partnership Agreements: Understanding Compensation Agreements, *University of Chicago Law Review*, 76: 161–218.

Lucchetti, Aaron and Matthew Karnitschnig. 2009. On Street, New Reality on Pay Sets In, *Wall Street Journal*, B1 (Jan. 31).

Metrick, Andrew. 2007. *Venture Capital and the Finance of Innovation*. Hoboken NJ: Wiley.

Milne, Richard. 2010. IMF Economists Criticise CDS Model, *Financial Times*, 19 (Aug. 25).

Peng, Lin and Alisa Roell. 2008. Managerial Incentives and Stock Price Manipulation, manuscript, available at http://ssrn.com/abstract=1321903.

Perry, Tod and Mark Zenner. 2001. Pay for Performance? Government Regulation and the Structure of Compensation Contracts, *Journal of Financial Economics*, 62: 453–88.

Personick, Martin E. 2005. IRRC Governance Research Service 2005 Background Report A: Management Proposals on Executive Compensation Plans.

Reinhardt, Carmen and Kenneth S. Rogoff. 2009. *This Time Is Different: Eight Centuries of Financial Folly*. Princeton NJ: Princeton University Press.

Rose, Nancy L. and Catherine Wolfram. 2002. Regulating Executive Pay: Using the Tax Code to Influence Chief Executive Officer Compensation, *Journal of Labor Economics*, 20: S138–S175.

Schizer, David M. 2000. Executives and Hedging: The Fragile Legal Foundation of Incentive Compatibility, *Columbia Law Review*, 100: 440–504.

Seligman, Joel. 1995. *The Transformation of Wall Street* (rev. ed.), Boston: Northeastern University Press.

Singh, Manmohan and Karim Youssef. 2010. Price of Risk—Recent Evidence from Large Financials, IMF Working Paper WP/10/190.

Story, Louise. 2009. In Merrill's Failed Plan, Lessons for Pay Czar, *New York Times*, B1 (Oct. 8).

Suntheim, Felix. 2010. Managerial Compensation in the Financial Services Industry, manuscript, available at http://ssrn.com/abstract=1592163.

Treanor, Jill. 2009. Bankers Bow to Pressure on Bonuses: Darling Gets Agreement to G20 Rules a Year Early, *The Guardian*, 26 (Oct. 1).

Tung, Frederick. 2010. Pay for Banker Performance: Structuring Executive Compensation for Risk Regulation, manuscript, available at http://ssrn.com/abstract=1546229.

Walker, David I. 2009. The Challenge of Improving the Long-Term Focus of Executive Pay, Boston University School of Law Working Paper No. 09-22, available at http://ssrn.com/abstract=1396663.

Wei, Chenyang and David B. Yermack. 2010. Deferred Compensation, Risk and Company Value: Investor Reactions to CEO Incentives, NYU Working Paper No. FIN-09-020, available at http://ssrn.com/abstract=1519252.

Weisman, Jonathan. 2009. Obama Retakes Global Stage But With Diminished Momentum, *Wall Street Journal*, A6 (Sept. 1).

Weisman, Jonathan and Joann S. Lublin. 2009. Obama Lays Out Limits on Executive Pay, *Wall Street Journal*, A1 (Feb. 5).

Ydstie, John. 2010. Pay Czar Slams Bank Executives' Bonuses, available at http://www.npr.org/templates/story/story.php?storyId=128725677&ft=1&f=1003.

Yermack, David. 2009. Keeping the Pay Police at Bay, *Wall Street Journal*, W1 (Oct. 10–11).

8 How to avoid compensating the CEO for luck: the case of macroeconomic fluctuations

Lars Oxelheim,* Clas Wihlborg and Jianhua Zhang**

1 INTRODUCTION

Executive compensation is under scrutiny and there are calls for regulation and "codes of conduct" with respect to levels as well as forms of compensation. Although the level of compensation in Europe remains below that in the US, the level in most European countries has increased rapidly in the new millennium. According to Fernandes et al. (2008) the difference between Europe and the US can be explained to a large extent by the larger variable component of executive compensation in the US. The higher variability in the US seems to be associated with a risk-premium. This observation implies that levels and forms of compensation are not independent.

One common view in the current debate is that CEO compensation should be linked to "sustainable" profits that presumably are the result of skill and effort. Regulation seems to be emerging in many countries stating that the reward for improved performance should not be fully realized unless the improved performance is observed for a period of 3–5 years. Increased compensation would be linked to performance surpassing some benchmark for some duration. The argument behind such proposals would be that improved performance is likely to be caused by other factors than executive skill and effort if it does not exceed a benchmark for duration of time. The other factors could be earnings management by the executives and some sort of luck.

There are a number of difficulties associated with proposals of the type discussed if they are to provide appropriate incentives for managers. The concern with earnings management can be partly resolved by linking compensation to less manageable variables and by improved accounting standards. The issue of luck is more complicated (Bertrand and Mullainathan, 2001). One problem is to define a benchmark for performance representing a minimum level that would be achieved without particular skill and effort. A second problem is to determine when and how performance above (below) the benchmark should be rewarded (penalized) for being the result of skill and effort rather than luck. More fundamentally, what changes in performance are caused by good or bad luck in an environment characterized by a variety of shocks? Even with the benefit of hindsight this question could be hard to answer.

The contracting literature indicates that optimal incentive contracts are achieved by means of some kind of benchmarking for "normal" performance and the linking of

* Financial support from NASDAQ OMX Nordic Foundation to Lars Oxelheim is gratefully acknowledged.
** Financial support form VINNOVA (2010–02449) to Jianhua Zhang is gratefully acknowledged.

compensation to a performance measure reflecting skill and effort with as little noise as possible.[1]

Analyzing the impact of luck on CEO compensation, Bertrand and Mullainathan (2000, 2001) define luck as performance beyond the CEO's control. As examples, they consider performance effects of fluctuations in oil prices in the energy sector, the impact of exchange rates in traded goods sectors and changes in performance around year to year changes in mean industry performance. Garvey and Milbourn (2006) use a market index and an industry index as proxies for stock price performance based on luck. In all cases the empirical results indicate that compensation depends strongly on luck. Garvey and Milbourn also find that executives are rewarded (penalized) more for good luck than for bad luck and that this asymmetry can be linked to corporate governance variables.

Accepting the premise from the contracting literature that lucky performance should not be rewarded there is an additional difficulty associated with the measurement of performance outside the control of management. As pointed out by Oxelheim and Wihlborg (2003) and Gopalan, Milbourn and Song (2010), the effect on performance of external shocks beyond management's control can be influenced by management's strategic choices as well as operational decisions in response to external shocks. If so, the incentives of management to take advantage of lucky external events and to dampen the effects of unlucky external events would be removed if compensation is not related to performance effects of lucky circumstances.

The implication of this discussion is that the appropriate definition of lucky performance depends on the nature of shocks and the technological ability to adjust strategy and operations to shocks within a certain time frame. The adjustment of strategy and operations can take the form of investment in flexibility or real options in an environment characterized by high uncertainty about external shocks, or adjustment may take the form of switching production and marketing efforts in response to anticipated and even current events. A restaurant business may be able to respond very quickly to lucky events by adding tables while a capital-intensive firm may need years to adjust production capacity.

Lack of sustainability of performance is not a good indication of luck in all industries. Macroeconomic fluctuations may be short-lived or last several years. The performance of a firm that can respond rapidly to macroeconomic fluctuations depends on skill and effort even in the short run. This calls for an approach that even in a shorter perspective can assess the sustainability of performance.

In this chapter we focus on the macroeconomic environment as a major source of changes in performance beyond management's control. Macroeconomic fluctuations affect almost all aspects of corporate performance but they cannot be influenced by management. However, as noted, the effect of macroeconomic fluctuations on corporate performance can be influenced by management if macroeconomic conditions can be forecast and operations can be adjusted within the period. For this reason we distinguish between anticipated and unanticipated macroeconomic conditions. Depending on firm-specific conditions, performance beyond management control may be explained either by all macroeconomic fluctuations or only by unanticipated fluctuations.

---

[1]   Milgrom and Roberts (1992) review the contracting literature on incentive effects of compensation schemes.

Our objective is to model the macroeconomic influence on CEO compensation and to estimate the macro economy's contribution to changes in this compensation. The empirical analysis in this study is based on Swedish companies and the period under investigation is 2001–07.[2] Most studies on CEO compensation are based on US firms and to some extent this choice is motivated by the easy access to detailed data for very long periods. However, our research question motivates the choice of a small open economy since a higher degree of openness may also mean higher exposure to macroeconomic factors influencing CEO compensation (Oxelheim and Randøy, 2005). Swedish firms are known to belong to the top-five league regarding financial as well as commercial internationalization (UNCTAD, 2008).

We ask how compensation for Swedish CEOs would have developed had macroeconomic influences on compensation been filtered out. Second, we distinguish between anticipated and unanticipated macroeconomic fluctuations to see how CEO compensation would have developed if only unanticipated macroeconomic influences were filtered out from compensation. Third, we ask whether there is an asymmetric impact on remuneration in any particular year in the sense that remuneration is particularly sensitive to favorable developments in variables affecting performance. The interest in asymmetry arises because it may reflect "skimming" of shareholders in the words of Bertrand and Mullainathan (2001) and because asymmetry affects incentives for risk management with respect to variables affecting compensation.

Compensation is typically not linked in a simple way to one well-defined performance measure. Macroeconomic effects on compensation can occur through a number of channels depending on what aspects of performance affect salaries, bonuses and other forms of CEO compensation. Therefore, we focus on the decomposition of compensation into "intrinsic" and macroeconomic components rather than on any one performance measure. Presumably, changes in compensation net on changes linked to macroeconomic factors represent compensation for changes in firms' "intrinsic" competitiveness. We control for industry factors as well.

In Oxelheim and Wihlborg (2003) the case of Electrolux was used in the context of value-based management (VBM) to illustrate how changes in performance can be decomposed into one "intrinsic" component and one component caused by macroeconomic developments. A set of domestic and foreign macroeconomic price variables (exchange rates, interest rates, price levels) were used to filter out the macroeconomic component from total changes in performance from quarter to quarter. One reason for using price variables is that they can be observed without a long lag. Therefore, they can be used in practice to decompose very recent changes in performance and, thereby, to adjust compensation.

In the empirical part of this chapter, macroeconomic price variables are also used as indicators of macroeconomic fluctuation. The period 2001–07 is determined by data availability. Industry factors are also included to the extent possible in the relatively small Swedish economy. After estimating the impact of macroeconomic factors we ask how salaries and bonuses would have developed for the average firm during the estimation

---

[2]   Oxelheim, Wihlborg and Zhang (2008) present a more limited analysis of macroeconomic influences on cash compensation for a shorter time period.

period had they been independent of total and unanticipated macroeconomic fluctuations, respectively.

The chapter is organized as follows. In Section 2, the data set for compensation in the form of salary, bonus, option awards and pension payments is described. Relevant performance variables explaining compensation are identified in Section 3. The contribution of macroeconomic factors to compensation and performance measures is estimated in Section 4 using cross-section and panel analyses. In Section 5 we decompose compensation each year into an "intrinsic" component and a component caused by macroeconomic factors, distinguishing between the total impact of the macro economy and the unanticipated impact. In Section 6 we test whether remuneration is asymmetric in response to macroeconomic factors, in particular. The total compensation each year is divided into symmetric and asymmetric components. Concluding comments follow in Section 7.

2   THE COMPENSATION DATA

Our dataset covers compensation for CEOs and contains two samples: cash disbursements (salaries and bonus) from 2001–07, and total compensation (i.e. salaries, bonus, stock option awards, and pensions) from 2004–07. Data have been collected from annual reports for all Swedish firms listed on the stock exchange as Large-Cap, Mid-Cap, and Small-Cap[3] firms during the period 2001–07. The firm-specific factors are collected from DataStream, while the macroeconomic factors are obtained from EcoWin (Reuters) database.

Table 8.1 reports mean (in million SEK), standard deviation, as well as growth index (Index = 100 in 2001) for cash disbursement levels for the CEOs in 127 Swedish firms on the Stockholm Stock Exchange during the period 2001–07.[4] We can see that in panel C of the table, the compensation levels in the form of total cash disbursements increased during this period. On average, salary plus bonus increased 58 percent. A distinction is made between salary and bonus in panels A and B. The year 2001 is excluded here because we could not separate the bonus from the salary for this year. The table shows that bonus payments increased much faster than salary payments. Bonus payments increased 183 percent, while salaries increased only 30 percent. The former figure takes into account both that average bonus payments increased and that the number of firms paying bonus increased.

In Table 8.2 compensation in the form of option awards and contributions to pensions are added. Since the option and pension data are only available as of 2004, the descriptive statistics in this table refer to the period 2004–07 (with index 100 in 2004). In Panel C we can see that compensation in the form of option awards increases by 725 percent over the period. The variation is substantial. Pension awards are stable and increase only 9

---

[3]   It is grouped according to the market capitalization of the firm. "Large-Cap" refers to firms with market capitalization greater than 1bn euros. "Mid-Cap" firms have market capitalization between 150m and 1bn euros, while firms denoted "Small-Cap" have market capitalization below 150m euros.
[4]   There is no publicly available database for executive compensation as in the US but the availability of data is limited to annual reports of firms specifying compensation to CEO. As of January 2005, the implementation of the International Financial Reporting Standards (IFRS) improved disclosure and access to detailed compensation data.

Table 8.1   Compensation levels: salary and bonus

Year	2001	2002	2003	2004	2005	2006	2007
Panel A: Salary							
Mean	–	3.263	3.579	3.582	3.764	3.975	4.270
Std.	–	2.462	3.112	2.683	2.812	3.051	3.290
Index	–	100	110	110	115	121	130
Panel B: Bonus							
Mean	–	0.684	0.822	1.306	1.774	1.944	1.932
Std.	–	1.553	1.672	2.205	2.868	2.941	3.128
Index	–	100	120	191	259	284	283
Panel C: Salary + Bonus							
Mean	3.918	3.947	4.401	4.888	5.538	5.919	6.202
Std.	4.059	3.494	4.104	4.335	4.961	5.388	5.586
Index	100	101	112	125	141	151	158

Note: This table displays mean, standard deviation for compensation levels (salary and bonus) (Million SEK), as well as the growth index for the CEOs in 127 Swedish firms during the period 2001–07.

percent. Both options and pensions decreased in 2006. If we add all the components, i.e. Salary + Bonuses + Options + Pensions, we can see that the total increased 29 percent from 2004 to 2007.

3   EXPLAINING COMPENSATION WITHOUT MACROECONOMIC FACTORS

Early US studies of executive compensation across firms focused on the relation between CEO compensation and measures of firm performance (Coughlan and Schmidt, 1985; Murphy, 1985, 1986; Abowd, 1990; Jensen and Murphy, 1990; Leonard, 1990), while other studies analyzed whether CEOs are rewarded for performance relative to a market or industry benchmark (Antle and Smith, 1986; Gibbons and Murphy, 1990; Bebchuk and Grinstein 2005). The US evidence indicates that benchmarking is not practiced much.

In this section we ask which measures of firm performance explain CEO compensation across the Swedish sample of firms. The analysis in the following sections of the impact of macroeconomic factors is similar to analysis of benchmarking but it allows macroeconomic factors to have a general as well as a firm-specific impact on CEO compensation.

Cash compensation (salary plus bonus) is used as the main measure of CEO compensation but we also analyze whether the results are likely to generalize to a wider measure of compensation. After eliminating the missing values in the firm performance sample, our final sample contains different numbers of firms in different years. Thus, the panel is unbalanced with a maximum of 127 firms and a minimum of 109 firms during the period 2001–07.

We begin by analyzing how the cross-section variation of cash compensation levels (salary plus bonus) for the CEOs depends on a number of firm- and industry performance

Table 8.2   Compensation levels: salary, bonus, options, and pensions

Year	2004	2005	2006	2007
Panel A: Salary				
Mean	3.582	3.764	3.975	4.270
Std.	2.683	2.812	3.051	3.290
Index	100	105	111	119
Panel B: Bonus				
Mean	1.306	1.774	1.944	1.932
Std.	2.205	2.868	2.941	3.128
Index	100	136	149	148
Panel C: Options				
Mean	0.094	0.432	0.272	0.782
Std.	0.456	3.004	0.882	3.292
Index	100	462	290	825
Panel D: Pensions				
Mean	1.707	2.020	1.780	1.861
Std.	2.368	2.921	3.053	2.617
Index	100	118	104	109
Panel E: Salary + Bonus				
Mean	4.888	5.538	5.919	6.202
Std.	4.335	4.961	5.388	5.586
Index	100	113	123	129
Panel F: Salary + Bonus + Options				
Mean	4.982	5.970	6.191	6.984
Std.	4.313	6.853	5.119	7.177
Index	100	120	124	140
Panel G: Salary + Bonus + Options + Pensions				
Mean	6.659	7.942	7.601	8.571
Std.	6.023	6.452	7.160	8.661
Index	100	119	114	129

Note: This table displays mean, standard deviation for compensation levels (salary, bonus, options, and pensions) (Million SEK), as well as the growth index for the CEOs in 127 Swedish firms during the period 2004–07.

measures, and we ask whether the cross-section pattern is stable over the data period. The following regression is estimated in cross-section for each year, as well as pooled:

$$Log(Compensation_{i,t}) = \alpha_0 + \alpha_1 Log(Sales_{i,t}) + \alpha_2 Log(Performance_{i,t})$$
$$+ \sum_{i=3}^{8} \alpha_i Industry\ dummies_i + \varepsilon_{i,t} \tag{8.1}$$

The firm's total sale is used as a proxy for firm size. Whether CEO compensation is more closely tied to firm size (sales) or firm profits is controversial due to a multicollinearity problem among the independent variables in the regressions (Ciscel and Carroll, 1980; Rosen, 1992). In order to minimize this problem, we focus on variables and ratios that exhibit relatively little correlation with each other. A number of performance variables were tested in equation (8.1) to find which one(s) explain(s) compensation the best. The variables were return on assets, return on equity, and Tobin's Q. We found that Tobin's Q (measured as market value relative to book value) had the most explanatory power. Therefore, Tobin's Q is used as the performance proxy from now on. Seven industry dummies are used to control for industry factors.[5]

All the variables in the regressions in this study are in logarithms. Thus, the regression coefficients are interpreted as "compensation-performance elasticities." One of the advantages of the elasticity approach is that it produces a better "fit" in terms of marginal effects. Another advantage is that the elasticity is relatively invariant to firm size while sensitivities vary monotonically with firm size (larger firms having smaller betas) (Gibbons and Murphy, 1992; Murphy 1999).

Table 8.3 shows the results for equation (8.1) for each year and for pooled data. It can be seen that the elasticity with respect to sales remains fairly constant from year to year. The elasticity with respect to Tobin's Q is also stable except for the relatively low elasticities for the years 2001 and 2002. The only industry showing a significant difference from the average is industry 4 (health care). The compensation level in this industry has increased relatively fast.

Table 8.4 shows the results for equation (8.1) for the pooled data by using different compensation measures as dependent variables: 1) Salary plus Bonus, 2) Salary plus Bonus plus Options, and 3) Salary plus Bonus plus Option plus Pensions. This sample covers the period 2004–07. We want to check whether the coefficients for the firm-specific variables depend on the scope of the compensation measure. Table 8.4 shows that the estimated coefficients remain very much the same when we add options and pension awards to salary plus bonus as the dependent variable. Since we have several more years of observations for salary plus bonus alone we will use this measure of compensation in the decomposition below.

Using the sample 2001–07 and the above firm-specific factors, we estimate two random effects models with industry dummy variables in one and industry plus time dummy variables in the other.[6] The results are reported in Table 8.5. The results for the random effects Model 1 with industry factors is very similar to the results for pooled data in Table 8.3 except that the dummy for industry 6 is not significant. Thus, competitive conditions in particular industries do not seem to influence compensation much.

The time dummy variables are highly significant in the second column of Table 8.5. The coefficients increase each year from 2001 to 2007. The time pattern could be caused by macroeconomic influences and provides motivation to analyze the role of these influences.

Are the patterns for salary and bonus different? It can be expected that the bonus

---

[5] The industries are: 1) consumer goods, 2) information technology, 3) financials, 4) health care, 5) industrials, 6) others, 7) materials.

[6] The random effects model is compared to pooled linear regressions and the fixed effects model in the next section where macro variables are introduced. See footnote 7 below.

Table 8.3 *Pooled and cross-sectional regressions without macro variables*

Year	2001–07	2001	2002	2003	2004	2005	2006	2007
Log (Sales)	0.277***	0.293***	0.266***	0.235***	0.290***	0.300***	0.275***	0.285***
	(29.21)	(12.43)	(11.92)	(9.74)	(11.88)	(11.66)	(9.67)	(9.78)
Log (Tobin's Q)	0.236***	0.094	0.070	0.205***	0.286***	0.309***	0.277***	0.202***
	(7.28)	(1.17)	(0.84)	(1.98)	(2.91)	(3.29)	(2.91)	(2.20)
Industry Dummy 1	0.051	0.210	0.049	0.083	0.040	0.032	-0.036	0.094
	(0.54)	(0.86)	(0.229)	(0.32)	(0.17)	(0.13)	(-0.13)	(0.33)
Industry Dummy 2	0.053	0.324	0.053	-0.047	0.060	0.072	-0.058	0.064
	(0.59)	(1.41)	(0.26)	(-0.19)	(0.26)	(0.30)	(-0.23)	(0.25)
Industry Dummy 3	0.174***	0.318	0.058	0.239	0.347	0.298	-0.052	-0.016
	(2.01)	(1.44)	(0.28)	(1.03)	(1.61)	(1.32)	(-0.20)	(-0.06)
Industry Dummy 4	0.564***	0.762***	0.552***	0.559	0.437	0.587***	0.641**	0.673***
	(4.98)	(2.65)	(2.10)	(1.78)*	(1.53)	(1.99)	(1.91)	(2.03)
Industry Dummy 5	0.125	0.265	0.091	0.090	0.094	0.035	0.156	0.229
	(1.52)	(1.26)	(0.48)	(0.41)	(0.45)	(0.16)	(0.65)	(0.94)
Industry Dummy 6	0.425***	0.425	0.324	0.342	0.312	0.482	0.544	0.554
	(3.02)	(1.21)	(0.98)	(0.90)	(0.88)	(1.30)	(1.33)	(1.35)
Constant	10.743***	10.221***	10.910***	11.372***	10.514***	10.425***	10.887***	10.787***
	(63.41)	(24.26)	(27.74)	(26.33)	(24.23)	(22.62)	(21.29)	(20.74)
Observations	846	122	127	127	127	127	111	109
Adjusted R^2	55%	60%	58%	48%	56%	54%	52%	53%

Notes:
This table reports the parameter estimations from both pooled and cross-sectional regressions from equation (8.1). The dependent variable is Log (Compensation). The industries are: 1) consumer goods, 2) information technology, 3) financials, 4) health care, 5) industrials, 6) others, and 7) materials. The dummy 7 is dropped in the model.
t-values are in round parentheses.
*, **, *** denote significance at the 0.10, 0.05 and 0.01 level or better.

Table 8.4   Pooled regression using salary plus bonus, or salary plus bonus plus options, or salary plus bonus plus options plus pensions as dependent variable

	Log (Salary + Bonus)	Log (Salary + Bonus + Options)	Log (Salary + Bonus + Options + Pensions)
Log (Sales)	0.279***	0.287***	0.309***
	(21.63)	(21.34)	(23.43)
Log (Tobin's Q)	0.246***	0.270***	0.275***
	(5.70)	(5.99)	(6.22)
Industry Dummy 1	0.001	0.011	−0.030
	(0.01)	(0.08)	(−0.24)
Industry Dummy 2	0.057	0.060	−0.037
	(0.50)	(0.50)	(−0.32)
Industry Dummy 3	0.125	0.163	0.033
	(1.11)	(1.39)	(0.29)
Industry Dummy 4	0.629***	0.632***	0.530***
	(3.94)	(3.81)	(3.25)
Industry Dummy 5	0.127	0.138	0.027
	(1.20)	(1.25)	(0.25)
Industry Dummy 6	0.451***	0.468***	0.348**
	(2.53)	(2.52)	(1.91)
Constant	10.802***	10.682***	10.709***
	(47.16)	(44.74)	(45.72)
Observations	438	438	438
Adjusted R^2	57%	56%	61%

Notes:
This table reports the parameter estimations from three pooled models to identify compensations. The dependent variable is Log (Salary + Bonus), Log (Salary + Bonus + Options), or Log (Salary + Bonus + Options + Pensions). The industries are: 1) consumer goods, 2) information technology, 3) financials, 4) health care, 5) industrials, 6) others, and 7) materials. The industry dummy variable 7 is dropped in the models. The time period is 2004–07.
t-values are in round parentheses.
*, **, *** denote significance at the 0.10, 0.05 and 0.01 level or better.

component of compensation is more sensitive than the salary component to performance-variation over time and across firms. Therefore the model with industry dummies is also tested for Salary and Bonus separately. The results are shown in Table 8.6. There are fewer observations for Salary and Bonus separately than for the sum of these components, because all observations of zero Bonus are excluded. The Salary component is explained mainly by sales, while Tobin's Q has a strong effect on Bonus but little effect on Salary. Clearly and not surprisingly, compensation in the form of bonus is much more sensitive to performance from a shareholder perspective than salary compensation. The table also shows that the results for Salary plus Bonus are similar to the results for Bonus alone, although the coefficients for the total are generally smaller. Since the results are so similar, and since we have twice as many observations for total compensation as for Bonus alone, we focus on total compensation in the following analysis of macro-factors.

Table 8.5   Random effects model with industry or industry and time dummy variables

	Model 1	Model 2
Log (Sales)	0.260***	0.233***
	(15.28)	(13.34)
Log (Tobin's Q)	0.189***	0.083***
	(6.19)	(2.55)
Industry Dummy 1	0.121	0.120
	(0.62)	(0.61)
Industry Dummy 2	−0.006	0.002
	(−0.03)	(0.01)
Industry Dummy 3	0.185	0.186
	(1.03)	(1.02)
Industry Dummy 4	0.524***	0.556**
	(2.21)	(2.30)
Industry Dummy 5	0.125	0.141
	(0.71)	(0.79)
Industry Dummy 6	0.406	0.374
	(1.31)	(1.18)
Year Dummy 2002	–	0.082***
	–	(2.06)
Year Dummy 2003	–	0.172***
	–	(4.44)
Year Dummy 2004	–	0.219***
	–	(5.63)
Year Dummy 2005	–	0.300***
	–	(7.64)
Year Dummy 2006	–	0.319***
	–	(7.73)
Year Dummy 2007	–	0.360***
	–	(8.87)
Constant	11.027***	11.270***
	(33.98)	(34.66)
Observations	846	846
Log likelihood-ratio test	−418.44***	−364.90***
	[0.000]	[0.000]

Notes:
This table reports the parameter estimations from two random effects models for the period 2001–07. The dependent variable is Log (Compensation). In the first model the industry dummies are used, while in the second model both industry and time dummies are used. The industries are: 1) consumer goods, 2) information technology, 3) financials, 4) health care, 5) industrials, 6) others, and 7) materials. The time dummies are the years 2001–07. The industry dummy variable 7 is dropped in the first model, while the industry dummy variable 7 and time dummy variable for the year 2001 are dropped in the second model.
t-values are in round parentheses, and *p*-values are in square parentheses.
*, **, *** denotes significance at the 0.10, 0.05 and 0.01 level or better.

Table 8.6   Random effects model using salary, bonus or salary plus bonus as dependent variable

	Log (Salary)	Log (Bonus)	Log (Salary plus Bonus)
Log (Sales)	0.239***	0.352***	0.286***
	(4.81)	(8.84)	(15.06)
Log (Tobin's Q)	0.005	0.623***	0.162***
	(0.14)	(6.31)	(4.40)
Industry Dummy 1	0.185	0.031	0.168
	(1.14)	(0.08)	(0.88)
Industry Dummy 2	0.115	0.322	0.242
	(0.74)	(0.88)	(1.32)
Industry Dummy 3	0.175	1.185***	0.492***
	(1.13)	(3.22)	(2.65)
Industry Dummy 4	0.690***	1.094***	0.890***
	(3.28)	(2.21)	(3.54)
Industry Dummy 5	0.093	0.386	0.190
	(0.64)	(1.13)	(1.10)
Industry Dummy 6	0.429*	0.706	0.529**
	(1.78)	(1.24)	(1.84)
Constant	11.245	7.651***	10.670***
	(38.76)	(10.77)	(31.20)
Observations	456	456	456
Log likelihood-ratio test	−117.37***	−622.68***	−157.82***
	[0.000]	[0.000]	[0.000]

Notes:
This table reports the parameter estimations from three random effects models. The dependent variable is Log (Salary), Log (Bonus), or Log (Salary plus Bonus). The industries are: 1) consumer goods, 2) information technology, 3) financials, 4) health care, 5) industrials, 6) others, and 7) materials. The industry dummy variable 7 is dropped in the models. The time period is 2002–05. The regressions are based on the sample that firm pays bonus for the year.
t-values are in round parentheses, and *p*-values are in square parentheses.
*, **, *** denotes significance at the 0.10, 0.05 and 0.01 level or better.

4   CEO COMPENSATION AND MACROECONOMIC FACTORS

In this section we turn to an analysis of the macroeconomic influences on CEO compensation. These influences can occur through the performance variables in equation (8.1) or through other variables influencing compensation. We investigate whether macroeconomic variables affect compensation independently of variation in Q and Sales, and we analyze macroeconomic influences on Q and Sales. The total macroeconomic influence on compensation is the sum of these effects.

   Macroeconomic conditions can be identified using either quantity variables like GDP, GDP growth, investments and employment, or price variables like interest rates, inflation and exchange rates. Although the former group of variables describes macroeconomic conditions, they are typically observed with a substantial lag. Price variables, on the other hand, can be seen as easily observable signals of underlying macroeconomic shocks and developments. A shock would have a certain effect on a group of price variables as well as on GDP, employment, etc. but only the former would be observable at the time a shock occurs. Therefore, these signals can be useful tools for a firm wishing to decompose compensation and performance into "intrinsic factors" and macroeconomic factors. Another advantage of using price variables like interest rates and exchange rates in the decomposition is that they adjust rapidly to both domestic and foreign conditions affecting a firm's performance. For these reasons we prefer to use only price variables as proxies for macroeconomic conditions in the following.[7] Specifically, we use exchange rates, interest rates, inflation and the market return in the stock market.

It is likely that each firm's performance is sensitive to its specific set of variables but here we employ one set to explain changes in compensation across firms and time. Thus, we obtain estimates for the macroeconomic impact on compensation for the average firm. Dummy variables for firm characteristics could have been introduced in the analysis if the data set had covered a longer time period. We restrict the use of dummies to identification of industry effects on levels of compensation. In addition, we use a dummy to identify relatively export-dependent firms.

The first step in the analysis of macroeconomic influences on compensation is to determine effects of macroeconomic influences controlling for variation in the performance variables Q and Sales. The latter variables will explain only a part of changes in compensation if corporate boards use varying criteria to determine compensation. The following random effects model is estimated:

$$
\begin{aligned}
Log(Compensation_{i,t}) &= \alpha_0 + \alpha_1 Log(Sales_{i,t}) + \alpha_2 Log(Tobin's\ Q_{i,t}) \\
&+ \alpha_3 Log(1 + Anticipated\ interest\ rate_{i,t}) \\
&+ \alpha_4 Log(1 + Unanticipated\ interest\ rate_{i,t}) \\
&+ \alpha_5 Log(1 + Anticipated\ \Delta exchange\ rate_{i,t}) \\
&+ \alpha_6 Log(1 + Unanticipated\ \Delta exchange\ rate_{i,t}) \\
&+ \alpha_7 Log(1 + Anticipated\ \Delta CPI_{i,t}) + \alpha_8 Log(1 + Unanticipated\ \Delta CPI_{i,t}) \\
&+ \alpha_9 Log(Exchange\ rate_{i,t-1}) \\
&+ \sum_{i=10}^{15} \alpha_i Industry\ dummies_i + u_i + \varepsilon_{i,t}
\end{aligned}
\tag{8.2a}
$$

All variables are defined in log levels. The macro variables are the Swedish one-year interest rate, the exchange rate (SEK/USD) and the Swedish consumer price index (CPI). The stock market index has been removed from the equation. It does not add explanatory power to the interest rate. Table 8.7 shows that the correlation between the market index and the interest rate is −0.88.

---

[7]   A similar analysis of macroeconomic influences has been developed for purposes of exposure management in Oxelheim and Wihlborg (2008). An alternative formulation including GDP as well as price variables was tested. The explanatory power of this formulation including GDP was much lower than the present formulation. This result supports the idea that price variables serve as useful signals of macroeconomic conditions.

Table 8.7 Correlations

	Log (Salary and Bonus)	Log (Sales)	Log (Q)	Log (1+Market return)	Log (1+Anti. int. rate)	Log (1+Unanti. int. rate)	Log (1+Anti. Δex. rate)	Log (1+Unanti. Δex. rate)	Log (1+Anti. ΔCPI)	Log (1+Unanti. ΔCPI)
Log (Salary and Bonus)	1									
Log (Sales)	0.7046 (0.000)	1								
Log (Tobin's Q)	0.0629 (0.067)	-0.1845 (0.000)	1							
Log (1+Market return)	0.1782 (0.000)	0.0425 (0.216)	0.2106 (0.000)	1						
Log (1+Anti. interest rate)	-0.1791 (0.000)	-0.0524 (0.128)	-0.2031 (0.000)	-0.8878 (0.000)	1					
Log (1+Unanti. interest rate)	0.1057 (0.002)	0.0489 (0.155)	0.0248 (0.471)	0.2539 (0.000)	-0.5223 (0.000)	1				
Log (1+Anti. Δexchange rate)	-0.0517 (0.132)	-0.0421 (0.221)	-0.0572 (0.096)	0.0361 (0.294)	0.2512 (0.000)	-0.7383 (0.000)	1			
Log (1+Unanti. Δexchange rate)	-0.0137 (0.690)	0.0252 (0.464)	0.0561 (0.102)	-0.1854 (0.000)	-0.1024 (0.002)	0.2449 (0.000)	-0.7339 (0.000)	1		
Log (1+Anti. ΔCPI)	-0.1056 (0.002)	-0.0429 (0.212)	-0.2071 (0.000)	-0.4207 (0.000)	0.6399 (0.000)	-0.2803 (0.000)	0.5952 (0.000)	-0.6984 (0.000)	1	
Log (1+Unanti. ΔCPI)	0.0091 (0.791)	0.0222 (0.519)	0.0331 (0.336)	-0.2990 (0.000)	0.0176 (0.608)	0.4451 (0.000)	-0.8655 (0.000)	0.6674 (0.0009)	-0.5689 (0.000)	1

Notes:
This table reports the correlation coefficients of all the variables. The time period is 2001–07.
p-values are in parentheses.

Table 8.8   Random effects model with firm specific factors and interest rate, exchange rate and inflation as macroeconomic factors

	Model 1	Model 2	Model 3	Model 4
Log (Sales)	0.234***	0.234***	0.226***	0.226***
	(13.43)	(13.42)	(12.67)	(12.68)
Log (Tobin's Q)	0.072***	0.075***	0.075***	0.075***
	(2.27)	(2.37)	(2.37)	(2.37)
Log (1+Anti. interest rate)	−5.495**	−5.222**	−5.295**	−5.293**
	(−2.19)	(−2.14)	(−2.18)	(−2.17)
Log (1+Anti. Δexchange rate)	−0.009	–	–	–
	(−0.01)	–	–	–
Log (1+Unanti. Δexchange rate)	−0.681***	–	–	–
	(−4.51)	–	–	–
Log (1+Δexchange rate)	–	−0.703***	−0.660***	−0.703***
	–	(−4.89)	(−3.57)	(−4.89)
Log (1+Unanti. ΔCPI)	3.482	2.483**	2.508**	2.507**
	(1.34)	(1.76)	(1.77)	(1.77)
Log (Exchange rate $_{t-1}$)	−0.547***	−0.540***	−0.542***	−0.542
	(−3.18)	(−3.15)	(−3.17)	(−3.17)
Export Dummy	–	–	0.179**	0.182**
	–	–	(1.91)	(1.95)
Export Dummy × Log (1+Δexchange rate)	–	–	−0.821	–
	–	–	(−0.36)	–
Constant	12.776***	12.757***	12.737***	12.735**
	(27.77)	(27.83)	(27.97)	(27.97)
Observations	846	846	846	846
Log likelihood-ratio test	−366.05***	−366.16***	−364.20***	−364.27***
	[0.000]	[0.000]	[0.000]	[0.000]

Notes:
This table reports the parameter estimations from four random effects models. The dependent variable is Log (Compensation). The industry dummy variables are included in all the models but not reported here. The time period is 2001–07.
t-values are in round parentheses, and *p*-values are in square parentheses.
*, **, *** denote significance at the 0.10, 0.05 and 0.01 level or better.

Since compensation may be affected to different degrees by anticipated and unanticipated levels and changes in the macro-variables, we distinguish between the anticipated levels of the interest rate and the exchange rate, and the unanticipated changes in these variables from the previous year.

The anticipated exchange rate level in period *t* is further divided into the level last period and the anticipated change from last year. Thereby, the exchange rate can influence compensation in three ways: the level from the previous period, the anticipated change from previous period, and the unanticipated change.

We assume that compensation is potentially influenced by inflation rather than by the price level. Since Sales are in nominal values the price level is accounted for in this variable. Inflation is also divided into an anticipated and an unanticipated component.

Before discussing the results in Table 8.8 it is important to clarify how anticipated and unanticipated changes in the macro variables have been constructed. The following time line illustrates the average yearly observations of interest rates, exchange rates, and consumer prices. On the time line period t is 2002.

Year 2000	Year 2001	Year 2002	Year 2003
$t-2$	$t-1$	t	$t+1$

The expected interest rate in the next period is equal to the current interest rate. Thus, all interest rate changes from year to year are assumed to be unanticipated.

$$Anticipated\ interest\ rate_t = i_{t-1}$$

$$Unanticipated\ interest\ rate_t = i_t - i_{t-1}$$

The return on the one-year Government bond is used as the interest rate. The expected exchange rate change over the next year is reflected in the current one-year interest rate differential (uncovered interest rate parity). Thus,

$$Anticipated\ \Delta exchange\ rate_t = i_{t-1}^{SEK} - i_{t-1}^{USD}$$

$$Unanticipated\ \Delta exchange\ rate_t = [(SEK/USD)_t - (SEK/USD)_{t-1}] - [i_{t-1}^{SEK} - i_{t-1}^{USD}]$$

The exchange rate is SEK/US Dollars. All the changes are in percent. The expected inflation over the next year is equal to the inflation last year. Thus,

$$Anticipated\ \Delta inflation_t = cpi_{t-1} - cpi_{t-2}$$

$$Unanticipated\ \Delta inflation_t = [cpi_t - cpi_{t-1}] - [cpi_{t-1} - cpi_{t-2}]$$

Estimating equation 8.2a we find that the unanticipated interest rate and the anticipated inflation rate, as specified above, are insignificant and, therefore, dropped. The following specification is estimated. The result is presented in Table 8.8, Model 1.

$$
\begin{aligned}
Log(Compensation_{i,t}) = {} & \alpha_0 + \alpha_1 Log(Sales_{i,t}) + \alpha_2 Log(Tobins\ Q_{i,t}) \\
& + \alpha_3 Log(1 + Anticipated\ interest\ rate_{i,t}) \\
& + \alpha_4 Log(1 + Anticipated\ \Delta exchange\ rate_{i,t}) \\
& + \alpha_5 Log(1 + Unanticipated\ \Delta exchange\ rate_{i,t}) \\
& + \alpha_6 Log(1 + Unanticipated\ \Delta CPI_{i,t}) \\
& + \alpha_7 Log(Exchange\ rate_{i,t-1}) \\
& + \sum_{i=8}^{13} \alpha_i Industry\ dummies_i + u_i + \varepsilon_{i,t}
\end{aligned}
\tag{8.2b}
$$

The correlation between the anticipated and the unanticipated exchange rate changes is -0.74 as shown in Table 8.7 and the estimated effect of the former is very small in

Model 1. For this reason we include the total exchange rate change in Model 2 in Table 8.8 and the remainder of the paper.

Sales and Tobin's Q are significant in all the models in Table 8.8 and their coefficients are insensitive to the specification.[8] In comparison with Tables 8.3 and 8.4 the coefficient for Tobin's Q, in particular, is substantially smaller as a result of correlation between this variable and macroeconomic factors. Thus, it seems that macroeconomic influences occur through Q and Sales, as well as through other channels. CEO compensation changes by about 2.30 percent for each 10 percent change in firm size, and it changes about 1 percent for each 10 percent change in firm performance as measured by Q. The former finding is consistent with some findings from the US markets. Bebchuk and Grinstein (2005) find in a US sample for the period 1993–2003 that a 10 percent change in the firm size results in a 2.14 percent change in CEO compensation. They also find that a 10 percent change in performance leads to a 2.11 percent change in compensation. Our results before controlling for macroeconomic factors in Table 8.4 are consistent with these figures, but when we control for macroeconomic factors the compensation effect of a change in Tobin's Q in Table 8.8 is less than a third of the effect in Table 8.5.[9] This result indicates that Q also depends on macroeconomic factors. We return to this issue.

The anticipated (lagged) interest rate is strongly significant, negative and almost the same in the four specifications. A one percentage point increase in the interest rate leads to a five percent decline in compensation. Since we control for inflation the interest rate can be considered real.

The lagged level of the exchange rate is significant in the four models, with a negative coefficient indicating that a weaker SEK is associated with a decline in compensation. The unanticipated exchange rate change during the last year has an even stronger negative effect. The coefficients for the total exchange rate change in Models 2–4 are almost the same. A one percent depreciation of the SEK leads to a 0.7 percent decline in compensation. The negative coefficient may seem surprising but it must be remembered that the coefficients include not only the direct effects of the macro-economic price variables but the also the effects of underlying shocks causing the changes in the exchange rate and the other macro variables. For example, a depreciating exchange rate is often the result of a weak macro economy with negative effects on performance and compensation.

In Model 3 the interaction between the exchange rate change and the export dummy is insignificant. Therefore only the export dummy is kept in the final Model 4.[10]

---

[8]   The robustness of the random effects model, Model 4, is further tested by using two alternative specifications, i.e. pooled linear regression model or fixed effects model. The random effects exist based on the Breusch and Pagan Lagrangian Multiplier test (χ^2 (1) =1049.11, Prob >χ^2 = 0.000). Furthermore, based on the Hausman test (χ^2 (5) =11.57, Prob >χ^2 = 0.024), the random effects model is rejected at 5 percent level of significance, but it cannot be rejected at 1 percent level of significance. In addition, in order to detect multicollinearity among all the factors, the variance inflation factors (VIF) are estimated by using the pooled regression. The average VIF is 2.67, and the individual VIF is within the range 1.36–4.74. Therefore, multicollinearity does not seem to be a problem in the final model.

[9]   Test for simultaneity between performance and compensation (not presented here) indicates that the results are not seriously affected by simultaneity.

[10]   The compensation for the CEOs in the export firms is about 20 percent (which is ($e^{0.18}-1$)*100) higher than in the non-export firms.

Table 8.9 *Random effects model with Tobin's Q or sales as dependent variable and interest rate, exchange rate and inflation as macroeconomic factors*

	Q Equation	Sales Equation
Log (Sales)	−0.031*	–
	−(1.70)	–
Log (Tobin's Q)	–	−0.044
	–	(−1.04)
Log (1+Anti. interest rate)	−1.096	−3.725
	−(0.40)	(−1.20)
Log (1+Δexchange rate)	0.064	0.204
	(0.40)	(1.11)
Log (1+Unanti. ΔCPI)	0.405	2.316
	(0.26)	(1.28)
Log (Exchange rate $_{t-1}$)	−1.063***	−0.624***
	−(5.69)	(−2.85)
Export Dummy	0.036	1.402***
	(0.38)	(3.88)
Constant	2.967***	16.231***
	(6.31)	(19.15)
Observations	846	846
Log likelihood-ratio test	−441.32***	−722.50***
	[0.000]	[0.000]

Notes:
This table reports the parameter estimations from two random effects models. The industry dummy variables are included in both models but not reported here. The time period is 2002–07.
t-values are in round parentheses, and p-values are in square parentheses.
*, **, *** denote significance at the 0.10, 0.05 and 0.01 level or better.

We turn now to the impact of macroeconomic factors on the performance measures, Sales and Q, which systematically affect compensation. We regress these two perform-ance variables on the set of macroeconomic and dummy variables used in Model 4 in Table 8.8. In addition, Log (Tobin's Q) is an independent variable in the regression for log Sales and vice versa.

Table 8.9 shows that Sales has a small but significant negative effect on Q when con-trolling for macroeconomic factors. This result indicates that sales generally are higher than what value maximization would call for. As expected, Tobin's Q does not affect Sales.

The only macroeconomic variable that significantly explains Tobin's Q and Sales is the lagged level of the exchange rate. A depreciation of the SEK leads to a decline in both variables. None of the other macroeconomic variables has a significant effect on Tobin's Q but effects on Sales cannot be ruled out although the coefficients are not significant on conventional levels. An exchange rate depreciation has a positive effect on Sales while in Table 8.8 a depreciation affected compensation negatively. The export dummy variable is also positive and significant indicating that the sales from export-oriented firms are larger than sales from other firms.

In the next section the above estimates of macroeconomic influences on Sales, Q-values, and on compensation at constant levels of Sales and Q will be used to decompose compensation into one component explained by macroeconomic factors and one component explained by "intrinsic" factors.

5   FILTERING OUT MACROECONOMIC INFLUENCES ON COMPENSATION

How would compensation have developed if the impact on compensation of macroeconomic factors would have been filtered out? Table 8.10a shows the impact on compensation of the total change in the macro variables for the period 2001–07, while Table 8.10b displays the impact of unanticipated changes in macro variables.

In each of the Tables 8.10a and 8.10b column (1) shows the percent of salary plus bonus caused by macroeconomic variables each year at constant levels of Q and Sales. In Table 8.10a the column shows the effects of total changes in macroeconomic variables while in Table 8.10b the effects of unanticipated changes are presented. Columns (2) and (3) show the percent of changes in Q and Sales explained by the same variables. Column (4) presents the sum of the effects in columns (1)–(3) using the coefficients in Table 8.8 Model 4 as weights. Thus, column (4) shows the percent change in salary plus bonus each year explained by macroeconomic factors. In columns (5) and (6) we show the macroeconomic effects as percent of bonus payments only.

Table 8.10a   Contribution of the anticipated and unanticipated macroeconomic factors to compensation (interest rate, exchange rate, and inflation)

Year	Macro effects in the compensation equation; Salary plus Bonus, given Q and Sales	Macro effects in the Q equation	Macro effects in the sales equation	Total macro effects to Salary and Bonus $(1) + w_1 \times (2) + w_2 \times (3)$	Macro effects in the compensation equation to Bonus only	Total macro effects to Bonus only $(5) + w_1 \times (2) + w_2 \times (3)$
	(1)	(2)	(3)	(4)	(5)	(6)
2001	−11.61%	0.04%	1.30%	−11.31%	–	–
2002	1.09%	−1.38%	−4.95%	−0.13%	6.31%	5.09%
2003	7.26%	−2.40%	−8.35%	5.19%	38.88%	36.81%
2004	3.96%	−0.96%	−4.70%	2.83%	14.84%	13.70%
2005	3.11%	1.23%	4.16%	4.15%	9.72%	10.76%
2006	10.47%	3.78%	4.57%	11.78%	31.87%	33.19%
2007	9.98%	1.09%	3.46%	10.84%	32.03%	32.90%
Average	3.47%	0.20%	−0.64%	3.35%	22.28%	22.07%

Note: This table reports the predicted anticipated and unanticipated macro effects in different years as well as the whole period 2001–07 using Model 4 in Table 8.8, and the models in Table 8.9. The macroeconomic factors are interest rate, exchange rate, and inflation. In column (4) and column (6), w_1 and w_2 are the coefficients for the variables Log (Tobin's Q), and Log (Sales) in Table 4.2, Model 4.

Table 8.10b   *Contribution of the unanticipated macroeconomic factors to compensation (exchange rate, and inflation)*

Year	Unanticipated macro effects in the compensation equation; Salary plus Bonus, given Q and Sales (1)	Unanticipated macro effects in the Q equation (2)	Unanticipated macro effects in the sales equation (3)	Total unanticipated macro effects to the Salary and Bonus $(1) + w_1 \times (2) + w_2 \times (3)$ (4)	Unanticipated macro effects in the compensation equation to Bonus only (5)	Total unanticipated macro effects to Bonus only $(5) + w_1 \times (2) + w_2 \times (3)$ (6)
2001	−4.83%	1.33%	5.56%	−3.48%	–	–
2002	4.65%	−0.62%	−2.28%	4.09%	26.85%	26.29%
2003	11.94%	−1.31%	−4.48%	10.83%	63.91%	62.80%
2004	2.67%	−1.24%	−5.69%	1.29%	9.98%	8.60%
2005	−1.82%	0.21%	0.74%	−1.64%	−5.70%	−5.51%
2006	4.15%	2.31%	−0.48%	4.22%	12.64%	12.71%
2007	7.72%	0.58%	1.77%	8.17%	24.79%	25.24%
Average	3.50%	0.18%	−0.69%	3.35%	22.08%	21.69%

Note: This table reports the predicted unanticipated macro effects in different years as well as the whole period 2001–07 using Model 4 in Table 8.8, and the Models in Table 8.9. The macroeconomic factors are interest rate, exchange rate, and inflation. In columns (4) and (6), w_1 and w_2 are the coefficients estimated from Model 4 in Table 4.2 for the variable Log (Tobin's Q) and Log (Sales), respectively.

Macroeconomic effects are calculated based on deviations from mean levels of the macro variables during the period times the coefficients in Table 8.8, Model 4. The procedure for calculating macroeconomic effects on Q and Sales is the same, but the coefficients are obtained from Table 8.9. The mean levels of unanticipated changes are zero. The effects of changes in the exchange rate do not include effects of changes in the lagged level of the exchange rate.

Column (4) in Table 8.10a reveals that the macroeconomic factors through all three channels had a large negative effect on compensation in 2001 (−11.3 percent). The macroeconomic factors had an increasingly positive effect on compensation each year through 2006 when macroeconomic factors added nearly 12 percent to compensation. In 2007 macroeconomic factors added 11 percent to compensation. The average share of compensation explained by macroeconomic factors is around three and a half percent. This small average effect is the result of our assumption that macroeconomic effects occur when the variables deviate from their mean values.

Another way to look at these figures is to calculate how compensation would have changed in a stable and average macroeconomic environment. Applying the results in Table 8.10a on the index figures for salary plus bonus in Table 8.1, the compensation adjusted for macroeconomic factors in 2001 would have been higher at index 113 (100/ (1−0.113) while the compensation in 2006 would have been lower at index 135 (151/1.118). In 2007 the adjusted compensation would have been at index 143 (158/1.108). In other words, in a stable macroeconomic environment the compensation would have increased by 19 percent (from index 113 to index 135) through 2006 and then increased in 2007 to a level 27 percent above 2001. Instead we have observed a 58 percent increase in compensation.

The total macro effects in column (4) are dominated by the independent effects in column (1) although the macro effects on both Q and Sales are substantial.

The total macroeconomic effects each year as percent of bonus payments only are presented in column (6). Since bonus is only a fraction of total compensation, increasing from 21 percent to 45 percent of salary plus bonus, the macroeconomic effects here are much larger. Table 8.10a shows that in 2007 macroeconomic factors contributed to compensation an amount equal to 33 percent of the bonus payments.

The contributions of unanticipated macroeconomic effects are shown in Table 8.10b for the period 2001–07. The unanticipated changes in macro variables include effects of exchange rate changes and inflation under the assumption that all exchange rate changes are unanticipated.

The contribution of unanticipated macroeconomic factors to compensation is smaller than the total effects in the previous table. The time pattern is also very different. Table 8.10b Column (4) shows that the largest positive impact of unanticipated macro factors on compensation occurred in 2003 (+10.8 percent). The lowest effect occurred in the year 2001 (−3.5 percent). Clearly, it would make a substantial difference whether compensation levels would be adjusted for total macroeconomic influences or only unanticipated influences.

The unanticipated macroeconomic effects on compensation are quite large relative to bonus payments in some years as shown in column (6). In 2003 the compensation due to unanticipated macroeconomic effects amounted to 63 percent of the bonus payments.

6   ASYMMETRIC MACROECONOMIC EFFECTS

Since the macroeconomic effects could be asymmetric, Model 4 in Table 8.8 is re-estimated by including interaction terms capturing up or down periods. We define one dummy variable for each of the independent variables. Thereby, we analyze whether different sources of changes in performance have different asymmetric effects on compensation. In this case there is a Q dummy, a sales dummy, an anticipated interest rate dummy, an exchange rate change dummy and an unanticipated inflation dummy.[11] The dummy for the particular variable takes the value one when the variable is increasing relative to the previous year. The sample period is 2002–07 since the year 2001 is lost in the creation of dummies for change. Table 8.11 shows the estimated parameters after dropping the change in the exchange rate. This variable and its interaction term turn out to be far from significant when asymmetries are introduced. The remaining macro factors with asymmetry dummies in Table 8.11 are the anticipated interest rate and unanticipated inflation.

---

[11]   An alternative way to test for asymmetry is to use the same dummy for all the variables. In this case the interactive 0/1 dummy for all variables is set to one in years when the performance variable Q increases. Using this approach the interaction terms were not significant and the test for asymmetry effects of all variables on compensation did not reveal significant asymmetry. The result of this test is not shown.

Table 8.11   Test for the asymmetric macroeconomic effects

	Model
Log (Sales)	0.211***
	(8.64)
Log (Tobin's Q)	0.049
	(1.15)
Log (1+Anti. interest rate)	14.637
	(0.61)
Log (1+Unanti. ΔCPI)	4.366
	(1.36)
Log (Exchange rate $_{t-1}$)	−1.158
	(−1.16)
Sales Dummy×Log (Sales)	0.004*
	(1.82)
Q Dummy×Log (Tobin's Q)	0.055**
	(1.95)
Anti. Interest Rate Dummy×Log (1+Anti. interest rate)	−0.662
	(−0.22)
Unanti. Inflation Dummy×Log (1+Unanti. ΔCPI)	11.475
	(0.72)
Export Dummy	0.216**
	(1.98)
Constant	13.625***
	(9.69)
Observations	719
Wald test	−377.29***
	[0.000]

Notes:
This table reports the parameter estimations from the random effects model testing for the asymmetric macroeconomic effects. The dependent variable is Log (Compensation). The industry dummy variables are included in the model but not reported here. The time period is 2002–07.
t-values are in round parentheses, and *p*-values are in square parentheses.
*, **, *** denote significance at the 0.10, 0.05 and 0.01 level or better.

The F-test for joint significance of the interaction terms for the exchange rate, unanticipated inflation plus Q and sales is $\chi^2 = 8.22$ (*p*-value 0.0839). Thus the symmetric model is rejected at the 10 percent significant level. In Table 8.11 the interactive terms with asymmetry dummies for Sales and Q turn out to be significant and positive. The coefficients without interaction terms in Table 8.11 show the effects of falling values of the variables. The effect of a rising value for each variable is obtained as the sum of the two coefficients for the variable. Thus, the coefficient for a decline in Sales is 0.211 while the coefficient for an increase is 0.215 (0.211 + 0.004). In spite of the significant coefficient this asymmetry seems to be negligible. The corresponding coefficients for Q are 0.049 and 0.104 (0.049 + 0.055). Thus, an increase in Q increases compensation twice as much as a decrease reduces compensation.

Turning to the asymmetric effects of the macroeconomic variables in addition to effects through Q and Sales, we can observe that the coefficient for the interactive asymmetry dummy for the interest rate is insignificant and negligible. The coefficient for a decline in inflation is 4.4 while the coefficient for an increase in inflation is as large as 15.8 although the large coefficient (11.5) for the interactive term is not significant.[12] We conclude that significant asymmetric effects of macroeconomic variables occur primarily through effects on Tobin's Q.

Fluctuations in Q depend primarily on fluctuations in the firm's share price which in turn depends on macroeconomic factors. The asymmetry of changes in compensation to changes in Q can be explained by bonus payments being linked to firms' share prices. As noted in Tables 8.9, 8.10a and 8.10b, changes in bonus payments depend strongly on macroeconomic factors.

Another implication of the asymmetry result is that CEOs' incentives to manage firms' macroeconomic exposure is weakened by the likelihood that improved macroeconomic conditions lead to larger bonus payments while the "penalty" for worse macroeconomic conditions is relatively small.

7 CONCLUSIONS

The "optimal" CEO compensation contract in terms of sensitivity and asymmetry to macroeconomic factors from shareholders' point of view depends on a number of firm-specific factors in addition to ability to forecast macroeconomic developments and risk-aversion of managers. Firms differ with respect to adjustability of structure, capacity and operations, and they differ in terms of their sensitivity to macroeconomic fluctuations. Thus, although macroeconomic fluctuations are beyond management's control, their impact on performance may not be the result of luck alone. If management cannot do much to benefit from positive macroeconomic developments or to dampen the effects of negative developments, contract theory suggests that management should not be rewarded (penalized) for performance it cannot influence. This argument presumes that it does not lie in the shareholders' interest to induce management to reduce exposure to macroeconomic fluctuations.

No matter how the optimal incentive contract looks there is little doubt that macro-economic fluctuations have a powerful impact on CEOs' compensation in Sweden on the average in spite of the fact that the variable part of compensation is lower than elsewhere (Fernandes et al., 2008).

Analysis of the dependence of a particular firm's performance and CEO compensation on macroeconomic conditions requires data for performance, compensation, and relevant macroeconomic data for a substantial period. Lacking such data we were restricted to ana-lyzing macroeconomic influences on CEO compensation in 127 Swedish firms for the period 2001–07 using the same set of macroeconomic factors for all firms. Using pooled data we identified the average impact of macroeconomic factors on Swedish firms. Industry-level analysis is also constrained by an insufficient number of firms within each industry.

---

[12]   The F-test for joint significance of the interaction terms for the anticipated interest rate and unanticipated inflation is $\chi^2 = 0.095$ with the p-value $= 0.6213$.

One set of macroeconomic variables was used in the decomposition for all firms. Thereby, the macroeconomic influences on performance in many firms could be underestimated, since the appropriate set of variables is likely to be firm-specific.

Three channels of macroeconomic influences on compensation were identified. Macroeconomic factors affect sales and Q-values, and they affect compensation through other variables that affect compensation in a less systematic way than sales and Q. The macroeconomic factors we claimed as important for the aggregate performance and compensation in the Swedish firms were the exchange rate, the interest rate and the inflation rate. These macroeconomic price variables can be viewed as signals of underlying macroeconomic shocks. As such, they are easily observable and useful for decomposing performance and compensation into an "intrinsic" component and a macroeconomic component.

After estimation of the sensitivities of performance variables and compensation to the macroeconomic factors, we used the coefficients in combination with macroeconomic developments each year to calculate how compensation would have developed had macroeconomic influences been filtered out for each of the years 2001 through 2007. The calculations showed that in a neutral and stable macroeconomic environment, compensation would have increased by 27 percent rather than by the observed 58 percent. Thus, if compensation had been based on intrinsic factors alone, CEO compensation would have increased by less than half of the actual increase.

Unanticipated macroeconomic factors explain a smaller part of compensation. In 2003 and 2007 these factors increased compensation by 11 and 8 percent while in 2005 the same factors reduced compensation by almost 2 percent. As percent of bonus payments the largest effect of unanticipated factors, amounting to 55 percent, occurred in 2002.

The analysis of asymmetric effects on compensation of positive and negative changes in performance and macroeconomic variables indicated that the effect of an increase in Q is twice as large as the effect of a decrease in Q. This result supports the findings of Garvey and Milbourn (2006) and may explain the mechanism behind their findings. Asymmetric effects of macroeconomic variables appear to take place primarily through changes in Q. The asymmetric effects of increases and decreases in sales appear to be small.

The main recommendation of this chapter for corporate remuneration policy and for regulators is to capture the "sustainable" performance worth a reward by filtering out the impact of macroeconomic factors in accordance with the approach developed above and not by waiting three to five years as suggested by policy-makers to see if the improved performance is still observable. In the latter case, luck in one way or the other will still be present.

REFERENCES

Abowd, John, 1990. Does Performance-Based Managerial Compensation Affect Corporate Performance? *Industrial and Labor Relations Review*, 43(3), 52–73.

Antle, Rick and Smith, Abbie, 1986. An Empirical Investigation of the Relative Performance Evaluation of Corporate Executives. *Journal of Accounting Research*, 24(1), 1–39.

Bebchuk, Lucian and Grinstein, Yaniv, 2005. The Growth of Executive Pay. *Oxford Review of Economic Policy*, 21(2), 283–303.

Bertrand, Marianne and Mullainathan, Sendhil, 2000. Agents With and Without Principals. *American Economic Review*, 90(2), 203–8.
Bertrand, Marianne and Mullainathan, Sendhill, 2001. Are CEOs Rewarded for Luck? The Ones Without Principals Are. *Quarterly Journal of Economics*, 116(3), 901–32.
Ciscel, David and Carroll, Thomas, 1980. The Determinants of Executive Salaries: An Econometric Survey. *Review of Economics and Statistics*, 62(1), 7–13.
Coughlan, Anne and Schmidt, Ronald, 1985. Executive Compensation, Management Turnover, and Firm Performance: An Empirical Investigation. *Journal of Accounting and Economics*, 7(1–3), 43–66.
Fernandes, Nuno, Ferreira, Miguel A., Matos, Pedro P. and Murphy, Kevin J., 2008. The Pay Divide: (Why) Are U.S. Top Executives Paid More?, mimeo, University of Southern California.
Garvey, Gerald T. and Milbourn, Todd T., 2006. Asymmetric Benchmarking in Compensation: Executives Are Rewarded for Good Luck but not Penalized for Bad. *Journal of Financial Economics*, 82(1), 197–225.
Gibbons, Robert and Murphy, Kevin J., 1990. Relative Performance Evaluation for Chief Executive Officers. *Industrial and Labor Relations Review*, 43(3), 30–51.
Gibbons, Robert and Murphy, Kevin J., 1992. Optimal Incentive Contracts in the Presence of Career Concerns: Theory and Evidence. *Journal of Political Economy*, 100(3), 468–505.
Gopalan, Radhakrishnan, Milbourn, Todd and Song, Fenghua, 2010. Strategic Flexibility and the Optimality of Pay for Sector Performance. *Review of Financial Studies*, 23(5), 2060–98.
Jensen, Michael C. and Murphy, Kevin J., 1990. Performance Pay and Top-Management Incentives. *Journal of Political Economy*, 98(2), 225–64.
Leonard, Jonathan S., 1990. Executive Pay and Firm Performance. *Industrial and Labor Relations Review*, 43(3), 13–29.
Milgrom, Paul and Roberts, John, 1992. *Economics of Organization and Management*. Prentice Hall, Englewood Cliffs, New Jersey.
Murphy, Kevin J., 1985. Corporate Performance and Managerial Remuneration: An Empirical Analysis. *Journal of Accounting and Economics*, 7(1–3), 11–42.
Murphy, Kevin J., 1986. Incentives, Learning, and Compensation: A Theoretical and Empirical Investigation of Managerial Labor Contracts. *Rand Journal of Economics*, 17(1), 59–76.
Murphy, Kevin J., 1999. Executive Compensation, in: Ashenfelter, Orely and Card, David E. (eds), *Handbook of Labor Economics*, 3, 2485–563. North-Holland, Amsterdam.
Oxelheim, Lars and Randöy, Trond, 2005. The Anglo-American Financial Influence on CEO Compensation in Non-Anglo-American Firms. *Journal of International Business Studies*, 36(4), 470–83.
Oxelheim, Lars and Wihlborg, Clas, 2003. Recognizing Macroeconomic Fluctuations in Value Based Management. *Journal of Applied Corporate Finance*, 15(4), 104–10.
Oxelheim, Lars and Wihlborg, Clas, 2008. Corporate Decision-making with Macroeconomic Uncertainty. *Performance and Risk Management*. Oxford University Press, New York.
Oxelheim, Lars, Wihlborg, Clas and Zhang, Jianhua, 2008. Executive Compensation and Macroeconomic Fluctuations, in: Oxelheim, Lars and Wihlborg, Clas (eds), *Markets and Compensation for Executives in Europe*, 233–61. Emerald Group Publishing.
Rosen, Sherwin, 1992. Contracts and the Market for Executives, in: Werin, Lars and Wijkander, Hans (eds), *Contract Economics*, 181–211. Blackwell Publishers.
Smith, Clifford W. and Stulz, Rene M., 1985. The Determinants of Firms' Hedging Policies. *Journal of Financial and Quantitative Analysis*, 20(4), 391–405.
UNCTAD, 2008. *World Investment Report*, Geneva.

9 CEO compensation and stock options in IPO firms
Salim Chahine and Marc Goergen

1 INTRODUCTION

"Pay without performance", "rent appropriation", or pay "under the radar". Despite the economic crisis and significant collective pay cuts, the chief executives of the 500 biggest companies in the US received an average $8 million per head in 2009.[1] Over the last two or three decades, the compensation of executives and in particular CEOs of mature firms has been the subject of a debate fuelled by corporate-governance activists and academics. As a result, there is now a substantial body of research on the determinants of executive compensation and its association with firm performance.

Several studies have linked the design of executive compensation to organizational and institutional characteristics (see e.g. Balkin and Gomez-Mejia, 1987). More recently, developments of the principal–agent theory have examined the motivation behind and the incentives created by executive compensation from a behavioral perspective. Specifically, agency problems might occur from the divergence of interests between the agent (the CEO, i.e. the decision-maker) and the principal (the shareholders, the risk-bearers) resulting in the former taking advantage of the latter. However, despite extensive research on CEO compensation in mature firms, as yet little attention has been given to the role and design of executive pay in firms going public.

An initial public offering (IPO) is a cornerstone in the life of a corporation and is characterized by information asymmetries between the management and outside investors and thus potentially substantial agency problems. The IPO consists of the first public offer of the company's equity shares. It typically results in the exit of key shareholders – such as the company's founder – or at least the dilution of their ownership stake. Due to this dilution, the managers' incentives tend to be worse than before the IPO. Hence, after the IPO there is a need for the use of other corporate governance devices such as executive pay in order to realign the incentives of the managers with those of the owners.

Prior research suggests that CEOs have a strong influence on firm performance (Daily and Johnson, 1997), and even more so in small firms where they are the locus of control and decision making (Daily et al., 2002). Prior research suggests that executive compensation can be used to alleviate conflicts of interests between shareholders and managers (Jensen and Meckling, 1976). In particular, it may be used to alter the risk-taking incentives of the CEO, who may otherwise be too conservative and shy away from risky but shareholder-value creating investments (Coles et al., 2001). An executive pay package typically consists of the following four basic components: a base salary, an annual bonus, stock options, and long-term incentive plans (including restricted stocks and multi-year

---

[1] Scott DeCarlo, "What the Boss Makes", Forbes.com, April 28 2010.

accounting-based performance plans). Executives also often receive benefits in kind such as life insurance and retirement plans.

The main focus of this chapter is on CEO stock options in IPO firms. Stock options are securities that give their holders the right to buy a specific number of the company's shares at a predetermined price over a predetermined period. Stock options do not incur cash outlays until they are exercised, which results in limited downside risk compared to equity (Certo et al., 2003), thus inducing risk taking. In other words, stock options are likely to provide CEOs of IPO firms with "upside potential" (Sanders, 2001), increasing their propensity to take risks (Beatty and Zajac, 1994), which in turn may result in higher firm performance (Hall and Liebman, 1998). However, stock options may also be a means for powerful CEOs to expropriate the (other) pre-IPO shareholders. By discussing the two possible impacts of stock options on firm performance for IPOs, this chapter contributes to the current debate on the potentially excessive levels of managerial compensation and possibly flawed incentive systems.

The remainder of the chapter is structured as follows. First, we review the theoretical literature and existing empirical evidence for the case of mature firms. Specifically, we present an overview of prior research related to executive compensation paradigms, and discuss the theoretical role played by equity-based compensation schemes, i.e. stock ownership versus stock-option ownership, within an agency framework. We also review empirical evidence on the association between executive compensation on the one hand, and risk-taking and firm performance on the other hand. Second, we focus on the case of CEO stock options in initial public offerings. We review the IPO event and the contrasting effects of stock options when there is CEO entrenchment and they may serve as a means to expropriate the shareholders, and when there is no CEO entrenchment and they are likely to realign the CEO's interests with those of the shareholders. We further survey recent evidence on the differential effect of corporate governance and venture capital firms on the association between CEO stock-option grants and IPO performance.

2   EXECUTIVE COMPENSATION IN MATURE FIRMS

Although executive pay requires the approval of the board of directors, whose role is to represent the shareholders, executives, and mainly the CEO, frequently have a major influence on both the level and structure of their pay.[2] It is thus crucial to understand the theoretical framework related to the determinants of the pay level and structure and its relationship with firm value. Hereafter, we present the theoretical background related to executive compensation in general and the association between executive compensation and agency theory in particular.

---

[2]   Murphy (1999) explains that initial recommendations for pay levels are typically issued by the company's human resource department. These recommendations are usually sent to top managers for approval and subject to revision before being sent to the compensation committee, and then to the board of directors.

2.1   Theoretical Framework

2.1.1   The different executive compensation paradigms

According to neoclassical theory, employee compensation should be at a level such that the marginal increase in compensation is equal to the worker's marginal revenue product. In order to provide the right degree of incentives, reward systems should then structure compensation in such a way that a worker's expected utility increases with observed productivity. Neoclassical theory has advanced several explanations about the determinants and the role of executive pay. These include managerialism, agency theory, structural theory, and human capital theory.

Managerialism is based on the premise that there is a separation of ownership and control in the company (Penrose, 1995). Managerialists argue that executives are often self-serving, i.e. their actions are at the expense of the shareholders. Accordingly, managers are viewed as risk-averse agents who prefer compensation that rises when the company is doing well, but does not drop when the company is performing poorly. Hence, company performance is only a minor determinant of the level of executive compensation. Indeed, managerialism suggests that managers prefer to adopt strategies that increase company size rather than increase company profits, as the former will improve the company's visibility, and in turn create a reason for higher managerial compensation. Since much incentive-based pay is short term in nature, this theory argues that executives are tempted to make decisions that will benefit the company in the short term, but perhaps not so in the long term.

Similar to managerialism, agency theory assumes that there is a separation of ownership and control within the company (Jensen and Meckling, 1976). As a result, executives have a great deal of discretionary power which enables them to make decisions that may be in conflict with the shareholders' interests. Hence, since the interests of both parties may not always be aligned, the managers, who have more knowledge about the company, will generally do what maximizes their utility (Pauly, 1974). Managers should thus be monitored and must be given incentives, e.g. via their compensation package, to realign their interests with those of the shareholders of the company (Jensen and Murphy, 2010).

Unlike the agency and managerialism theories, structural theory is, as the name implies, structured with little room for variation in executive pay. In other words, executive compensation is determined by "requirements of internal consistency of the salary scale with the formal organization and by norms of proportionality between salaries of executives and their subordinates" (Simon, 1957, p. 34). Hence, an executive's pay depends on the pay of those above and below him/her in the hierarchy of the company, i.e. the organizational hierarchy.

Human capital theory proposes human characteristics as the main determinants of pay. The acquisition of human capital over time, i.e. the individual's experience, skills, and education, is compensated according to how valuable it is to the company (Scarborough and Elias, 2002).

In addition, Lazear and Rosen (1979) propose the tournament theory whereby the level of compensation is determined by the individual's relative position within the firm. Lazear and Rosen argue that, since the differences in the level of output between individuals might be quite small, promotion-based incentives are less costly and more effective than bonus-based incentive schemes. However, Baker, Jensen and Murphy (1988) argue that the incentives generated by promotion opportunities depend on the probability of promotion as well as the rate at which the organization is growing. For example, promotion incentives depend on the identity and expected horizon of the incumbent superior. They also work better in growing firms than in shrinking firms.

2.1.2   Agency theory and compensation theory

From an agency perspective, there are several reasons that may lead managers to use their control over the operations of the firm to extract private benefits rather than maximize shareholder value. First, conflicts of interests between managers and shareholders may result from the inability of the former to run the firm well. Managers are thus likely to seek control as a means to protect their jobs and to remain in power. Second, while a typical shareholder holds a well-diversified portfolio of shares, managers have the majority of their human capital (and probably also their financial wealth) tied up in the firm they work for. Managers have thus much more to lose if a project fails than does the typical shareholder, and this creates the potential for conflicts of interests with regard to investment policy. While well-diversified shareholders favor investing in all positive net present value (NPV) projects, managers, especially those who are risk averse, may be concerned about how likely a project's failure is and how costly the failure may be for themselves. Third, managers are supposed to pay the free cash flow of the firm out to the shareholders, i.e. the cash generated by the firm in excess of the amount required to fund all available positive NPV projects (Jensen, 1986), reinvest it into new or existing projects, or hold onto it. While shareholders do not want free cash flow to be wasted on negative NPV projects and prefer to have it returned if there are no positive NPV projects to invest in, managers may have the exact opposite preferences.

In order to mitigate agency problems, shareholders might need to ensure that their firm benefits from good corporate governance practices. Corporate governance is the "amalgam of mechanisms which ensure that the agent (the management of the corporation) runs the firm for the benefit of one or multiple principals (shareholders, creditors, suppliers, customers, employees and other parties with whom the firm conducts business" (Goergen and Renneboog, 2005, p. 285). Shareholder monitoring may be such a mechanism. However, as most firms are widely held, there is likely to be a lack of shareholder monitoring. Hence, there is a need for other corporate governance mechanisms, such as institutional and market mechanisms to induce managers to maximize shareholder value. Contracts may accomplish this goal. However, it is impossible for a contract to cover every possible eventuality and specify what action the manager should take in each situation. Hence, at best contracts only provide a partial and incomplete solution to agency problems.

As both contracts and shareholder monitoring are likely to be deficient, the role of the independent members on the board of directors is to ensure that the managers act in the interests of the shareholders. The board of directors, appointed by the shareholders, is expected to provide oversight over the managers hired to run the company. However, the effectiveness of the board may be reduced as its size increases, given the greater difficulty of having open and clear communications. As a result, larger boards may be dominated by the CEO, thus ultimately leading to less scrutiny of executive behavior. In addition to board size, board independence may also be an important determinant of the quality of monitoring. However, similar to the managers, the independent directors are ultimately agents acting on behalf of the principals, i.e. the shareholders. Hence in turn, they may suffer from agency problems. For example, boards are dependent on managers for pertinent information (Guthrie and Sokolowsky, 2009). In addition, independent directors are sometimes only independent by job title, and may still have social ties with the CEO which may cloud their objectivity (Chidambaran et al., 2009).[3] Therefore, agency theory suggests that compensation plans should be designed as a means to align the interests of the risk-averse and self-interested managers with those of the shareholders. Agency theorists predict that managerial equity compensation schemes, which include equity shares as well as stock options, should help achieve this objective.

Despite the growing use of stocks and stock options, these two components of managerial compensation packages however have very different risk properties and their use is also not quite as simple as it may sound. While equity ownership often induces risk aversion, stock options improve risk taking (Sanders, 2001). Indeed, compared to stock option grants, the rewards from direct stock ownership are linear, hence incentivizing executives to avoid risks that their diversified shareholder base may wish them to take. Conversely, stock options have a convex payoff function that induces managers to be less risk averse and to make optimal investment decisions.[4] Finally, since there are different payoffs associated with each instrument, they are also likely to have different effects on firm value.

2.2   Empirical Evidence

The performance benchmarks that executive compensation is based on may vary across industries. For example, industries that put emphasis on operating results may use accounting measures as benchmarks whereas compensation may be based on stock returns in industries that focus on stock performance (Nikbakht et al., 2007). Executive tenure also affects compensation as executives with longer tenure tend to earn more than those with shorter tenure. In addition, older executives earn more than younger ones and those with stock ownership make more than those without (Weber and Dudney, 2003). Executive compensation is thus a complex system as it is associated with risk taking, firm performance, corporate governance and the manager's profile.

2.2.1   Executive compensation and risk taking
Since the financial upside of managers without equity-based compensation, i.e. stocks and stock options, is capped, such managers are likely to focus on short-term accounting profits to secure their jobs and to have better bargaining power. Managers without equity-based compensation may thus prefer investments with stable cash flows and a lower return, over risky but more profitable investments.

---

[3]   Consistent with this argument, Chidambaran et al. (2009) find that the greater the connection of the CEO with the directors of the firm, the weaker the governance structure.

[4]   However, there are cases where stock options may not increase risk taking. For example, the increase in stock option-based compensation reduces the diversification level of the executive's personal portfolio, thus inducing greater risk aversion. This is more significant in firms granting at-the-money stock options, where managers are exposed to some downside risk in the value of the option ex-post. See Ross (2004) for further discussion on the conditions under which stock options induce optimal risk-taking.

Based on an agency perspective, Jensen and Meckling (1976) argue that stock ownership aligns the interests of managers with those of the other shareholders, and thus results in strategies that optimize risk. However, Cheng and Warfield (2005) provide empirical evidence contradicting this theoretical argument: managers holding equity are not as tolerant of stock volatility and hence tend to smooth earnings, i.e., stock ownership increases abnormal accruals.[5] This suggests that since risk taking may reduce the value of the shares, executives holding stocks, as part of their incentive package, are likely to shy away from risk-taking behavior.

Similarly, Jensen and Meckling (1976) expect that executives who are paid with stock options will do what it takes to maximize the value of their options even at the expense of the shareholders. However, contrary to stock, the returns on options are more volatile and executives paid with stock options will likely take more risks since they tend to operate with a "nothing to lose" mentality given that options may increase an executive's wealth, but cannot decrease it (Certo et al., 2003). Since they have nothing to lose, executives may take excessive risks. While this may harm the firm, the value of the stock options still increases. Accordingly, Cohen et al. (2000) find higher stock volatility for firms using executive stock options. Rajgopal and Shevlin (2002) find that their proxy for exploration risk increases with the sensitivity of the value of the CEO's options to stock return volatility in the oil industry. They conclude that stock options increase the incentives of the managers to invest in high-risk high-return projects.

However, Carpenter (2002) and Ross (2004) argue that the relationship between options and risk taking is more complex and depends on the individual's propensity to take risks. Indeed, the optimal level of volatility may be lower for managers with higher numbers of stock options (Carpenter, 2002). This suggests that managers are likely to avoid risks when their wealth is at stake, i.e. mainly when their stock options are far in the money. In other words, the association between stock options and risk taking depends on "the wealth effect of the options; increasing the wealth of the executive may move into more or less risk-averse portions of the utility function. In addition, depending on the amounts, options by themselves could have an important (marginal) magnification effect that could actually lead to more risk aversion" (Ross, 2004, p. 224).

To conclude, existing studies provide conflicting evidence as to the link between stock options and risk taking. This suggests that there are *specific* conditions under which stock option grants mitigate agency problems via encouraging risk taking behavior and providing incentives for optimizing long-term performance. Further research is needed to identify those specific conditions.

2.2.2   Compensation design and firm performance

Since stock markets may act as an ultimate monitor of managers, Fama (1980) argues that stock performance should be used as a determinant of executive pay. However, prior

---

[5]   Bergstresser and Philippon (2006) find that the use of discretionary accruals to manipulate reported earnings is more pronounced for firms where the CEO's potential total compensation is more closely tied to the value of stock and option holdings. Burns and Kedia (2006) show that the sensitivity of the CEO's option portfolio to the stock price is positively related to the propensity to misreport. Financial misreporting is also more likely in firms where CEOs are paid with stock options (Chidambaran et al., 2009).

research fails to provide convincing evidence as to the sensitivity of executive pay to stock price performance. For example, Jensen and Murphy (1990), who examine the association between managerial wealth and firm performance in large publicly listed US firms from 1974 to 1986, find low CEO pay–performance sensitivities as CEO wealth increases by only $3.25 for every $1,000 increase in firm value. This mere fraction however hides the large changes in the absolute value of managerial wealth. This is even more significant in more recent periods characterized given the increasing use of stock option grants. For example, Hall and Liebman (1998) indicate that "between 1980 and 1994 the direct compensation (salary, bonus, and the value of annual stock option grants) of CEOs increased by 136 percent at the median and 209 percent at the mean in real terms" (p. 655). They demonstrate that the use of stock option grants also increased the median elasticity of CEO compensation with respect to firm value from 1.2 to 3.9 between 1980 and 1994, which is about 30 times larger than previously reported salary and bonus elasticities, which ignore the sensitivity generated by stocks and stock options (see also Murphy, 1999).

Overall, the empirical research suggests that executives are no longer paid as "bureaucrats", as stated by Jensen and Murphy (1990). It also indicates that, while low pay–performance sensitivity can be observed for the 70s and 80s, the increase in the use of stock options in the 90s has increased the sensitivity. Stock options and other equity grants are thus likely to align top executives' interests with those of the shareholders, as long as these are monitored to ensure that the positive association between executive pay and performance is maintained.

2.3 Brief Summary

Prior research reports great diversity in the composition of CEO compensation packages and highlights the complexity of assessing their effects on risk taking and firm performance. Compared to stock options, there is evidence of a low sensitivity of cash compensation to firm performance, and mixed results on the ability of direct stock ownership to incentivize executives to increase risk and increase shareholder value. Conversely, there is a consensus that stock options are better at providing CEOs with upside potential, with a limited downside. In other words, they add convexity to managers' payoff functions, and are thus likely to mitigate agency problems and encourage a higher propensity to take risks, which may result in higher firm performance.

3   CEO STOCK OPTIONS AND IPO PERFORMANCE

While the CEO is typically the most powerful executive within a corporation (see e.g. Harrison et al., 1988), his power is even greater in small firms, which typically lack the constraints associated with the more rigid organizational systems and structures found in larger firms (Daily and Dalton, 1992). Further, problems of agency and informational asymmetry tend to be highest at the IPO. It is also believed that these problems may explain the extent to which IPO firms are underpriced, i.e. they have a closing price on the first day of trading that is higher than the offer price of the shares in the IPO.

In what follows, we first discuss the role of stock options at the IPO. Specifically, we present the IPO context and a review of the existing empirical evidence on the mixed role stock options play in IPO firms. As such, we discuss their effects on realigning the interests of the managers in IPO firms and we contrast this with the perverse role they may fulfill which consists of serving as a means to expropriate the firm's shareholders. Given the potentially perverse role played by stock options, we then move on to discussing the impact of CEO power on the role of stock option grants. As such, we provide evidence that corporate governance devices mitigate this negative effect of stock options, as well as evidence on the potentially important role played by venture capital firms in IPO firms.

3.1   The Role of CEO Stock Options at the IPO

The high levels of IPO underpricing observed in the late nineties have prompted a debate in academia. The focus of the debate is on the increasing number of IPO firms witnessing severe underpricing while their insiders seem unconcerned about limiting it. This trend becomes even more puzzling when one takes into account the huge amounts of revenues foregone as a result of the underpricing. For example, Ritter and Welch (2002), who study 6,249 US IPOs between 1980 and 2001, find that around 70 percent of them are underpriced, with an average first-day return of 18.8 percent, increasing to an average of 65 percent during the "bubble period" of 1999–2000.

Due to the advantage they hold over other forms of compensation, stock options may then play an important role in realigning the interests of the CEO with those of the shareholders, thereby increasing IPO performance and reducing underpricing.

3.1.1   The initial public offering context
An IPO is typically the reflection of the initial owners' desire to raise equity capital and create a public market in the shares of their firm. In addition, the IPO is also likely to enhance the firm's reputation and to offer the initial owners the possibility to sell part of their shares or fully to exit from their firm. However, the IPO is also a complex and costly process. In particular, the initial owners require the services of an investment bank in order to place the IPO with heterogeneous outside investors. Hence, the IPO generates not only benefits, but also costs. It also usually raises questions as to the motivations of the initial owners for taking their firm public, which is likely to affect the pricing of the IPO shares adversely.

Many theories have been proposed to explain IPO underpricing. Some of these theories assert that underpricing is the result of the informational asymmetry that exists between the insiders and the outsiders at the IPO. For example, underpricing may act as a credible signal of firm quality. It may also be a way to leave a good taste in the mouth of investors while its cost can be recouped through future offerings (Welch, 1989). Underpricing may also compensate outside investors for sharing their knowledge about the value of the IPO firm with the issuer, or it may be a form of compensation to uninformed investors who participate in all offerings compared to informed investors who participate in high quality offerings only (Rock's, 1986, "winner's curse hypothesis"). Finally, underpricing may be the consequence of agency problems between the issuer and the underwriter, as the former may have to accept some underpricing in order to induce the latter to provide the required effort to market its shares, or it may compensate the underwriter for the costly marketing expenditure.[6]

More recently, empirical research has focused on the means that may mitigate agency problems around the IPO and in turn reduce underpricing. While prior research mainly focused on disclosure practices in the IPO prospectuses (Chahine and Filatotchev, 2008a), board characteristics (Daily et al., 1999; Chahine et al., 2011), and ownership structure (Bruton et al., 2010), little is known about the monitoring role played by stock options in the IPO. Stock options are likely to align CEO interests with those of the shareholders (Jensen and Meckling, 1976) and provide IPO firms with upside potential (Sanders, 2001). The ability of CEOs to time stock option grants and determine the exercise price may however create its own agency problems. In the next section, we discuss prior research on the pros and cons of stock options in IPO firms.

3.1.2 CEO stock options: alignment versus entrenchment

Since outside investors do not have any prior experience with the IPO firm, the IPO process is usually characterized by high levels of uncertainty. CEO compensation schemes may play an important role in signaling the level of alignment of the interests of the executives with those of the shareholders. Equity and stock option based compensation schemes permit the CEOs to receive part of the gains they generate and are thus valuable signals to investors about how well insiders are incentivized. Moreover, large equity holdings mitigate the potential agency problems between managers and executives (Jensen and Meckling, 1976).

Certo et al. (2001) report average CEO ownership of 13 percent in IPO firms, which is extremely high when compared to the average 1 percent reported by Carpenter (2002) for mature firms. However, despite the signaling and agency roles attributed to equity holdings, the CEO's stake in the IPO firm is likely to increase the CEO's risk aversion, and adversely affect the alignment of his interests with those of the outside investors. Accordingly, the empirical evidence does not provide support for a positive association between IPO performance and CEO equity ownership (see e.g., Dalton et al., 2003). The reason for this may be that large equity holdings cause the CEO to become entrenched, and use his power to extract private benefits of control (Shleifer and Vishny, 1997). In addition, given the lack of portfolio diversification, the CEO may try to minimize the riskiness of his portfolio by choosing low risk projects and thereby fail to maximize shareholder value (Amihud and Lev, 1981; Wright et al., 1996).

---

[6] In addition to explanations of underpricing based on asymmetric information, there are several alternative explanations. For example, high underpricing may reduce the likelihood of a lawsuit by investors who bought the IPO shares (Tinic, 1988). Underpricing may increase when the wealth gains from the shares retained by the insiders exceed the wealth losses from the IPO underpricing (the prospect theory of Loughran and Ritter, 2002). It may also increase as a result of the analysts of the investment bank which underwrote the IPO deliberately boosting the share price and maintaining it at a high level until the expiration of the lock-up period after which the insiders may sell significant amounts of their shares (see the sweet escape hypothesis of Martin, 2008; and the collaboration hypothesis of Hoberg and Seyhun, 2009).

Further, the effect of CEO ownership on the IPO firm's valuation may be simultaneously related to whether the CEO holds stock options. Certo et al. (2003) find that stock options have more effect on IPO valuation in firms where the CEO holds a large percentage of ownership. They explain this result by the upside potential created by the stock options which cancels out the risk averseness created by the CEO having most of his personal wealth and human capital tied up in a single firm. Conversely, Certo et al. (2003) find that the effect of stock options on IPO valuation is less significant in IPO firms where CEOs own less equity, and are therefore much more inclined to take risk. More generally, this suggests that the role played by stock options in IPO firms may be related to the presence and effectiveness of other corporate governance mechanisms. In the next section, we focus on the impact of corporate governance on the link between CEO power and CEO remuneration.

3.2   CEO Power and CEO Compensation

Given the potentially perverse incentives created by stock options, outside investors may insist on additional monitoring mechanisms to ensure that the CEO has the right incentives to maximize firm value. CEO power, and thus the effectiveness of the use of stock options, may be counterbalanced by corporate governance devices and the presence of professional investors, such as venture capital firms. Further we provide a discussion of recent empirical evidence on the association between CEO stock options and both corporate governance and venture capital at the IPO.

3.2.1   CEO stock options and corporate governance

Despite the positive role attributed to stock options, Yermack (1997) has a more cynical view based on the premise that executives are self-serving. He argues that executives are able to influence the timing of option grants and are likely to receive options that are already "in the money" just prior to releasing news that increases their company's share price, thereby maximizing their option gains.[7] Powerful CEOs are more likely to be entrenched and take actions that are not likely in the best interest of the shareholders (Hermalin and Weisbach, 1998).[8] For example, powerful CEOs should be able to set their own compensation packages at the IPO. They should also be able to time their option grants to coincide with their firm's IPO and to set the options' exercise price equal to a deliberately low offer price so as to maximize their option gains (Lowry and Murphy, 2007). As such, CEOs granting themselves IPO options at favorable terms may expropriate the firm's pre-IPO shareholders not only via these IPO options grants, but also via higher levels of underpricing.

---

[7]   Aboody and Kasznik (2000) show that forecasts issued during the three months prior to the scheduled awards of CEO stock options are significantly less optimistically biased than forecasts issued during the other months. Moreover, CEOs who receive their options before the earnings announcement date are significantly more likely to issue bad news forecasts, and less likely to issue good news forecasts, than CEOs who receive their awards after the earnings announcement date, which is consistent with the opportunistic timing of voluntary disclosures around scheduled awards.

[8]   CEO power reflects the CEO's ability to change the behavior of a person or a group in an intended way (Bach and Smith, 2007).

Lowry and Murphy (2007) test the above argument on 854 US companies going public over the period 1996–2000. However, their results suggest that IPO underpricing is related neither to the existence nor to the magnitude of IPO stock option grants.[9] Chahine and Goergen (2011a) examine a sample of 435 US firms going public during 1997–2004. They find that CEOs receive stock options around the IPO date in 24 percent of the firms. Based on the first-day underpricing, the IPO options provide CEOs with an average gross gain of $693,901, which represents about 1 percent of the average IPO gross proceeds. They also find evidence that stock option grants are not limited just to the short period surrounding the IPO. Indeed, the vast majority of issuing firms, i.e. 70 percent or 304 IPOs, grant their CEOs stock options during the period before the IPO. CEOs hold on average 432,556 stock options (i.e. 2 percent of the total number of shares outstanding) in these 304 firms by the time the company decides to go public. In detail, 49 percent of the firms (214 IPOs) grant an average of 418,354 stock options to their CEO during the year prior to the IPO, and around 20 percent of the firms (90 IPOs) grant on average 293,958 stock options during the period *before* the year prior to the IPO. Moreover, Chahine and Goergen find that the total gains using the SEC option pricing method reach an average of $16.43 million per CEO.[10]

Further, Chahine and Goergen (2011a) find higher underpricing in firms with stock option grants when CEO power is strong, i.e. the CEO is the founder, the chairman of the board of directors, or both. However, they report that while underpricing typically increases with stock options granted at the IPO or during the year prior to the IPO date, the sign of this effect is reversed in firms with high board independence. Controlling for direct and indirect connections between board members and both the IPO firm and venture capital investors, they provide empirical support that good corporate governance, such as high board independence, counteracts the power of the CEO. This suggests that board independence ensures that CEO stock options fulfill their incentivizing role, and avoids potential misuse of stock options to expropriate the shareholders.[11]

3.2.2 CEO stock option and venture capital firms

During the last two decades, VCs have been increasingly recognized as important risk-financiers in the life-cycle of IPO firms. Yet, our understanding about the effects of VC involvement on firm performance remains limited (Chahine and Filatotchev, 2008b).

On the one hand, VC power and board representation may have a positive effect on firm performance via the positive role VC firms play in their portfolio companies. Although they are not normally involved in the day-to-day management of the latter, they typically provide management guidance, networking opportunities for strategic

---

[9] Frequently, CEOs sell a large amount of their shares in the IPO immediately and/or during the first year after the IPO date. However, Kim and Pukthuanthong (2006) find no evidence that managers selling their stocks or exercising their options in the first year after the IPO are doing so to exploit the company's other shareholders and to obtain personal advantages.

[10] The SEC method takes into account the maturity of the option and assumes a constant 10 percent increase p.a. in the price of the underlying stock.

[11] Beatty and Zajac (1994) report a negative association between board independence and the use of stock options in US IPO firms. They argue that board independence may act as a substitute for the need to incentivize the management with stock options grants.

alliances (Hellmann and Puri, 2002), and financial support (Gorman and Sahlman, 1989; Gompers and Lerner, 1999). Moreover, VCs help their firms design their organizational structure, build their teams, and develop their market share (Hellmann and Puri, 2002). They are also active investors and they put in place mechanisms aimed at monitoring the management (Cornelli and Yosha, 2003). All of this helps alleviate moral hazard and adverse selection problems between the insiders and the outside investors (Kaplan and Strömberg, 2003), resulting in an increase in firm value.

On the other hand, VCs may misuse their power by pushing through decisions which are in their own interests but not in the interests of the other shareholders. Such decisions may consist of grandstanding, i.e., taking their portfolio companies public prematurely to enhance their own reputation (Gompers, 1996). Young VCs, i.e., those without a track record of startup firms that have been successfully taken public, may find it difficult to obtain further financing. One way of improving their access to financing is to rush their portfolio firms to the stock market. While grandstanding generates tangible benefits for the VCs, it also causes a significant cost to the other shareholders of the portfolio firm in the form of higher underpricing (Gompers, 1996; Lee and Wahal, 2004). The power of VCs may thus increase rather than reduce investors' concerns about the risk of adverse selection, thus increasing underpricing.

Accordingly, there is mixed evidence on the role played by VCs. For example, Megginson and Weiss (1991) find lower underpricing for VC-backed IPOs. Hamao et al. (2000) and Chahine and Goergen (2011b), however, find that VC-backed IPOs are associated with higher underpricing. Still, Barry et al. (1990) show that there is no significant difference between VC-backed and non-VC-backed IPOs. Similarly, the empirical evidence is mixed as to the impact of VCs on long-term performance. For example, Jain and Kini (1995) report that, in line with findings by Brav and Gompers (1997), US VC-backed IPOs have a higher operating performance than non-VC-backed IPOs over the three-year period following the IPO date. Hamao et al. (2000), however, find that the long-term performance of Japanese VC-backed IPOs is no better than that of other Japanese IPOs.

The presence of VC firms may also affect executive compensation via their representation on the board of directors and via their leadership. Hellmann and Puri (2002) find that VC backing is related to the adoption of stock option plans. The granting of IPO options is also more likely when VCs are on the board of directors (Fried et al., 1998). As mentioned above, powerful VCs may also have an influence on CEO compensation. For example, VCs may issue IPO options to the CEOs of their investee firms with an exercise price equal to a deliberately low offer price in order to bribe or compensate the CEOs for their support for an early IPO. Chahine and Goergen (2011a) find support for this argument as CEO stock option grants increase underpricing in firms with young VCs sitting on their board, which is consistent with the grandstanding hypothesis.

3.3   Brief Summary

Since CEOs are more powerful at the time of the IPO, outside investors are likely to question CEO behavior in general and be concerned about the latter's exploitation of private benefits of control. Indeed, as argued by the proponents of managerialism, CEOs may influence the timing and terms of their stock option arrangements. Therefore, outside investors may require high risk compensation, in the form of higher IPO under-pricing, when there are stock option grants at the IPO. Empirical evidence however indicates that the corporate governance characteristics of the IPO firm ultimately deter-mine which of the effects of CEO stock options dominates. For example, good govern-ance practices, such as board independence, that are able to counterbalance the power of CEOs may cause a better alignment of the interests of the CEOs with those of the shareholders via the stock option grants. In contrast, the presence of venture capital investors, especially young ones, is likely to encourage CEO rent seeking around the initial public offering.

Overall, prior research confirms the complexity of the role played by CEO stock options in IPO firms, which are usually characterized by severe agency problems and information asymmetries.

4 CONCLUSION

Despite an extensive body of research on stock options, there is as yet no clear evidence on the role they play in mature firms. Even less is known about their role in IPO firms. Indeed, this chapter identifies the contrasting effects of stock options on IPO perform-ance. On the one hand, stock options may incentivize the CEO to take the optimal amount of risk, i.e. the amount of risk that maximizes shareholder value. In other words, in the absence of stock options the CEO is likely to be too risk averse as most of his wealth and human capital are tied up in a single firm. Stock options may be a means to address this issue by providing the CEO with an upside combined with a limited downside. On the other hand, CEO stock options in IPO firms may just be a means to expropriate the other pre-IPO shareholders via excessive underpricing. In other words, the CEO may benefit from the excessive underpricing at the IPO by grant-ing himself stock options with an exercise price set equal to the deliberately low offer price of the shares.

Overall, prior research suggests that the role played by stock options depends on the presence and the effectiveness of corporate governance, i.e. monitoring mechanisms. The latter are even more important in IPO firms where agency problems and information asymmetries are more pronounced than in mature firms. The effect of CEO stock options on firm performance at the IPO is thus likely to be the outcome of a complex game of power involving the various parties participating in the IPO process. These parties include venture capital firms, the board of directors (and in particular independent direc-tors) alongside the CEO. All in all, the existing literature suggests that both CEO power and VC power is likely to bring out the negative effects of CEO options on firm perform-ance and in particular IPO underpricing whereas the incentivizing effect of stock options dominates in the presence of strong boards.

REFERENCES

Aboody, David and Kasznik, Ron, 2000. CEO stock option awards and the timing of corporate voluntary disclosures. Journal of Accounting and Economics 29, 73–100.

Amihud, Yakov and Lev, Baruch, 1981. Risk reduction as a managerial motive for conglomerate mergers. Bell Journal of Economics 12, 605–17.

Bach, Seung B. and Smith, Anne D., 2007. Are powerful CEOs beneficial to post-IPO survival in high technology industries? An empirical investigation. Journal of High Technology Management Research 18, 31–42.

Baker, George, Jensen, Michael C., and Murphy, Kevin J., 1988. Compensation and incentives: practice vs. theory. Journal of Finance XLIII, 593–616.

Balkin, D. and Gomez-Mejia, L., 1987. Toward a contingency theory of compensation strategy. Strategic Management Journal 8, 169–82.

Barry, Christopher B., Muscarella, Chris J., Peavy, John W., and Vetsuypens, Michael, 1990. The role of venture capitalists in the creation of a public company. Journal of Financial Economics 27, 447–71.

Beatty, Randolph P. and Zajac, Edward J., 1994. Managerial incentives, monitoring, and risk bearing: a study of executive compensation, ownership, and board structure in initial public offerings. Administrative Science Quarterly 39, 313–35.

Bergstresser, Daniel and Philippon, Thomas, 2006. CEO incentives and earnings management. Journal of Financial Economics 80, 511–29.

Brav, Alon and Gompers, Paul A., 1997. Myth or reality? The long-run under-performance of initial public offerings: evidence from venture and nonventure capital-backed companies. Journal of Finance 52, 1791–821.

Bruton, Garry, Filatotchev, Igor, Chahine, Salim, and Wright, Mike, 2010. Ownership concentration and performance of IPO firms: the impact of different types of private equity investors and legal institutions in two European nations. Strategic Management Journal 31, 491–509.

Burns, Natasha and Kedia, Simi, 2006. The impact of performance-based compensation on misreporting. Journal of Financial Economics 79, 35–67.

Carpenter, Jennifer N., 2002. Does option compensation increase managerial risk appetite? The Journal of Finance 55, 2311–31.

Certo, S. Trevis, Covin, Jeffrey G., Daily, Catherine M., and Dalton, Dan R., 2001. Wealth and the effects of founder management among IPO-state new ventures. Strategic Management Journal 22, 641–58.

Certo, S. Trevis, Daily, Catherine M., Cannella, Albert A., Jr., and Dalton, Dan R., 2003. Giving money to get money: how CEO stock options and CEO equity enhance IPO valuations. Academy of Management Journal 46, 643–53.

Chahine, Salim and Filatotchev, Igor, 2008a. Information disclosure, corporate governance and performance of IPOs. Journal of Small Business Management 46, 219–41.

Chahine, Salim and Filatotchev, Igor, 2008b. The effects of venture capitalist affiliation to underwriters on short- and long-term performance in French IPOs. Global Finance Journal 18, 351–72.

Chahine, Salim and Goergen, Marc, 2011a. The two sides of CEO option grants at the IPO. Journal of Corporate Finance, 17 (4), 1116–31.

Chahine, Salim and Goergen, Marc, 2011b. VC board representation and performance of US IPOs. Journal of Business Finance and Accounting, 38 (3&4), 413–45.

Chahine, Salim, Filatotchev, Igor, and Zahra, Shaker, 2011. Building perceived quality of founder-involved IPO firms: founders' effects on board selection and stock market performance. Entrepreneurship: Theory and Practice, 35 (2), 319–35.

Cheng, Qiang and Warfield, Terry D., 2005. Equity incentives and earnings management. The Accounting Review, 80, 441–76.

Chidambaran, N.K., Kedia, Simi, and Nagpurnanand, R. Prabhala, 2009. CEO–director connections and corporate fraud. Working Paper.

Cohen, Randolph B., Hall, Brian J., and Viceira, Louis M., 2000. Do executive stock options encourage risk-taking? Harvard Business School, working paper (Harvard University, Boston, MA).

Coles, Jerilyn W., McWilliams, Victoria B., and Sen, Nilanjan, 2001. An examination of the relationship of governance mechanisms to performance. Journal of Management 27, 23–50.

Cornelli, Francesca and Yosha, Oved, 2003. The staging of venture capital financing: Milestones vs. rounds. Review of Economic Studies 70, 1–32.

Daily, Catherine M. and Dalton, Dan R., 1992. Financial performance of founder-managed versus professionally managed corporations. Journal of Small Business Management 30, 25–34.

Daily, Catherine M. and Johnson, Jonathan L., 1997. Sources of CEO power and firm financial performance: a longitudinal assessment. Journal of Management 23, 97–117.

Daily, Catherine M., Johnson, Jonathan L., and Dalton, Dan R., 1999. On the measurements of board composition: poor consistency and a serious mismatch of theory and operationalization. Decision Sciences 30, 83–106.

Daily, Catherine M., McDougall, Patricia P., Covin, Jeffrey G., and Dalton, Dan R., 2002. Governance and strategic leadership in entrepreneurial firms. Journal of Management 28, 387–412.

Dalton, D.R., Daily, C.M., Certo, S.T., and Roengpitya, R., 2003. Meta-analyses of corporate financial performance and the equity of CEOs, officers, boards of directors, institutions, and blockholders: fusion or confusion? Academy of Management Journal 46, 13–26.

Fama, Eugene F., 1980. Agency problems and theory of the firm. The Journal of Political Economy 88, 288–307.

Fried, Vance H., Bruton, Garry D., and Hisrich, Robert D., 1998. Strategy and the board of directors in venture capital-backed firms. Journal of Business Venturing 13, 493–503.

Goergen, Marc and Renneboog, Luc, 2005. Corporate governance in Germany, in: Keasey, Kevin, Thompson, Steve and Wright, Mike (eds.), *Corporate Governance: Accountability, Enterprise and International Comparisons*. Chichester: John Wiley & Sons, 285–326.

Gompers, Paul A., 1996. Grandstanding in the venture capital industry. Journal of Financial Economics 42, 133–56.

Gompers, Paul A. and Lerner, Josh, 1999. *The Venture Capital Cycle*. Cambridge (MA): MIT Press.

Gorman, Michael and William Sahlman, 1989. What do venture capitalists do? Journal of Business Venturing 4, 231–48.

Guthrie, Katherine and Sokolowsky, Jan, 2009. CEO compensation and board structure revisited. Working Paper.

Hall, Brian J. and Liebman, Jeffrey B., 1998. Are CEOs really paid like bureaucrats? Quarterly Journal of Economics 113, 653–91.

Hamao, Yasushi, Packer, Frank, and Ritter, Jay R., 2000. Institutional affiliation and the role of venture capital: evidence from initial public offerings in Japan. Pacific-Basin Finance Journal 8, 529–58.

Harrison, J. Richard, Torres, David L., and Kukalis, Sal, 1988. The changing of the guard: turnover and structural change in the top-management position. Administrative Science Quarterly 33, 211–32.

Hellmann, Thomas and Puri, Manju, 2002. Venture capital and the professionalization of start-up firms: empirical evidence. Journal of Finance 57, 169–97.

Hermalin, Benjamin E. and Weisbach, Michael S., 1998. Endogenously chosen boards of directors and their monitoring of the CEO. American Economic Review 88, 96–118.

Hoberg, Gerard and Seyhun, Hasan Nejat, 2006. Do underwriters collaborate with venture capitalists in IPOs? Implications and evidence. AFA Boston Meetings Paper.

Jain, Bharat A. and Kini, Omesh, 1995. Venture capitalist participation and the post-issue operation performance of IPO firms. Managerial and Decision Economics 16, 593–606.

Jensen, Michael C., 1986. Agency costs of free-cash-flow, corporate finance, and takeovers. American Economic Review 76, 323–9.

Jensen, Michael C. and Meckling, William H., 1976. Theory of the firm: managerial behavior, agency costs and ownership structure. Journal of Financial Economics 3, 305–60.

Jensen, Michael C. and Murphy, Kevin J., 1990. CEO incentives: it's not how much you pay, but how. Harvard Business Review 68, 138–53.

Jensen, M.C. and Murphy, K.J., 2010. CEO incentives: it's not how much you pay, but how. Journal of Applied Corporate Finance 22, 64–76.

Kaplan, Steven and Strömberg, Per, 2003. Financial contracting theory meets the real world: an empirical analysis of venture capital contracts. Review of Economic Studies 70, 281–315.

Kim, Jaemin and Pukthuanthong, Kuntara, 2006. IPO firm executives, compensation, and selling. The Journal of Entrepreneurial Finance and Business Ventures 11, 23–41.

Lazear, Edward P. and Rosen, Sherwin, 1979. Rank-order tournaments as optimum labor contracts. Working Paper No. 401, National Bureau of Economic Research.

Lee, Peggy M. and Wahal, Sunil, 2004. Grandstanding, certification and the underpricing of venture backed IPOs. Journal of Financial Economics 73, 375–407.

Loughran, Tim and Ritter, Jay R., 2002. Why don't issuers get upset about leaving money on the table in IPOs? Review of Financial Studies 15, 413–43.

Lowry, Michelle and Murphy, Kevin J., 2007. Executive stock options and IPO underpricing. Journal of Financial Economics 85, 39–65.

Martin, Jens, 2008. Sweet escapes: analysts' recommendations and the lockup period. Working Paper.

Megginson, William L. and Weiss, Kathleen A., 1991. Venture capitalist certification in initial public offerings. Journal of Finance 46, 879–903.

Murphy, K.J., 1999. Executive compensation, in Orley Ashenfelter and David Card (eds.), *Handbook of Labor Economics*, Vol. 3b. Elsevier Science North Holland, chapter 38, 2485–563.

Nikbakht, Ehsan, Shahrokhi, Manuchehr, and Martin, Robert, Jr., 2007. IPO pricing and executive compensation. International Journal of Business 12, 311–24.

Pauly, Mark V., 1974. Overinsurance and public provision of insurance: the roles of moral hazard and adverse selection. Quarterly Journal of Economics 88, 44–62.

Penrose, Edith, 1995. *The Theory of the Growth of the Firm* (third ed.). New York: Oxford University Press.

Rajgopal, Shivaram and Shevlin, Terry, 2002. Empirical evidence on the relation between stock option compensation and risk taking. Journal of Accounting and Economics 33, 145–71.

Ritter, Jay R. and Welch, Ivo, 2002. A review of IPO activity, pricing, and allocations. The Journal of Finance 44, 1795–828.

Rock, Kevin, 1986. Why new issues are underpriced. Journal of Financial Economics 15, 187–212.

Ross, Stephen A., 2004. Compensation, incentives, and the duality of risk aversion and riskiness. The Journal of Finance 59, 207–25.

Sanders, W. Gerard, 2001. Behavioral responses of CEOs to stock ownership and stock option pay. Academy of Management Journal 44, 477–92.

Scarborough, Harry and Elias, Juanita, 2002. *Evaluating Human Capital*. London: Chartered Institute of Personnel and Development.

Shleifer, Andrei and Vishny, Robert W., 1997. A survey of corporate governance. Journal of Finance 52, 737–83.

Simon, Herbert A., 1957. The compensation of executives. Sociometry, 20, 32–5.

Tinic, Seha M., 1988. Anatomy of initial public offerings of common stock. Journal of Finance 43, 789–822.

Weber, Marsha and Dudney, Donna, 2003. A reduced form coefficients analysis of executive ownership, corporate value, and executive compensation. The Financial Review 38, 399–434.

Welch, Ivo, 1989. Seasoned offerings, imitation costs, and the underpricing of initial public offerings. The Journal of Finance 44, 421–49.

Wright, M., Wilson, N., and Robbie, K., 1996. The longer term effects of management-led buy-outs. Journal of Entrepreneurial and Small Business Finance 5, 213–34.

Yermack, David, 1997. Good timing: CEO stock option awards and company news announcements. Journal of Finance 52, 449–76.

10 Corporate governance going astray: executive remuneration built to fail*

Jaap Winter

1 BONUSES OF CONTENTION

Most of the modern academic thinking on corporate governance starts from the understanding that in public companies with dispersed ownership an agency relation exists between the managers as agents whose decisions affect the shareholders as principals. Corporate governance and underlying company law mechanisms are very much about addressing the issues triggered by this relationship, seeking to ensure that managers act in the interests of shareholders. Classic company law tools such as appointment and dismissal rights, disclosure, monitoring through supervisory or non-executive directors, can all be seen as mechanisms that aim to address the agency problems. A relatively new corporate governance mechanism, introduced in the 1990s, is to align the interests of managers with the interests of shareholders through the remuneration of executive directors. This was done by making remuneration of executives dependent upon certain performance targets having been met and by paying executives in stock options and shares of the company.

Scholars in the US claimed that the problem of executive remuneration was not that CEOs received too much pay, but that their pay was not related to the performance of companies (Jensen and Murphy 1990). The US government stimulated performance-based pay in 1993 by providing that non-performance-related compensation in excess of $1 million was no longer deductible as an ordinary business expense for corporate income tax purposes (Omnibus Budget Reconciliation Act of 1993). The result was, first, that many companies increased non-performance-based cash compensation to $1 million and then began to add on performance-based pay that satisfied the new tax act (Jensen and Murphy 2004). Performance-based pay primarily took the form of stock options, based on the belief that stock options did not present a cost to the company. Europe was quick to catch up with performance-based pay. Large cash bonuses, stock option and share awards have become common features of remuneration packages of executive directors of EU listed companies.

Performance pay, popularly captured under the now ominous term "bonuses", in the meantime has become highly contentious in the wake of the financial crisis. Many believe extreme variable pay schemes have led executives, managers and traders of financial institutions to excessive risk taking with short-term private benefits for themselves and the risks shifted to the institutions. Public outrage has been triggered even more by the continuation of excessive bonus payments by some financial institutions while they and

---

* This chapter builds on an earlier version which is included in the Festschrift for Professor Klaus J. Hopt, Walter de Gruyter, Berlin, 2010, pp. 1521–35.

other institutions with which they trade have received billions and billions of aid from governments, paid for by taxpayers' money (Sandel 2009). Although performance-based pay did receive criticism before the financial crisis (Bebchuk and Fried 2004, Jensen and Murphy 2004), the public and political outrage after the crisis go way beyond such criticism and have caused a major rift between financial institutions, and perhaps the business community at large, and the rest of society. Both the public outrage and the lack of responsiveness from the industry preclude a sensible debate about the effectiveness of performance-based pay.

My sense is that we can only return to normal if both sides of the debate would focus on what performance-based pay is actually doing. This article seeks to contribute to such a debate. The key argument is that performance-based pay for executives not only suffers from the original criticism of bad governance and poor design, but that it cannot be made to work because people behave differently than performance-based pay assumes. I think we have shot ourselves in the foot with a governance mechanism that was supposed to mitigate the agency problem but has aggravated it instead. My argument is not of a legal nature but is concerned primarily with the reality of being human that underlies our rules and practices. It precedes the legal judgments we make of what we should regulate and how.

I make two provisos. The first is about scope. This chapter is about performance-based pay for executive directors of listed companies, as a governance response to the perceived agency problem of well informed managers who are in control and may not always act in the interest of less or uninformed dispersed shareholders. I am not making the claim that performance-based pay never works in any setting, although I do believe the evidence presented here may also be relevant for the effectiveness of performance-based pay in other settings. The second proviso is that I am not certain of the conclusions that I draw from the arguments in this chapter. We are often fooled by our own belief of knowing something to be true (Burton 2008, Schulz 2010). The arguments and underlying evidence presented here appear to make sense to me and sit with me more comfortably than arguments that seek to support performance-based pay for executives. I also acknowledge that I am not objective, or at least not more objective than average. I come from a background, I have had experiences, I have studied materials and I have discussed, all of which create and reinforce a basis for being more comfortable with the arguments presented here. I trust that others with different backgrounds, experiences and acquired understandings will bring their arguments to the table. Only our dialogue will bring matters forward.

2   INITIAL CRITICISM: THE GOVERNANCE AND DESIGN OF EXECUTIVE REMUNERATION

Criticism of performance-based pay systems to reward executives is not new. In 2004 Bebchuk and Fried published their book *Pay without Performance: The Unfulfilled Promise of Executive Compensation* (Bebchuk and Fried 2004). The core element of their argument is that performance-based pay for executives assumes that a company's board of directors negotiates pay arrangements at arm's length from executives, which does not happen in reality:

Directors have had various economic incentives to support, or at least go along with, arrangements favorable to the company's top executives. Various social and psychological factors – collegiality, team spirit, a natural desire to avoid conflict within the board team, and sometimes friendship and loyalty – have also pulled board members in that direction. Although many directors own shares in their firms, their financial incentives to avoid arrangements favorable to executives have been too weak to induce them to take the personally costly, or at the very least unpleasant, route of haggling with their CEOs. Finally, limitations on time and resources have made it difficult for even well-intentioned directors to do their pay-setting job properly. (p. 4)

Bebchuk and Fried suggest a number of improvements both to pay schemes (for example, reducing windfall profits) and to the governance and transparency of performance-based pay schemes, including requiring shareholder approval of equity based plans.

After having promoted performance-based pay as a means to mitigate the principal–agent problem, Jensen and Murphy have reviewed actual pay practices in 2004, concluding that the design is often poor (for example on performance targets) and that boards typically simply ratify executives' remuneration initiatives (Jensen and Murphy 2004). Directors should be much less dependent on the CEO, boards should be chaired by a person who is not the CEO and remuneration committees should take full control over the process and should seldom, if ever, use compensation consultants for executive compensation purposes who are also used by the firm for actuarial or lower-level employee remuneration assignments.

Regulation of executive remuneration until now also primarily focused on the governance of remuneration: the role of independent non-executive directors, shareholder votes on remuneration policy or remuneration reports and on share-based schemes of remuneration, independence of remuneration consultants, disclosure of individual director pay, etc.[1] Some of these elements have been laid down in mandatory regulation, other elements have been included in corporate governance codes (for an overview see Ferrarini et al. 2009). More recently some attention has been given to the design of remuneration schemes, in particular seeking to mitigate the short term incentive provided by variable pay and to limit severance pay, certainly in case of non-performance. Regulation, as the initial criticism, assumes that performance-based pay can be made to work if only it would be designed and governed better. If we succeed in providing for a better design and governance, the thinking is that performance-based pay would be desirable, or acceptable at the least.

3   CAN WE HANDLE EXECUTIVE PERFORMANCE-BASED PAY?

Research from a wider field of cognitive sciences seriously questions whether performance-based pay for executives can ever be made to work. The nature of the challenges has

---

[1]   See for example the Recommendations of the EU Commission relating to executive remuneration of 14 December 2004, Fostering an Appropriate Regime for the Remuneration of Directors of Listed Companies, and of 29 April 2009, Completing the Recommendation of 14 December 2004 and the Recommendation of 15 February 2005 [on the role of non-executive directors]; see http://ec.europa.eu/internal_market/company/directors-remun/index_en.htm.

everything to do with who and how we are as human beings. The evidence provided comes from new research into how we make decisions and choices, our biases, our blind spots, our self-serving nature and our perceptions of fairness, in short, as Bazerman and Moore call it: our bounded rationality, our bounded awareness and our bounded ethicality (Bazerman and Moore 2009). Somehow little of the findings of this research has found its way to the debate on performance-based pay for executives. The basic assumption still is that if executives have monetary incentives to produce enterprise value which eventually flows to shareholders they will indeed do so. The implicit assumption for promoting performance-based pay is that executives are insufficiently motivated to produce enterprise value for the benefit of shareholders without explicit monetary incentives. These assumptions ignore what effects such incentives in reality have. They also ignore the effects of the incentive system we have designed on our preferences, our thinking and our behavior. The two key elements of this system are the setting of performance targets and benchmarking with peers. In the following sections I will discuss what we know about incentives, target setting and benchmarking and why this, at least for me, destroys the validity of our assumptions underlying performance-based pay for executives. It appears that we simply cannot handle performance-based pay.

4   INCENTIVES AND BEHAVIOR

Economic theory has long held that monetary incentives improve performance. Since the governance crisis at the start of this millennium it has been recognized that in particular stock options as the mechanism that was introduced to reward executives may provide perverse incentives. Coffee explained how the surge in stock option schemes in the 1990s has led to a proportionate surge in restatements of annual accounts by listed companies in the US (Coffee 2003). Shares acquired under stock option schemes could be sold immediately, which led executives to drive up the stock price through aggressive earnings forecasts, which they then satisfied by premature earnings recognition thus sustaining higher market valuations. This game went on mostly unnoticed as it was played during a sustained bull market in the 1990s, causing investors, analysts, auditors and other gatekeepers to suspend their usual skepticism. The 2007–08 financial crisis has spurred more criticism on variable-pay schemes in the form of cash bonuses, in particular for the asymmetry between risk and reward ingrained in cash bonus schemes: the immediate reward of a cash bonus is for the executive while the long term risk caused by the actions that have led to meeting short term turnover and profitability targets lies solely with the financial institution. A requirement to defer a substantial part of the cash bonus for three or four years, as the EU Commission Recommendation of 29 April 2009 suggests, is intended to reduce this asymmetry.[2]

But the problem with monetary incentives lies much deeper. A growing body of psychological research raises serious questions about the effects of monetary incentives. An important phenomenon that is now widely evidenced is *crowding out*. Monetary incentives appear to have the effect that the intrinsic motivation of people to perform a certain

---

[2]   See sec 3.3 of the Recommendation of 29 April 2009, see fn 1 above.

task well is displaced by the extrinsic monetary incentive. This often has the effect that people actually perform less than without the monetary incentive. An often-cited example of the crowding out effect are the fines that a day care center in Israel imposed on parents who arrived late to pick up their children, which resulted in more parents coming late. The fine was quickly perceived as a price to be paid for additional services, which replaced the feeling of guilt or obligation parents may have had towards their children and their care-takers (Gneezy and Rustichini 2000). The crowding out effect has also been widely researched in relation to incentives for blood donors. Some results indicate that giving financial incentives actually reduces the number of donors, while more recent research indicates that different incentives such as free cholesterol testing may have positive effects.[3] Some economists have questioned the relevance of the psychological evidence of crowding out effects in pro-social environments (day care centers, blood banks) to economic relations where people expect to be paid for their efforts (Prendergast 1999, Fehr and Falk 2002). Nonetheless there is evidence that also in economic relations the crowding out effect occurs (Frey and Jegen 2000, Fehr and Gächter 2002). Various theories explain the crowding out effect. One explanation offered by Fehr and Gächter is that without explicit incentives, agents perceive their contracts to contain an implicit obligation to provide efforts, based on social norms of cooperation and reciprocity (Fehr and Gächter 2000). Once an explicit incentive is introduced the perception may shift to the understanding that effort is only required because of and according to the incentive, and the social norms as a basis for providing effort are forgotten. Ariely offers a variety of examples, among which is the example of lawyers who generally refuse to offer services for retirees at a very low rate of $30 an hour, but overwhelmingly agree to offer those services for free (Ariely 2008). The low fee signals that the activity is governed by market norms with sharp-edged exchanges and no place for pro-social behavior. Without the fee being offered the perception is that the activity is governed by social norms, based on our need for community and mutual help. Based on cognitive evaluation theory James provides a different explanation, holding that an extrinsic incentive may provide intrinsic satisfaction if the incentive indicates competence, but it will not do so if it is perceived as controlling (James 2004). When the size of the incentive is large it will primarily be perceived as controlling, as it rationally compels the agent to attribute his efforts to the incentive rather than to his own preferences.

The crowding out effect is not all. A different strand of research indicates that monetary incentives have a negative impact on creative, non-mechanical tasks. In 1945 Duncker conducted an experiment, giving participants a candle, a box of thumbtacks and a book of matches and asking them to fix the candle to the wall so that it would not drip on the table below. Many participants tried to fix the candle to the wall with the thumbtacks, or to glue it to the wall by melting it, neither of which works. Only a few found the solution: to empty the box of the thumbtacks and fix the box to the wall with the tacks, as a platform for the candle to stand on. Duncker has called this phenomenon functional fixedness: we fail to see that the box can be used for anything else than to hold the thumbtacks.[4]

---

[3] Goette and Stutzer (2008).
[4] See http://en.wikipedia.org/wiki/Functional_fixedness and http://en.wikipedia.org/wiki/The_Candle_Problem.

Glucksberg reported in 1962 that participants who were told they would receive a reward for solving the candle problem faster were actually slower in solving the problem than participants who were only told they were being timed in order to find out how quickly people could solve the problem (Glucksberg 1962). The reward narrows the cognitive focus, blocking creativity. This is in line with conclusions drawn by Condry and Chambers in 1978 that rewards often distract attention from the process of task activity to the getting of a reward (Condry and Chambers 1978). In other words, the carrot in front of our eyes blinds us, in particular when we need to perform complex tasks, requiring assessment of complex information. This is a cognitive analogy to limitations in our visual perception called inattentional blindness. We have a tendency to see only what we are looking for and to miss what we are not looking for, even when we are staring directly at it. This has been established over and over again with short films of two basketball teams in black, and white, outfits. When asked to count the number of times the white team passes a ball people typically miss the bear moonwalking between the players.[5] Pink concludes that incentives only work for straight-forward, mechanical tasks, and not for anything that requires more than a minimum of cognitive skills (Pink 2010).

Perverse incentives, crowding out and narrowing of cognitive focus: the evidence from modern research is that the effect of monetary incentives on the performance of complex cognitive jobs is likely to be negative. The job of an executive is a complex one, requiring not only strong analytical skills but also an awareness of and an openness to yet unknown or uncertain factors and information and the ability to weigh opportunities and risks in light of these uncertainties. The alignment theory as a justification for performance-based pay in itself is a strong signal that the performance-contingent incentive is intended to be controlling, seeking to ensure that the executives as agents perform in the interests of shareholders as principals, which they, apparently, would not do otherwise. The insistence by shareholders that executives should only be paid if there is clear, measurable performance gives the same signal. The variable part of total pay of the executive has increased substantially over the last decade and a half. This has enforced the crowding out effect and at the same time has narrowed the cognitive focus of executives to ensuring that targets will be met and the performance-based pay is actually paid.

5   TARGET SETTING, GAMING AND CHEATING

A crucial element of performance-based pay for executives is setting targets in advance and measuring if and to what extent these targets have been met. The pay-out is then related to the actual achievement in relation to the pre-set targets. Based partly on experience and partly on perception, shareholders and code regulators have insisted that the targets to be set should be objective and measurable and should be disclosed to the extent that they are not competition-sensitive. This should help shareholders to assess whether there indeed has been performance that should be rewarded. It should also limit the scope for rigging the system of performance-based pay by executives.

---

[5]   See http://www.break.com/index/awareness-test.html. See also the colour-changing card trick on http://www.youtube.com/watch?v=voAntzB7EwE.

I leave aside here that the targets often used in performance-based pay systems offer only a one-sided, often short term perspective on performance that is to be rewarded, typically produced by financial performance indicators that happen to be available. Regulation attempts to deal with this by insisting that longer term targets and non-financial targets should be used to measure performance that is to be rewarded. But target setting has a number of negative side effects that are completely ignored in the discussion on executive remuneration. As Ordonez et al. write on the basis of a study of literature on goals setting and performance, target setting can narrow focus, motivate risk-taking, lure people into unethical behaviour, inhibit learning, increase competition, and decrease intrinsic motivation (Ordonez et al. 2009). Jensen describes the same phenomenon for the other example of goal setting we are so completely accustomed to: budgeting. Jensen calls budgeting a game that pays people to lie twice, both at the setting of the budget and when measuring whether the budget has been met or not. "Tell a manager that he or she will get a bonus when targets are realised and two things are sure to happen. First, managers will attempt to set targets that are easily reachable, and once the targets are set, they will do their best to see that the targets are met even if it damages the company to do so" (Jensen 2003). Performance indicators corrupt immediately when they become targets that need to be met in order to receive a certain reward. Jacob and Levitt conducted research into the cheating by teachers in Chicago public schools, which increased when the Chicago school district introduced a new system for holding schools accountable for student learning, including the right to close down schools that consistently under-performed (Jacob and Levitt 2004). Schwartz describes the ultimate effect of financial incentives: more and more incentives destroy our moral will, our will to do right (Schwartz 2009).

The cheating that goes on in target-setting and measurement in business is ubiquitous and at the same time accepted as a matter of fact. Paradoxically, most people engaged in this process do not see themselves as being dishonest. People typically value honesty; it activates our internal reward system. Cheating may provide a material gain, but it reduces our positive self-concept. Mazar et al. have developed a theory explaining how people who generally perceive themselves to be honest, nonetheless can engage in cheating (Mazar et al. 2008). The ability to combine cheating with a view of ourselves as honest increases when we can categorize our actions and find rationalizations that allow us to reinterpret our actions in a self-serving manner. This ability reduces when we pay more attention to honesty standards. One powerful self-serving rationalization that is often used is that others do it too. In corporate life this cheating has become very much the norm when it comes to target setting for budgeting purposes, in particular when performance-based pay is related to such targets, with very little or no attention at all to standards of honesty and integrity. The result is that target setting defeats its purpose of ensuring that only real and objectively measurable performance is rewarded.

6   (BAD) LUCK

Another, related problem with performance-based pay is that it tends to reward windfall profits, increases in performance which are just a result of general market developments rather than real performance of executives. The solution is to try to single out the individual performance of a company as compared to general market trends. But even if we are able to do so, the isolated performance of the company is not a straightforward indication of the performance of executives. In his well known book *The Black Swan* Nassim Taleb describes how we typically overestimate our own influence on success and ignore factors which are often more relevant: timing, circumstances and pure luck (Taleb 2007). We tend to create narratives to find meaning in events and we tend to do so in a self-serving way, ignoring that reality is mostly more complex, fuzzy and messy. Similarly, we underestimate our influence on failure and are all too quick to blame circumstances outside our control. This correlates to an opportunistic shift of perception of what is supposed to be rewarded, value or merit. When times are good, the creation of value by the company is perceived as the performance that should be rewarded, regardless of how much value was actually created by the specific performance of the executives. When times are not so good and little or no value is created, the "extraordinary efforts" of the executives need to be rewarded. This is confirmed by research indicating that executive pay is most sensitive to industry or market benchmarks when such benchmarks are up but much less so when they are down. Executives are paid for good luck, but not punished for bad luck (Garvey and Milbourn 2003).

The tendency to overestimate our performance fits into a pattern in which we generally view ourselves in a more positive light than is objectively accurate. The basis for this tendency is our motive to affirm self-worth. People react to negative information about themselves by making more self-serving attributions that affirm their worth. When we find our self-worth affirmed, we feel less need to make self-serving judgments (Bazerman and Moore 2009). An old saying from the northern part of the Netherlands where I come from is that when you fall when ice-skating the cause "is either the ice or the skates". Our need to continuously affirm our self-worth in a self-serving way creates *cognitive dissonance* when performance targets have not been met. We will look for other reasons outside our own performance to explain the failure to reach targets. To preserve our self-worth we then explain that we worked very hard in a difficult market, which justifies that we receive our bonus. Or we start to cheat to ensure that targets will be met, to the possible detriment of the company, or to show that targets have indeed been met while in reality they have not.

7   BENCHMARKING FOR FAIRNESS AND STATUS

A final essential feature of modern executive remuneration schemes is the benchmarking of the performance of the company to the performance of other companies in a peer group. Similar to the insistence on objective and measurable targets, benchmarking was introduced to provide for a more objective standard of the company's performance and, possibly, to exclude windfall profits. And as with performance targets, the composition of peer groups has been widely manipulated in order to ensure that executive remuneration would go up regardless of performance. But the heart of the problem is much more pervasive. Benchmarking is an expression of the human reality that we perceive the fairness of our income in relative terms, relative to what others make for similar or different jobs. Not only executives compare their incomes, we all do, secretaries, truck drivers, doctors, lawyers and professors. If we see that others doing a similar job receive more than we do, we feel treated unfairly if we do not receive more as well (Layard 2005).

One particular element of the benchmarking of executive remuneration warrants special attention. Remuneration policies typically provide that the company will reward its executives above the median, or sometimes in the top quartile of the peer group. The argument for this has generally been that a company with an ambition to be successful cannot afford to pay its executives only in the lower 50 per cent of the companies it compares itself with. The result is well known: the remuneration of executives of all companies will go up structurally. If a company is not yet paying its executives in the upper half, it will have to increase remuneration to get above the median. As a result another company will drop from the upper half and will have to increase its executive remuneration to get back above the median and so on and so forth. Benchmarking with executives of other companies and paying above the median have an autonomous effect of pushing executive remuneration up, unrelated to any increase in performance of any of the companies. A German executive once said at a conference: "I know I am being overpaid, but the benchmark shows I am not being overpaid enough!" This effect has been ubiquitous across business over the last decade and a half: executive remuneration has gone up steeply compared to the performance of companies which did not go up proportionally and sometimes did not go up at all. Recent research conducted by the Central Planning Bureau of the Netherlands shows that the average income of executives of listed companies in the Netherlands increased 9 per cent annually between 1999 and 2005 (with the years of excess still to come), while economic value added and profits did not on average increase during the same period. Of the 9 per cent, 4.8 per cent can be explained as a result of inflation, increase in scale and aging, but the additional rise cannot be explained (Centraal Plan Bureau 2010). Many blame the disclosure of individual directors' pay, which has been made mandatory in many EU member states in the last few years (Ferrarini et al. 2009), as the root cause of this effect on executive pay. I do not think it is the main cause. Benchmarking would have taken place also without disclosure of individual director pay. It is the core business of remuneration consultants advising companies and their non-executive directors on pay levels and structures. Paying above the median as a remuneration policy, regardless of performance, is the real culprit. Interestingly, the Dutch Banking Code, adopted by the Dutch association of banks, the NVB, in the wake of the financial crisis, provides that it is best practice to reward bank executives just below the median.[6] If everybody would follow this practice as meticulously as rewarding above the median was practiced, executive remuneration of bank executives should approach zero over time.

The fairness of executive remuneration as executives perceive it themselves is closely related to social status. In our world of financial capitalism, remuneration has become the key measure for the status of executives. It is the same with fund managers, investment bankers, management consultants, doctors and lawyers. High remuneration signals high social status among peers. The problem with social status is that it is a zero-sum game: if you have more status than I have, then I should get more by receiving even higher pay, after which your status will have been reduced and you need to get paid more in order to

---

[6]   See par. 6.3 of the Dutch Banking Code, see http://www.nvb.nl/index.php?p=16248.

get more status etc (Layard 2005). We see it at all levels in society, in particular when comparing material goods. It explains conspicuous consumption, a term first used by Veblen in 1899 to indicate the lavish spending on goods and services mainly for the purpose of displaying income or wealth (Veblen 1899).The same social-status sensitivity explains why frequently people prefer an absolute lower income for themselves provided their relative position as compared to neighbors or peers improves (Solnick and Hemenway 1998). The Russian peasant whose neighbor has a cow, when asked by God how He can help, answered: "Kill the cow" (Layard 2005). We all continuously need to "keep up with the Joneses" and executives are no different. The status factor is probably even more important than the actual income derived from pay schemes as such. Most executives when asked admit that they do not need the high income they receive and would be willing to cut back but only when others accept a cut-back too. This fits with other research indicating that the only situation where we may accept a pay cut is when others are doing the same (Bewley 1999). The annual executive pay rankings that newspapers produce and that often cause certain levels of aversion among the public, paradoxically at the same time serve as a status signal to the executives concerned, pushing them to demand even higher pay. Executives in a way are trapped in a rat race of all against all that nobody can ever win.

8   REGULATION WILL NOT HELP

The research described here indicates that the difficulties with executive remuneration are much more fundamental than previously discussed. Financial incentives often work counterproductively, in particular when the incentives are large and the job to be done is cognitively complex. Performance-based pay on the basis of pre-set targets induces manipulation and cheating, while our self-serving nature allows us to maintain that we are honest, deserve the pay, and to ignore the cost of lack of integrity. With remuneration as the key indicator of status for executives, they are all trapped in an upward-spiraling race that no one can ever win. I very much doubt that any new design or better governance of executive pay schemes can solve these fundamental problems of performance-based pay for executives. Additional design elements are likely to enhance the control-nature of the incentives, targets and wider conditions of performance-based pay. They will have precisely the unintended effect of crowding out executives' intrinsic motivation to perform well and will provide ever more incentives to cheat and manipulate and to not feel bad about it. It is an illusion to think that non-executive directors, let alone shareholders, will ever be as sophisticated as executives in understanding what performance targets really mean and what levers can be pulled to ensure that targets will be met. A solution would be for executives to simply all agree to cut back and abstain from counterproductive, ever-increasing remuneration. But executives have a collective-action problem; there are simply too many players who would need to agree.

A typical response in such a situation would be to regulate executive remuneration, prohibit performance-based pay or at least restrict it substantially. The prospects of such regulation however are slim if not only executives, non-executives and shareholders of listed companies, but human resource thinking in commercial and non-commercial organizations generally, including more and more in the public sector, hail performance-based pay as the mechanism to enhance performance of managers and employees. Regulation will never be realistic if we do not fundamentally reconsider the pros and cons of performance-based pay. Also, the problem of ineffective and counterproductive executive pay in essence is a private problem, the consequences of which are suffered by companies and shareholders in the first place. Specific regulation may be justified in view of public interests, such as risk management and fair treatment of customers of financial institutions, or as a response to the generally felt unfairness of bankers cashing in bonuses while financial institutions worldwide have been saved with trillions of taxpayers' money. Other than that, I see little scope for the state in regulating executive remuneration. Regulation of executive pay will not change the fundamental beliefs that people have created about the benefits of performance-based pay. In all likelihood regulation will have precisely the opposite of the intended effect. The more we regulate, the more our responsibility focuses on compliance rather than on the effect of our behavior. The more rules we make the more we care only about following the rules and think that within the rules we are free to do whatever suits us best, regardless of the consequences for others (Winter 2010).

Companies and their shareholders will have to come to their senses: performance-based pay for executives is not a solution for the alignment problem, not because of the design or governance but because of who we are.

9   A PARADIGM CHANGE

Coming to our senses is easier said than done. The business community and the financial industry within it have created a strong belief that performance-based pay is the right way to remunerate executives. With executives being on the bonus drip for almost two decades and remuneration consultants depending on creating benchmarks and designing complex performance-based pay systems, there are powerful vested interests to maintain the current remuneration paradigm. So what should we do? I offer three things: deconstruct the myths surrounding performance-based pay, build a new narrative, and present some lessons for the key actors: shareholders, non-executives and executives. None of this is rule- or incentive-based. And none of this is of a quick-fix nature.

9.1   Deconstructing Myths

The business community (companies and their shareholders) has created a cascade of myths surrounding performance-based pay that its members have massively started to believe in. The myths include:

- Performance-based pay for executives actually enhances overall performance of companies
- the more performance-based pay the better the performance of the company
- executives personally create success for their companies
- when executives lead companies to higher performance they are entitled to receive part of the gains

- executives only perform well when they have "skin in the game"
- substantial performance-based pay is essential to retain first class managers in an international market for executive talent
- financial rewards are the key indicators of personal success.

The combination of these myths leads to *worldviews* and *frames of reference* that have come to dominate the business community and how it behaves. Erhard et al. describe worldviews and frames of reference as "the network of unexamined ideas, beliefs, biases, prejudices, social and cultural embeddedness and taken for granted assumptions through which an individual interprets and interacts with the world, other people and himself or herself [worldview] or with a given specific something in his or her world [frame of reference]" (Erhard et al. 2010). They are the lenses through which we view the world and specific things within it. They constrain and shape what we see and perceive, both the world as such and specific things in it, and therefore they also constrain and shape the way we are and relate to the world and specific things in it. The problem with worldviews and frames of reference is that it is very hard to see them. They are like water to the fish, invisible to us who have them. Our worldviews and frames of reference are stored as representations in our brain through vast amounts of memory that are recalled to deal with the present and immanent. These neural representations of what we are dealing with shape our perception of what is really there, which shapes a prediction of the way it works which in turn generates a pattern of action consistent with that prediction. The pattern of action that follows may not be consistent at all with what is actually there. Here is an example of how it works.

David de Cremer, a Rotterdam-based professor of Behavioural Business Ethics, recently interviewed fifteen executives of Dutch banks, with some revealing results (De Cremer 2010). They all believed that others in the banking world find bonuses more important for performing well than they themselves did. Our self-serving bias in full operation. The conviction that others need bonuses to perform well is the basis for the myth that the industry must offer bonuses in order to retain their executives. De Cremer continues by asking the executives to make a choice between two types of bankers to manage their personal wealth. Type A banker only works for his personal financial incentive, type B banker has a genuine interest in banking matters and wants to provide service to customers. All executives said they would bring their money to banker B. The self-created myth about what sort of remuneration is needed to retain talent leads banking executives to hire the people they would not entrust with their own money. Who is fooling whom?

As long as the unexamined biases, prejudices, assumptions etc. that build the worldview and frames of reference of executives, non-executives and shareholders remain unchallenged, the current folly of substantial executive performance-based pay is destined to continue. Our standard legal (i.e. rules prohibiting or prescribing behaviour) and economic (i.e. incentives determining the behavior of rational subjects) approaches will not challenge the myths surrounding performance-based pay, they are based on these myths. They need to be fundamentally renewed with the input of modern cognitive sciences. Only then we can expect to dilute and break down the myths of executive performance-based pay. This requires lawyers and economists to be open to the knowledge gathered outside their own disciplines and cognitive scientists to take an interest in the specifics of executive performance-based pay as a fundamental governance problem. Insight into what really makes us tick is the crucial starting point for any transformation.

9.2   Building a New Narrative

Deconstructing the myths surrounding executive performance-based pay will also require that an alternative remuneration narrative be built. The new narrative should include a few key elements.

9.2.1   Make remuneration less significant

Rather than using remuneration as a primary instrument to steer executive behavior we should reduce the importance of remuneration. Money is a threshold motivator: it motivates only up to a baseline, beyond that it does not do much and likely more harm than good. Companies should remunerate their executives in such a way that remuneration is no longer an issue. People can then focus on their work and performance, which are no longer just perceived as factors that determine income.

9.2.2   Benchmark internally instead of externally

The crucial factor that can move remuneration off the table is fairness. Fairness here is relative fairness, compared to what others receive for similar or different jobs. As long as people perceive that their remuneration is unfair in light of what others receive, remuneration will remain an issue. Our current model is set to focus excessively on external fairness, in relation to peers in the industry. At the same time internal fairness is often ignored completely, with executive remuneration becoming ever higher multiples of average employee pay.[7] Refocusing benchmarks on internal fairness will help to stop the upward spiraling that is the result of automatic benchmarking with external peers, pushing remuneration up without any connection to underlying performance. Internal benchmarking in reality is much more relevant than external. The position of executives in different companies is difficult to compare in detail, certainly for companies in different countries and across Channels and Atlantics. Benchmarking remuneration details with those of other companies is over-simplifying the different realities of companies. The so-called market for international talent in practice is rather limited; most executives will not be able or willing or asked to move to other countries to work there as executives. By focusing on external benchmarking with peer groups we exaggerate the external fairness component to the detriment of internal fairness. A refocusing on internal fairness is needed, as the most important benchmark to satisfy fairness concerns. The Dutch Corporate Governance Code now provides as best practice that executive remuneration should take into account the remuneration ratios within the company.[8] This would avoid another negative effect of external benchmarking, which is to suggest that executives are in fact mercenaries: they will come for the money and they will go for the money. Most

---

[7]   See for example http://www.aflcio.org/corporatewatch/paywatch/pay/index.cfm#_ftn1, indicating that while CEO pay in the US was 42 times average employee pay in 1980, it rose to 525 times in 2000, and then fell back to 263 in 2009.

[8]   Best practice provision II.2.2.

companies need executives who are committed more to the company's future than to their own remuneration. The external benchmark at best should be a sanity check on the remuneration of executives, not the primary factor determining it, applied with wisdom and sometimes simply ignored when enough is enough.

9.2.3   Reduce variable pay substantially and use a wide set of collective targets

Executive variable pay today often doubles or triples fixed pay. This triggers the cognitive focus on everything that can ensure the desired outcome regardless of the risks or costs involved. Variable pay should be reduced substantially as part of overall compensation. When the Dutch Corporate Governance Committee, of which I was a member, in 2003 suggested that as a matter of best practice variable pay should not exceed fixed pay, we were derided by all as it was going against the established myths. After the financial crisis the same provision has become part of the Dutch Banking Code, a specific corporate governance code that was developed to apply to banks on top of the Corporate Governance Code in order to restore public trust in banks. The same now applies to insurance companies.[9] Under these provisions the executives can still double their income through variable pay, a big carrot right in sight. It would probably be better to reduce performance-based pay even further, so that it is only an extra to express true appreciation for results achieved, not based on previously set targets. As long as performance-based pay systems are used the target setting should include a wide set of measures, indicating the company's performance in a number of areas that are critical for its success in the future, including non-financial indicators. Any particular measure can be manipulated, but gaming all of the variety of measures is going to be more difficult. The scope for cheating and gaming would reduce further if the core of the measures would focus on collective performance of the company as a whole, rather than on individual targets.

9.2.4   Our real motivation

Remuneration should not be allowed to destroy our real motivation to do well at our jobs. Pink has researched extensively what truly motivates us and three factors stand out: autonomy, mastery and purpose (Pink 2010). A sense of autonomy has a powerful effect on individual performance, as a number of behavioral studies indicate (Csikszentmihalyi 1975). Autonomy is not the same as independence. Autonomy is about willful choice; we can be autonomous and choose to co-operate with and depend on others. Its opposite is control. Autonomy requires trust on both sides, from the person who should do the job and from the person who has the hierarchical position to assess the performance. Autonomy leads to engagement, which enhances the ability of people to take responsibility for the job they should perform. Performance-based pay is doing precisely the opposite as it seeks to exercise control over performance by rewarding achievement of pre-established targets and takes distrust as its starting point.

The second element is striving for mastery. The urge to master something new and

---

[9]   See for the Dutch Banking Code http://www.nvb.nl/ and for the Governance Principles adopted by the Verbond van Verzekeraars (Association of Insurers) http://www.verzekeraars.nl/ Publicaties.aspx?publicatieid=200.

engaging appears to be a strong predictor of productivity. If the challenges are set right, not too high – when the fear of failing creates anxiety, or too low – when we get bored, people can get into flow, continuously improving their mastery. Work becomes play and self-fulfilling: the activity is its own reward.

Purpose is the third element. People become particularly motivated if they can contribute to something that is larger than themselves. Chasing personal profit goals and reaching them does not satisfy us, while striving to reach purposes beyond ourselves has a lasting effect on our happiness. Modern happiness studies all indicate that finding purpose in something larger than ourselves is a crucial factor contributing to happiness. Seligman describes transcendence as one of the six virtues endorsed by almost all religious and philosophical traditions (Seligman 2008). Haidt describes the elevation that stirs a warm emotion in us when we witness moral beauty (Haidt 2006). It is also the source of power and passion that leaders need (Erhard et al. 2010). And again, performance-based pay is doing precisely the opposite: it makes our own direct pay-off the driving force of our actions, rather than the larger purposes we could be striving for.

9.2.5   Integrity

Substantial performance-based pay leads to ubiquitous cheating, which people grow to no longer recognize as such. This is partly because they believe they have acted within the rules and therefore all is fine. This is ignoring a vital element of effectiveness and performance, and that is integrity. Integrity in the sense developed by Erhard, Jensen and Zaffron, meaning whole and complete. People have integrity when their word to others is whole and complete. This requires honoring your word, which is either to keep your word and do what you said you would do (at the time and in the manner you said or implied you would) or, as soon as it becomes clear that you will not keep your word (because you cannot or no longer want to keep your word), tell the other who relies on your word that you will not keep it and deal with the problem that you have created for the other by not keeping your word. By honoring your word it remains credible and as a person you remain effective. The same is true for an organization. Acting with integrity enhances productivity and creates value (Erhard et al. 2009). Lack of integrity can exist within the boundaries of any set of given rules and also then has the effect of reducing effectiveness and productivity. Substantial performance-based pay creates a blind spot for breaches of integrity within the rules. Detailed compliance systems have the same effect: as long as we stay within the rules and procedures we fail to see that there may be massive integrity problems. Removing the blind spot allows us to focus on integrity as an essential ingredient of performance.

9.3   Lessons for Shareholders, Executives and Non-executives

Shareholders as principals can suffer when executives as agents ignore their interests. The lesson that performance-based pay for executives in its current form provides to shareholders is that it does not reduce the agency problem but exacerbates it. Substantial performance-based pay increases the focus of executives on their personal interests to the detriment of all other interests, including the interests of shareholders. Alignment of financial interests has proven to be an illusion.

So what is the alternative for shareholders? The idea that executives of public companies cannot be trusted to take the interests of shareholders sufficiently into account is deeply rooted in the shareholder community and is the key driver for their interest in corporate governance. But it would help if shareholders could see that one of the core reasons for the lack of trust between them and executives is their own lack of engagement with the companies in which they invest. We can debate long about the causes for their lack of engagement – I believe that the predominant investment theory, the Modern Portfolio Theory, which requires widespread diversification of portfolios, is one of the culprits (Winter 2011). Regardless of the causes, the fact that shareholders are unwilling to engage more deeply and closely is probably as much to blame for the distrust between shareholders and executives as the behavior of executives themselves. Investing in engagement is a much more promising avenue for shareholders to secure the value of their investments than relying on performance-based pay for executives to create an illusory alignment of financial interests.

Seeing our worldviews and frames of reference that guide our perception and actions is difficult for all of us. If you also have a strong material interest in maintaining them, as executives have with performance-based pay, it becomes all the more difficult. It is therefore no surprise to see that executives struggle to listen, understand and appreciate the criticism on their remuneration and not dismiss it outright; there is simply too much worldview and self-interest in the way. More regulation restricting remuneration in form and scope will not help executives to see their self-created myths on remuneration, it will only confirm them in their view that the politicians, media, trade unions and the public in general don't know what they are talking about. Many theories about leadership have been developed over time, but a crucial commonality is that leadership is not about the success of the leader but of the organization he leads. It is precisely this shift of attention from oneself to the purpose beyond oneself that also gives the leader access to a much deeper level of enduring satisfaction and happiness. This finding is so basic and yet so easy to ignore, certainly in the face of large personal gains that can be made. "You only see it when you get it," is how Johan Cruijff, the famous Dutch soccer player, describes it (Winsemius 2005). It takes courageous leaders to acknowledge that the focus on personal income has not worked well and to develop new, truly motivating stories.

Courage is also what non-executives need. Corporate governance regulation has put them in charge of setting the remuneration of executives. Even if shareholders decide on remuneration policies,[10] it is typically for non-executive directors to design the policy for adoption by shareholders. Non-executives have the authority to transform executive pay and substantially reduce performance-based pay. It will be difficult for them to do so as long as both shareholders and executives insist on substantial performance-based pay for executives. On the other hand, getting remuneration off the table and ending the constant internal strife with executives over targets, achievements and peer groups and ending the ever growing external criticism of their decisions should make the job of the average non-

---

[10]   In the Netherlands shareholders adopt the remuneration policy for executive directors: art. 2: 135 Dutch Civil Code. In other jurisdictions shareholders have an advisory vote on the remuneration report which reports on the actual remuneration of executives, such as the UK and, recently, the US following the Dodd-Frank Wall Street Reform and Consumer Protection Act of 2010.

executive a whole lot more attractive. That prospect may lead them to start to deconstruct the myths of performance-based pay and build new remuneration narratives with a primary focus on the company's strategy and sustainable performance, on true motivation and integrity. If non-executives can take on this big leadership role, corporate governance will prosper for it.

REFERENCES

Ariely, Dan, 2008. *Predictably Irrational: The Hidden Forces that Shape Our Decisions.* Harper Collins Publishers.
Bazerman, Max and Moore, Don, 2009. *Judgment in Managerial Decision Making.* John Wiley & Sons.
Bebchuk, Lucian and Fried, Jesse, 2004. *Pay without Performance: The Unfulfilled Promise of Executive Compensation.* Harvard University Press.
Bewley, Truman, 1999. *Why Wages Don't Fall During a Recession.* Harvard University Press.
Burton, Robert, 2008. *On Being Certain: Believing You Are Right Even When You're Not.* St. Martin's Press, New York.
Centraal Plan Bureau, 2010. Hoge Bomen in de Polder. Globalisering en Topbeloningen. CPB document 199.
Coffee, Johan, 2003. What Caused Enron? A Capsule Social and Economic History of the 1990s. Columbia Law School, the Center for Law and Economic Studies, Working Paper Series no 214, see http://papers.ssrn.com/sol3/papers.cfm?abstract_id=373581.
Condry, J. and Chambers, J., 1978. Intrinsic Motivation and the Process of Learning, in: M. Lepper and D. Greene (eds), *The Hidden Costs of Reward: New Perspectives on the Psychology of Human Motivation.* Lawrence Erlbaum Associates, Hillsdale, NJ.
Csikszentmihalyi, Mihaly, 1975. *Beyond Boredom and Anxiety: Experiencing Flow in Work and Play,* San Francisco, Jossey-Bass.
De Cremer, David, 2010. *Als goede mensen slechte dingen doen. Op zoek naar de psychologie achter de financiële crisis* [When good people do bad things. Looking for the psychology behind the financial crisis]. VOC Uitgevers.
Erhard, Werner, Jensen, Michael and Zaffron, Steve, 2009. A New Model of Integrity: An Actionable Pathway to Trust, Productivity and Value. Harvard NOM Research Paper No. 07-01, see http://papers.ssrn.com/sol3/papers.cfm?abstract_id=932255.
Erhard, Werner, Jensen, Michael, Zaffron, Steve and Granger, Karl, 2010. Introductory Reading For Being a Leader and the Effective Exercise of Leadership: An Ontological Model. Harvard NOM Research Paper No. 09-022, October 2010, see http://papers.ssrn.com/sol3/papers.cfm?abstract_id=1585976
Fehr, Ernst and Falk, Armin, 2002. Psychological Foundations of Incentives. Institute for the Study of Labor IZA, Working Paper no 507, see http://ssrn.com/abstract_id=294287.
Fehr, Ernst and Gächter, Simon, 2000. Do Incentive Contracts Crowd out Voluntary Cooperation? Working paper no. 34, Institute for Empirical Research in Economics, University of Zurich.
Fehr, Ernst and Gächter, Simon, 2002. Do Incentive Contracts Crowd Out Voluntary Cooperation? USC Center for Law, Economics and Organization, Research Paper no C01-3.
Ferrarini, Guido, Moloney, Niamh and Ungureanu, Maria Cristiana, 2009. Understanding Directors' Pay in Europe: A Comparative and Empirical Analysis, ECGI Law Working Paper 126/2009, see http://papers.ssrn.com/sol3/papers.cfm?abstract_id=1418463.
Frey, Bruno and Jegen, Reto, 2000. Motivation Crowding Theory: A Survey of Empirical Evidence. CESifo Working Paper no 245, see http://papers.ssrn.com/sol3/papers.cfm?abstract_id=203330.
Garvey, Gerald and Milbourn, Todd, 2003. Asymmetric Benchmarking in Compensation: Executives are Paid for (Good) Luck But Not Punished for Bad. See http://papers.ssrn.com/sol3/papers.cfm?abstract_id=392701.
Glucksberg, Sam, 1962. The Influence of Strength of Drive on Functional Fixedness and Perceptual Recognition. Journal of Experimental Psychology 63, 36–44.
Gneezy, Uri and Rustichini, Aldo, 2000. A Fine is a Price. Journal of Legal Studies 29, 1–17.
Goette, Lorenz and Stutzer, Alois, 2008. Blood Donations and Incentives: Evidence from a Field Experiment. Research Center for Behavioral Economics and Decision Making, Federal Reserve Bank of Boston, Working Paper Series no 08-3.
Haidt, Jonathan, 2006. *The Happiness Hypothesis.* Arrow Books.
Jacob, Brian and Levitt, Steven, 2004. To catch a cheat: the pressures of accountability may encourage school

personnel to doctor the results from high-stakes tests. Here's how to stop them – Research, see http://findarticles.com/p/articles/mi_m0MJG/is_1_4/ai_111734754/pg_6/?tag=content;col1.

James, Harvey, 2004. Why Did You Do That? An Economic Examination of the Effect of Extrinsic Compensation on Intrinsic Motivation and Performance. Revision of CORI Working Paper no 2003-01, see http://papers.ssrn.com/sol3/papers.cfm?abstract_id=476542.

Jensen, Michael, 2003. Paying People to Lie: The Truth about the Budgeting-Process. European Financial Management 379–206, see http://papers.ssrn.com/sol3/papers.cfm?abstract_id=267651.

Jensen, Michael and Murphy, Kevin, 1990. CEO Incentives: It's Not How Much You Pay, But How. Harvard Business Review 68, No 3, 138–53, see http://ssrn.com/abstract=146148.

Jensen, Michael and Murphy, Kevin, 2004. Remuneration: Where We've Been, How We Got There, What Are the Problems, and How We Fix Them. ECGI Finance Working Paper no 44/2004, see http://ssrn.com/abstract=561305.

Layard, Richard, 2005. *Happiness: Lessons from a New Science*. Penguin Books.

Mazar, Nina, Amir, On and Ariely, Dan, 2008. The Dishonesty of Honest People: A Theory of Self-Concept Maintenance. Journal of Marketing Research, 633–44, see http://papers.ssrn.com/sol3/papers.cfm?abstract_id=979648.

Ordonez, Lisa, Schweitzer, Maurice, Galinsky, Adam and Bazerman, Max, 2009. Goals Gone Wild: The Systemic Side-Effects of Over-Prescribing Goal Setting. Harvard Business School Working Paper 09-083, see http://papers.ssrn.com/sol3/papers.cfm?abstract_id=1332071.

Pink, Daniel, 2010. *Drive: The Surprising Truth about What Motivates Us*. Canongate, http://www.ted.com/talks/dan_pink_on_motivation.html.

Prendergast, C., 1999. The Provision of Incentives in Firms. Journal of Economic Literature, XXXVII, 7–63.

Sandel, Michael, 2009. *Justice: What's the Right Thing to Do?* Farrar, Straus and Giroux.

Schulz, Kathryn, 2010. *Being Wrong: Adventures in the Margin of Error*. Harper Collins Publishers.

Schwartz, Barry, 2009. TED talk on our loss of wisdom. February, http://www.ted.com/talks/lang/eng/barry_schwartz_on_our_loss_of_wisdom.html.

Seligman, Martin E.P., 2008. *Authentic Happiness*. Nicholas Brealy Publishing.

Solnick, S. and Hemenway, D., 1998. Is More Always Better? A Survey on Positional Concerns. Journal of Economic Behaviour and Organisation 37, 373–83.

Taleb, Nassim, 2007. The *Black Swan: The Impact of the Highly Improbable*. Random House.

Veblen, Thorstein, 1899. *Theory of the Leisure Class: An Economic Study in the Evolution of Institutions*. 1994 Penguin Classics edition.

Winsemius, Pieter, 2005. *Je gaat het pas zien als het doorhebt. Over Cruijff en leiderschap* [You only see it when you get it. On Cruijff and Leadership]. Balans.

Winter, Jaap, 2010. Geen regels maar best practices [No rules but best practices], in: Willems Wegen, essay for prof. mr. J.H.M. Willems, Series Van der Heijden Instituut no. 102, Kluwer, 459–67.

Winter, Jaap, 2011. Aandeelhouder engagement en stewardship [Shareholder engagement and stewardship], in: Samen werken in het Ondernemingsrecht, Series Instituut voor Ondernemingsrech no. 7, Kluwer.

PART III

CORPORATE GOVERNANCE AND EXECUTIVE COMPENSATION

11 Regulating executive remuneration after the global financial crisis: common law perspectives

Jennifer G. Hill[1]

1 INTRODUCTION

Executive pay has become a regulatory flashpoint of the global financial crisis. In contrast to the traditional non-interventionist approach to executive remuneration, it has galvanized regulators around the world to search for effective responses to the perceived problem of executive remuneration.

Executive remuneration first became a prominent aspect of corporate governance in the 1990s. A radical paradigm shift occurred at that time. Executive pay, which had until that time been treated as a corporate governance problem associated with breach of fiduciary duty (Yablon 1999, 279–80), was famously re-interpreted by Jensen and Murphy as an issue of misalignment between managerial and shareholder interests (Jensen and Murphy 1990). This transformation envisaged pay for performance as a self-executing mechanism, which could achieve alignment of incentives. Executive remuneration had, in effect, evolved from corporate governance problem to solution.

The primary focus under this paradigm shift became the design and structure of optimal remuneration contracts (Bebchuk et al 2002; Core et al 2003). Other issues, such as the pay-setting environment, managerial power and compensation levels were rendered either minor themes or invisible (Hill and Yablon 2002). The transformation also served to legitimise executive pay, by adopting a "just deserts" approach to remuneration, offering the prospect of reward for superior performance and penalties for inferior performance (Jensen and Murphy 1990; *cf* Frydman and Saks 2008, 2, 33).

Since the heyday of performance-based pay in the 1990s, there have been two major shocks to financial markets. The first involved the collapse of Enron, and analogous international corporate scandals, around the turn of the last decade (Coffee 2004; Miller 2004; Hill 2005). The second was the global financial crisis from 2007 onwards. Puzzling differences emerge in the international regulatory responses to these two sets of events. Professor John Coffee considered that executive remuneration was a possible cause of the Enron collapse (Coffee 2004). Yet, international regulatory responses to the issue of executive remuneration were at that time curiously muted, certainly in contrast to the reaction to the global financial crisis.

[1] This chapter builds on earlier research work on executive compensation and on a conference paper presented at the 2009 Annual Supreme Court of New South Wales Conference on Directors in Troubled Times. I would like to thank Randall Thomas and Ron Masulis, who are my co-researchers on a broad comparative research project on US and Australian remuneration contracts. Thanks also go to Alice Grey and Maria Leonor Jardim for their excellent research assistance, and to the Australian Research Council and Sydney Law School for financial support for this research.

Although, in keeping with Jensen and Murphy's "alignment of interests" paradigm, there has been much research on the determinants of executive pay (Core et al 2003), there was far less on policies to control executive remuneration (Dew-Becker 2009). The global financial crisis has altered this. Executive remuneration is once again portrayed as a corporate governance problem in search of a solution (BIS 2010, 25), prompting a complex array of regulatory developments around the world. The aim of this chapter is to examine some of these developments in three common law jurisdictions: the United States, United Kingdom and Australia.

2   CORPORATE CRISES AND EXECUTIVE PAY – POST-ENRON REGULATORY RESPONSES

Historically, there has been a strong link between corporate crises and increased regulation (Coffee 2004, 278; Hill 2005, 375). This is hardly surprising - as one commentator recently noted a "crisis is a terrible thing to waste" (Begg 2009; Lannoo 2009).

Certainly, there is little evidence that the global financial crisis has been wasted as a catalyst for change in relation to executive pay. However, the issue of executive remuneration received relatively little attention under post-Enron legislation in the United States. Only two provisions of the Sarbanes-Oxley Act of 2002 ("Sarbanes-Oxley Act") addressed the issue directly. The most prominent of these, s 304, is a claw-back provision, permitting recovery of bonuses, incentives-based or equity-based compensation received by the CEO or CFO, if the corporation is required to restate earnings due to material noncompliance with financial reporting requirements, as a result of misconduct (Simmons 2009, 347–9). Enforcement of s 304 has been problematical with very few successful actions under the provision (Schwartz 2008, 2, 13–15). The provision's effectiveness has been undermined by a range of factors (Schwartz 2008, 2, 13–15; J. Gordon 2009, 334), including initial uncertainty as to whether the requisite "misconduct" must be attributable to the defendant executive (Schwartz 2008, 15*ff*; Simmons 2009, 347). However, in the recent decision in *SEC v Jenkins*,[2] the court stated that s 304 does not require personal misconduct of the executive, merely of the issuer, in order to ground recovery (Savarese 2010). The other section in the Sarbanes-Oxley Act relating to executive remuneration is s 402, which imposes a prohibition on personal loans to directors or executive officers. (Romano 2005, 1538).

Notably absent from the Sarbanes-Oxley Act was any legislative attempt to grant shareholders stronger powers in relation to corporate governance matters, such as executive pay or director elections (Chandler and Strine 2003, 999). This gap provided an interesting contrast to post-Enron reforms in Australia and the United Kingdom, where legislative rhetoric focused on the need to strengthen shareholder participation rights in corporate governance (Hill 2008, 826). One of the clearest manifestations of this goal was the introduction of a non-binding shareholder vote on executive pay. In Australia, the relevant provision, s 250R(2) of the Corporations Act 2001 (Cth) ("Corporations Act"), requires shareholders of an Australian listed company to pass a non-binding advisory

---

[2]   No CV 09-1510-PHX-GMS (D. Ariz., 9 June 2010).

vote at its annual general meeting, indicating whether they adopt the directors' remuneration report (Chapple and Christensen 2005; Hill 2005, 413–14). This provision was based on an analogous provision introduced two years earlier in the UK (Ferran 2005, 24–8).

Many other post-Enron reforms relating to executive pay were introduced in Australia under the Corporate Law Economic Reform Program (Audit Reform and Corporate Disclosure) Act 2004 (Sheehan 2009, 275–6). These included enhanced remuneration disclosure, modification of provisions relating to termination pay (Stapledon 2005; Sheehan and Fenwick 2008), and the introduction of a specific non-binding Remuneration Principle under the Australian Securities Exchange (ASX) Corporate Governance Council's *Principles of Good Corporate Governance and Best Practice* exhorting companies to "remunerate fairly and responsibly" (ASX 2003, Principle 9; ASX 2007, Principle 8; Ablen 2003).

3 TWO INTERESTING CURRENT QUESTIONS

3.1 Is Excessive Executive Pay an "American Problem"?

Jurisdictions around the world, including the United States, Australia and the United Kingdom, are again grappling to find an appropriate response to the issue of executive remuneration in the light of the global financial crisis. Two interesting background questions have emerged in this regard.

The first question has particular resonance in the Australian context. The Australian Government Productivity Commission ("Productivity Commission") in its 2009 Issues Paper explicitly raised the issue whether corporate excess, including excessive executive remuneration, is a problem for Australia, or whether it is a "foreign phenomenon" (AGPC 2009, 4). This expression appeared to be code for an "American problem".

Although there have been many strongly convergent trends in executive remuneration in recent years (Ferrarini and Moloney 2005), it is nonetheless an area where culture matters (Levitt 2005). Cultural differences between various jurisdictions are reflected in the design of executive contracts (Hill et al 2011), levels of pay, societal tolerance for income inequality (Henrekson and Jacobsson 2010, 16; Conyon and Murphy 2000, F646–7), and attitudes to remuneration disclosure (Ferrarini and Moloney 2005).

Social norms concerning executive pay can also change across time in a single jurisdiction. It appears, for example, that events such as the Great Depression and World War II greatly affected contemporaneous US social norms regarding income inequality (Piketty and Saez 2003, 34–5; Frydman and Saks 2008). It has been suggested that changes to those norms may explain the steep rises in executive compensation, wealth concentration and income inequality in recent decades (Dew-Becker 2009, 434; Saez 2009, 2; *cf* R.J. Gordon 2009, 31). Some commentators, however, argue that rising inequality has now ceased in the United States (R.J. Gordon 2009, 32).

US executive remuneration rose steadily from the 1970s onwards (Piketty and Saez 2003; Frydman and Saks 2008), but skyrocketed in the 1990s. Between 1993 and 2003, the average CEO compensation at S&P 500 firms increased by 146 percent. During this period, average CEO compensation at S&P 500 firms rose from US$3.7 million to US$9.1 million and the average compensation of the top five executives increased 125 percent from US$9.5 million to US$21.4 million (Bebchuk and Grinstein 2005). The increase in CEO pay levels in real terms greatly outpaced increases in the pay of average US workers. There was a 45 percent growth in CEO pay, compared to 2.7 percent for the average worker (Ebert et al 2008). Pay levels for CEOs have tended to be vastly higher in the United States than in other jurisdictions (R.S. Thomas 2004, 1173–5; *cf* Conyon et al 2011). Commentators have offered a variety of explanations to explain this fact from the divergent standpoints of the arm's length bargaining model and managerial power model of executive pay (Bebchuk and Grinstein 2005, 298–302).

How do levels of executive compensation in the US compare with those in Australia and the United Kingdom? In Australia, the disparity in growth of CEO pay compared to average worker pay was less pronounced. During the last decade, executive salaries in Australia rose approximately three times the amount of ordinary full-time employee wages (Shields 2005, 303). From 2001–07, both the median fixed remuneration (ie non-performance-based elements of Australian CEO pay) and the median total remuneration increased by around 96 percent in total (ACSI 2008). This compared to a 32 percent increase in average Australian adult weekly earnings during the same period (ACSI 2008; AGPC 2009, 9). Nonetheless, there has still been a significant escalation in CEO packages in Australia. The average CEO pay in the top 100 listed Australian companies increased from A$3.77 million in 2005 to A$5.53 million in 2007 (ACSI 2008), though there has been a slight decline in median total disclosed CEO pay since 2007 (ACSI 2010, 5). A common explanation for the steep rise in executive pay is the fact that increasingly, Australian companies need to compete internationally, and now appoint executives from a "mobile worldwide executive talent pool" (Tarrant 2009). Another potentially relevant factor is firm size. Recent US empirical research suggests that, since the mid-1970s, American CEO pay has been strongly correlated with increases in market capitalization (Frydman and Saks 2008; Gabaix and Landier 2008). There has been a dramatic increase in the market capitalization of a number of Australian companies in the last decades. The current market capitalization of BHP Billiton, for example, is $200 billion, compared to $16 billion in 1989 (AGPC 2009a, xviii).

In the United Kingdom, executive pay increased almost four-fold between 1998 and 2009, rising from an average of £1m to £3.7m during that period. CEO remuneration in FTSE100 companies increased by an average of 13.6 percent each year between 1999 and 2009, and has continued to rise in the top UK corporations notwithstanding the global financial crisis (BIS 2010, 26). Although CEO pay in the United States has traditionally been much higher than in the United Kingdom, that gap has narrowed over the last decade (BIS 2010, 27; Conyon et al 2011, 409).

In 2007 the average executive manager in the largest fifteen US firms earned around 500 times more than an average employee in 2007 (International Institute for Labour Studies 2008, 3). The 2008 annual reports of Australia's top fifteen companies revealed that, excluding share-based compensation, the CEOs earned approximately 135 times more than the average Australian employee (Tarrant 2009). In the United Kingdom, from 2002 onwards, CEO remuneration was more than 100 times that of an average employee (BIS 2010, 5–26).

3.2 Did Executive Pay Cause or Contribute to the Global Financial Crisis?

The second interesting current question about executive remuneration is the extent to which it actually caused, or contributed to, the global financial crisis.

Although there was certainly evidence to suggest that executive remuneration practices had played a significant role in the earlier Enron collapse (Coffee 2004, 273–4, 297–8), the widely held view, confirmed by the US regulatory response at that time, was that audit failure was the real culprit (J. Gordon 2002, 1237*ff*; Coffee 2004a, 321*ff*).

If there was scant recognition of the role of executive remuneration in that first financial market shock, the same cannot be said of the current financial crisis. Many commentators have argued that remuneration schemes directly contributed to the crisis by rewarding short-term profit that encouraged excessive risk-taking, particularly in the banking sphere (Avgouleas 2009, 42–5; Bebchuk and Spamann 2010, 255–68; Crotty 2009, 565), although some dissenting voices have now emerged (Core and Guay 2010, 12–13; Fahlenbrach and Stulz 2010; Ferrarini and Ungureanu 2010).

The Australian and US governments have also suggested that a close nexus exists between executive compensation and the global financial crisis. In 2008, the Australian Prime Minister, Kevin Rudd, described the financial crisis as a consequence of "extreme capitalism", characterized by "[o]bscene failures in corporate governance which rewarded greed without any regard to the integrity of the financial system" (Bartlett 2008). The following year, the US Secretary of the Treasury, Timothy Geithner, expressed the view that perverse incentives for short-term gain in compensation contracts had "overwhelmed the checks and balances" designed to address the risk of excessive leverage (Braithwaite 2009). In the United Kingdom, however, the Turner Review was more circumspect. It considered that executive remuneration was a far less important theme in the global financial crisis than other factors, such as inadequate regulation of capital, accounting and liquidity (FSA 2009, 80; AGPC 2009a, 13). The majority report of the recent US Financial Crisis Inquiry Commission viewed the prime factors leading to the crisis as excessive borrowing, high risk investments and lack of transparency, with executive compensation schemes as an important element of general governance failure (FCIC 2011, xix, xxvi).

4　GLOBAL AND NATIONAL REGULATORY DEVELOPMENTS REGARDING EXECUTIVE PAY IN THE GLOBAL FINANCIAL CRISIS ERA

The global financial crisis has generated an unprecedented response to the issue of executive pay at a global level. In 2008, at its first summit on the financial system, the Group of 20 (G-20 2009) stressed the need for greater international co-ordination in monitoring systemic risk and implementing financial market reforms, including in the area of executive compensation (G-20 2009, 32–5).

The reconstituted Financial Stability Board (FSB) (Carrasco 2010) undertook this task, releasing its *Principles for Sound Compensation Practices* for translation into national prudential standards for financial institutions (FSB 2009; G-20 2009, 32–3). The FSB appealed for urgent and coherent action in major financial centres, to "prevent a return to the compensation practices that contributed to the crisis" (FSB 2009a, 1). Increased cross-border regulatory harmonization also offered the promise of reduced risks of regulatory arbitrage (G-20 2009, vi; Basel Committee, 2010, 4). International regulators, such as the G-20 and FSB among others (Pan 2010, 249–58), which have played an important role in the financial crisis, are exemplars of "'regulation beyond the state" (Black 2010, 28), yet there are significant challenges to the effective implementation of this kind of global co-ordinated regulation (Brummer 2011, 290–95).

There has also been a wide array of regulatory responses to perceived problems in executive remuneration at a national level, including in common law jurisdictions, such as the United States, Australia and the United Kingdom. The following section outlines some of the current responses to executive pay and the perceived problem of "extreme capitalism" in these jurisdictions (Bartlett 2008).

4.1　The US Response

In the United States, the reform agenda relating to executive pay has been somewhat byzantine. Although the US response was originally rapid and highly targeted towards institutions receiving federal financial assistance, it later expanded to encompass the corporate sector generally. The US reform proposals, which over time became increasingly complex and overlapping, culminated in the executive compensation provisions of the Wall Street Reform and Consumer Protection Act of 2010 ("Dodd-Frank Act").

The early US reforms were closely tied to emergency federal funding assistance to prevent the failure of financial institutions and restore confidence in US financial markets. Between October 2008 and February 2009, a raft of legislation and guidelines were introduced by the US Treasury and Congress, aimed at controlling executive pay at institutions receiving federal financial assistance under government bail-out programs. These included new rules on executive compensation for participating institutions created in programs under the Emergency Economic Stabilization Act of 2008 ("EESA") (Davis Polk 2008). In February 2009, the US government released guidelines under the EESA, restricting executive pay at companies receiving future federal financial assistance (US Department of the Treasury 2009; Davis Polk 2009) and also enacted the American Recovery and Reinvestment Act of 2009, commonly referred to as the "stimulus bill". Provisions in this Act included additional limitations on executive compensation, demanded by Congress, for institutions participating in the Troubled Asset Relief Program ("TARP"), including a limitation on bonus payments to one third the value of total annual compensation (Bachelder 2009; Morphy 2009).

Another US regulatory approach adopted in the bail-out context was the introduction of governmental pay oversight. In June 2009, the US government appointed Kenneth Feinberg as Special Master for TARP Executive Compensation, or soi-disant "Pay Czar", with authority to review and approve the pay of senior executives at institutions receiving federal financial assistance (Labaton 2009; Office of the Special Master for TARP Executive Compensation 2010). Some commentators have questioned the constitutionality of the appointment (McConnell 2009; Sholette 2010, 237–40), which was described by the financial press as a "hard-to-believe turn" for the US "market economy" (Opinion 2009), and evidence of the federal government's "increasingly visible hand in corporate affairs" (Story and Labaton 2009).

From mid-2009 onwards, US reform proposals broadened, in both their scope and application. These later reform proposals related not only to executive pay, but also to the issues of shareholder power and corporate governance generally, and their application was not restricted to institutions receiving bail-out funding. The earlier TARP reforms had proved to be merely the tip of the regulatory iceberg, serving as a blueprint for more general reforms in the corporate sector.

Shareholder empowerment was a central, and particularly divisive, aspect of these recent US corporate governance reforms (Hill 2010). The need to restore market trust after the global financial crisis emerged as a rationale for stronger shareholder rights (Bratton and Wachter 2010, 656–7). This new policy thread underpinned several reform proposals in 2009, such as the Shareholder Bill of Rights, which sought to increase shareholder powers to counteract extreme risk-taking and excessive executive compensation (Schumer 2009). Some provisions of the Shareholder Bill of Rights related directly to executive remuneration in public companies, such as a mandatory annual non-binding shareholder vote on executive compensation. Others, including elimination of staggered boards, separation of the position of CEO and chairman, and presence of a risk committee, were more general in nature (US Senate 2009). Some, but not all, of these provisions found their way into the Restoring American Financial Stability Acts of 2009 and 2010 (Davis Polk 2009a, Sandler 2010). The problem of risk-taking in financial organisations was also addressed in a remuneration guidance, *Guidance on Sound Incentive Compensation Policies*, issued by the Federal Reserve in co-operation with other US banking agencies in June 2010 (Federal Reserve et al 2010). This guidance is principles-based and accords with the FSB's *Principles for Sound Compensation Practices* (Federal Reserve et al 2010, 9–10).

Another high profile general reform proposal involved granting shareholders access to the company's proxy materials to nominate directors (Bebchuk 2003). This reform proposal was included in the Shareholder Bill of Rights, and received Securities and Exchange Commission (SEC) endorsement in a vote by Commissioners in May 2009 to propose Rule 14a-11 (SEC 2009). The debate surrounding this particular reform has been aptly described as a "knockdown, drag out political brawl" (Grundfest 2010, 378). The brawl is an ongoing one. After the SEC released its final rules conferring limited proxy access in August 2010 (SEC 2010; SEC 2010a), US business groups commenced legal proceedings against the SEC to have the rules overturned (Eaglesham 2010; US Chamber of Commerce 2010). This was in spite of the fact that many commentators considered that the SEC's final rules would deliver only negligible benefits to shareholders (Editorial 2010; Plender, 2010).

The compensation provisions of the Dodd-Frank Act, which was signed into law on 21 July 2010, represent the statutory finale to these reform developments. Key features of this Act's reforms include: a "say on pay" provision, requiring a periodic advisory shareholder vote on executive pay (s 951); new disclosure rules for golden parachute payments in connection with certain change-of-control transactions, together with a non-binding shareholder vote on such payments (s 951);[3] a clawback provision (s 954); and disclosure requirements concerning policies on hedging by directors and employees (s 955). The Dodd-Frank Act also affirmed the SEC's power to adopt proxy access rules (s 971), which, as noted above, became the subject of a strong legal challenge (Lipton 2011).

These provisions of the Dodd-Frank Act have, predictably, elicited criticism. Some commentators have condemned the Act on the basis that it empowers shareholder activists, interferes with board discretion, and continues an illegitimate trend of federal encroachment into the traditionally state-based domain of US corporate law (Bainbridge 2010; Lipton 2011). Yet, the Act is in fact a substantially diluted version of earlier reform proposals, and relatively modest in its regulatory constraints compared to trends in Australia and the United Kingdom. In contrast to those jurisdictions, for example, the Dodd-Frank Act does not require an annual advisory shareholder vote on executive pay. Rather, shareholders may determine that the vote occur every one, two or three years, and must have the opportunity to cast a vote on this frequency issue at least once every six years. Also, some crucial corporate governance reform proposals appeared to evaporate along the legislative path to the Dodd-Frank Act. Unlike earlier reform proposals, the Act contains no majority voting requirement or constraints on staggered boards. These striking omissions have led one commentator to describe the Dodd-Frank Act as a "triumph of business lobbying" (Plender 2010).

4.2   The Australian Response

Australia's response to the issue of executive compensation has been broad and multifaceted (Hill 2009, 104–5), in spite of the fact that the global financial crisis has had a far less serious effect on the Australian economy than in many other Western jurisdictions (AGPC 2009a, 34; Ferran 2010, 10).

The first significant regulatory response was undertaken by the Australian Prudential Regulation Authority ("APRA"), which is the prudential supervisor for deposit-taking and other financial institutions under Australia's "twin peak" regulatory structure (Trowbridge 2009). This response was designed to implement the FSB Principles and involved an extension of APRA's existing prudential standards to impose additional requirements on boards of financial institutions concerning executive compensation (APRA 2008; APRA 2009).

The APRA guidelines on executive remuneration (APRA 2009a) are principles-based, and constitute a more intense form of government monitoring of executive pay than has applied in Australia to date (Sheehan 2009). The policy justification for the guidelines is to ensure that risks associated with executive pay are prudently managed (APRA 2009a, 3), yet it has been suggested that the problem of excessive risk-taking in the finance indus-

---

[3]   The SEC issued proposed rules on 18 October 2010 implementing the "say on pay" and provisions regarding golden-parachute payments under s 951 of the Dodd-Frank Act, which adds s 14A to the Securities Exchange Act of 1934 (SEC 2011). On 25 January 2011, the SEC introduced its final rules, which closely tracked the contours of the proposed rules, with some minor modifications (SEC 2011, SEC 2011a).

try was far less pronounced in Australia than in many other countries (AGPC 2009a, xxv).

The APRA guidelines introduce industry-specific regulation of executive pay. In a related initiative, the Productivity Commission undertook a more general review of the remuneration framework for directors and executives under the Corporations Act. The Productivity Commission's final report, *Executive Remuneration in Australia*, was released in December 2009 (AGPC 2009a). The Productivity Commission made seventeen recommendations in total, the majority of which relate to ensuring procedural integrity of the pay-setting process and to shareholder approval, increased disclosure and reporting requirements (Banks 2009).

One interesting issue addressed by the Productivity Commission was the non-binding shareholder vote under s 250R(2) of the Corporations Act. Although this provision was controversial and strongly opposed by the business community at the time of its introduction in 2004 (AGPC 2009a, 281), the Productivity Commission considered that it had been successful in the goal of fostering "more productive engagement between shareholders and boards" (AGPC 2009a, 277, 282).

Significant shareholder protest votes tended to be far more common in Australia than in the United Kingdom, at least until the onset of the global financial crisis (Hill 2008, 829–37; Burgess and Steen 2009), and there are many examples of Australian companies that have amended their remuneration practices in response to such votes (AGPC 2009a, 282). Nonetheless, the Productivity Commission expressed concern that some companies continued to be non-responsive to shareholder views. In 2008–09, for example, approximately 5 percent of ASX 200 companies received consecutive "no" votes of 25 percent or more (AGPC 2009a, 283). The Productivity Commission sought to strengthen the consequences of a significant "no" vote, via a "two strikes and re-election resolution" recommendation (AGPC 2009a, xl, 294*ff*). Under this proposed reform, a 25 percent "no" vote on the remuneration report would trigger a formal obligation on the board to explain how shareholder concerns were being addressed (AGPC 2009a, 295). Two consecutive "no" votes of 25 percent or more would activate a separate "re-election" resolution, which, if successful, would require all elected directors who signed the remuneration report to submit to re-election at an extraordinary general meeting to be held within 90 days (AGPC 2009a, xxxii).

In April 2010, the Australian government responded to the Productivity Commission, supporting virtually all its recommendations, including the controversial "two strikes and re-election resolution" proposal. The government recommended further strengthening of the proposals relating to the legitimacy of the non-binding remuneration vote, and also announced that it would consider the introduction of an additional claw-back provision (Minister for Financial Services 2010). The government referred certain matters raised by the Productivity Commission to the Corporations and Markets Advisory Commission ("CAMAC") for further consideration. These matters related to the effect of complexity and lack of transparency in relation to reporting requirements under the Corporations Act and also in the context of intricate performance-based pay schemes (CAMAC 2010, 1–2).

The approach of the Productivity Commission and the Australian government to addressing perceived problems with executive pay provides a sharp regulatory contrast to that of the Australian Institute of Company Directors in guidelines on executive pay

("AICD guidelines") released in early 2009 (AICD 2009). These guidelines reflected a strong preference by the business sector for self-regulation (AICD 2009, 5), and were clearly an attempt to forestall more intense government regulation. The AICD guidelines focused predominantly on the process for determining executive remuneration, and on the terms and structure of compensation packages (AICD 2009, 6, 12–25). The Australian Shareholders' Association also released a policy statement on executive remuneration at that time, predicting greater government intervention in the event of failure by the corporate sector to respond to public concerns over executive pay (ASA 2009).

Finally, Australia has introduced a number of specific legislative reforms and reform proposals in relation to executive pay. The Corporations Amendment (Improving Accountability on Termination Payments) Act 2009 was passed to address concerns about "golden handshakes" (Sheehan and Fenwick 2008; Paatsch and Lawrence 2008). This Act provides greater constraints on such payments, by capping a director's termination pay at one year's average base salary – a significant reduction from the previous seven year threshold – unless shareholder approval is obtained. In December 2010, the Federal government released an exposure draft of the Corporations Amendment (Improving Accountability on Director and Executive Remuneration) Bill 2011, implementing several recommendations of the Productivity Commission, including the controversial "two strikes and re-election resolution" recommendation. The explicit goal of this Bill was to provide more power to shareholders and to enhance "transparency, disclosure and accountability" in the area of executive pay (Parliamentary Secretary to the Treasurer 2010). In conjunction with release of the Bill, which was subsequently enacted into law in mid-2011, the government also published a discussion paper on a claw-back proposal for executive remuneration (Australian Government 2010).

4.3 The UK Response

In the period prior to the global financial crisis, the London Stock Exchange had acquired considerable cachet as a centre for international capital raising (Furse 2006). The Financial Services Authority ("FSA") was admired for its "light touch" style of regulation, which had elevated principles-based supervision to "a regulatory art form" (Black 2010a, 3; *cf* Cunningham 2007; Kershaw 2005). The rise of London as a financial centre led to intense US–UK regulatory competition (Pritchard 2009, 24*ff*; Black 2010a, 12). The challenge to New York's historical dominance caused consternation in the United States, and prompted several reviews to consider the decline of US competitiveness in financial markets (Committee on Capital Markets Regulation 2006, xi; McKinsey 2007).

Yet, by 2008, the picture had altered fundamentally. The collapse of Northern Rock (FSA 2008) sent regulatory shock-waves around UK financial markets (Black 2010a, 15). It tarnished London's much vaunted principles-based regulatory system, (Masters 2008; Begg 2009, 1108; Ferran 2010, 3) and prompted the FSA to shift towards a more intensive, "outcome based" system of oversight (Black 2010a, 3, 13–19; Ferran 2010, 17–18, 26; Sants 2010, 1).

The UK regulatory response to the global financial crisis initially focused particularly on the banking and financial sector, which required massive government funding to avert collapse (HM Treasury 2009). Two influential reviews commissioned by the government at that time set the tone for many subsequent UK regulatory developments.

The first of these reports was the Turner Review into the global banking crisis (FSA 2009). This review was established to assess whether regulatory deficiencies were a contributing factor to the financial crisis and to make reform proposals. According to the review, the global financial crisis challenged a central assumption concerning the market's efficiency, rationality and ability to self-regulate that had underpinned prior financial law (Avgouleas 2009a; FSA 2009, 39*ff*; Benjamin 2010; Ferran 2010, 8; *cf* Boettke 2010, 373–74). The review, which has been described as a watershed for UK finance (Wolf 2009), recommended radical strengthening of financial system regulation and supervision, including increased capital requirements. Executive compensation constituted an important feature of the Turner Review. The review considered that in the past bank regulators around the world had paid insufficient attention to remuneration structure and its potential for creating unacceptable incentives for risk-taking (FSA 2009, 79–81). In conjunction with the Turner Review, the FSA also released a draft code on remuneration practice (FSA 2009a). This Remuneration Code was subsequently finalized, and applied from early 2010 onwards to approximately 26 of the largest banks, building societies and broker dealers operating in the United Kingdom (FSA 2009b).

The second important UK report was the Walker Review, which was released in late 2009 (Walker Review 2009). This report focused on improving general corporate governance in the banking and financial sector, with specific measures to strengthen boards (Walker Review 2009, 14–17) and to increase institutional investor activism as a protective mechanism (17–19). The Review recommended the adoption of a Stewardship Code to enhance dialogue between institutional investors and their companies, and to reduce the danger of future financial market collapses (Walker Review 2009, 153).

These two reviews have formed the basis for many important subsequent UK reform initiatives. Some recommendations of the Walker Review, for example, have been realized by the FRC's implementation in 2010 of the UK Stewardship Code (FRC 2010; FRC 2010a) and the UK Corporate Governance Code for listed companies (FRC 2010b). These two codes operate on a principles-based, "comply or explain" basis (FRC 2010b, 4–5). Shareholder participation in corporate governance occupies a central role in these reforms.

The Stewardship Code (FRC 2010; FRC 2010a) comprises seven principles that seek to place greater monitoring responsibility on shareholders (Black 2010a, 16; Plender 2010), although the code makes clear that compliance with its directives by shareholders "does not constitute an invitation to manage the affairs of investee companies" (FRC 2010, 1). The code also provides that institutional investors should establish clear guidelines for escalating activism and be prepared to act collectively (FRC 2010, 7–8). In spite of its worthy aspirational goal of producing more engaged shareholders, some commentators are sceptical of the Stewardship Code's ability to achieve this in view of modern shareholder fragmentation and the high proportion of foreign investors in the UK equity market (Cheffins 2010; Plender 2010; Reisberg 2010).

Greater shareholder engagement and dialogue is also an important feature of the Corporate Governance Code (FRC 2010b, 1), which replaces the earlier 2008 Combined Code on Corporate Governance (FRC 2010c). Enhanced shareholder power has generally been a far less contentious issue in the United Kingdom than in the United States. Yet, one provision in the Corporate Governance Code has proven particularly controversial in this respect. Code provision B.7.1 states that all directors of FTSE 350 companies should be submitted for re-election annually (FRC 2010b, 17), further strengthening the position of shareholders in the director selection process (FRC 2010c, 3–5). The Corporate Governance Code also includes new provisions specifically relating to executive pay levels, components and pay-setting procedures (FRC 2010b, 22–24, 27).

A related statutory reform was the Financial Services Act 2010 (FSA 2010). This Act gave the FSA a new regulatory objective of promoting financial stability (s 1(3A)). Other significant provisions include a section empowering the Treasury to make regulations about preparation and disclosure of executives' remuneration reports (s 4), thereby extending the prior UK disclosure regime, which was limited to directors of quoted companies. The Act expanded the FSA's rule making and enforcement powers in relation to executive pay, requiring the FSA to ensure that firms have, and comply with, remuneration policies that are consistent with effective risk management. In particular, the Act gave the FSA authority to prohibit specified types of remuneration and to void contracts or contractual provisions that violate its rules (s 6). Interestingly, when these reforms were originally proposed, the UK business community raised similar arguments to those used in the US context following the enactment of the Sarbanes-Oxley Act, forecasting the decline of UK competitiveness in financial markets (Groom 2009).

These UK reform initiatives have had a cumulative effect. They have also been shaped by international and European developments, in the push for jurisdictional harmonization (Black 2010a, 21–2). In December 2010, the FSA published revisions to its remuneration code ("Revised Remuneration Code"). These revisions were designed to take account of a range of developments such as the Walker Review, the Financial Services Act 2010, and the need to comply with the European Parliament's Capital Requirements Directive ("CRD III"),[4] in conjunction with related guidelines of the Committee of European Banking Supervisors ("CEBS Guidelines on Remuneration Policies and Practices") (CEBS 2010).

The scope of the UK remuneration code was drastically altered by the December 2010 revisions. Whereas the previous code governed only around 26 large financial institutions, the Revised Remuneration Code applies to around 2,700 financial firms, including all banks, building societies and investment firms (FSA 2010b). The Revised Remuneration Code establishes four different tiers of firm, for which different minimum compliance expectations will apply (Cleary Gottlieb 2010, 3; FSA 2010a, [3.23]–[3.24]). More stringent requirements attach to certain persons classified as "Code Staff", who have a major influence on the firm or significant impact on its risk profile (Cleary Gottlieb 2010, 4–5; FSA 2010a, [1.15]). The Revised Remuneration Code also includes certain specific restrictions on remuneration design (Cleary Gottlieb 2010, 5–6).

The relentless interest in executive remuneration in the United Kingdom seems unlikely to abate any time soon. In October 2010, the UK Secretary of State for Business announced a review into short-termism and market failures in UK equity markets, with executive remuneration as one of the key issues on the table for discussion (BIS 2010; Rigby and Barker 2010; Thomson and MacDonald 2010).

One surprising casualty of the global financial crisis is the FSA, which played such a

---

[4]   CRD III implements the FSB's *Principles for Sound Compensation Practices* (Cleary Gottlieb 2010; FSA 2010a, 5; Murphy and Masters 2010).

prominent role in responding to the disaster (Moore 2009). In mid-2010, the UK government announced its intention to transfer overall control of prudential regulation of financial markets to the Bank of England (HM Treasury 2010; HM Treasury 2010a), in a regulatory overhaul that signified a "dramatic fall from grace" for the FSA (Ferran 2010, 3). In spite of the FSA's original commitment to principles-based regulation, its ultimate legacy in responding to the global financial crisis, aided by EU requirements, is an intensive, rules-based form of market supervision in the United Kingdom (Sants 2010, 3).

5   CENTRAL REGULATORY THEMES

A number of central themes emerge from the panoply of regulatory responses and reform proposals outlined above. These themes, many of which are interconnected, include: (i) risk-based approach to executive pay; (ii) long-term focus and sustainability; (iii) re-evaluation of the concept of interest alignment in executive pay; (iv) re-evaluation of performance measures; and (v) income inequality.

5.1   Risk and Executive Pay

Risk has become a hallmark of the global financial crisis (IMF 2008, ix*ff*; Schwarcz 2008; Department of the Treasury 2009, 5, 19). It has been claimed that specific risk-related problems included use of financial innovation to detach risks from returns (IMF 2008, xii; Benjamin 2010, 812) and to create excessive leverage (Department of the Treasury 2009, 5, 19; Blair 2010), which distorted incentives (Carmassi et al 2009). The shift in recent decades from public to private pension or superannuation funding for retirement has magnified the public's exposure to financial market risk (Benjamin 2010, 800).

Risk is also a major theme in contemporary regulatory debate concerning executive compensation. This is particularly the case in relation to financial institutions, which have been singled out as representing a special case under a risk-based approach. Professor Lucian Bebchuk has argued, for example, that enhanced regulation of pay in financial institutions is justified on the basis of moral hazard concerns, and because failure of such institutions imposes substantial costs on taxpayers (Bebchuk 2009). An analogous argument was used in 2009 by the Chancellor of the Exchequer to justify a temporary bank payroll tax in the United Kingdom, on the basis that:

> [I]f banks choose to make awards that are not consistent with a prudent approach to risk, it is only fair that they contribute more to the public finances in a year when profits have been facilitated by significant taxpayer support of the banking sector as a whole. (HM Treasury 2009a, 44)

The current reassessment involves the idea that executive pay, rather than being a corporate governance tool, has itself become a risk management problem. Both the Australian Productivity Commission and the UK Turner Review alluded to the dangers posed by remuneration packages with design features that create unacceptable incentives for risk-taking (AGPC 2009a, iv; FSA 2009a, 79–81). This message also pervades the

CEBS Guidelines on Remuneration Policies and Practices (CEBS 2010, 37–8), and the Revised Remuneration Code (FSA 2010a, 8).

In the United States, the Dodd-Frank Act requires appropriate Federal regulators to jointly prescribe regulations prohibiting any type of incentive arrangement that the regulators determine encourages "inappropriate risks" by covered financial institutions in certain circumstances (s 956(2)(b)). According to the *Guidance on Sound Incentive Compensation Policies* issued by the Federal Reserve and other US banking agencies, "it is important that incentive compensation arrangements at banking organizations do not provide incentives for employees to take risks that could jeopardize the safety and soundness of the organization" (Federal Reserve et al 2010, 7).

5.2   Short-Termism Versus Long-Termism

Many recent regulatory responses and proposals relate to the theme of short-termism, which is closely allied with that of risk (Hill 1999, 1123–5; Federal Reserve et al 2010, 3, 23). Here, the concern is that the design of executive remuneration, particularly in the banking industry, created incentives for short-term profit while simultaneously creating long-term organisational risks (Federal Reserve et al 2010, 3, 23; *cf* Ferrarini and Ungureanu 2010).

The Walker Review perceived short-term performance pressures to be a significant and growing problem in the United Kingdom (Walker Review 2009, 27). The search for a solution to the problem of short-termism in the context of executive pay is central to the BIS consultation paper, *A Long-Term Focus for Corporate Britain* (BIS 2010). In Australia, the Productivity Commission, although acknowledging the danger of short-term incentives, considered the problem to be less pervasive in Australia than in some other jurisdictions (AGPC 2009a, xxv).

Promotion of sustainable corporate performance is, therefore, the new goal in executive remuneration. The UK Corporate Governance Code introduces a provision stipulating that performance conditions in executive pay should promote long-term corporate success (FRC 2010b, 22, 27). According to the Walker Review, executive pay can be designed to foster this goal by, for example, increasing the portion of total remuneration tied to long-term outcomes, and ensuring redress via claw-backs for bonuses based on inaccurate financial data (Walker Review 2009, 27).

Recent academic literature has also stressed the need for executives to be compensated on a long-term basis, and has called for mandatory holding periods of equity-based compensation (Bhagat and Romano 2009; Bebchuk and Fried 2010). This approach is adopted in a number of recent reforms. The UK Corporate Governance Code, for example, supports phased and deferred vesting of shares and options, stating that normally such forms of remuneration should not vest or be exercisable in less than three years, and that directors should be encouraged to hold stock for a further period after vesting (FRC 2010a, 27). Under the UK Revised Remuneration Code, a firm should not pay variable remuneration unless at least 40 percent (or 60 percent for variable remuneration over £500,000) is deferred for not less than three to five years (FSA 2010b, Appendix 1, 25).

Claw-backs, another regulatory constraint on short-termism, appear as a regulatory mechanism in many recent reforms. The UK Corporate Governance Code, for example, provides that consideration should be given to use of claw-back provisions "in exceptional circumstances of misstatement or misconduct" (FRC 2010b, 27; FRC 2010c, 8). Section 954 of the Dodd-Frank Act requires the SEC to ensure that all listed public companies have a claw-back policy, irrespective of whether fraud or misconduct is involved (s 954; Bainbridge 2010, 26–7; Lublin 2010; H. Thomas 2010). The introduction of a claw-back requirement is also on the regulatory drawing board in Australia (Australian Government 2010; Kitney 2010).

Finally, there is increased recognition of the dangers of hedging, and its ability to subvert incentives and "just deserts" in the design of executive pay (Bebchuk and Fried 2010, 1951*ff*). Section 955 of the Dodd-Frank Act introduces disclosure requirements concerning issuer policies on hedging by directors and employees. Australia's 2011 remuneration reforms go further, however, by actually prohibiting hedging in relation to executive compensation packages (Parliamentary Secretary to the Treasurer 2010).

5.3   Re-evaluation of the Concept of Interest Alignment in Executive Pay

The "alignment of interests" paradigm for executive pay, which became dominant over the last two decades, sought to solve the agency problem between management and shareholders by using remuneration techniques to align their interests.

Following the global credit crisis, however, the rhetoric accompanying the alignment goals of executive remuneration has shifted, and alignment with shareholder interests is no longer necessarily treated as the sole touchstone. The US Treasury, for example, stated that the EESA guidelines were designed to ensure that remuneration of executives in the financial community be aligned not only with the interests of shareholders and financial institutions, but also with the interests of taxpayers providing financial assistance to those institutions (US Department of the Treasury 2009). The US *Guidance on Sound Incentive Compensation Policies* explicitly rejects the adequacy of a shareholder-centred approach to interest alignment in financial institutions, on the basis that shareholders may tolerate a higher level of risk than accords with the organization's soundness (Bebchuk 2009; Federal Reserve et al 2010, 2).

The Australian government's response to the global financial crisis is explicitly based on the need to promote a regulatory framework which better aligns managerial interests with the interests of shareholders and "the community" (AGPC 2009, iv; Minister for Financial Services 2010). The AICD Guidelines also reflect this rhetorical shift. They note the importance of gauging public sentiment concerning executive pay, and considering whether remuneration packages are publicly defendable and affect corporate reputation (AICD 2009, 29–31).

There is a potential tension between this broader, public approach to interest alignment and the increasing focus on shareholder power as a regulatory technique under, for example, "say on pay" reforms and the UK Stewardship Code.

5.4   Re-evaluation of Performance Measures

As a corollary to the burgeoning risk-based/long-term approach to executive pay, there has been a re-evaluation of appropriate measures of performance. The current regulatory responses to the issue of executive pay strongly favour the adoption of demanding performance measures that promote long-term and sustainable goals, with an increased focus on non-financial performance criteria. The UK Corporate Governance Code states that performance hurdles should, where appropriate, include use of non-financial metrics (FRC 2010b, 27). Performance measurement also features prominently in the CEBS Guidelines on Remuneration Policies and Practices, which assert that institutions should use both quantitative (financial) and qualitative (non-financial) criteria in performance assessment. According to the CEBS Guidelines, negative qualitative performance, such as unethical behaviour, should trump positive financial performance (CEBS 2010, 52, 53). In Australia, the AICD guidelines contemplate performance assessment on both financial and non-financial criteria, and use improved workplace safety as an example of a non-financial performance metric that might be appropriate for some companies (AICD 2009, 19).

There is also a trend toward simplifying executive remuneration disclosure to ensure that there is a demonstrable link between executive pay and performance. The BIS consultation paper, *A Long-Term Focus for Corporate Britain*, alludes to concern that provision of overly detailed information about executive pay may, in fact, create a barrier to effective disclosure (BIS 2010, 28). The Productivity Commission considered that the length and complexity of remuneration reports in Australia had compromised their utility to investors (AGPC 2009, xxx), and this matter is currently under review for possible reform (CAMAC 2011).

5.5   Income Inequality

The issue of income inequality arises in a number of the regulatory responses to executive pay. The Australian Shareholders' Association has stated that the gap between the pay of Australian CEOs and the general workforce has become "huge", and is the subject of justifiable criticism (ASA 2009). The Productivity Commission raised the prospect that large internal disparities between executives' pay and average earnings might "demotivate" employees and affect the wider community (AGPC 2009a, 12).

The issue of income disparity also has great resonance in the United Kingdom, with the Corporate Governance Code cautioning that the remuneration committee should be "sensitive to pay and employment conditions elsewhere in the group" (BIS 2010, 28; FRC 2010b, 22). A recent UK interim report, the *Hutton Review of Fair Pay in the Public Sector*, suggests that there is a strong case, on a fairness rationale, for the introduction of a maximum pay multiple, such as 20:1 for public sector organizations, and there have been calls for the review to be extended to cover the private sector (Hutton Review 2010, 11; Pickard and Rigby 2010).

New SEC disclosure rules also touch on this issue. Under s 953 of the Dodd-Frank Act, the SEC must require companies regularly to disclose the ratio of median annual pay of all employees to that of the CEO, a reform that potentially creates incentives for outsourcing (Business Life 2010; Eaglesham 2010a).

6   CONCLUSION

We are in the midst of a complex, and developing, story about executive remuneration, corporate governance and regulation generally. The current focus on executive pay reflects the fact that, as a result of the global financial crisis, business once again has "a legitimacy problem" (Plender 2008). The crisis has also prompted a remarkable level of government intervention in financial markets, particularly in the United States and United Kingdom.

An unprecedented range of reforms concerning executive pay have been introduced, or are in train, around the world. Yet, regulation is not a one way street. Rather, it is a dynamic and relational process (Milhaupt and Pistor 2008, 6; Skeel 2008, 696), and these remuneration developments will inevitably engender some forms of strategic commercial pushback (Hill 2010). There is also new upward pressure on executive pay on Wall Street, with an overall 5 percent increase in executive pay in the US financial services industry in 2010 (Craig 2010). It is, as yet, too soon to tell whether the regulatory responses to the global financial crisis will result in a long-term cultural shift in relation to executive pay in the common law jurisdictions discussed in this paper.

REFERENCES

Ablen, David. 2003. Remunerating "Fairly and Responsibly" – the "Principles of Good Corporate Governance and Best Practice Recommendations" of the ASX Corporate Governance Council, *Sydney Law Review* 25: 555–66.
ACSI. 2008. Australian Council of Super Investors, Media Release, *Top 100 CEO Pay Research Released.*
ACSI. 2010. Australian Council of Super Investors, *CEO Pay in the Top 100 Companies: 2009.*
AGPC. 2009. Australian Government Productivity Commission, Issues Paper, *Regulation of Director and Executive Remuneration in Australia.*
AGPC. 2009a. Australian Government Productivity Commission, Productivity Commission Inquiry Report No. 49, *Executive Remuneration in Australia.*
AICD. 2009. Australian Institute of Company Directors, *Executive Remuneration: Guidelines for Listed Company Boards.*
APRA. 2008. Australian Prudential Regulation Authority, Media Release No 08-32, *APRA Outlines Approach on Executive Remuneration.*
APRA. 2009. Australian Prudential Regulation Authority, Discussion Paper, *Remuneration: Proposed Extensions to Governance Requirements for APRA-Regulated Institutions.*
APRA. 2009a. Australian Prudential Regulation Authority, *Prudential Practice Guide: PPG 511 – Remuneration.*
ASA. 2009. Australia Shareholders' Association, *Executive Remuneration, ASA Policy Statement.*
ASX. 2003. Australia Securities Exchange (ASX) Corporate Governance Council, *Principles of Good Corporate Governance and Best Practice Recommendations.*
ASX. 2007. Australia Securities Exchange (ASX) Corporate Governance Council, *Revised Corporate Governance Principles and Recommendations* (2nd edition).
Australian Government. 2010. Discussion Paper, *The Clawback of Executive Remuneration Where Financial Statements are Materially Misstated.*
Avgouleas, Emilios. 2009. The Global Financial Crisis, Behavioural Finance and Financial Regulation: In Search of a New Orthodoxy, *Journal of Corporate Law Studies* 9: 23–59.
Avgouleas, Emilios. 2009a. The Global Financial Crisis and the Disclosure Paradigm in European Financial Regulation: The Case for Reform, *European Company and Financial Law Review* 6: 440–75.
Bachelder, Joseph E. 2009. Executive Compensation under TARP, *The Harvard Law School Forum on Corporate Governance and Financial Regulation*, 28 April.
Bainbridge, Stephen M. 2010. Dodd-Frank: Quack Federal Corporate Governance Round II, UCLA School of Law, Law-Econ Research Paper No. 10-12, available at SSRN: http://papers.ssrn.com/sol3/papers.cfm?abstract_id=1673575.

Banks, Gary. 2009. Australian Government Productivity Commission, *Executive Pay: Economic Issues from the Commission's Report, Speech to the Economics Society of Australia.*

Bartlett, Lawrence. 2008. Global crisis "failure of extreme capitalism": Australian PM, Agence France Presse, 15 October.

Basel Committee on Banking Supervision. 2010. The Joint Forum, *Review of the Differentiated Nature and Scope of Financial Regulation: Key Issues and Recommendations.*

Bebchuk, Lucian. 2003. The Case for Shareholder Access to the Ballot, *Business Lawyer* 59: 43–66.

Bebchuk, Lucian. 2009. Regulate Financial Pay to Reduce Risk-taking, *Financial Times* (UK), 4 August, p. 7.

Bebchuk, Lucian and Jesse Fried. 2010. Paying for Long-Term Performance, *University of Pennsylvania Law Review* 158: 1915–59.

Bebchuk, Lucian and Yaniv Grinstein. 2005. The Growth of Executive Pay, *Oxford Review of Economic Policy* 21: 283–303.

Bebchuk, Lucian and Holger Spamann. 2010. Regulating Bankers' Pay, *Georgetown Law Journal* 98: 247–87.

Bebchuk, Lucian, Jesse Fried and David Walker. 2002. Managerial Power and Rent Extraction in the Design of Executive Compensation, *The University of Chicago Law Review* 69: 751–846.

Begg, Iain. 2009. Regulation and Supervision of Financial Intermediaries in the EU: The Aftermath of the Financial Crisis, *Journal of Common Market Studies* 47: 1107–28.

Benjamin, Joanna. 2010. The Narratives of Financial Law, *Oxford Journal of Legal Studies* 30: 787–814.

Bhagat, Sanjai and Roberta Romano. 2009. Reforming Executive Compensation: Focusing and Committing to the Long-Term, *Yale Journal on Regulation* 26: 359–72.

BIS. 2010. Department for Business Innovation & Skills, *A Long-Term Focus for Corporate Britain: A Call for Evidence.*

Black, Julia. 2010. Empirical Legal Studies in Financial Markets: What Have We Learned? LSE Law, Society and Economy Working Papers 4/2010, available at: www.lse.ac.uk/collections/law/wps/wps1.htm.

Black, Julia. 2010a. The Rise, Fall and Fate of Principles Based Regulation, LSE Legal Studies Working Paper No. 17/2010, available at SSRN: http://papers.ssrn.com/sol3/papers.cfm?abstract_id=1712862.

Blair, Margaret M. 2010. Financial Innovation, Leverage, Bubbles, and the Distribution of Income, Vanderbilt Public Law Research Paper No. 10-40, available at SSRN: http://papers.ssrn.com/sol3/papers.cfm?abstract_id=1693913.

Boettke, Peter. 2010. What Happened to "Efficient Markets"? *The Independent Review* 14: 363–75.

Braithwaite, Tom. 2009. US will Appoint "Pay Tsar" to Vet Executive Packages, *Financial Times* (UK), 11 June, p. 6.

Bratton, William W. and Michael L. Wachter. 2010. The Case Against Shareholder Empowerment, *University of Pennsylvania Law Review* 158: 653–728.

Brummer, Chris. 2011. How International Financial Law Works (and How It Doesn't), *Georgetown Law Journal* 99: 257–327.

Burgess, Kate and Michael Steen. 2009. Shell's Executive Pay Plan Voted Down in Shareholder Rebellion, *Financial Times*, 20 May, p. 15.

Business Life. 2010. Should Companies Be Forced to Reveal CEO Pay Ratios? *Financial Times* (UK), 8 September, p. 14.

CAMAC. 2010. Corporations and Markets Advisory Committee, Information Paper, *Executive Remuneration.*

CAMAC. 2011. Corporations and Markets Advisory Committee, Report, *Executive Remuneration.*

Carmassi, Jacopo, Daniel Gros and Stefano Micossi. 2009. The Global Financial Crisis: Causes and Cures, *Journal of Common Market Studies* 47: 977–96.

Carrasco, Enrique. 2010. The Global Financial Crisis and the Financial Stability Forum: The Awakening and Transformation of an International Body, *Transnational Law & Contemporary Problems* 19: 203–20.

CEBS. 2010. Committee of European Banking Supervisors, *Guidelines on Remuneration Policies and Practices.*

Chandler, William B. and Leo E. Strine Jr. 2003. The New Federalism of the American Corporate Governance System: Preliminary Reflections of Two Residents of One Small State, *University of Pennsylvania Law Review* 152: 953–1006.

Chapple, Larelle and Blake Christensen. 2005. The Non-Binding Vote on Executive Pay: A Review of the CLERP 9 Reform, *Australian Journal of Corporate Law* 18: 263–87.

Cheffins, Brian R. 2010. The Stewardship Code's Achilles Heel, *The Modern Law Review* 73: 1004–25.

Cleary Gottlieb. 2010. *The Revised FSA Remuneration Code.*

Coffee, John. 2004. What Caused Enron? A Capsule Social and Economic History of the 1990s, *Cornell Law Review* 89: 269–309.

Coffee, John. 2004a. Gatekeeper Failure and Reform: The Challenge of Fashioning Relevant Reforms, *Boston University Law Review* 84: 301–64.

Committee on Capital Markets Regulation. 2006. *Interim Report of the Committee on Capital Markets Regulation* (revised version released 5 December 2006).

Conyon, Martin and Kevin Murphy. 2000. The Prince and the Pauper? CEO Pay in the United States and United Kingdom, *The Economic Journal* 110: F640–F671.

Conyon, Martin J., John E. Core and Wayne R. Guay. 2011. Are US CEOs Paid More Than UK CEOs? Inferences from Risk-adjusted Pay, *The Review of Financial Studies* 24: 402–38.

Core, John E. and Wayne R. Guay. 2010. Is There a Case for Regulating Executive Pay in the Financial Services Industry? Working Paper, available at SSRN: http://papers.ssrn.com/sol3/papers.cfm?abstract_id=1544104.

Core, John E., Wayne R. Guay and David Larcker. 2003. Executive Equity Compensation and Incentives: A Survey, *Economic Policy Review* 9: 27–50.

Craig, Susanne. 2010. Wall Street Gets Its Groove Back, and Big Pay, Too, *New York Times*, 4 November, p. 1.

Crotty, James. 2009. Structural Causes of the Global Financial Crisis: A Critical Assessment of the "New Financial Architecture", *Cambridge Journal of Economics* 33: 563–80.

Cunningham, Lawrence. 2007. A Prescription to Retire the Rhetoric of "Principles-Based Systems" in Corporate Law, Securities Regulation, and Accounting, *Vanderbilt Law Review* 60: 1411–93.

Davis Polk & Wardell. 2008. *Executive Compensation Rules under the Emergency Economic Stabilization Act of 2008*.

Davis Polk & Wardell. 2009. *New Executive Compensation Restrictions under the Emergency Economic Stabilization Act of 2008*.

Davis Polk & Wardell. 2009a. Davis Polk Client Memorandum, *Dodd Bill would Affect Corporate Governance and Executive Compensation Processes for All US Public Companies*.

Department of the Treasury. 2009. *Financial Regulatory Reform. A New Foundation: Rebuilding Financial Supervision and Regulation*.

Dew-Becker, Ian. 2009. How Much Sunlight Does it Take to Disinfect a Boardroom? A Short History of Executive Compensation Regulation in America, *CESifo Economic Studies* 55: 434–57.

Eaglesham, Jean. 2010. Business Groups Sue SEC on "Proxy Access", *Financial Times* (UK), 30 September, p. 4.

Eaglesham, Jean. 2010a. Mind the Gap, Warn Critics of Pay Disclosure, *Financial Times* (UK), 31 August, p. 15.

Ebert, Franz Christian, Raymond Torres and Konstantinos Papadakis. 2008. International Institute for Labour Studies, Discussion Paper DP/190/2008, *Executive Compensation: Trends and Policy Issues*.

Editorial. 2010. Their Investors' Voice, *New York Times*, 28 August, p. 18.

Fahlenbrach, Rudiger and Rene M. Stulz. 2010. Bank CEO Incentives and the Credit Crisis, Charles A Dice Center Working Paper No. 2009-13, available at SSRN: http://papers.ssrn.com/sol3/papers.cfm?abstract_id=1439859.

FCIC. 2011. Financial Crisis Inquiry Commission, *The Financial Crisis Inquiry Report: Final Report of the National Commission on the Causes of the Financial and Economic Crisis in the United States*.

Federal Reserve, Federal Deposit Insurance Corporation, Office of the Comptroller of the Currency, Office of Thrift Supervision. 2010. *Guidance on Sound Incentive Compensation Policies*.

Ferran, Eilis. 2005. Company Law Reform in the UK: A Progress Report, European Corporate Governance Institute Law Working Paper No. 27/2005, available at SSRN: http://ssrn.com/abstract=644203.

Ferran, Eilis. 2010. The Break-up of the Financial Services Authority, University of Cambridge Faculty of Law, Legal Studies Research Paper Series no. 10/04, available at SSRN: http://ssrn.com/abstract=1690523.

Ferrarini, Guido and Niamh Moloney. 2005. Executive Remuneration in the EU: The Context for Reform, *Oxford Review of Economic Policy* 21: 304–23.

Ferrarini, Guido and Maria Cristina Ungureanu. 2010. Economics, Politics and the International Principles for Sound Compensation Practices: An Analysis of Executive Pay at European Banks, European Corporate Governance Institute Law Working Paper No. 169/2010, available at SSRN: http://papers.ssrn.com/sol3/papers.cfm?abstract_id=1707344.

FRC. 2010. Financial Reporting Council (UK), *The UK Stewardship Code*.

FRC. 2010a. Financial Reporting Council (UK), *Implementation of the UK Stewardship Code*.

FRC. 2010b. Financial Reporting Council (UK), *The UK Corporate Governance Code*.

FRC. 2010c. Financial Reporting Council (UK), *Revisions to the UK Corporate Governance Code (Formerly the Combined Code)*.

Frydman, Carola and Raven E. Saks. 2008. Executive Compensation: A New View from a Long-Term Perspective, 1936–2005, NBER Working Paper No. 14145, available at SSRN: http://ssrn.com/abstract=1152686.

FSA. 2008. Financial Services Authority (UK), *The Supervision of Northern Rock: A Lessons Learned Review*.

FSA. 2009. Financial Services Authority (UK), *The Turner Review: A Regulatory Response to the Global Banking Crisis.*

FSA. 2009a. Financial Services Authorities (UK), *FSA Draft Code on Remuneration Practices.*

FSA. 2009b. Financial Services Authorities (UK), Media Release FSA/PN/108/2009, *FSA Confirms Introduction of Remuneration Code of Practice.*

FSA. 2010. Financial Services Authority (UK), *Financial Services Act 2010.*

FSA. 2010a. Financial Services Authority (UK), Policy Statement 10/20, *Revising the Remuneration Code: Feedback on CP 10/19 and Final Rules.*

FSA. 2010b. Financial Services Authority (UK), Press Release, *FSA Publishes Revised Remuneration Code.*

FSB. 2009. Financial Stability Board, *FSF Principles for Sound Compensation Practices.*

FSB. 2009a. Financial Stability Board, *FSB Principles for Sound Compensation Practices: Implementation Standards.*

Furse, Clara. 2006. Sox is Not to Blame – London is Just Better as a Market, *Financial Times* (UK), 18 September, p. 19.

G-20 Working Group 1. 2009. *Enhancing Sound Regulation and Strengthening Transparency: Final Report.*

Gabaix, Xavier and Augustin Landier. 2008. Why Has CEO Pay Increased So Much? *Quarterly Journal of Economics* 123: 49–100.

Gordon, Jeffrey. 2002. What Enron Means for the Management and Control of the Modern Business Corporation: Some Initial Reflections, *The University of Chicago Law Review* 69: 1233–50.

Gordon, Jeffrey. 2009. "Say on Pay": Cautionary Notes on the UK Experience and the Case for Shareholder Opt-In, *Harvard Journal on Legislation* 46: 323–68.

Gordon, Robert J. 2009. *Misperceptions about the Magnitude and Timing of Changes in American Income Inequality*, NBER Working Paper No. 15351, available at SSRN: http://ssrn.com/abstract=1475543.

Groom, Brian. 2009. City Voices Competitiveness Fears, *Financial Times* (UK), 19 November, p. 3.

Grundfest, Joseph A. 2010. The SEC's Proposed Proxy Access Rules: Politics, Economics, and the Law, *Business Lawyer* 65: 361–94.

Henrekson, Magnus and Ulf Jacobsson. 2010. The Swedish Corporate Control Model: Convergence, Persistence or Decline? IFN Working Paper No. 857, available at SSRN: http://ssrn.com/abstract=1734149.

Hill, Jennifer G. 1999. Deconstructing Sunbeam: Contemporary Issues in Corporate Governance, *University of Cincinnati Law Review* 67: 1099–127.

Hill, Jennifer G. 2005. Regulatory Responses to Global Corporate Scandals, *Wisconsin International Law Journal* 23: 367–416.

Hill, Jennifer G. 2008. Regulatory Show and Tell: Lessons from International Statutory Regimes, *Delaware Journal of Corporate Law* 33: 819–43.

Hill, Jennifer G. 2009. New Trends in the Regulation of Executive Remuneration, in *Directors in Troubled Times*, 100–123, 4th edition, R. P. Austin and A. Y. Bilski eds, Ross Parsons Centre of Commercial, Corporate and Taxation Law.

Hill, Jennifer G. 2010. The Rising Tension Between Shareholder and Director Power in the Common Law World, *Corporate Governance: An International Review* 18: 344–59.

Hill, Jennifer G. and Charles M. Yablon. 2002. Corporate Governance and Executive Remuneration: Rediscovering Managerial Positional Conflict, *University of New South Wales Law Journal* 25: 294–319.

Hill, Jennifer G., Ron Masulis and Randall Thomas. 2011. Comparing CEO Employment Contract Provisions: Differences between Australia and the US, forthcoming, *Vanderbilt Law Review.*

HM Treasury (UK). 2009. *Speech by the Financial Services Secretary to the Treasury, Paul Myners, to the Association of Foreign Banks.*

HM Treasury (UK). 2009a. *Securing the Recovery: Growth and Opportunity. Pre-Budget Report.*

HM Treasury (UK). 2010. *Speech at the Lord Mayor's Dinner for Bankers & Merchants of the City of London by the Chancellor of the Exchequer, the Rt Hon. George Osborne MP, at Mansion House.*

HM Treasury (UK). 2010a. *A New Approach to Financial Regulation: Judgement, Focus and Stability.*

Hutton Review. 2010. *Hutton Review of Fair Pay in the Public Sector.*

IMF. 2008. International Monetary Fund, *Global Financial Stability Report, Containing Systemic Risks and Restoring Financial Soundness.*

International Institute for Labour Studies. 2008. Executive Summary, *World of Work Report 2008: Income Inequalities in the Age of Financial Globalization.*

Jensen, Michael C. and Kevin J. Murphy. 1990. CEO Incentives: It's Not How Much You Pay, But How, *Harvard Business Review* 68: 138–49.

Kershaw, David. 2005. Evading Enron: Taking Principles Too Seriously in Accounting Regulation, *Modern Law Review* 68: 594–625.

Kitney, Damon. 2010. Super Funds Push to Claw Back Executive Bonuses, *The Australian*, 21 December.

Labaton, Stephen. 2009. Treasury to Set Executives' Pay at 7 Ailing Firms, *New York Times*, 11 June, p. 1.

Lannoo, Karel. 2009. Centre for European Policy Studies Commentary, *A Crisis is a Terrible Thing to Waste*.

Levitt, Arthur. 2005. Corporate Culture and the Problem of Executive Compensation, *Journal of Corporation Law* 30: 749–53.

Lipton, Martin. 2011. Some Thoughts for Boards of Directors in 2011, *The Harvard Law School Forum on Corporate Governance and Financial Regulation*, 18 January 2011.

Lublin, Joann S. 2010. Law Sharpens "Clawback" Rules for Improper Pay, *Wall Street Journal* (on-line version), 25 July.

Masters, Brooke. 2008. Northern Rock Woes Take Toll on City's Reputation, *Financial Times* (UK), 27 August, p. 3.

McConnell, Michael W. 2009. The Pay Czar is Unconstitutional, *Wall Street Journal*, 30 October 2009, p. A25.

McKinsey & Company. 2007. *Sustaining New York's and the US' Global Financial Services Leadership*, Report to Michael R. Bloomberg and Charles E. Schumer.

Milhaupt, Curtis J. and Katharina Pistor. 2008. *Law and Capitalism: What Corporate Crises Reveal about Legal Systems and Economic Development around the World*, Chicago: University of Chicago Press.

Miller, Geoffrey P. 2004. Catastrophic Financial Failures: Enron and More, *Cornell Law Review* 89: 423–55.

Minister for Financial Services. 2010. Minister for Financial Services, Superannuation & Corporate Law & Minister for Human Services, Joint Media Release, *Government Responds to the Productivity Commission Report on Executive Remuneration*.

Moore, James. 2009. The End of the Road for the FSA? *The Independent* (UK), 21 July, p. 40.

Morphy, James. 2009. Economic "Stimulus" Legislation to Impose New Executive Compensation Restrictions, *The Harvard Law School Forum on Corporate Governance and Financial Regulation*, 16 February.

Murphy, Megan and Brooke Masters. 2010. FSA Unveils Tough New Pay and Bonus Code, *Financial Times* (on-line version), 30 July.

Office of the Special Master for TARP Executive Compensation. 2010. *Final Report of Kenneth R. Feinberg*.

Opinion. 2009. The New Wage Controls: One More Sign that the Levelers are Now in Charge, *Wall Street Journal*, 15 June, p. A13.

Paatsch, Dean and Martin Lawrence. 2008. Money for Nothing, *Business Spectator*, 17 July.

Pan, Eric J. 2010. Challenge of International Cooperation and Institutional Design in Financial Supervision: Beyond Transgovernmental Networks, *Chicago Journal of International Law* 11: 243–84.

Parliamentary Secretary to the Treasurer. 2010. Media Release n. 017, *More Power to Shareholders on Executive Remuneration*.

Pickard, Jim and Elizabeth Rigby. 2010. Cable on Collision Course With High Earners, *Financial Times* (UK), 29 October, p. 3.

Piketty, Thomas and Emmanuel Saez. 2003. Income Inequality in the United States, 1913–1998, *Quarterly Journal of Economics* 118: 1–39.

Plender, John. 2008. Mind the Gap: Why Business May Face a Crisis of Legitimacy, *Financial Times* (UK), 8 April, p. 9.

Plender, John. 2010. Rules of Engagement, *Financial Times* (UK), 12 July, p. 7.

Pritchard, Adam C. 2009. London as Delaware? *Regulation* 32: 22–8.

Reisberg, Arad. 2010. The Notion of Stewardship From a Company Law Perspective: Re-Defined and Re-Assessed in Light of the Recent Financial Crisis? Forthcoming 2011 *Journal of Financial Crime*.

Rigby, Elizabeth and Alex Barker. 2010. Cable to Take a Swipe at City Greed, *Financial Times* (UK), 22 September, p. 1.

Romano, Roberta. 2005. The Sarbanes-Oxley Act and the Making of Quack Corporate Governance, *Yale Law Journal* 114: 1521–612.

Saez, Emmanuel. 2009. Striking it Richer: The Evolution of Top Incomes in the United States (Update with 2007 estimates), available at: elsa.berkeley.edu/~saez/saez-UStopincomes-2007.pdf.

Sandler, Richard J. 2010. Corporate Governance and Executive Compensation in the New Dodd Bill, *Harvard Law School Forum on Corporate Governance and Financial Regulation*, 17 March.

Sants, Hector. 2010. Speech by Hector Sants, Chief Executive, FSA Reuters Newsmakers Event, *Reforming Supervisory Practices: Progress to Date*.

Savarese, John F. 2010. Sarbanes-Oxley "Clawback" Developments, *The Harvard Law School Forum on Corporate Governance and Financial Regulation*, 24 June.

Schumer, Charles E. 2009. Press Release, *Schumer, Cantwell Announce "Shareholder Bill of Rights" to Impose Greater Accountability on Corporate America*.

Schwarcz, Steven L. 2008. Systemic Risk, *Georgetown Law Journal* 97: 193–249.

Schwartz, Rachel E. 2008. The Clawback Provision of Sarbanes-Oxley: An Underutilized Incentive to Keep the Corporate House Clean, *Business Lawyer* 64: 1–35.

SEC. 2009. US Securities and Exchange Commission. Press Release, *SEC Votes to Propose Rule Amendments to Facilitate Rights of Shareholders to Nominate Directors*.

SEC. 2010. US Securities and Exchange Commission. *Facilitating Shareholder Director Nominations: Final Rule.*

SEC. 2010a. US Securities and Exchange Commission. Press Release, *SEC Adopts New Measures to Facilitate Director Nominations by Shareholders.*

SEC. 2011. US Securities and Exchange Commission. *Shareholder Approval of Executive Compensation and Golden Parachute Compensation: Final Rule.*

SEC. 2011a. US Securities and Exchange Commission. Media Release 2011-25, *SEC Adopts Rules for Say-on-Pay and Golden Parachute Compensation as Required Under the Dodd-Frank Act.*

Sheehan, Kym. 2009. The Regulatory Framework for Executive Remuneration in Australia, *Sydney Law Review* 31: 273–308.

Sheehan, Kym and Colin Fenwick. 2008. Seven: *The Corporations Act 2001* (Cth), Corporate Governance and Termination Payments to Senior Employees, *Melbourne University Law Review* 32: 199–241.

Shields, John. 2005. Setting the Double Standard: Chief Executive Pay the BCA Way, *Journal of Australian Political Economy* 56: 299–324.

Sholette, Kevin. 2010. The American Czars, *Cornell Journal of Law and Public Policy*, 20: 219–41.

Simmons, Omari Scott. 2009. Taking the Blue Pill: the Imponderable Impact of Executive Compensation Reform, *SMU Law Review* 62: 299–365.

Skeel, David A. 2008. Governance in the Ruin, *Harvard Law Review* 122: 696–743.

Stapledon, Geof. 2005. Termination Benefits for Executives of Australian Companies, *Sydney Law Review* 27: 683–714.

Story, Louise and Stephen Labaton. 2009. Overseer of Big Pay Is Seasoned Arbitrator, *New York Times*, 11 June, p. B1.

Tarrant, Deborah. 2009. Payday Paralysis, *Intheblack* 79: 28–31.

Thomas, Helen. 2010. US Companies in Pay Clawback Moves Ahead of Shake-Up, *Financial Times* (UK), 9 August, p. 19.

Thomas, Randall S. 2004. Explaining the International CEO Pay Gap: Board Capture or Market Driven, *Vanderbilt Law Review* 57: 1171–268.

Thomson, Ainsley and Alistair MacDonald. 2010. UK's Cable Shines Light on Business "Short-termism", *Wall Street Journal* (on-line version), 22 September.

Trowbridge, John. 2009. The Regulatory Environment: A Brief Tour, Paper Presented at the National Insurance Brokers Association (NIBA) Conference, Sydney, Australia.

US Chamber of Commerce. 2010. Press Release, *US Chamber Joins Business Roundtable in Lawsuit Challenging Securities and Exchange Commission.*

US Department of the Treasury. 2009. Press Release, *Treasury Announces New Restrictions On Executive Compensation.*

US Senate. 2009. 111th Congress, S. 1074, *A Bill to Provide Shareholders with Enhanced Authority over the Nomination, Election and Compensation of Public Company Executives.*

Walker Review (UK). 2009. *A Review of Corporate Governance in UK Banks and Other Financial Industry Entities: Final Recommendations.*

Wolf, Martin. 2009. Why the Turner Report is a Watershed for Finance, *Financial Times* (UK), 20 March, p. 11.

Yablon, Charles M. 1999. Bonus Questions: Executive Compensation in the Era of Pay for Performance, *Notre Dame Law Review* 75: 271–308.

12 Institutional investor preferences and executive compensation
Joseph A. McCahery and Zacharias Sautner

1 INTRODUCTION

Over the last two decades, institutional investing has become an important component of financial markets (e.g., Gillan and Starks (2007)). The increase in institutional ownership has been accompanied by an enhanced role played by institutions in monitoring the corporate governance behavior of companies. Among other things, institutional investors ascertain whether companies comply with the best practice standards elaborated in the guidelines established by corporate governance bodies, pursue proxy voting challenges at annual meetings or conduct coordinated shareholder activism.

Prior research has studied the participation of institutional investors in targeting poorly performing firms and pressuring boards of directors to improve corporate performance. In recent years, activist institutions in the United States (US) have made use of a federally mandated privilege to submit shareholder proposals included in the management's annual proxy statement for a vote at the annual general meeting (see Thomas and Cotter (2007)). The proposal process provides a mechanism for shareholders to raise corporate governance and performance concerns and to pressure boards to implement the proposed changes. Most proposals submitted by investors (other than hedge funds) relate to the elimination of anti-takeover devices, executive compensation, the board of directors and voting rules. In the last decade, hedge funds have embraced activist strategies, taking investment stakes in underperforming firms and directly engaging management to undertake changes that are favorable for outside shareholders and their financial agenda (e.g., Brav et al. (2008)).

The evolving role of institutional investor participation in corporate governance is likely to continue and its growth is driven by investor strategies which have changed significantly. In this chapter, we investigate the attitudes of institutional investors, such as hedge funds, insurance companies, mutual funds and pension funds, towards a key corporate governance mechanism, namely executive compensation. The purpose of this study is to document the preferences they have about both the level and structure of executive compensation. Our analysis takes a comparative approach as we ask investors to reveal their preferences for firms both in the US and in The Netherlands. Further, we selected these two countries because they have different legal origins, investor protection regimes, and ownership characteristics. In particular, the United States is an English common law country that is generally considered to have high investor protection, low ownership concentration, and high institutional ownership, whereas The Netherlands is a French civil law country that is viewed as having low investor protection, high ownership concentration, and low institutional ownership.

Our analysis further sheds light on who should decide on executive pay, thereby contributing to the recent debate on shareholder involvement in executive pay ("say on pay"). Finally, we study investors' views on the most important and largest component of executive pay, executive stock options, and investigate what preferences they have when it comes to the design of such options. To investigate these issues, we make use of a new dataset from a survey of 118 large institutional investors, including mutual funds, hedge funds and insurance firms.

Based on our survey responses, we find that a majority of investors prefer a reduction of the level of severance payments (golden handshakes) when CEOs leave, for portfolio firms both in The Netherlands and in the US. This is consistent with the view that the granting of extravagant pay packages reflects poor corporate governance and a strong CEO bargaining position. Interestingly, the majority of investors do not think that overall CEO pay should be reduced in The Netherlands. Moreover, a (small) majority believes that the compensation of Dutch CEOs should be more equity-based (i.e. more stock options or restricted shares). While overall CEO pay in The Netherlands is generally not considered as being too high, almost half of the investors believe that CEO pay in the US should be reduced.

Agency theory and optimal contracting theory posit that shareholders should make the pay decision in order to limit the moral hazard problem caused by low ownership stakes of CEOs and to provide incentives to motivate CEOs to maximize shareholder wealth. Our analysis reveals that shareholders prefer to be responsible for deciding about the structure and level of CEO pay. We find, moreover, no evidence that the differences in the one-tier versus two-tier board system have an effect on shareholder preferences for CEO pay decisions being delegated to the compensation committee (one-tier system) or non-executive members of the board (two-tier system).

As regards institutional investors' preferences for the design of executive stock options, we find that investors are sensitive to a transparent disclosure of option compensation, relative operating and stock price benchmarks (benchmarks that managers need to fulfill before they are eligible to exercise their options) and long vesting periods. In addition, absolute stock price benchmarks are considered relatively unimportant, which is consistent with optimal contracting models (Holmström (1979, 1982)).

The remainder of the chapter is organized as follows. In Section 2, we provide a review of selected evidence on the role of institutional investors in executive compensation. Section 3 contains the data sources and summary information about the investors in the sample. Section 4 presents the empirical results of our study on the preferences of institutional investors regarding executive compensation. Section 5 summarizes our findings.

2   INSTITUTIONAL INVESTORS AND EXECUTIVE COMPENSATION

Previous research has shown that institutional investors can influence the structure and level of executive compensation. We consider two possible views on the role of institutional investors on executive compensation.

The first view arises from agency theory research and highlights the monitoring benefits of institutional investors, i.e. their role in ensuring that CEO pay is properly designed. This view implies, for example, that the pay-for-performance sensitivity of CEO pay, a measure of how well incentives of CEOs and shareholders are aligned, should be positively related to the concentration of institutional investor ownership (Jensen and Murphy 1990). Providing support for this standpoint, the empirical work by Hartzell and Starks (2003) shows that with an increase in institutional investor ownership, CEO pay levels decrease but pay-for-performance sensitivities increase.

A second view highlights potential conflicts of interests arising from business ties between institutional investors and CEOs of their portfolio firms. This perspective suggests that institutional investors with more conflicts of interests from business ties are less likely to contribute to the monitoring of CEO pay (Brickley, Lease and Smith (1988)). Moreover, this work suggests important differences between pressure-resistant institutional investors, who have greater incentives to influence the level of CEO pay, and pressure-sensitive institutional investors, who because they must continue to maintain their business relationships are unlikely to invest in active monitoring. Recent research finds evidence in support of the role that different groups of institutional investors play in influencing total CEO pay. For example, Shin and Seo (2010) show the different effect of public pension funds and mutual funds on the level of CEO pay and pay-for-performance sensitivity for CEO pay, thus observing a negative association of pension fund ownership with CEO pay and a positive association for mutual fund ownership and total CEO pay.

Institutional investors not only influence executive compensation directly, but also indirectly through their trading. Trading may affect executive pay through its effect on the value of the options and stock holdings of executives. Recent evidence demonstrates the important role of trading behavior of investors. Sias, Starks and Titman (2002) show that stock returns are correlated with changes in institutional ownership, which is due to the informed trading of institutional investors. The enforcement of insider trading rules creates dangers for institutional investors which can reduce this effect (Maug 2002).

In response to the above-stated views, a new line of research has integrated the implicit assumption that institutional investors are heterogeneous in their effects on CEO compensation structure and looks to their preferences to explain the different pay outcomes for CEOs. For example, Bushee and Noe (2000) show that improved disclosure rankings increase the attractiveness to transient institutional investors who are more likely to act as traders, which can greatly influence the share price of the portfolio company. In contrast with institutions with a longer investment horizon and concentrated holdings (dedicated investors) who invest in monitoring and attempt to introduce changes in the strategies of portfolio firms, transient investors are more likely to sell the firms' shares in reaction to poor firm performance or to force CEO turnover. This increases the willingness of portfolio companies to adopt CEO pay packages that transient investors' prefer in order to ensure that investors maintain their holdings in the company's stock.

3 DATA DESCRIPTION

We exploit in this study a new dataset from a survey of institutional investors to better understand the preferences of institutional investors about CEO compensation. We use our survey to assess their views about three important aspects of executive pay, namely (i) whether adjustments to the level and structure of pay are necessary, (ii) who should decide on pay, and (iii) how executive stock option plans should be designed.

The survey questions were developed based on the existing executive pay literature. Before conducting the survey, we circulated it among academics and investor relations research experts to get their feedback and suggestions on the survey design and execution. Our survey recipients were selected from the FactSet/LionShares database, which defines institutional investors as professional money managers with discretionary control over assets. Because we ask our survey respondents to assess executive pay in the United States and The Netherlands, we need to ensure that they have at least some knowledge of CEO pay in The Netherlands. Consequently, we restrict the survey to those institutions in the database that have at least 5 percent of their assets under management invested in Dutch companies. Asking questions about pay in The Netherlands and the US allows us to benchmark and compare the situation in both countries. The scope of our survey includes all important investor-types, i.e. pension funds, mutual funds, insurance companies and hedge funds.

Our survey was sent by email to the chief investment officers of a total of 1,178 institutional investors on November 1, 2007. To maximize the response rate additional reminders were sent and individual phone calls made in the last weeks of December 2007 and the last responses were received in the first weeks of January 2008. We received a total of 118 surveys, a response rate of about 10 percent. We are able to match the identity of the institutional investors and hence the survey responses with data from FactSet/LionShares on institutional investor characteristics such as assets under management or share turnover for 90 of these 118 investors.

The original survey also contained a wide set of questions on the preferences of institutional investors for country-level investor protection, firm-level corporate governance mechanisms, and shareholder activism. An extensive analysis of these questions is provided in McCahery, Sautner and Starks (2011).

Table 12.1 shows in Panel A that the average institutional investor in our sample has about 623m USD assets under management. The largest 5 percent of investors in our sample have invested assets worth more than 3.5bn USD. The average investor further has an annual share turnover of 16 percent and holds 89 firms in its portfolio. The fraction of assets invested by the investors in The Netherlands and the US is approximately 10 percent and 9 percent, respectively. See also the explanatory note at the end of the table.

Panel B reports the breakdown of the investors by type of institution. As can be seen, by far the most institutions in the sample are mutual funds (63 percent), but our sample also includes hedge funds, insurance firms and pension funds. Panel C shows that our respondents come from a wide range of countries, but a majority comes from The Netherlands and other European countries.

In the survey, we also asked the investors to what extent they make use of proxy voting advisors such as ISS or Glass Lewis for voting at an annual meeting. We included this question to examine to what extent investors delegate their voting decisions, for example on potential executive pay issues, to external advisors. The data, reported in Panel D of Table 12.1, suggests that over half of the institutions in our sample do not employ proxy voting advisory services at all. Of those investors that use proxy voting firms to some extent, most use the advice of these firms to determine their own position vis-à-vis the

Table 12.1 Institutional investor characteristics

Panel A: Institutional investor characteristics

Investor characteristic	Mean	Median	STD	5%	95%	Obs.
Assets under management (in 1000 USD)	623,000	140,000	1,260,000	9,540	3,550,000	90
Fraction of assets invested in NL (in %)	10.38%	6.85%	13.96%	0.00%	33.38%	90
Fraction of assets invested in US (in %)	9.21%	0.00%	18.93%	0.00%	48.23%	90
Share turnover	0.16	0.13	0.13	0.04	0.32	87
Number of firms in portfolio	89	60	135	20	292	89

Ownership position in portfolio firms	Mean	Median	STD	5%	95%	Obs.
Percentage ownership stake (in %)	0.131	0.006	0.573	0.000	0.534	7919
Value of ownership stake (in 1000 USD)	6,103	841	20,100	44	29,400	7919

Panel B: Type of institution

	All investors		Hedge fund		Insurance		Mutual fund		Pension fund		Other investors	
	Number	Percent	Number	Percent	Number	Percent	Number	Percent	Number	Percent	Number	Percent
Questionnaire responses	118	100%	7	5.9%	9	7.6%	74	62.7%	7	5.9%	21	17.8%

Table 12.1 (continued)

Panel C: Investor origin (actual seat)

	All investors		Hedge fund		Insurance		Mutual fund		Pension fund		Other investors	
	Number	Percent	Number	Percent	Number	Percent	Number	Percent	Number	Percent	Number	Percent
The Netherlands	12	13%	2	50%	0	0%	7	11%	1	33%	2	14%
UK	12	13%	0	0%	1	14%	7	11%	1	33%	3	21%
Germany	8	9%	0	0%	1	14%	7	11%	0	0%	0	0%
France	9	10%	0	0%	2	29%	5	8%	0	0%	2	14%
Luxembourg	3	3%	0	0%	0	0%	1	2%	0	0%	2	14%
Other European Countries **	33	37%	1	25%	3	43%	26	42%	0	0%	3	21%
US	9	10%	0	0%	0	0%	6	10%	1	33%	2	14%
Other North American (Canada, Caymans)	4	4%	1	25%	0	0%	3	5%	0	0%	0	0%
Total	90	100%	4	100%	7	100%	62	100%	3	100%	14	100%

**Note: Each European country in this category (BE, CH, NO, IE, IT, FI, ES) has five or fewer investors in the sample

Panel D: Importance of proxy voting advisors

Usage of proxy voting advisors	Always	That depends on the company	That depends on the agenda item	That depends on the circumstances	Never	Sum	Obs.
Percent of responses	17%	10%	7%	13%	53%	100%	118

Manner of usage of proxy voting advice	Always follow advice fully	Use advice to determine own position	Use advice in case of own doubts	Others	Sum	Obs.
Percent of responses	9%	65%	13%	13%	100%	55

Note: Panel A of this table summarizes descriptive statistics of the main characteristics of the institutional investors that returned our questionnaires (total of 118 responses). It contains information on the assets under management of the investors (value of equity portfolio measured in 1000 USD), on the fraction of shares which are invested in firms listed in The Netherlands (in %) as well as in the US (in %), and on the share turnover of the investors. The share turnover is measured as the value of all buy and sell transactions in a quarter divided by the market value of the equity portfolio. The data source for these investor characteristics is FactSet/LionShares. The number of observations varies and is smaller than 118 due to limited data availability in FactSet/LionShares. Panel A further reports data on the size of the equity stakes (in %) that the institutional investors hold in their portfolio firms and reports the market values (in 1000 USD) of these stakes. This data is also from FactSet/LionShares. Panel B shows the distribution of the 118 survey respondents by investor-type. The investor-type categorization is based on self-reported information in the returned questionnaires. Panel C reports the national origins of the investors (actual seat and not legal seat). This information is hand-collected. Panel D records whether and to what extent the institutional investors make use of external proxy voting advisors when determining how to vote in a Dutch annual meeting (AGM). Conditional on using such firms (i.e. if the answer is not 'Never'), the panel also contains information on the extent to which the advice of the proxy voting firms is used. The data source for this information is also the returned questionnaires. The FactSet/LionShares variables are calculated for the year-end 2007.

portfolio company of interest. Overall, this suggests that our investors show substantial levels of involvement when it comes to issues such as executive pay. More detailed characteristics about the investors can be found in McCahery, Sautner and Starks (2011).

4   EXECUTIVE COMPENSATION PREFERENCES

Having supplied a general description of the characteristics of the investors in our sample, we will provide, in the next section, an analysis of their preferences with regard to different aspects of executive compensation.

4.1   The Structure and Level of Executive Compensation

The rise of executive compensation is partially the result of a perceived need to bring about change in corporate performance and to establish a link between the pay and wealth of executives and shareholder value (Hall and Liebman (1998)). Much research has documented a strong correlation between pay and corporate size, typically measured by reference to sales (Murphy (1999)). Top executive pay levels vary not only by corporate size, but also differ substantially according to industrial sector, performance and a firm's growth opportunities. Pay-to-sales sensitivities are much higher in manufacturing industries than in financial services and utilities, a phenomenon which is similar across countries.

There is evidence of increasing convergence of top executive pay levels and of remuneration structures resulting from the emergence of an international market for top managers, the abolition of legal prohibitions on executive stock options, and the use of peer groups to determine competitive levels of compensation. However, comparative research shows that the total level of CEO pay in the US is roughly double that in any other country, even allowing for differences in purchasing power and taxation of direct pay and perquisites (Fernandes et al. (2010)). Interestingly, this substantial discrepancy between the United States and all other countries is only observed at the level of the CEO and does not extend down to lower-level management. Notice also that executive pay in the US significantly outpaces the pay practices of The Netherlands.

A number of explanations have been offered for the dramatic rise in CEO compensation in the US compared to other countries. First, contrasting compensation levels may reflect the difference in firm size between the US and other OECD countries. Second, the high level of executive pay may be due partly to the substantial gap in stock market performance across the 1990s. Nevertheless, even if stock options are taken into account, the differences in compensation practices between Europe and the US are still substantial. Third, the divergence in practice may be due to the degree of influence the CEO has over the board of directors (Bebchuk and Fried 2003). Finally, the difference may also be due to the risk premium that needs to be paid if firms predominantly pay their managers using stock options, as is the practice in most large US firms (Fernandes et al. (2010)).

In light of the general increases in executive pay and the substantial differences that arguably exist between CEO pay in US and Dutch firms, Figure 12.1 a–b presents

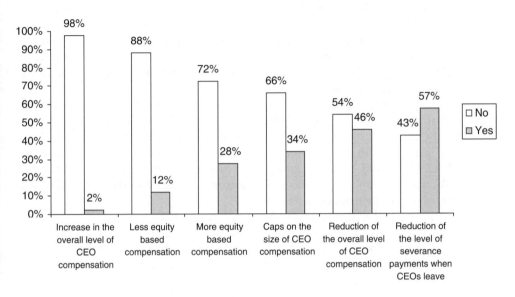

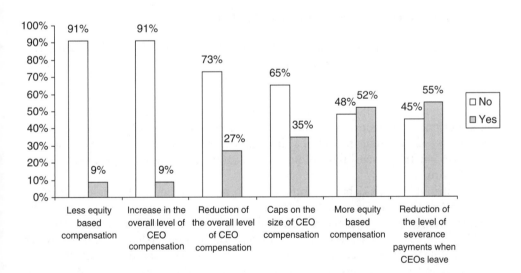

Note: This figure reports the views of institutional investors about the structure and level of executive compensation in the US and The Netherlands. The data source for this information is the returned questionnaires.

Figure 12.1 a–b   The structure and level of executive compensation

information about whether institutional investors deem adjustment in the level and structure of CEO compensation in the US and The Netherlands necessary. We sought to elicit their preferences on the level of pay by asking, separately for the US and The Netherlands, whether they think that CEO pay is too high or too low, whether reduction in severance pay is considered necessary, and by asking whether they have a preference for caps on the overall level of CEO compensation. Similarly, we attempted to measure their preferences on the structure of pay by asking whether they think that CEOs should be more or less compensated with equity-based pay.

Turning to the Netherlands, we find that a majority, 55 percent, of investors prefer a reduction of the level of severance payments (golden handshakes) when CEOs leave. Interestingly, the majority of investors do not think that overall CEO pay should be reduced in The Netherlands. Moreover, a (small) majority believes that the compensation of Dutch CEOs should be more equity-based (i.e. more stock options or restricted shares). We will discuss the preferences of investors with regard to the design of equity-based pay, in particular stock options, below.

For the US, we find that respondents have a similar view with regard to reducing the level of severance pay, with 57 percent of the respondents being in favor of reducing the levels of severance packages. Interestingly, while overall CEO pay in The Netherlands is generally not considered as being too high, 46 percent of the investors believe that CEO pay in the US should be reduced.

Overall, the data indicate that a large number of investors are dissatisfied with the overall level of executive compensation in the US but not so much in The Netherlands. This result is in line with the above mentioned differences in the observed levels of CEO pay in The Netherlands and in the US.

4.2   Decision-making Around Executive Compensation

Public discontent over pay packages of top executives in the US and Europe has triggered a debate in politics, academia, and among the public at large on whether shareholders should have more influence on the pay setting process ("say on pay"). Providing support for this view, it is noteworthy that recent empirical research suggests that shareholder voting indeed can serve as a check against greater compensation for managers, but mainly in poorly governed firms (Cai and Walking (2011)). Based on this evidence, we expect that institutional investors would have a preference for deciding themselves on the design and volume of executive compensation packages in their portfolio firms.

To contribute to this debate, Figure 12.2 a–b reports views about whether investors prefer having shareholders decide over executives' remuneration at the annual general meeting (AGM). We report their responses separately for firms with a one-tier or two-tier board system, to determine whether their preferences may be related to the board system in place. Note that in the one-tier board system, a firm has one board of directors consisting of both executive and non-executive directors (as in the United States). With a two-tier board system, a firm has two separate boards, namely, a management board, which is responsible for the day-to-day management of the firm, and a supervisory board, which monitors the management board (as in Germany). Dutch firms have a choice between the two board structures.

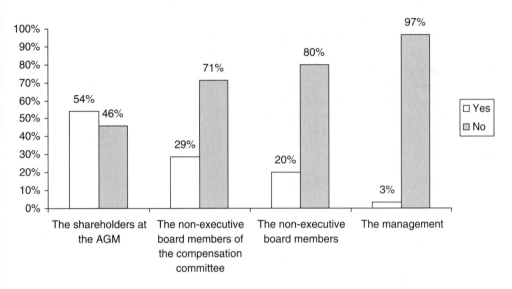

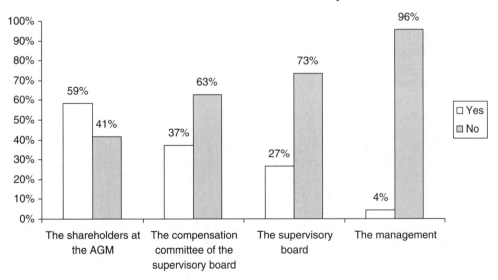

Note: This figure reports the views of institutional investors about the decision-making around executive compensation. The data source for this information is the returned questionnaires.

Figure 12.2 a–b   Decision-making around executive compensation

We find that most respondents (in terms of the no votes) are opposed to giving management power over executive compensation (97 percent where a firm has a one-tier and 96 percent where a firm has a two-tier board). Similarly, we find negative associations with delegating pay decisions to non-executive board members (80 percent), or members of a supervisory board (73 percent) in the case of a two-tier system. Furthermore, the majority of institutional investors are not inclined to entrust board committees with deciding on executive pay. However, the data indicate a majority response to the suggestion of allocating shareholders with decision-making authority over executive compensation, both in the one-tier and in the two-tier system.

Overall, these figures give strong support to our hypothesis that institutional investors prefer to have the decision-making power over executive pay in their own hands at the annual general meeting.

4.3 Designing Executive Stock Options

Executive stock options constitute the largest component of CEO pay. At the same time, they are probably also the most difficult component of executive pay when it comes to their design, as poorly designed option plans can trigger dysfunctional managerial behavior such as excessive risk taking. It is therefore crucial to understand the views of institutional investors on how such option plans should be designed. Industry codes of good practice typically endorse the adoption of disclosure of option characteristics and the volumes granted, long vesting periods, relative performance benchmarks, and subjecting pay schemes to shareholder approval.

In order to understand the option design preferences of institutional investors, we used our survey to ask them to assess the importance of a set of key design features incorporated in option plans, namely (1) relative stock performance benchmarks; (2) relative operating performance benchmarks; (3) absolute stock market performance benchmarks; (4) absolute operating performance benchmarks; (5) exercise prices that are in the money; (6) exercise prices that are out of the money; (7) long vesting periods; (8) long time to maturities; and (9) disclosure of option characteristics. The investors could indicate on a scale from 1 (not important at all) to 7 (very important) how they assess these different design features.

The results, reported in Figure 12.3, are consistent with the features of good governance codes. In particular, investors consider sufficient disclosure, long vesting periods, and relative operating and stock performance benchmarks as key design features of properly designed option plans. We find less evidence in favor of linking compensation to absolute stock performance benchmarks, which is in line with the suggestions of optimal contracting models (e.g., Holmström (1979, 1982)). Interestingly, Figure 12.3 reveals that there is little difference between the weight given to disclosure and the absolute stock performance benchmarks in the vesting conditions. Finally, we find that institutional investors apparently do not find options that are designed with exercise prices in the money very important (such options could be used as a way to reduce incentives for risk taking).

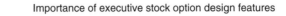

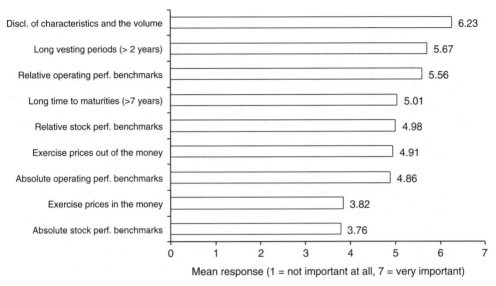

Note: This figure reports the views of institutional investors about the design of executive stock option plans. The data source for this information is the returned questionnaires.

Figure 12.3   Designing executive stock options

5   CONCLUSION

In this chapter, we analyzed a new dataset that is constructed based on a survey among 118 institutional investors and that elicits their preferences about various aspects of executive compensation. In particular, we used our survey to understand their views about (i) whether adjustments to the level and structure of executive compensation are necessary, (ii) who should decide on executive pay, and (iii) how executive stock options should be designed.

We show that a majority of investors want to reduce the size of firms' severance packages to departing CEOs. Furthermore, the majority of investors do not think that overall CEO pay should be reduced in The Netherlands. Moreover, a (small) majority believes that the compensation of Dutch CEOs should be more equity-based. While overall CEO pay in The Netherlands is generally not considered as being too high, almost 50 percent of institutional investors believe that CEO pay in the US should be reduced.

Our study also reveals that shareholders prefer to be responsible for the design and volume of executive pay. Finally, our study recognizes the differences in investors' preferences in the design of executive stock options. In terms of the order of importance, we show that institutional investors prefer disclosure of option compensation, relative operating and stock price benchmarks that managers need to fulfill before they are eligible to exercise their options, and long vesting periods.

REFERENCES

Bebchuk, Lucian and Jesse Fried, 2003, Executive compensation as an agency problem, *Journal of Economic Perspective* 17(3), 71–92.

Brav, Alon, Wei Jiang, Frank Partnoy, and Randall Thomas, 2008, Hedge fund activism, corporate governance, and firm performance, *Journal of Finance* 63, 1729–55.

Brickley, James, Ronald Lease, and Clifford Smith, 1998, Ownership structure and voting on antitakeover amendments, *Journal of Financial Economic* 20, 267–92.

Bushee, Brian and Christopher Noe, 2000, Corporate disclosure practices, institutional investors, and stock return vitality, *Journal of Accounting Research* 73, 305–33.

Cai, Jie and Ralph A. Walking, 2011, Shareholders' say on pay: Does it create value? *Journal of Financial and Quantitative Analysis* 46, 299–339.

Fernandes, Nuno G., Miguel A. Ferreira, Pedro P. Matos, and Kevin J. Murphy, The pay divide: (Why) are US top executives paid more? ECGI – Finance Working Paper No. 255/200.

Gillan, Stuart and Laura Starks, 2007, The evolution of shareholder activism in the United States, *Journal of Applied Corporate Finance* 19(1), 55–73.

Hall, Brian J. and Jeffrey B. Liebman, 1998, Are CEOs really paid like bureaucrats? *Quarterly Journal of Economics* 113, 653–91.

Hartzell, Jay and Laura Starks, 2003, Institutional investors and executive compensation, *Journal of Finance* 58, 2351–74.

Holmström, Bengt, 1979, Moral hazard and observability, *Bell Journal of Economics* 10, 74–9.

Holmström, Bengt, 1982, Moral hazard in teams, *Bell Journal of Economics* 13, 324–40.

Jensen, Michael and Kevin Murphy, 1990, Performance pay and top-managerial incentives, *Journal of Political Economy* 98, 225–64.

Maug, Ernst, 2002, Insider trading legislation and corporate governance, *European Economic Review* 46(9), 1569–97.

McCahery, Joseph, Zacharias Sautner and Laura Starks, 2011, Behind the scenes: The corporate governance preferences of institutional investors, ECGI Finance Working Paper No. 235/2009.

Murphy, Kevin, 1999, Executive compensation, in Ashenfelter and Orley, David Card, eds: *Handbook of Labor Economics* Vol. 3 (North Holland), Amsterdam.

Shin, Jae Yong and Jeongil Seo, 2010, Less pay and more sensitivity? Institutional investor heterogeneity and CEO pay, *Journal of Management*, forthcoming.

Sias, Richard, Laura Starks, and Sheridan Titman, 2006, Changes in institutional ownership and stock returns: Assessment and methodology, *Journal of Business* 79, 2869–910.

Thomas, Randall and James Cotter, 2007, Shareholder proposals in the new millennium: Shareholder support, board response, and market reaction, *Journal of Corporate Finance* 13, 368–91.

13 Say on pay and the outrage constraint
Kym Sheehan

Say on pay is an important regulatory innovation in the area traditionally dominated by disclosure-based regimes as a targeted transparency policy (Fung et al 2007). That said, say on pay's success as a regulatory technique depends upon a number of factors, and how it fits within the overall regulatory framework for executive remuneration in any particular jurisdiction can make a major difference to its operation. Improving board of director accountability for executive remuneration decisions – the reason cited to justify regulatory intervention by government into board decision-making on remuneration (HM Treasury 2009a; Productivity Commission 2009) – is not an end in and of itself: *improved remuneration practices* are. Understanding how the vote fits within a regulatory framework highlights how the 'say' relates to the practice of 'pay', in the process identifying those levers which can be pulled by shareholders and those that are left for governments in an attempt to achieve this end game of improved remuneration practices.

This chapter examines 'say on pay' in the first three years after its introduction into law in the UK and in Australia. Section 1 presents the theoretical framework for the study. It begins in section 1.1 by examining the framework for executive remuneration in terms of the economic theories that justify executive remuneration and its regulation. Section 1.2 maps the 'regulatory space' (Hancher and Moran 1989) within which four activities (practice, disclosure, engagement and voting) occur in an annual cycle. Using the regulatory space device presents an important departure from previous literature that places more emphasis on the economic rationales for executive remuneration and its regulation (eg Bebchuk and Fried 2004), rather than devoting attention to the nature of the rules themselves. My work seeks to map the regulation of 'say on pay' as it is authentically experienced.

Section 2 presents the empirical study of its operation in the UK and Australia. By taking shareholder voting on the advisory vote as evidence of and thus a proxy for 'outrage' (Bebchuk and Fried, 2004), I investigate whether there is any pattern of changes that can be linked to this outrage. If Bebchuk and Fried are correct, outrage by shareholders should 'constrain' executive remuneration. Using content analysis[1] I identify what changes are made to remuneration practices as a result of the advisory vote. Unlike other studies that are based on regression analysis (Carter and Zamora 2008; Ferri and Maber 2008; Alissa 2009; Conyon and Sadler 2010), my study is a *qualitative analysis* of

---

[1] Content analysis is 'a careful, detailed, systematic examination and interpretation of a particular body of material in an effort to identify patterns, themes, biases and meanings': Berg 2007, pp. 303–4. It adds value through the qualitative and interpretative information it provides, even though content analysis is reported using count data and thus appears quantitative. It is both inductive and deductive (Strauss 1987), although Berg argues it is largely inductive because the method of selecting criteria for analysis presents the perceptions of 'others' whose texts are being analysed (Berg 2007).

changes to remuneration practice. Section 2.1 presents the findings of the study and examines empirical evidence of the first three years of its operation in the UK and section 2.2 presents the results for Australia. Section 2.3 compares these empirical findings and identifies three factors that contribute to the different experience in the UK over the initial three years of the advisory vote when compared with Australia. Section 3 concludes.

1   THEORETICAL JUSTIFICATIONS FOR EXECUTIVE REMUNERATION AND ITS REGULATION

In the absence of efficient markets, the economic theories derived from agency theory recognize the need for regulation to, at best, permit executive remuneration to operate as conceptualized, so that higher performance and thus higher economic benefits for shareholders are achieved. Regulating executive remuneration to facilitate these outcomes requires an understanding of the dynamic interplay between the various actors operating within the regulatory spaces that exist for executive remuneration. Accountability in this model becomes not the role of one group (the board of directors) but instead requires some kind of extended accountability between the various regulators and their targets (Scott 2001). To evaluate the effectiveness of the government's actions in mandating the remuneration report and advisory vote requires the map of the regulatory space to be drawn, so that these initiatives are seen in their context as one set of rules that seeks to influence the remuneration paid by listed companies to their senior executives. However, regulatory space does not offer its own normative explanations for regulation. Before examining the regulatory space for executive remuneration, I begin by examining the optimal contract and managerial power theories and how these influence the regulation of executive remuneration.

1.1   Optimal Contract and Managerial Power Theories

One way to 'solve' the agency problem created by the separation of ownership of listed companies from their control, typically in large public companies (Berle and Means 1933; Fama and Jensen 1983), is through executive remuneration contracts that provide an ex ante incentive for managers to create shareholder value by allowing the manager to share ex post in the gains thus obtained (Holmström 1999). Where optimal contract differs from the managerial power theory is in whether remuneration contracts solve or exacerbate the problem.

Optimal contract theory posits that executive remuneration can solve the agency problem (Jensen and Meckling 1976; Shavell 1979) by paying the manager his or her reservation value[2] plus a share of the 'profits' to maximize the utility of the manager and the owner, and apportion the risk of non-performance efficiently between them. The

---

[2]   The amount that the manager could receive in another job in the market as a 'guaranteed' or fixed sum, otherwise the manager, being a rational economic actor, will choose to work elsewhere (Diamond and Verrechia 1982; Moore 1985; Oyer 2004).

optimal contract is the *best contract in the circumstances*, not the perfect contract (Core, Guay and Larcker 2003). The manager is assumed to be risk adverse (Holmström and Milgrom 1987; Moers and Peek 2005). As a risk-adverse agent he or she will demand a risk premium if confronted with a high risk situation (Moers and Peek 2005). Unlike the risk-neutral owner who can diversify his or her portfolio to mitigate firm-specific risk, managers are not typically permitted to take their remuneration in the shares of another company to achieve the same end. Instead, managers typically receive a significant interest in the company's shares (in the form of options over shares or else rights to shares) to provide an alignment of interests (Hart 1983). However, the optimal contract designed to pay the manager his or her ex ante marginal products makes no adjustment ex post to recognize the manager's failure to achieve the performance targets. Where the risk of non-performance falls onto the executive, he or she will demand a higher salary to account for this risk. The labour market is theoretically said to provide ex-post settling up (Fama 1980) by adjusting the salary in the executive's next position upwards or downwards to reflect its assessment of the executive's performance (Desai, Hogan and Wilkins 2006). The provision of sign-on bonuses (Dickersin Van Wesep 2010) as well as golden parachute payments (Lambert and Larcker 1985) to executives on leaving the firm suggests such settling up is not guaranteed in practice (Trade and Industry Committee 2003; Stapledon 2005).

By way of contrast, the managerial power thesis (MP thesis) posits that an optimal contract, while theoretically possible, cannot be achieved in practice because the board of directors, the owners' agent for settling the terms of the contract with the manager, is effectively captured by the manager (Bebchuk and Fried 2004). The only constraint on the remuneration package is outrage by relevant outsiders to the remuneration package. To avoid outrage, the board will collude with the CEO or else the CEO will keep the true information from the board. Either way, steps will be taken to camouflage the true remuneration from outsiders' observation. Bebchuk and Fried suggest the CEO will be more powerful than the board when either the board lacks independence from management and is thus weak or ineffectual, or the company's shareholder base lacks significant institutional shareholders who, as a coalition, have an incentive to monitor both the board and senior management (Bebchuk and Fried 2003). While there is evidence to support the claim that more powerful CEOs command higher salaries (Bertrand and Mullainathan 2001), some question whether 'outrage and camouflage', key components of the managerial power thesis, are empirically testable (Murphy 2002; Snyder 2003; Jensen and Murphy 2004; Bainbridge 2005; Core, Guay and Thomas 2005; Gordon 2005). However, support for the managerial power thesis exists (for example see Singh 2006; Kuhnen and Zwiebel 2007; Ruiz-Verdu 2008). Its appeal lies in the recognition of the human factors that can bedevil attempts to regulate behaviour in the boardroom which is crucial if director accountability for their remuneration decisions is to result in 'better' remuneration practices. Controversially, Bebchuk and Fried explicitly state they would be happy with *higher* levels of remuneration than those seen commonly in the USA if the remuneration outcome results from the manager achieving superior performance measured as superior shareholder return (Bebchuk and Fried 2004). If outrage functions as a constraint, firms attracting outrage should either modify their practices to avoid future outrage, or else camouflage their true practices to obtain shareholder support.

1.1.1   Regulation justified by optimal contract and managerial power theories

Both theories accept that market mechanisms play an important role in setting remuneration levels (Holmström 1981; Bebchuk and Fried 2004), so any regulation should not interfere with the efficient operation of these mechanisms. However, to the extent that these market mechanisms are inefficient and do not operate as intended, there is scope for a range of rules to regulate different aspects of remuneration.

The traditional regulatory strategy of *disclosure laws* can enhance market efficiency (by facilitating price discovery) as well as corporate governance (by facilitating monitoring) (Moloney 2008). Both the optimal contract and managerial power theories will primarily seek disclosure-based regulation. For the optimal contract such disclosures enable performance measurement and monitoring (eg the provision of information on performance) to ensure that the contract has allocated the fruits of performance efficiently as between the owners and manager. This will require disclosures to redress the information asymmetry in favour of the manager to give the owners information on performance. Specifying the information about performance in detailed rules allows for inter-firm comparisons because each firm is disclosing the same items of information (Corporations and Markets Advisory Committee – CAMAC 2010). Optimal contract theory also justifies rules to permit owners to establish each manager's reservation value, to calculate the utility of owners and managers, and finally to assess the manager's risk in performing to achieve owners' desired performance outcomes. The remuneration committee might have to explicitly ask the manager for this information, thus justifying some involvement of the manager in setting his or her remuneration (beyond the manager providing information about company performance and strategy). The remuneration committee will need to obtain information from remuneration consultants to price the reservation value of the manager in the broader labour market.

The MP thesis seeks different disclosure rules because it is suspicious of managers' power over the board of directors (Bebchuk and Fried 2004). Hence the company's process for setting remuneration and disclosure of that process are fundamental requirements in any disclosure-based regulation. For example, the thesis will justify a rule that allocates the task of settling the remuneration contract to an independent remuneration committee of the board of directors. It will also justify a rule that gives the committee the right to appoint remuneration consultants who will advise it exclusively and will therefore perform no other work for the company (Bebchuk and Fried 2004). Furthermore, it will justify rules that limit how much control managers can wield over the board of directors (for example by requiring information on the process for selecting board members), as well as rules to diminish that power (for example, rules that prohibit the executive sitting on the remuneration committee). The MP thesis will also demand disclosure laws that diminish the potential for camouflage (such as full disclosure of pension entitlements and full disclosure of performance) and increase the potential for outrage by full expensing of all remuneration items, together with rules that prohibit certain remuneration practices (such as golden parachutes). Disclosures should expose the true value of remuneration, such as accounting standards on valuing share-based payments, and there should be disclosure laws that mandate detailed information on remuneration items including current financial year expense and accumulated earnings (Bebchuk and Fried 2004).

Both theories also suggest content for rules about *remuneration structures and forms* (for example cash, shares, options, superannuation/pension). Optimal contract theory also seeks rules that describe the relationship between the pay outcomes and the firm's performance, to write a contract that allocates risk efficiently and meets the utilities of owners and managers. Given that owners' utility is measured in terms of dividends received (the owners' share of the profit), the optimal contract justifies remuneration practice rules that endorse absolute shareholder return. It justifies some fixed remuneration, so as to meet the executive's reservation value, although most remuneration would be provided by variable remuneration (annual bonus and long term incentives). As lower performance means lower utility for owners, rules that reduce managers' pay when performance has not satisfied the owners' utility reflect the optimal contract. As the optimal contract aligns interests, rules that require some 'skin in the game' in the form of a shareholding requirement for senior executives appear consistent with this theory, although, strictly speaking, any gain does not come from firm profit, but from the market. The MP thesis justifies rules to allow owners to write a part of the contract because their agent, the board of directors, cannot be relied upon to negotiate terms that work in the owners' favour (Bebchuk and Fried 2004). It justifies additional rules to prohibit some forms of payment that allow for payments unlinked to performance (Bebchuk and Fried 2004). The MP thesis would punish non-performance by making termination of employment more likely (Bebchuk and Fried 2004), and would reduce the size of any payment made on termination (Bebchuk and Fried 2004). It justifies rules that give a high potential level of performance-related remuneration and less fixed remuneration (Bebchuk and Fried 2004).

A say on pay is more readily justifiable via the managerial power theory than it is through optimal contract theory. This is because optimal contract theory appears to assume that, once information asymmetries can be reduced, if not eliminated, both the owners and manager as profit maximizers will be able to agree on the best contract. That is, it does not explicitly factor in the further agency relationship that exists between the shareholders (owners) and their agent in these negotiations, the board of directors. Irrespective of its economic justification, it is important to understand how say on pay fits with other forms of regulation aimed at influencing directors' decisions on executive remuneration.

1.2 The Regulated Remuneration Cycle

Examining the regulation of executive remuneration through the analytic frame of regulatory space provides a holistic view of the various rule types and regulators as a system of regulation for each particular activity (Scott 2001). It also emphasizes that non-legal authority can be just as effective in regulating and ensuring compliance with standards of good remuneration practice. Other approaches that describe the regulation of executive remuneration as a layer of rules (Villiers 2006; Farrar 2008) or which present the framework in terms of the silos of rule-making authority (for example, see Productivity Commission 2009), shift the focus away from the activity being regulated onto who is regulating by describing the framework in terms of the individual regulators. As such they can overstate the case for government regulation via legal rules. Law does not invariably trump other forms of regulation of executive remuneration: in many areas or activities there are no *legal rules* that seek to regulate the particular activity (see Sheehan 2009). Thus the particular value of regulatory space lies in recognizing the non-hierarchical

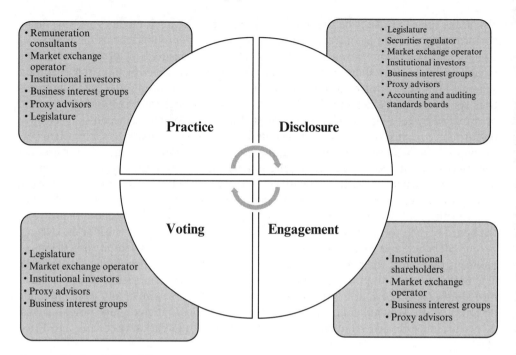

Source: Sheehan 2009, p. 278.

Figure 13.1   The regulated remuneration cycle

conception of regulation which authentically represents 'the space' for executive remuneration.

The regulated remuneration cycle pictured in Figure 13.1 represents the regulatory space for executive remuneration in the UK and Australia as an annual cycle of four activities: remuneration practice within the individual firm, disclosure of that practice to the market, shareholder engagement of boards and remuneration committees on the practices disclosed and, finally, shareholder voting on remuneration. The nature and extent of regulation of each activity varies considerably. There are limits on the extent to which legislation can directly dictate *remuneration practice*. The list of 'regulators' attached to practice in Figure 13.1 includes the 'usual suspects' of the legislature and market exchange operator, as well as persons who are not traditionally regarded as 'regulators'. Legislatures have, to date, been persuaded that market mechanisms operate on executive remuneration practice and these should be left largely unhindered (Dine 2006). In other words, governments should leave it up to 'the market' to regulate the social practice of executive remuneration with any formal regulation designed to ensure the efficiency of the market (Hill 1996; Cheffins 1997). Thus formal regulation by government is limited to disclosure initiatives and to prescribing voting rights which assign particular remuneration decisions to shareholders, such as the advisory vote on the remuneration report in the UK and Australia which consists of legislation mandating *disclosure* via a remuneration report and an annual *vote* on that report.

Given limited government intervention in the area of remuneration practice, institutional investors are the primary regulators of good remuneration practices within listed companies.[3] The notion that shareholders 'regulate' executive remuneration may at first seem unsettling. Shareholders are, after all, participants in the company through share ownership. However they are not insiders in those large listed corporations that have a dispersed pattern of share ownership. Nor are they involved in making the primary decision on remuneration. This is a decision of the board of directors. Shareholders make rules in the form of practice guidance, about what a 'good' remuneration structure looks like. How they control the decisions of directors is through their engagement and voting activities. In doing so, they 'regulate' board conduct. The further notion that shareholders act in an enforcement role might appear to depart from more typical analyses of the relationship between shareholders and the company. John Armour notes that shareholder voting should not be thought of as 'governance' in this context, but as informal, private enforcement (Armour 2008).

The regulated remuneration cycle acknowledges that shareholders and boards deal with matters informally behind closed doors via engagement. Thus, the interpretations and negotiations of the remuneration practice rules can be thought of as regulatory 'conversations' (Black 2002). They can occur at the *micro-level* as conversations between a remuneration consultant and a remuneration committee, or a remuneration committee and an institutional investor (Pendelton 2005); or at a more *formal level* as discussions about the formulation and reformulation of rules and policies. These regulatory conversations can involve a number of players both in one-on-one (remuneration committee and chief executive, remuneration committee and one shareholder) and in two- or three-way conversations (remuneration committee with remuneration consultants and chief executive and a number of institutional investors, proxy advisors and perhaps even the media, if the firm's remuneration practices have attracted some notoriety).

Understanding the micro-level at which much of the regulation of executive remuneration 'happens' is crucial to appreciating how executive remuneration decisions are regulated in practice. The quality of these micro-level regulatory conversations is therefore critical to the rules applied and hence the quality of the decision made. Poor conversations are likely to result in sub-optimal application where the principles, standards and guidance surrounding executive remuneration are narrowly interpreted as rules to be followed to the letter, irrespective of whether that practice is actually appropriate for the company, given its circumstances: the 'principles paradox' (Black 2008). Furthermore, that say on pay is acknowledged as leading to increased engagement (Gilshan and PIRC

---

[3]   While many writers view proxy advisors as driving the decisions of institutional investors (Larcker and Tayan 2010), their role may simply be boosting the *regulatory capacities of individual institutional shareholders* by providing resources such as information and expertise to facilitate shareholder actions to enforce their own guidance. As one well-known Australian proxy advisor says, 'We don't fire the bullets. We make them' (Chessell and Kitney 2010). My own interview research confirms that institutional investors are more likely to follow without question a recommendation to vote 'for' the remuneration report. A recommendation to vote 'against' the resolution will be flagged within the fund manager/pension or superannuation fund (depending on who has the voting right per the terms of the mandate between the pension/superannuation fund), and the decision made internally.

Ltd 2009; Productivity Commission 2009) does not mean better decisions are being made by boards of directors and their remuneration committees.

With this understanding of the regulatory framework within which say on pay operates in the UK and Australia, section 2 presents empirical evidence of its initial period of operation in the UK over the period from 2003 until 2005. While this study is not specifically seeking to measure the outrage constraint, but to detect what effect the advisory vote had on subsequent remuneration practice, it is possible to use the advisory vote as a proxy for the outrage constraint identified by Bebchuk and Fried. If the vote is effective in constraining executive remuneration, it should be possible to detect a change in remuneration practices following a level of shareholder dissent that approaches 'outrage'.

2   EMPIRICAL STUDY

There were two phases to this study: an analysis of voting results in two samples of companies, one drawn from the FTSE 100 and the other drawn from the S&P ASX 200 and the content analysis of changes in remuneration practices as disclosed by these two samples for the initial three years of the operation of say on pay (2003–05 for the UK, 2005–08 for Australia).[4] Based on the voting results, I split the sample into two groups, an outrage group and a control group. Measuring the level of changes, as well as the nature of the changes for each group using content analysis to detect these changes, and then comparing the results between the two groups would allow me to account for changes in executive remuneration practice generally (both groups would make the change at the same rate), as well as identifying those changes that can be attributed to the outrage expressed by shareholders via the Non-binding Shareholder Vote on the Directors' Remuneration Report (NBSV) (the level of changes in the outrage group would be higher). Once the sample is split into two groups based on the relevant threshold results at the 2003 AGM, *the groups do not change for the remaining two years.*[5]

Analyses were conducted using three different cut-off points: the *median level of outrage* at AGM 2003, the *10 per cent level of outrage* at AGM 2003 and the *25 per cent level of outrage* at AGM 2003. To determine the magnitude of 'outrage', the actual votes for and against the resolution were re-weighted to take account of votes withheld (where these were separately disclosed), an approach consistent with the Pensions Investment

---

    [4]   The Australian financial year runs from 1 July to 30 June. Thus the first year of the Australian study is FY05/06 and the last is FY07/08.

    [5]   An alternative approach would be to reconstitute the groups each year and base the analysis on two years' data (year of outrage, year of response), with the periods being AGM 2003/2004 and AGM 2004/2005. Reconstituting the 10 per cent outrage group based on the AGM 2004 results would result in a group of 25 companies, of which 20 were in the original 2003 10 per cent outrage group. Repeating the same task based on the 2005 AGM results would result in a group of 12 companies, of which 11 were in the original 2003 outrage group. Based on the observations from the initial sample that a response could take up to two years to eventuate, it was decided not to adopt this alternative approach.

Research Consultants (PIRC) methodology (Pensions Investment Research Consultants, 'Directors' Remuneration to the Trade and Industry Committee', 2003). The votes against and votes withheld were summed as the outrage vote.[6] Proxy instructions to vote at the discretion of the proxy were ignored and not taken into consideration.

The choice of 10 per cent outrage reflects not only evidence of institutional investors using the vote abstain as a 'yellow card' but also comments made to me by institutional investors that '10 per cent' against the remuneration report was the level at which remuneration committees would think about changing practices, while '25 per cent against' was the level at which a change to these practices would be required. While 10 per cent and 25 per cent votes against were also used as thresholds in my analysis, I adopted 10 per cent and 25 per cent outrage as the relevant thresholds to report, consistent both with the PIRC approach mentioned, as well as the evidence of strategic use of the abstain vote. The threshold of 25 per cent also reflects a benchmark set by the UK government in responding to the global financial crisis (HM Treasury 2009 (recommendation 36)), as well as the policy position of the Australian Government in accepting the recommendation of the Productivity Committee (Australian Government 2010).

2.1 UK Study

Proxy voting instructions or poll voting data for the sample of FTSE 100 companies for the period 2003–07 were obtained either from the company's website or from the Regulatory Notice Service offered by the London Stock Exchange. The voting results are presented in Table 13.1 and show that a median outrage vote on the remuneration report at the 2003 AGMs in the sample of 73 FTSE 100 companies was 16 per cent (average 17.79 per cent), with the spread between median and average reflecting the existence of some high levels of outrage. The highest outrage vote reported in 2003 was 63 per cent achieved by GlaxoSmithKline. By the 2004 AGMs, the general level of shareholder outrage was muted (median of 7 per cent) and was further silenced in the 2005 AGMs to a median of 5 per cent. Clearly, shareholders' sentiments towards company remuneration practices altered over this three year period, even though the maximum outrage values reported in Table 13.1 indicate that investors were willing to resort to an outrage vote at both the 2004 and 2005 AGMs.[7] The change in shareholder sentiment is also reflected in the declining level of abstaining votes: shareholders no longer needed to resort to this nuanced voting preference by 2005 to send a message to remuneration committees.

---

[6] The outrage vote represents the proportion of all proxy intentions that were against management, either as a vote against, or a vote withheld or abstained. That is, Outrage vote = (proxy instructions against + proxy instructions withheld/abstain) ÷ total number of proxy votes cast.

[7] A point noted by the NAPF in relation to contract length: National Association of Pension Funds, *Voting Guidelines and Statements of Good Practice for the 2004 NAPF Corporate Governance Policy* (2005), (principle K.6) and for change in control clauses in executive service contracts: NAPF 2005 (principle K.8). In both instances, the NAPF warns that failure to comply with good practice may lead to a recommendation to vote against the re-election of the remuneration committee chairman or another member of the committee.

Table 13.1 Summary proxy statistics, FTSE 100 sample, AGMs 2003–2005

Summary statistics	AGM 2003				AGM 2004				AGM 2005			
	For	Abstain	Oppose	Outrage	For	Abstain	Oppose	Outrage	For	Abstain	Oppose	Outrage
Total sample¹	73											
Median	84.00	7.00	8.00	16.00	93.00	1.00	3.42	7.00	94.1	2.00	3.00	5.00
Average	82.41	8.31	11.87	17.79	90.58	4.78	5.31	9.5	92.92	2.81	4.54	7.12
Minimum value	37.00	0	1.00	1.00	61.00	0	0	1.00	63.0	0	0	1.0
Maximum value	99.00	25.0	49.00	63.00	99.00	14.00	28.00	39.00	99.00	28.00	34.00	37.00

Note: 1. The total sample is calculated on the votes 'for' and 'oppose'. Due to a lack of consistent disclosure of the votes abstained or votes withheld, the sample for the abstaining votes varies by AGM year (52, 64 and 67 in years 2003, 2004 and 2005 respectively).

Table 13.2   Categories of observed changes to remuneration practice

Term	Description
Governance changes	
Change	Overall change to policy disclosed; new policy to apply for next year (does not apply in year of vote)
Consultation	Disclosure of consultation with major shareholders on remuneration strategy
Contract	Changes to contract made
Review	Review disclosed in advance, to occur post AGM
Shareholding	New shareholding requirements introduced
Quantum changes	
Opportunity	Increase in size of annual grant for a short term incentive scheme
Opportunity L	Increase in size of annual grant for a long term incentive scheme
Structural changes	
Comparator L	Introduce use of a peer comparator group for existing long-term plans or change existing comparator group
Performance	Change to performance criteria from those used for existing short terms plans
Performance L	Change to performance criteria from those used for existing long term plans
Retests	Removal of re-testing provisions from LTI plans (so that performance is measured over a defined period, rather than a rolling period)

2.1.1   Content analysis of changes to practice

The criteria of analysis[8] used in the UK study were initially developed from the first two years of the FTSE 100 annual reports for a group of 28 companies identified in a submission to the 'Rewards for Failure' inquiry. Companies disclosed various aspects of their remuneration practice in a similar manner, which led me to investigate further to see if there was any relationship between the advisory vote outcomes and the changes in practice.

The views of good practice expressed in the relevant guidelines issued by institutional investors and others as the criteria of analysis can be further categorized into *governance* rules (rules about how to make executive remuneration decisions so as to mitigate the principal–agent problem and managerial power) and *structural* rules (rules that describe characteristics evident in 'best' executive remuneration practices). These are summarized below in Table 13.2: categories of observed changes to remuneration practice. A further two categories were added to measure changes to the quantum of remuneration and are classified as quantum changes.[9]

I then reviewed the directors' remuneration reports (DRRs) for each of the three

---

[8]   Criteria of analysis are simply categories based on words or phrases in the remuneration report.

[9]   A fuller explanation of these categories can be found in Sheehan 2007.

Table 13.3   Changes to remuneration practice by number of firms, FTSE 100 sample,
2003–2005 AGMs

Type of change	Number (%) of firms making change		
	AGM 2003	AGM 2004	AGM 2005
Governance changes			
Change	5 (6.85%)	24 (32.88%)	25 (34.25%)
Consultation	3 (4.11%)	14 (19.18%)	16 (21.92%)
Contract	7 (9.59%)	21 (28.77%)	3 (4.11%)
Review	11 (15.07%)	18 (24.66%)	16 (21.92%)
Shareholding	6 (8.22%)	9 (12.33%)	11 (15.07%)
Quantum changes			
Opportunity	10 (13.70%)	20 (27.40%)	26 (35.62%)
Opportunity L	9 (12.33%)	22 (30.14%)	23 (31.51%)
Structural changes			
Comparator L	6 (8.22%)	16 (21.92%)	19 (26.03%)
Performance	4 (5.48%)	10 (13.70%)	18 (24.66%)
Performance L	10 (13.70%)	34 (46.58%)	27 (36.99%)
Retests	3 (4.11%)	25 (34.25%)	20 (27.40%)

Note: Total sample is 73 companies.

years to identify changes between the remuneration policies and practices as disclosed
in the year 1 DRR (the DRR voted on at the 2003 AGM) with those disclosed in years
2 (the DRR voted on at the 2004 AGM) and 3 (the DRR voted on at the 2005 AGM).
Changes were classified into the above categories, based upon observed changes to
practice.

Table 13.3 shows the number of companies within the sample that made changes to
each of these 11 remuneration practices over the years 2003–05. Results are reported
below for the 10 per cent outrage threshold (Table 13.4) and 25 per cent outrage threshold
(Table 13.5). Each of the tables show the number of companies in the group (outrage or
control) making the change, as well as the percentage of each group that disclosed the
particular change in the remuneration report voted on at that year's AGM. In interpreting the results below, a comparison of the percentage of the group making that particular
change is most relevant because it takes into consideration the differing group sizes for
the 10 per cent and 25 per cent thresholds.

2.1.2   Governance changes

The changes observed in executive director service contracts ('Contract') have been
noted elsewhere (Deloitte 2004; Thompson 2005), reflecting what has been an important
issue over many years (PricewaterhouseCoopers 1999). A strong response by the
outrage group evident in 2004 across the 10 per cent and 25 per cent thresholds (37.5
per cent and 47.06 per cent respectively) should not overshadow the fact that some
companies in the control group at the 10 per cent and 25 per cent level also amended
contracts in 2004 (that is after the 2003 AGM) to comply with best practice guidelines

Table 13.4   *Changes made to remuneration, FTSE 100 sample, AGMs 2003–2005 (outrage and control groups based on 10% outrage on NSBSV AT 2003 AGM)*

Type of change	AGM 2003		AGM 2004		AGM 2005	
	Outrage (% group)	Control (% group)	Outrage (% group)	Control (% group)	Outrage (% group)	Control (% group)
Governance changes						
Change	4 (8.33%)	1 (4.00%)	18 (37.50%)	6 (24.00%)	19 (39.58%)	6 (24.00%)
Consultation	2 (4.17%)	1 (4.00%)	13 (27.08%)	1 (4.00%)	9 (18.75%)	7 (28.00%)
Contract	3 (6.25%)	4 (16.00%)	18 (37.50%)	3 (12.00%)	3 (6.25%)	0
Review	4 (8.33%)	7 (28.00%)	9 (18.75%)	9 (36.00%)	10 (20.83%)	6 (24.00%)
Shareholding	3 (6.25%)	3 (12.00%)	8 (16.67%)	1 (4.00%)	7 (14.58%)	4 (16.00%)
Quantum changes						
Opportunity	3 (6.25%)	7 (28.00%)	12 (25.00%)	8 (32.00%)	15 (31.25%)	11 (44.00%)
Opportunity L	5 (10.42%)	4 (16.00%)	13 (27.08%)	9 (36.00%)	16 (33.33%)	7 (28.00%)
Structural changes						
Comparator L	4 (8.33%)	2 (8.00%)	9 (18.75%)	7 (28.00%)	15 (31.25%)	4 (16.00%)
Performance	2 (4.17%)	2 (8.00%)	6 (12.50%)	4 (16.00%)	9 (18.75%)	9 (36.00%)
Performance L	6 (12.50%)	4 (16.00%)	24 (50.00%)	10 (40.00%)	19 (39.58%)	9 (36.00%)
Retests	2 (4.17%)	1 (4.00%)	20 (41.67%)	5 (20.00%)	18 (37.50%)	2 (8.00%)

Note: N(outrage) = 48; N(control) = 25; total sample = 73 companies.

Table 13.5   *Changes made to remuneration, FTSE 100 sample, AGMs 2003–2005 (outrage and control groups based on 25% outrage on NBSV at 2003 AGM)*

Type of change	AGM 2003		AGM 2004		AGM 2005	
	Outrage (% group)	Control (% group)	Outrage (% group)	Control (% group)	Outrage (% group)	Control (% group)
Governance changes						
Change	3 (17.65%)	2 (3.57%)	10 (58.82%)	14 (25.00%)	4 (23.53%)	21 (37.50%)
Consultation	1 (5.88%)	2 (3.57%)	7 (41.18%)	7 (12.50%)	3 (17.65%)	13 (23.21%)
Contract	1 (5.88%)	6 (10.71%)	8 (47.06%)	13 (23.21%)	1 (5.88%)	2 (3.57%)
Review	3 (17.65%)	8 (14.29%)	2 (11.76%)	16 (28.57%)	5 (29.41%)	11 (19.64%)
Shareholding	1 (5.88%)	5 (8.93%)	5 (29.41%)	4 (7.14%)	1 (5.88%)	10 (17.86%)
Quantum changes						
Opportunity	1 (5.88%)	9 (16.07%)	7 (41.18%)	13 (23.21%)	5 (29.41%)	21 (37.50%)
Opportunity L	3 (17.65%)	6 (10.71%)	5 (29.41%)	17 (30.36%)	3 (17.65%)	20 (35.71%)
Structural changes						
Comparator L	2 (11.76%)	4 (7.14%)	4 (23.53%)	12 (21.43%)	3 (17.65%)	16 (28.57%)
Performance	2 (11.76%)	2 (3.57%)	4 (23.53%)	6 (10.71%)	1 (5.88%)	17 (30.36%)
Performance L	4 (23.53%)	6 (10.71%)	12 (70.59%)	22 (39.29%)	5 (29.41%)	22 (39.29%)
Retests	1 (5.88%)	2 (3.57%)	6 (35.29%)	19 (33.93%)	7 (41.18%)	13 (23.21%)

Note: N(outrage) = 17; N(control) = 56; total sample = 73 companies.

(12 per cent and 23.31 per cent at the 10 per cent and 25 per cent thresholds respectively). In other words, something more than a non-compliant contract was required to attract a NBSV sanction at the 2003 AGM. These remuneration committees might have engaged with shareholders prior to the AGM. This could be captured by 'Consultation'. However, that category was used predominantly by companies in the outrage group at the 2004 AGM (27.08 per cent and 41.08 per cent for 10 per cent and 25 per cent thresholds).[10]

Alternatively, companies in the control group might have used the promise of a review of remuneration practices to occur after the AGM as a way of garnering shareholder support. 'Review' is higher in the control group for AGM 2003 at the 10 per cent threshold (but not the 25 per cent threshold), however both 'Change' and 'Review' are higher in AGM 2004 and AGM 2005 across both groups. Based on this analysis, 'Change' and 'Review' indicate that the remuneration committee appreciates its policies need to be revisited in a major review of remuneration practices that occurs alongside the annual review. This signal can be used strategically by companies to obtain shareholder support for the current year's DRR, where shareholders might otherwise have voted against or voted 'abstain' on this resolution.

2.1.3   Quantum changes

An interesting finding is the incidence of increases in *annual bonus opportunity* ('Opportunity') and *long term incentive scheme opportunity* ('OpportunityL') across both groups and over the whole period examined. This is consistent with remuneration consultant survey data showing growth in maximum bonus potential for chief executives of FTSE100 companies between years 2004 (KPMG 2004) and 2005 (Sjostrom and Shammai 2005). The high levels of companies making increases to 'Opportunity' and 'OpportunityL' for control group companies across all thresholds during the three years of the study (28, 32 and 44 per cent for the 10 per cent threshold, 17.07, 23.21 and 37.50 per cent for the 25 per cent threshold), and the higher incidence of these same changes for outrage companies in AGM 2004 and AGM 2005 (25 and 31.35 per cent for the 10 per cent threshold, 41.18 and 29.41 per cent for the 25 per cent threshold), suggest that companies complying with best practice guidelines for the structure of remuneration can, within limits, increase remuneration without attracting shareholder dissent. The basis on which shareholders will assess the increase, the proxy advisors' reports on comparative market data, will typically show a number of companies making a similar increase. Given shareholder guidelines encourage companies to pay market rates of remuneration (for example see ABI 2002), and that quantum is not necessarily of concern to shareholders, there is no basis on which shareholders can label the increase as unjustified, abusive or egregious.[11]

---

[10]   There is also evidence of 'Consultation' in both groups leading up to the 2005 AGM. However, given the groups do not change over the three years of the study, it may be that companies in the control group attracted shareholder wrath at the 2004 AGM for their practices. However, as noted above in note 5, only five companies in the control group (based on 2003 outrage) attracted outrage of more than 10 per cent against their remuneration report at the 2004 AGM.

[11]   While my methodology does not allow me to examine this, a regression analysis to detect the impact of the advisory vote on the quantum of remuneration should factor in market levels of increases.

2.1.4   Structural changes

The explosive growth in companies making 'PerformanceL' changes over 2004 and 2005 (per Table 13.3, 46.58 and 36.99 per cent of companies in the overall sample made these changes) and the high level of 'PerformanceL' changes in both groups, particularly the outrage group in AGM 2004 (50 and 70.59 per cent for the 10 per cent and 25 per cent thresholds respectively) are both consistent with increasing numbers of share plan resolutions in 2004 and 2005.[12] It is also consistent with remuneration consultant data (Birla 2005, p. 5). Companies can be very surprised when share plans endorsed by shareholders within the previous couple of years are 'suddenly' no longer acceptable to them (Halliwell Consulting 2005). Companies adopting a new vehicle to deliver long term incentives are likely to make this particular change. While the choice of performance criteria for long term incentive plans is cyclical (Buck et al. 2003), such criteria are specified in detail in the pertinent shareholder guidance. Non-compliance is highly visible to both proxy advisory services and institutional investors.

Finally, the overall level of changes to 'Retests' is high in 2004 AGM and 2005 AGM (per Table 13.3, 34.25 and 27.40 per cent of the overall sample of 73 companies) and reflects a change of position from where retests were unnecessary and needed to be justified to be acceptable to shareholders (but could be acceptable), to a position of no retests in the 2004 guidelines (ABI 2004 (guideline 8.1); NAPF 2005 (guideline L.10)).

2.1.5   Conclusion on UK study

Evidence of changes made to remuneration in AGM 2004 by companies in the control group support Eilis Ferran's hypothesis that institutional investors use the *threat* of a negative vote to enforce compliance (Ferran 2005). As noted by one UK-based corporate governance manager in an interview with the author in 2008: 'A company knows that if it gets a New Bridge Street [remuneration consultant] plan with 50 per cent TSR and 50 per cent EPS it will get through on the nod.' 'Getting through on the nod' means that companies are being driven towards one model of best practice: the model that reflects shareholders' views of what constitutes good remuneration practice. We shall see in the next subsection that the Australian experience of say on pay was very different in its first three years of operation.

2.2   Australian Study

Voting data for the 109 companies in the S&P/ASX 200 sample was obtained from company disclosures of proxy voting and poll outcomes to the ASX.[13] To determine outrage, the voting results were analysed for any results which separated out those proxies that permitted voting at the proxy's discretion and excluded these from the

---

[12]   There were 36 at the 2004 AGM and 32 at the 2005 AGM, compared with 12 resolutions at the 2003 AGM.

[13]   Disclosure is required under the *Corporations Act 2001* (Cth), s 251AA. Unlike the UK sample where disclosure of votes withheld did not become standard practice until 2005/06, most Australian listed companies comply with this requirement. Thus there is no need to draw a sub-sample as was the case with the UK study.

calculations of votes for and total votes.[14] The voting results for the Australian sample are shown in Table 13.6. The median outrage vote in the year 1 sample was 6.19 per cent (average 9.14 per cent), decreased in year 2 (4.38 per cent) but increased again in year 3 (5.21 per cent). However, unlike the UK study results reported in Table 13.1 the maximum value of outrage increased over the three years of the Australian study. The effect of these large outrage votes is reflected in the spread between the median and average outrage votes reported in Table 13.6 which increased from year one to year three.

2.2.1   Content analysis of RRs

Observed changes were classified into a number of the same categories as those used in the UK study. To capture observed local practices and practice guidance, some new categories were added: A-Contract, Hedging, Retention, MD Loans and Remco. These terms are summarized in Table 13.7.

Table 13.8 shows the number of companies within the sample that made the various types of changes over each of the three years. The overall level of activity in years 2 and 3 is markedly lower than that observed in the FTSE 100 sample in its second and third years (see Table 13.3). To allow comparison with the UK study results, the same three thresholds were used to determine outrage and thus split the sample into an outrage group and a control group. Table 13.9 reports the results for the 10 per cent outrage vote at the year 1 AGM, with the 25 per cent outrage vote threshold reported in Table 13.10. With only a few exceptions, the nature and percentage of the sample making a change is the same for both groups as the 109-company sample. *That is, splitting the Australian sample into an outrage and a control group does not indicate that companies attracting shareholder sanction via the Remuneration Report Vote (RRV) in year 1 amended their practices in year 2 more frequently, or in very particular ways, compared with companies that did not attract such a sanction.* There are some differences observed in the 25 per cent outrage group; however the size of the 25 per cent outrage group is very small, with 8 companies, or just over 5 per cent of the full 109-company sample falling into this category.

2.2.2   Governance changes

The category 'A-Contract' (a change to the termination provisions in the employment contract) is low, with only 16 of the 109 companies making changes to the MD/CEO's remuneration contract over the period, despite detailed shareholder guidance since July 2005 on the issue (ACSI 2005, principle 14.1). The ASX CG Council guidance on termination provisions in the 2003 edition of its corporate governance guidelines does not seek to describe what an acceptable termination payment looks like (such as 12 months' base salary) (cf Financial Reporting Council 2003, B.1.6). This position is the same in its revised guidance that influenced year 3 of the study (ASX Corporate Governance Council 2007).

Even the general categories 'Change' and 'Review' are low over the three years, with 28 companies disclosing 'Change' and 19 companies disclosing 'Review'. These results

---

[14]   There is much variation in the level of open instructions. The average (median) level of instructions in the sample group of 109 companies was 10.07 per cent (2.78 per cent) in year 1, 6.29 per cent (2.73 per cent) in year 2 and 6.24 per cent (2.73 per cent) in year 3.

Table 13.6 *Summary proxy statistics, RRV sample S&P/ASX 200, AGMs 2005–2007*

Summary statistics	AGM year 1				AGM year 2				AGM year 3			
	For	Abstain	Oppose	Outrage	For	Abstain	Oppose	Outrage	For	Abstain	Oppose	Outrage
Total sample	109											
Median	93.81%	0.97%	4.24%	6.19%	95.62%	0.57%	3.15%	4.38%	94.79%	0.67%	3.81%	5.21%
Average	90.86%	2.80%	6.34%	9.14%	92.10%	1.33%	6.57%	7.90%	91.60%	1.35%	7.05%	8.40%
Minimum value	51.49%	0	0.03%	0.05%	45.59%	0.03%	0.13%	0.34%	30.76%	0.00%	0.42%	0.42%
Maximum value	99.95%	27.89%	45.39%	48.51%	99.66%	18.39%	52.61%	54.41%	99.58%	11.93%	64.88%	69.24%

271

Table 13.7   Additional categories of observed changes to remuneration practices in Australia[1]

Term	Description
Governance changes	
A-Contract	Change to termination provisions in employment contract
Hedging	Company's share trading policy includes provision prohibiting hedging of unvested share-based payments
RemCo	Remuneration committee consists solely of independent non-executive directors
MD Loans	Long term incentive scheme funds purchase of shares on market through the provision of a company loan to the managing director
Quantum changes	
Retention	Disclosure of special payment made as a retention device

Note: 1.   It is important to note that two categories, 'MD Loans' and 'RemCo', do not represent a change from previous practice: 'MD Loans' is the number of companies where there is a loan given by the company to the MD, while 'RemCo' represents the number of companies with a fully independent remuneration committee.

suggest Australian companies did not need to try to avoid a shareholder sanction by indicating in the remuneration report that major changes to the remuneration practices had either been made ('Change') or that the policy was under examination over the next year ('Review'). 'Consultation' was rarely used by companies in the Australian sample. This does not of course mean that Australian remuneration committees were not consulting with shareholders. Interviews with remuneration committee chairmen, remuneration consultants and institutional investors in 2009 confirmed that it was common practice for Australian remuneration committees to engage with fund managers or their proxy advisors about remuneration, even though the conversation did not necessarily resolve the differences of opinion.

The low levels of governance changes in general do not mean that the Australian sample companies were not responsive to changing views of best remuneration practice. The levels of change with 'Hedging' over the three years of the study are a good example of how effective shareholder guidance can be in achieving changes to remuneration and governance practices. By year 3, 52 companies or 48 per cent of sample companies disclosed that the company prohibited hedging of unvested share-based remuneration rewards. ACSI's guidance has been against hedging since 2003 (ACSI 2003, guideline 13.7). The major institutional investors' representative organisation, IFSA, only adopted this stance in 2007, in line with changes in the revised ASX Corporate Governance Council's *Principles of Corporate Governance and Practice Recommendations* issued in 2007.

The change with 'RemCo' differs in its character. Neither the ASX corporate governance principles nor shareholder guidance recommend that the remuneration committee consist only of independent non-executive directors. Thus the movement towards a fully independent remuneration committee evident over the three years of the Australian study as measured by 'RemCo' cannot be attributed to local shareholder expectations. Rather it reflects the influence of practice statements from the Australian Institute of Company

Table 13.8   Number of companies making changes in Australian sample, 2005/06–2007/08[1]

Type of change	Number (%) of firms making change		
	AGM YEAR 1	AGM YEAR 2	AGM YEAR 3
Governance changes			
A-Contract	1 (0.92%)	7 (6.42%)	8 (7.34%)
Change	9 (8.26%)	11 (10.09%)	8 (7.34%)
Consultation	1 (0.92%)	3 (2.75%)	2 (1.83%)
Hedging	5 (4.59%)	30 (27.52%)	17 (15.60%)
MD Loans[2]	18 (16.51%)	22 (20.18%)	18 (16.51%)
RemCo[3]	57 (52.29%)	60 (55.05%)	65 (59.63%)
Review	8 (7.34%)	6 (5.50%)	5 (4.59%)
Shareholding	4 (3.67%)	2 (1.83%)	2 (1.83%)
Quantum changes			
Opportunity	12 (11.01%)	20 (18.35%)	21 (19.27%)
Opportunity L	9 (8.26%)	15 (12.84%)	10 (9.17%)
Retention	2 (1.83%)	4 (3.67%)	8 (7.34%)
Structural changes			
Comparator L	3 (2.75%)	6 (5.50%)	6 (5.50%)
Performance	0	18 (16.51%)	18 (16.51%)
Performance L	10 (9.17%)	29 (26.61%)	23 (21.10%)
Retests	3 (2.75%)	4 (3.67%)	3 (2.75%)

Notes:
1. Total sample = 109 companies.
2. MD Loans is recorded as '1' if the company has entered into a loan agreement with the MD/CEO. Thus the details here do not strictly represent a change.
3. RemCo is recorded as '1' if the company has a remuneration committee consisting only of independent directors. Thus the details here do not strictly represent a change.

Directors who advise boards to adopt a fully independent remuneration committee to avoid perceptions of a conflict of interest (AICD 2004; AICD 2009).

2.2.3   Quantum changes

The quantum measures 'Opportunity' and 'OpportunityL' are stronger in years 2 and 3 than in year 1 and reflect analysis from RiskMetrics showing an average increase in STIs for the ASX 100 of 11.1 per cent in each of years 1 and 2, and an increase of 32.6 per cent in year 3 (ISS Proxy Australia, 2005; ISS 2006; RiskMetrics (ISS Governance Services) 2007; RiskMetrics (ISS Governance Services) 2008). Increases to the LTI via 'OpportunityL' are stronger in the control group than the outrage group at all thresholds. The number of firms disclosing this particular change is less than the number of firms seeking shareholder approval for an issue of securities under ASX Listing Rule 10.14.[15]

---

[15]   The number of resolutions that approved the issue to the CEO/MD was 41 (year 1), 42 (year 2) and 46 (year 3). That shareholder approval is typically sought for grants over a two to three year

Table 13.9   Changes made to remuneration, ASX 200 sample 2005–2007 (outrage and control groups based on 10% outrage on RRV at AGM year 1)

Type of change	AGM year 1		AGM year 2		AGM year 3	
	Outrage (% group)	Control (% group)	Outrage (% group)	Control (% group)	Outrage (% group)	Control (% group)
Governance changes						
A-Contract	0	1 (1.35%)	2 (5.71%)	5 (6.76%)	3 (8.57%)	5 (6.76%)
Change	2 (5.71%)	7 (9.46%)	5 (14.29%)	6 (8.11%)	4 (11.43%)	4 (5.41%)
Consultation	0	1 (1.35%)	2 (5.71%)	1 (1.35%)	1 (2.86%)	1 (1.35%)
Hedging	2 (5.71%)	3 (4.05%)	8 (22.86%)	22 (29.73%)	7 (20.00%)	10 (13.51%)
MD Loans	9 (25.71%)	9 (12.16%)	11 (31.43%)	11 (14.86%)	10 (28.57%)	8 (10.81%)
RemCo	15 (42.86%)	42 (56.76%)	16 (45.71%)	44 (59.46%)	20 (57.14%)	45 (60.81%)
Review	0	8 (10.81%)	2 (5.71%)	4 (5.41%)	1 (2.86%)	4 (5.41%)
Shareholding	0	4 (5.41%)	0	2 (2.70%)	0	2 (2.70%)
Quantum changes						
Opportunity	3 (8.57%)	9 (12.16%)	7 (17.14%)	13 (17.57%)	5 (14.29%)	16 (21.62%)
Opportunity L	1 (2.86%)	8 (10.81%)	2 (5.71%)	13 (17.57%)	3 (8.57%)	7 (9.46%)
Retention	0	2 (2.70%)	0	4 (5.41%)	3 (8.57%)	5 (6.76%)
Structural changes						
Comparator L	0	3 (4.05%)	0	10 (13.51%)	2 (5.71%)	4 (5.41%)
Performance	1 (2.86%)	7 (9.46%)	6 (17.14%)	12 (16.22%)	8 (22.86%)	10 (13.51%)
Performance L	4 (11.43%)	8 (10.81%)	10 (28.57%)	19 (25.68%)	6 (17.14%)	17 (22.97%)
Retests	0	3 (4.05%)	1 (2.86%)	3 (4.05%)	0	3 (4.05%)

Note: N(outrage) = 35; N(control) = 74; total sample = 109 companies.

2.2.4   Structural changes

The relevant guidance for the configuration of short-term incentive schemes, 'Performance', suggests the performance measures and targets should be clear (ACSI 2005, principle 14.5(b)). However, the internal budgets against which performance is measured are commercial secrets, which shareholders do not expect to be disclosed (ACSI 2005, principle 14.5(c)). Companies also have a lot of flexibility in designing short-term incentives. These latter two factors best explain the low but consistent incidence of this type of change in years 2 and 3 of the study. Opaque disclosure requirements surrounding STIs also mean that it is possible the performance criteria are changed more frequently by more companies than detected in this study.

The level of 'PerformanceL' changes in years two and three is significant: Table 13.9 shows that just over 26 per cent of the total sample made changes to the long-term incentive scheme performance measures in year two of the study, with just over 21 per cent of the total sample making a change to these measures in year 3 of the study. Shareholder guidance on the structure of long-term incentive schemes is detailed, with ACSI releasing

cycle is a plausible explanation for the lower rate of change for 'OpportunityL' compared with the UK sample.

Table 13.10   *Changes made to remuneration, ASX 200 sample 2005–2007 (outrage and control groups based on 25% outrage on RRV at AGM year 1)*

Type of change	AGM year 1		AGM year 2		AGM year 3	
	Outrage (% group)	Control (% group)	Outrage (% group)	Control (% group)	Outrage (% group)	Control (% group)
Governance changes						
A-Contract	0	1 (0.99%)	1 (12.50%)	6 (5.94%)	1 (12.50%)	7 (6.93%)
Change	0	9 (8.91%)	2 (25.00%)	9 (8.91%)	1 (12.50%)	7 (6.93%)
Consultation	0	1 (0.99%)	1 (12.50%)	2 (1.98%)	0	2 (1.98%)
Hedging	1 (12.50%)	4 (3.96%)	3 (37.50%)	27 (26.73%)	2 (25.00%)	15 (14.85%)
MD Loans	2 (25.00%)	16 (15.84%)	3 (37.50%)	19 (18.91%)	3 (37.50%)	15 (14.85%)
RemCo	3 (37.50%)	54 (53.47%)	3 (37.50%)	57 (56.44%)	6 (75.00%)	59 (58.42%)
Review	0	8 (7.92%)	1 (12.50%)	5 (4.95%)	0	5 (4.95%)
Shareholding	0	4 (3.96%)	0	2 (1.98%)	0	2 (1.98%)
Quantum changes						
Opportunity	0	12 (11.88%)	1 (12.50%)	19 (18.91%)	2 (25.00%)	19 (18.91%)
Opportunity L	0	9 (8.91%)	1 (12.50%)	14 (13.86%)	0	10 (9.90%)
Retention	0	2 (1.98%)	0	4 (3.96%)	1 (12.50%)	7 (6.93%)
Structural changes						
Comparator L	0	3 (2.97%)	0	10 (9.90%)	1 (12.50%)	5 (4.95%)
Performance	0	8 (7.92%)	0	18 (17.82%)	1 (12.50%)	17 (16.83%)
Performance L	0	12 (11.88%)	5 (62.50%)	24 (23.76%)	2 (25.00%)	21 (20.79%)
Retests	0	3 (2.97%)	0	4 (3.96%)	0	3 (2.97%)

Note: N(outrage) = 8; N(control) = 101; total sample = 109 companies.

new guidance in July 2005 and July 2007, and IFSA revising its 2000 guidance in 2007. While evidence in 2009 to the Productivity Commission suggests that Australian LTI practices have converged towards a single view of best practice (Productivity Commission 2009), it did not reach this end state in the first three years of the advisory vote.

2.2.5   Conclusion on the Australian study

The Australian experience over the first three years of the 'remuneration report plus advisory vote' is very different to the UK experience described earlier. Particular types of structural changes are relevant to establishing a clear link between performance of the company and the pay outcomes of the executive (for example, Performance and PerformanceL). Somewhat imprecise shareholder guidance on the attributes of a robust pay-for-performance incentive scheme allows for the flexibility of approach to incentive schemes observed amongst the Australian sample companies during the period studied. While flexible principles suggest that there are many ways to structure the performance hurdles for a long-term incentive scheme, such principles cannot achieve a meaningful pay-for-performance link if companies interpret the principles in ways that undermine the principles. 'Three years' for performance is not necessarily 'three years from 1 July

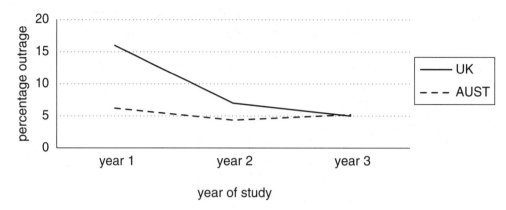

Figure 13.2   Comparison of FTSE 100 outrage with S&P/ASX 200 outrage (median values)

2005 to 30 June 2008'. It can be interpreted as 'any three years within a 10 year period' if retesting is allowed. Clearly these are very different performance criteria.

2.3   Comparative Analysis

The outcomes of the two studies above illustrate that a similar regulatory regime of a 'remuneration report plus advisory vote' operated very differently in these two jurisdictions over the first three years of its operation. Three concurrent reasons explain the difference: the different voting behaviour of institutional shareholders in year 1, the credible threat of government law-making in the 'Rewards for Failure' initiative in the UK that coincided with the first year of the NBSV, and the differences in shareholder guidance, not only in the practices preferred by institutional investors, but in how the guidance is written, monitored and enforced.

2.3.1   Voting behaviour
The different voting outcomes on the NBSV and RRV respectively, illustrated in Figure 13.2, indicate that the general level of outrage in the first year of the regime in the UK (median of 16 per cent) was not achieved at all during the first three years of the regime in Australia. Shareholders in Australian companies largely supported management in the first three years of the RRV: a median of 6.19 per cent in year 1 reduced to 4.38 per cent in year 2, increasing slightly to 5.21 per cent in year 3.

However, Figure 13.3 shows that the level of non-support increased in the Australian sample over the three years of the study. The maximum value of outrage in year 1 (48.51 per cent) increased to 54.41 per cent in year 2 and 69.24 per cent in year 3. In the FTSE 100 sample, the highest level of outrage was in year 1 (63 per cent) *reducing* to 39 per cent in year 2 and 37 per cent in year 3.

Australian shareholders were prepared to signal disagreement with remuneration practices, as evident in the maximum outrage votes illustrated in Figure 13.3. The results of voting on an issue of securities to the managing director in the sample of 109 ASX 200 companies over the same three years are shown in Figure 13.4. This resolution recorded

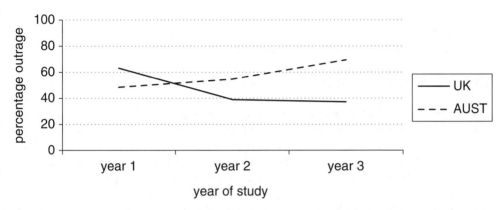

Figure 13.3   Comparison of highest level of outrage: FTSE 100 and S&P/ASX 200

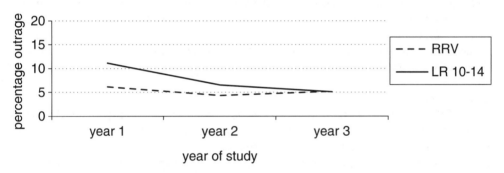

Figure 13.4   RRV outrage cf ASX Listing Rule 10-14 outrage (median values)

a median outrage in year 1 of 11.12 per cent (compared with 6.19 per cent for the RRV), which decreased in year 2 to 6.53 per cent (compared with 4.38 per cent for the RRV) and decreased further in year 3 to 5.12 per cent (compared with 5.21 per cent for the RRV). Institutional investors in Australian companies appear comfortable with voting against the remuneration for a particular executive director, unlike their UK counterparts who, according to my interviews with them in 2008, prefer the de-personalized nature of the advisory vote on the remuneration report to signal dissent.

The incentive for companies to change practices reflects these voting behaviours. The high level of NBSV dissent at 2003 AGMs indicates shareholders took the opportunity created by the NBSV to signal disagreement with remuneration practices that could not be resolved via engagement alone. It explains the higher level of changes made to remuneration in the following two years of the study shown in Tables 13.3–13.5. Forty per cent of respondents to a survey by the Chartered Secretaries of Australia in 2005 believed the board would respond to a vote against the remuneration report, with 48 per cent suggesting the board would respond if they received 20 per cent of votes against (Chartered Secretaries of Australia 2005). Eighty-eight companies (81 per cent of the sample) did not reach the 10 per cent votes against 'tipping point', while only eight companies reached the 20 per cent vote 'tipping point' at the AGM in year 1. This is reflected in the low rates of changes reported in

Tables 13.8–13.10. By way of contrast, the 10 per cent tipping point is reached by 33 companies in the FTSE 100 sample (45 per cent of the sample) in the first year, with the 20 per cent tipping point being reached by 15 companies (21 per cent of the sample) in that same year.

2.3.2   The credible threat of government law making

The lack of momentum for changes to remuneration in Australia over this period can also be explained by the lack of any equivalent to the 'Rewards for Failure' initiative in the UK. The early success of the combination of a credible threat of (undesirable) government intervention combined with a shareholder action via the NBSV forced FTSE 100 companies to make changes to executive service agreements. While problems with termination payments in Australian companies were highlighted in 2005 (Stapledon 2005) and the problems with the relevant legislative provisions were highlighted in 2008 (Commonwealth of Australia 2008; Fenwick and Sheehan 2008; Sheehan and Fenwick 2008), it was not until 2009 that the government passed legislation amending the relevant legislative provisions.[16] Evidence from 2008 suggests companies could side-step negative shareholder sentiment with relative ease (Vaughan 2008). The results of this study confirm there was little pressure on Australian sample companies to conform to shareholder requirements, even though the contracts within companies did not comply with the more stringent shareholder guidelines.

2.3.3   Principles or rules?

Most of the rules for remuneration practices come from shareholder guidance that oscillates between tightly worded, prescriptive rules, and more flexible principles. While companies want to have flexibility in choosing practices that best suit the company's circumstances, the extremes of approach in the guidance can work against shareholders in two ways: companies will adopt clear and specific statements of preferred practices to the letter (so if the preferred practices are poor, company practices will be poor) and companies will exploit any principle that allows for flexibility to adopt their preferred arrangements (so principles should be crafted carefully to allow for variations, but only variations that comply with shareholder-preferred arrangements).

This is illustrated by the guidance on 'Retests'. 'Retests' (the removal of retesting provisions for performance in LTI plans) are very low in the Australian study, with only 10 companies making this change over the whole three years of the study. The importance of rule character (Black 1995) is indicated by the guidance on the issue: retests may be either acceptable or unacceptable depending on the circumstances (ACSI, 2005, principle 14.6(f)). An identical position was adopted by the proxy advisor ISS Proxy Australia in the initial round of RRV in 2005 (ISS Proxy Australia 2005). As the Australian shareholder guidance does not take a clear stance on the practice, companies can argue that the retesting provisions should remain. The FTSE 100 sample results show that by AGM 2005 (year 3) all companies in the sample had removed retests from their long-term incentive schemes. This reflects the opposition to retesting evident in shareholder guidance from the ABI and the NAPF (ABI 2002, guideline 8.1; ABI 2004, guideline 8.1; NAPF 2005, guidelines L.10).

---

[16]   Corporations (Improving Accountability on Termination Payments) Act 2009 (Cth).

It is also confirmed by Australian evidence on 'Hedging'.[17] The shareholder guidance in relation to hedging is unequivocal, whereas that given for 'Retests' is ambivalent. Likewise, the persistence of 'MD Loans' as a means of financing the CEO's shareholdings under incentive plans is supported by evidence that proxy advisors adopt a similar stance to that of shareholders: the practice is assessed on a case-by-case basis, so it may be acceptable (Institutional Shareholder Services 2006; RiskMetrics (Australia) Pty Ltd 2008). If many of the rules in shareholder guidance and proxy advisor voting guidance are applied flexibly by proxy advisors (on a 'case by case' basis) and thus by shareholders, remuneration committee chairpersons and remuneration consultants are justified in not feeling constrained by the guidance.

3   CONCLUSION

The new initiative of the remuneration report and advisory vote indeed 'had an effect' on remuneration practice. Soft-law rules in the form of best practice can influence practice upwards towards shareholder-preferred practices in terms of structure. This is consistent with the operation of the regulated remuneration cycle presented above in Figure 13.1 and a close analysis of the rules relating to remuneration practice.[18] Constraining the quantum of remuneration through the advisory vote is more likely for an ad hoc payment such as a termination payment (because shareholders successfully constrained the terms of the contract) than it is for ongoing market rates of increases or short term incentives. Thus governments seeking to introduce a say on pay as a way of lowering the overall quantum of executive remuneration may be disappointed when it fails to deliver any constraint on the growth of executive remuneration. This outcome is a consequence of the endorsement of market-based levels of remuneration by institutional investors. It is therefore little surprise that the regression results reported in the few studies to date of say on pay in the UK have not found there to be any constraint on the quantum of CEO pay following a poor outcome on the advisory vote (however 'poor' is defined).

Of deeper concern is the evidence, particularly in the UK sample, that shareholders appeared to reward remuneration committees for being *responsive* to shareholders' concerns (suggested by the use of 'Consultation' and 'Review' in years 2003 and 2004; see Table 13.3) before waiting to see what companies actually did in response.[19] This allows companies to 'game' the vote by indicating their willingness to reconsider their remuneration practices ('Review') and that they have consulted with shareholders about their remuneration practices ('Consultation') before they actually need to signal 'Change'. Even with 'Change', it is possible to delay changing practices for a further year. In year 1 of the vote, a company can signal 'Review'; in year 2, they could signal 'Consultation', noting that the 'Review' was ongoing; and in year 3 they could signal 'Change', with the

---

[17]   For a discussion on hedging in executive remuneration in Australia see Ali and Stapledon 2000 and Productivity Commission 2009.
[18]   For the Australian results of that analysis see Sheehan 2009. The UK results are on file with the author.
[19]   This is also confirmed by my own interviews with institutional investors in 2007 and 2008 in the UK.

change to apply for year 4. In other words, from a poor voting outcome in year 1, the company may not implement actual change until year 4. This inertia has been noted in Australia (Productivity Commission 2009, pp. 296–7) and used to justify a 'two-strikes' rule whereby the board of a company attracting a vote of more than 25 per cent against the remuneration report for two consecutive years will be up for re-election (notwithstanding that such directors typically have three-year terms in Australia).

Finally, the analysis in this chapter is inconclusive as to whether the changes observed actually led to better remuneration practices. Best practice is a contested term (Bender and Moir 2006) and the adoption of best practice itself could simply be a form of camouflage (Singh 2006) to avoid outrage. Given that most of the rules for remuneration practice are found in guidance issued by shareholders, this chapter suggests that institutional investors need to carefully describe remuneration practices in their guidance and consider how best to engage with companies if *better remuneration practices* – and not just more activity in the form of ever more detailed disclosures, increased levels of engagement and higher levels of shareholder voting – *are the desired outcome of the say on pay*.

REFERENCES

Ali, Paul and Geof Stapledon. 2000. Having Your Options and Eating Them Too: Fences, Zero-cost Collars and Executive Share Options, *Company & Securities Law Journal* 18: 277–82.
Alissa, Walid. 2009. Boards' Response to Shareholders' Dissatisfaction: The Case of Shareholders' Say on Pay in the UK, Working Paper, http://ssrn.com/abstract=1412880.
Armour, John. 2008. Enforcement Strategies in UK Corporate Governance: A Roadmap and Empirical Assessment, Law Working Paper no. 106/2008, European Corporate Governance Institute.
Association of British Insurers (ABI). 2002. Guidelines on Executive Remuneration.
Association of British Insurers (ABI). 2004. Principles and Guidelines on Remuneration.
ASX Corporate Governance Council. 2007. Corporate Governance Principles and Recommendations.
Australian Council of Super Investors Inc (ACSI). 2003. Corporate Governance Guidelines for Superannuation Fund Trustees and Corporations.
Australian Council of Super Investors Inc (ACSI). 2005. Corporate Governance Guidelines: A Guide for Superannuation Trustees to Monitor Listed Australian Companies.
Australian Government. 2010. *Australian Government Response to the Productivity Commission's Inquiry on Executive Remuneration in Australia*.
Australian Institute of Company Directors (AICD). 2004. Remuneration Committees: Good Practice Guide.
Australian Institute of Company Directors (AICD). 2009. Executive Remuneration: Guidelines for Listed Company Boards.
Bainbridge, Stephen. 2005. Executive Compensation: Who Decides? *Texas Law Review* 83: 1615–62.
Bebchuk, Lucian and Jesse Fried. 2003. Executive Compensation as an Agency Problem, *Journal of Economic Perspectives* 17: 71–92.
Bebchuk, Lucian and Jesse Fried. 2004. *Pay Without Performance: The Unfulfilled Promise of Executive Compensation*, Cambridge MA: Harvard University Press.
Bender, Ruth and Lance Moir. 2006. Does 'Best Practice' in Setting Executive Pay in the UK Encourage 'Good Behaviour'? *Journal of Business Ethics* 76: 75–91.
Berg, Bruce. 2007. *Qualitative Research Methods for the Social Sciences*, 6th edition, Boston: Pearson/Allyn & Bacon.
Berle, Adolph and Gardiner Means. 1933. *The Modern Corporation and Private Property*, New York: Macmillan Co.
Bertrand, Marianne and Sendhil Mullainathan. 2001. Are CEOs Rewarded for Luck? The Ones Without Principals Are, *Quarterly Journal of Economics* 116: 901–32.
Birla, Renu. 2005. Performance Share Plans, in KPMG, *FTSE 100 Directors' Compensation 2005*.
Black, Julia. 1995. Which Arrow? Rule Types and Regulatory Policy, *Public Law* 94–117.
Black, Julia. 2002. Regulatory Conversations, *Journal of Law and Society*, 29: 163–96.

Black, Julia. 2008. Forms and Paradoxes of Principles-Based Regulation, *Capital Markets Law Journal* 3: 425–57.

Buck, Trevor, Alistair Bruce, Brian Main and Henry Udueni. 2003. Long Term Incentive Plans, Executive Pay and UK Company Performance, *Journal of Management Studies* 40: 1709–27.

Carter, Mary Ellen and Valentia Zamora. 2008. Shareholder Remuneration Votes and CEO Compensation Design, Working Paper, Boston College.

Chartered Secretaries of Australia. 2005. Survey on the Non-Binding Shareholder Vote on Remuneration Reports in the Top 200 Companies.

Cheffins, Brian. 1997. *Company Law: Theory, Structure and Operation*, Oxford: Clarendon Press.

Chessell, James and Damon Kitney. 2010. Proxy Advisors Earn Their Place in the Sun. *The Australian* on-line edition, August 21.

Commonwealth of Australia. 2008. Parliamentary Debates, Senate, 4 December.

Conyon, Martin and Graham Sadler. 2010. Shareholder Voting and Directors' Remuneration Report Legislation: Say on Pay in the UK, *Corporate Governance: An International Review*, 18: 296–312.

Core, John, Wayne Guay and David Larcker. 2003. Executive Equity Compensation and Incentives: A Survey, *Federal Reserve Bank of New York Economic Policy Review* 9: 27–50.

Core, John, Wayne Guay and Randall Thomas. 2005. Is US CEO Compensation Inefficient Pay Without Performance? Working paper, Vanderbilt University Law School, Law & Economics Working Paper Series, No. 05-05.

Corporations and Markets Advisory Committee (CAMAC). 2010. *Executive Remuneration: Information Paper*.

Deloitte. 2004. Report on the Impact of the Directors' Remuneration Report Regulations: A Report for the Department of Trade and Industry.

Desai, Hemang, Chris Hogan and Michael Wilkins. 2006. The Reputational Penalty for Aggressive Accounting: Earnings Restatements and Management Turnover, *The Accounting Review* 81: 83–112.

Diamond, Douglas and Robert Verrecchia. 1982. Optimal Managerial Contracts and Equilibrium Security Prices, Papers and proceedings of the 40th Annual Meeting of the American Finance Association, Washington, 28–30 December 1981, *Journal of Finance* 37: 275–87.

Dickersin Van Wesep, Edward. 2010. Pay (Be)for(e) Performance: The Signing Bonus as an Incentive Device, *The Review of Financial Studies* 23: 3812–48.

Dine, Janet. 2006. Executive Pay and Corporate Governance in the UK: Slimming the Fat Cats?, *European Company Law* 3(2): 75–85.

Fama, Eugene. 1980. Agency Problems and the Theory of the Firm, *Journal of Political Economy* 88: 288–307.

Fama, Eugene and Michael Jensen. 1983. Separation of Ownership and Control, *Journal of Law and Economics* 26: 301–25.

Farrar, John. 2008. *Corporate Governance: Theories, Principles and Practice*, 3rd edition, South Melbourne: Oxford University Press.

Fenwick, Colin and Kym Sheehan. 2008. Share-based Remuneration and Termination Payments to Company Directors: What Are the Rules? *Company & Securities Law Journal* 26: 71–92.

Ferran, Eilis. 2005. Company Law Reform in the UK: A Progress Report, Working paper no. 27/2005, European Corporate Governance Institute.

Ferri, Fabrizio and David Maber. 2008. Say on Pay Vote and CEO Compensation: Evidence from the UK, Working Paper, http://ssrn.com/abstract=1160446.

Financial Reporting Council (UK). 2003. *The Combined Code*.

Fung, Archon, Mary Graham and David Weil. 2007. *Full Disclosure: The Perils and Promise of Transparency*, New York: Cambridge University Press.

Gilshan, Deborah and PIRC Limited. 2009. Say on Pay Six Years On: Lessons from the UK Experience.

Gordon, Jeffrey. 2005. Executive Compensation: If There's a Problem, What's the Remedy? The Case For Compensation Discussion and Analysis, *Journal of Corporation Law* 30: 675–702.

Halliwell Consulting. 2005. Build Your Own Executive Share Scheme.

Hancher, Leigh and Michael Moran. 1989. Organizing Regulatory Space, in Leigh Hancher and Michael Moran, eds, *Capitalism, Culture and Economic Regulation*, Oxford: Clarendon Press.

Hart, Oliver. 1983. Optimal Labour Contracts Under Asymmetric Information: An Introduction, *Review of Economic Studies* 50: 3–36.

Hill, Jennifer. 1996. 'What Reward Have Ye?' Disclosure of Director and Executive Remuneration in Australia, *Company and Securities Law Journal* 14: 232–47.

HM Treasury. 2009. A Review of Corporate Governance in UK Banks and Other Financial Industry Entities: Final Recommendations.

HM Treasury. 2009a. A Review of Corporate Governance in UK Banks and Other Financial Industry Entities.

Holmström, Bengt. 1981. Contractual Models of the Labor Market, *The American Economic Review* 71(2): 308–13.
Holmström, Bengt. 1999. Managerial Incentive Problems: A Dynamic Perspective, *Review of Economic Studies* 66: 169–82.
Holmström, Bengt and Paul Milgrom. 1987. Aggregation and Linearity in the Provision of Intertemporal Incentives, *Econometrica* 57: 303–28.
Institutional Shareholder Services (ISS). 2006. CEO Pay in the Top 100 Companies: 2005.
Institutional Shareholder Services ISS Proxy Australia. 2005. CEO Pay in the Top 100 Companies: 2004.
Investment & Financial Services Association Ltd (IFSA). 2007. Executive Equity Plan Guidelines, IFSA Guidance Note no. 12.00.
Jensen, Michael and William Meckling. 1976. Theory of the Firm: Managerial Behavior, Agency Costs and Ownership Structure, *Journal of Financial Economics* 3: 305–60.
Jensen, Michael and Kevin Murphy. 2004. Remuneration: Where We've Been, How We Got to Here, What Are the Problems and How to Fix Them, Working paper, European Corporate Governance Institute.
KPMG. 2004. 2004 Survey of FTSE 100 Directors' Compensation.
Kuhnen, Carmelia and Jeffrey Zwiebel. 2007. Executive Pay, Hidden Compensation and Managerial Entrenchment, Working Paper, http://ssrn.com/abstract-972622.
Lambert, Richard and David Larcker. 1985. Golden Parachutes, Executive Decision-making and Shareholder Wealth, *Journal of Accounting and Economics* 7: 179–203.
Larcker, David and Brian Tayan. 2010. 'RiskMetrics: The Uninvited Guest at the Equity Table, Standard Graduate School of Business, Closer Look Series, CGRP-01.
McKnight, Phillip and Cyril Tomkins. 2002. Executive Stock Options and Shareholder Return: Empirical Evidence from the UK, Working paper, http://ssrn.com/abstract=350820.
Moers, Frank and Erik Peek. 2005. An Empirical Analysis of the Role of Risk Aversion in Executive Compensation Contracts, MARC Working Paper No. 3/2000-07, http://ssrn.com/abstract=249571.
Moloney, Niamh. 2008. *EC Securities Regulation*, 2nd edition, Oxford: Oxford University Press.
Moore, John. 1985. Optimal Labour Contracts When Workers Have a Variety of Privately Observed Reservation Wages, *Review of Economic Studies* 52: 37–68.
Murphy, Kevin. 2002. Explaining Executive Compensation: Managerial Power Versus the Perceived Cost of Stock Options, *University of Chicago Law Review* 69: 847–69.
National Association of Pension Funds (NAPF). 2005. Voting Guidelines and Statements of Good Practice for the 2004 NAPF Corporate Governance Policy.
Oyer, Paul. 2004. Why Do Firms Use Incentives that Have No Incentive Effects? *Journal of Finance* 59: 1619–49.
Pendelton, Andrew. 2005. How Far Does the United Kingdom Have a Market-based System of Corporate Governance? A Review and Evaluation of Recent Developments in the United Kingdom, *Competition and Change* 9: 107–26.
PricewaterhouseCoopers. 1999. Monitoring of Corporate Governance Aspects of Directors' Remuneration.
Productivity Commission (Cth). 2009. Executive Remuneration in Australia: Productivity Commission Inquiry Report No. 49.
RiskMetrics (ISS Governance Services). 2007. CEO Pay in the Top 100 Companies: 2006.
RiskMetrics (ISS Governance Services). 2008. CEO Pay in the Top 100 Companies: 2007.
RiskMetrics (Australia) Pty Ltd. 2008. Australia Voting Guidelines.
Ruiz-Verdu, Pablo. 2008. Corporate Governance When Managers Set Their Own Pay, *European Financial Management* 14: 921–43.
Scott, Colin. 2001. Analysing Regulatory Space: Fragmented Resources and Institutional Design, *Public Law*, Summer: 329–53.
Shavell, Stephen. 1979. Risk Sharing and Incentives in the Principal and Agent Relationship, *Bell Journal of Economics* 10: 55–73.
Sheehan, Kym. 2007. Is the Outrage Constraint an Effective Constraint on Executive Remuneration? Evidence from the UK and Preliminary Results from Australia, Working Paper, http://ssrn.com/abstract=974965.
Sheehan, Kym. 2009. The Regulatory Framework for Executive Remuneration in Australia, *Sydney Law Review* 31: 239–72.
Sheehan, Kym and Colin Fenwick. 2008. Seven: the *Corporations Act 2001* (Cth), Corporate Governance and Termination Payments to Senior Employees, *Melbourne University Law Review*, 32: 199–241.
Singh, Ravi. 2006. Board Independence and the Design of Executive Compensation, Working paper, http://ssrn.com/abstract=673741.
Sjostrom, Carl and David Shammai. 2005. Overview of Remuneration, in KPMG, FTSE 100 Directors' Compensation 2005.

Snyder, Franklin. 2003. More Pieces of the CEO Compensation Puzzle, *Delaware Journal of Corporate Law* 28: 129.

Stapledon, Geof. 2005. Termination Benefits for Executives of Australian Companies, *Sydney Law Review* 27: 683–714.

Strauss, Anselm. 1987. *Qualitative Analysis for Social Scientists*, New York: Cambridge University Press.

Thompson, Steve. 2005. The Impact of Corporate Governance Reforms on the Remuneration of Executives in the UK, *Corporate Governance: An International Review* 13: 19–25.

Trade and Industry Committee, House of Commons (UK). 2003. *Rewards for Failure: Sixteenth Report of Session 2002–03*, HC 914 (September).

Vaughan, Michael. 2008. Michelmore Must Go to the Buy Side, *The Australian Financial Review* (Melbourne) 22 August, p. 56.

Villiers, Charlotte. 2006. *Corporate Reporting and Company Law*, Cambridge: Cambridge University Press.

14 Taxing executive compensation
Glen Loutzenhiser

The primary goal of any tax system is to raise money to pay for the services provided by the State. Ideally, in so doing, the tax system should operate in an efficient and fair way that does not favour certain taxpayers or economic activities over others, and the rules should be easy for taxpayers to comply with and government to administer. Tax systems can be (and are) used to advance other goals as well, such as redistributing wealth from the better off to the less well off in society. Tax also can be a powerful macro-economic tool – taxes can be raised to cool a charging economy, or, as witnessed recently in the US,[1] taxes can be cut to stimulate investment and consumer spending. Finally, the tax system can be used as a tool of social policy, providing tax incentives to encourage desirable behaviour (eg tax credits for investing in 'green' technology) and tax penalties to discourage other behavior (eg 'sin taxes' on tobacco and alcohol). The price to be paid for pursuing social goals through the tax system, however, is a tax regime that inevitably is less coherent, more detailed and more complicated than it otherwise would be.

Employment taxation is one area of tax law that has been particularly susceptible to political tinkering in the pursuit of goals other than raising revenue in the most simple, fair and economically efficient way possible. The UK employment tax regime, for example, contains a host of rules aimed at changing employee and employer behaviour for the greater good. Concerned about the environment and climate change? Under the UK tax rules an employee's taxable benefit from using a company car is calculated according to the car's level of CO_2 emissions. Want to promote computer literacy in the general population? The UK formerly provided a tax exemption to encourage employers to provide computers to their employees for use at home. This exemption was repealed when it became apparent that the definition of 'computer' in the tax legislation arguably was broad enough to include video game consoles, which apparently was not the sort of computer literacy policymakers had in mind. Worried about sky-rocketing levels of executive compensation and associated corporate governance failures, particularly in the financial sector? Perhaps there is a tax solution to these problems as well.

In this chapter I consider what role (if any) the tax system can play in controlling the level of executive pay generally and in the financial sector in particular. In the UK, the Governor of the Bank of England, the Deputy Prime Minister, the Business Secretary and other prominent figures have recently called on the financial sector to show restraint in paying bonuses.[2] Since the depths of the financial crisis in 2008,

---

[1]   The American Recovery and Reinvestment Act of 2009. Roughly two thirds of the $787 billion stimulus package represented new government spending; the other third was tax cuts.

[2]   Christopher Hope, 'Bank of England governor Mervyn King attacks bank bonuses and excessive pay' *Telegraph* (London: 15 Sept 2010); James Tapsfield, 'Nick Clegg warns banks on "unjustified" bonuses' *The Independent* (London: 21 September 2010); Elizabeth Rigby and Alex Barker 'Cable unrepentant over attack on greed' *Financial Times* (London: 22 September 2010).

which in the UK led to the nationalization of two banks and the part-nationalization of two others, the UK's major banks have made tens of thousands of mostly lower-paid staff redundant and boosted their profit margins on mortgages, loans and credit cards. These banks are now predicted to make large profits in 2010.[3] The prospect of those profits translating into large banker bonuses is especially galling for many because the rest of the UK economy is not faring nearly as well, in part because the banks have sharply restricted access to credit for small businesses and first-time home buyers. To make matters worse, the Government announced large cuts in public spending in its October 2010 spending review, which is expected to lead to widespread job losses in the public sector and related industries. Business Secretary Vince Cable has been a particularly harsh critic of the bank bonus culture, and recently summed up the mood of many:

> At a time of austerity when an awful lot of people are faced with a very difficult future, people in the banking community are going to be walking away with outrageously large sums despite the fact that that sector caused the crisis that caused the hardship. . ... If there are unacceptable bonuses, the Government has an obligation to intervene. [There must be] a deterrent to banks which are preparing to undertake unacceptable bonuses.[4]

Whether the compensation paid to bankers and other executives should be subject to some form of legislative oversight is the matter of keen academic debate.[5] Assuming for present purposes that government intervention is desirable and necessary to address the problem of excessive executive compensation in the financial sector and elsewhere, are changes to the tax system an appropriate and useful legislative response?

In the first section of this chapter I advance a policy framework for evaluating the taxation of employee compensation in general. The traditional tax policy objectives of equity and neutrality support taxing compensation in the same way irrespective of the legal form that it takes – be it salary, bonus, pension, shares or stock options. This may be easier said than done, and there are additional considerations as well, including administration and compliance issues and the ever-present spectre of tax avoidance. The example of non-cash benefits or 'perks' will be used to illustrate some of the difficulties faced in pursuing these objectives. Tax incidence – who ultimately bears the economic burden of a tax – is another important consideration in this area.

In the second section, I examine examples of tax measures adopted in the US and the UK for the express purpose of restricting executive pay, and evaluate those measures against the policy framework outlined in section 1. Since 1993 the US federal tax regime has denied a corporate income tax deduction for annual compensation in excess of $1 million paid to senior executives of public companies. In 2009 the UK introduced a one-off 'banker bonus' tax of 50 percent, intended to discourage banks from paying large bonuses to their employees so soon after the taxpayer-funded bailouts of the financial

---

[3] 'Vince Cable criticised over "odd" and "emotional" attack on bankers' *Daily Telegraph* (London: 22 September 2010). The major banks' 2010 profits are estimated to be in the range of £28 billion.

[4] 'Vince Cable criticised over "odd" and "emotional" attack on bankers' *Daily Telegraph* (London: 22 September 2010).

[5] Discussed elsewhere in this book.

sector. Tax measures like these may make good politics but do they make good tax policy?

Section 3 concludes.

1   CRITERIA OF GOOD TAX DESIGN

In assessing tax policy, commentators and theorists generally recognize that good tax design must take into account a range of often conflicting factors.[6] Equity or fairness is an important objective for a tax system, both on the moral view that it is right and proper (like equality before the law is right), and also because taxpayers are more likely to comply with a tax system they believe is fair than one that is not (Tiley 2008, 10). Fairness or equity in tax design is difficult to define precisely, but is generally analyzed as two distinct concepts – *horizontal equity* and *vertical equity* (Meade 1978, 12; Stiglitz 1988, 399). Horizontal equity requires that persons in a similar situation pay a similar amount of tax, whilst vertical equity requires those with a greater ability to pay to pay more tax. Treating similarly situated taxpayers differently is not only horizontally inequitable, but it may also constitute discrimination under constitutional principles or human rights law. Although intuitively attractive, taxing in accordance with ability to pay is a difficult concept to implement in practice. No matter how described, ability to pay always turns out to be very difficult to define and to be a matter on which opinions will differ rather widely (Meade 1978, 14; Banks and Diamond 2010, 555). For this reason and others, some tax commentators question whether equity should be a relevant consideration in tax design,[7] although most of these critics ultimately accept equity has a role to play.[8]

A system in which Executive A who receives £200,000 in salary pays the same amount of tax as Executive B who receives a painting, the use of a company-owned apartment, or shares in his employer, each also worth £200,000, is horizontally equitable – taxing like alike. For many years, however, the UK taxed non-cash benefits only if the benefit was convertible into money or money's worth – the 'convertibility principle' from *Tennant v Smith*.[9] The amount subject to tax was then the convertible, or second-hand, value. Thus, in *Wilkins v Rogerson*[10] an employee given a suit by his employer was taxable if the suit could be sold on, but only at the low second-hand value of say £5; an employee given £15 by his employer to buy a new suit was taxable on the full £15. A very different tax result for economically equivalent transactions, and a clear violation of the horizontal equity principle.

In some cases, identifying whether the employee has received a 'benefit' that could be said to be equivalent to cash compensation and deserving of the same tax treatment is not a straightforward exercise. Salary, bonuses and other cash payments to employees are

---

[6]   See eg Meade 1978, pp 7 et seq.

[7]   Eg, optimal tax theory proponents such as Kaplow 2008 and Banks and Diamond 2010.

[8]   For a recent, robust defence of equity in tax design see Kay 2010. Ultimately even Banks and Diamond concede a role for horizontal equity in 'providing limitations on the set of allowable tax policies' (at 555).

[9]   [1892] AC 150 (HL).

[10]   [1961] Ch 133.

relatively easy to spot, although payments to reimburse employees for expenses incurred in the course of performing their employment duties create some difficulties. In the case of non-cash benefits, however, it can be difficult to distinguish between, on the one hand, an employee being provided with the tools, equipment, and other support necessary to do the job – or do the job better – and, on the other hand, an employee deriving a personal benefit from that which the employer is providing. Consider the example of the CEOs of the Big Three automakers who recently raised the ire of US lawmakers when they flew on company-owned private jets to Washington in search of government bailout funds,[11] or the $1.2 million spent by Merrill Lynch redecorating CEO John Thain's office.[12] Although these executives may derive a personal benefit from flying about in a private jet or working in a luxuriously appointed office, should these benefits be subject to tax, and, if so, on what amount? Tiley suggests that a tax system, if it is of a puritanical disposition, may seek to levy tax (Tiley 2008, 268); however, most tax jurisdictions are not of such a disposition. In other cases the employee may derive no benefit at all from what may appear to others to be a desirable perk, as in Simons' famous example of an employee who is given free tickets to a Wagner opera by his employer but who hates opera (Simons 1938, 53).

Neutrality is another guiding principle of taxation – a well-designed tax system should not distort decisions, except where intended to do so, as in the case of taxes on tobacco meant to discourage smoking for public health reasons (Meade 1978, 7–11; Stiglitz 1988, 328–31). The taxation of executive compensation will be neutral if the tax system provides neither tax incentives nor disincentives for any particular form of compensation over another. If the tax rules are neutral, the level and type of compensation will be driven by commercial factors relevant to the particular business concerned and negotiation between employer and employee, rather than by tax considerations. Neutral taxation in this context has the added advantage of being fair. A system in which Executive A who receives £200,000 in salary pays the same amount of tax as Employee B who receives a non-cash benefit such as shares in his employer worth £200,000 is not only horizontally equitable, but it also provides no tax reason for paying salary instead of shares (or vice versa). It is often the case that tax rules are not neutral; sometimes deliberately and some-times not. When the UK taxed employees only on benefits that could be converted into money or money's worth, this created an obvious incentive for employees to prefer, and employers to offer, non-cash benefits instead of salary and bonuses.

Administration and compliance costs are also important considerations from a tax policy perspective because they represent pure social loss from the total goods and serv-ices available to the community (Shaw, Slemrod and Whiting 2010, 1105). Governments need to hire tax inspectors and others to administer the system. Taxpayers and third parties charged with assisting in the administration of the system (eg employers required to withhold and remit employment taxes) spend time and effort fulfilling their respective tax compliance obligations, perhaps employing outside advisors to help them do so. These costs can vary dramatically depending on the nature of the tax involved and are generally lower for simpler taxes – those with fewer rates, borderlines and reliefs.

---

[11]   Dana Milbank, 'Auto Execs Fly Corporate Jets to D.C., Tin Cups in Hand' *Washington Post* (Washington DC: November 20, 2008).
[12]   Discussed in Salley (2009) at 765.

Employment taxes are amongst the easiest taxes for government to administer as much of the burden of collection and remittance is placed on employers. Larger employers can take advantage of economies of scale, but complying with these obligations can be quite burdensome on smaller employers. The UK's employment tax withholding system, Pay As You Earn (PAYE), is more complicated than the system used in many jurisdictions. It is a cumulative system designed to take into account an employee's earnings not just in the current pay period but in the entire tax year to date. The aim of PAYE is to ensure the correct amount of income tax is withheld, with the result that most employees in the UK do not need to file an annual tax return. Social security contributions (called national insurance contributions or NICs) are also collected under PAYE, but are levied on a pay-period and non-cumulative basis, which further complicates matters. PAYE's complicated nature and ambitious aim make it susceptible to errors, particularly for those employees with multiple employments or other sources of income such as pensions. In 2010 HMRC and its top officials came under intense public and political pressure following the embarrassing revelation that nearly six million UK taxpayers had had the wrong amount of tax withheld under the PAYE system in the preceding two tax years; some received refunds, others received letters demanding additional tax of on average £2,000.[13]

Returning to the example of non-cash benefits, these perks raise a host of difficult administrative and compliance issues. First, tax cannot be assessed and collected easily at source since by definition the benefit is not paid in cash; rather, there must be some other source of cash against with the tax can be withheld, or, failing that, a year-end reconciliation must be done with the appropriate payment made when the tax return is due. Second, valuation may be difficult, such as for shares in closely held companies. When the UK introduced new rules to supplement the convertibility principle that in most cases make the employee taxable on the cost to the employer of providing the benefit, even this seemingly straightforward test gave rise to a difficult issue in *Pepper v Hart*[14] as to whether the employer's 'cost' meant the employer's average cost or marginal cost.

Complexity and lack of clarity in tax law generally increases administrative and compliance costs (Shaw, Slemrod and Whiting 2010, 1119). This is a particular concern when tax rules are introduced to advance social goals. Highfield (2010) argues that the political dimension to tax policy sometimes results in decisions that give little or no regard to, or even fly in the face of, administrative or compliance cost considerations. For Highfield, this political factor, coupled with the use of tax systems for a plethora of objectives unrelated to their primary revenue-raising role, in part explains why tax systems in advanced economies such as the US and the UK have become so complex and costly to administer (2010, 1174). These concerns are especially relevant to the present discussion on using the tax system to restrain excessive compensation. Tax rules, like legal rules generally, also should be certain, clear and easy to understand. Taxpayers should be able to know their tax liability, where and when to pay it, and tax should be levied at a time and in the manner that is most likely to be convenient for taxpayers to

---

[13]   See eg 'HMRC chief forced to apologise over tax bills' *Telegraph* (London: 11 Sept 2010).
[14]   [1993] AC 593 (HL).

pay (Meade 1978, 18–19). Whilst certainty is an important objective, however, some vagueness in law is inescapable and tax law in particular will never be completely certain. This is a reflection of the nature of law generally and tax law specifically (Freedman 2004, 345).

Finally, tax avoidance is an ever-present concern in employment taxation. In the UK, as in many jurisdictions, there has been an ongoing cat-and-mouse game between, on one side, clever taxpayers and their well-paid advisors designing employment tax and NIC avoidance schemes intended to fall within the letter of the law if not always within the spirit, and, on the other side, tax legislators introducing a near-continuous stream of amendments (including, in the UK, threats of retroactive legislation) to plug the loopholes as soon as they appear. Non-cash benefits were an early, popular way to compensate employees in a more tax-efficient manner than ordinary salary or cash bonus. At one point, a significant number of employees were compensated in very non-traditional ways – including gold, platinum sponge, diamonds and fine wine – in order to save tax and NICs. More recent avoidance schemes have sought to exploit the different tax treatment of income and capital using shares and stock options, or to exploit gaps in the taxation of international activity through payments into offshore trusts – all in an attempt to reduce the UK tax bill for high earners including footballers and City bankers.

2 TAXING 'EXCESSIVE' EXECUTIVE COMPENSATION

In March 2009, when it came to light that insurance company American International Group (AIG) had paid $165 million in bonuses to executives of the unit that helped lead the insurance giant to the brink of collapse, the US House of Representatives quickly approved a bill to impose a 90 per cent tax on bonuses awarded by companies bailed out by the US government.[15] Those who received bonuses of more than $125,000 would pay a special income tax of 90 per cent on the payments.[16]

In this section of the chapter I consider whether tax measures like those passed by the US House of Representatives aimed at restraining excessive executive compensation represent good tax policy, taking into account the criteria of good tax design and policy considerations just outlined. As with the example of the UK's rules on home computing, the real challenge with tax measures aimed at curbing excessive executive compensation is ensuring the law is effectively targeted and has the desired effect. Four types of tax measures are considered: (2.1) raising taxes on high-earners generally, (2.2) restrictions on tax deductions for excessive compensation, (2.3) super taxes on recipients of certain types of compensation, and (2.4) special taxes on bonus payers.

---

[15] Shailagh Murray, Paul Kane and David Cho, 'Congress Moves to Slap Heavy Tax on Bonuses: 90% Levy for Biggest Payouts at Bailed-Out Firms' *Washington Post* (Washington: March 20, 2009) and discussed in Zelinsky 2009, 637.

[16] H.R.1586 – To impose an additional tax on bonuses received from certain TARP recipients. 111th Congress, 1st Session (March 19, 2009). The bill (and later incarnations) never reached President Obama's desk, however.

2.1   Higher Taxes for all High-Earners

One response to high levels of executive compensation is simply to tax it at increasing rates – the 'if you can't beat them, you might as well tax the hell out of them' approach. As do most jurisdictions, the UK levies personal income tax at increasing, progressive rates – 0 per cent on income below £6,475 (this is covered by the taxpayer's personal allowance), 20 per cent on the next £37,400 and 40 per cent thereafter. Beginning in April 2010, the UK system became even more progressive with the introduction of a new top marginal income tax rate of 50 per cent on taxable income over £150,000. Personal allowances were also reduced by £1 for every £2 of income over £100,000; tax relief for child care and pension contributions was restricted for higher-rate taxpayers as well. Capital gains formerly subject to one flat 18 per cent tax rate are, from June 2010, taxable at 28 per cent for higher-rate taxpayers. Although these tax increases were not directed specifically at high-earning executives, this group is certainly feeling the pinch. Increasing the tax burden on high earners can be supported on vertical equity grounds and does not unfairly single-out particular taxpayers (ie executives or bankers) for harsher treatment than other, similarly situated taxpayers. On the other hand, as all high earners are affected – including those with investment or business income – this approach does not explicitly signal governmental disapproval of excessive executive compensation. Without this signal, firms may well continue to pay high bonuses, perhaps even higher bonuses to compensate their executives for the additional income tax they pay.

Increasing tax rates across the board has a number of other disadvantages. First, progressivity tends to increase the complexity of a tax system. Section 4 of the Taxation of Chargeable Gains Act setting out the flat 18 per cent tax rate on capital gains was one short line of text; the amending legislation introduced to give effect to the additional new 28 per cent top rate ran to five pages.[17] Second, high marginal tax rates also can be non-neutral – as marginal tax rates rise, so too does the incentive for taxpayers (especially women with young children) to forgo paid work for time at home (the 'substitution effect') or for the internationally mobile executive to relocate to a lower-tax jurisdiction. Third, the redistributive effect may be insignificant. Even the UK Government expects higher earners to avoid much of the impact of the new top rate; the 50 per cent tax rate is admitted to be as much about the Government being seen to be fair and spreading the pain than actually raising much additional revenue from high-earners.

As marginal tax rates rise, the incentive to avoid or evade income tax also increases, as does the motivation for government to crack down on avoidance. Unsurprisingly this is exactly what is now happening in the UK. Along with the massive cuts to public spending announced in the October 2010 spending review, the Government launched a £900 million program aimed at raising £7 billion annually from cracking down on tax avoidance and evasion. The Government is specifically targeting high-income professionals, including compensation schemes for City bankers and footballers involving shares and payments into offshore trusts (as mentioned above). Funds held by UK residents in offshore bank accounts, and the tax avoidance practice of large banks, are also under the

---

[17]   Finance (no 2) Act 2010 Sch 2.

microscope. A five-fold increase in criminal prosecutions is planned, and the introduction of a statutory general anti-avoidance rule is under consideration.

The substantial difference in the top tax rates on income (50 per cent) versus capital gains (28 per cent) also provides an obvious incentive to turn highly taxed income into more lightly taxed capital gains wherever possible – a violation of both equity and neutrality. For example, for many years in the UK the returns on private equity were subject to a very low capital gains tax rate of 10 per cent. The newspapers ran frequent articles criticizing the tax regime for allowing private equity managers to pay a lower tax rate than their office cleaners.[18] A similar situation occurred in the US, though the comparison commonly drawn was with their office secretaries rather than their cleaners.[19] The 28 per cent rate was introduced partly in response to this public outcry, but this only narrowed the gap between income and capital gains taxation, it did not eliminate it.

Finally, the magnitude of the rising income-tax burden on high earners in the UK has been sharply criticized in some quarters. In July 2010 the OECD warned that the UK's top rate of personal income tax was 'substantially above the OECD average and likely to adversely affect work incentives and entrepreneurship'.[20] For now at least, the much-discussed 'banker exodus' from the City of London has failed to materialize, though a number of high-earning (and formerly high tax paying) hedge fund employees reportedly have left the UK for Switzerland.[21] The significantly higher tax burden faced by executives is one reason (along with comparatively high corporate tax rates) why some large multinationals including Shire Pharmaceuticals and the WPP advertising group recently have moved their head offices out of the UK; others are considering making the move.[22] The UK tax environment is now viewed as quite unattractive by many executives and their employers. The perilous state of the UK's public finances, however, makes it unlikely that the UK coalition government will reduce taxes on high-earning executives any time soon.

2.2 Restrictions on Tax Deductibility of Executive Compensation

A second tax approach to address excessive executive compensation is a more targeted option: restrict the amount that employers can claim as a tax deduction for compensation. This could involve the application of general tax rules limiting deductions to 'reasonable' amounts, or specific legislation setting a maximum limit on deductible

---

[18]   See eg Christine Buckley and Siobhan Kennedy, 'Brown signals private equity could face tax crackdown' *The Times* (London: 6 June 2007).

[19]   See eg Warren Buffett's criticism of the US tax system in Tom Bawden, 'Buffett blasts system that lets him pay less tax than secretary' *The Times* (London: 28 June 2007).

[20]   Organisation for Economic Cooperation and Development, *United Kingdom: Policies for a Sustainable Recovery* (Paris: July 2010) 24–5.

[21]   Megan Murphy, 'Banker exodus fails to hit City' *Financial Times* (London: 15 October 2010); Jamie Dunkley, 'Treasury "will lose hundreds of millions of pounds" in tax as hedge funds move abroad' *Daily Telegraph* (London: 2 Oct 2010).

[22]   See eg BBC News Online, 'Diageo hits out at UK tax regime' (London: 11 February 2010) available at http://news.bbc.co.uk/1/hi/business/8510025.stm and Julia Kollewe, 'McDonald's to move European head office to Switzerland' *Guardian* (London: 13 July 2009).

compensation. As between these two options, a specific number cap has the advantage of more certainty than a general reasonableness test. Specific caps are also easier for tax authorities to administer and taxpayers to comply with, although some degree of uncertainty will remain in determining exactly what compensation is caught by the cap and what is not. Even a reasonableness test, however, is not likely to be so uncertain as to be unworkable so long as appropriate administrative and judicial guidance is available.

Beginning with the general rule option, US Internal Revenue Code s. 162(a)(1) provides that 'there shall be allowed as a deduction all the ordinary and necessary expenses paid or incurred during the taxable year in carrying on any trade or business, including . . . a *reasonable* allowance for salaries or other compensation for personal services actually rendered' (emphasis added). An argument can be made that excessively large compensation paid to executives is unreasonable. In fact, a related provision (IRC s. 260G) specifically denies a deduction for 'excess' golden parachutes payments on change of control; such payments effectively are deemed 'unreasonable' unless proven otherwise (Mullane 2009, 516).

In practice, however, the IRS has limited the application of s. 162(a)(1) to closely held private companies – notwithstanding the fact that the provision is not so limited on its face – on the presumption that the salaries of public company executives are negotiated at arm's length by an independent, profit-maximizing board of directors (Conway 2008, 391–2; Mullane 2009, 508–9; Zelinsky 2009, 637–8). The UK has had a similar experience with HMRC's application of the requirement that expenses be incurred 'wholly and exclusively for the purposes of the trade' in order to be tax-deductible.[23] Zelinsky (2009) criticizes the IRS' hands-off approach to public companies as inequitable in comparison with its approach to private companies. He contends that excessive executive compensation at public companies also should be open to scrutiny under this provision because some publicly traded companies may lack the appropriate oversight and incentive infrastructure to set executive compensation reasonably.[24] In Zelinsky's view the underlying purpose of IRC s. 162(a)(1) is to preserve the corporate tax base from erosion by self-rewarding managers (640–41). Salley notes that this differential treatment might encourage companies to remain private (2009, 763–4) – a violation of the neutrality tax policy objective.

An alternative to a general 'reasonability test' is to place a specific statutory limit on the amount of compensation that can be deducted in respect of any one employee. The US federal tax code has for some time imposed a $1 million cap on the deduction of non-performance-related annual compensation paid by public companies to their CEOs and certain other executives (IRC s. 162(m)). More recently, a $500,000 deductibility limit was introduced in 2008 and extended in 2009 in respect of compensation paid to any one of a

---

[23]   Formerly Income and Corporation Tax Act 1988 s. 74 and now rewritten in Corporation Tax Act 2009 s. 54 and Income Tax (Trading and Other Income) Act 2005 s. 34.

[24]   Zelinsky's view is based on recent scholarship on management power, which disputes traditional optimal contracting theory claims that any size payment approved by a publicly traded corporation's board is prima facie reasonable, and contends instead that executives exercise influence over the board to set their own compensation levels in a manner inconsistent with shareholder preferences.

small number of listed senior executives of entities taking assistance under the Troubled Asset Recovery Program (TARP) for as long as that assistance remains outstanding.[25]

Capping the deductibility of compensation, either through a specific cap or a reasonability test, has some appeal. The government's disapproval of excessive compensation is clearly evident, particularly with a specific statutory cap. Zelinsky also argues that public IRS challenges and judicial determinations of excessive executive compensation have the potential to reduce excessive executive pay through shaming the companies and their boards (Zelinsky 2009, 645). He contends that the threat of future derivative action will provide a further check on excessive compensation. On the other hand, imposing caps on TARP entities may drive valuable employees away from troubled entities when those employees' services are most needed. Caps may also remove incentives for employees to participate in the recovery process at these entities.

The real question is whether tax measures restricting the deductibility of executive compensation will have the deterrent effect intended by government. As already noted, the US and UK general reasonability tests have not been applied to public companies so have had no impact. The evidence to date on the US $1 million deductibility cap indicates that it has had an effect on how executive pay has been structured, but has been remarkably ineffective at restraining executive compensation overall, for a number of reasons. First, companies paying salaries below the threshold quickly moved up to the $1 million mark – clearly not the intended result at all (diFilipo 2009, 274; Mullane 2009, 522–3). In effect Congress implicitly gave its approval to any salary up to that amount, and provided boards with a defence to shareholder challenges to larger executive pay packages (diFilipo 2009, 274). Second, as the cap excludes deferred payments and performance-based pay, unsurprisingly the use of these forms of compensation, and particularly stock options, became more widespread after the introduction of the cap (diFilipo 2009, 273; Mullane 2009, 523–4)). The risk premium attached to performance-related pay combined with the rapid rise in stock markets in the late 1990s generated financial gains for some executives far in excess of the $1 million cap. Again, clearly not the result the politicians had in mind. In fact, some argue that s. 162(m), by encouraging companies to rely more on stock options and executives to focus on short-term stock price appreciation, contributed to such corporate scandals as the collapse of Enron (Markham 2007, 293–9; Conway 2008, 411; Mullane 2009, 525). The obvious incentives to use complex, offshore tax avoidance schemes to shield taxation are another, completely expected result (Salley 2009, 764).

Even if an effective compensation deductibility cap or reasonableness test can be implemented, such an approach may still not be desirable. The key question, and one that Conway (2008) and Zelinsky (2009) do not address but other commentators including Mullane do, is the *incidence* of tax deductibility limits – who ultimately bears the burden of these measures. Whilst a taxpayer may be formally or legally obligated to pay a tax, if the tax can be passed on to another (eg a business customer through higher prices), that other person is said to bear the *economic* incidence of the tax. For example, economists generally believe the burden of a payroll tax such as employer NICs in the UK will ultimately fall on employees, at least in the long term. Employers are concerned with the

---

[25]   See the Emergency Economic Stabilization Act of 2008 (EESA) and the American Recovery and Reinvestment Act of 2009 (ARRA).

overall bottom-line cost of an employee, and not with individual components, be it salary, pension or a payroll tax. If payroll taxes rise, all things being equal, employees will bear the real incidence, through lower wages or reduced employment (Adam and Loutzenhiser 2007, 23).

When it comes to other taxes on companies, including taxes on the company's profits, the economic incidence is less clear. Although companies are formally subject to a myriad of taxes, to an economist companies are mere artificial entities, a nexus of contracts, and thus cannot bear tax. If we accept the proposition that only humans ultimately bear the burden of taxes in the form of reduced consumption and reduced leisure, the question becomes does the burden of a tax on a company fall on the company's shareholders (including domestic residents, foreigners, and investment entities such as employee pension plans), employees, customers, suppliers, or some combination? At first glance it seems logical to assume that the company shareholders will bear the brunt of higher company taxes brought on by limits on the deductibility of executive compensation, as less profits will be available for dividends. This may well be the case for a private company where the burden from the denial of a deduction under s. 162(a)(1) is more likely to fall on a small number of easily identifiable shareholders. The most recent economic literature, however, suggests that in an open economy with mobile capital, taxes on large multinational companies most likely ultimately are borne by the workforce in the form of reduced wages.[26]

In summary, whilst either a general reasonability test or a specific statutory limit on executive compensation may sound desirable in theory, neither approach has been successful in practice. The US experience indicates that those companies concerned about limits on the deductibility of executive compensation are very adept at getting around caps. Alternatively, some companies simply are willing to pay the tax penalty under IRC s. 260G or s. 162(m) in order to have the freedom to pay their executives how and how much they want. These companies do not economically bear the tax penalty they formally incur, but most likely shift the burden not onto the executives concerned, but the broader workforce instead (Mullane 2009, 517). Ultimately, even Zelinsky does not advocate IRS oversight under s. 162 'as the lead mechanism for purifying the muddled world of executive compensation', acknowledging that it will likely require coordinated action by a variety of governmental and nongovernmental actors (Zelinsky 2009, 645).

2.3 Super Taxes on Recipients of Certain Types of Compensation

A third option is to impose a super tax on executives (rather than their employers) who are in receipt of certain types or amounts of compensation that policymakers consider 'undesirable'. For example, US IRC s. 4999 levies a 20 per cent tax on recipients of excess parachute payments in addition to the usual payroll and income taxes; as mentioned above, the payer is also denied a tax deduction by IRC s. 260G. The UK has not adopted specific rules taxing certain payments to executives of this nature, choosing instead (as discussed earlier) to increase the top marginal income tax rate for all high-income taxpayers to 50 per cent and reduce tax reliefs.

---

[26] Reviewed in Arulampalam, Devereux and Maffini 2009 and also in Mullane 2009.

Super taxes payable by executives on some elements of their compensation clearly send a message that government disapproves, but do these tax measures have the intended deterrent effect? Incidence is again the key consideration. Even a tax levied on an individual may be shifted to another, eg under an indemnity agreement between an executive and corporate employer that requires the employer to make good any taxes the executive is legally obliged to pay on a particular form of remuneration (sometimes called a 'gross up' provision). Just as some companies are willing to forgo a tax deduction on excess parachute payments due to the operation of s. 260G, many of those companies also may be willing to gross-up the payments to the executive to shield him or her from the charge under s. 4999 (Conway 2008, 417; Mullane 2009, 517–8). Thus, the end result of imposing super taxes on executives may ultimately be the same as rules limiting the employer's ability to claim a tax deduction – the executive's extra tax is shifted first to the employer and then to the employer's overall workforce. If tax penalties formally imposed on executives are in fact merely shifted to other 'innocent' parties – as seems likely – this obviously defeats the social policy purpose of levying a super tax on the executives in the first place.

2.4   Special Taxes on Bonuses

Recently, governments have tried a fourth approach – levying special taxes on bonuses. The US House of Representatives bill previously mentioned is one example. Unlike the US, the UK Government actually did go so far as to introduce a 'banker bonus tax' following on from its bailout of the UK banking sector, which saw the Government take a controlling interest in several large financial institutions including the Royal Bank of Scotland and Northern Rock. As these and other banks returned to profitability, and announced plans to pay large bonuses, the political furore grew as well. In response, in the December 2009 Pre-Budget Report, the then Labour Government announced it was levying a 50 per cent tax on excessive bankers' bonuses, on top of existing income tax and NIC charges.

The bank payroll tax (BPT) ultimately introduced in the Finance Act 2009 applied to banks and building societies (not the employees) on awards of bonuses and other performance-based variable compensation over £25,000 to employees during the chargeable period, which began on 9 December 2009 and ended on 5 April 2010. The tax was payable in August 2010 and was not deductible for corporation tax purposes. Because the bonuses remained subject to income tax and NICs, this resulted in effective marginal rates on the bonuses of up to 64 per cent (IMF 2010, 39). According to the Explanatory Notes accompanying the implementing legislation, the Government wanted 'to encourage the development of sustainable long-term remuneration policies that take greater account of risk and facilitate the build-up of loss-absorbing capital'. It was thought that the BPT 'would encourage banks to consider their capital position and make appropriate risk-adjustments when settling the level of bonus payments'. A similar tax was imposed by the French Government.[27]

The BPT was clearly intended to be a short-term measure; the Government expected that in the longer term the remuneration practices would change as a result of

---

[27]   Discussed in Bachellerie, Boynes and Message (2010) and IMF (2010, 39–40).

corporate-governance and regulatory reforms. It now appears that the tax will be much more successful at raising money than at stopping banks from using profits to pay large bonuses. The tax is expected to generate about £3 billion for the Treasury – more than five times the £550 million predicted when the tax was announced.[28] The initial revenue estimate assumed that introduction of the tax would radically curb bonus payments, and thus that the burden of at least a large part of the tax would ultimately be borne by bank employees; however, as the IMF concluded, 'experience appears to have been otherwise' (IMF 2010, 39). When given the choice between paying bonuses and a tax, on the one hand, and paying lower bonuses with no tax, on the other hand, most banks chose to pay the bonuses and incur the tax penalty. Given the US experience with tax penalties on excessive compensation perhaps this result was predictable. In any event, the impact on bank profits and capital was substantial. This again raises the issue of incidence, though in this particular case it appears that the one-off BPT primarily induced the banks to pay the gross cost of the bonuses, effectively passing on the cost of the tax to the bank's shareholders (Devereux, Fuest, and Maffini 2010, 5).

In addition to failing in its primary purpose – to limit the amount of banker bonuses paid – the BPT can be criticized on tax policy grounds as non-neutral and horizontally inequitable to the point of being discriminatory. The tax fell on a very small number of taxpayers in one particular sub-sector of the economy; the vast majority of the tax was paid by fewer than five banks. The application of the tax also was arbitrary in many ways, beginning with the £25,000 threshold – why not £10,000 or £50,000 or £250,000? Even more troubling, because banks pay bonuses at different times of the year, those bonuses falling within the December–April chargeable period were subject to tax whilst other bonuses that happened to be paid before December 2009 fell outside the net. Finally, as I argued earlier in this chapter, employee compensation in whatever form should be taxed in the same way on equity and neutrality grounds. Singling out large bonuses for extra taxation whilst ignoring salary and equity-based compensation is non-neutral and horizontally inequitable. Some have even argued that the arbitrariness of the BPT made the tax discriminatory, although Athanassiou (2010) argues that the BPT would most likely withstand a challenge under human rights law.

Most recently, tax policy experts have turned their focus away from narrow banker bonus taxes towards a range of broader-based taxes on financial institutions. The primary aim of these proposals is not to restrict compensation payments per se, but rather to curb excessive risk-taking generally to avoid another crisis in the financial system. A report prepared by the IMF for the G-20 leaders meeting in June 2010 analyzed a range of options countries have adopted or are considering as to how the financial sector could contribute toward the cost of past and future government bailouts for the banking system. The report proposed an insurance-type levy called a financial services contribution (FSC) with any necessary further contributions in the form of a financial activities tax (FAT) on the sum of the profits and remuneration of financial institutions (IMF 2010).

---

[28] HM Treasury, Budget June 2010, Table C11.

Although quite different in the form of operation, the FAT is very similar to a value-added tax (VAT), and can be justified on the grounds that the financial sector is generally not subject to VAT (IMF 2010, 22). As Devereux points out, whilst the FAT gets around some of the problems of applying VAT to financial services, other implementation issues, most importantly international co-ordination, will need to be worked out (Devereux 2010, 2). In the June 2010 budget (the first of the new Conservative–Liberal Democrat coalition), Chancellor of the Exchequer George Osborne announced that the Government, working with its 'international partners', was exploring a FAT on profits and remuneration as part of that action, along the lines of the IMF proposal.[29]

3   CONCLUSION

Tax systems can take on a myriad of roles, from raising revenue and managing the economy to signalling desirable consumer behaviour, and, perhaps, placing curbs on excessive executive compensation. As the UK's tax exemption for employer-provided home computers discussed in the introduction to this chapter illustrates, however, the pursuit of social goals through the tax system sometimes can lead to badly targeted, ill-defined, inequitable, non-neutral, overly complicated and ineffective tax legislation that clever taxpayers and their advisors find all too easy to plan around or exploit. The tax measures governments in the US and the UK have implemented to date aimed at restraining executive pay have suffered this same fate. Moreover, to the extent that tax charges have arisen under these measures, the economic incidence appears to have fallen in large part on parties other than the executives intended to bear the tax.

Although there is some support in academic circles for attacking the deductibility of executive pay under general tests requiring tax-deductible expenses to be reasonable, tax authorities in the US and UK so far have failed to pursue this approach in relation to payments by public companies. Specific statutory limits on certain forms of executive remuneration – such as annual cash compensation – have fared little better. The US rule in IRC s. 162(m) actually raised executive pay to the $1 million cap for some, and is non-neutral in that it encourages companies to pay executives in forms of compensation not covered by the legislation, including stock options, which led in some cases to even more exorbitant returns. The UK banker bonus tax was in many ways arbitrary and inequitable, and failed in its primary objective to limit the payment of bonuses. On the other hand, the tax was extremely successful at raising revenue. Arguably a more horizontally equitable approach is to increase the tax burden on high-income earners generally rather than target a particular sector, which the UK has also done.

Thus, on the basis of the UK and US experience to date, it appears that tax measures are unlikely to be particularly effective at curbing excessive executive compensation. To the extent that government intervention is indeed considered necessary and desirable in this area, non-tax regulation may prove a more fruitful avenue to pursue.

---

[29]   HM Treasury, Budget June 2010, para 1.99.

REFERENCES

Adam, Stuart and Glen Loutzenhiser. 2007. Integrating Income Tax and National Insurance: An Interim Report, IFS Working Paper WP21/07, London: The Institute for Fiscal Studies.

Arulampalam, Wiji, Michael P. Devereux and Giorgia Maffini. 2009. The Direct Incidence of Corporate Income Tax on Wages, Oxford: Oxford University Centre for Business Taxation Working Paper WP 09/17.

Athanassiou, Phoebus. 2010. The Taxation of Bankers' Bonuses as a Human Rights Issue: A Tale of Two Schemes, *Journal of International Banking Law and Regulation*, 275.

Bachellerie, Pierre-Antoine, Nicolas De Boynes and Nicolas Message. 2010. The 50 per cent French Bank Bonus Tax, *International Business Law Journal*, 306.

Banks, James and Peter Diamond. 2010. The Base for Direct Taxation, in *Dimensions of Tax Design*, James Mirrlees and others (eds), London: The Institute for Fiscal Studies, 548.

Conway, Meredith R. 2008. Money for Nothing and the Stocks for Free: Taxing Executive Compensation, *Cornell Journal of Law and Public Policy*, 17: 383–429.

Devereux, Michael. 2010. *Tax Advisor* (June 2010) 12.

Devereux, Michael, Clemens Fuest and Giorgia Maffini. 2010. Taxing Banks: A Briefing Note, Oxford: Oxford University Centre for Business Taxation.

diFilipo, Michael. 2009. Regulating Executive Compensation in the Wake of the Financial Crisis, *Drexel Law Review*, 2: 258–312.

Freedman, Judith. 2004. Defining Taxpayer Responsibility: In Support of a General Anti-Avoidance Principle, *British Tax Review*, 332.

Highfield, Richard. 2010. Administration and Compliance: Commentary, in *Dimensions of Tax Design*, James Mirrlees and others (eds), London: The Institute for Fiscal Studies, 1172.

International Monetary Fund. 2010. A Fair And Substantial Contribution by the Financial Sector: Final Report for the G-20. Washington: IMF.

Kaplow, Louis. 2008. *The Theory of Taxation and Public Economics*. Princeton: Princeton University Press.

Kay, John. 2010. The Base for Direct Taxation: Commentary, in *Dimensions of Tax Design*, James Mirrlees and others (eds), London: The Institute for Fiscal Studies, 656.

Markham, Jerry W. 2007. Regulating Excessive Executive Compensation – Why Bother? *Journal of Business & Technology Law*, 2: 277–348.

Meade, James (ed.). 1978. *The Structure and Reform of Direct Taxation*, London: George Allen and Unwin.

Mullane, Joy Sabino. 2009. Incidence and Accidents: Regulation of Executive Compensation through the Tax Code, *Lewis & Clark Law Review*, 13: 485–552.

Organisation for Economic Co-operation and Development. 2010. *United Kingdom: Policies for a Sustainable Recovery*, Paris: OECD Publishing.

Salley, Stephen M. 2009. 'Fixing' Executive Compensation: Will Congress, Shareholder Activism, or the New SEC Disclosure Rules Change the Way Business Is Done in American Boardrooms? *Ohio State Law Journal*, 70: 757–95.

Shaw, Jonathan, Joel Slemrod and John Whiting. 2010. Administration and Compliance, in *Dimensions of Tax Design*, James Mirrlees and others (eds), London: The Institute for Fiscal Studies, 1100.

Simons, Henry. 1938. *Personal Income Taxation: The Definition of Income as a Problem of Fiscal Policy*, Chicago: University of Chicago Press.

Stiglitz, Joseph E. 1988. *Economics of the Public Sector*, 2nd edn, New York: W.W. Norton & Company.

Tiley, John. 2008. *Revenue Law*, 6th edn, Oxford: Hart Publishing.

Zelinsky, Aaron S.J. 2009. Taxing Unreasonable Compensation: § 162(A)(1) and Managerial Power, *Yale Law Journal*, 119: 637–46.

15 Insider trading and executive compensation: what we can learn from the experience with Rule 10b5-1

M. Todd Henderson

Executive compensation experienced something akin to a Glorious Revolution in the past thirty years with the change from primarily cash compensation to primarily equity-based compensation. (Such compensation, in the form of stock options of various kinds, today accounts for nearly 70 percent of total pay, compared with less than 5 percent just 20 years ago.) Paying corporate executives with firm stock helps align the interests of shareholder–owners and managers, and therefore is believed to give stronger incentives for shareholder wealth creation (Jensen & Murphy 1990). It is, in short, a method of reducing the problems created by the separation of ownership and control inherent in the modern firm (Berle & Means 1932).

But compensating executives with firm stock has costs too, one of which—trading by insiders—is the subject of this chapter. There are two potentially large costs from insider trading. The first is what we might call short-termism. Executives looking to maximize the value of their shares may engage in conduct that increases the stock price in the short run at the expense of the long term so that they can profit from trading in firm stock. This cost is not dependent on the managers having private information when they trade, but is instead premised simply on different time horizons between managers and shareholders. This type of "fraud" is, of course, only possible if markets work imperfectly and enforcement against accounting manipulations, disclosure misstatements, and so on is also costly and imperfect. For instance, managers in final periods may believe the trading profits greatly exceed the reputational and legal consequences of any fraud.

The easiest solution to these potentially value-destroying possibilities is to require executives to refrain from selling stock they are given for some period of time, perhaps until retirement or departure from the firm. Vesting requirements, restricted stock, and other techniques can be used to align manager and shareholder investment horizons, but these have costs too. Over-accumulation of firm equity in a manager's portfolio can induce excess risk on executives, whose human capital is also invested in the firm. Since risk-averse insiders tend to prefer diversified portfolios, one can expect most insiders to want to sell shares with some regularity to minimize the amount of firm stock they hold. Firms could forbid trading and compensate managers for these risks, but then this would just alter the bargain to something like a world of primarily cash compensation. One can imagine reaching an equilibrium in which the first-best employment contract is used for executives, but this has yet to be discovered or implemented anywhere known.

The second potentially large cost thus becomes apparent. If insiders are permitted to sell their shares at their discretion, they may take advantage of private information to perpetrate a "fraud" against those who buy from or sell their shares to the manager. This is what we generally think of as "insider trading," and there is a long-running debate about whether permitting managers to make informed trades is good or bad from a social welfare perspective. The Securities and Exchange Commission (SEC) has long taken the position that any trades based on informational asymmetries are fraudulent, but recognized the need for sales.[1] The SEC's ideal situation would be a system that allowed managers to sell shares for diversification and consumption reasons but prevent them from selling based on private information. The SEC believes it can achieve this harmonious result through regulation.[2] This chapter is about its latest attempt to do so with Rule 10b5-1.

Prior to 2001, the SEC attempted to prevent informed trading by banning certain types of trades (e.g., the short-swing profit rule banning buying and selling within six months for certain insiders), and policing all trades for "fraud" (i.e., trades based on informational asymmetries). Importantly, the SEC brings very few cases of insider trading (fewer than 40 per year) and most of these are against securities professionals instead of corporate insiders. The SEC relies mostly on highly imperfect private lawsuits, specifically securities class actions, to deter insider trading by managers. Also of interest, the SEC has chosen not to adopt regulations that would seem to solve this problem easily. One simple way would be an automated trading program designed to remove any potential for timing or gaming of trades or disclosures. Insiders could, for example, tell the SEC or some third party a dollar amount to sell per year (as needed for consumption or portfolio rationalization), and then those trades could be scheduled randomly over a year period.

Firms also have incentives to reduce fraudulent trading. Not only does insider trading potentially increase firm capital costs (by making buyers of equity reluctant), but it also increases legal risks either from the SEC or private parties in securities class actions. Firms therefore have tried to reduce the possibility of informed trading by contract. As discussed below, firms use "blackout windows" to restrict the times when managers can trade to those in which they are least likely to have informational advantages.

The SEC was not content with a private contractual solution, however, since firms might not fully internalize the costs of insider trading. The SEC promulgated Rule 10b5-1, which allows insiders to trade at any time so long as they committed to the trade when they did not possess an informational advantage. The SEC believed it could write a rule that would improve on private contracts by allowing insiders more freedom to trade within blackout windows but without giving them opportunities to trade on inside information. The results show that this was a failure.

Not only did Rule 10b5-1 not work as intended, it increased the opportunities for insiders to profit (at lower legal risk) from informed trades by unwinding firm contractual restrictions. It made things worse. Or did it? Certainly from the perspective of the SEC it did, since its announced policy has for decades been to reduce informed trading. But as a normative matter, the SEC's failed rule may have been a success.

There is a long-running debate about whether the benefits from informed trading exceed the costs. These trades provide information to the market about the true value of a security from the persons best positioned to know that value (Manne 1966). They also

---

[1]   Importantly, the courts have pushed back and confined illegal trades to those involving a breach of fiduciary duties or property rights.

[2]   This, of course, accepts to some extent the risks of the first type of fraud, which the SEC believes it can police through other means.

provide information within the firm to decision makers about the value of the firm, potential misconduct, and the firm's competitive position (Abramowicz & Henderson 2007). In addition, informed profits are a useful compensation device for firms, since current shareholders are paying executives with funds from future shareholders. This sounds like fraud, but so long as buyers of firm stock know about the potential for insider trading, these "savings" should thus be embedded in stock prices. That firms tolerate trading by insiders shows the benefits are greater than the costs for firms, but it doesn't tell us anything about the social costs and benefits, since firms could, in an imperfect equilibrium, be externalizing some costs. The normative questions are not yet answered.

At the end of the day, the chapter argues that government attempts to regulate insider trading have failed and new evidence supports the laissez-faire view of insider trading proposed by Henry Manne, as it seems there may be significant benefits and low costs from allowing insiders to trade. The chapter first summarizes some basic insider-trading law, then describes the SEC's latest attempt to allow trading while reducing informed trades, and then finally presents new evidence on the effectiveness of these regulations.

1   INSIDER TRADING LAW

1.1   Law

The legality of insider trades is based on a vague statute, rules and interpretations of the SEC, and a body of case law interpreting these. Section 10(b) of the Securities Exchange Act of 1934 is the wellspring of this body of law: "It shall be unlawful for any person . . . [t]o use or employ, in connection with the purchase or sale of any security . . ., any manipulative or deceptive device . . . ." Since the statute is ambiguous on the question of whether trades based on asymmetric information on an anonymous exchange are "manipulative or deceptive," the statute delegates to the SEC the authority to write rules to implement the statute for "the public interest or for the protection of investors."

The relevant SEC rule is not a model of clarity either. Rule 10b-5 makes it unlawful to use interstate commerce to, among other things, "employ any . . . scheme . . . to defraud . . . in connection with the purchase or sale of any security." The result of executive agency ambiguity layered on top of Congressional ambiguity is judicial power to decide what is and what is not illegal. The law of insider trading is effectively federal common law or, as Chief Justice Rehnquist wrote, "a judicial oak which has grown from little more than a legislative acorn."[3]

As the chief prosecutor of these cases, the SEC's point of view has considerable influence. The SEC has fairly consistently taken the view (also taken by a minority of states[4]) that insiders have a duty to disclose all material information available to them before trading—the so-called "disclose or abstain" rule. The rule was first announced in *Cady, Roberts & Co.*, an enforcement proceeding in 1961.[5] The SEC found liability

---

[3]   *Blue Chip Stamps v. Manor Drug Stores*, 421 U.S. 723 (1975).
[4]   See *Oliver v. Oliver* (Ga. 1903).
[5]   *Cady, Roberts & Co.*, 40 S.E.C. 907 (1961).

in the case of an outside director who tipped his partner in a brokerage business about an upcoming dividend cut. Relying on two separate theories—first, that the director expropriated corporate information for personal use; and second, that there is "inherent unfairness" in trading on information knowing it is not known by the other side—the SEC declared that an insider in possession of material, nonpublic information (hereinafter "inside" information) must disclose such information before trading or abstain from trading.

The Second Circuit endorsed this view several years later, holding in *SEC v. Texas Gulf Sulphur*, that insiders of a mining company trading in advance of public disclosure of a favorable geology report violated Rule 10b-5.[6] The court specifically blessed the disclose-or-abstain rule the SEC announced in *Cady, Roberts*, noting this rule "is based in policy on the justifiable expectation of the securities marketplace that all investors trading on impersonal exchanges have relatively equal access to material information."[7]

The practical impact of all this is a de facto rule of mandatory abstention for insiders in possession of material information unknown to outsiders. The other option, disclosure, is unavailable since the information is likely unknown to outsiders for a (corporate) reason. Taking the information for personal use would be both a violation of an insider's fiduciary duties (to not profit against the corporation or its shareholders) and, according to the SEC, unfair to market traders outside of the firm, and thus degrading of the public's confidence in public securities markets.

Mandatory abstention from trading is undoubtedly overinclusive. A rule of this nature would unnecessarily deter insiders from making trades even at times when insiders do not have inside information or are not using it to inform a trading decision. As a result, firms will face additional and unnecessary costs from having to compensate managers for bearing more firm-specific risk. (Insiders will value shares they cannot trade freely less than those they can.)

Some courts recognized this problem, and accepted an "I-would-have-traded-anyway" defense. In *SEC v. Adler*, the Eleventh Circuit held that the government had to prove not only that an insider "possessed" inside information at the time of trading, but also the insider "used" the information to make the trading decision.[8] The prototypical case was an insider claiming she planned to make a trade on the date in question some time before she came into possession of inside information, and the timing of the trade was a coincidence. These cases routinely include a reason for the planned sale, such as the expiration of a mandatory holding period following an IPO. The SEC, supported by other circuit courts, continued to claim the statute banned trading while merely in "possession" of inside information, and its burden was only to show this.[9]

Before turning to the SEC's attempted resolution of this dispute with the courts, it is worth detouring to consider the private ordering that operates in the background of these legal rules.

---

[6]   401 F.2d 833 (2d Cir. 1968).
[7]   Id.
[8]   137 F.3d 1325 (11th Cir. 1998).
[9]   See, for example, *United States v. Teicher*, 987 F.2 112 (2d Cir. 1993).

1.2 Private Ordering

The SEC's disclose-or-abstain rule strongly deters trades by insiders, so firms are forced to find a way of providing trading opportunities for insiders, while minimizing the potential firm costs of such trades. The biggest potential cost from trades is the litigation risk of fraud suits. Insider stock sales are frequently used as evidence of "scienter," a necessary element of any securities fraud case, especially when they are unusual in time or amount. All else being equal, insider sales that show managers benefited monetarily from trades made during the time when alleged misrepresentations affected the firm's stock price will increase the firm's litigation risk.

The primary mechanism for limiting firm risk from insider sales is the use of contracts limiting the time and manner of insider sales. Firms impose blackout windows that restrict the times when insiders can trade to those when insiders are least likely to have access to inside information.[10] This widespread practice means that there are very limited "trading windows" outside of which transactions are prohibited (Bettis et al. 2000). Research suggests that, prior to Rule 10b5-1, insiders of firms with blackout windows dramatically reduce the trading within these windows (Bettis et al. 2000).

These restrictions are imperfect for several reasons. First, the restrictions are only a crude proxy for when insiders might actually possess inside information—for example, within 30 to 45 days of earnings announcements—and thus are likely to be both overinclusive and underinclusive. Trading outside of designated trading windows is *verboten*, even if the insider does not possess an informational advantage, and likewise, trading inside is likely to have some litigation prophylactic benefits, even if the insider does so based on material, non-public information.

Second, the restrictions greatly reduce the times at which insiders can trade, thus concentrating sales and raising the stakes for each sale. This may give insiders incentives to manipulate other aspects pertaining to the trade, such as the timing of the release of firm information, in ways that skirt the contractual restrictions. Studies show insiders are able to strategically time disclosures to avoid the restrictions of trading windows: managers about to receive options disclose negative news and withhold good news in order to increase the options' value (Aboody & Kasnik 2000).

Finally, boards do not have great information about the private trading habits of insiders, since boards' ability to oversee the private trading of insiders is both impractical and not legally required.[11] Insiders are compensated in options to align their incentives with shareholders, but insiders need to convert these options to cash, and would like to do so more often than shareholders would prefer. Trading windows are thus likely to force obfuscation of insider diversification, as much as compliance with insider trading policies.

---

[10] Another version of this would be to require executives to put all firm equity into a blind trust. The costs of such a strategy are sufficiently large as to make this an unacceptable condition for executives. A more modest version of this is the use of pre-commitment trading plans discussed below.

[11] See, for example, *Beam v. Martha Stewart Living Omnimedia, Inc.*, 833 A.2d 961 (Del. Ch. 2003) (finding no duty for board to monitor or police sales of stock in private portfolio of CEO).

In light of these problems and the uncertainty created by the split of authority on the "use" versus "possession" issue, the SEC promulgated Rule 10b5-1 to broaden the trading opportunity set for insiders' trades (thus providing incentives for firms to relax constraints from firm-imposed blackout windows), but trying to limit insiders' ability to use private information to their advantage. We turn now to a brief examination of the Rule.

2   RULE 10B5-1

The SEC established Rule 10b5-1 plans as a defense to allegations of illegal insider trading in October 2000, after it adopted a broad interpretation of the "on the basis of" language in Rule 10b-5. The SEC formally codified the "knowing possession" standard, making federal prosecutions of insider trading significantly easier. Recognizing that this tightening of the legal standard put even more pressure on executives trying to execute uninformed diversification trades, the SEC provided insiders with a new affirmative defense for trades planned at a time when the insider was uninformed, regardless of whether the insider was informed when the trades executed. The Rule was designed to walk the razor's edge of insider trading—trying to allow firms to permit insiders to optimize their wealth portfolios (and thus make the most efficient labor bargain) and trying to reduce the social costs of insider trading.

The Rule provides that insiders trade "on the basis of" when they are "aware of material nonpublic information when [they] made the purchase or sale."[12] This definition is subject to an affirmative defense if the insider can show that "before becoming aware of the information" the insider entered into a plan committing to trade at a certain future date.[13] There is a requirement that the executive not deviate from the plan. This could be read as limiting the ability of an insider to selectively cancel plans based on inside information; however, the SEC does not take this position. Believing there can be no securities fraud without an actual purchase or sale transaction, the SEC stated that canceling a plan based on private information is not inconsistent with the Rule.[14]

---

[12]   *See* 17 CFR § 240.10b5-1(b).

[13]   "(1) entered into a binding contract to purchase or sell the security; (2) instructed another person to purchase or sell the security for the [insider's] account, or (3) adopted a written plan for trading securities," put in the plan "(1) . . . the amount of securities to be purchased or sold and the price at which and the date on which the securities were to be purchased or sold; (2) . . . a written formula or algorithm . . . for determining the amount of securities to be purchased or sold and the price at which and the date on which the securities were to be purchased or sold; or (3) [did] not permit the [insider] to exercise any subsequent influence over [transactions]"; and did not "alter[] or deviate[] from the contract, instruction, or plan to purchase or sell securities (whether by changing the amount, price, or timing of the purchase or sale), or enter[] into or altered a corresponding or hedging transaction or position with respect to those securities." Rule 10b5-1(c).

[14]   *See* SEC Division of Corporation Finance, Manual of Publicly Available Telephone Interpretations, Fourth Supplement, Rule 10b5-1, Question 15 (issued May 2001). The logic is that a canceled sale is not the "purchase or sale" of a security. This view has appeal. After all, it would be impossible to police trades planned in the mind of executives but canceled based on an informational advantage.

The SEC did state, however, that canceling a plan in this way could raise questions about whether the plan was entered into in good faith. Hence another requirement: the Rule includes a catchall provision intended to avoid manipulation that complies with the letter but not spirit of the Rule. Plans that are not entered into in "good faith" or are entered into "as part of a plan or scheme to evade" the Rule do not get the benefit of the affirmative defense.[15] As shown below, this safety valve is not likely effective in both theory and practice. It is not clear that this good faith requirement can be readily enforced by the SEC (perhaps because it is procedurally very difficult), and empirically, insiders appear to retain a strategic advantage.

Returning to the strategies firms can use to allow trading yet limit costs, firms could require (or simply allow) executives to make certain or all trades pursuant to pre-commitment trading plans pursuant to SEC Rule 10b5-1(c).[16] These plans could serve as substitutes for trading windows or other contractual restrictions. An insider with no legally significant information possession as of January 1st could enter into a trading plan on that day, agreeing to buy or sell shares pursuant to a set schedule, a pre-set trading algorithm, or merely designate authority to a broker. Thus, in June when the insider obtains posses-sion of inside information, purchases or sales are still possible. According to the Rule, the June sales are not "on the basis of" inside information because of the pre-commitment. These plans are often explicit substitutes for compliance with trading windows, meaning that sales can be made under these plans at any time. (They are often adopted during open windows, however, as this helps meet the Rule's requirement that the plan be entered into in "good faith" at a time when the insider does not have any inside information.)

The Rule as promulgated did not require disclosure of any kind. In April 2002, the SEC proposed mandatory disclosure, through 8-K filings, of insiders' use of Rule 10b5-1 trading plans. There was, however, widespread criticism of the proposal on the ground that disclosure might send erroneous signals to the market about the insiders' intent in entering into the plan.

3   THE USE OF 10B5-1 TRADING PLANS

Executives appear to be embracing the Rule. Rule 10b5-1 trading plans have been adopted widely—at least 600 firms and over 1000 individual insiders have disclosed that they used these plans between 2001 and 2007.[17] Trading volume is high too. Executives at Fortune 500 firms sold about $8.5 billion in stock through these plans in 2006, a 60 percent increase from 2004 (Searcey & Scannell 2007).

But what can we learn about insider trading and executive compensation from the use of the Rule to date? There are empirical and theoretical insights from several recent studies of the Rule. The first shows how insiders can abuse the Rule to retain or even increase their trading advantage, and this highlights the futility of trying to regulate

---

[15]   Rule 10b5-1(c)(ii).
[16]   Rule 10b5-1(c)(1)(C).
[17]   Since disclosure is not required and brokers who manage plans estimate that thousands of them are not disclosed, this number likely materially underestimates the actual number in use.

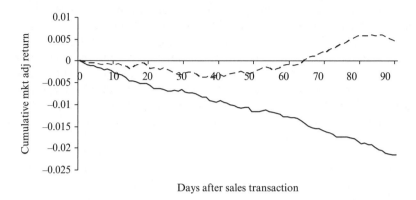

Source: Jagolinzer 2009, Figure 1, Panel C.

Figure 15.1   Returns to firm stock following sales in plans (solid line) and outside plans (dotted line)

insider trading. The second shows how disclosure, which is thought to be a disinfectant, can actually be used as a weapon by insiders hoping to hide informed trades. The third shows how boards and managers "bargain" over the results of the first two studies in a way that should make us feel less worried about insider trading.

3.1   Insiders Abuse the Rule

Alan Jagolinzer found sales executed within Rule 10b5-1 plans earn returns that are, on average, greater than returns earned by the market index and also returns earned by insiders who execute sales outside of Rule 10b5-1 plans (Jagolinzer 2009). The study finds that "insiders' sales systematically follow positive and precede negative firm performance, generating abnormal forward-looking returns larger than those earned by non-participating colleagues" (Id.). After rejecting several possible innocent explanations for this finding,[18] the study concludes that "trading within the Rule does not solely reflect uninformed diversification" (Id.).

More specifically, the study examines over 100,000 10b5-1 trades by more than 3000 insiders at over 1000 firms. These trades beat the market average by over 3.6 percent over a six-month period, compared with less than 0.3 percent for insiders trading outside 10b5-1 trading plans. See Figure 15.1. According to the study, this result is statistically very unlikely, and can be explained only as a result of some aspects of the Rule or the way

---

[18]   The benign explanations considered and rejected by the data are: (1) mean reversion; (2) market reaction to sales by insiders; and (3) abnormally negative returns for the firm in question. Explanation (1) was rejected because a control group of firms with similar run-ups in prices did not show a similar magnitude mean reversion over the same period. Explanation (2) was tested and rejected using a 3-day abnormal return, which showed no extraordinary returns. Explanation (3) was rejected after looking at a comparison of returns across industry SIC code, and finding no bear market to speak of in these firms. *See id.*

in which plans are being used. The SEC expected the Rule to reduce insider abnormal returns, but the opposite happened.

3.2 Disclosure as Weapon, not a Disinfectant

The Jagolinzer study does not isolate the exact mechanism by which insiders are able to exploit the current formulation of the Rule, but a follow-on study by Todd Henderson, Alan Jagolinzer, and Karl Muller suggests disclosure is the mechanism that allows insiders to earn abnormal returns (Henderson et al. 2011). Disclosure provides extra litigation protection by allowing insider-trading cases to be won at the motion-to-dismiss phase. Although nothing within the Rule limits its application to cases in which the trading plan was disclosed prior to the trade or the filing of the complaint, the peculiarities of civil procedure and the typical course of this class of cases make such disclosure an important element of any risk reduction strategy.

As a matter of practice, the vast majority of class action lawsuits alleging securities fraud are won or lost at the "motion to dismiss" phase of the litigation. In every case, defendants file a motion to dismiss pursuant to Federal Rule of Civil Procedure 12(b)(6), arguing that even if plaintiffs' allegations are true, relief cannot be granted on the face of the complaint. If the motion is not granted, the litigation proceeds to discovery, which is likely to be costly to defendants, in real dollar terms, in distraction and opportunity costs, and in potential piggyback litigation based on materials uncovered during the process. Hence, nearly all cases in which such a motion is not granted settle, often for many millions of dollars. According to a lawyer specializing in these cases we spoke with, "the game is won or lost with the motion to dismiss."[19]

A key issue on which these motions routinely turn is scienter. Under the revised pleading standards of the Private Securities Litigation Reform Act of 1995 (PSLRA), to survive a motion to dismiss, a plaintiff must plead with "particularity facts giving rise to a strong inference that the defendant acted with knowledge or recklessness."[20] This is usually done through claims that defendants profited from alleged misrepresentations by buying or selling the stock at artificially high or low prices. A trading plan can provide a counterpoint to such a claim, since it is arguably more difficult for insiders to profit from a misrepresentation when a trading plan is in place.

But the litigation prophylactic works well (if at all) only when the existence of the plan is publicly disclosed. This is because when ruling on a motion to dismiss, courts generally do not consider materials other than the pleadings, taking the facts alleged in the complaint as true; defendants may not rebut factual allegations at this stage in the process.[21] Publicly available documents, however, may be considered in securities fraud cases "as long as they are integral to the statements within the complaint."[22] "Integral" means basically related to the issues, and publicly available and accurate,[23] so courts routinely take

---

[19] This is widely accepted, but is confirmed by lawyers who try these cases. In an interview with lawyer Jim Kramer, we heard this refrain again and again. Interview conducted in June 2008.

[20] *In re Cardinal Health Inc. Sec. Litig.*, 426 F.Supp.2d 688, 718 (S.D. Ohio 2006).

[21] See, e.g., *Weiner v. Klais & Co.*, 108 F.3d 86, 88-89 (6th Cir.1997).

[22] *In re Cardinal Health Inc. Sec. Litig.*, 426 F.Supp.2d at 712.

[23] See Fed. Rule of Evid. 201(b).

judicial notice of SEC filings, prospectuses, analysts' reports, and other publicly available documents relating to a firm's financial statements, even if not part of the complaint.[24] This point highlights the need for defendants to make the existence of 10b5-1 trading plans public, either through press release or filing with the SEC.[25]

The lesson from the case law is that the greater the amount of disclosure, the more powerful the litigation protection. Bare-bones disclosure gives insiders a chance of winning early when litigation is still cheap, while detailed disclosure makes this more likely. Non-disclosure provides no litigation deterrent or opportunity for early victory, but does still allow an insider to win later on. But disclosure is costly because it allows front-running, which makes potential trades less valuable since trading counterparties can anticipate the advantage of insiders' planned trades, and take profits in advance of them.

If well calibrated, the costs of disclosure should offset the gains, thereby minimizing the potential opportunism capable from the Rule. But there are two ways in which insiders can nevertheless abuse the Rule to earn abnormal returns. One, what we call "insider insurance," involves making bare-bones or "limited" disclosures; the other, what we call "hiding in plain sight," involves making more detailed or "specific" disclosures. Let's consider them in turn.

3.2.1 "Insider insurance"

The most obvious way for insiders to abuse the Rule is to opportunistically cancel planned trades, based on private information. As noted above, under prevailing SEC interpretations, trading plans may be canceled even based on inside information. This gives insiders a valuable real option on future firm performance. In effect, the Rule gives insiders a put option—the right to sell shares at a given price—on the firm's future performance. So if the insider believes there is some chance that the firm's stock will fall in the future, she can pick the price at which she will sell (the strike price of the put) and plan sales periodically between the initiation of the plan and the expected bad news. If the bad state of the world happens, the insider exercises the put, and sells the shares under the plan. If not, she cancels the plan (equivalent to letting the put expire) and retains the shares. In effect, the Rule can turn the decision to sell based on inside information into a decision not to terminate based on inside information, only the former of which is illegal by the Rule. The strategy is likely to be extremely effective where the knowledge of the insider when the plan is executed is less than 50 percent, since this is the time when the SEC will have to prove knowledge.

Importantly, the Rule, coupled with case law, the relevant statute, and the rules of civil procedure, makes the embedded option costless or nearly so. As shown above, "disclosed" plans can provide limited information—such as, "sales will be made each month up to or exceeding 1000 shares each month" or, simply, "the CEO is trading all shares pursuant to a Rule 10b5-1 trading plan"—and courts have dismissed cases involving

---

[24]   See, e.g., *In re Royal Appliance Sec. Litig.*, 1995 WL 490131, at *2 (6th Cir. Aug.15, 1995).
[25]   This seems to represent the consensus view not only among courts, but also among corporate advisors. Institutional Shareholder Services, the largest proxy advising firm for institutional shareholders, concludes, "such plans should be filed in some form with the SEC so that [they] . . . can be considered at the motion to dismiss stage" (ISS 2006). Lawyers advising firms on securities fraud litigation matters also think disclosure is a prerequisite to risk reduction: "[t]he adoption of the Rule 10b5-1 trading plans . . . should be publicly disclosed" to reduce the risk of litigation (Roberts & Porritt 2004).

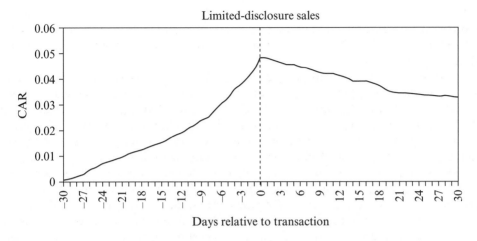

Source: Henderson et al. 2011, Figure 2, Panel B.

Figure 15.2   Stock price before and after limited disclosure sales

plans like this at the motion to dismiss stage. Such disclosures would not allow traders to predict trading behavior of insiders, since they do not give any details about the timing, price, or volume of future sales. This means the cost of disclosure, in terms of forgone profits, is negligible. Thus insiders have nearly guaranteed loss avoidance, which is just another way of saying guaranteed profits in excess of those outsiders can earn.

If canceling planned sales had a significant cost, then this would be the cost of the put option. For example, if an insider disclosed a plan to sell shares at a certain future time but then disclosed that she was canceling the planned sales, the market might interpret this as an attempt at manipulation, and impose a cost through the firm's stock price. The same would be true even if there were no disclosure of the cancellation, since the market is likely to observe any mismatch between disclosed trades and announced trades in Form 4 filings. But because firms do not have to disclose the details of trades or their cancellation, the costs of this strategy are likely to be very low.

The termination option that makes insider insurance valuable is traded off against reduced litigation risk reduction benefits, since the discussion above showed that these benefits are increasing in disclosure specificity. In other words, an insider who is confident in the need for litigation protection (because she knows she will be selling) would opt for the benefits of specific disclosure (discussed next), and an insider who is less confident would perhaps opt for the option of termination.

The data show insiders using this strategy. Sales within "limited disclosure" 10b5-1 plans, on average, precede negative firm performance relative to the market. As shown in Figure 15.2, these firms experienced an average of about −6 percent market-adjusted returns in the six-month period following sales by insiders making limited disclosures.[26] These results are statistically significant at the 1 percent level.

---

[26]   The median was −5 percent return.

If these trades were uninformed, the abnormal returns after sales should be zero in expectation (that is, a flat line to the right of the "0" in Figure 15.2[27]).[28] The fact that insider sales following limited disclosures systematically precede drops in firm value suggests abuse of the Rule.

But such abuse may actually be efficient. To see why what we can call "insider insurance" embedded in Rule 10b5-1 plans might be efficient and desirable for shareholders, consider the following example. Sue, the CEO of Acme, Inc., has 100 shares of vested stock; the stock is trading at $10 per share. Sue has the choice of two projects: Project A has a 70 percent chance of increasing the stock price to $15 in one year, and a 30 percent chance of decreasing the stock price to $8 over the same period; Project B has a 70 percent chance of increasing the stock price to $20, and a 30 percent chance of decreasing the stock price to zero. Diversified, risk-neutral shareholders prefer Project B, since its expected value ($14) exceeds that of Project A ($13). Sue, however, prefers Project A, since the 30 percent chance of failure in Project B will result in not only economic losses, but also likely her job. Here we see classic agency cost problems—managers interests are not fully aligned with those of shareholders, even with substantial equity compensation.

The early termination option embedded in Rule 10b5-1, however, can help align these incentives by increasing the economic returns to Sue from choosing Project B, perhaps enough to overcome the potential of losing her job. To see this, consider Sue's payoffs from the sale of all her stock at the end of one year. Pre-Rule, Sue would earn $290 from Project A and $400 from Project B. Although based on purely stock profits Sue would prefer Project B (along with shareholders), as noted above, Sue's risk aversion with respect to her job may mean this monetary difference is insufficient to persuade her to choose Project B. With the Rule, however, Sue can earn more from Project B, maybe even enough to overcome her expected losses from employment. Her payoffs increase to $350 from Project A but even more so to $700 from Project B. This is because she can avoid any losses from the 30 percent bad states of the world by planning sales trades in advance and then letting them execute in the bad states of the world or terminating them in the good states of the world. In other words, choosing Project B increases Sue's expected payoffs by 38 percent in the pre-Rule world, but over 100 percent in the world with the Rule. Whether or not this increased economic return will be sufficient to overcome a CEO's risk aversion with respect to employment will vary by firm, by individual, and over time, but *ceteris paribus*, the existence of the Rule helps align shareholder and manager interests.

3.2.2   "Hiding in plain sight"

Insiders who do not need the option arising from the ability to terminate may opt for specific disclosures to enhance litigation prophylaxis. As suggested by a recent court's reluctance to grant a motion to dismiss on a bare-bones 10b5-1 plan, the more information available in a plan, the more likely it will be an effective defense at the motion-to-

[27]   This is the result for the non-disclosure group.

[28]   As shown in Figure 15.2, the decline in stock price performance following insider trades for firms making limited disclosures occurs after a run up in the stock price. This is expected because increases in firm stock price lead to a greater percentage of insider wealth being held in firm stock, which under normal circumstances would result in sales under most plans.

dismiss stage.[29] This is especially the case because not all trades need be made pursuant to plans, and, since plan trades and non-plan trades will be hard to distinguish, the former can masquerade as the latter if need be. So, identifying particular trades to be made at particular times in the future makes it much more likely that a court will be able to conclude that the trades in question in the litigation were ones covered by the plan. Disclosures about dates, price targets, volume of shares traded, and so on can provide valuable information to courts to match suspected illegal trades with precommitments.

But disclosure of this specificity raises the cost of terminating because market participants can do the same ex ante to ex post matching the court can do, and thereby impose reputational or other costs on the firm or individual executive. Opportunistic termination may also raise the possibility of government sanctions, either civil or criminal. Insiders will therefore only use this approach when highly confident about the future state of the world—where termination is very unlikely. Where the tradeoff of costs and benefits reaches its maximum for any firm or individual in a given factual setting is likely to vary widely by the details of the case, making any generalizations quite difficult.

To see how this strategy might work, consider the CEO of a small biotech firm. On January 1st, she sees confidential reports from doctors conducting clinical trials on her firm's key drug suggesting the drug is likely (say, 90 percent likely) to be rejected by the FDA when it makes a decision in September. Wanting to profit from this information, the CEO can trade now on the news or she can put in place a plan to trade on the news sometime in the future, as the decision date is closer. These two courses are seemingly of equal risk. The inquiry into the possession of inside information centers on the same day—January 1st—when the trade was made or the plan to trade was made.

The latter course is, however, likely to be more profitable for two reasons. First, it allows the insider to profit from any increase in the stock price from January until September. Delaying trading without a plan for some time would also have this benefit, but in the pre-Rule world, any delay increases the likely litigation risk. The Rule thus allows the insider the riskless option (compared with the pre-Rule sale on January 1st) of earning any stock price appreciation between the time of the knowledge and the time of the sale. Importantly, an insider can do this without risk (compared with the trade-immediately strategy), since the plan can bake in price floors at which sales are automatically triggered.

Second, it allows insiders to sell more shares with the same legal risk, since sales can be spaced out over time in a way that may reduce the attention of either private lawyers or the government. Large sales in advance of bad news look suspicious, while smaller sales on a regular basis look more like random, diversification trades. Plaintiffs' lawyers and prosecutors have limited resources and are likely to focus on the most vulnerable potential defendants; this type of concealment is bound to distinguish insiders using hiding in plain sight in a way that deters suits.

The data show that sales within "specific disclosure" 10b5-1 plans, on average, precede large negative firm performance relative to the market. The average cumulative abnormal return in the six months after the first trade for companies making specific disclosures is

---

[29]   *Miss. Pub. Employ. Retire. Sys. v. Boston Scientific Corp.*, 523 F.3d. 75 (1st Cir. 2008).

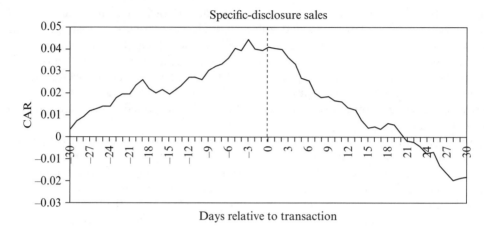

Source: Henderson et al. 2011, Figure 2, Panel A.

Figure 15.3   Stock price before and after specific disclosure sales

−12 percent.[30] This result is statistically significant at the 1 percent confidence level. As shown in Figure 15.3, there is a large decline in stock price performance following insider trades for firms making specific disclosures.

Consistent with the strategic use of disclosure, insiders making specific disclosures also appear to be trying to hide their trades by spacing them deliberately in time between the plan initiation and the revelation of bad news. Insiders making specific disclosures trade much more often than other insiders, averaging about 25 trades within their plans compared with about 5 for insiders making no disclosures and 10 for insiders making limited disclosures (Henderson et al. 2011). The average size of each transaction is also much smaller for insiders making disclosures: non-disclosing insiders' trades were six times larger than those of insiders making specific disclosures (Id.). These trades are less likely to garner negative attention, because of both their smaller size and their pattern, which both suggest random, diversification trades.

3.3   Implicit Compensation

The use of Rule 10b5-1 can also reveal something about the broader issues of insider trading as executive compensation. After all, the Rule allows firms and managers to effectively unwind blackout window restrictions and trade more liberally than before the Rule. Since we know that disclosure choices are correlated with different levels of expected profit from 10b5-1 trades, we can use this data to test whether firms reduce compensation to offset the expected increase in trading profits from use of these plans and, if they do, whether this offset includes expected gains from informed trades.

---

[30]   The median firm returns were −7 percent for the six months following the first sales transaction.

3.3.1   Data

New research tries to answer these questions (Henderson 2011). This study examined firms using Rule 10b5-1 plans from 2000 to 2006 and compared the pay at firms making explicit disclosures of 10b5-1 usage and firms for which the use of plans is implied. This difference is crucial for the analysis, because insiders making explicit disclosures earn significantly greater abnormal returns than insiders not making disclosures of 10b5-1 usage (Henderson et al. 2011).

Henderson 2011 makes two significant findings. First, the evidence suggests that executives whose trading freedom is increased experience reductions in other forms of pay to offset the potential gains from trading. This result is consistent with (and the flipside of) a study by Darren Roulstone, finding firms that restrict trading increase compensation to offset the lost opportunities from trading (Roulstone 2003). While Roulstone finds that firms restricting trading pay more, the data show that firms liberalizing trading pay less. From this, we can conclude that boards take executives' ability to trade profitably in firm stock into account when setting their pay, and, importantly, it is a two-way street. This should not be surprising, since if it were not true it would mean executives were systematically overpaid, earning more pay when trading is limited but not earning less when it is freed up. This result is, however, inconsistent with the managerial power theory of executive compensation. Lucian Bebchuk and others claim executives use undisclosed trading profits to enrich themselves at the expense of shareholders (Bebchuk et al. 2002). The data presented in this study call the strong form of this claim into doubt, since it seems shareholders are including such expected profits into CEO pay packages.

Second, the data also suggest that some of the reduction in pay that boards impose as a result of liberalizing trading opportunities is to offset expected gains from trades based on material, non-public information. Firm disclosure choice about Rule 10b5-1 plans provides two groups of firms that sort by expected trading profits based on informed trades, and this allows one to test whether boards anticipate these profits and deduct them from executive compensation. The evidence suggests they do.

The way the study reaches this conclusion is by examining the pay of firms disclosing 10b5-1 plans and firms not disclosing them in the years before and after the first use of a 10b5-1 plan. As noted above, Henderson et al. show that disclosing firms earn significantly higher profits from trading than non-disclosure firms (Henderson et al. 2011). So if trading profits are taken into consideration in setting pay of executives, firms with executives disclosing 10b5-1 plans should see their pay reduced (or increased less), compared with firms not disclosing their use of 10b5-1 plans. The study finds that the total pay for the CEOs of nondisclosure firms rises nearly 10 percentage points above the total pay for the CEOs of disclosure firms (Id.).

This difference could be explained, however, by factors unrelated to the fact that during the intervening year the firm authorized executives to use Rule 10b5-1 trading plans and the chief executive officer of the company first used a trading plan to make a trade. For instance, it is possible that small variations in economic performance could explain differences in pay across the disclosure partition.

A first way of testing the potential confounding effects of economic performance is to examine the average and median changes in performance across the disclosure partition. If changes in firm economic performance are the reason why disclosure firms saw smaller pay increases relative to nondisclosure firms, then we should expect to see the change in economic performance for disclosure firms to be worse than for nondisclosure firms. The opposite is true. The average and median disclosure firm performs as well as or outperforms the average and median nondisclosure firm across all economic performance metrics (Id.). In fact, disclosure firms experienced larger increases in market value, operating income, earnings per share (EPS), and net income than nondisclosure firms (Id.).

The results of an ordinary-least-squares linear regression support the proposition that disclosure is negatively correlated with the change in pay (Id.). Disclosure of Rule 10b5-1 trading plans is a statistically significant determinate of the change in pay (95 percent confidence interval). The coefficient on the disclosure dummy variable is negative, meaning the use and disclosure of a Rule 10b5-1 trading plan is associated with negative changes in the amount of pay for CEOs. Since disclosure choice is associated with greater expected insider trading profits (especially from informed trades), this means the data suggest changes in pay are negatively correlated with expected insider trading profits. Firms where insiders are likely to earn significant abnormal returns from informed trading (in addition to those from optimization trades) see smaller increases in pay than firms where insiders are likely to engage only in optimization trades.

In order to test the robustness of the main finding—firms where expected trading profits are greater see significantly different and negative changes in pay relative to firms where expected trading profits are less—Henderson 2011 compared the pay of these two groups of firms in periods before the adoption of Rule 10b5-1 trading plans. If the adoption and disclosure of a Rule 10b5-1 plan is a significant event and causes an observable difference in the change in pay between the two groups, the change in pay in periods before the adoption of such trading plans should not be statistically different between the two groups. Instead, the change in pay should be driven by economic factors, such as change in market value or firm income. This is what Henderson 2011 finds.

3.3.2   Discussion

The existence of bargaining about trading profits appears to offer a powerful counterargument to the claim by some scholars that, on average, boards and executives do not bargain at arm's length about pay. The ability of CEOs to earn undisclosed profits from insider trading is a central component of Lucian Bebchuk and Jesse Fried's managerial power theory of executive compensation (Bebchuk et al. 2002). Bebchuk and Fried observe that executives earn money by selling shares, and then claim executives "camouflage [insider trading] transactions" from the board and shareholders in order to earn compensation beyond what they deserve (Id.). They argue: "These [insider-trading] profits . . . provide extra value to executives that does not show up in any of the firm's accounting information or compensation figures disclosed to shareholders. . . . Thus, the cost of these hidden insider trading profits to shareholders is likely to go unnoticed" (Id.).

According to the managerial power theory, the board does not know about insider-trading profits, and therefore cannot take them into consideration in setting the executive's wage. The result is the board may systematically overpay executives. Bebchuk and Fried claim the existence of insider-trading profits is "difficult to explain from an optimal contacting perspective, [but] is easily explained under the managerial power approach" (Id.).

For the existence of trading profits to support the managerial-power hypothesis, their claim must be that the board does not take even the possibility of insider-trading profits into account when setting executive pay. If the board does take the profits into account, the existence of insider-trading profits does not implicate the validity of the pay-setting process, since the board would in fact be bargaining with the executive, at some degree of arm's length. The insider-trading profits may raise issues about the firm's compliance with accounting and disclosure requirements of state corporate law and federal securities laws, but they do not, without more, say anything about whether the board did a good job for shareholders in bargaining over executive pay.

The data presented above is some evidence that boards are aware of insiders' trading proclivities and ability to earn abnormal returns, and bargain (albeit perhaps imperfectly) about these gains. This bargaining is, however, not generally disclosed and may in fact be surreptitious given the potential negative implications of the underlying conduct. Although it may be rational for the board to engage in this bargaining, disclosing it may be irrational, as it would expose the executive and the firm to costs they do not otherwise have to bear. This obviously raises issues about the completeness of firm disclosures about pay and the efficacy of existing pay disclosure rules.

The managerial power theory may have some traction if bargaining is not complete or even nearly so. But we can, based on this data, reject the strong form of the managerial power thesis. For the strong form to be true, there would have to be no difference in pay across disclosure partitions. If there were no difference, we could conclude that boards did not rationally reduce pay based on the ability to earn abnormal returns. The evidence presented above suggests the boards did know and did offset executive pay to account for some of these profits. So the strong form of the managerial power thesis seems less plausible.

A weaker version of the managerial-power theory, however, might argue that bargaining exists but is incomplete, perhaps woefully so. Say an insider is able to earn implicit compensation of $100 from Rule 10b5-1 trades, but sees total explicit pay reduced by only $10. This might suggest some managerial power over the pay-setting process, although there are other competing explanations. So what we need for a test of the completeness of bargaining is some measure of the amount of implicit compensation (that is, the amount of expected insider-trading profits) and the reductions in pay.

Henderson et al. 2011 report that the average insider sold about $8 million in shares in the one-year period following the first observed disclosure of a 10b5-1 plan trade (Henderson et al. 2011, Table 2). These are actual observed sales in the marketplace. Henderson et al. also find the average insider was able to earn abnormal returns of about 12 percent over a one-year period on these sales. This means the average insider could earn about $1 million in abnormal returns from these 10b5-1 trading plan sales. This is roughly equal to the amount of compensation offset against pay suggested by the regression coefficient for disclosure choice in Henderson 2011. The coefficient on the disclosure dummy (variable = 1 or 0) is −1219, which means disclosure (variable = 1) is associated with a reduction in pay of about $1.2 million (Henderson 2011).

There is some imprecision in both the estimate of the average trading profits and the regression coefficient, so these estimates can be said to be roughly equal. This back-of-the-envelope calculation is not conclusive evidence, and the estimates are very rough. But the magnitudes are suggestive that the offset in compensation is within the range of expected profits that insiders earn. It is much less likely in light of this data that the offset is far less than the profits insiders earn from informed trading. This suggests that the claims about camouflaged profits being evidence of executive dominance of the pay-setting process are much weaker than they appear.

The reductions in pay to offset trading profits seem consistent with the well-accepted board goal of maximizing firm value. As mentioned above, the board is reducing payments by current shareholders (and thus increasing firm value by that amount) as a result of the ability of executives to earn profits from trades against outsiders. The optimization component of implicit compensation, what Roulstone estimates at about 13 percent of total pay, is unobjectionable from any perspective. Giving executives the ability to trade, and offsetting their pay in an amount equal to their expected gains, is a Pareto improvement, since current shareholders pay less for executive talent and future shareholders receive shares in a bargain in which no side to the transaction is expected to outperform the other. The SEC had this win-win situation in mind when it passed Rule 10b5-1.

The inability to limit Rule 10b5-1 to optimization trades, however, complicates board decision-making. From the perspective of current shareholders the payment of implicit compensation for informed trades may not only make economic sense but it may be an imperative. Allowing insiders to trade, including on inside information, may be the cheapest way to pay, considering all costs, including potential legal costs. This may be because the board makes the deliberate calculation of the costs and benefits of restricting trading, or it may simply be because the board believes it is powerless to prevent insiders from trading, since there are no legal duties for it to monitor executives' private behavior and, in any event, such attempts may be very expensive and fruitless. In either case, if the board is aware that executives are earning abnormal returns from trading and the board is unable to efficiently prevent them from doing so, it is perfectly rational for the board to reduce the expected costs of such trading (that is, authorize the use of 10b5-1 trading plans) and to offset pay as a result of expected gains.

The problem arises because the board is arguably complicit in illegal activity by the executives. For instance, we wouldn't defend a board decision for a pharmaceutical firm to sell heroin, even if it was based on a business judgment that the benefits exceeded the costs. The same would be true of board actions designed to conceal the CEO's hobby of robbing banks. In this case, the board is not necessarily aiding and abetting the illegal trades, but it does have the power to make such trades much less likely. The board could, for instance, have a policy banning the insider from trading or from using a 10b5-1 plan, either of which would make it much less likely (but not impossible) that the insider would be able to earn abnormal returns from informed trades. This decision would undoubtedly raise the costs of management talent for current shareholders, but it would reduce the probability that future shareholders would be defrauded. As mentioned above, this may be a bargain that even future shareholders might not want. This is because diversified shareholders are as likely to be current shareholders as future ones, and implicit compensation may encourage the optimal level of risk taking.

If the insider were engaging in this conduct without board approval, it would unquestionably be illegal under the classical theory of insider trading. By agreeing to implicitly pay executives with profits from trading against outsiders with less information, the board is in effect paying the executive with cash from future shareholders instead of from current ones. And, arguably, taking "unfair advantage" of them to reduce the cash expenses of current shareholders. The Supreme Court has held that the executive's role of trust and confidence "gives rise to a duty to disclose [or abstain from trading] because of the 'necessity of preventing a corporate insider from . . . tak[ing] unfair advantage of . . . uninformed . . . stockholders.'"[31]

But there is something interesting about the fact that the board authorized the trading and took it into account when setting the executive's pay. These are not secret profits. The board disclosed the fact that the executive was given shares, that the executive was free to trade the shares, and that the trades would be given extra protection against insider trading liability by virtue of the application of the affirmative defense provided by Rule 10b5-1. One could argue that outsiders who traded in firm stock were on notice about the possibility of informed trading by insiders. If this is true, then it seems more difficult to say the insider was trading against "uninformed stockholders." To be sure, the people they trade against are uninformed about the specific facts—e.g., a key drug will not be approved and therefore the stock price will likely fall—but they are arguably informed about the possibility of trading on this information deficit. Prospective shareholders should thus be willing to pay less for the shares based on the probability of trading at an information disadvantage, and therefore the advantage of the insiders would not be unfair, but would be paid for in advance.

This is just a way of saying that if the firm is internalizing the costs of insider trading, say by seeing its shares traded in less liquid markets because of the risk of insider trading and therefore seeing its cost of capital rise, then it is more difficult to make out the case for regulation. There is some support for this in the Supreme Court's insider-trading jurisprudence. In interpreting the "misappropriation theory" of insider trading, the Court suggested that board authorization might convert illegal into legal trading.[32] The misappropriation theory covers cases where the trader, such as a lawyer working for the firm, could be deemed to have taken property that belonged to the firm, in this case the information about the price decline, for personal use. In *United States v. O'Hagan*, a case involving a lawyer using information from a partner about a pending corporate takeover, the Court remarked in a footnote:

> [T]he textual requirement of deception precludes § 10(b) liability when a person trading on the basis of nonpublic information has disclosed his trading plans to, or obtained authorization from, the principal—even though such conduct may affect the securities markets in the same manner as the conduct reached by the misappropriation theory.[33]

The case imagined in *O'Hagan* is not even as strong as that of implicit compensation, because in the former the world need not know about the authorization, while in the latter it does.

There is no obvious reason why the authorization theory in *O'Hagan* should not insulate classic trading as well. There is arguably no deception in a case in which the firm discloses that insiders are likely to be trading based on informational advantages. In fact, the classical theory requires that insiders disclose or abstain from trading. Although the disclosure element is typically thought to require disclosure of the facts underlying the trade, for example, the discovery of an ore deposit, as discussed above, the generic

---

[31]   *Chiarella v. United States*, 445 U. S. 222, 228–9 (1980).
[32]   See *United States v. O'Hagan*, 521 US 642, 652–3 (1997).
[33]   Id. at 659 n. 9.

disclosure about insider propensity to trade on inside information may achieve the same kind of price adjustment and cost internalization on average. There will be cases in which the ex-ante price difference will not turn out to be a sufficient compensation for the informational advantage in the particular case, but the outsiders would, on average, be compensated for this risk. The argument for authorization as a prophylactic here is thus economic instead of statutory.

This is especially true for diversified shareholders. As noted above, paying implicit compensation is simply a wealth transfer from future shareholders of the firm to current shareholders of the firm. Diversified shareholders are as likely to be current shareholders of a firm as they are future shareholders of the firm, and therefore there should be no systematic wealth effects. Shareholders who have to pay less for executive talent in one firm have to pay more in another firm, simply by virtue of when they enter the shareholder pool. On average, shareholders should be indifferent.

The other typical objection to insider trading is it will make markets less liquid and efficient because individual shareholders will not trust the market to be fair, viewing it instead as a place for privileged individuals to extract wealth from less privileged ones. This argument is weaker, however, in a world where the possibility of trading is disclosed ex ante. If traders know about the potential for informed insiders to be on the other side of a transaction, this risk should be priced by the market, and the firm should internalize these costs. In addition, the unfairness is ameliorated by the fact that the insiders are paying for any insider trading gains by reducing other forms of compensation in approximately equal amounts.

4   CONCLUSION

This chapter has demonstrated some significant weaknesses in the use of Rule 10b5-1 to replace the private restrictions on insider trading used by firms. Although the Rule seems to have been used by insiders in ways inconsistent with its intended use by the SEC, at the end of the day, the impact on firms and investors is likely slight. Boards seem to be taking expected trading profits into consideration, including informed trading profits, and this ameliorates any negative impact on investors as a group.

REFERENCES

Aboody, David & R. Kasnik. 2000. CEO Stock Option Awards and the Timing of Corporate Voluntary Disclosures, *Journal of Accounting & Economics*, 29: 73.
Abramowicz, Michael B. & M. Todd Henderson. 2007. Prediction Markets for Corporate Governance, *Notre Dame Law Review*, 82: 1343.
Bebchuk, Lucian A., Jesse M. Fried & David I. Walker. 2002. Managerial Power and Rent Extraction in the Design of Executive Compensation, *University of Chicago Law Review*, 69: 751, 831.
Berle, Adolf & Gardiner Means. 1932. *The Modern Corporation and Private Property*. New York, Macmillan.
Bettis, J. Carr, Jeffrey L. Coles & Michael L. Lemmon. 2000. Corporate Policies Restricting Trading by Insiders, *Journal of Financial Economics*, 57: 191.
Henderson, M. Todd. 2011. Insider Trading and CEO Pay, *Vanderbilt Law Review*, 64: 505.
Henderson, M. Todd, Alan Jagolinzer & Karl Muller. 2011. Strategic Disclosure of 10b5-1 Trading Plans, University of Chicago Law & Econ. Working Paper, available at http://papers.ssrn.com/sol3/papers.cfm?abstract_id=1137928.

Institutional Shareholder Services, Securities Litigation Watch. 2006. More on Trading Plans/Restrictions and Motions to Dismiss: Monterey Pasta Co. and Rayovac Corp., available at http://slw.issproxy.com/securities_litigation_blo/2003/11/index.html (last visited August 29, 2006).

Jagolinzer, Alan D. 2009. SEC Rule 10b5-1 and Insiders' Strategic Trade, *Management Science Quarterly*, available at http://ssrn.com/abstract=541502.

Jensen, Michael C. & Kevin J. Murphy. 1990. CEO Incentives: It's Not How Much You Pay, But How, *Harvard Business Review*, 138–53.

Manne, Henry. 1966. Insider Trading and the Stock Market, The Free Press.

Roberts, Lyle & Nicholas Porritt. 2004. Individual Trading Plans Can Help Defend Securities Fraud Claims, *Compliance Week* (July 7).

Roulstone, Darren. 2003. The Relation Between Insider-Trading Restrictions and Executive Compensation, *Journal of Accounting Research*, 41: 525.

Searcey, Dionne & Kara Scannell. 2007. SEC Now Takes a Hard Look at Insiders' "Regular" Sales, *Wall Street Journal* (April 4).

16 Executive compensation consultants
Ruth Bender

Executive compensation in listed companies is, in many jurisdictions, determined by a compensation committee comprising independent directors. In most large companies, that committee is advised by one or more compensation consultants. The consultants provide advice on the appropriate level of pay and on the types of plan that will be suitable. They model likely outcomes, and advise on a variety of other matters including tax, accounting treatments, regulation and investor sentiment. This use of independent advisors to the compensation committee is not mandatory, but is encouraged by regulators.

This chapter discusses the role of compensation consultants, and summarizes research into how they have impacted executive pay. It is structured in three sections.

Firstly, we review the role of the executive compensation consultant, considering the reasons that companies use them: their expertise, and their impact in legitimizing the compensation committee's decisions. In doing so, we examine how the consultants operate, and the factors influencing companies' choice of consulting firm.

In the second section we consider executive compensation consulting as an industry, and review the forces affecting the business of consulting, and the effect that these have on the consulting firms, their clients, shareholders and regulators. The industry is dominated by a few large firms, of which most are multi-business organizations, earning fees from other activities in addition to advice on executive compensation. The main factor determining a firm's ability to attract executive compensation assignments is its reputation, enhanced by expertise and proprietary knowledge. However, reputation may be damaged due to two potential conflicts of interest: the consultants' desire to retain an assignment in future years, and their wish to cross-sell other services. Investors and regulators perceive that these conflicts of interest can lead to the firms shaping their advice to favour the client's executives, which is damaging the reputation of the industry.

These operational matters give a context to the final part of the chapter, in which we review research on the impact that the use of consultants has had on the level and structure of executive compensation in the USA, UK and Canada, the three main jurisdictions in which studies have been undertaken. This research demonstrates that companies using consultants have higher pay levels and more equity-based compensation than do others. However, the reasons for these differences are unclear. Furthermore, contrary to common perceptions, research is equivocal as to whether there is evidence that pay structures do indeed reflect a conflict of interest between the firms and their clients.

1 THE ROLE OF COMPENSATION CONSULTANTS

According to Crystal (1991) executive compensation consulting as a profession dates back to the 1950s, but it only took off in the early 1980s, triggered by movements in the stock market which led to a greater sophistication in compensation schemes. As plans have become more complex, the use of consultants has grown, itself resulting in further complexity. In this section we consider what consultants do, and how and why they are appointed.

The first reason for using consultants is the need for their expertise. The process of determining executive compensation includes establishing an appropriate level of pay based on some sort of 'market' indicator, and determining suitable incentive plans for the short and long term. In doing this, account needs to be taken of current market trends, tax and accounting treatments, regulatory requirements and investors' preferences. The compensation committee charged with this task is staffed by outside directors, with neither the time nor the experience to undertake this task. Accordingly, they look to consultants for advice and assistance.

A second reason for employing consultants, and one which is fundamental to their activities, is the role that advisors have in legitimizing the committee's remuneration decisions. Executive pay is a high-profile subject, and there is no one right answer to the question, 'How much should we pay the executives?' Accordingly, there is always the danger for the committee members that they will be seen as making pay decisions that favour their executive colleagues. It can be argued that the use of an independent advisor will result in a more optimal contract. Thus, committees obtain legitimacy for their decisions by seeking advice from consultants.

1.1   The Consultant as an Expert

The consultants' expertise is harnessed both in determining the level of pay, and in devising a suitable pay scheme. It is also important in managing the presentation of the plans to, and liaising with, key investors.

It is customary for executive pay levels to be determined with reference to appropriate comparators amongst the company's peers. One area of expertise for the consultancies is through maintaining proprietary databases which collect comparative data on pay levels and structures in different industries and sizes of business. These, supplemented by surveys conducted by the consulting firms, are used in benchmarking 'market' levels of pay. Companies often use several firms to supply such data for their remuneration decisions, perhaps taking generic published data from some and commissioning bespoke analysis from others. Frequently, the lead consultant will provide advice to the committee on which comparators should be used (Bender, 2003). Given that this selection will set the yardstick for executive pay, the choice is critical, and the consultants' advice will have considerable influence on the level of pay.

In addition to the level of pay, decisions need to be taken on the structure of the schemes to be used. Structures have become increasingly complex over the last two decades, with companies using various types of short- and long-term incentive. With this complexity and variety, the need for consultants' advice has grown. They provide input on plan design, modelling the possible pay outcomes for a range of different profitability scenarios, and they advise on tax and accounting consequences. In this, the consulting firms display their technical knowledge of the different types of plan that are possible, their understanding of different valuation methodologies for equity-based plans, their market knowledge of what is acceptable to shareholders, and their experience of successful implementation. They also work with clients on existing compensation plans, helping to provide data on, for example, comparative shareholder return, in order to establish whether executives have met performance targets.

Whereas companies will use several consultancy firms to provide benchmark data on pay levels, it is less common to use more than one advisor to determine the structure of pay. If two advisors work on different parts of the pay package, there is a danger that they will produce something that is not coherent as a whole, and the incentives they design might drive different behaviours, or could produce too rich a reward for the executive. Nevertheless, there are instances where companies choose to use different consultants for different parts of the package. Alternatively, companies may employ two firms of consultants because one is being used to review existing schemes to provide an opinion on whether they are still appropriate (Bender, 2011; Kabir and Minhat, 2009; Murphy and Sandino, 2010).

It is worth noting that the consultants' role is to provide both information and advice. In theory, the comparator data are merely information, free of value-judgements and given to committees to help them determine an appropriate pay level. However, in producing the figures, the consultants take a view on what data to include and exclude from the comparators they use. This act of selection effectively blurs the boundary between information and advice on pay levels. Furthermore, the consultants do more than advise clients on 'best practice' in scheme design – they also help create that practice. In an example of normative isomorphism, the practices they follow are promulgated around the various companies they advise, until often they become seen as best practice (Bender, 2003; Conyon et al., 2000; Conyon et al., 2009b; Hodak 2005; Thorley Hill and Stevens, 1995). Thus, their influence permeates the market.

Compensation consultants clearly have a lot of influence over the outcome of the pay-setting process in the companies they advise. But it is worth noting that all they are doing is *advising*, they do not actually make the compensation decisions. The decision rests with the remuneration committee, which could if it wished ignore their advice, although the psychological impact of the numbers the consultants produce leads to an anchoring effect that might be difficult to overcome (Bender, 2003). Research by Bender (2011) highlighted committee members' awareness of the limitations and possible biases in the data supplied to them. That research was not able to determine whether committees did in fact act independently of the consultants' recommendations.

1.2   The Consultant as an Intermediary

The level and structure of executive compensation have to be tolerable to shareholders. In some jurisdictions this is more important to the board than others. For example, in the UK shareholders have had a non-binding vote on the annual remuneration report since 2002. This practice was adopted in the following few years by several European countries and Australia (Hodgson, 2009). In 2010, the Canadian Coalition for Good Governance brought in a recommendation on 'say on pay'. And the passing of the Dodd-Frank Act of 2010 means the practice of regular 'say on pay' will become compulsory in the USA as well. Accordingly, the views of investors have become more important to compensation committees, and consultants who can moderate these discussions can add value for their clients.

One advantage of using consultants as intermediaries is that they understand, and can explain to the shareholders, all the technical details of the schemes they have devised. More importantly, they have experience in liaising between companies and their investors, and understand the investors' approach. Research in the UK (Bender, 2011) shows that this expertise is one of the key reasons behind a company's choice of advisor. In addition to giving their clients an understanding of the institutional viewpoint, the consultants often play an active part in the dialogue, attending meetings with investors, or drafting correspondence. For the consultants, this reinforces their institutional network and, of course, generates fees. For the compensation committees it gives comfort that the task is being handled in an appropriate manner. However, investors often prefer to see the directors themselves, rather than having the conversation conducted through their advisors.

1.3 Legitimizing the Committee's Decisions

In addition to the stated objective of advice on structuring packages, an important reason for using consultants is to create legitimacy for the committee's decisions on executive pay (Suchman, 1995).

On a board, the executives and directors will work closely together, which leads many observers to suggest that the directors cannot then be totally unbiased in determining the compensation of their executive colleagues, and that, consciously or unconsciously, they will be predisposed towards high awards (Murphy, 1999, p2518). The use of an external, independent advisor can help provide some comfort in the objectivity of these decisions (Bender, 2003). This phenomenon was illustrated by Wade et al. (1997), examining how compensation committees justified CEO pay to shareholders. They found that companies frequently legitimized their executive compensation practices by citing the role of consultants in the process. Similarly, Barkema and Gomez-Mejia (1998, p141) referred to "judgments of the committee members, legitimized by the opinions of external consultants". In a situation where the decision cannot be proved to be 'right', such legitimation is valuable to boards.

This potential bias means that regulators also see the need for independent advice to the committee. This has been the situation for many years: for example in 1995 the UK's Greenbury Study Group stated, "The committee may need to draw on outside advice. This should combine quality and judgement with independence" (para 4.17). Since then, regulation has strengthened in all jurisdictions, emphasizing the need for independent advice. An example of such regulation is in the Dodd-Frank Wall Street Reform and Consumer Protection Act (2010), which views factors influencing consultants' independence as including: the provision of other services to the company; the level of fees for the assignment as a percentage of the consultant's total fee income; procedures in place to prevent conflicts of interest; and any business or personal relationships with committee members, or shareholdings in the company.

The employment of independent consultants is seen as protecting stakeholders. Accordingly, it can act as a form of risk-management by the company; advice from consultants can be used by the committee and the board to justify any decisions that are later challenged. However, this legitimacy is an intangible that can only be achieved if the consultants are perceived to be independent. Thus, the challenge to their independence posed by their potential conflicts of interest could have a detrimental impact.

1.4   Hiring Consultants

The length of tenure of advisors to the compensation committee is not governed by rules or guidance. Some companies retain the same consulting firm for many years; others change advisors regularly. Changes might occur as a matter of good practice (for example, because the advisors are becoming too close to management), or because the committee is not satisfied with the advice given. Dissatisfaction can arise for several reasons, one illustration being that the advice was felt to be insufficiently tailored to the particular company.[1] However, advisors might also be removed because the outcome of a scheme was less than the anticipated level of executive reward (Bender, 2011).

Bender (2011), reporting work done in the UK in 2001–2003, found that the selection of consultants to advise the committee took into account the reputation and expertise of the consulting firm. This makes sense, given the need for both advice and legitimacy from the appointment. Furthermore, she found that the choice of consultant was often influenced by personal recommendation: with a preference for shortlisting a consulting firm that was known to the non-executive directors, either due to another appointment, or because they had put on seminars which the directors had attended. Firms were shortlisted based on the knowledge of the remuneration committee members, and also that of their internal advisors in the company's human resources department. Those internal advisors were sometimes influential in making the decision as to which firms to employ.

2   EXECUTIVE COMPENSATION CONSULTING AS AN INDUSTRY

Academics and regulators view executive compensation consultants through a corporate governance lens, examining their impact on the compensation landscape. But for those involved, consultancy is first and foremost a business. Accordingly, it is worth discussing the business of consultancy, and how it makes its money. In doing this we commence with a brief industry analysis before looking at the mechanisms adopted by consultants to protect their franchise. We also consider the threat to their business due to their potential conflicts of interest, and how this is being addressed.

2.1   Industry Analysis

In common with most management consultants, executive compensation consulting can be expensive. In large companies, where the resources are available and where pay

---

[1]   Consultants sell their services partly on their ability to match solutions specifically to the needs of the company. However, there is a need for the plans to be acceptable, and therefore recognizable to their clients and to the rest of the corporate world. It is an odd fact of the consultancy industry in general that whilst consultants claim to produce novel recommendations, and clients claim to employ them so to do, a consultant producing something far removed from accepted practice will be treated with suspicion, and so fresh ideas can be stifled. The way in which consultants balance this tension is discussed by Sturdy (1997) and Hodak (2005).

decisions are high-profile and thus high-risk for the directors, this is seen as a necessary and affordable cost. However, the expense is less justifiable in smaller companies, and such organisations make less use of the advisors (Cadman et al., 2010; Conyon et al., 2009b; Goh and Gupta, 2011; Voulgaris et al., 2009). The industry analysis that follows reflects the consulting market for the larger listed companies, as does the majority of academic research on the subject.

In the major jurisdictions studied by researchers – the USA, Canada and the UK – there is an oligopoly, with a handful of large firms dominating.[2] Conyon (2010) summarized the basic market structure in each jurisdiction, noting then that six major firms dominated the market. Merger activity meant that his data, extracted from earlier studies, became quickly out of date. Adjusting for this, the major players, present in all three jurisdictions, are: Towers Watson, Mercer Human Resources Consulting, and Hewitt New Bridge Street, all global, diversified consultancies.[3]

In the USA, there are two other significant players, Pearl Mayer and Frederic W. Cook & Co., both focusing just on compensation. Thus in the USA, the five leading firms are all consultancies.[4] This differs from the situation in the UK, where accounting firms such as PricewaterhouseCoopers and Deloitte also have a significant profile in the market.

The classic way to analyse an industry is Michael Porter's five forces analysis (1998). Applying this model, as set out in Table 16.1, gives a context for understanding industry behaviour.

Given the analysis above, the main factors impacting a firm's ability to compete are its reputation and expertise. These are closely linked.

For a firm to be successful there are two prerequisites. To undertake the assignments the consultant needs to have expertise; to win assignments, it needs to *appear* to have expertise. The consultants' actual expertise is evidenced in their advice. This will include their understanding of what is acceptable to the market, technical knowledge of what might be appropriate and how it will work, and their ability to implement the resultant schemes. But the appearance of expertise is vital in convincing potential clients to consider them for the work in the first place. Impression management techniques, used in all areas of management consultancy, are relevant here. A firm's reputation will be signalled through its blue chip client base; the words used to describe its expertise; and its website, literature and presentations. These are all seen as indicators of the quality of the advice and, ultimately, are used to signal that their clients are adopting 'best practice' (Bender, 2011).

The value of the consulting firm in legitimizing its client's decisions will be reduced if the firm itself is not seen as independent. Thus we now need to consider ways in which this has affected consultants and the committees they advise.

---

[2] For example, Cadman et al. (2010), reporting 2006 data, noted that 76 percent of their S&P 500 sample employed one of the large consultants, and the remaining companies used one of 63 smaller consulting firms.

[3] Conyon (2011) notes that the industry in Australia appears to share similar attributes to these other jurisdictions.

[4] See Conyon (2011) for a full analysis of consultant engagement presence in the USA over the S&P 1500, S&P 500 and Russell 3000.

Table 16.1   Forces impacting the executive compensation consulting industry

Force	Implication
Threat of new entrants	
A low threat, reduced by barriers to entry in the form of reputation, proprietary databases, contacts and expertise.	Although there are many firms of consultants, a few dominate. New entrants are disadvantaged by having less access to proprietary and market information. Also, companies are unlikely to risk employing an unknown firm, as it may not give their decisions the legitimacy they require.
Substitutes	
Minimised due to the use of independent consultants being seen as 'best practice'.	Regulatory expectations mean that companies choosing not to employ compensation consultants will be queried. Tighter regulations, on advisors and on compensation plans, have led to more work for the consultants.
Rivalry	
Although there are many consultants, at the top end the industry is an oligopoly with strong competition.	Mergers between firms have reduced numbers, but rivalry is still strong.
Buyer power	
Individual clients have few switching costs in moving between the major consultancies.	Clients have some power over the consultancy firm, as the impact on a consultancy of losing clients could be a loss of reputation, potentially damaging future income. Such buyer power could be evidenced in schemes which are favourable to the company's executives.
Supplier power	
The main suppliers to the consulting firms are the consultants themselves.	Not a constraint on the industry. Some individuals have a personal reputation, but the importance of firm brands outweighs individuals'.

2.2   Who is the Client? Conflicts of Interest and How they are Addressed

Sturdy (1997, p406) argues that in every field of consultancy the consultant has two goals: to complete the assignment, and to gain repeat business. In executive compensation consulting this tension is exacerbated. A compensation consultant could potentially earn fees from three types of assignment for a company. He could advise the compensation committee (or board) on their executive compensation schemes; he could advise the executives on the executive compensation schemes;[5] and he could advise the executives on compensation in other parts of the organization or on wider business issues. This gives rise to

---

[5]   The use of consultants to advise executives on their packages is less common in the UK than in the USA.

three possible areas for conflict of interest between the consulting firm's duty to its compensation committee client, and its own financial benefit.

One of these potential conflicts should seldom arise. There would be an unavoidable conflict of interest if a firm of consultants were to advise both the executives and the committee on the same issue. Committees and consultants are aware of this, and it is not usual practice, certainly not on a formal, fee-earning basis. However, other areas are of more concern. Although the consulting firm should be formally instructed by the compensation committee, if in practice the executives have power or influence over this decision the consultants could be tempted to design packages that are more rewarding than appropriate. In this way one might assume that the consultants would gain favour with the executives, and thus retain their advisory position.

There is also potential for conflict if the committee's consultants are, or wish to become, advisors to the company on its other compensation and human resource issues, or wider business matters. For any major consulting firm, the potential fee income from this other business will significantly exceed that from advising the compensation committee.[6] Accordingly, in addition to the sell-on of other executive compensation consulting, there is potentially a conflict of interest for the consultant, who might be swayed into recommending packages that favour a CEO who has influence over the award of other work. Thus, the pull of obtaining new work is added to the desire to retain the original assignment.

Against this backdrop, many have suggested that consultants tend to produce schemes structured to favour the company's executives. For example, Crystal (1991, p9) commenced his thesis on why CEO pay had increased by stating, "The first culprits in what will be a litany of culprits are compensation consultants. . ." Others have taken similar views (e.g. Bebchuk and Fried, 2006; Hodak, 2004; Liberman, 2003).

One way in which regulators have sought to limit the impact of this potential conflict of interest is by requiring companies to disclose the names and interests of their compensation committee advisors. In doing so, the intention is to give prominence to potential threats to the advisors' independence. For example, the UK's Directors' Remuneration Report Regulations (Department of Trade and Industry, 2002) demanded disclosure of the names of advisors, the nature of their involvement, and whether or not they were appointed by the committee itself. It is possible that this disclosure, by highlighting whether consultants were working for the company as well as for the committee, led to more separation of these roles; this may be one reason why the use of multiple consultants is more prevalent in the UK than the USA, where regulation came later (Conyon et al., 2009a; Kabir and Minhat, 2009). Table 16.2 summarizes the relevant disclosure requirements in the UK, Canada and the USA, to date the only large regimes requiring such public information.[7]

---

[6]   The multi-business consulting firms provide advice on all aspects of remuneration, pensions and benefits throughout the company, but also on wider employment matters, outsourcing, aspects of mergers and acquisitions, risk management, and investment management. Using US data, Waxman (2007, p4) reported that the ratio of 'other' fees to fees from executive compensation advice to the board averaged almost 11:1 and in some cases was over 100:1. There is thus a powerful financial incentive to win and retain this business, which could compromise independence from management.

[7]   Within the European Union, although there is a Recommendation that the remuneration committee should ensure that its consultant does not at the same time advise the human resources

Table 16.2   Regulation on disclosure of advisor information

Regulation or Recommendation	UK	Canada	USA[1]
	Directors' Remuneration Report Regulations	National Instrument 58–101	Regulation S-K, Item 407(e)
First year for which disclosure made	2002	2005	2006
Names of all advisors to the committee	Yes	Yes	Yes
Information about their appointment / mandate (detail varies by country)	Yes	Yes	Yes
Nature of any other work done for the company by the advisors	Yes	Yes	No
Fees earned for advising the committee	No	Yes[2]	No
Fees earned for other work for the company	No	Yes[3]	No

Notes:
1. Disclosures in the USA have been enhanced following the passing in 2010 of the Dodd-Frank Wall Street Reform and Consumer Protection Act, which strengthened the requirements of the independence of the committee's consultants.
2. Fee disclosure arises under best practice guidelines issued by the Canadian Coalition for Good Governance.
3. Fee disclosure arises under best practice guidelines issued by the Canadian Coalition for Good Governance.

As will be seen in the final part of this chapter, although the potential conflict of interest is widely discussed, it has not been unequivocally demonstrated through academic research. Nevertheless, it is a live issue, addressed by regulators. For example, in the UK, the House of Commons Treasury Committee, examining the role of executive compensation practices in the financial crisis, concluded in its final report (2009, para 82):

> We have received a body of evidence linking remuneration consultants to the upward ratchet of pay of senior executives in the banking sector. We have also received evidence about potential conflicts of interest where the same consultancy is advising both the company management and the remuneration committee. Both these charges are serious enough to warrant a closer and more detailed examination of the role of remuneration consultants in the remuneration process.

Likewise the Waxman committee (2007) in the USA concluded that "[c]ompensation consultant conflicts of interest are pervasive", and recommended that the consultant retained by the board should not perform other work for the company. And in Australia, the Productivity Commission Inquiry (2009) also thought it necessary to recommend ways in which such conflicts could be minimized or avoided.

---

department or executives of the company, only the UK and Ireland require disclosure of the other services that a consultant provides for the company. German and Italian governance codes require that the committee's consultants be independent (Shearman & Sterling, 2009).

The consulting firms themselves are actively taking measures to reduce the perception of a conflict of interest. They argue that it is against their interest to succumb to these pressures: were they to do so, it would damage their market reputation for independence and thus harm their chances of obtaining future work, either from that client or from others.[8] In evidence to the Waxman committee they explained measures taken to prevent conflicts of interest clouding their advice, such as implementing Chinese walls between different parts of their business (Waxman, 2007, p8). Taking this one step further, in the USA the consultant Pay Governance LLC was spun out of Towers Watson with the specific aim of picking up executive compensation work from those of Towers Watson's clients who wished to demonstrate the independence of their board advisors.[9]

Another outcome of such regulatory interest, in the UK, was the formation in 2009 of the Remuneration Consultants Group. The sole aim of this group, which represents executive remuneration consultancy firms advising UK listed companies, was to develop "a voluntary Code of Practice that clearly sets out the role of executive remuneration consultants and the professional standards by which they advise their clients, which for the most part are Remuneration Committees". The five principles behind the Code are: Transparency, Integrity, Management of Conflicts to Ensure Objectivity, Competence and Due Care, and Confidentiality.[10]

3   RESEARCH FINDINGS ON THE IMPACT OF COMPENSATION CONSULTANTS

Until relatively recently, there were few studies on the impact of executive compensation consultants, due to the lack of available data. However, regulatory changes in three jurisdictions led to mandatory disclosure, summarized above in Table 16.2, which triggered academic research into the subject.

The nature of the available data has driven the research agenda. Some studies have examined the structure of the industry, dominated by a few key players (e.g. Conyon et al., 2009a for the USA and UK; Murphy and Sandino, 2010 for the USA and Canada; Conyon, 2011 for the USA). More have investigated the impact of using consultants on the level of executive compensation and the nature of schemes adopted. A particular concern has been whether there is evidence that executive pay is impacted by the potential for conflict of interest in the consultancy firms.

---

[8]   These same arguments have been used in the past by credit ratings agencies (who are paid by the companies on which they report) and by the auditors to Enron and other high-profile failures. The threat of reputational damage is not always sufficient to prevent independence being compromised.

[9]   However, Towers Watson has stated that it will continue to work with compensation committees that are comfortable with the company's existing protocols on independence.

[10]   www.remunerationconsultantsgroup.com. This came about as a direct result of the various enquiries into the role played by bankers' pay structures in causing the financial crisis. The members of the Remuneration Consultants Group, listed on its website, are all firms advising at least one FTSE 350 company on their executive remuneration.

Most of the studies, particularly those concerning conflict of interest, have examined the data through the lens of managerial power theory and rent extraction (for example Goh and Gupta, 2011; Murphy and Sandino, 2010; Voulgaris et al., 2009). However, Conyon et al. (2009b) used a multi-theoretical approach which also included institutional and social comparison theories, to explore how practices are transmitted, and executive pay becomes homogenized. Institutional theory is also used by Bender (2011), who additionally takes an impression management perspective. The majority of the research uses quantitative methodologies, but Bender (2003, 2011) and Kostiander and Ikäheimo (2012) have both adopted an interview-based approach.

3.1   Level and Structure of Compensation Schemes

Researchers have sought to determine the impact on executive pay, if any, of committees taking advice from compensation consultants. Although there are differences in research approach (set out in detail by Conyon, 2011), the results of many of these studies are similar, finding that, after controlling for the size of company, the use of compensation consultants correlates to higher pay levels for the CEO (e.g. Armstrong et al., 2008; Conyon et al., 2009a; Conyon, 2011; Voulgaris et al., 2009). Armstrong et al. suggest that governance differences between the companies explain this correlation, arguing that CEOs of companies with weaker governance use consultants to extract higher pay. Conyon et al. (2009a) suggest several potential reasons for the finding, including differences in the characteristics of firms employing consultants from those not doing so. They point out that the use of pay consultants is endogenous, and this precludes a causal explanation of the correlation. Conyon (2011) concludes that "establishing a statistical relationship between CEO pay and consultants may indeed be sensitive to the type of method used".

Using consultants also has an implication for plan design; companies advised by consultants tend to adopt a higher level of equity-based incentives in their pay packages than do companies which do not use such advice (Conyon et al., 2009a and 2009b; Voulgaris et al., 2009). This finding could be explained in two different ways. It may be that companies seeking to use equity-based plans realize that this is a complex area and thus decide to employ consultants to advise and implement them (Conyon et al., 2009b). Alternatively, it could be because, as suggested by Hodak (2004), consultants have a natural bias towards complexity. Hodak points out that, quite apart from the higher fees generated by designing and implementing complex plans, implementing more sophisticated schemes enables the advisor to resolve conflicting agendas amongst the stakeholders and such schemes can sometimes be used to prevent 'gaming' of the outcomes by management. On the other hand, Kostiander and Ikäheimo (2012), in a study of Finnish state-owned enterprises, find that complex plans are deliberately adopted in order to exploit loopholes to benefit management.

In considering the outcome of the consultants' advice, the constituent parts of the compensation cannot be considered in isolation. The design of compensation plans is holistic, with fixed and variable elements being balanced to meet the company's and individual's needs. So, although the use of consultants correlates with increased pay, Conyon et al. (2009a) and Voulgaris et al. (2009) both point out that this makes sense in terms of balancing risk and return for the executive: the increased amounts of pay compensate for the greater risk due to the volatility of the equity-based elements.

Other studies have examined different aspects of the consultants' impact. Both Goh and Gupta (2011) and Kabir and Minhat (2009) use time series data in investigating the ways in which UK companies use multiple consultants. Neither study finds evidence that the use of multiple consultants leads to higher executive pay. Goh and Gupta also consider the effect on compensation of a change in advisors. Their results are mixed, but overall, they find some evidence that opinion-shopping (i.e. changing the lead consultant) leads to higher executive salaries and less pay-risk. Cadman et al. (2010) tested the impact of adding or dropping a consultant, and found no impact on pay. Likewise, they reviewed the data by consultant and, although there was some variation, they found no significant differences in median executive pay between clients of different consulting firms.

3.2 Conflicts of Interest

Waxman (2007), using proprietary data, found that at least 45 percent of Fortune 250 companies used their executive pay advisors to provide other services as well. Murphy and Sandino (2010) returned a lower estimate, but this may be understated due to the limitations of available data. Their Canadian data showed about 47 percent providing other services. UK research by Conyon et al. (2009a) found that some 45 percent of companies used their executive pay consultants to supply other services. No data are published on the level of fees paid to UK compensation consultants, but for Canada, where there is such disclosure, Murphy and Sandino's sample put the ratio of 'other' fees to executive compensation advice fees at approximately 13:1. This is similar to the average for the US from Waxman's proprietary data, which showed ratios averaging almost 11:1.

There is little doubt that consultants' multiple business relationships can result in a conflict of interest. The important issue is whether this conflict biases their advice in favour of the CEO and executives, causing them to recommend higher pay awards, or to reduce the level of risk in a scheme.

Much has been written about this problem. For example, a survey of US boards by Lawler and Finegold (2007) found that directors believed that the most important cause of rising executive compensation was the actions of compensation consulting firms. Likewise, the governance commentator Robert Monks (1998, p37) stated:

> A critical question of corporate legitimacy is whether CEOs set their own pay. 'Best practice' has decreed an elaborate 'ritual' through which the board of directors creates a Compensation Committee consisting entirely of 'independent' directors. . . . Likewise, when the independent members of the Compensation Committee appoint an independent executive compensation consultant to assist them, one need suspend disbelief as to the appetite of personal service organizations to bring unwelcome advice to their clients.

Some research evidence has been found which supports this view. The Waxman committee found a correlation between the extent of a consultant's conflict of interest and the level of CEO pay. Also, a qualitative study by Kostiander and Ikäheimo (2012) reported consultants' bias in favour of management. Kabir and Minhat (2009) found that consultants' market share was significantly related to CEO compensation, consistent with the authors' hypothesis that consultants are concerned with the risk of losing business. Nonetheless, the bulk of the extant research is equivocal, either showing no evidence of conflict of interest or only slight correlations.

One measure used to proxy conflict of interest is the use of multi-business consultancies, where it can be assumed that there might be a desire to cross-sell services to clients. Testing for this, Armstrong et al. (2008) found no support for claims that CEO pay is higher in companies advised by multi-business firms. Nor did Cadman et al. (2010). Likewise, Conyon et al. (2009a) also reported no evidence that this potential conflict of interest affected contract design (although Conyon et al. (2009b) did find some evidence consistent with conflict of interest). However, Murphy and Sandino (2010), using several measures of potential conflicts of interest, had different results. In some of their analyses, for the USA and Canada, they found evidence that pay was higher in companies where the consultants supplied other services. Also, for their Canadian sample, they reported that the level of pay was correlated with the size of the consultants' fees for 'other' services. As regards the other type of conflict of interest, the desire for repeat business, they hypothesized that pay would be higher when consultants were employed by the CEO rather than the committee. They found the opposite to be true: CEO pay was about 13 per cent higher in US companies where the consultant worked exclusively for the committee, rather than for the management.

Conyon (2011) reviews this literature, setting out details of the samples and methodologies in these studies, and concludes that there is no clear-cut evidence of the effect of a conflict of interest. He argues that the choice of methodology affects the robustness of the studies' results, and advises caution in interpreting the research findings due to selection effects and the possibility of reverse causality. Table 16.3 sets out an overview of the main studies.

4   THE FUTURE?

Compensation consultants provide advice and expertise in the increasingly complex area of executive pay. They are part of the governance landscape, and their use appears likely to continue. Indeed, as more jurisdictions introduce regulation on independence and disclosure, it seems probable that the use of advisors will increase.

If they are perceived as independent, they also serve a role in legitimizing the decisions of the remuneration committee. Although their independence has been queried, due to the existence of areas for conflict of interest, regulation in many jurisdictions is being enhanced to try to strengthen their independence, or to ensure fuller disclosure of their activities. This growth in disclosure will also drive developments in the research agenda, and over the next decade we can anticipate further revelations on how consultants are employed, and what they do.

Table 16.3 An overview of research studies

Study	Sample	Key findings
QUANTITATIVE STUDIES ON EXECUTIVE COMPENSATION		
Armstrong, Ittner and Larcker (2008)	USA: 2116 publicly traded companies with fiscal years ending on or after 2006.	Differences in pay levels are not statistically significant when companies are matched on governance.
	Russell 3000, plus selected smaller companies.	No support for claims that CEO pay is higher in conflicted consultants that also offer additional services.
Cadman, Carter and Hillegeist (2010)	USA: 755 firms from the S&P 1500, for 2006.	No widespread evidence of higher levels of pay or lower pay–performance sensitivities where consultants have potential conflicts of interest.
		Differences in average pay but no significant differences in median pay between clients of different consultancies.
Conyon, Peck and Sadler (2009a)	USA: 308 companies drawn from the S&P 500 in 2006.	CEO pay is generally greater in firms using consultants, as is the amount of equity used in the CEO compensation packages.
	UK: about 230 companies drawn from the FTSE 250 in 2003.	Little evidence that using consultants with potential conflicts of interest leads to greater CEO pay or the adverse design of pay contracts.
Conyon, Peck and Sadler (2009b)	UK: about 230 companies drawn from the FTSE 250 in 2003.	Consultant use is positively associated with firm size and the equity pay mix.
		CEO pay is positively associated with peer firms with high board and consultant interlocks.
		Some evidence that where firms supply other business services to the firm, CEO pay is greater.
Conyon (2010)	UK: about 230 companies drawn from the FTSE 250 in 2003.	Some evidence that pay is higher in firms using consultants. Less evidence that conflicts of interest increase pay.

Table 16.3 (continued)

QUANTITATIVE STUDIES ON EXECUTIVE COMPENSATION

Study	Sample	Key findings
Conyon (2011)	USA: 308 companies drawn from the S&P 500 in 2006. UK: about 230 companies drawn from the FTSE 250 in 2003.	CEO pay is higher in firms using consultants. Slight evidence that pay is higher when consultants face conflicts of interest. No evidence that changing consultants leads to higher levels of CEO pay.
Goh and Gupta (2011)	UK: FTSE 350, 2002–8. 1359 firm-years covering 420 unique firms. Includes CEOs and other executives.	Level of pay and equity-based pay are higher if consultants retained. Mixed evidence on whether companies undertake opinion-shopping. Changing the number of consultants does not increase pay.
Kabir and Minhat (2009)	UK: 175 FTSE 350 companies (700 firm-year observations) 2003–6.	No support for the hypothesis that CEO pay is higher when firms employ multiple compensation consultants. Market share of compensation consultants is significantly related to CEO compensation.
Murphy and Sandino (2010)	USA: 1,046 firms from S&P 500, MidCap 400, SmallCap 600, and others. Canada: 124 of largest Canadian firms by market capitalization, fiscal year 2006.	Pay was higher where the consultant provided other services. In Canadian sample, pay was higher where consultants had high fees for other services. In US sample, tests for conflict of interest due to 'repeat business' were negative: CEO pay was higher when consultant worked for the board rather than for management.

Tosi and Gomez-Mejia (1989)	USA: survey of Chief Compensation Officers (175 usable replies).	Using consultants influences CEO pay to a greater extent in manager-controlled firms than in owner-controlled firms.
Voulgaris, Stathopoulos and Walker (2009)	UK: 500 firms from FTSE 100, 250 and Small Cap indexes, 2006 data.	Large firms are more likely to use consultants. Consultant use is positively associated with CEO total pay, mainly due to increase in equity based compensation.

QUALITATIVE STUDIES ON EXECUTIVE COMPENSATION

Bender (2003)	UK: 10 interviews conducted 2001–2 with protagonists in the pay-setting decision in 2 FTSE 350 utility companies.	Discusses the detailed reports produced by consultants, and the processes used.
Bender (2011)	UK: 40 interviews conducted 2001–3 with protagonists in the pay-setting decision in 12 FTSE 350 companies.	Discusses how consultants are chosen; their roles as expert, intermediary and legitimating device; conflicts of interest. Also, why companies choose not to use consultants.
Kostiander and Ikäheimo (2012)	Finland: 40 interviews conducted 2006–7 and 2009 with protagonists in pay-setting in 23 state owned enterprises.	Remuneration consultants are not independent of management, and work creatively to increase remuneration. Competition between consultancies influences the forms, levels, and structures of remuneration designs.

QUANTITATIVE STUDY ON OUTSIDE DIRECTOR COMPENSATION

André, Khalil and Magnan (2010)	Canada: 130 firms adopting a deferred share unit plan over the period 1997–2005.	Likelihood of adopting a deferred unit share plan for outside directors is greater when using compensation consultants.

REFERENCES

André, P.M., Khalil, S. and Magnan, M. (2010). The Adoption of Deferred Share Unit Plans for Outside Directors: Economic and Social Determinants, *Journal of Management and Governance*, DOI: 10.1007/s10997-010-9142-5.

Armstrong, C.S., Ittner, C.D. and Larcker, D.F. (2008). *Economic Characteristics, Corporate Governance, and the Influence of Compensation Consultants on Executive Pay Levels*, http://ssrn.com/abstract=1145548.

Australian Government Productivity Commission (2009). *Executive Remuneration in Australia*, accessed from http://www.pc.gov.au/__data/assets/pdf_file/0008/93590/executive-remuneration-report.pdf on 13 August 2010.

Barkema, H.G. and Gomez-Mejia, L.R. (1998). Managerial Compensation and Firm Performance: a General Research Framework, *Academy of Management Journal*, 41(2), 135–45.

Bebchuk, L.A. and Fried, J.M. (2006). Pay without Performance: An Overview of the Issues, *Academy of Management Perspectives*, 5–23.

Bender, R. (2003). How Executive Directors' Remuneration is Determined in Two FTSE 350 Utilities, *Corporate Governance: An International Review*, 11(3), 206–17.

Bender, R. (2011). Paying for Advice: The Role of the Remuneration Consultant in UK Listed Companies, *Vanderbilt Law Review*, 64(2), 361–98.

Cadman, B.D., Carter, M.E. and Hillegeist, S.A. (2010). The Role and Effect of Compensation Consultants on CEO Pay, *Journal of Accounting and Economics*, 49(3), 263–80.

Canadian Coalition for Good Governance (2010). *Model Shareholder Engagement And 'Say On Pay' Policy For Boards Of Directors*, available from www.ccgg.ca.

Conyon, M.J. (2010). Compensation Consultants and Executive Compensation, Chapter 15 in *Corporate Governance: A Synthesis of Theory, Research, and Practice*, H.K. Baker and R. Anderson (eds), Wiley.

Conyon, M.J. (2011). Executive Compensation Consultants and CEO Pay, *Vanderbilt Law Review*, 64(2), 399–430.

Conyon, M.J., Peck, S.I., Read, L.E. and Sadler, G.V. (2000). The Structure of Executive Compensation Contracts: UK Evidence, *Long Range Planning*, 33(4), 478–503.

Conyon, M.J., Peck, S.I. and Sadler, G.V. (2009a). Compensation Consultants and Executive Pay: Evidence from the United States and the United Kingdom, *Academy of Management Perspectives*, 23(1), 43–55.

Conyon, M.J., Peck, S.I. and Sadler, G.V. (2009b). New Perspectives on the Governance of Executive Compensation: An Examination of the Role and Effect of Compensation Consultants, *Journal of Management and Governance*, DOI 10.1007/s10997-009-9117-6.

Crystal, G.S. (1991). Why is CEO Compensation So High?, *California Management Review*, 34(1), 9–29.

Department of Trade and Industry (2002). Statutory Instrument 2002 No. 1986: The Directors' Remuneration Report Regulations 2002, London, DTI.

Goh, L. and Gupta, A. (2011). Executive Compensation, Compensation Consultants, and Shopping for Opinion: Evidence from the UK, *Journal of Accounting, Auditing and Finance*, 25(4), 607–44.

Greenbury, Sir Richard (1995). *Directors' Remuneration: Report of a Study Group Chaired by Sir Richard Greenbury*. London, Gee.

Hodak, M. (2004). Alignment Exposed: How CEOs are Paid, and What Their Shareholders Get for It, *Journal of Applied Corporate Finance*, 16(2/3), 111–21.

Hodak, M. (2005). Letting Go of Norm: How Executive Compensation Can Do Better Than 'Best Practices', *Journal of Applied Corporate Finance*, 17(4), 115–24.

Hodgson, P. (2009). *A Brief History of Say on Pay*, 1st October, accessed from http://blog.thecorporatelibrary.com/blog/2009/10/a-brief-history-of-say-on-pay.html.

House of Commons Treasury Committee (2009). *Banking Crisis: Reforming Corporate Governance and Pay in the City*. 12 May.

Kabir, R. and Minhat, M. (2009). *The Role of Compensation Consultants on UK CEO Pay*, Edinburgh Napier University Working Paper.

Kostiander, L. and Ikäheimo, S. (2012). 'Independent' Consultants' Role in the Executive Remuneration Design Process under Restrictive Guidelines, *Corporate Governance: An International Review*, 20(1), 64–83.

Lawler, E.E. III and Finegold, D. (2007). CEO Compensation: What Board Members Think, *Center for Effective Organizations*, CEO PUBLICATION G 07-8 (518).

Liberman, V. (2003). It's Not Our Fault – Usually, *Across the Board*, http://www.conference-board.org/publications/atb/articles/03marLiberman_02.cfm accessed 28 Mar 2003.

Monks, R.A.G. (1998). Executive and Director Compensation – 1984 REDUX, *Corporate Governance: An International Review*, 6(3), 135–9.

Murphy, K.J. (1999). Executive Compensation. In: *Handbook of Labor Economics, Volume 3B*, O. Ashenfelter and D. Card (eds) Amsterdam: Elsevier.

Murphy, K.J. and Sandino, T. (2010). Executive Pay and 'Independent' Compensation Consultants, *Journal of Accounting and Economics*, 49(3), 247–62.

Porter, M. (1998). *Competitive Strategy: Techniques for Analyzing Industries and Competitors*, Free Press.

Shearman & Sterling LLP (2009). *Corporate Governance of the Largest US Public Companies: Director and Executive Compensation*, accessed from www.shearman.com/corporategovernance.

Sturdy, A. (1997). The Consultancy Process: An Insecure Business?, *Journal of Management Studies*, 34, 389–413.

Suchman, M. (1995). Managing Legitimacy: Strategic and Institutional Approaches, *Academy of Management Review*, 20, 571–610.

Thorley Hill, N. and Stevens, K.T. (1995). CEO Compensation and Corporate Performance, *Journal of General Management*, 20(4), 65.

Tosi, H.L. Jr. and Gomez-Mejia, L.R. (1989). The Decoupling of CEO Pay and Performance: An Agency Perspective, *Administrative Science Quarterly*, 34, 169–89.

Voulgaris, G., Stathopoulos, K. and Walker, M. (2009). *Compensation Consultants and CEO Pay: UK Evidence*, http://ssrn.com/abstract=1293864.

Wade, J.B., Porac, J.F. and Pollock, T.G. (1997). Worth, Words, and the Justification of Executive Pay, *Journal of Organizational Behavior*, 18, 641–64.

Waxman, Henry A. (et al.). (2007). *Executive Pay: Conflicts Of Interest Among Compensation Consultants*, United States House of Representatives Committee On Oversight And Government Reform Majority Staff, December.

PART IV

INTERNATIONAL PERSPECTIVES ON EXECUTIVE PAY

17 Lessons from the rapid evolution of executive remuneration practices in Australia: hard law, soft law, boards and consultants

Randall S. Thomas[1]

1 INTRODUCTION

Executive remuneration is a hot topic in US corporate governance circles today. Hardly a day goes by without a prominent press report about the details of a particularly large compensation or severance package. Often the reporter's theme is that American investors are at the mercy of an out-of-control process and that the legal and corporate governance systems in this country have completely broken down when it comes to CEO pay. For that reason, it is important to carefully examine the legal and corporate governance systems in other industrialized, wealthy nations to see how they have treated executive pay in the last decade, to determine if there is a better model available.

Australia provides a particularly interesting comparison to the American system. Australia is one of the few western nations that was largely untouched by the global financial crisis of 2008–09, with its industrial and mining base left unscathed and the Australian dollar leaping impressively in value. Economic news has been largely good for the local economy. Nevertheless, the country chose to closely scrutinize executive remuneration and to enact many changes to its executive pay system that increased investor involvement in the process, some of which have been copied in the Dodd-Frank legislation recently passed by the US Congress.

This chapter gives a dynamic overview of the key Australian corporate governance and legal rules that impact on executive remuneration practices at publicly traded Australian corporations. It has a special focus on the role of compensation consultants and their current practices, using interview data collected by the author. By documenting the current system and its rapid evolution in the past several years, it hopes to offer some insights into where pay practices in the US may be going in the future and why.

[1] Many thanks to the Sloan Foundation for their financial support for this research, to Professors Jennifer Hill and Kym Sheehan at the University of Sydney Law School for their kind words of encouragement and patient guidance, and to Katie Waite for her diligent and excellent research assistance.

2   OVERVIEW OF THE AUSTRALIAN REGULATORY AND CORPORATE GOVERNANCE SYSTEM FOR EXECUTIVE COMPENSATION

2.1   Legal and Regulatory System for Corporations

The Australian legal and regulatory system governing their corporations is a complex mix of rules, regulations, and standards, including statutory law (the Corporations Act), Australian Stock Exchange (ASX) rules that bind listed companies, prudential regulation of financial institutions and soft law in the form of corporate governance principles and recommendations from the ASX's Corporate Governance Council (CGC). The breadth and flexibility of these sources illustrate the Australian view that executive remuneration should generally be restrained by the market, and that black letter law should be designed only to ensure the efficiency of the market (Sheehan 2009 at 273–4). This is largely accomplished through the extensive use of "soft law" principles and guidelines that guide behaviors that require discretion and are therefore not easily addressed by legal sanctions. However, recent actions taken by the Australian government indicate a move away from this approach towards greater government interaction in the executive remuneration sphere. This section provides an overview of how this system works and recent and pending changes to the system.

2.1.1   The Corporations Act 2001 (Cth)

The Corporations Act is the principal statutory basis for corporate regulation in Australia. Australian corporate law, while once the province of the states and territories, is now national law pursuant to states' and territories' referral of their powers on corporations and securities to the Commonwealth. The Corporations Act covers the registration of companies, membership and internal management (including the duties of directors), financial reporting and disclosure, takeovers, fund raising and financial services/markets. These provisions apply in varying degrees to all public and private companies. Many provisions of the Act are considered replaceable rules, which means that companies may, and often do, replace the rule with an alternative rule in their constitutions (Corporations Act 2001 § 135(2)).[2] Because of the nature of legislation, the Act primarily deals with disclosure requirements, shareholders' rights, prohibitions and restrictions on termination payments, directors' duties, and other areas that can be remedied through legal sanctions. The actual setting of remuneration policy and levels is more appropriately governed by broader governance principles (Sheehan 2009 at 280).

Under the Corporations Act, unless provided otherwise in their constitutions, companies are to be managed by, or under the direction of, the directors on behalf of the share-

---

[2]   For example, Section 198A is a replaceable rule – so companies can replace this rule with an alternative in their constitution. Section 198A, Powers of directors:
  (1) The business of a company is to be managed by or under the direction of the directors.
      Note: See section 198E for special rules about the powers of directors who are the single director/shareholder of proprietary companies.
  (2) The directors may exercise all the powers of the company except any powers that this Act or the company's constitution (if any) requires the company to exercise in general meeting.

holders (Corporations Act 2001 § 198A). Directors have a wide set of powers under the statute and are required to exercise them in the best interests of the company. The board of directors is responsible for appointing the managing director (CEO) and deciding the composition of the CEO's and other senior officers' remuneration packages (Corporations Act 2001 §§ 201J, 202A, 204F), unless otherwise provided in the company's constitution. It may, but does not have to, refer compensation matters to a committee of the board, the remuneration committee (Corporations Act 2001 § 198D). However, recently the ASX Listing Rules have been amended to require companies in the S&P/ASX 300 to have a remuneration committee, effective from 1 July 2011.[3] When the board, or remuneration committee, initiates its pay discussions concerning any senior executive, it will likely consider a host of factors, including: the skills, experience and suitability of the executive; labor market conditions; cost; disclosure requirements; tax and accounting issues; community, shareholder and market expectations; and the job requirements (Productivity Commission 2009 at 170). It may, but does not have to, employ the services of a compensation consultant to assist it in its work. Because of this discretion given to boards under the Corporations Act, many aspects of executive remuneration are governed by guiding principles, rather than specific legislation.

For a listed company, once the board, or remuneration committee, has determined the pay level and structure for the executives' compensation, it must disclose the details of this package to its shareholders in its annual directors' report (Corporations Act 2001 § 300A). This document will contain the company's remuneration report, prepared in accordance with applicable accounting standards, including a valuation of share-based payments. The applicable disclosure requirements for executive compensation have evolved substantially since 1986.[4] The required disclosures have become much more extensive over the past twenty-five years. As discussed below, the Australian government is currently undertaking a review of these disclosure requirements in an effort to simplify the remuneration report and make it more accessible to investors.

Today, the Corporations Act § 300A requires that for the five highest paid company executives and the five highest paid group executives, the company must disclose a wide variety of information in a section of the annual report, including extensive details about equity-based pay, certain details concerning any employment contract that may exist between the company and the executives, salary, bonuses, post-employment benefits, and termination benefits. The company must also disclose its policies for determining compensation and the relationship between company performance and compensation. The detailed information that is relevant to the selected individual employees will comprise the bulk of the disclosures (Productivity Commission 2009 at 245). The Productivity Commission recommended changes to some of these aspects and they are currently under discussion in the government (Corporations and Market Advisory Committee: CAMAC 2010).

In addition to disclosure requirements, the Corporations Act also provides shareholders with certain rights in relation to executive remuneration. Since 2004, a company's remuneration report has been subject to a non-binding shareholder vote (Corporations

---

[3]   Under the Corporations Act, however, a remuneration committee is not mandatory.

[4]   For a full description of the evolution of these disclosure requirements, see the Productivity Commission Report, at 37.

Act 2001 § 250R), although, until recently, very few remuneration reports have attracted majority opposition (Productivity Commission 2009 at 95). Recent proposed legislation, discussed below, could make this an even more powerful tool for investors. In addition, a binding shareholder vote is required on termination payments above a certain level and on the issuance of certain equity grants (Corporations Act 2001 § 200B). If the compensation paid to non-executive directors is not considered reasonable, then the shareholders must also vote on the non-executive directors' compensation (Corporations Act 2001 §§ 208, 211). Hence the practice of remuneration committees is to seek a 'reasonableness certification' from the board's remuneration consultant.

2.1.2   Australian Stock Exchange listing rules

The Australian Stock Exchange sets additional rules for companies trading on their market. These ASX listing rules apply to all companies listed on the ASX (ASX 2010 Listing Rules Introduction). Compliance is mandatory for all listed firms and non-compliance can result in sanctions against the company, enforceable by a court (Corporations Act 2001 §§ 793C, 1101B). The rules set out requirements for corporations generally (von Nessen 2003). These rules range from disclosure requirements to shareholder consent on major decisions (von Nessen 2003). Rules regarding financial disclosure requirements also come mostly from the ASX listing rules (von Nessen 2003). ASX listing rules date from 1987, the date of the formation of the Australian Stock Exchange, but have evolved substantially over time (Productivity Commission 2009 at 130).

A listed company must comply with the continuous disclosure requirement in ASX Listing Rule 3.1, the main rule governing continuous disclosure, which states that "once an entity is or becomes aware of any information concerning it that a reasonable person would expect to have a material effect on the price or the value of the entity's securities, the entity must immediately tell ASX that information." This effectively requires continuous disclosure of all material facts about a company by corporate boardrooms, although in practice, management still seems to retain a good deal of discretion in timing of disclosure (Hill & Yablon 2003). Even some unlisted companies must inform the Australian Securities & Investments Commission (ASIC) for similar reasons (von Nessen 2003).

Under these rules, a company must immediately disclose to the ASX the contractual terms of any appointment of a senior executive at the time of his appointment (ASX 2010 Listing Rule 3.1). Companies must also disclose the extent to which they have complied with the ASX Corporate Governance Council's recommendations, and if they have not complied, then disclose why they have not complied (ASX 2010 Listing Rule 4.10.3). Other important listing rules that affect executive compensation are rules relating to the issuance of shares to related parties (including directors) (ASX 2010 Listing Rule 10.11), voting on non-executive director remuneration (ASX 2010 Listing Rule 10.17), and prohibitions on senior executives receiving termination payments due to a change in control of the company (ASX 2010 Listing Rule 10.18). As noted above, a recent amendment to the ASX Listing Rules requires all listed companies to have a remuneration committee comprised solely of independent directors (ASX Listing Rule 1.1 Condition 16).

2.1.3   Australian Prudential Regulation Authority (APRA)

APRA is the prudential regulator for the financial services industry, which includes banks, insurance companies and the pension (superannuation) industry. The financial services industry is regulated separately because of the risks of losses to society from failures that have a systemic effect on the wider financial system. Though APRA regulations apply only to the financial services industry, there has recently been talk about extending some of their new regulations to corporations generally, through legislation (Productivity Commission 2009 at xxviii). However, while all companies are regulated by ASIC, only some companies are also regulated by APRA.

Generally speaking, APRA leaves the board of directors responsible for remuneration decisions, with some exceptions. The most important exceptions are that APRA requires regulated firms to have a remuneration committee comprised solely of non-executive directors and to have remuneration policies that take into account risk management issues (APS 510 Governance (ADIs); GPS 510 Governance (General insurance); LPS 510 Governance (life insurance); see also the Prudential Practice Guide PPG 511 Remuneration). These rules were implemented in April of 2010.

2.1.4 ASX Corporate Governance Council's Principles and Recommendations (2003 and 2007 revision)

The CGC is recognized as a group of experts comprised of a mix of 21 business, investment and shareholder groups. It was established in 2002 to provide a practical guide for listed companies and investors. The Council's make-up and rigorous procedure for developing and implementing guidelines lends credibility to the guidelines (Sheehan 2009 at 290). The Council's Corporate Governance Principles and Recommendations constitute a soft law set of principles and recommendations, which are considered a "code" of best practice, and have significant regulatory force. Under the ASX listing rules, listed companies must comply with the CGC's recommendations, or disclose why they have not done so (ASX 2010 Listing Rule 4.10.3).[5]

In March 2003, the ASX Corporate Governance Council elected to lay out The Principles of Good Corporate Governance and Best Practice Recommendations, ten "essential principles 'that [it] believes underlie good corporate governance'." The relevant principles for corporate governance with respect to executive remuneration are numbers 4, 5, 6, and 9. These specified that a company must take part in accurate financial reporting, make timely disclosure, respect the rights of shareholders, and remunerate fairly and responsibly (Ablen 2003). Using these principles, in 2003, the CGC laid out 28 separate, non-binding recommendations as key guidelines for the best corporate processes (Ablen 2003).

CGC issued revised principles and recommendations in 2007. Principle 8 states that "companies should ensure that the level and composition of remuneration is sufficient and reasonable and that its relationship to performance is clear." This principle has three recommendations: boards should establish remuneration committees; boards should distinguish between executive remuneration and non-executive director remuneration; and boards should disclose: the names of the members of the compensation committee, or if there is no committee, how those functions are performed; the company's policy on hedging unvested performance pay; and the terms of any retirement plans for non-executive directors (ASX CGC 2007 Principle 8).

---

[5] They do not, however, need to do so if the CGC only suggests that the company do something.

The CGC has left a central role in setting pay to the board of directors. In an effort to bring about more independent decision-making and effective boards, it has defined an independent director as a non-executive director who is free of any business or other relationship that could materially interfere with the independent exercise of their judgment, or appear to do so (CGC 2007 Principle 2). It instructs boards to consider a variety of factors in determining if a director is independent, including whether they have previously been employed by the company, been a consultant or adviser to the company, or had significant relationships with the company such as being a supplier or had material contractual relationships with it (CGC 2007 Principle 2). APRA has adopted a much stricter definition of independence for the firms that it regulates.

2.2 Changes

The legal and regulatory framework for executive remuneration in Australia has changed dramatically over the past 25 years. Many changes have occurred relatively unnoticed because of the flexibility of the framework that is afforded by the substantial use of "soft law" principles. Changes came slowly, but still consistently, from the mid-1980s to the early 2000s. Beginning in 2003, the Australian government introduced new legislation to drastically alter the existing framework. More recently, following the global financial crisis, the government has again examined the topic of executive remuneration. While rejecting more extreme legislative measures, such as pay caps or binding shareholder votes, and generally maintaining that executive remuneration should largely be left to board discretion and market forces, in the past decade the Australian government has shown some willingness to enter into this area, mainly through legislation and regulation related to disclosure requirements and shareholder rights.

2.2.1 CLERP 9

After a slow evolution of the executive remuneration regulatory landscape from the mid-1980s, in 2003, the Australian government introduced the Corporations (Audit Reform and Corporate Disclosure) Bill 2003 (Cth) ('CLERP 9') with the objectives of promoting transparency, accountability, and shareholder activism (Sheehan 2009 at 275). Consistent with Australian policy on executive remuneration, this legislation (whose provisions became effective in July 2004) aimed not to dictate specific actions, but rather to improve the operation of the market and included mechanisms to achieve these objectives in relation to executive remuneration (Productivity Commission 2009 at 130). Nonetheless, this legislation provided for some important checks on executive remuneration. Most notably, Section 300A of the Corporations Act was modified to require a remuneration report to be included in the directors' report and to give shareholders a non-binding advisory vote on the report at each annual general meeting (Sheehan 2009 at 275). Other modifications were made, including a shareholder vote on termination payments (Productivity Commission 2009 at 129). Guiding these modifications was the idea that shareholders should be given a more effective voice in relation to levels of executive remuneration and pay–performance link (Sheehan 2009 at 276). As is the case with much of the regulation of executive remuneration in Australia, much of the success of the CLERP 9 amendments is aligned with guiding principles provided by various regulatory groups.

2.2.2   2009 Golden handshake changes

In 2009, Australia introduced new legislation relating to termination benefits. Prior to these reforms, corporations could give up to seven years' salary in termination benefits without shareholder approval. The new legislation lowered the threshold to one year's base salary before approval is required (Australian Government 2010 at 3).

2.2.3   Government's response to Productivity Commission recommendations

In the aftermath of the financial crisis, the Australian Government asked the Productivity Commission to study the existing regulatory framework around the remuneration of directors and officers of Australian corporations (Productivity Commission 2009 at iv). On December 19, 2009, the Productivity Commission issued a lengthy report on the results of its inquiry. Overall, the Commission determined that, unlike in some other countries, mainly the United States and the United Kingdom, executive remuneration in Australia was not a widespread failure (Productivity Commission 2009 at 357). Instead of overhauling the entire system and taking away some of the board's discretion in setting executive remuneration policy and levels, the Commission recommended several changes focused on improving corporate governance (Productivity Commission 2009 at xxviii).[6] These changes focused primarily on avoiding conflicts of interest and improving account-ability of boards. Four months later, the Australian Government published a response to the Commission's report. In its response, the government agreed to implement, or encourage other responsible bodies to implement, almost all of the Commission's recom-mendations.[7] While many of the Productivity Commission's recommendations extend beyond the scope of this chapter, we discuss a few of them here briefly.[8]

Conflicts of interest occur when executives influence the process of setting their own remuneration. This can happen if executives have too much control over the compensa-tion contracting process, or if interested parties serve on the remuneration committee or if remuneration consultants are under the influence of management, as opposed to the board. Many of the Commission's recommendations had already been implemented by the APRA in the financial sector, but would now have wider application (Productivity Commission 2009 at xxviii). To address these perceived problems with conflicts of interest in the remuneration-setting process, the Productivity Commission recommended a variety of measures, ranging from corporate governance principles to legislation.

One important recommendation is a complete prohibition on executives hedging unvested equity remuneration or vested equity that is subject to holding period restrictions (Productivity Commission 2009 at xxxiv). The perceived need for legislation was based on the apparent lack of a comprehensive ban on this practice from other sources. Thus, the Productivity Commission noted that, while in the past, the hedging of unvested equity inter-ests had been prohibited by some companies through their executive share trading policies (Productivity Commission 2009 at 226), only about one-half of the ASX 200 companies

---

[6]   Chapter 11 of the Productivity Commission Report contains the Commission's recommen-dations and explanations for why it is making them (Productivity Commission 2009 at 357–94).

[7]   The Government Response lists the Productivity Commission's recommendations and its responses to them (Australian Government 2010 at 5–7).

[8]   We defer until the next section our discussion of the recommendations that directly relate to compensation consultants.

surveyed reported that their share trading policy covered this practice. Furthermore, it found that while the Corporations Act requires the company's remuneration report to discuss board policy on hedging, this disclosure requirement was only created in 2007 and does not prohibit the practice (Productivity Commission 2009 at 227). Finally, the Productivity Commission observed that the CGC discourages hedging of unvested equity interests but does not formally recommend against it (Productivity Commission 2009 at 227). The Commission therefore recommended a straight ban on hedging of unvested equity interests by executives. In response to the Commission's recommendation, the Government agreed to support the recommendation by seeking to amend the Corporations Act (Australian Government 2010 at 10).

By contrast, the Productivity Commission did not seek to eliminate nonrecourse loans to executives for the purchase of stock in their companies. These loans are not very common in Australia with only two percent of Australian executives receiving them (Productivity Commission 2009 at 221). The main argument in their favor is that they facilitate alignment between executives and shareholders by helping officers to purchase shares, but they may also limit the downside risk in executives' pay. The Commission also noted that they must be fully disclosed to shareholders (Productivity Commission 2009 at 225). Additional recommendations regarding conflicts of interest within recommendation committees and with remuneration consultants are addressed in Section 4, infra.

Another major concern of the Productivity Commission that was supported by the government was the complexity and accessibility of remuneration reports because of the existing disclosure requirements. As part of its effort to improve disclosure requirements, the government requested that the Corporations and Market Advisory Committee (CAMAC) review the existing disclosure requirements under the Corporations Act in an effort to simplify the remuneration report (Australian Government 2010 at 12). CAMAC provided an informational paper in July 2010 outlining the current framework and asking for submissions (CAMAC 2010). On its own initiative, the government also asked CAMAC to examine current incentive components of executive remuneration in an effort to better align executive remuneration with company performance and to simplify incentive pay (Australian Government 2010 at 12). Some of the potential changes, including disclosing the actual value of equity awards that vested in the current year or disclosing the fair value of rewards provided as a result of the year's performance, are discussed in Section 3, infra. These efforts are designed to make the information more easily accessible and understandable by shareholders, as well as simplifying some of the accounting procedures for the company. Any changes that come from CAMAC's review will be in addition to the requirement that remuneration reports include a plain English summary and report actual remuneration received and total shareholdings of the individuals named in the report (Moodie 2010).

The government, also on its own initiative, has introduced legislation that would claw back bonuses that were awarded based on misstatements in a company's financial statements (Saulwick 2010). In December 2010, it circulated a discussion paper for feedback and comments to be submitted by March 30, 2011 (Australian Government Dec. 2010). Under the current framework, shareholders must institute legal proceedings to recover overstated bonuses (Australian Government Dec. 2010). The proposed legislation aims to remove the onus from the shareholders and to simplify the process of recovery (Australian Government Dec. 2010). Several companies have voluntarily included claw-back provisions in their constitutions in the past few years, but the government believes this is not enough (Australian Government Dec. 2010). The discussion paper seeks input on how the provisions should be implemented, to whom they should apply, and when they should be triggered (Australian Government Dec. 2010).

The one area where the Productivity Commission's recommendations were rejected by the Government related to the taxation of equity compensation. At present, executives and other employees are taxed on options as of the date that they leave the firm, even if these options are unvested at the time (Productivity Commission 2009 at 325). This can create disincentives for executives to defer equity compensation into the future because they will still face immediate tax liability. As a result, the Commission recommended changing the current practice so that tax liability was incurred upon the earlier of the vesting of the equity-based payments or seven years after the employee acquires the interest. The Government, however, was unwilling to change current practices. Many, including the APRA and the Productivity Commission, argue this refusal to change the existing law serves as a disincentive to keep a long-term investment in the business, thereby making it more difficult to align executive and shareholder interests (Kehoe, Durkin & Hepworth 2010).

3   BACKGROUND FACTS ABOUT EXECUTIVE REMUNERATION IN AUSTRALIA

As noted above, the Corporations Act 2001 mandates disclosure of executive compensation. Public compensation data are taken from the directors' annual report that details the compensation packages granted to directors or any of the five top-paid officers, as well as the board's policy for determining this compensation (Corporations Act 2001, § 300(1)(a)(i), (d)(iii)). One aspect of these disclosures is that they provide information about the independence of directors on the boards of Australian corporations. Looking at the largest 300 Australian companies in 2007–08, three quarters of all of their directors were non-executive directors, which increases to eighty percent for the top 50 companies.[9] However, only a little over half of board members were independent directors at these top 300 companies, again with a somewhat larger percentage for the top 50 firms (Productivity Commission 2009 at 93, 143–4). In addition, around eighty percent of Australian listed firms separate the roles of board chair and CEO with an even greater percentage at the largest 150 firms (Productivity Commission 2009 at 143). In the remainder of this section, we discuss the trends in executive compensation levels and practices, then issues surrounding stakeholder power related to the compensation setting process and outcomes and finish up with an examination of some of the current issues in the field of Australian executive compensation.

---

[9]   Australian terminology groups directors into three categories that are slightly different from the ones that Americans use, but whose correspondence can roughly be given as follows: executive directors (inside directors in US parlance); independent non-executive directors (independent directors in US terms); and non-independent non-executive directors (gray directors in America). While the precise definitions of independence vary among the different regulators and across the two countries, they are similar in concept.

3.1   Trends in Pay

In the last two decades, there has been a dramatic shift in the way corporations compensate employees, specifically executives. Both in response to large gains and to serve as a governance technique, companies began providing compensation plans that were linked to performance as a means of aligning executives' interests with shareholders' (Hill 2007). Performance-based pay was viewed as a legitimizing device, intending to reward those who had earned it, and discipline those who did not (Hill & Yablon 2003). Secondly, option packages became central in compensation plans, which led to a sharp escalation in pay during this period, most noticeably in the United States (Hill 2007).

Looking at Australia, publicly available data show that executive compensation at ASX 100 firms increased on average by 6–7 percent annually in real terms from 1993 to 2009 (Productivity Commission 2009 at 41). However, executive pay grew most rapidly in the 1990s, increased at a slower rate from 2000–07, peaked in 2006–07, and then fell significantly over the next two years. By 2008–09, average executive pay levels had dropped to their 2004–05 levels.

In 2008–09, the 20 largest ASX firms paid their CEOs $7.2 million ASD in total compensation, which was about 50 percent higher than the average total compensation figures for the next 20 largest ASX firms ($4.7 million ASD) (Productivity Commission 2009 at 57). In general, the largest companies demonstrated the highest levels of pay with compensation levels dropping off progressively as firm size decreased (Productivity Commission 2009 at 41, 48–9). These figures illustrate the strong positive relationship between firm size and pay level (Productivity Commission 2009 at 57, 429).

CEO pay packages can be divided into fixed pay and performance-based pay. Fixed pay is comprised of base salary, superannuation payments by the company, perquisites and termination pay (Productivity Commission 2009 at 190). Termination pay includes a monetary component, accelerated share vesting benefits, accrued leave entitlements and retirement benefits (beyond the superannuation payments previously mentioned) (Productivity Commission 2009 at 190). Performance-based pay covers short term incentive payments and long term incentive payments, both of which are paid only if the executive meets certain conditions. Under both types of plan, satisfaction of the attached conditions can lead to payments that include cash bonuses, options and shares. Share grants can take several different forms,[10] including performance rights,[11] deferred shares,[12] share appreciation rights,[13] and loan-funded shares.[14]

At ASX 100 firms, over the time period from 2002 to 2008, options were used by

---

[10]   'Free' shares, which are shares granted without any condition attached to them, constitute a very small additional form of incentive pay. We will not discuss them further as they are of negligible value overall.

[11]   These are grants of shares conditional on the executive meeting certain performance hurdles.

[12]   These are like restricted stock in the US because the grant is conditional on the executive remaining employed at the company for a specified period of time.

[13]   These are designed to track the payouts from options without the executive having to actually buy the option to receive a benefit.

[14]   These are shares that the executive purchases from the company using the proceeds of a company loan, which may either be a recourse loan or a non-recourse loan (Productivity Commission 2009 at 190).

between 40 and 55 percent of companies each year. Their grant date value ranged from 6 to 11 percent of these CEOs' total compensation over that time period (Productivity Commission 2009 at 195). Historically, performance rights were less commonly used than options. However, in 2008, more ASX 100 CEOs received performance rights than options. Their value increased dramatically as well, rising from only 4 percent of total CEO pay in 2002 to 12 percent in 2008. By comparison, the usage and value of deferred shares and loan-funded shares remained relatively flat over the same time period. This trend may be changing, however, as many companies are giving up the use of options because of recent tax changes to employee share schemes following concerns about undeclared income (Durkin July 2010). Macquarie group was among the first companies to move away from options back to performance rights (Durkin July 2010).

Although it is becoming more common in the US, Australian firms use performance hurdles on performance-based pay much more often than their American counterparts (Hill 2007; Hill, Masulis and Thomas 2010). The CGC supports the use of relative performance measures, such as relative total shareholder return,[15] so that the company's performance relative to a specific group of peer firms or broader stock market index is used to determine if the target is satisfied (Productivity Commission 2009 at 200). This makes it difficult to value Australian equity-based incentives and therefore companies usually value them at grant date using accounting value. As many options never vest, and market conditions may change dramatically from the time of grant to the time of exercise, value at exercise may be very different from the value reported to the company's shareholders at the time of issuance (Productivity Commission 2009 at 45–7). This has led the Australian Institute of Company Directors to argue that these numbers should not have to be disclosed in remuneration reports and that instead the report should be framed in "actual pay" terms (Australian Institute of Company Directors: AICD 2010 at 14). Actual pay would be determined by when the remuneration vests, not when it is originally awarded (AICD 2010 at 15). The value would be calculated by adding fixed pay to the value of equity and other incentive awards that have vested during that year (Walsh 2010). CAMAC is considering this potential change in its examination of remuneration disclosure requirements. However, many of the accounting problems related to calculating incentive pay could still be present in determining actual pay. In addition, companies that have deferred incentives may have to report rewards from several years past (Walsh 2010).

Performance-based pay has played a significant role in CEO pay and its increase in recent years. For example, since 2004, most growth of Australian executive pay came from the increased growth in the value of incentive-based pay (Productivity Commission 2009 at 41, 54–5). Larger companies have been more affected by this trend than smaller ones. At the same time, average base pay fell by about 10 percent in real terms from 2003 to 2009 (Productivity Commission 2009 at 54).

In terms of international comparisons, CEO pay in Australia is relatively high. For example, Towers and Perrin, a leading international consulting company, released a global survey in 2001 placing Australia third in the world for highest paid executives, with

---

[15]   This is measured in terms of stock price changes, adjusted for dividend payments, relative to the appropriate benchmark group (Productivity Commission 2009 at 200).

the average CEO's pay package increasing by 73 percent in the previous two years (Hill & Yablon 2003). However, data contained in the Productivity Commission Report show that CEO pay levels are much lower than in the US (Productivity Commission 2009 at 41, 79–82). In 2008, for instance, US CEOs at the 500 largest American firms received approximately $13.4 million ASD whereas Australian CEOs at the ASX 200 firms averaged $2.9 million ASD. Overall, Australian CEOs were paid comparably to those at companies in several of the smaller European countries (Productivity Commission 2009 at 79–80).

If Australian firms were to go into the international market to hire top executives that are US nationals, this could have an upward impact on local CEO pay if firms match the pay these executives received from their former American employers. Although it is not completely clear, there is some evidence that the dramatic increases in the use of incentive-based pay at American firms may have pushed up Australian CEO pay (Productivity Commission 2009 at 110–11). This is consistent with findings that a significant number of Australian executives were recruited from overseas.

Another trend that is raising executive salaries in Australia is known as the ratchet effect. This occurs because very few companies want to pay below the median salary, so each year everybody tries to pay median or above, thereby ratcheting up the median salary for the next year. One compensation consultant points to several sources of the ratchet effect, including the required disclosure of executive remuneration data, and a blind obedience to the data, even when it is not for a comparable company (Compensation Consultant 3 2009). He argues that this effect often goes unnoticed and unquestioned by investors and boards because it is acceptable to pay the median (Compensation Consultant 3 2009). What they fail to realize is that the median is increasing every year because of the practice. He points to a role for compensation consultants in addressing this problem by suggesting and testing alternative remuneration structures that may involve lower fixed pay and higher at-risk pay (Compensation Consultant 3 2009). This could keep the median lower, while still allowing companies to structure their remuneration to attract talent. He argues that it is important that the government does not prescribe median compensation, and that it allows for these alternative structures (Compensation Consultant 3 2009). Another consultant focuses on the importance of boards not relying too heavily on data and making sure the data they do use is for comparable companies (Compensation Consultant 1 2009).

3.2   The Effects of Shareholder Power and Social Norms on Australian Executive Pay

Two important influences on executive pay practices are the importance of shareholder participation in the corporation and social norms against strong levels of income inequality in society (Thomas 2009). Both factors appear to have an important influence on Australian executive compensation practices. First, with regard to shareholder power in Australia, we note that shareholders have significant influence over pay levels. Australian institutional investors hold 36 percent of listed shares and other equity of ASX companies. Their ownership is relatively concentrated compared to US levels, and in addition, foreign investors hold another 42 percent of ASX listed firms' shares (Productivity Commission 2009 at 31–2). Institutional shareholders have a larger role in oversight and in setting pay (Hill 2007).

Under Australian corporate governance practices, shareholders have been given a role in the actual pay setting (Hill 2007). Shareholders' role in the compensation process is governed by a non-binding shareholder vote requirement (Hill 2007). Companies cannot ignore the requirement and must inform shareholders of the vote, even though it is non-binding (Hill 2007). Also, companies have to explain how they will respond to a rejection of a remuneration report, which illustrates the potential power of the shareholder vote (Hill 2007). In practice, at the top 200 listed companies in 2005, only one company experienced a majority vote against the remuneration report (Hill 2007). However, at least one-third of the largest corporations had a protest "no" vote of more than ten percent. Institutions, in particular, have been active in this area. For example, the Australian Council of Superannuation Investors (ACSI) advised its members to vote against the remuneration recommendations of thirty-five companies (Hill 2007). While many argue that the advisory vote has had an important and positive impact on shaping boards' behavior, one director claims that the vote negatively impacts the remuneration process because of its potential for misuse and the added costs associated with justifying pay practices (Director 2 2009). This view has clearly been rejected by the Australian government, which continues to strengthen the shareholders' vote.

Following the global financial crisis, shareholders have been more active in exercising their right to vote against a remuneration report. During the Annual General Meeting season from October to December 2009, 30 ASX 200 companies out of 157 holding meetings received a no vote of 25 percent or more, with an additional 65 companies receiving a protest vote of 10 percent or more (Prudence Holds Sway on Pay, Jan. 2010). This trend continued into the 2010 AGM season, with several companies experiencing very large "no" votes (Wiggins 2010). Some companies, including mining services providers Boart Longyear, and paper manufacturer Paperlinx, witnessed a no vote of greater than 50 percent (Wen 2010). In response to the Productivity Commission Report, the Australian Government strengthened this shareholder right by providing for an automatic and simultaneous vote on a resolution to spill the board to be triggered by two consecutive "no" votes over 25 percent (Connors 2010). If a majority votes for the resolution, an extraordinary general meeting must be held within 90 days to determine whether to "spill," that is to remove, the entire board (Connors 2010). This vote is separate from the vote on the remuneration report itself to avoid a minority wielding disproportionate influence through the non-binding remuneration report vote and large shareholders voting for a bad remuneration report simply to avoid spilling the board (Connors 2010).

As mentioned earlier, the Australian Government recently strengthened shareholder power to reject excessive termination payments to CEOs. The amount of termination payments is not directly regulated by the Corporations Act, but there is a shareholder approval requirement in some cases if the prescribed multiple of the executive's remuneration exceeds a certain threshold. While the prior threshold was 7 times total remuneration, this was dropped to 1 times base salary in November of 2009 (Productivity Commission 2009 at 232, 234). This legislation also expanded the scope of the persons covered by the vote requirement to include senior executives of the firm (Australian Government 2010 at 3). It is still early to determine the consequences of this legislation, but many companies have tried to get around its effects by either increasing fixed pay or getting shareholder approval for higher termination payments in advance (Durkin May 2010).

Why do many Australian shareholders harbor negative feelings toward high levels of executive pay? Australians often claim that their society manifests a negative feeling about high executive pay. One common metaphor relates to "tall poppies," and how they should be cut down to the same size as others. Such a social norm may exercise a strong pressure against executive pay levels that are perceived as being "too high." If the law reflects these social norms, and "community concerns about executive pay led to a lack of confidence in corporate governance more generally, this could have negative implications for capital raising by companies and ultimately, the economic wellbeing of the community itself" (Productivity Commission 2009 at 14).

One compensation consultant interviewed for this study acknowledged this potential influence on executive pay. He pointed to the social democratic undertones in Australian culture and their impact on remuneration committees. He admitted that, within companies, the pressure is not overwhelming, and it is generally accepted that pay should be based on performance. However, where he did see an impact is in government behavior, particularly in risk management and tax schemes, which exerts external pressure on remuneration committees (Compensation Consultant 1 2009). He also noted that corporate shame attached to excessive pay often acts as a restraint on salaries, and pointed out that, even if the culture within corporations is not exactly egalitarian, fairness is central to remuneration practice at the majority of companies (Consultant 1 2009).

4   REMUNERATION COMMITTEES AND REMUNERATION CONSULTANTS IN THE AUSTRALIAN PAY-SETTING PROCESS

Evident in the Productivity Commission's findings is the growing importance of remuneration committees and remuneration consultants in the remuneration-setting context. With the complexity of the executive remuneration system, especially with the increasing use of performance-based incentive pay, it is becoming more important than ever to have knowledgeable remuneration committees and consultants. The Productivity Commission critically examined their roles in its recommendations as did the Australian government in its response to the Productivity Commission Report. Notwithstanding these actions, remuneration committees and consultants play central roles in the remuneration-setting process. This section describes those roles from a variety of perspectives.[16]

---

[16]   In this section, we draw on information contained in the Productivity Commission Report and the various submissions to that body both before and after the initial publication of its report, as well as scholarly articles that have been written by several academic scholars. In addition to the information contained in the various reports and articles, the author interviewed ten participants in the Australian executive compensation area to gather more detailed information about compensation consultants' practices. In particular, five compensation consultants, three corporate directors and two attorneys were interviewed for several hours each. The interviews were done on a confidential basis, with an agreement that the identity of the interviewee would not be disclosed. They were also tape recorded with the permission of the interviewees. These tapes were subsequently transcribed, proofread and sent to the participants for correction. The interviews were designed to cover many of the same questions in an effort to gain a richer understanding of the differences in the participants' views about the market for compensation consultants, the services

4.1   Remuneration Committees

Australian listed firms are free to, but not required to, have a compensation committee (Corporations Act 2007 § 198D(a); Hill 2007). Recommendation 8.1 of the ASX Principles of Good Corporate Governance goes further and recommends that firms have a remuneration committee. It also suggests that firms appoint a compensation committee that has at least three members, is chaired by an independent director, and is composed of a majority of independent directors, but this suggestion does not require firms to justify their practices (ASX CGC 2007). By comparison, the UK's Combined Code, which has a "comply or explain" policy similar to the ASX Principles, recommends that compensation committees be made up of independent non-executive directors (UK Combined Code 2008 § B.2.1). Similarly, but on a mandatory basis, the US NYSE requires listed firms to set CEO pay via a compensation committee made up entirely of independent directors (NYSE 2008 § 303(A)(5)(a)).

According to the Australian Productivity Commission Report on executive remuneration, most large Australian companies have remuneration committees: 55 percent of all listed companies in 2007–08 had remuneration committees (Productivity Commission 2009 at 174). This average figure has been virtually constant since 2003–04. The larger listed companies are much more likely to have remuneration committees: 98 percent of the top 50 companies by market capitalization have remuneration committees, while 85 percent of the top 250 companies have such a committee.

In terms of the composition of the committees, around 75 percent of remuneration committees at large firms have only non-executive directors and a majority of remuneration committees of top 400 firms have a majority of independent non-executive directors and an independent chair (Productivity Commission 2009 at 94, 175). But a significant minority of remuneration committees are still comprised solely of executive directors (Productivity Commission 2009 at 94). In this regard, it is important to note that a high percentage of Australian listed firms separate the positions of chairman of the board and CEO, with about 80 percent of all listed companies separating these positions (Productivity Commission 2009 at 143,175). By comparison, in the US about 75 percent of the top 200 firms have combined the two positions (Productivity Commission 2009 at 144).

A lack of independence is not the only potential shortcoming of a remuneration committee. According to one compensation consultant, remuneration committees are often made up of former CEOs with varying levels of experience with remuneration matters (Compensation Consultant 2 2009). While most of these directors have had some experience in dealing with remuneration in certain circumstances, that experience was usually in the context of one specific company, rather than from a market perspective (Compensation Consultant 2 2009). This often leads members of the remuneration committee to settle on what worked for their prior company, even if it is inappropriate under the circumstances (Compensation Consultant 2 2009). However, consultants have

---

that consultants provide to their clients, the market for CEO services, issues relating to risk alignment and CEO retention, and the role of other corporate constituencies in the pay setting process. Significantly, these interviews were conducted in the summer of 2009, prior to the Productivity Commission's work.

recently noticed a positive change in this area. One points to a recent trend of specialization on remuneration committees (Compensation Consultant 1 2009) while another focuses on the presence of the committee chair who often sits on several boards and thereby builds a broad base of knowledge on the subject (Compensation Consultant 2 2009).

Consistent with the rest of the executive remuneration framework, remuneration committees are evolving. The Productivity Commission recommended that the ASX Corporate Governance Council should introduce an "if not, why not" recommendation that committees be made up of at least three members, who are non-executive directors, a majority of which are independent; be chaired by an independent director; and have a formal procedure addressing procedures for non-members attending their meetings (Productivity Commission 2009 at 389). The Australian government supported this recommendation, but noted that it is a matter for the ASX Corporate Governance Council, and not for the legislature (Australian Government 2010 at 9). In conjunction with the CGC recommendation, the Commission recommended that there should be a new ASX listing rule requiring all ASX 300 to have a remuneration committee comprised solely of non-executive directors (Productivity Commission 2009 at 370). Although inconsistent with a move toward greater director independence on remuneration committees, a Mercer remuneration specialist argues that CFOs are now taking a more active role in the remuneration-setting process, and will likely be members of remuneration committees (Drummond 2010). This change is said to be largely driven by the importance of incentive schemes in managing risk. While the CFO previously was involved in the financial side of remuneration policies, they will now claim to be more active in understanding the behaviors and risks associated with the incentive schemes through their membership on the remuneration committee (Drummond 2010).

4.2   Remuneration Consultants

The AICD guidelines on remuneration committees endorse boards obtaining independent advice on compensation matters. They also provide numerous examples of good practice procedures for listed company boards. These include such matters as "ensuring the Board maintains control of negotiations with CEO candidates, and where appropriate, other executives," and "obtaining appropriate expert advice, independent of management, when entering into employment contracts with executives and setting their remuneration" (Productivity Commission 2009 at 180).

There are good reasons for directors to seek the advice of remuneration consultants. Remuneration committee members may not have the time, expertise, and access to data, to allow them to perform all of their assigned duties. Given the highly technical nature of many compensation plans, and the complexities associated with them, compensation consultants can serve an important role in assisting directors on the remuneration committee. Remuneration committees appear to seek such external advice from compensation consultants quite commonly, and the Productivity Commission Report states that between 67 and 83 percent of boards are estimated to use their services (Productivity Commission 2009 at 180–1). As discussed below, these consultants can perform a variety of services for their clients.

At the time this chapter was written, Australian corporate law did not require the disclosure of the use of compensation consultants, which limits the amount of publicly available information on that subject (Sheehan 2009). Presently, firms are neither required to reveal their use of consultants, nor required to identify the consultants they used. This is in marked contrast to practices in the US and UK, which both require listed firms to disclose the use of compensation consultants (Regulation S-K 2008 17 C.F.R. 229.402(b)(2)(xiv), (xv)); Directors' Remuneration Report Regulations 2002 § 9, Schedule 7A, Part 2, 2.(1)(b)). The UK requires companies to disclose which compensation consultant they used (Productivity Commission 2009 at 184; Directors' Remuneration Report Regulations 2002 § 234B, Schedule 7A, Part 2, 2.(1)(b)), and the Securities and Exchange Commission recently adopted amendments to its executive compensation and governance disclosure requirements that include mandatory disclosure of certain information relating to the use of compensation consultants (Securities and Exchange Commission 2010 Final Rule (D)(3)).

This will soon change. The Productivity Commission Report Recommendation 10 states that the ASX Corporate Governance Council should issue a recommendation that companies should "disclose the expert advisors they have used in relation to the remuneration of directors and key management personnel, who appointed them, who they reported to and the nature of other work undertaken for the company by those advisors" (Productivity Commission 2009 at 379). In addition, the Commission Report Recommendation 11 recommends amendments to the ASX listing rules to require that "where an ASX 300 company's remuneration committee (or Board) makes use of expert advisors on matters pertaining to the remuneration of directors and key management personnel, those advisors be commissioned by, and their advice provided directly to, the remuneration committee or board, independently of management" (Productivity Commission 2009 at 379). Listed companies would need to disclose these arrangements in their remuneration report to their investors.

In December 2010 the Australian Government released its exposure draft of the Corporations Amendment (Improved Accountability on Director and Executive Remuneration) Bill 2011. This Act, set to commence on July 1, 2011, addresses the recommendations of the Productivity Commission. Proposed section 206K states that remuneration consultants must be engaged only by non-executive directors. Proposed section 206L requires remuneration consultants to report to and give advice directly to non-executive directors or members of the remuneration committee, not to executives of the company. Both of these provisions address the concerns about potential conflicts of interest that may arise when a remuneration consultant is working closely with a company's executives. Proposed section 300A (1)(h) provides disclosure requirements related to the use of remuneration consultants. Under this section, the disclosing entity must disclose the name of the consultant, the name of each director who engaged the consultant, the name of each person to whom the consultant gave advice, a summary of the nature of the advice, the amount and nature of the consideration under the consulting contract, the nature of any other work performed by the consultant, and the amount and nature of consideration paid to the consultant for any other work performed for the company.

Some Australian firms already report their use of compensation consultants despite the fact that they are not required to do so. There are two major reasons for them to do this. First, disclosing the use of a consultant adds legitimacy to the company's pay decisions.

For example, Caltex, the only oil refining and marketing company listed on the ASX, reported in its 2008 annual report that it used an external consultant to perform a detailed review of its long term incentive plan (LTIP) (Caltex 2008). Second, some firms are dually listed. These firms may be subject to the additional disclosure rules of their listing countries. For example, BHP Billiton is "the world's largest diversified resources company," specializing in natural resources.[17] It is dually listed on the ASX in Australia and the London Stock Exchange in the UK. In its 2008 Annual Report, BHP Billiton disclosed its use of an independent compensation consultant solely to set executive compensation (BHP Billiton 2008). It also offered a detailed explanation of each consultant it hired (BHP Billiton Advisors 2008).[18]

Who are the principal participants in the compensation consultant business in Australia? The Big Four accounting firms – Deloitte, E&Y, KPMG, and PwC – and two management and governance advisory firms – Hay Group and Mercer – are major participants in the compensation consulting business. These firms provide advice to both boards and management (Productivity Commission 2009 at 181). Other consultants provide executive compensation information only to boards. Egan Associates, Godfrey Remuneration Group and Guerdon Associates are prominent so-called boutique firms. Corporate boards, particularly at larger listed companies, may seek advice from a range of consultants to assist them in their duties (Productivity Commission 2009 at 181).

4.2.1   Services provided by remuneration consultants

What type of services do compensation consultants provide in Australia? Remuneration consultants provide boards with market data (from their own sources as well as from other companies' remuneration reports) and insights into remuneration trends, assist boards to produce appropriate pay structures and performance hurdles, and provide insight into tax, legal and accounting matters relating to remuneration (Productivity Commission 2009 at 180). Each of the major consulting firms advertises its services to the corporate director community. The Big Four accounting firms offer a wide range of services. They frame their services around managing risk and executive pay by addressing both the amount of compensation and its structure. They are best known for their tax and accounting advice, including compliance and regulatory advice.

Hay Group describes itself as a "global management consulting firm" that focuses its corporate clients on "develop[ing] a strategic approach to remuneration; design[ing] reward plans and programs that support the business strategy; understand[ing] the real responsibilities and value of jobs in a consistent and objective way; develop[ing] executive reward policies and practices that are consistent with the long term needs of the organization; and understand[ing] the competitive remuneration environment by providing valid and reliable market data on current pay practice" (Hay Group Nov. 2009). Hay Group's job evaluation system is viewed as a very strong product by many companies.

---

[17]   BHP Billiton, at http://www.bhpbilliton.com/bb/aboutUs/companyOverview/ourProfile.jsp.

[18]   However, as BHP Billiton is dual listed on the ASX and the LSE, these disclosures were likely made in response to requirements in the UK to disclose any material advisors to the remuneration committee.

Mercer states that its executive remuneration principals "provide advice on the design and implementation of executive pay programs in support of aligning executive performance with the company's business strategy and shareholder interests. These principals fulfill two primary roles in relation to the work of the committee: first they assist the committee to establish an overall philosophy of executive pay as a platform for specific program design; and second they provide objective and expert analysis, advice and information to support the committee in its decision-making" (Mercer May 2009). Mercer also markets to companies its well-known services in the superannuation area.

Egan Associates, by comparison, describes its consultants' services as relating to: appointing executives; acting as an independent advisor for the remuneration committee; conducting annual market reviews of executive remuneration; reviewing incentive-based plans; preparing the company's remuneration report; noticing and or attending annual and general meetings; responding to investors, proxy advisors, etc.; advising on remuneration implications of restructuring, merging, etc.; and reviewing the work of other advisors and providing an independent perspective (Egan Associates Sept. 2009). John Egan is viewed by many as the founder of the executive compensation consulting industry in Australia.

Godfrey Remuneration Group is also a boutique consultancy firm that primarily provides remuneration consulting for non-executive directors and for the managing director. They benchmark data by selecting comparative groups, analyzing the data, and making recommendations. They also work closely with an executive search firm in two primary roles. First, they help to match packages that a potential executive is currently receiving, by providing technical and analytical information to help sway the executive. Second, they provide data to the company to convince them to pay whatever is necessary to get the desired executive.

Guerdon Associates is another independent consulting firm and provides director and executive compensation services only to boards. They advise on pay for performance, other performance-related issues, provide data on comparable companies, and give advice and recommendations on technical issues relating to design and implementation of LTI plans, including modeling their implications.

Like their peers throughout the developed world, Australian companies frequently seek advice from compensation consultants to attract and retain key employees. As part of this process, the firms seek to learn what the market pay level is for each of their employees. Annual pay surveys are the most basic service that compensation consultants offer. Some consultants only offer their proprietary surveys for sale to firms that contribute data. For example, Hewitt CSI's website states that the firm's "Australian Top Executive Remuneration Report [is] made available to contributing organizations on an annual basis."[19] Towers Perrin's website indicates that "only survey participants can purchase our survey data."[20] Other firms rely on market data about CEOs that they have compiled from public filings by firms over the years (interview, Compensation Consultant 4).

---

[19]   Hewitt CSI, *at* http://www.csirem.com.au/Surveys/Australian/TopExec/index.htm.

[20]   Towers Perrin, *at* http://www.towersperrin.com/tp/showhtml.jsp?url=global/service-areas/research-and-surveys/tpdata/compdata.htm&country=global.

In a confidential interview with the author conducted prior to the Productivity Commission Report's preparation, Director 1 offered several insights into some of the services that consultants provide companies. In the case of hiring a new CEO, the consultant first gives some idea of what the market is like for someone with a comparable skill set. This provides a very broad starting point for the board's process. For internal CEOs, consultants will often provide periodic reviews to make sure their remuneration is still where it should be relative to the market. In addition, boards commission remuneration consultants to review scheme design and to advise on related best practices. This includes modeling implications of any suggested plans.

Director 2 in a similar interview added some additional thoughts on the services that companies need from consultants. This interviewee stated that remuneration consultants are often used when dealing with foreign remuneration policy issues with which the remuneration committee is unfamiliar. In addition, after determining what they are looking for in a CEO, the board will consult a remuneration advisor for comparisons with similarly situated companies, or benchmarking. Consultants may also provide advice about incentive plans and design, particularly LTI plans, but the committee itself does the scenario planning around the advice so they can include stress testing in their scenarios. This information is then discussed with the consultants in an interactive process.

Director 1 was clear that consultants will recommend a range of pay levels for the CEO, but they are very reluctant to recommend an actual number. This is consistent with statements in the Productivity Commission Report on executive remuneration in Australia that say it is rare in Australia for consultants to recommend an actual amount of pay for the CEO. Instead, their role appears to be to recommend how the desired amount of pay is structured (Productivity Commission 2009 at 180).

4.2.2   Potential conflicts of interest

When compensation consultants are retained by companies, two kinds of potential conflict of interest issues arise. First, did the CEO hire the consultant to advise the board on the CEO's pay? And second, is the consultant providing more than one kind of service to the company? (Productivity Commission 2009 at 182). The first issue relates to the consultant's line of reporting: are they reporting directly to the remuneration committee or is the consultant's work flowing through the human resources department and management's hands? A remuneration consultant's principal contact can be the board, senior management or the company's human resources department depending on what type of services they are providing to the company. When they are being employed to consult with the board on executive compensation matters, the different firms take different approaches. In a confidential interview with the author conducted prior to the Productivity Commission Report's preparation, Compensation Consultant 1 stated that recently boards have more frequently hired compensation consultants who are answerable to the board, as opposed to management or Human Resources. Although one cannot be sure what has caused this recent trend, this interviewee suggested that recent talk about changes in the Corporations Act has forced boards to become more active in the process, rather than sitting back and taking advice from Human Resources and management. This doesn't necessarily mean that they have separate consultants from management and Human Resources. Rather, it is the board which is in control of the relationship with the consultants and which gets the information from the consultants, without it being filtered through Human Resources and management.

Compensation Consultant 2 had a different perspective in a similar interview. This interviewee stated that the principal contact often varies based on the client. Though it is not entirely possible, they try to give balanced advice regardless of the client. At large companies, the principal contact is primarily HR or management. However, at midsize companies, the advisors often deal directly with the board or the remuneration committee. Compensation Consultant 3 stated that consultants only provide services to the board. Not surprisingly, each of these consultants worked for different types of compensation consulting firms. Compensation Consultant 5, however, stated that the head of Human Resources was normally the principal contact, but that the interviewee reported directly to the remuneration committee.

Director 1 looked at things in another way when interviewed. This interviewee said that the relationship between the company and the consultant is often handled by management and that most contacts are between Human Resources and the consultant. When boards do communicate directly with the remuneration consultant, it is often to discuss a report that was commissioned by management, rather than at the onset of the engagement. Ideally, boards might take a more proactive role with the consultants, but practical matters, such as access to the necessary information, make dealing with management more convenient. The interviewee did opine that the current financial crisis may provide boards with the opportunity to take more control of the process at an earlier stage. Director 2 stated that consultants are always retained directly by the remuneration committee, and not by management or Human Resources. It seems apparent from comparing the statements made in the different interviews that a wide variety of approaches are taken by different participants in the pay setting process. The legislation will require that all consultants be retained either by non-executive directors or by the remuneration committee (Corporations Amendment Bill 2011 § 206K).

The second issue, the provision of multiple services, may create the appearance that the content of the consultants' work on executive compensation is influenced by their interest in receiving requests from management to provide other consulting services. While it is appropriate that consultants have discussions with executives when framing their advice, as such interactions are likely to lead to more informed discussions with the board, a number of potential strategies can be used to reduce these potential conflicts of interest. For example, the remuneration committee may retain consultants that solely provide remuneration advice to boards. Alternatively, the consultant may agree to provide advice to the board only on executive and/or director remuneration, although many of the big firms would likely be hesitant to choose this option because other services are typically much more lucrative. A third strategy is to limit the individual consultants responsible for advising the board on executive remuneration to working only on those matters, while other employees of the consulting firm are responsible for the other services provided to the company (Productivity Commission 2009 at 182). In this situation, consultants should develop in-house policies such as "Chinese walls" to protect against potential conflicts. For financial services businesses, APRA states that the remuneration committee should not engage an advisor who is acting concurrently or recently on behalf of management (APRA Prudential Standard 51).

Prior to the issuance of the Productivity Commission Report, Australian remuneration consulting firms took different approaches to potential conflicts of interest. Hay Group described its conflict of interest procedures for executive remuneration assignments as follows. Its consultants give advice only from the standpoint of the board, not of management. Regarding CEO pay, they only provide advice and information directly to the board. Preferably, the board hires them directly, although this often does not happen. Any consultant advising on executive remuneration is not responsible for any other advice provided to the company. Further, there are quality assurance processes in place to assure advisers follow the clear principles Hay Group has regarding executive remuneration advice (Hay Group June 2009; Hay Group Nov. 2009). Mercer states that its consultants deal only with the directors or executives in charge of determining remuneration for an individual, never with the individual himself regarding his own pay. It discloses any relationship with or other services provided to the client in the engagement letter for executive remuneration services, including fees. It voluntarily adopted Global Business Standards to address this problem and includes these standards in its engagement letters. They also have rules about providing information to management and clear reporting procedures for information between the adviser and the remuneration committee and there is no incentive pay for selling other services to executive-remuneration clients. Further, reporting is limited to the specific line of business; no remuneration consultants report to other members of the firm. Consultants are also required to report any attempts by management to influence their advice about executive remuneration (Mercer Nov. 2009).

The author asked his interviewees how different types of firms handled potential conflicts of interest. Compensation Consultant 1 told him that accounting firms have strict procedures for their audit clients who ask them to also perform compensation consulting services. An accounting firm could not provide pay advice to an audit client. In particular, the source referred to accounting firm [A] and stated that it has an internal audit independence procedure that must be followed before they submit a proposal for other work for an audit client. This procedure makes it impossible to set up a code for the new work to be done for the client without going through the process, meaning that they cannot get paid without going through it. These procedures are rigidly enforced for audit clients.

Companies also are keenly aware of the potential for conflicts of interest and take actions to deal with them. BHP Billiton reports that its "Remuneration Committee receives specialist advice from an external firm. The Adviser is directly accountable to the Remuneration Committee, and does not provide any other services to the company" (BHP Billiton May 2009). Woolworths says that it "is prudent in their choice of consultants, choosing to use different consultants for non-executive directors and senior executives. [It] has a rigorous review process to determine the appropriateness of consultants used for providing this type of information and have noted no conflict of interest" (Woolworths June 2009). Potential conflicts of interest are generally disclosed to the remuneration committee. Mercer, for instance, states that they disclose to their remuneration committee clients Mercer's relationship with the client organization, including fees and services (Mercer Nov. 2009). Director 1 confirmed that consultants must disclose all consulting services that they are performing to the remuneration committee and that this information often appears in the company's annual report.

The Productivity Commission addressed this issue in Recommendations 10 and 11.

Recommendation 10 calls for a CGC recommendation requiring disclosure of any consultants used in the remuneration setting process, who appointed them, and the nature of their work (Productivity Commission 2009 at 379). The government not only supported this recommendation, but greatly strengthened its effect by putting it into legislation, as opposed to a CGC recommendation, and by also requiring disclosure regarding the amount and nature of payment that the consultant receives (Corporations Amendment Bill 2011 § 300A(1)(h)). The Commission also recommended that any remuneration consultants be commissioned by and report directly to the board, as opposed to management (Productivity Commission 2009 at 379). Again, the government not only supported the recommendation, but strengthened it by implementing it through legislation instead of the recommended ASX listing rule (Australian Government 2010 at 14). The government also extended its reach to cover all listed companies, and not only the ASX 300 (Australian Government 2010 at 14). Both of these recommendations and the government's response illustrate the importance of transparency and accountability in the use of remuneration consultants.

4.2.3 Defining the relevant comparable companies within the market

Another key issue that arises for remuneration committees and compensation consultants is how to determine the appropriate comparator group of firms when they are trying to gauge the market level of compensation for executives. Essentially, this process is equivalent to figuring out the market wage level for different types of officers and employees. For employees below the CEO level, firms cannot rely solely on job title, and therefore may use industry, size/complexity of the organization, and responsibilities of the role to determine comparable types of employees (Hay Group June 2009). However, for the CEO, this process requires companies and their consultants to consider what other firms are comparable. Some consultants focus on firm size, industry sector, international reach, and comparative performance rankings in advising boards about what might be comparable firms (Mercer May 2009).

My interviewees opined that there are several factors that they consider when benchmarking companies. Often the consulting firm begins with the size and the sector of the firm. After the consultants come up with an initial group, they use several additional factors to exclude companies from the group. Most important among these factors is market capitalization. In addition, they might consider number of employees, assets, and profitability. Other relevant factors include whether the company is going through any type of corporate change, such as a takeover, and whether the company has had any substantial growth or decline in recent years. The consultants also consider things such as whether the company is public or private, whether it is a multinational company with only a small presence in Australia, and whether there is one shareholder with a large stake in the company. This helps to exclude companies that are similar based on the other factors, but that are actually not comparable in terms of remuneration. The thinness of the Australian market makes it difficult to find a lot of comparable companies. Egan notes that, "boards representing shareholder interests, particularly on companies with a significant international footprint, need to inform themselves on a regular basis on the extent to which international reward trends are proving to be a detriment to their ability to either attract or retain top talent" (Egan Associates Sept. 2009). Companies understand the importance of having some market based information about compensation levels. For example, Woolworths has stated that, "The Board of Directors, assisted by a subcommittee of the Board, reviews all remuneration relative to the rest of the Australian workforce and on appropriate international benchmarks" (Woolworths June 2009).

Compensation consultants differ slightly about how much input companies have into the list of comparable firms that they generate. Compensation Consultant 1 stated that as a starting point, companies give input about who they believe their comparable companies are. Often, after the advisors review the client's list, many of the companies will be excluded because they are significantly too large or too small. Even though the client gives input as to their comparable companies though, they do not dictate the results to the advisors.

However, Compensation Consultant 2 was of the view that it is the consulting firm that determines the comparable companies. Through the benchmarking factors listed above, the consultant develops a list of comparable companies and shares that list with the client. The client is welcome to comment on the list, and sometimes they will suggest a couple of companies who are not on the list but should be. However, if the consultant has reason to exclude the company suggested by the client, it will exclude it, or add in an additional company to neutralize the effect of adding the company. Director 1 agreed that the consultants usually develop the list of comparable companies and the board may discuss other possibilities after the list has been generated.

While compensation surveys are used in the compensation setting process (Mercer May Submission), they are not determinative of the final pay package. Director 2 remarked that in the end, it is really a judgment call. Using the factors to come up with comparables provides a good start, but it is not definitive. As the Hay Group further explained, "It is tempting for boards – and CEOs – to presume they can set the CEO package by reference to market data only. But benchmarking provides a point of reference, not an absolute answer. Market data may reveal how much competitors paid in bonuses, but not what targets had to be reached, or whether the scheme in question actually worked to drive value creation. Ultimately, no data is perfect and boards need to consider market data as one input into a CEO pay strategy rather than the determining factor" (Hay Group June 2009). In this regard, Compensation Consultant 4 viewed the consultant's role as providing the board with sufficient information, including different scenarios based on possible performance outcomes, to show the range of possibilities rather than a particular number.

Importantly, my interview sources reported, Australia differs from the US in its reliance on the market to set salaries. While the market plays a factor in both countries, in the US being competitive relative to the market is almost determinative, even if it leads to a ludicrous level of executive pay. However, in Australia, as in the UK, companies will set a reasonable amount beyond which they will not go, even if it might be below a competitive market rate.

4.2.4   Interactions with stakeholders

In certain situations, compensation consultants may have a role to play in assisting the remuneration committee in its interactions with corporate stakeholders. Compensation Consultant 1 stated that while they would love to talk with investors, they almost never go on their own to speak to large investors. It might happen that a consultant would go with a member of the remuneration committee to meet with specific investors or advisory groups, but never alone. However, they do regularly talk with third party voting advisors, such as RiskMetrics, but often not on behalf of clients. Rather, it is a way to keep the dialogue open. RiskMetrics is viewed as the leader in the area. Compensation Consultant 2 though was emphatic that this was not part of their role as compensation consultants. Director 2 agreed – generally the chairman of the board or the CEO will talk with proxy voting advisors about remuneration as well as many other issues.

Compensation Consultant 3 stated that consultants interact with both investors and proxy advisors, but primarily with proxy advisors. The interactions may be on behalf of the client, but they may also be solely on behalf of the consultant firm. Generally, the consultants will present their point of view to the proxy advisors for discussion before the board moves forward. With investors, they take more of a secondary role by accompanying the board or the remuneration committee to speak to investors. This allows them to be there to answer any technical questions, but gives the board members control of the process. Compensation Consultant 4 said that he had frequent interactions with RiskMetrics in order to gather information for clients, but that it was rare to speak to them on behalf of a client, and then only on a no-name basis.

Director 1 was clear that it is important for consultants to educate proxy advisors because they can potentially have a lot of influence over voting, and they often don't understand what they are voting on and generally do not want to engage with the board. However, when consultants do interact with these proxy advisor groups, it is generally just to educate them, and not on behalf of the client. Companies do not use consultants, Director 1 said, to interact with investors though.

4.2.5 Internal pay equity

Another consideration is the difference in pay between the CEO and other employees of the firm. Some consultants believe that internal pay equities play an important role in employee satisfaction. Guerdon Consulting, for one, claims that "research on internal pay equity reveals that the most important factor for employee satisfaction is an assessment of pay relativity with co-workers of the same level, and secondly themselves relative to their supervisor" (CGI Glass Lewis & Guerdon Associates June 2009). Companies may therefore consider internal pay equity in determining the level of CEO pay. BHP Billiton, for example, considers any increases in pay for the general employees in determining adjustments to the base salary of senior executives in the same market. Because the market for employees and the market for senior executives are different, however, this is only the starting point for setting executive pay. Any additional adjustments are justified by a change in the role the executive plays in the company, or a change in the market rate for comparable executives (BHP Billiton May 2009). Macquarie also says that there is some relationship between executive remuneration and remuneration of other employees. However, differences in remuneration levels reflect differences in role, skills, and value brought to the company (Macquarie May 2009).

Compensation Consultant 1 noted that consultants may consider internal pay relativities to make sure their proposal is reasonable. However, this use is limited in the work that they do. Rather than on equity, the focus is more on who can drive performance in the company. It is more important to appropriately reward those top performers, than to have equity in payment. Compensation Consultant 3 opined that this is not very important in Australia because the disparity between the top paid executive and the next highest paid executive is not huge, as it often is in the United States. Compensation Consultant 4 said the focus is on the difference between the CEO and the next executive in the management hierarchy and that one rule of thumb was that the CEO would get twice as much as that person. Director 2 remarked that companies do look at internal pay equity, both for lower levels of the company and for the CEO.

5   CONCLUSIONS

Australia has experienced a vigorous regulatory and soft law response to domestic critics' complaints about executive remuneration practices. Although the dominant view continues to be that markets should determine pay levels, and that law serves a subordinate role of ensuring the market's efficiency, recent changes should increase investor input into the pay process with uncertain effects. In particular, the nonbinding advisory vote adopted earlier and, more recently, the 2009 legislation requiring a binding shareholder vote on termination payments in excess of one times base salary, should give investors a greater voice at companies. These changes may be seen as part of the more concentrated stock ownership patterns and stronger institutional investor oversight of compensation levels in Australia.

Concentrated investor power may play a role in keeping pay levels lower in Australia than in the US. For instance, in comparison to the US, executive pay levels have been lower and equity compensation practices more restrictive than those that American CEOs face (Hill, Masulis and Thomas 2010). New rules prohibiting hedging of insiders' equity interests in Australia are also tougher on executives than those in place in the States. In addition, the widespread practice at Australian firms of separating the roles of chairman of the board and CEO may have an effect on pay levels. Oddly, Australian boards of directors appear to have a lower percentage of independent directors on them, and less commonly use separate and independent remuneration committees than in the US. Most corporate governance experts would argue that this could lead to less monitoring of executive pay levels.

With respect to remuneration consultants, Australian rules have evolved substantially and continue to do so. New disclosure requirements will result in much more information being available in Australia than was previously the case. Furthermore, consultant practices are quite different: consultants do not generally provide remuneration committees or boards with a suggested compensation number for executives, but largely restrict themselves to advice concerning the structure of executive pay. This is quite different from the US scenario, where consultants normally do offer direct advice about CEO pay levels.

Clearly Australia has carefully studied the US experience as well as the UK experience. While the share ownership patterns in the US and Australia are quite different, and the size of Australian firms is on average smaller than that of American firms (Hill, Masulis & Thomas 2010), the US could learn much from studying the Australian experience. Its unique combination of hard law, soft law, and market-responsive practices, seems to be capable of rapid and effective evolution.

REFERENCES

Ablen, David. 2003. Remunerating "Fairly and Reasonably" – The "Principle of Good Corporate Governance and Best Practice Recommendations" of the ASX Corporate Governance Council, *Sydney Law Review*, 25: 555–66.

APRA, Prudential Practice Guide PPG 511 Remuneration, at http://www.apra.gov.au/ADI/upload/PPG511_REM_revised-Dec-09.pdf.

ASX. 2010. Listing Rules, at www.asx.com.au/supervision/rules_guidance/listing_rules1.htm.

ASX Corporate Governance Council (CGC). 2003. Principles of Good Corporate Governance and Best Practice Recommendations, at http://www.shareholder.com/visitors/dynamicdoc/document.cfm?documenti d=364&companyid=ASX.

ASX Corporate Governance Council (CGC). 2007. Corporate Governance Principles and Recommendations, at http://asx.ice4.interactiveinvestor.com.au/ASX0701/Corporate%20Governance%20Principles/EN/body. aspx?z=1&p=-1&v=1&uid=.

Australian Government. Dec. 2010. Discussion Paper: The Clawback of executive remuneration where financial statements are materially misstated.

Australian Government. 2010. Response to the Productivity Commission's Inquiry on Executive Remuneration in Australia, at http://mfsscl.treasurer.gov.au/Ministers/ceba/Content/pressreleases/2010/attachments/033/ 033.pdf.

Australian Institute of Company Directors (AICD). June 4, 2010. Position Paper No. 15: Remuneration Reports, at http://www.companydirectors.com.au/NR/rdonlyres/7E8EFA43-9331-444B-8FAA-E93A65 AE0D57/0/PositionPaper_No15RemunerationReports_4June2010.pdf.

Australian Prudential Regulation Authority (APRA). 2009. Prudential Standard APS 510 Governance, at www.apra.gov.au.

BHP Billiton. 2008. Advisors to the Remuneration Committee, at http://www.bhpbilliton.com/bbContentRe-pository/docs/200905advisorsToRemunerationCommittee.pdf (BHP Billiton Advisors).

BHP Billiton. 2008. Annual General Report 139, at http://www.bhpbilliton.com/bbContentRepository/docs/ annualReport2008.pdf.

BHP Billiton. May 2009. Submission to the Productivity Commission's Inquiry Into Regulation of Director and Executive Remuneration in Australia, at http://www.pc.gov.au/__data/assets/pdf_file/0003/89472/ sub045.pdf.

Caltex. 2008. Directors' Report: Remuneration Report, at http://www.caltex.com.au/annualreports/2008/fully-ear/2008_financial_report/remuneration_report.html.

CGI Glass Lewis & Guerdon Associates. June 2009. Regulation of Director and Executive Remuneration in Australia, Submission to the Productivity Commission, at http://www.pc.gov.au/__data/assets/pdf_ file/0003/89751/sub080.pdf.

Compensation Consultant 1. 2009. Interview with Randall Thomas.

Compensation Consultant 2. 2009. Interview with Randall Thomas.

Compensation Consultant 3. 2009. Interview with Randall Thomas.

Compensation Consultant 4. 2009. Interview with Randall Thomas.

Compensation Consultant 5. 2009. Interview with Randall Thomas.

Connors, Emma. Jan. 4 2010. "Two Strikes" Exec Pay Plan Softened. *Australian Financial Review*.

Corporations Act 2001 (Australia).

Corporations Amendment (Improved Accountability on Director and Executive Remuneration) Bill. Dec. 2011. Exposure Draft.

Corporations and Market Advisory Committee (CAMAC). July 2010. Executive Remuneration Paper, at http://www.camac.gov.au/camac/camac.nsf/byHeadline/PDFDiscussion+Papers/$file/Executive_rem_info_ paper_Jul10.pdf.

Director 1. 2009. Interview with Randall Thomas.

Director 2. 2009. Interview with Randall Thomas.

Directors' Remuneration Report Regulations. 2002, at http://www.legislation.gov.uk/uksi/2002/1986/regula tion/1/made.

Drummond, Shaun. Oct. 2010. Pay Change on the Way. *Australian Financial Times*.

Durkin, Patrick. May 2010. More Heat on Executive Pay. *Australian Financial Review*.

Durkin, Patrick. July 2010. Companies Opt Out of Option Rewards. *Australian Financial Review*.

Egan Associates. Sept. 2009. Submission to Productivity Commission Enquiry on Director and Executive Remuneration in Australia, at http://www.pc.gov.au/__data/assets/pdf_file/0004/91408/sub105. pdf.

Financial Reporting Council. 2008. Combined Code on Corporate Governance (UK Combined Code).

Hay Group. June 2009. Regulation of Director and Executive Remuneration in Australia: Hay Group

Submission to the Productivity Commission, at http://www.pc.gov.au/__data/assets/pdf_file/0011/89813/sub084.pdf.

Hay Group. Nov. 2009. Submission in Response to Productivity Commission's Findings and Recommendations, at http://www.pc.gov.au/__data/assets/pdf_file/0019/92251/subdd132.pdf.

Hill, Jennifer 2007. Regulating Executive Remuneration: International Developments in the Post-Scandal Era, Vanderbilt Law and Economics Research Paper No. 06-15.

Hill, Jennifer & Charles Yablon. 2003. Corporate Governance and Executive Remuneration: Rediscovering Managerial Positional Conflict, Vanderbilt Law and Economics Research Paper No. 03-02.

Hill, Jennifer, Ronald Masulis & Randall Thomas. 2010. Comparing CEO Employment Contract Provisions: Differences between Australia and the US, 64 *Vanderbilt Law Review* 559.

Kehoe, John, Patrick Durkin & Annabel Hepworth. Apr. 19, 2010. Executive Pay Verdict a Taxing Point. *Australian Financial Review*.

Macquarie Group Limited. May 2009. Submission to the Productivity Commission, at http://www.pc.gov.au/__data/assets/pdf_file/0006/89484/sub052.pdf.

Mercer. May 2009. Submission to the Productivity Commission on the Executive Remuneration Inquiry, at http://www.pc.gov.au/__data/assets/pdf_file/0006/89448/sub041.pdf.

Mercer. Nov. 2009. Executive Remuneration in Australia: Submission on Productivity Commission Discussion Draft, at http://www.pc.gov.au/__data/assets/pdf_file/0008/92258/subdd139.pdf.

Moodie, Ann-Maree. June 8, 2010. Remuneration Changes. *Australian Financial Review*.

New York Stock Exchange (NYSE). 2008. Listed Company Manual.

Productivity Commission. 2009. Executive Remuneration in Australia, Report No. 49, Final Inquiry Report, Melbourne.

Prudence Holds Sway on Pay. Jan. 2010. *Australian Financial Review*.

Regulation S-K. 2008. United States.

Saulwick, Jacob. April 17, 2010. Business Welcomes Exec. Pay Outcome. *Sydney Morning Herald*.

Securities and Exchange Commission (SEC). 2009. Proxy Disclosures Enhancements, 17 CFR Parts 229, 239, 240, 249 and 274, at http://www.sec.gov/rules/final/2009/33-9089.pdf.

Sheehan, Kym. 2009. The Regulatory Framework for Executive Remuneration in Australia, *Sydney Law Review*, 31: 273–308.

Thomas, Randall. 2009. International Executive Pay: Current Practices and Future Trends, in Kenneth G. Dau-Schmidt, Seth D. Harris & Orly Lobel (eds), *Labor and Employment Law and Economics*, 183–234.

Von Nessen, Paul. 2003. Corporate Governance in Australia: Converging with International Developments, *Australian Journal of Corporate Law*, 15: 1–36.

Walsh, Katie. Aug. 2010. Executive Pay Changes Not So Simple. *Australian Financial Review*.

Wen, Philip. 2010. Chairman Retires Amid Pay Backlash. *Sydney Morning Herald*.

Wiggins, Jenny. Oct. 30, 2010. Investors Attack Executive Salaries. *Australian Financial Review*.

Woolworths Limited. June 2009. Productivity Commission Inquiry into Executive Remuneration, at http://www.pc.gov.au/__data/assets/pdf_file/0006/89898/sub091-part1.pdf.

18 Presidents' compensation in Japan

Katsuyuki Kubo[1]

1 INTRODUCTION

The purpose of this chapter is to examine recent changes in executive compensation in Japan. We will focus mainly on three topics. First, we review recent changes in the institutional framework for executive pay. In particular, we discuss the new rules on disclosure of executive compensation, which require firms to disclose the salaries of their presidents if their pay exceeds a certain amount after 2010. However, this new rule is not applicable to most presidents as the threshold, US$1 million, is higher than the salary of most executives.

Second, we describe changes in the level of presidents' salaries, using a sample of 179 firms taken from the Nikkei 225 Stock Index between 2000 and 2007. As individual compensation of presidents is not disclosed, we adopt the Kubo and Saito (2008) calculations and show rapid increases in presidents' salaries after 2000.

Third, we examine change in pay–performance sensitivity (PPS), which shows the relationship between presidents' wealth and firm performance, and attempt to examine whether presidents have a financial incentive to maximize shareholder value. It is shown that pay–performance sensitivity has been increasing during this period. However, this pay–performance sensitivity is much weaker than in the U.S. In other words, presidents in Japan have much less financial incentive to maximize shareholder value compared to their American counterparts.

There are several reasons why it is important to examine executive compensation in Japan. First, it might explain differences in firm behavior between Japan and other countries. It is often considered that the behavior of Japanese firms is different from that of their Western counterparts (Abegglen and Stalk, 1985; Aoki, 1988). At the same time, top managers are considered to have little incentive to maximize shareholder value. Instead, they emphasize employees' interests, as shown in a questionnaire survey by Yoshimori (1995). By examining executive compensation, we might be able to explain the behavior of these firms.

Second, it is of importance to generate stylized facts on executive compensation outside the UK and U.S., where there has been relatively more research on this subject. International differences in corporate governance practices have received increasing attention during the 1990s. In particular, many scholars have focused on the differences in ownership structure and monitoring mechanisms.[2] However, there are relatively few

[1] I acknowledge the financial support of a Grant-in-Aid for Scientific Research (19530292) from the Japanese Ministry of Education, Science, Sports and Culture and Waseda University Grant for Special Research Projects (Project number: 2009A-502).

[2] See Allen and Gale, 2000, Barca and Becht, 2002, La Porta et al., 1999 among others.

international comparisons of top executive compensation (Abowd and Bognanno, 1995; Conyon and Murphy, 2000; Kaplan, 1994). There are several reasons why it is important to generate stylized facts on executive compensation in different countries. To start with, there are complementarities between executive compensation and the various monitoring mechanisms. By establishing stylized facts on international differences, we may be able to understand the interaction between institutions and the financial incentives of top managers. Another reason is the globalization of the managerial labor market. For example, the increasing number of foreign-born presidents in Japanese companies, including Mr. Carlos Ghosn at Nissan Motor, have attracted interest from academics and practitioners regarding relative differences in executive compensation between Japan and other countries. To understand international differences in managers' financial incentives, it is important to establish stylized facts on executive compensation under different environments.

The remainder of the chapter is structured as follows. In Section 2, we describe recent changes in corporate governance in Japan, with particular emphasis on board structure. In Section 3, we provide an account of how directors' compensation is set and disclosed. Section 4 presents our data and descriptive statistics and in Section 5 we calculate pay–performance sensitivity using these data. The chapter concludes with a discussion in the final section.

2   CORPORATE GOVERNANCE IN JAPAN

2.1   Traditional Board Style

Since 1997, when Sony changed its board style, broad changes have taken place in the board structure of large Japanese firms. Traditionally, there had been several distinctive features of boards of directors in Japan. First, board size was quite large; for example, there were 67 directors of the Bank of Tokyo Mitsubishi in 1997. Second, most board members were insiders; typically, there were no outside directors. By examining changes in the board structure of large listed firms, Saito (2010) shows that the number of outside directors is very small. In 1997, only 33 percent of firms had at least one outside director, increasing to 53 percent in 2008. Many of the directors are ex-employees of the firm who have spent many years with the firm. Of the 30 directors of Toyota in 2008, not one was an outside director, and 29 of the directors joined Toyota just after leaving university and spent their career with the firm.[3]

Third, there were hierarchies of chains of command within the board. In addition to the president, chairperson and vice-presidents, directors have such titles as senior executive director, junior executive director and executive director. Each director is assigned

---

[3]   Kato and Rockel (1992) compared the determinants of top executive pay in Japan and the U.S. In particular, they focused on the effect of working experience of top executives on their compensation. They show that executives in the U.S. who have experience working outside the firm they manage receive higher compensation than those without such experience. But in Japan those executives with outside experience receive lower salaries. It is conjectured that Japanese firms emphasize the value of human capital that is accumulated within the firm.

Table 18.1   Salaries of directors of various ranks

	Monthly pay	Annual bonus thousand yen	Cash salary	Ratio President = 1
Chairperson	4220	7580	58220	1.009
President	4050	9050	57650	1
Vice president	3330	5550	45510	0.789
Senior executive	2340	6180	34260	0.594
Junior executive	1940	5350	28630	0.496
Director	1770	3290	24530	0.425
Statutory auditor	1620	1050	20490	0.355

certain tasks in the company and reports to the president. Table 18.1 shows the amount of salary for each director title.[4] It shows that higher rank directors earn more than those of lower rank. For example, a president typically receives 4.05 million yen (US$40,500) per month,[5] senior executive directors receive 2.34 million yen (US$23,400), while an untitled director receives 1.77 million yen (US$17,700) per month.

2.2   Board Reform

These characteristics of boards of directors suggest that they have little incentive to monitor their presidents. It is often argued that a lack of monitoring might explain the declining performance of large Japanese firms during long recessions. In response to these criticisms, many firms have changed their boards of directors.

Sony was one of the first firms to reform its board of directors. Table 18.2 shows changes in Sony's board structure. Sony's board reform started in 1997 when it introduced an 'executive officer system'. First, Sony reduced the number of directors drastically from 38 in 1996 to 10 in 1997. Second, it created new positions called 'executive officer' in an attempt to differentiate between the roles of monitoring and management. Executive officers are supposed to conduct day-to-day operations and each executive officer has a specific responsibility within the firm. In contrast, the board of directors is supposed to focus on decision making for important issues and on monitoring performance.

In response to the change in company law in 2003, Sony again reformed its board of directors. The company instituted a committee system and introduced a number of outside directors. The amendment of company law in 2003 made it possible for firms to choose between board structures of two types, the traditional board and a committee system. Firms that adopt the committee system are required to have compensation, nomination, and audit committees. In addition, at least half the members of these committees

---

[4]   As will be described in Section 3, Japanese firms do not disclose the amount each director receives. Data in Table 18.1 are obtained by questionnaire survey (Romu Gyosei Kenkyusyo, 2008) and are based on survey results of 44 large firms that have more than 1000 employees.

[5]   We calculate figures in U.S. dollars using the exchange rate of US$1 = 100 Japanese yen.

Table 18.2   Evolution of Sony's board structure

Year	Board style	Board size	No. of outside directors	No. of foreign directors
1994	Traditional	37	0	3
1995	Traditional	38	0	3
1996	Traditional	38	0	2
1997	Executive officer system	10	0	1
1998	Executive officer system	9	0	1
1999	Executive officer system	10	0	2
2000	Executive officer system	12	0	2
2001	Executive officer system	12	0	3
2002	Executive officer system	11	3	2
2003	Committee style	17	8	3
2004	Committee style	17	8	3
2005	Committee style	12	8	3
2006	Committee style	14	10	4
2007	Committee style	14	11	3
2008	Committee style	15	12	4

are required to be outside directors. Sony increased the number of its outside directors from three to eight. The proportion of outside directors increased from 27 percent to 47 percent in 2003, and to 80 percent (12 outside directors out of 15) in 2008.

Many large Japanese firms followed in reforming their board structure. Typically, they reduced the number of directors and introduced the executive officer system. However, not many firms adopted the committee system; according to Saito (2010), only 11 firms of 418 in the Nikkei 500 market index adopted the committee system.

3   HOW DIRECTORS' COMPENSATION IS DETERMINED AND DISCLOSED

3.1   How Compensation is Set

According to Japan's company law, the determination of directors' compensation varies according to the board style each firm chooses. As noted above, most firms use the traditional board system. In such firms, directors' compensation must be fixed by a resolution at a shareholder meeting, unless it is prescribed in the articles of incorporation (Article 361).[6] This holds for all types of compensation, including pay, bonuses, stock option grants and retirement bonuses. In practice, current management teams propose 'the

---

[6]   If a firm adopts the committee system, it is not required that the amount of directors' compensation be approved by a shareholders' meeting; instead it is determined by the compensation committee (Articles 404(3) and 409).

maximum pay bill for directors' that the company can pay and then it is approved by the shareholder meeting. It should be noted that the 'maximum pay bill' is the amount that the company is able to pay, and may or may not be the same as the pay bill that the company pays in reality. The pay bill is usually larger than the amount actually paid, so that the current management team does not have to have their pay bill approved by a shareholders' meeting every year. It was legally difficult for firms to grant stock options to their executives until 1997.[7]

Traditionally, most firms paid retirement bonuses to their directors, but now 60 percent of firms listed in the First Section of the Tokyo Stock Exchange have abolished directors' retirement bonuses, according to the Nikkei newspaper.[8] In the future, more firms will discontinue retirement bonuses because the tax deductibility of directors' retirement bonuses is set to be abolished in 2012. Some firms introduced stock options to replace retirement bonuses and it is often the case that firms grant a 'one yen option'—where the exercise price is just one yen. The Nikkei newspaper also revealed that of 383 firms that introduced stock options from July 2009 to June 2010, 171 offered the 'one yen option'.

3.2   Information on Presidents' Salaries

One of the difficulties in studying executive compensation in Japan is that before 2010 there was no disclosure rule requiring firms to disclose individual directors' salaries; consequently, there were very few firms that disclosed levels of individual salaries. Instead, they typically disclosed the total amount of the directors' base pay and annual bonus for directors as a whole.[9] Only a few firms, for example, AEON and Nikko Cordial Group, disclosed the individual pay packages of their top managers.

It is essential to obtain information on executive compensation to examine various aspects of financial incentives of top directors. Previous studies used several methods to deal with this problem. Kato and Kubo (2006) use data that is based on a questionnaire survey conducted by a major compensation consulting firm. Other studies (Kato and Rockel, 1992; Kato, 1997) estimate presidents' income using income tax data. Until 2005, the National Tax Agency disclosed a list of top taxpayers and the amounts of tax paid for those whose income tax exceeded 10 million yen (US$100,000). It is possible to estimate presidents' incomes once the amount of income tax is disclosed. The problem with this method is that income that is unrelated to the business, such as income from real estate, may be included. In addition, only managers with a certain amount of executive compensation would be on the list. Personal incomes would be typically 33.3 million yen

---

[7]   Kato et al. (2005) find a positive abnormal return on firms' announcements of stock options in Japan.

[8]   *Yakuin Taishoku Iro Kin no Kazei Kyoka, Haishi Kento no Kigyo Aitsugu, Kabusiki Konyuken no Katsuyomo* (The more firms discontinue directors' retirement bonus due to abolition of tax deduction, the more firms offer stock options); Nikkei newspaper, 26th January 2011.

[9]   Traditionally, directors' base pay (*yakuin hosyu*) and their bonus (*syoyo*) were treated as different accounting items. That was because base pay was tax deductible while the bonus was not, and they were therefore disclosed separately. After the introduction of the new commercial code in 2005, firms have to disclose the amount of directors' salary that includes both base pay and bonus, as the distinction between base pay and bonus was abolished.

(approximately US$333,333) if their income tax was 10 million yen each, which is not a very large figure. However, there are some presidents whose income is not included on the list, which shows that their salaries are relatively small.

The list of top taxpayers in 2005, the last year this list appeared, reveals several interesting figures. Many presidents are listed, including Tadashi Yanai, the president and chairman of Fast Retailing, with an estimated income of 2.9 billion yen (US$29 million). There were 26 managers and owners whose income exceeded one billion yen (US$10 million).[10]

Some previous studies used directors' average base pay and their average bonus, instead of presidents' salaries, as dependent variables (Kaplan, 1994; Xu, 1997)[11] and calculated directors' average base pay and bonuses by dividing total compensation for directors by the number of directors. Kubo and Saito (2008) extend this method and calculate presidents' salary by dividing the total amount of board compensation by the number of directors, weighted by their rank. We will describe their calculation in detail in a later section.

3.3   The New Disclosure Rule

The Financial Services Agency (FSA) has implemented the new system of mandatory disclosure of directors' remuneration since it came into effect in March 2010.[12] First, listed firms are required to disclose the amount of pay on an individual basis in their annual securities reports (*yuka shaken hokokusyo*) filed with the FSA if it exceeds 100 million yen (US$1 million). Firms are also required to report a breakdown by the type of remuneration (e.g., base pay, bonus, stock option and retirement bonus). This is the first time that firms have been required to report individual directors' pay. In addition, firms are required to report their compensation policy if such a policy is in place.

Because of this new rule, firms are now disclosing their top executives' remuneration. Around 280 executives have been reported as receiving compensation exceeding 100 million yen, according to Jiji Press.[13] It is sometimes the case that a firm discloses the salaries of several executives. Sony and Nomura Holdings, a securities firm, have the largest number of executives, seven each, whose pay is above the threshold. There are five such executives at Nissan Motor, Fanuc, Nintendo, Mizuho Financial Group and Daiwa Securities Group. Those who receive the highest remuneration include Carlos Ghosn of

---

[10]   It should be noted that these amounts are not just the amount of compensation from the firm. Instead, it is often the case that they receive dividends as they are large shareholders. It is sometimes the case that they also sell a large amount of stock. For example, Ikuo Kimura, president of INVOICE Inc., sold stock worth approximately 3.82 billion yen (US$38.2 million) of his own company one year; therefore, it can be assumed that a large portion of his income came from this sale. He also received 120 million yen (US$1.2 million) in dividends.

[11]   Kato (1997) discusses extensively the difference between data based on annual reports and those based on income tax reports.

[12]   Details of the rule can be found at the FSA's website; retrieved 18 February 2011 from http://www.fsa.go.jp/en/news/2010/20100219-2/01.pdf.

[13]   *Ichi Okuen Ijo, 280 nin cho ni: Joi ha Gaikokujin ya Choki Zainin no Keieisya Yakuin Hosyu* (There are more than 280 executives whose pay exceeds 100 million yen. Those who receive the highest pay include foreign directors and those who stay in the same position for many years); retrieved 18 February 2011 from http://www.jiji.com/jc/v?p=ve_eco_company-yakuinhousyu20100630o-01-w500.

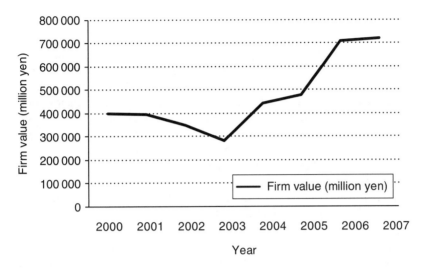

Figure 18.1   Median firm value 2000–2007 in million yen

Nissan Motor who receives 890 million yen (US$8.9 million) and Howard Stringer of Sony who receives 814 million yen (US$8.14 million). Yoshitoshi Kitajima of Dai Nippon Printing is the highest paid Japanese executive, receiving 787 million yen (US$7.87 million). It should be noted that these amounts do not include dividends from their shares in the firms they manage.

It should also be noted that at around 280 the number of executives whose pay is disclosed is relatively small, considering that there are around 1800 firms that hold shareholders' meetings in June. In other words, most top directors receive less than 100 million yen (US$1million), showing that the new mandatory rule applies to only a small proportion of the executives of listed firms.

4   LEVEL OF EXECUTIVE PAY

4.1   Sample

First, we describe the sample we use to examine the change in the level of presidents' pay and their pay–performance sensitivity. Our sample comprises a panel of 1432 observations of 179 firms during the period 2000–2007. The firms were selected from the 225 firms that constituted the Nikkei 225 Stock Index. The Nikkei Stock Average is the benchmark Japanese stock index, corresponding to the U.S. S&P Index. It is composed of 225 major firms on the First Section of the Tokyo Stock Exchange. We excluded financial institutions and firms for which we could not obtain the total board compensation data. Figure 18.1 shows changes in firm share value (median) between 2000 and 2007. We can see that firm value increased during this period: median firm value was 400.658 billion yen (US$ 4006.58 million) in 2000, and 720.24 billion yen (US$7202.4 million) in 2007. In other words, firm value increased by around 80 percent during this period.

4.2 Calculating Presidents' Pay

In this study, we examine changes in presidents' pay. In particular, we analyze presidents' financial incentives generated by various mechanisms, such as cash salary, stock option grants, changes in stock value and changes in the value of stock options they hold. To examine presidents' financial incentives, it is necessary to estimate their cash salary, as that is not disclosed. Although many previous studies use average directors' salary as the dependent variable, it is generally more desirable to use presidents' salaries rather than directors' average salary. For example, the pay–performance sensitivity for the average director may be smaller than that for a president because the directors' average salary is smaller than that of a president.

We follow Kubo and Saito (2008) in calculating presidents' pay. In particular, we use information on the pay-gap ratio between directors in each rank—i.e., the proportion of vice-presidents' salaries compared with presidents' salaries. It is assumed that this pay gap is constant across time and firms.[14] Therefore, once we obtain information on the pay-gap ratio and board composition—i.e., the number of vice-presidents and senior directors—we can calculate presidents' salaries by dividing the total amount of board compensation by the number of directors, weighted by their rank. Information on directors' total salary is obtained from the Nikkei NEEDS database. Information on pay gaps between directors in each rank is obtained from Table 18.1. The board's composition—i.e., the number of directors in each rank—is obtained from *Yakuin Shikiho* (Directory of Executives), which is published by Toyo Keizai. Using this information, we calculate presidents' cash salaries.[15] Financial data were also obtained from the Nikkei NEEDS database.

4.3 Descriptive Statistics: Presidents' Financial Incentives

Selected descriptive statistics of the sample firms for 2000–2007 are presented in Table 18.3. We can see that the mean market value of firms is 1.019 trillion yen (US$10.19 billion) while the median value is 476.9 billion yen (US$4.76 billion). The mean value of the change in firm market value is 73.6 billion yen (US$736 million) while the median is 18.4 billion yen (US$184 million). There is a large variation in the change in firm value. The 25th percentile of the change in firm value is –48.1 billion yen (–US$481 million) while the 75th percentile is 140.5 billion yen (US$1.405 billion). The median value of stock

---

[14] This assumption may have some bias. For instance, studies on rank-order tournaments suggest that pay gaps among directors depend on board composition (Lazear and Rosen, 1981; Main et al., 1993).

[15] For example, suppose that a board is composed of one president, one vice-president and ten directors. Assume also that total compensation for all directors is 200 million yen. Then, presidents' pay is calculated as follows.

$$\text{Presidents' pay} = \frac{200 \text{ million}}{1 + 0.789 + 10*.425} = \frac{200 \text{ million}}{6.039} = 33.12 \text{ million yen.}$$

Table 18.3   Data summary: firms

	Observation	Mean	S.D.	25th percentile	50th percentile	75th percentile
Firm value (million yen)	1413	1018781	1937834	197493	476917.8	1072000
Change in firm value (million yen)	1411	73622.36	731876.6	−48085.66	18377.44	140510.5
Stock return (%)	1413	9.717693	44.95775	−19.42369	2.151284	27.77778

returns is 9.71 percent while the mean is 2.15 percent. The 25th percentile of stock returns is −19.4 percent while the 75th is 27.8 percent.

Basic statistics on presidents' financial incentives in 2000 and 2007 are shown in Table 18.4. Presidents' financial incentives derive from various sources. These include cash salary, stock option grants, and changes in the value of stockholdings and stock options. Presidents' shareholdings are collected from the Annual Securities Report.

Data needed to calculate the value of stock option grants and stock option holdings are also taken from Annual Securities Reports. Stock option values are based on the Black–Scholes formula for valuing European call options. To calculate precisely the incentives from presidents' stock option holdings, we construct a president's total holdings of stock options by adding options granted that year to those granted in previous years and by excluding matured options. Unfortunately, firms do not report when and how many stock options are exercised. Therefore, we assume that each president holds and does not exercise their stock options until maturity. This assumption might be strong. However, we can calculate the upper bound of pay–performance sensitivity, i.e., how much presidents' wealth changes according to fluctuations in their firms' performance.

According to Table 18.4, in 2000 the median president received 39.66 million yen (US$396,600) as cash salary, while the mean value was 51.5 million yen (US$515,000). Median salary increased to 69.11 million yen (US$691,100), a 74.3 percent increase, in 2007. Presidents typically received no stock options in 2000 or 2007. Median values of stock options granted at each year were zero. The mean value of the stock option grant was 4.115 million yen (US$41,150) in 2000 and 2.821 million yen (US$28,210) in 2007. It should be noted that these figures are calculated for all presidents including those who received no stock options.

Table 18.4 also exhibits a stock option dummy, which is defined as 1 if the president is granted a stock option in the year, and 0 otherwise. It is shown that the proportion of presidents who receive an option is increasing, though most presidents do not receive one. 17.9 percent of them received stock options in 2000 and 20.7 percent in 2007. Descriptive statistics of those who received stock options are also shown. In 2000, the mean value of stock options granted to presidents was 23.02 million yen (US$230,200) while the median value was 9.623 million yen (US$96,230). The median value in 2007 was 11.09 million yen (US$110,900). It is suggested that there is no tendency for firms to use stock options as their main incentive device.

Presidents' wealth changes according to the change in value of the stocks they hold. On

Table 18.4   Data summary: presidents

Panel A (2000)	Observation	Mean	S.D.	25th percentile	50th percentile	75th percentile
Cash salary (1000 yen)	138	51504.82	57522.3	31115.27	39657.36	52047.83
Option value (1000 yen)	179	4115.343	16874.29	0	0	0
Change in the value of stock (1000 yen)	170	−241100.8	2328587	−4727	298.75	3700
Change in the value of stock option (1000 yen)	179	−1669.844	9667.265	0	0	0
Presidents' total wealth change (1000 yen)	133	−252577.3	2630638	27841.41	39927.8	57943.49
Presidents' ownership (%)	172	0.3391594	4.068253	0.002331	0.0059251	0.0130206
Value of presidents' stock holding (1000 yen)	170	1856197	19100000	10400	17746.5	41583
Stock option grant dummy	179	0.1787709	0.3842352	0	0	0
Value of option (only for those who receive 1000 yen)	32	23020.2	34434.52	4419.493	9623.678	24344.61
Panel B (2007)						
Cash salary (1000 yen)	176	76602.9	61103.92	40696.45	69114.02	93189.54
Option value (1000 yen)	179	2821.474	7093.119	0	0	0
Change in the value of stock (1000 yen)	176	684624.4	9386950	−23116	−10860	−4965.5
Change in the value of stock option (1000 yen)	179	−3456.669	11775.66	0	0	0
Presidents' total wealth change (1000 yen)	174	768345.4	9444527	18574.19	56705.1	79750.91
Presidents' ownership (%)	178	0.1651461	1.998679	0.0024761	0.0066788	0.0145109
Value of presidents' stock holding (1000 yen)	176	1186451	14500000	22558	49617	87168.5
Stock option grant dummy	179	0.2067039	0.4060771	0	0	0
Value of option (only for those who receive 1000 yen)	37	13649.83	9841.52	5695.121	11091.87	19406.22

average, the change in the value of stock holdings in 2000 was –241.1 million yen (US$2.411 million), and the median was 298,800 yen (US$2,988). In 2007, the value of stock for a typical president decreased (median –10.86 million yen, –US$108,600). For most directors, the financial incentive generated by stock option holdings is very small. The 75th percentile of the change of the value of stock option holdings is zero in both 2000 and 2007. By combining information on cash pay, value of stock option grants, changes in the value of stock holdings and of stock option holdings, we can calculate the overall change in presidents' wealth. The median value of presidents' wealth change was 39.93 million yen (US$399,300) in 2000 and 56.71 million yen (US$567,100) in 2007. In other words, presidents were more likely to receive greater financial incentive during this period, with an increase of 42 percent.

Managerial ownership, combined with stock options, is often considered the most direct financial incentive aligning presidents' incentives with those of shareholders. However, Table 18.4 also shows that presidents' share of total ownership is very small. In 2000, the median president's ownership was 0.00593% and the 75th percentile's 0.013%. There was little change in 2007. The value of presidents' stock ownership is not large. The median was 17.75 million yen (US$177,500) in 2000. It increased to 49.62 million yen (US$496,200) in 2007. In addition, these figures are lower than those found in the U.S. by Hall and Liebman (1998), who report that CEOs' ownership was 2.15 percent (mean) and 0.14 percent (median). In other words, presidents in large Japanese firms have much weaker financial incentives from their shareholdings in their own firms than CEOs in the U.S.

One of the most striking features in Table 18.4 is that cash salary accounts for the major proportion of presidents' wealth changes. Another important feature is that changes in the level of presidents' wealth are small compared to those in the U.S. According to the Executive PayWatch website, CEOs of S&P 500 companies receive US$1.41 million as salary, US$203,000 as bonus, US$2.63 million as stock awards, US$2.28 million as stock options, US$1.79 million as nonequity incentive plan compensation, US$1.06 million as pension and deferred compensation earnings and US$235,000 as other compensation.[16] Overall, the average S&P 500 CEO receives US$9.25 million, which suggests that CEOs in the U.S. receive larger compensation than Japanese managers.

4.4 Changes in Presidents' Wealth 1977–2007

Figure 18.2 depicts the median value of presidents' income, classified as cash salary, stock option grant, change in the value of stock holdings and change in the value of stock option holdings for thirty-one years, from 1977 to 2007. It should be noted that the median value of stock option grants and that of the change in the value of stock option holdings is zero throughout the period. Therefore, this figure shows only cash salary and changes in the value of stock holdings. Data before 1999 are taken from Kubo and Saito (2008), whose sample is similar to ours but not identical. Their data are a balanced panel of 117 firms from the Nikkei 225 Stock Index; as our sample includes 177 firms, it is somewhat larger.[17]

One of the most striking features in Figure 18.2 is that presidents' cash salaries have increased dramatically since 2000. In contrast, the change in cash salary between 1977 and 1999 was not large. Another important characteristic of Figure 18.2 is that the change in the value of stock that presidents hold is not very large. Even in 1988, at the zenith of the 'bubble economy', the median change in the value of stock holdings was 20.65 million yen (US$206,500), which is smaller than the 37.09 million yen cash salary of that year. In many years, changes in the value of stock option holdings were negligible compared with cash salary.

---

[16] Retrieved 18 February 2010 from http://www.aflcio.org/corporatewatch/paywatch/pay/index.cfm.
[17] Their figures are adjusted to 1996 constant yen by using the consumer price index. Our figures are not adjusted to the price index because price changes in our sample are very small.

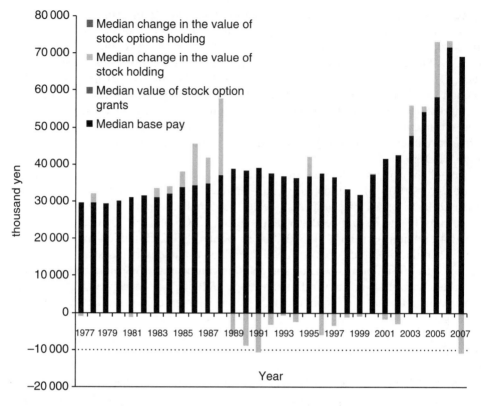

Figure 18.2   Presidents' median cash salary 1977–2007

5   DO PRESIDENTS HAVE INCENTIVES TO MAXIMIZE SHAREHOLDER VALUE?

5.1   Cash Compensation and Shareholder Value

One of the main issues in executive compensation is to examine whether there is a positive relationship between pay and performance. If this is the case, executives may have incentives to maximize shareholder value. First, we analyze the relationship between presidents' cash salaries and stock returns. Table 18.4 shows that cash salary comprises a significant proportion of presidents' wealth change. Therefore, it is of importance to examine the mechanism that aligns their interests with those of shareholders. To analyze the connection between each president's cash compensation and shareholder value, we estimate the determinants of the change in cash salary. The dependent variable is the change in cash salary (thousand yen). The independent variable is stock return (%) at year t. We estimate this equation using median regression so that the effect of a few outliers is not serious. The result is as follows. Figures in parentheses indicate standard errors.

$$\Delta\text{Cash Salary}_t = 1036.3 + 700.04 \text{ Stock Return}_t$$

$$(487.05)\ (234.27)$$

$$\text{No. Obs.} = 1366,\ \text{Pseudo R2} = 0.0003 \tag{18.1}$$

The coefficient of stock return is 700.04 but it is not statistically significant, suggesting that the relationship between shareholder value and cash salary is weak. The magnitude of the effect of stock return is not large. This coefficient shows that a 1 percent increase in stock return will lead to an increase of 700,000 yen (US$7,000) in presidents' cash salary. Even if good presidents improve their stock return by 10 percent, they will receive 7 million yen (US$70,000), which may not be a large financial incentive for such performance improvement; this result is consistent with the view that top managers in Japan have little financial incentive to maximize shareholder value.

5.2 Pay–Performance Sensitivity: Simulation

Cash salary is not the only source of financial incentive for presidents. Though not very significant, presidents hold some stocks and stock options. As the value of stock holdings and stock option holdings changes due to stock price performance, a financial incentive is generated by these holdings as well.

Table 18.5 shows the results of a simulation of how much presidents' total wealth changes for a given change in stock return, following Hall and Liebman (1998). Presidents' wealth change includes cash salary and changes in the value of stocks and stock option holdings. To obtain the standardized value of direct pay and change in presidents' wealth, we calculate the distribution of stock prices by pooling the annual stock returns in our sample. The first row of Table 18.5 shows that stock returns ranged from –36.1 percent (10th percentile) to 66.1 percent (90th percentile).

To obtain pay–performance sensitivity, we calculate how each component of presidents' earnings, such as cash salary, changes according to variation in performance. First, we calculate each president's cash salary at each decile. Cash salary at each performance is calculated using the equations below. Coefficients are obtained by results of the above regression analysis. The constant term at each year is the median value of the actual cash salary paid to presidents in each year.

Year 2000: Cash salary = 39547 + 700.04 (stock return at each decile)

Year 2007: Cash salary = 69114 + 700.04 (stock return at each decile)

Then, we calculate the change in the value of stocks and options for each president in each year given the stock return, as we have information on presidents' shareholding and stock option holdings. Table 18.5 and Figure 18.3 show the results. Each column in Table 18.5 shows the amount each president earns (median) for each stock return in 2000 and 2007. For example, column 3 in 2000 shows that presidents typically receive a cash salary of 39.544 million yen (US$395,440) if the firm's stock return is –16.1 percent (30th percentile) in 2000. At the same time, the change in the value of stock is –2.635 million yen (–US$26,350). Overall, presidents receive 33.959 million yen (US$339,590) for this poor

Table 18.5 Composition of compensation, assuming stock price performance at each decile

Year: 2000 Deciles	10%	20%	30%	40%	50%	60%	70%	80%	90%
Stock return (%)	−36.1168	−24.7361	−16.0882	−7.47883	1.891771	9.998382	20.84254	39.16182	66.07284
Cash salary (1000 yen)	39404.53	39484.2	39544.74	39605.01	39670.6	39727.35	39803.27	39931.51	40119.9
Change in the value of stock (1000 yen)	−5915.93	−4051.78	−2635.24	−1225.03	309.8721	1637.735	3414.009	6414.706	10800
Change in the value of stock option (1000)	0	0	0	0	0	0	0	0	0
Change in the value of stock and option (1000 yen)	−6623.1	−4536.11	−2950.25	−1371.47	342.2781	1809.007	3771.041	7085.548	12000
Total wealth change (1000 yen)	26865.5	30896.31	33959.25	37008.5	40322.75	43174.09	46988.32	53431.76	62919.9

Year: 2007 Deciles	10%	20%	30%	40%	50%	60%	70%	80%	90%
Stock return (%)	−36.1168	−24.7361	−16.0882	−7.47883	1.891771	9.998382	20.84254	39.16182	66.07284
Cash salary (1000 yen)	68861.19	68940.86	69001.4	69061.67	69127.26	69184.01	69259.93	69388.17	69576.56
Change in the value of stock (1000 yen)	−17800	−12200	−7920.2	−3681.83	931.3189	4922.204	10300	19300	32500
Change in the value of stock option (1000)	−5671.74	−3884.53	−2526.47	−1174.47	243.1396	1285.041	2678.785	5033.268	8492.004
Change in the value of stock and option (1000 yen)	−21800	−14900	−9717.24	−4517.21	1105.267	5841.555	12200	22900	39900
Total wealth change (1000 yen)	23589.44	37956.32	48837.49	59688.16	71406.99	81232.81	94438.71	116621.4	150468.6

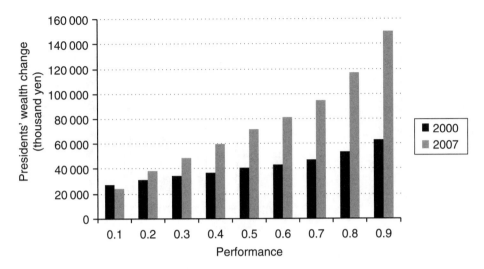

Figure 18.3 Presidents' cash salary in 2000 and 2007 assuming stock price performance at each decile

performance. Similarly, column 7 shows that a president typically receives 46.998 million yen (US$469,880) when firms achieve better performance, or 20.8 percent (70th percentile). In other words, columns 3 and 7 show that presidents would receive 13.029 million yen (=46.988−33.959), US$130,029, if they succeed in improving stock returns from −16.1 percent to 20.8 percent in 2000. Similarly, presidents' wealth changes by 6.67 million yen (=46.988−40.322), US$66,700, when they improve stock returns from the 50th percentile (1.89 percent) to the 70th percentile (20.8 percent) in 2000. This figure may not be very large considering the difficulty in improving stock returns.

Figure 18.3 shows these results graphically. The horizontal axis variable is the performance of each decile. The vertical axis shows how much presidents earn for each given performance. A steeper slope shows that the amount of presidents' income varies according to their stock return.

Figure 18.3 and the lower panel of Table 18.5 show the results in 2007. The relationship between stock returns and the change in presidents' wealth becomes stronger than in 2000. For example, a president receives 71.41 million yen (US$714,100) for the 50th percentile stock return (1.89 percent), and 94.44 million yen (US$944,400) for the 70th percentile stock return (20.8 percent). In other words, presidents' wealth changes by 23.03 million yen (= 94.44−71.41), US$230,300, when stock returns improve from the 50th percentile to the 70th percentile. This figure is larger than the 6.67 million yen in 2000 for the same performance improvement. However, considering that presidents are running very large firms, some may argue that this figure is not large enough. They may want to waste the firms' resources on a project that does not improve firm value because the loss of their own personal wealth is not large.

Table 18.5 and Figure 18.3 show that presidents do not have a strong financial incentive to maximize shareholder value. In addition, although the level of cash salary constitutes the larger part of presidents' earnings, their financial incentive is generated mostly

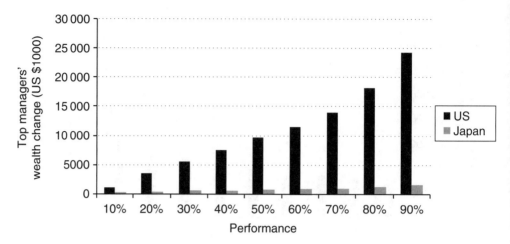

Figure 18.4   Top managers' cash salary in Japan and the U.S. assuming stock price performance at each decile

by their stock holdings. Cash salary does not change much with performance change, while the change in the value of managerial ownership is relatively large.

5.3   Pay–Performance Sensitivity: Comparison with the U.S.

Section 4 reveals that the level of compensation of CEOs in the U.S. is much larger than that in Japan. Next, we compare pay–performance sensitivity of the two economies. U.S. data are taken from Frydman and Saks (2010), which is based on a sample of three executives of each of the fifty largest firms for 2000–2005.[18] Figure 18.4 shows the results for Japan data based on our sample. As in Figure 18.3, Figure 18.4 shows how much top managers earn for a given performance in both countries. The horizontal axis is a stock market performance, shown at each decile. The vertical axis is the amount a top manager would receive for a given performance.

The most striking feature in Figure 18.4 is that the slope is much steeper in the U.S., indicating that pay–performance sensitivity is larger. In other words, top managers in the U.S. have a much stronger financial incentive to maximize stockholders' wealth. There, a CEO receives US$9.63 million for median stock return and US$13.95 million for 70th percentile performance. CEOs' income in the U.S. would increase by US$4.32 (=13.95–9.63) million if they succeeded in improving firms' stock return from the median to the 70th percentile. This figure is much larger than the corresponding figure in Japan, US$230,300. In other words, Japanese presidents have a much smaller financial incentive to maximize shareholders' value compared with the U.S.[19]

---

[18]   Median compensation for a top manager is US$9.2 million in their Table 18.3. In addition, their Table 18.6 shows that managers' wealth from their stock and option holdings increases US$227,881 for a 1 percent increase in stock return.

[19]   It should be noted that our sample and the U.S. sample are not completely comparable. Firms in the U.S. sample are larger than those in our sample.

6 DISCUSSION

Our results raise a number of interesting questions. One of the most fundamental is why pay–performance sensitivity is low. There are several possible explanations. First, it might be the case that there is little need to motivate top directors because they are well monitored by banks. The role of the 'main bank' or company group (*keiretsu*) in corporate governance in Japan has been much debated. Some emphasize positive aspects of the main bank relationship in helping firms in financial distress (Aoki and Patrick, 1994; Hoshi et al., 1990), while others show that there is no positive effect on firms with a main bank relationship (Hanazaki and Horiuchi, 2000). Kato (1997) shows that compensation of top managers of the firms that belong to financial *keiretsu* is 21 percent lower than that in firms without such a relationship. He suggests that banks play an important role in monitoring top management, preventing them from receiving excessive salaries. Murase (1998) shows managers' bonuses are more likely to decrease when firm performance deteriorates in a firm with larger ownership by financial institutions. In addition, the proportion of directors' bonuses to their total compensation is smaller if an ex-bank officer is on the board of directors (Abe et al., 2005). As the directors' bonuses are considered to be more performance related, it implies that directors have less financial incentive to maximize performance. Abe et al. suggest that managers in a firm with bank directors on boards are closely monitored by their main banks. Therefore, their effort would be greater even without financial incentive. These studies suggest that main banks play some monitoring role in directors' compensation.

Second, top managers are not expected to maximize shareholders' interest. Questionnaire surveys show that managers do not emphasize shareholder value; rather they maximize the interest of various stakeholders, such as employees (Yoshimori, 1995). Kubo (2003) emphasizes that there are several similarities in directors' compensation and employees' wages. Both directors and employees are paid monthly wages and bonuses. Both a director's salary and an employee's wage are affected by the firm's performance, such as its sales and profits. Thus, Kubo hypothesizes that directors' salaries are determined jointly with employees' wages. Consistent with this discussion, Kubo finds a positive and significant relationship between employees' wages and directors' salaries. He suggests that his result is consistent with the idea that top managers are managing the firm to maximize stakeholders' interest.

REFERENCES

Abe, Naohito, Gaston, Noel, and Kubo, Katsuyuki (2005), "Executive Pay in Japan: the Role of Bank-appointed Monitors and the Main Bank Relationship", Japan and the World Economy, 17, 371–94.

Abegglen, James and Stalk Jr., George (1985), Kaisha: The Japanese Corporation, New York, Basic Books.

Abowd, John and Bognanno, Michael (1995), "International Differences in Executive and Managerial Compensation" in Richard Freeman and Lawrence Katz eds., Differences and Changes in Wage Structure, National Bureau of Economic Research, Comparative Labor Market Series, Chicago: Chicago University Press.

Allen, Franklin and Gale, Douglas (2000), Comparing Financial Systems, Cambridge: MIT Press.

Aoki, Masahiko (1988), Information, Incentives, and Bargaining in the Japanese Economy, Cambridge: Cambridge University Press.

Aoki, Masahiko and Patrick, Hugh (eds.) (1994), The Japanese Main Bank System, Oxford: Oxford University Press.

Barca, Fabrizio and Becht, Marco (2002), The Control of Corporate Europe, Oxford: Oxford University Press.

Conyon, Martin and Murphy, Kevin (2000), "The Prince and the Pauper? CEO Pay in the United States and United Kingdom", Economic Journal, 110, F640–F671.

Frydman, Carola and Saks, Raven (2010), "Executive Compensation: A New View from a Long-Term Perspective, 1936–2000", Review of Financial Studies, 23, 2099–138.

Hall, Brian and Liebman, Jeffrey (1998), "Are CEOs Really Paid Like Bureaucrats?" Quarterly Journal of Economics, 113, 653–92.

Hanazaki, Masaharu and Horiuchi, Akiyoshi (2000), "Is Japan's Financial System Efficient?" Oxford Review of Economic Policy, 16, 61–73.

Hoshi, T., Kashyap, Anil, and Scharfstein, David (1990), "The Role of Banks in Reducing the Costs of Financial Distress in Japan", Journal of Financial Economics, 27, 67–88.

Kaplan, Steven (1994), "Top Executive Rewards and Firm Performance: A Comparison of Japan and the United States", Journal of Political Economy, 102, 510–46.

Kato, Hideaki, Lemmon, Michael, Luo, Mi, and Schallheim, James, (2005),"An Empirical Examination of the Costs and Benefits of Executive Stock Options: Evidence from Japan", Journal of Financial Economics, 78, 435–61.

Kato, Takao (1997), "Chief Executive Compensation and Corporate Groups in Japan: New Evidence from Micro Data", International Journal of Industrial Organization, 15, 455–67.

Kato, Takao and Kubo, Katsuyuki (2006), "CEO Compensation and Firm Performance in Japan: Evidence from New Panel Data on Individual CEO Pay", Journal of the Japanese and International Economics, 20, 1–19.

Kato, Takao and Rockel, Mark (1992), "Experiences, Credentials and Compensation in the Japanese and U.S. Managerial Labor Markets: Evidence from New Micro Data", Journal of the Japanese and International Economics, 6, 30–51.

Kubo, Katsuyuki (2003), "The Determinants of Executive Compensation in Japan and UK: Agency Hypothesis or Joint Determination Hypothesis?" in Fan, Joseph, Teranishi, Juro, and Hanazaki, Masaharu, eds., Designing Financial Systems in East Asia & Japan, London: Routledge.

Kubo, Katsuyuki and Saito, Takuji (2008) "The Relationship between Financial Incentives for Company Presidents and Firm Performance in Japan", Japanese Economic Review, 59(4), 401–18.

La Porta, Rafael, Lopez-de-Silanes, Florencio, and Shleifer, Andrei (1999), "Corporate Ownership Around the World", Journal of Finance, 54(2), 471–517.

Lazear, Edward and Rosen, Sherwin (1981), "Rank-Order Tournaments as Optimum Labor Contracts", Journal of Political Economy, 89(5), 841–64.

Main, Brian, O'Reilly III, Charles, and Wade, James (1993), "Top Executive Pay: Tournament or Teamwork?" Journal of Labor Economics, 11(4), 606–28.

Murase, Hideaki (1998), "Equity Ownership and the Determination of Managers' Bonuses in Japanese Firms", Japan and the World Economy, 10, 321–31.

Romu Gyosei Kenkyusyo (2008), "Yakuin Hosyu Syoyo Taisyoku Irokin to Yakuin Kaikaku no Saishin Zittai [Directors' pay, bonus, retirement bonus and recent development in board reform]" Rosei Ziho, 3739, 2–31.

Saito, Takuji (2010), "The Determinants of Board Composition when Managers Control Director Selection: Evidence from Japan", working paper, Kyoto Sangyo University.

Xu, Peng (1997), "Executive Salaries as Tournament Prizes and Executive Bonuses as Managerial Incentives in Japan", Journal of the Japanese and International Economics, 11, 319–46.

Yoshimori, Masaru (1995), "Whose Company Is It? The Concept of the Corporation in Japan and the West", Long Range Planning, 28, 33–44.

19 Top executive pay in China
Michael Firth, Tak Yan Leung and Oliver M. Rui

1 INTRODUCTION

This Handbook analyzes various facets of top management pay and provides an extensive review of the latest research in the area of executive compensation. However, most of the evidence we have on executive pay practices is from the developed economies, most notably the U.S. economy. The purpose of this chapter is to describe top executive pay in the world's largest transitional economy, the People's Republic of China. In doing so, we provide some empirical evidence on the levels of pay, the role of corporate governance in setting executive pay, and other determinants of compensation. China's unique approach to economic reform and corporate restructuring means that research findings on executive pay in developed countries cannot be automatically imputed to firms in China. We compare and contrast top executive pay in China with management compensation in the U.S. and other developed countries.

We begin our chapter with a brief review of China's economic reforms and its recent economic performance. This section discusses how the corporate sector has evolved and describes the regulatory environment. Then we discuss how compensation is set in China and reference the relevant legal and disclosure requirements that pertain to top management pay. We then present some detailed statistics on the levels of executive pay in listed companies and show how pay has changed over time. We analyze the determinants of compensation and calculate pay–performance sensitivities and elasticities. These analyses are compared with findings from other countries. We pay special attention to the type of controlling shareholder and its influence on executive pay. The role of a firm's internal governance in determining pay is also examined. Finally, we discuss the challenges in determining optimal compensation contracts in China and likely future developments in setting top management pay.

2 CHINA'S ECONOMIC REFORMS

In the late 1970s, China began to reform its moribund economy. Two of the main planks of the reforms were the introduction of a free enterprise system where prices are set in markets, and the corporatization and subsequent privatization of state owned enterprises (SOEs). In contrast to Russia and some other countries, China's reforms have been gradual and they are still evolving after some 30 years of change. The gradualist approach to reform is a reflection of the conservative stance of China's leaders and their quest to maintain the communist party's grip on power.

Except for certain 'strategic industries', most SOEs have now been reorganized. The reorganization has involved hiving off the operating units of the SOEs into corporate firms with share capital. The non-operating units (e.g., hospitals, schools) are retained by the SOE. Initially, all the shares were owned by the state (i.e., owned by central, provincial, or city level government or ministries). Subsequently, many of the firms sold shares to the public (i.e., privatization) with the state often keeping a significant or controlling share of the issued capital. These shares are listed on the stock market. There are two stock markets, one in Shanghai (opened in 1990) and one in Shenzhen (opened in 1991). By February 2012, there are more than 2,300 listed companies in China and the combined market capitalization of the two exchanges exceeds 3.5 trillion U.S.\$, making it the second largest stock market in the world after the U.S.

The state (via central or regional government) is the major shareholder in more than 60 percent of listed companies. Thus, the state has a significant influence on firms and this extends to the selection of top managers. There are relatively few non-state institutional investors in China and the market for corporate control is very inactive. Small private shareholders tend to hold relatively small stakes and they frequently trade their shareholdings. Professional managers' shareholdings are very low. The pattern of share ownership in Chinese firms is very different from the patterns of firms in developed countries and this has the potential to have an impact on top management pay.

The reform of the SOEs was intended to change the incentives and rewards of managers as well as to raise private finance for the firms. By adopting a corporate form with private shareholders, the government hopes to impose market discipline on the firm and its top managers. Slowly but surely, top managers have become more professional and fewer of them are former government bureaucrats or old-guard SOE bureaucrats. This has led to changes in the ways managers are recruited and rewarded.

From 2001, listed companies have had to comply with the *Code of Corporate Governance for Listed Companies in China* issued by the China Securities Regulatory Commission (CSRC), which is the regulator of listed firms and the securities markets. The Code is based on international norms (e.g., Cadbury Report 1992; Hempel 1998; OECD 1999) and has provisions relating to the rights of shareholders, the duties of controlling shareholders, responsibilities of the board of directors, and assessing the performance of directors and top executive management. The Code is *de facto* law. As with many of the economic reforms, company law and corporate governance rules adopt what are perceived as the best practices from the developed countries.

At the macro level, China's reforms have been very successful. The reform of SOEs into listed firms and the encouragement of a vibrant non-listed company sector have led to unparalleled growth, burgeoning exports, and a growing middle class. Annual GNP growth rates have averaged 10 percent in the last two decades, there is a large positive trade gap (where exports greatly exceed imports), foreign exchange reserves are the second largest in the world after Japan, and China is the second largest economy after the U.S. Despite China's enviable growth, the benefits have not always flowed through to the corporate sector. Return on assets, profit growth, and stock market valuations are anemic in many cases (Chen et al. 2006). It appears that firms have emphasized growth over profitability. This emphasis on growth has come from pressure from the state, which, as we described earlier, is the single largest investor in many firms. The state emphasizes growth to meet its socio-economic objectives (e.g., full employment). An interesting research question is whether this striving for growth results in low pay-for-performance sensitivities.

2.1 Ownership

In the standard principal–agent models, firms develop compensation packages to hire, retain, and motivate top executives to maximize stockholder wealth (Mirrlees 1976; Holström 1979; Murphy 1999).[1] If the directors or shareholders can directly monitor and discipline top management then incentive compensation schemes become less necessary. Thus, compensation incentives and monitoring activities can be viewed as substitute mechanisms (Hermalin and Weisbach 1998, 2003). A large investor in a firm may find it cost effective to directly monitor the top managers and in these cases there is less need for incentive pay to make the managers work hard. In contrast, there is a greater need for carefully designed compensation incentive systems in widely held companies. While these arguments are widely articulated in developed countries, they may be less applicable in China. This follows because China has unique ownership structures, which we detail below.

Almost all of China's listed firms have a dominant shareholder whose share ownership far exceeds that of the second largest owner. On average, the largest shareholder owns 34 percent of a firm's outstanding shares while the second largest has about 9 percent (Chen et al. 2009). These investors typically have board representation and may even have a majority of seats on it. The power and responsibilities of the dominant investor is enshrined in the *Code of Corporate Governance*.

We identify three major types of owner control. These are central government controlled firms, local government controlled firms, and privately controlled firms. Large firms with national operations are typically controlled by the central government. These firms are often in strategic industries and may be subject to controls over the prices they charge to consumers. Central government control is usually exercised by state asset management bureaus (SAMBs). State firms that are located in specific cities or provinces tend to be controlled by the local government. Privately controlled listed firms are majority owned by an individual and her/his family. Sometimes a former SOE may have been acquired by a private individual. In other cases, a private individual may have started a business from scratch and built it up into a listed firm. Over time, there has been a move towards private control. In 2002, about 27 percent of listed firms had a private investor as the largest shareholder. This figure increased to 35 percent by 2008.

Privately controlled listed firms have the strongest motive to maximize shareholder wealth as they are not encumbered with achieving social or political objectives. In most cases, the controlling investor is actively engaged in managing the company (they are the founder of the listed firm) and so the manager–principal agency problem is non-existent. The investor earns rewards through share ownership and so cash compensation may be less of a concern for the owner-manager. Arguably, incentive reward systems are less necessary in privately controlled listed firms. However, in some cases, the privately controlled firms hire professional managers to take up the chairperson or CEO positions and they search for the best talent available.

The bureaucrats at the SAMBs who look after the central government's ownership of

---

[1] This Handbook provides an extensive coverage of the principal–agent model and how efficient compensation contracts can mitigate agency problems.

listed firms do not enjoy the cash flow rights from the investment. Instead, the cash flows (e.g., dividends) flow to the Ministry of Finance. These bureaucrats are not allowed to have a direct involvement in the management of the firms (Cao 2000) and they are selected through the political process, with little regard for their business acumen or business experience (Qian 1998; Zhang 1998). This may lead to weak monitoring of the firms they control. Furthermore, state controlled listed firms may have non-profit objectives thrust upon them and so the monitoring that does take place may focus on the achievement of many objectives. This suggests that the officials of the SAMBs will be less likely to impose pay for (economic) performance systems on the listed firms they control. Cao et al. (2011) make similar comments.

Local government controlled firms are likely to fall in between privately controlled and SAMB controlled firms in terms of objectives and monitoring. Close physical proximity makes it easier for local government controlled firms to be monitored (vis-à-vis SAMB controlled firms) and this may weaken the need for pay-for-performance systems. On the other hand, dividends paid by firms controlled by local government flow through to the local government. For this reason, local government controlled firms may face more discipline and there should be more emphasis on efficiency and profitability. This could result in these firms being more likely to have incentive based pay schemes.

2.2   Regional Development

China's reforms have led to rapid developments in the legal and social environments and in economic freedoms. However, these advances have not occurred at the same pace throughout the country. In fact, there are major disparities in wealth, employment, law enforcement, corruption, education, etc., across the different cities and regions of the country. While China's leaders are aware of the dangers of such disparities, they have so far been powerless to reverse the trends that have emerged. Several studies have shown that regional disparities in economic and institutional development have an impact on the governance and performance of firms (Wang et al. 2008; Firth et al. 2010). The monitoring of management and the design of compensation systems could vary depending on where a company is located. For example, the coastal regions tend to be more developed and the ethos of corporate governance and the willingness to introduce new management concepts might be stronger for companies located in these areas. Thus, compensation practices could differ between firms located in more developed regions and firms located in less developed regions.

3   SETTING COMPENSATION

China's Company Law 1993 (as amended in 1999) states that the general shareholders' meeting has the ultimate authority in making major decisions including those that relate to the appointment of directors and senior executives (article 103 of the Company Law). The *Code of Corporate Governance* sets out guidelines and rules about the duties and responsibilities of directors, chairpersons, CEOs, and shareholders. The *Code* states that the controlling shareholder makes a recommendation on the appointment of directors and the shareholders' meeting votes on the recommendation. Since 2003, at least one-third of the directors should be independent and take no part in the day-to-day management of the company. Note, however, that the major shareholder has a strong influence on the appointment of directors, including the independent directors.

The board of directors is responsible for hiring the CEO and the upper echelon of senior management. The compensation of the CEO and chairperson are decided by the board. Some firms have a remuneration committee that recommends compensation and incentive schemes for top management but the final decision is made by the board. The chairperson of the remuneration committee should be an independent director and the majority of the committee members should also be independent directors. Shareholders do not vote on the compensation of the CEO and chairperson. The major shareholder has the capacity to influence top management pay.

Up until the mid-1990s, the pay of the chairperson and CEO was often based on the civil service pay grades. This is because the CEO or chairperson of the listed firm was often the general manager of the firm when it was part of the 100 percent government owned SOE and they were paid a salary according to their seniority on the civil service scale. CEOs' and chairpersons' compensation typically did not have a performance based pay component during this time period.

As the economic reforms unfolded, China recognized the need to move away from a fixed pay scale that depended on the equivalent civil service rate of pay. The state encouraged SOEs to include performance related pay and this slowly took hold (Ministry of Labor 2000). The move away from the civil service pay structure is a natural outcome of the change to a market-based economy and the increased mobility of management. CEOs are no longer automatically recruited from within the firm or from the civil service bureaucracy. The rapid rise of a labor market for top management is witnessed by high CEO turnover. Firth et al. (2006a) report that CEO tenure in China averages about four years. The state has continued to issue directives to encourage listed state controlled firms to relate compensation to performance (SASAC 2003, 2004, 2006a, 2006b, 2010).

Although companies are often reluctant to disclose the different components of salary and bonus pay, there is reason to believe that bonus pay is becoming more prevalent. *The Code of Corporate Governance* states that top management should be selected on the basis of open competition and compensation should include an element based on the firm's performance.

While we argue that there has been a move towards market prices for top management talent during the past decade, we also recognize there is some evidence of performance related pay in SOEs in the 1980s and early 1990s, prior to privatization and corporatization (Groves et al. 1994, 1995; Mengistae and Xu 2004). Survey evidence in Liu and Otsuka (2004) shows that more than 80 percent of respondents claim that their firms have incentive based pay at some level in their work force. Yueh (2004) documents the increased use of variable pay for rank and file workers based on the achievement of meeting pre-specified targets. O'Connor and Deng (2005) discuss the detailed incentive pay structure of sales managers in a Chinese telecom company. Fleisher and Wang (2003) report that incentive pay systems exist in some (non-listed) township cooperative ventures. Thus, there is some evidence of performance related pay from earlier periods, non-listed firms, and from lower levels of the organizational hierarchy.

3.1   Disclosure of Top Management Pay

Listed companies are obliged to disclose the pay of top management. These disclosures, required by the CSRC regulation "Regulations for the Contents and Format of Public Firms' Information Disclosure: Content and Format of Annual Reports", have become more detailed over time. Until 2005, firms were required to disclose the aggregate pay of the three highest paid executives although the names of these people were not disclosed. However, the three highest paid executives would normally include the chairperson, the CEO, and another executive director. From 2005, the compensation of the individual directors and top managers has been disclosed including that of the chairperson and the CEO. Compensation includes salaries and bonuses. Until recently, most firms did not distinguish between salary and bonus in their annual report disclosures and, instead, reported the aggregate pay. Change in total compensation from one year to the next is used as a proxy for change in bonus pay in our empirical tests.

Executive stock options were not allowed in China until 2006. The Company Law explicitly prohibited firms incorporated in mainland China (i.e., excluding Hong Kong and Macau) from issuing employee stock options. Another reason is that share repurchases were not allowed and it is very difficult to get approval from the CSRC to issue new shares. As a consequence, there was no source of shares for the share option scheme. Since 2006, however, many listed firms have offered stock options to their top executives. Many features of the option schemes are similar to those used in developed countries and the accounting treatment of options (from 2007) accords with international financial reporting standards (IFRS). Thus, the value of the executive stock options is expensed. Chinese firms incorporated and listed on the Stock Exchange of Hong Kong or in foreign countries have been able to issue stock options for some time. Chen et al. (2010) investigate stock options issued by Chinese firms listed in Hong Kong. They conclude that the stock options do not appear to induce better performance. However, based on evidence in Magnan and Li (2009) and Conyon and He (2010), this negative view of options might not transfer to mainland-domiciled firms. Conyon and He concluded that the granting of equity-based pay depends on a firm's performance.

4   SAMPLE AND RESEARCH DESIGN

4.1   Sample

To aid our description of top management pay in China we make use of a comprehensive database covering non-financial companies listed on the Shanghai and Shenzhen stock exchanges over the period 2001 to 2008. We start in 2001 as that is the year that firms were required to publish executive pay information; prior to 2001, some firms did not disclose this information even though they were strongly recommended to do so. We exclude financial firms because they are heavily regulated.[2] This results in omitting just 40 firm-year observations as there are very few listed banks.

---

[2]   The compensations of chairperson and CEOs at financial institutions are very high. The

The data on compensation and company characteristics come from the CSMAR database and annual reports. The CSMAR database is marketed by GTA Corporation, one of the largest and most established data vendors of security prices and accounting data in China. Our sample is 7,580 firm-year observations. The CSMAR database has missing values for compensation for many firms in 2001. Thereafter, the coverage of listed firms is very high.

4.2 Research Design

We use regression models to test the determinants of management pay. Our basic model is a regression of compensation on a selection of independent variables. The model builds on prior China-based research (Firth et al. 2006a, 2007; Kato and Long 2006; Li et al. 2007). The model is:

$$\text{LnCOMP} = \beta_0 + \beta_1\text{RET(or ROA)} + \beta_2\text{SDRET(or SDROA)} + \beta_3\text{LnBoard} + \beta_4\text{IndDir}$$
$$+ \beta_5\text{DUAL} + \beta_6\text{Private} + \beta_7\text{LocalGov} + \beta_8\text{LnAssets} + \beta_9\text{LnCost} + \beta_{10}\text{LnAGE}$$
$$+ \beta_{11}\text{DA} + \beta_{12}\text{MB} + \beta_{13}\text{DirHold} + \beta_{14}\text{FOREIGN} + \beta\text{IND} + \beta\text{YEAR} \qquad (19.1)$$

Compensation is the log of the average pay of the top three executives (i.e., the aggregate pay of the three highest paid earners divided by three). The independent variables include those used in previous studies in developed countries as well as some that relate specifically to the China setting.

We use stock returns (RET) and return on assets (ROA) as measures of performance.[3] Risk is measured as the standard deviation of stock returns (SDRET) and standard deviation of return on assets (SDROA). There are arguments for risk having positive and negative associations with compensation and prior empirical research in the U.S. has reported mixed findings (Core et al. 2003; Prendergast 2002a, 2002b). Log of board size (LnBoard), the proportion of independent directors (IndDir), duality of chairperson and CEO (DUAL), and directors' shareholdings (DirHold) are included as governance variables. Directors with high shareholdings may be emboldened in the boardroom and have an even greater influence on the decisions regarding top management pay. Log of total assets (LnAssets) is our measure of a firm's size. Firm size is theoretically and empirically linked to top management pay (Gabaix and Landier 2008). The firm's market to book ratio (MB) is used to capture growth opportunities. If firms with high growth are more complex to manage then there will be a demand for better qualified managers who will receive higher compensation (Smith and Watts 1992; Core et al. 1999). Moreover, the Chinese government stresses the need for growth and consequently managers of high growth firms may be rewarded for growth. Leverage (DA) is total debt divided by total assets. Leverage can have an effect on management pay (Hernan 2007). LnAGE is added as a control for a firm's age.

---

government, via the Ministry of Finance, has recently ordered that the compensation at finance companies be cut (SCMP 2010). Financial firms (banks, insurance, securities brokers) are usually majority owned by the state.

[3]   In supplementary tests we use return on sales as an alternative measure of performance. The results are similar to those for ROA and so we do not discuss them further.

We include three ownership variables in our regression equation. Private is a dummy variable that is coded one (1) if the firm's major investor is a private individual or entity. In many cases, the private dominant shareholder is the CEO or chairperson and they could either pay themselves high compensation or, alternatively, they may pay themselves low cash compensation so as to avoid negative publicity or to set an example to others (Cheng and Firth 2006). LocalGov is a dummy variable that is coded one if a firm is controlled by the local government. This allows us to distinguish between central government control and local government control. Some firms have foreign shareholders and we control for this. Foreign is a dummy variable set equal to one (1) if a foreign shareholder is one of the top ten shareholders in the firm. Foreign shareholders may demand better qualified managers who will have a higher equilibrium wage. We include a variable (LnCost) which represents the cost of living for the city or region where the firm is located. The cost of living for an average family in a specific city or region is taken from the official government statistics. A higher cost of living may lead to higher top management pay.

We run the regressions with both contemporaneous and lagged independent variables. The results are very similar for both specifications and so we just report the results using contemporaneously measured independent variables. We do not use panel models because some variables (e.g., ownership) are time invariant and their impact will wash-out in panel models. We use robust standard errors to correct firm clustering, heterogeneity, and autocorrelation (Petersen 2009).

To examine the relation between pay and performance in more detail, we follow Murphy (1999) and calculate sensitivities and elasticities. The forms of the models are:

$$\Delta COMP = \beta_0 + \beta_1 \Delta PERF \qquad (19.2)$$

$$\Delta LnCOMP = \beta_0 + \beta_1 \Delta LnPERF \qquad (19.3)$$

Δ denotes change and Ln is the log transformation. Equation (19.2) examines sensitivities while equation (19.3) measures elasticities. Firm performance (PERF) is shareholders' wealth (SW) or operating income (OI).

To examine whether there are differences across more and less developed regions we make use of a development index constructed by China's National Economic Research Institute (NERI). The index captures the following items: (1) the relations between government and markets, such as the role of markets in allocating resources and enterprise burden in addition to normal taxes; (2) the development of non-state business, such as the ratio of industrial output by the private sector to total industrial output; (3) development of product markets, including considerations such as regional trade barriers; (4) development of factor markets such as FDI and mobility of labor; and (5) development of market intermediaries and the legal environment (e.g., the protection of property rights). A high index score signifies a province with a strong and well established market development (good law enforcement, strong institutional investors, etc.). Fan and Wang (2003) give an extensive description of the index.

Based on the NERI index, we call a province with an above-median score a "more developed region" and, in supplementary tests, firms in these provinces are examined separately from firms in provinces with below-median market development scores ("less developed region").

5   RESULTS

5.1   Summary Statistics

Tables 19.1 and 19.2 and Figures 19.1 and 19.2 (see Appendix) show the basic statistics on top executive pay in China's listed firms. Pay is the aggregate of salary, bonus, pension contributions, and stock option expenses. Table 19.1, Panel A, shows the aggregate pay of the three highest paid executive directors for each year from 2001 to 2008. The numbers are in renminbi (RMB), which is the Chinese currency.[4] It is quite clear that there has been a very large increase in mean and median pay, with compound growth rates of 23 percent and 24 percent, respectively. The mean pay of the three highest paid managers in 2008 is ¥966,760 (i.e., ¥322,253 per person), which is 447 percent higher than in 2001. The standard deviations in Table 19.1, Panel A also show that there is a wide variability in pay across firms. Figure 19.1, which shows a graph of the mean pay for each year, vividly illustrates the strong growth in compensation.

From 2005 onwards, firms also disclose the individual pay of the chairperson and the CEO. Note that in China the chairperson is normally different from the CEO. Chairpersons in China's companies are usually executive positions and they are the highest point on the management hierarchy (higher than the CEO). Table 19.1, Panel B, shows the summary statistics of the chairperson's and CEO's pay. The median chairperson's pay in 2008 is ¥316,600, which is equivalent to $46,814 U.S. (using the current exchange rate). The maximum pay is ¥72,370,000 (equivalent to $10,721,481 U.S.). Clearly, executive pay in China is just a small fraction of the top management compensation in U.S. firms and other developed countries' firms.[5] In 2005, the chairperson's compensation is about six times higher than a firm's average workers' pay (Firth et al. 2010) and the comparable figure for 2008 is about eight. This relative pay of the chairperson/CEO to the average worker is much lower than in the U.S. (Kim and Lu 2009), although it is something the Chinese government is still very concerned about. The CEO's compensation is similar to that of the chairperson. When comparing Panel A with Panel B it is clear that the chairperson and the CEO are the two highest paid executives in Chinese listed firms.

Table 19.1, Panel C, shows the chairperson and CEO's shareholdings. The mean shareholding of 5.80 percent (for the chairperson in 2008) compares with a median of 0.03 percent. So, for the majority of firms, the chairman's shareholdings are negligible. Nevertheless, there has been a growth in shareholdings over time. The CEO's shareholding is usually smaller than the chairperson's shareholding.

As discussed earlier, in section 2.1, Chinese listed firms have distinct ownership features and the different types of major shareholders could have an influence on top executive pay. To examine this question, we present top management pay by the type of owner

---

[4]   At the end of 2010, the exchange rate was ¥6.75 per one U.S. dollar. During most of our sample period, the exchange rate was closer to ¥8 per one U.S. dollar. The exchange rate is set by the Chinese government. The RMB is not a freely convertible currency. The RMB is also known as the yuan (¥).
[5]   As a comparison, the average pay of CEOs in the U.S. (S&P 1500 firms) is about $1,400,000 (cash compensation) and $3,600,000 (cash and stock-based compensation).

(Table 19.2). The three ownership types are privately owned (the largest owner is a private individual or non-state company), central government (administered by SAMBs), and local government. The sample size by year for each type of owner is shown in Panel A. The differences in aggregate pay of the three highest paid directors across the three ownership types are quite small (Panel B). There is no evidence that privately owned firms pay more than central or local government controlled firms. Panel C shows similar evidence for chairpersons and CEOs; that is, there is no clear evidence that privately owned firms pay more to their top executives. Figure 19.2 shows the mean pay by year. Pay increases over time for all three types of firm.

We show the average chairperson and CEO stockholdings across ownership type in Table 19.2, Panel D. This shows quite clearly that the chairperson and CEO have higher shareholdings in privately controlled listed firms. In many cases, the chairperson or CEO is the controlling shareholder (or is a member of the family of the private controlling shareholder). Chairperson and CEO shareholdings in state controlled firms are very low.

Table 19.3 and Figure 19.3 (see Appendix) show the pay of the three highest paid directors by the region where the firm is located. Here we use pay data from 2001 to 2008. Pay is highest in the more developed cities and provinces. For example, pay is highest in Guangdong (Guangdong is the province that adjoins Hong Kong), followed by Zhejiang (located next to Shanghai), Beijing, and Shanghai. The higher cost of living and the higher average workers' pay in these places may be used to justify the higher top management pay. Table 19.4 and Figure 19.4 (see Appendix) show the pay of the three highest paid directors by industry. There are large differences in pay across industries and for this reason we add industry controls to our regression models.

Table 19.5 (see Appendix) shows descriptive statistics of the variables used in the regressions. The average compensation is ¥214,300 (this is the pay of the three highest paid directors divided by three). SW, the market capitalization of equity, has a mean value of 3.97 billion RMB. The mean operating income, OI, is 171 million RMB. RET has a mean of 10.58 percent but a median of −7.33 percent. Stock returns are highly variable across firms and are volatile over time. ROA is quite small with a mean of 2.74 percent. Although China has very strong economic growth this does not translate to strong corporate profitability or high stock returns. About 87 percent of firms have separate people as chairperson and CEO. Approximately one-third of directors are independent and this is consistent with the minimum threshold specified by the CSRC. The mean board size is 9.8 directors (the median is 9).

The central government controls about 18 percent of firms over the period 2001 to 2008, local government about 52 percent of firms, and a large private investor controls about 29 percent of firms. As discussed earlier, private control has grown over time. Total debt is about 48 percent of total assets. The mean market to book ratio, MB, is quite high at 2.98, which reflects the high growth opportunities of Chinese firms.

5.2   Regression Results

Table 19.6 (see Appendix) shows the regression results for the levels analysis. Panel A refers to the full sample while Panels B and C refer to the firms in the more developed regions and less developed regions, respectively. Compensation is positively and significantly related to both performance measures in all three panels.[6] Similar results have been reported in other studies using China data (Kato and Long 2006; Conyon and He 2010; Firth et al. 2010). However, studies using earlier data found that stock returns were not associated with compensation (Firth et al. 2006b). Risk is negatively related to compensation, and, in the case of stock return risk and the debt ratio, it is statistically significant. As expected, top management pay is higher in large firms. Also as expected, firms located in high labor cost regions pay higher top executive compensation. Growth (MB) has a positive relation with pay.

Several board variables are significant.[7] Firms with large boards pay higher compensation. There is some evidence that firms where the chairperson doubles as the CEO have lower compensation. Here, the dual chairperson/CEO may have anticipated criticism of high pay by deliberately receiving lower compensation. Firms with high director shareholdings pay higher top executive compensation. Directors with large shareholdings have more power and they take advantage of this by awarding themselves higher pay.

Privately controlled firms and local government controlled firms pay higher compensation than central government firms. These firms hire top executives in the labor market whereas firms controlled by the central government tend to hire civil service bureaucrats who have lower pay. There is some evidence that foreign invested firms pay their top executives more. The foreign investors pressure firms to hire very well-qualified top managers who, in turn, demand higher compensation.

In untabulated sensitivity tests, we repeat regression equation (19.1) for (i) the years 2001 to 2004 and 2005 to 2008 and (ii) the chairperson and CEO compensation for 2005 to 2008. From 2005, firms had to show the compensation paid to named individuals. This increased disclosure could have an impact on the way top executives are remunerated. However, we find that the regression results for the 2001–2004 sample are similar to the results for the 2005–2008 samples. Thus, increased compensation disclosures have no discernible impact on the way top managers are paid. The regression results for the chairperson and the CEO regressions are both similar to those for the average director shown in Table 19.6. However, the R-square is higher for the CEO regression.

Panels B and C show similar results for firms located in the more developed and less developed regions. Thus, the economic and institutional development of a region has little impact on the way top executives are paid.

5.3 Pay–Performance Sensitivities and Elasticities

Table 19.6 shows that profitability and stock returns are important determinants of the compensation levels. To obtain more insights into the pay–performance relation we follow Murphy (1999) and calculate pay–performance sensitivities and pay–performance

---

[6] We arrive at similar conclusions when we use industry-adjusted performance measures. To arrive at industry-adjusted numbers we subtract the industry-year median ROA or RET from the firm's ROA or RET.

[7] We also test other governance variables (e.g., the existence of a remuneration committee and its make-up). These other governance variables are not significant.

elasticities. In the pay–performance sensitivity analyses we regress change in compensation (ΔCOMP) for a 1000 RMB change in shareholder wealth (ΔSW) or a 1000 RMB change in operating income (ΔOI). Shareholder wealth is the market capitalization of the equity shares. Operating income is pretax profit from core operations.

Table 19.7 (see Appendix), Panel A, shows the pay–performance sensitivities. ΔSW and ΔOI have positive and significant coefficients. As ΔCOMP is in thousands and ΔSW is in billions, we interpret the coefficient of 2.5417 on ΔSW (in Panel A1, column 1) as implying the top manager receives an additional 0.00254 RMB in pay for a 1000 RMB increase in shareholder wealth. This compares with a sensitivity of $0.0138 per $1000 increase in shareholders' wealth in the U.S. in the 1990s (Murphy 1999). Thus the pay–performance sensitivity is much lower in China. Change in pay is also sensitive to changes in operating profit (ΔOI). A 1000 RMB increase in operating profit leads to an increase of 0.0389 RMB in the top manager's compensation (ΔOI is in millions). Sensitivities are lower and less significant for firms in less developed provinces.

We add ownership variables, Private and LocalGov, to see if they have an impact on the sensitivities and elasticities. As discussed earlier, there are arguments for and against a privately controlled firm using performance-based pay systems. The results show that the ownership interactions are not significant. Thus, there is no evidence that private firms are more likely to use performance (change in shareholder wealth and change in operating income) in determining pay.[8]

Panels A2 and A3 show the results from the analyses conducted on firms located in more developed and less developed regions. The performance sensitivities are higher for firms in more developed provinces. This result seems to be attributable to the central government controlled firms in the less developed provinces. In contrast, private and local government controlled firms appear to have similar shareholder wealth-based sensitivities as firms in more developed regions.

Table 19.7 Panel B shows the elasticities. The coefficients on ΔLnSW and ΔLnOI are positive and significant. A one percent increase in shareholders' wealth leads to a .1338 percent increase in top executive compensation, while a one percent increase in operating income leads to a .0253 percent increase in pay. The shareholder wealth elasticities are significant in Panels B2 and B3, while the operating income elasticities are significant in Panel B2.

In untabulated sensitivity tests we find that the results do not differ significantly from the earlier period (2001 to 2004) to the later period (2005 to 2008). Thus, more detailed disclosures of who received what pay do not have a significant effect on pay–performance sensitivities and elasticities. Separate analyses of chairperson and CEO pay–performance sensitivities and elasticities yield results that are similar to those shown in Table 19.7.

---

[8]   Ke at al. (2012) find that different types of state controlled firms (those incorporated inside China and those incorporated outside) have similar pay–performance sensitivities. Thus, the legal domicile of a firm does not seem to matter for state controlled firms.

5.4 Perquisites

Another form of compensation is perquisites where managers receive the personal use of company cars, excessive entertainment and travel allowances, housing and education benefits. While some easily identifiable benefits such as housing and children's education allowances should be added to compensation, other perquisites are more difficult to identify and they are not added to compensation. For example, distinguishing between personal and work use of cars, travel, and entertainment is very difficult. Some preliminary studies have been conducted but they have mixed results. Firth et al. (2010) found no relation between perquisite consumption and a firm's performance. In contrast, Adithipyangkul et al. (2011) found a positive relation between perks and performance.

6 CONCLUDING REMARKS

There is a large literature on the determinants of top management compensation. However, most of the empirical evidence comes from the U.S. and some other developed countries. In contrast, there is a dearth of information on executive compensation in emerging economies. We hope our chapter helps fill this void in the literature.

The economic reforms in China have borrowed what are perceived as best management practices from developed countries. This extends to top executive pay. Pay levels have grown rapidly and there is an embryonic labor market for managers. The determinants of executive compensation mirror those in the U.S. although on a much smaller scale. For example, pay is related to economic performance and there are positive pay–performance sensitivities and elasticities.

Our review is a first step in understanding top level compensation in China's firms. More research is needed to gain a deeper knowledge of pay incentive schemes. Some of this future research will require data that we currently do not have. For example, companies' disclosure of stock option grants and stock appreciation rights is brief and lacks consistency across firms. Hopefully, there will be improved compensation disclosures in the future that will allow us greater insights into top management pay in China.

REFERENCES

Adithipyangkul, P., I. Alon, and T. Zhang. 2011. Executive perks: Compensation and corporate performance in China. Asia-Pacific Journal of Management 28 (2), 401–25.

Cadbury, A. 1992. *Report of the Committee on the Financial Aspects of Corporate Governance*. Gee Publishing, London.

Cao J., X. Pan, and G. Tian. 2011. Disproportional ownership structure and pay–performance relationship: Evidence from China's listed firms. Journal of Corporate Finance 17, 818–33.

Cao, L. 2000. Chinese privatization: Between plan and market. Law and Contemporary Problems 63 (4), 13–62.

Chen, G. M., M. Firth, and O. M. Rui. 2006. Have China's enterprise reforms led to improved efficiency and profitability? Emerging Markets Review 7, 82–109.

Chen, G. M., M. Firth, and L. Xu. 2009. Does the type of ownership control matter? Evidence from China's listed firms. Journal of Banking and Finance 33, 171–81.

Chen, Z., Y. Guan, and B. Ke. 2010. Does managerial stock option compensation increase shareholder value in state-controlled Chinese firms listed in Hong Kong? Working Paper. Pennsylvania State University.

Cheng, S. and M. Firth. 2006. Family ownership, corporate governance, and top executive compensation. Managerial and Decision Economics 27 (7), 549–61.
Conyon, M. and L. He. 2010. Executive compensation in China. Working Paper. ESSEC.
Core, J., R. Holthausen, and D. Larcker. 1999. Corporate governance, chief executive officer compensation, and firm performance. Journal of Financial Economics 51(3), 371–406.
Core, J., R. Holthausen, and D. Larcker. 2003. Executive equity compensation and incentives: A survey. FRBNY Economic Policy Review, 27–50.
Fan, G. and X. Wang. 2003. *NERI Index of Marketization of China's Provinces*. Economic Science Press, Beijing (in Chinese).
Firth, M., P. M. Y. Fung, and O. M. Rui. 2006a. Corporate performance and CEO compensation in China. Journal of Corporate Finance 12, 693–714.
Firth, M., P. M. Y. Fung, and O. M. Rui. 2006b. Firm performance, governance structure, and top management turnover in a transitional economy. Journal of Management Studies 43, 1289–330.
Firth, M., P. M. Y. Fung, and O. M. Rui. 2007. How ownership and corporate governance influence chief executive pay in China's listed firms. Journal of Business Research 60 (7), 776–85.
Firth, M., T. Y. Leung, and O. M. Rui. 2010. Justifying top management pay in a transitional economy. Journal of Empirical Finance 17 (5), 852–66.
Fleisher, B. M. and X. Wang. 2003. Potential residual and relative wages in Chinese township and village enterprises. Journal of Comparative Economics 31, 429–43.
Gabaix, X. and A. Landier. 2008. Why has CEO pay increased so much? Quarterly Journal of Economics 123, 49–100.
Groves, T., Y. Hong, J. McMillan, and B. Naughton. 1994. Autonomy and incentives in Chinese state enterprises. Quarterly Journal of Economics 109, 181–209.
Groves, T., Y. Hong, J. McMillan and B. Naughton. 1995. China's evolving managerial labor market. Journal of Political Economy 103, 873–92.
Hempel, R. 1998. *Committee on Corporate Governance: Final Report*. Gee Publishing, London.
Hermalin, B. E. and M. S. Weisbach. 1998. Endogenously chosen boards of directors and their monitoring of the CEO. American Economic Review 88 (1), 96–118.
Hermalin, B. E. and M. S. Weisbach. 2003. Boards of directors as an endogenously determined institution: A survey of the economic literature. FRBNY Economic Policy Review 9 (1), 7–26.
Hernan, O. M. 2007. Executive compensation and capital structure: The effect of convertible debt and straight debt on CEO pay. Journal of Accounting and Economics 43 (1), 69–93.
Holmström, B. 1979. Moral hazard and observability. Bell Journal of Economics 10 (1), 74–91.
Kato, T. K. and C. Long. 2006. Executive compensation, firm performance, and corporate governance in China: Evidence from firms listed in the Shanghai and Shenzhen Stock Exchanges. Economic Development and Cultural Change 54 (4), 945–83.
Ke, B., O. M. Rui, and W. Yu. 2012. Hong Kong stock listing and the sensitivity of managerial compensation to firm performance in state-controlled Chinese firms. Review of Accounting Studies 17 (1), 166–88.
Kim, E. H. and Y. Lu. 2009. Compensation dispersion, work independence, and performance. Working Paper. University of Michigan.
Li, D., F. Moshirian, P. Nguyen, and L. Tan. 2007. Corporate governance and globalization: An analysis of CEO compensation in China. Research in International Business and Finance 21, 32–79.
Liu, D. and K. Otsuka. 2004. A comparison of management incentives, abilities, and efficiency between SOEs and TVEs: The case of the iron and steel industry in China. Economic Development and Cultural Change 52, 759–80.
Magnan, M. and S. T. Li. 2009. Equity-based compensation: An important determinant for Chinese cross-listed firms. Working Paper. Concordia University.
Mengistae, T. and L. X. C. Xu. 2004. Agency theory and executive compensation: The case of Chinese state-owned enterprises. Journal of Labor Economics 22 (3), 615–37.
Ministry of Labor. 2000. Overview of the current situation of enterprise wage structure in China. Ministry of Labor, Beijing.
Mirrlees, J. A. 1976. Optimal structure of incentives and authority within an organization. Bell Journal of Economics 7 (1), 105–31.
Murphy, K. J. 1999. Executive compensation, in O. Ashenfelter and D. Card (eds), *Handbook of Labor Economics*, vol. 3b, Amsterdam: North Holland, 2485–563.
O'Connor, N. G. and F. J. Deng. 2005. The structuring of formal incentive systems in China: A longitudinal empirical study. Working Paper. The City University of Hong Kong.
OECD. 1999. OECD Principles of Corporate Governance. Organisation for Economic Co-operation and Development (OECD), Paris.
Petersen, M. A. 2009. Estimating standard errors in finance panel datasets: Comparing approaches. Review of Financial Studies 22, 435–80.

Prendergast, C. 2002a. The tenuous trade-off between risk and incentives. Journal of Political Economy 110 (5), 1071–102.

Prendergast, C. 2002b. Uncertainty and incentives. Journal of Labor Economics 20 (2), S115–S137.

Qian, Y. 1998. Government control in corporate governance as a transitional institution: Lessons from China. Working Paper. Stanford University.

SASAC (State-Owned Assets Supervision and Administration Commission of the State Council). 2003. Interim regulations on the evaluation of the SOE affiliated to the central government top executive operating performance. SASAC, Beijing.

SASAC (State-Owned Assets Supervision and Administration Commission of the State Council). 2004. Interim regulations on the administration of top executive pay in SOEs affiliated to the central government. SASAC, Beijing.

SASAC (State-Owned Assets Supervision and Administration Commission of the State Council). 2006a. Interim regulations on the evaluation of the SOE affiliated to the central government top executive operating performance. SASAC, Beijing.

SASAC (State-Owned Assets Supervision and Administration Commission of the State Council). 2006b. Instructions on regulating top executive 'on-job' consumption in SOEs affiliated to central government. SASAC, Beijing.

SASAC (State-Owned Assets Supervision and Administration Commission of the State Council). 2010. Interim regulations on the evaluation of the SOE affiliated to the central government top executive operating performance. SASAC, Beijing.

SCMP. 2010. Beijing clips the wings of high-flying earners. South China Morning Post, April 11.

Smith, C. W. and R. L. Watts. 1992. The investment opportunity set and corporate financing, dividend, and compensation policies. Journal of Financial Economics 32 (3), 263–92.

Wang, Q., T. J. Wong, and L. J. Xia. 2008. State ownership, the institutional environment, and auditor choice: Evidence from China. Journal of Accounting and Economics 46 (1), 112–34.

Yueh, L. Y. 2004. Wage reforms in China during the 1990s. Asian Economic Journal 18, 149–64.

Zhang, W. 1998. China's SOE reform: A corporate governance perspective. Working Paper. Peking University.

APPENDIX

Table 19.1 Pay (¥000) by year

Panel A: Top three directors' pay (¥000) by year

Year	Mean	Median	Min	Max	Standard deviation
2001	216.11	148.80	10.34	1,176.00	198.09
2002	388.14	278.00	13.13	4,800.00	410.96
2003	479.78	341.11	15.00	9,600.00	538.56
2004	575.20	400.00	18.00	10,201.92	649.48
2005	566.01	399.20	10.90	7,150.00	584.95
2006	637.37	462.00	12.00	5,845.00	578.73
2007	823.37	591.00	11.40	10,990.00	803.00
2008	966.76	701.00	9.00	14,677.00	1,101.62

Panel B: Pay of chairperson and CEO (¥000) by year

Year	Chairperson's pay (¥000)					CEO's pay (¥000)				
	Mean	Median	Max	Min	Standard deviation	Mean	Max	Median	Min	Standard deviation
2005	261.28	191.00	2,092.44	0.01	256.57	235.68	2,098.10	182.94	10.50	209.70
2006	282.64	214.00	2,215.59	2.00	266.96	265.48	4,800.00	210.00	2.00	253.60
2007	373.46	280.00	4,850.00	1.00	375.08	357.89	7,105.30	275.50	4.80	381.64
2008	450.25	316.60	7,237.40	5.00	575.90	409.50	6,846.40	304.60	5.00	453.70

Panel C: Shareholding percentage of chairperson and CEO by year

Year	Chairperson's shareholding %					CEO's shareholding %				
	Mean	Median	Max	Min	Standard deviation	Mean	Median	Max	Min	Standard deviation
2005	2.17	0.01	42.89	0.00	7.18	0.75	0.01	25.23	0.00	2.82
2006	2.40	0.01	42.89	0.00	7.32	0.72	0.01	25.65	0.00	2.70
2007	3.51	0.01	49.66	0.00	8.39	0.95	0.01	21.67	0.00	2.96
2008	5.80	0.03	63.95	0.00	11.60	1.45	0.01	28.46	0.00	4.01

Table 19.2 Pay (¥000) by year and by type of firm

Panel A: Sample sizes by year and by type of control

Year	Privately owned	Central government	Local government
2001	73	40	142
2002	219	148	448
2003	235	160	509
2004	258	168	525
2005	309	195	589
2006	325	213	591
2007	375	229	577
2008	431	241	580

Panel B: Top three directors' pay (¥000) by year and type of firm

Year	Privately owned			Central government			Local government		
	Mean	Median	Standard deviation	Mean	Median	Standard deviat:on	Mean	Median	Standard deviation
2001	205.58	136.50	198.23	219.13	136.23	213.76	220.66	153.75	194.69
2002	407.00	246.92	572.69	376.79	307.00	330.82	382.68	281.50	333.70
2003	517.15	317.00	783.02	494.67	377.00	425.41	457.84	337.00	418.70
2004	623.33	412.85	858.09	589.40	402.58	650.65	546.99	400.00	516.42
2005	615.91	450.00	606.30	519.26	387.00	627.92	555.31	393.40	557.36
2006	665.50	500.00	602.38	614.44	450.00	652.05	630.16	450.00	536.30
2007	796.02	604.00	847.51	789.67	552.00	835.98	854.52	600.00	758.97
2008	976.39	728.60	1,099.05	897.87	642.00	935.88	988.23	714.20	1,165.94

Table 19.2 (continued)

Panel C: Pay of chairperson and CEO (¥000) by year and type of firm

	Year	Privately owned			Central government			Local government		
		Mean	Median	Standard deviation	Mean	Median	Standard deviation	Mean	Median	Standard deviation
Chairperson	2005	281.12	216.00	278.75	204.16	150.00	176.04	260.65	198.55	254.77
	2006	301.16	230.00	300.00	199.61	156.00	176.54	288.08	220.00	256.09
	2007	368.43	274.50	414.50	335.88	279.00	308.38	385.97	300.00	355.07
	2008	436.21	300.00	568.38	459.17	315.00	485.17	461.91	340.00	606.30
CEO	2005	236.08	177.00	230.01	251.29	210.00	176.49	230.36	180.00	208.99
	2006	246.06	200.00	207.89	336.26	250.60	406.52	250.39	200.00	193.34
	2007	324.06	239.40	337.32	446.15	314.90	607.83	343.57	276.00	271.19
	2008	369.91	255.50	401.08	479.49	360.00	570.94	406.11	305.00	427.42

Panel D: Shareholding percentage of chairperson and CEO by year and type of firm

	Year	Privately owned			Central government			Local government		
		Mean	Median	Standard deviation	Mean	Median	Standard deviation	Mean	Median	Standard deviation
Chairperson	2005	7.15%	0.05%	11.83%	0.10%	0.00%	0.40%	0.18%	0.01%	1.63%
	2006	6.79%	0.08%	11.22%	0.12%	0.00%	0.46%	0.19%	0.01%	1.69%
	2007	8.70%	2.16%	11.63%	0.09%	0.00%	0.40%	0.36%	0.01%	2.22%
	2008	12.61%	6.86%	14.67%	0.18%	0.01%	0.46%	0.42%	0.01%	2.17%
CEO	2005	2.61%	0.02%	4.92%	0.15%	0.00%	0.76%	0.03%	0.00%	0.20%
	2006	2.53%	0.04%	4.70%	0.13%	0.00%	0.65%	0.03%	0.01%	0.17%
	2007	2.81%	0.29%	4.66%	0.13%	0.00%	0.66%	0.03%	0.00%	0.16%
	2008	3.28%	0.36%	5.32%	1.00%	0.01%	4.42%	0.07%	0.01%	0.24%

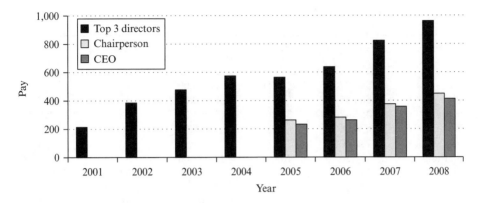

Figure 19.1   Pay (¥000) by year (2001–2008)

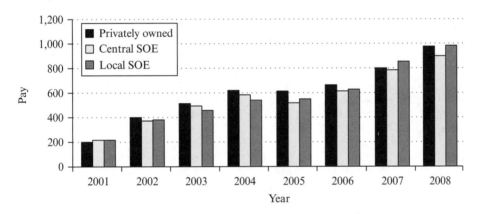

Figure 19.2   Pay (¥000) by year (2001–2008) and by type of firm

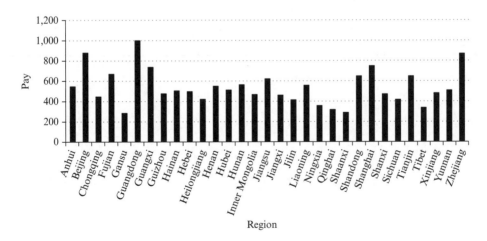

Figure 19.3   Top three directors' pay (¥000) by region

Table 19.3   Top three directors' pay (¥000) by region

Region	Mean	Median	Max	Min	Standard deviation
Anhui	544.97	359.50	2,358.00	17.10	492.87
Beijing	885.45	557.35	6,380.00	35.13	937.17
Chongqing	454.42	359.61	1,954.28	12.00	398.26
Fujian	674.08	416.80	3,833.80	46.92	636.26
Gansu	288.40	232.69	1,224.50	10.90	234.14
Guangdong	997.20	703.58	14,677.00	32.00	1,238.28
Guangxi	741.45	527.20	6,418.00	34.65	858.15
Guizhou	477.59	306.60	2,740.00	21.40	509.08
Hainan	509.70	384.70	2,593.52	28.00	464.55
Hebei	500.61	320.00	3,015.40	35.40	533.25
Heilongjiang	426.62	241.00	2,495.10	32.40	454.16
Henan	558.87	370.00	3,480.00	9.00	596.02
Hubei	520.29	380.00	11,191.00	23.10	691.92
Hunan	571.34	390.00	3,357.50	15.00	498.86
Inner Mongolia	473.80	251.60	4,970.00	26.00	633.48
Jiangsu	628.18	480.00	5,223.40	10.34	551.56
Jiangxi	469.50	323.00	3,551.40	12.00	552.60
Jilin	421.88	287.15	2,375.10	15.00	452.08
Liaoning	563.53	378.20	5,180.00	14.28	655.79
Ningxia	366.47	239.38	2,173.00	72.29	381.23
Qinghai	326.78	180.40	1,743.80	11.40	359.24
Shaanxi	298.62	237.60	1,016.70	56.00	191.69
Shandong	656.32	414.33	7,712.30	13.13	755.35
Shanghai	756.83	594.00	8,142.20	30.00	627.51
Shanxi	480.53	300.00	3,210.00	20.00	512.18
Sichuan	426.27	281.00	2,380.00	29.78	392.29
Tianjin	658.96	409.45	6,145.70	31.40	831.63
Tibet	344.82	273.30	880.00	140.00	191.98
Xinjiang	490.62	317.00	11,044.90	89.95	937.31
Yunnan	518.43	403.20	1,945.70	23.00	392.00
Zhejiang	882.18	676.50	4,230.00	75.00	689.14

Table 19.4 *Top three directors' pay (¥000) by industry*

Industry	Mean	Median	Max	Min	Standard deviation
Agriculture	394.87	303.20	2,368.40	45.60	322.74
Mining	645.63	497.05	3,260.00	53.40	528.64
Food and beverage	553.72	357.73	3,075.50	18.00	550.56
Textile and apparel	566.59	365.80	7,712.30	15.07	710.56
Furniture	533.52	517.20	1,053.10	108.00	305.42
Paper making and printing	633.30	399.60	5,251.00	12.00	802.10
Petroleum, chemicals and plastics	501.22	341.40	4,300.00	10.34	499.94
Electronics	800.05	645.00	5,223.40	21.40	734.12
Metal	583.72	370.00	7,105.30	10.90	686.20
Machinery and equipment	642.57	406.10	14,050.00	12.00	948.50
Medicine and biological products	710.29	501.90	11,191.00	11.40	796.65
Other manufacturing industries	521.04	350.00	1,874.50	15.00	414.80
Power, gas and water	559.15	456.00	2,495.10	24.97	410.02
Architecture	710.75	459.30	2,630.00	65.00	628.31
Transportation	711.72	468.00	6,145.70	28.00	732.63
Information technology	681.50	477.90	5,337.52	25.00	683.04
Retail	752.53	500.00	5,180.00	9.00	693.85
Real estate	1,040.94	648.00	14,677.00	30.00	1,361.20
Hotels and tourism	780.34	568.60	5,305.38	84.00	784.19
Communication	613.53	485.20	2,272.90	100.00	469.68
Conglomerates	646.00	480.00	4,150.00	15.00	538.02

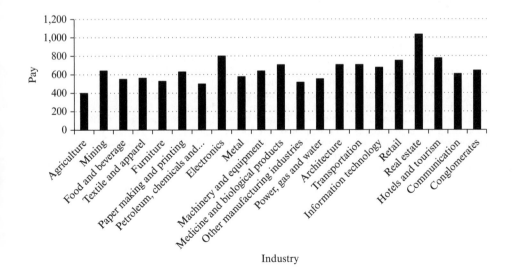

Figure 19.4 *Top three directors' pay (¥000) by industry*

Table 19.5   Descriptive statistics

	Mean	Median	Max	Min	Standard deviation
Comp(000)	214.3	145.1	4892.3	3.0	246.5
ΔComp(000)	30.3	12.3	3777.5	−4696.7	159.1
SW (billion)	3.9745	1.8342	332.4645	0.1995	9.9029
ΔSW (billion)	0.05	0.20	227.4	268.5	9.30
OI (billion)	0.1710	0.0506	23.32	−11.0712	0.7246
ΔOI	0.0098	0.0043	4.4924	−16.0641	0.3902
Net Income (million)	137.50	43.493	15,203.0	−9,260.29	544.582
RET	0.1058	−0.0733	5.9081	−1.0000	0.7012
SDRET	0.0312	0.0287	0.6977	0.0003	0.0157
ROA	0.0274	0.0284	1.7563	−0.8978	0.0695
SDROA	0.0337	0.0255	1.6528	0.0000	0.0529
Age	8.8401	9.0000	18	1	5.147
Dual	0.867	1			
Board	9.8317	9.0000	19.0000	4.0000	2.1495
IndRat	0.3226	0.3333	0.5000	0.0000	0.0824
DirHold	0.0120	0.0000	0.6748	0.0000	0.0639
Central Control (SAMB)	0.184	0			
LocalGov	0.523	1			
Private	0.293	0			
Foreign	0.0810	0			
Asset (billion)	3.3667	1.6566	368.3750	0.0768	8.0649
ΔAsset (billion)	0.4214	0.1140	19.7726	−8.8792	1.4030
DA	0.4805	0.4984	0.7992	0.0091	0.1699
MB	2.9842	2.1846	51.1014	0.3745	2.5901

Note: Comp is annual compensation (¥ 000) of the three highest paid directors divided by three. ΔCOMP is the change in average annual compensation of the three highest paid directors from one year to the next. SW (¥ billion) is stockholders' wealth, which is the beginning market capitalization. ΔSW is the change in stockholders' wealth (inclusive of dividends). OI is the operating income of the firm (¥ billion). ΔOI is the change in operating income. Net Income is the net income of the firm (¥ billion). RET is the annual stock return. SDRET is the standard deviation of the daily raw return for the year. ROA is net income divided by total assets. SDROA is the standard deviation of return on assets over five years. Age is the number of years the listed firm has been established. Dual is a dummy variable, which is coded 1 if the chairperson and general manager are different persons and 0 otherwise. Board is the number of board members. IndRat is the ratio of number of independent directors to the number of directors on the board. DirHold is the ratio of director shareholding to total number of outstanding shares. Central Control (SAMB) is a dummy variable, which is coded 1 if the controlling shareholder is the central government and 0 otherwise. LocalGov is a dummy variable, which is coded 1 if the controlling shareholder is the local government and 0 otherwise. Private is a dummy variable, which is coded 1 if the controlling shareholder is a private person or company. Foreign is a dummy variable, which takes the value of 1 if the firm has foreign investors. Asset is the total assets (¥000,000,000). ΔAsset is the change in total assets. DA is the debt to asset ratio. MB is the market to book value of equity.

Table 19.6 Determinants of compensation and relative compensation

	A More and less developed (7580)				B More developed (5244)				C Less developed (2336)			
	Coeff	t-value	Coeff	t-value	Coeff	t-value	Coeff	t-value	Coeff	t-value	Coeff	t-value
Intercept	-2.1107	-3.24	-1.2364	-1.85	-0.7910	-0.97	-0.2189	-0.26	-6.6123	-2.51	-4.7787	-1.84
RET	0.1462	5.07**			0.1204	3.54**			0.1968	3.62**		
SDRET	-3.0343	-3.01**			-3.4039	-2.76**			-2.5171	-1.93		
ROA			2.1663	8.03**			2.1147	6.31**			2.2897	5.91**
SDROA			-0.5485	-1.51			-0.6590	-1.47			-0.2258	-0.48
LnBoard	0.2258	3.22**	0.2161	3.09**	0.2725	3.41**	0.2630	3.27**	0.1711	1.43	0.1624	1.38
IndRat	0.4717	2.24*	0.4187	1.97*	0.4591	1.84	0.4433	1.76	0.5372	1.47	0.3922	1.07
Dual	-0.0885	-2.16*	-0.0884	-2.14*	-0.0512	-1.09	-0.0475	-0.99	-0.1539	-2.07*	-0.1509	-2.11*
Private	0.2584	5.13**	0.2372	4.67**	0.2333	3.95**	0.2130	3.57**	0.3114	3.43**	0.2957	3.27**
LocalGov	0.1584	3.65**	0.1486	3.46**	0.1376	2.70**	0.1304	2.60**	0.2284	3.02**	0.2129	2.83**
LnAsset	0.3538	18.32**	0.3125	15.53**	0.3495	15.27**	0.3112	13.30**	0.3537	9.31**	0.3017	7.85**
LnCost	0.7023	11.75**	0.6754	11.19**	0.5747	7.48**	0.5718	7.39**	1.1757	4.22**	1.0736	3.93**
LnAge	-0.1046	-4.47**	-0.0725	-2.35*	-0.1150	-4.18**	-0.0891	-2.42*	-0.0863	-2.13*	-0.0565	-1.04
DA	-0.2975	-3.18**	-0.0198	-0.20	-0.3764	-3.50**	-0.1105	-0.98	-0.1329	-0.77	0.1582	0.88

Table 19.6 (continued)

	A More and less developed (7580)				B More developed (5244)				C Less developed (2336)			
	Coeff	t-value	Coeff	t-value	Coeff	t-value	Coeff	t-value	Coeff	t-value	Coeff	t-value
MB	0.0131	2.05*	0.0084	1.42	0.0130	1.72	0.0073	1.07	0.0149	1.33	0.0123	1.16
DirHold	0.6774	3.40**	0.9684	4.26**	0.6772	3.15**	0.8976	3.44**	0.4819	1.30	1.2079	3.05**
Foreign	0.1682	2.61**	0.1827	2.89**	0.1226	1.83	0.1406	2.11*	0.6520	3.45**	0.6215	3.55**
Industry and Year Dummies included												
Adj R²	0.3588		0.3784		0.3474		0.3671		0.2950		0.3199	
F-statistics	116.89		121.80		77.28		80.32		27.69		30.02	
p-value	0.00		0.00		0.00		0.00		0.00		0.00	

Notes: LnCOMP is the dependent variable; it is the log value of the average annual compensation of the three highest paid directors. RET is the cumulative daily raw return for the year. SDRET is the standard deviation of the daily raw return for the year. ROA is return on assets. SDROA is the standard deviation of return on assets over five years. LnBoard is the log value of the number of directors on the board. IndRat is the percentage of the number of independent directors to the total number of directors on the board. Dual is a dummy variable, which is coded 1 if the chairperson and general manager are different persons and 0 otherwise. Private is a dummy variable, which is coded 1 if the listed firm is a privately controlled and 0 otherwise. LocalGov is a dummy variable, which is coded 1 if the controlling shareholder is the local government and 0 otherwise. LnAsset is the log value of total assets. LnCost is the log value of the living expenditure level of the province where the firm is located. LnAge is the log value of the number of years the listed firm has been established. DA is the debt to asset ratio. MB is the market to book value of equity. DirHold is the percentage of director shareholdings to total shares outstanding. Foreign is a dummy variable which takes the value of 1 if the firm has foreign investors. t-statistics are computed using robust standard errors.

* for significance at the 0.05 level.
** for significance at the 0.01 level.

410

Table 19.7 Pay and performance sensitivities and elasticities

Panel A: Sensitivities

	A(1) More and less developed (7580)				A(2) More developed (5244)				A(3) Less developed (2336)			
	Coeff (t-value)				Coeff (t-value)				Coeff (t-value)			
Intercept	0.0509 (9.85)	0.0511 (9.78)	0.0485 (8.58)	0.0485 (8.21)	0.0537 (8.35)	0.0537 (8.20)	0.0524 (7.21)	0.0522 (6.69)	0.0447 (5.21)	0.0448 (5.21)	0.0405 (5.05)	0.0402 (5.24)
ΔSW	2.5417 (3.10)**		2.6426 (2.04)*		3.1678 (3.21)**		3.7579 (2.44)*		1.2192 (2.15)*		0.3942 (1.71)	
ΔOI		0.0389 (3.24)**		0.0382 (2.66)**		0.0403 (2.88)**		0.0397 (2.63)**		0.0321 (2.36)*		0.0226 (1.30)
Private			0.0040 (0.88)	0.0035 (0.84)			0.0039 (0.66)	0.0034 (0.63)			0.0015 (0.35)	0.0004 (0.09)
ΔSW*Private			1.4101 (0.60)				0.7579 (0.23)				2.8099 (1.98)*	
ΔOI*Private				−0.0165 (−0.13)				−0.0495 (−0.26)				0.0633 (1.58)
LocalGov			0.0035 (0.94)	0.0030 (0.77)			0.0016 (0.34)	0.0013 (0.25)			0.0068 (1.35)	0.0063 (1.23)
ΔSW*LocalGov			−0.6373 (−0.45)				−1.9740 (−1.21)				2.1370 (2.03)*	
ΔOI*LocalGov				0.0046 (0.25)				0.0100 (0.48)				0.0033 (0.13)

411

Table 19.7 (continued)

Panel A: Sensitivities

	A(1) More and less developed (7580) Coeff (t-value)				A(2) More developed (5244) Coeff (t-value)				A(3) Less developed (2336) Coeff (t-value)			
Industry and Year Dummies included												
Adj R^2	0.0273	0.0143	0.0277	0.0139	0.0326	0.0135	0.0347	0.0136	0.0143	0.0112	0.0192	0.0117
F-statistics	11.62	6.48	9.64	5.46	9.84	4.59	8.54	4.02	2.69	2.32	2.82	2.15
p-value	0.00	0.00	0.00	0.00	0.00	0.00	0.00	0.00	0.00	0.01	0.00	0.00

Panel B: Elasticities

	B1 More and less developed (7580) Coeff (t-value)				B2 More developed (5244) Coeff (t-value)				B3 Less developed (2336) Coeff (t-value)			
Intercept	0.1246	0.1581	0.1150	0.1433	0.1389	0.1586	0.1331	0.1338	0.0970	−0.1812	0.0776	−0.1714
	(10.61)	(9.57)	(7.36)	(7.50)	(10.21)	(9.27)	(7.37)	(6.53)	(4.14)	(−0.87)	(2.38)	(−0.75)
ΔLnSW	0.1338		0.1526		0.1138		0.1358		0.1740		0.1863	
	(9.96)**		(6.64)**		(7.58)**		(5.00)**		(6.88)**		(4.46)**	
ΔLnOI		0.0253		0.0369		0.0220		0.0353		0.3660		0.3551
		(2.22)*		(3.62)**		(1.96)*		(4.06)**		(1.83)		(1.63)
Private			0.0134	−0.1152			0.0125	0.0800			0.0206	−0.3724
			(0.92)	(−0.22)			(0.75)	(0.14)			(0.66)	(−0.32)
ΔLnSW*Private			−0.0530				−0.0671				−0.0146	
			(−1.96)*				(−2.25)*				(−0.26)	

412

	(1)	(2)	(3)	(4)	(5)	(6)	(7)	(8)	(9)	(10)	(11)
ΔLnOI*Private				0.1160				−0.0616			0.3439
				(0.24)				(−0.12)			(0.33)
LocalGov			0.0100	0.0265			0.0039	0.0281		0.0222	0.0511
			(0.76)	(1.28)			(0.25)	(1.41)		(0.86)	(0.13)
ΔLnSW*LocalGov			−0.0032				0.0032			−0.0148	
			(−0.13)				(0.11)			(−0.31)	
ΔLnOI*LocalGov				−0.0264				−0.0294**			−0.0460
				(−1.80)				(−2.47)			(−0.13)
Industry and Year Dummies included											
Adj R^2	0.0203	0.0223	0.0228	0.0200	0.0188	0.0169	0.0201	0.0293	0.0289	0.0278	0.0273
F-statistics	8.78	11.72	9.75	7.38	7.23	5.25	6.33	5.36	4.44	4.31	3.70
p-value	0.00	0.00	0.00	0.00	0.00	0.00	0.00	0.00	0.00	0.00	0.00

Note: The dependent variable in the sensitivities regressions is ΔCOMP. ΔCOMP is the change in average annual compensation of the three highest paid directors from one year to the next. The dependent variable in the elasticities regressions is ΔLnCOMP. ΔLnCOMP is the change in the log of the annual compensation of the three highest paid directors from one year to the next. ΔSW is the change in stockholders' wealth (inclusive of dividends). Stockholders' wealth is the market capitalization. ΔOI is the change in operating income. ΔLnSW is the change in logSW. ΔLnOI is the change in logOI. Private is a dummy variable, which is coded 1 if the listed firm is privately controlled and 0 otherwise. LocalGov is a dummy variable, which is coded 1 if the controlling shareholder is the local government and 0 otherwise. t-statistics are computed using robust standard errors.

*   for significance at the 0.05 level.

**   for significance at the 0.01 level.

20 Executive compensation and pay for performance in China[1]

Martin J. Conyon and Lerong He

1 INTRODUCTION

We investigate executive compensation in China, the world's second largest economy. Relative to Western economies, empirical studies on CEO pay in China are scarce. From the 1990s Chinese firms began the transition process from state owned enterprises (SOEs) to modern enterprises. China has two stock exchanges, the Shanghai and Shenzhen Stock Exchanges. The Shanghai Stock Exchange (SSE) started operation in December, 2000. By the end of December 2009, there were 888 listed companies and a market capitalization of 18,465 billion RMB (or about US$2,715 billion). The Shenzhen Stock Exchange was founded in December, 2001. By the end of December 2009, a total of 830 firms were listed with a market capitalization of 5,928 billion RMB (or about US$872 billion). From an executive pay perspective, there are several important questions to address. Are Chinese executives paid in the same way as Western executives? Are the drivers of executive pay, such as firm performance and size, as important in socialist China as in the West? How does the Chinese state affect the provision of incentives in Chinese firms? To answer these and related questions we review the evidence amassed in the recent extant literature. In addition, we provide some further evidence on the determinants of executive pay in Chinese listed firms.

The institutional context of China is radically different from Western economies. China is a socialist economy and the state continues to play a dominant role in economic activity. This is manifested in the ownership and control of public firms. First, ultimate firm ownership is often in the hands of the state. This facilitates control and influence of the firm's activities. Second, ownership is highly concentrated, such that the single largest shareholder (state or non-state) may own in excess of forty percent of the firm. In addition, since the early 2000s China's regulatory bodies have embarked upon a series of corporate governance reforms, aimed at developing credibility in its capital markets. Against this background, it is not immediately obvious what form an optimal executive compensation should take. As such, a review of the evidence is salient and timely.

We find a number of important results. First, executive compensation, until very recently, was made up of salaries, bonuses and other stipends. Stock options and equity

[1]   Acknowledgements: We would like to thank Peter Cappelli, Ingolf Dittmann, Mahmoud Ezzamel, Simon Peck, William Forbes, Marc Goergen, Luc Renneboog, and David Yermack for comments. We are grateful to participants at the Managerial Compensation conference at Cardiff University (September 2010) and the Academy of Management 2010 conference for suggestions. Financial support from the Center for Human Resources at the Wharton School is gratefully acknowledged.

pay are a phenomenon in China only from 2006 onwards. Second, much of the extant literature finds that executive pay is positively correlated to measures of firm performance. Third, executive compensation is positively correlated to firm size; and the estimated pay elasticity is on a par with those found in Western studies. In this respect, the drivers of Chinese executive pay are similar to Anglo-Saxon governance studies. Fourth, the Chinese state has important influence on the patterns of executive pay. In general, the literature finds that the estimated pay-for-performance relation is weaker in state controlled firms or where there are opportunities for tunneling and rent extraction. We also present some new additional findings showing the pay-for-performance link is weaker in state controlled firms.

The remainder of this chapter is organized as follows. Section 2 provides an overview of the Chinese institutional context. Section 3 provides a review of recent extant studies on Chinese executive pay. Section 4 provides new results on the determinants of executive pay in China. Section 5 offers some conclusions.

2   INSTITUTIONAL CONTEXT

Little is known about executive compensation in China compared to Western economies (Kato and Long, 2006). There are only a handful of prior studies. Investigating Chinese executive pay and incentives is important for at least three reasons. First, China is now the second largest economy in the world, and has experienced several decades of sustained growth. Second, it is important to evaluate whether executive pay contracts are designed to promote managerial incentives, appropriate risk taking, and firm value. Third, given that China is still a socialist economy, it is important to appraise the role of the state in driving executive pay and incentives which ultimately lead to higher levels of value creation.

2.1   Capital Market Reforms

Since the late 1970s China's economy has transformed from a centrally planned system to a more market-oriented one. Reforms have been gradual rather than radical. They include increased autonomy for state-owned enterprises (SOEs), the opening up of the economy to foreign trade and investment, the development of domestic stock markets, and the rapid growth of the private sector. These have led to significant efficiency gains. Since 1978 China's GDP has increased more than tenfold. In 2010 China was the second-largest economy in the world after the USA. China's estimated 2010 GDP, at purchasing power parity, was about US$9.8 trillion. In the same year, China's economy (GDP) grew at about 10 percent.[2]

The China Securities Regulatory Commission (CSRC) regulates China's capital market. There are currently two domestic exchanges: the Shanghai and Shenzhen Stock Exchanges. Markets began trading in the 1990s, and the estimated market value of publicly traded

---

[2]   Source:https://www.cia.gov/library/publications/the-world-factbook/geos/ch.html(retrieved 4 February, 2011).

shares on December 31 2009 was about 24.39 trillion RMB. The value of China's stock market ranks third behind the United States and Japan. China's equity markets have grown significantly over time. In 1992 there were only 53 firms listed on the stock exchanges, but by 2000 there were 1088. The number of firms listed on the domestic exchanges has steadily increased and in 2009 there were a total 1718 firms listed on both stock exchanges.[3] At the same time proceeds from Initial Public Offerings (IPOs) have also increased.[4] Finally, the significance of capital markets reforms is reflected in the fact that the combined market capitalization of the Shanghai and Shenzhen stock market accounted for 73 percent of China's GDP in 2009. This compares to about 45 percent in 2001 and 18 percent in 2005.

2.2   Executive Compensation

Historically, Chinese executives receive only cash salaries, bonuses and stipends. Equity compensation in the form of stock options is rare, and is permissible only since 2006. In addition, Chinese executives receive perks from their companies, but the value of these is frequently difficult to assess. These are the rudiments of Chinese executive pay. In addition, executives may own shares in their own firms. Conyon and He (2011) document that CEOs at about fifty percent of public firms own shares. The notional value of such share ownership, though, is significantly greater than the value of annual cash compensation.

Disclosure of executive pay information is weaker than in many Western economies. The situation is improving with the passage of time, and the deepening market reforms. The China Securities Regulatory Commission (CSRC) regulates the disclosure of executive compensation information in publicly traded firms. Early regulation (pre-2001) did not require public firms to disclose information about executive pay in their annual reports (CSRC, 1998). Some firms did so on a voluntary basis. From 2001 the CSRC required public firms to report the aggregated sum of total compensation for the three highest-paid executives. Firms also had to report the total pay of the three highest-paid board members (including executive board members). The mix of salary, bonus and other remuneration was not divulged. Also, compensation disclosure was not required for each individual separately from 2001 to 2005 (CSRC, 2000, 2002, 2005b). Extant Chinese executive pay studies tend to use data from these periods.

From 2006 onwards publicly traded firms were required to report each individual board member and top management's total compensation separately as the sum of salary, bonus, stipends, and other benefits. Importantly, the CSRC provided a framework to introduce equity incentives at this time. In order to promote better incentives within public companies the CSRC promulgated the Trial Measures for the Administration of Equity Incentive Schemes of Listed Companies on January 1, 2006. Under these measures companies could propose the adoption of equity incentive plans, including restricted

---

[3]   Source: Chinese Securities Regulatory Commission Annual Report, 2009, http://www.csrc.gov.cn/pub/csrc_en/about/annual/201011/P020101105493830315968.pdf.

[4]   An example of the significance of IPOs in China is Agricultural Bank of China (ABC). On August 13, 2010, it completed the world's largest initial public offering. It raised a total of US$22.1 billion. The offering beat the one set by Industrial and Commercial Bank of China in 2006 of US$21.9 billion.

Source: "AgBank IPO officially the world's biggest", Financial Times. 13 August 2010.

stock and stock option plans (CSRC, 2005a, 2007). The total number of shares available for such incentive plans could not exceed ten percent of the total shares outstanding. In addition, independent directors were excluded from participating in such incentive plans. The independent directors gave their opinion on the fairness of such equity plans. Once the board of directors adopted the plan, and providing the CSRC did not object, the firm was able to convene a shareholder meeting to review, and then adopt, the equity plan. Overall, the direction of recent regulatory history suggests more information disclosure about executive pay and a move towards equity-based compensation.

2.3   Corporate Ownership Patterns

China has a highly distinctive pattern of corporate ownership and control, which has important implications for the configuration of executive pay. Two central features of public firm ownership stand out. First, the Chinese state is a major shareowner in many public firms, with stakes exceeding forty or fifty percent. Second, the ownership of shares is highly concentrated. Both of these facts contrast markedly with standard diffuse patterns of ownership in Anglo-Saxon economies.

There are three major classes of share ownership in China. First, the Chinese state owns shares, held through government agencies. Second, legal entities can own shares, held through state controlled legal persons, or privately controlled legal persons. Finally, individuals, institutions, and private businesses can own shares privately. When a state-owned-enterprise (SOE) is listed, only a small proportion of equity is sold to private investors in the IPO process. The state and parent SOEs still retain sufficient shares in the form of state shares or legal person shares to retain voting control, which typically accounts for two thirds of total shares outstanding (Qian, 1995). State shares and legal entity shares are (generally) non-tradable. There are circumstances when they can be exchanged, but the process is complex (Xu, 2004). Reforms began in 2005 to make all shares tradable. In addition, a Chinese company may also issue three types of tradable shares. Tradable "A" shares are listed on the two domestic exchanges (Shanghai and Shenzhen) to domestic investors and denominated in renminbi (RMB). "B" shares are issued to foreign investors and traded in either US dollars or Hong Kong dollars. Finally, a Chinese firm may also trade on the Hong Kong Stock Exchange and issue so called "H" share. Most Chinese executive pay studies deal with performance arising from the "A" shares traded on domestic stock exchanges.

The ownership of Chinese publicly traded firms is also highly concentrated. In most firms there is a single dominant shareholder whose large share ownership gives considerable power and influence over the way the firm is run. This is especially the case regarding the appointment and compensation of the CEO or the board. Typically, the largest shareholder owns about 43 percent of the firm's shares, the second largest about 9 percent, and the third largest about 4 percent. These figures are based on the data we report below, and they are consistent with those produced by Xu (2004).[5] China's ownership pattern

---

[5]   Xu (2004) finds the largest shareholder percentage is 46.23 percent, the second largest is 6.96 percent and the third largest is 2.85 percent. This is based on a study of Chinese firm ownership from 1996 to 2001.

stands in stark contrast to the US, where low concentration and ownership diffusion is the norm. It is rare for investors to own more than 10 percent of common equity in Anglo-Saxon firms.

Concentrated ownership has important consequences for the pattern of executive compensation. Agency theory predicts that when ownership is dispersed, individual owners have weak incentives to invest in monitoring and to exert influence over key corporate decisions (Fama and Jensen, 1983; Jensen and Meckling, 1976). The free-rider problem may be mitigated by concentrated share ownership by providing owners the incentives to monitor the potential entrenchment of insiders (Demsetz and Lehn, 1985; Jensen and Warner, 1988). Core et al. (1999) and Shivdasani (1993) thus hypothesize that large share stakes are negatively correlated with CEO compensation. Also, more concentrated ownership may suggest the optimal contract contains fewer financial incentives to motivate the CEO, especially if monitoring and equity incentives are substitutes. This suggests that CEO equity incentives are a decreasing function of ownership concentration. Set against the benefits of concentrated ownership are the costs associated with entrenchment and private benefits of control of a single large shareholder. Large shareholders may expropriate minority shareholders, or promote their own objectives over those of other shareholders. This may occur via tunneling or other rent extraction strategies (La Porta et al., 1998, 2000). The problem of expropriation by controlling shareholders is extremely severe in Chinese stock markets because of a more primitive disclosure system and weak corporate governance mechanisms (Ding et al., 2007). Another concern is that when the state is the firm's ultimate owner the CEO is more likely to be a bureaucrat or care about political actions (Firth et al., 2007). State controlled firms might pursue political or multiple objectives, such as employment growth, rather than profit maximization. Privately owned firms, therefore, are expected to set optimal contracts with greater pay-for-performance incentives.

2.4   The Board of Directors

China operates a two-tier board system consisting of a main board of directors and a supervisory board. Traditionally, the state has huge influence on the appointment of board and supervisory board members. An enduring concern is that state-appointed bureaucrats are ineffective in monitoring management (Fan et al., 2007; Hu et al, 2010). In response to shareholder pressure, and deepening market reforms, China's listed firms have increasingly adopted Anglo-Saxon style internal corporate governance structures (Allen, et al., 2005; Chen et al., 2010a; Jingu, 2007).

An important example of this is the Code of Corporate Governance issued by the China Securities Regulatory Commission (CSRC, 2002). This code required firms to add independent directors to the main board of directors and separate the posts of CEO and chairperson. The expectation is that one-third of the board should comprise independent directors. The Code defines director independence thus: "The independent director shall be independent from the listed company that employs them and the company's major shareholders." According to this definition, a non-executive director may not necessarily be independent. A non-executive director does not hold a position in the listed firm but may hold a position in the parent company or major shareholder of the firm. If these regulatory pressures reflect a tendency for increased quality of corporate governance, we would expect to observe different patterns of executive compensation and incentives. In short, we expect the pay-for-performance link to be stronger in firms that have a greater proportion of independent directors on the board.

3 PREVIOUS STUDIES ON CHINESE EXECUTIVE PAY

There are comparatively few studies investigating the determinants of CEO pay using Chinese data. Two fundamental research avenues have been pursued. First, a central focus is on the link between pay and performance. The connection is frequently interpreted as a measure of CEOs' incentives to promote firm value. Generally, Chinese studies have shown a positive correlation between pay and performance, although with some caveats. Second, studies focus on the role of the Chinese state. Researchers have investigated whether pay is higher or lower in state controlled firms and whether the connection between pay and performance is weaker in state controlled firms. Generally, studies find that the pay-for-performance sensitivity is weaker in such firms.

3.1 Executive Pay in Mainland Chinese Firms

Most literature on Chinese CEO compensation is built on principal–agent theories (Holmstrom, 1979; Jensen and Meckling, 1976; Mirrlees, 1976). The theoretical model posits a risk-neutral principal who designs an optimal contract for a risk- and effort-averse agent in the presence of a moral hazard problem. The resulting efficient contract is designed to motivate CEO effort (Murphy, 1999). Boards set CEO pay and incentives based on economic factors, the magnitude of agency problems, and monitoring difficulty in order to align shareholder and managerial interests (Core and Guay, 1999; Core et al., 2003; Jensen and Murphy, 1990; Murphy, 1985). Agency theory makes a number of predictions. First, executive pay is positively correlated to firm performance, reflecting CEO effort. It is, however, relatively silent on the functional form of the estimating equation and other types of variables to be included (Murphy, 1999). Holmstrom's (1979) "informativeness" principle is helpful as it predicts that any variable that is informative about CEO effort can be contracted upon. Second, agency theory predicts that the optimal contract is inversely related to CEO risk aversion. Too many incentives impose too high costs on a risk-averse CEO. Third, agency models predict that optimal contracts filter out shocks that are common across agents. Namely, relative performance evaluation should matter.

An early study by Mengistae and Xu (2004) examined CEO pay in approximately 400 Chinese state-owned enterprises in the 1980s using survey data. They find that CEO compensation is much less sensitive to firm performance the greater is the variance in enterprise performance. Indeed, they show the CEO pay sensitivity decreases with the variance of performance. In addition, Mengistae and Xu find that the CEO pay-for-performance sensitivity increases with the marginal productivity of executive action, which in turn has increased significantly in China's state enterprises following a series of state initiated reforms. Finally, they find little evidence of firms using relative performance evaluation criteria in setting executive compensation contracts. Overall, the determinants of CEO pay in China, according to this study at least, look very much like they do in Western firms. Mengistae and Xu (2004) do not examine the relation between pay and stock market performance because their study is based on previously State Owned Enterprises (SOEs). Neither does the study examine directly the effects of concentrated ownership structure on the determination of pay, nor how internal governance structures such as independent directors influence executive pay. However, it does control for firm and managerial fixed effects. This is important because, especially in China, there may be significant heterogeneity in managerial and firm quality that is not measured by the right hand side model variables.

Kato and Long (2006) investigated a sample of 937 publicly traded firms in China from 1998 to 2002. The study augments Mengistae and Xu (2004) in important respects. First, they use data from a later period after China's market reforms had been initiated. Second, they study listed firms, rather than State Owned Enterprise (SOEs). The authors measure compensation as the average pay of the top three executives. It includes cash and bonus pay, but excludes stock options as these are not used in this period. There are several key findings. First, they find that executive cash compensation is positively related to firm performance. The authors perform a regression of the change in the logarithm of compensation on the change in the logarithm of shareholder wealth: the elasticity approach to retrieving the pay-for-performance sensitivity. Implicitly this approach filters out firm fixed effects in the corresponding underlying levels model. Second, they find evidence that the pay-for-performance link is weaker in firms with a high concentration of government ownership. They interact the percentage of company shares owned by the government with shareholder return measures, and find that the sign is negative and significant. The implication is that the pay-for-performance relation is weaker in state controlled firms. The paper does not study the effect of independent directors on the pay-for-performance link, because independent directors are still rare in the study period of 1998 to 2002. The analysis also does not examine the role of CEO share ownership. Although stock options are not issued in this period the firm's CEOs do receive some form of company shares, and the authors note that this may be an important source of incentives.

This study also emphasizes that the role of the state is important in setting pay and incentives (pay-for-performance). Kato and Long (2006) show that state involvement can lead to inefficient executive compensation practices, arising from bureaucratic procedures and rigid institutional structures. They illustrate the complexities of the interactions between various state departments and the need to integrate social objectives with economic determinants of executive pay in China:

> [T]he existing institutional arrangements make it more difficult for state-controlled listed firms to reform. Specifically, the bureaucratic structure used until very recently for managing government shares in listed firms involves at least three separate government agencies. The CCP's Department of Organization (DO), the State Economic and Trade Commission or the Industrial Commission (SETC), and the Ministry of Finance (MOF) were in charge of the personnel, daily operations, and asset management of the listed firms, respectively. Since each agency has its own line of duties and there is not much communication among them, the determination of executive compensation, which is mainly under the authority of the DO, rarely depends on the firm's performance, which is evaluated by the SETC and MOF. Instead, in determining the level of compensation for top executives, the DO uses the compensation level for government officials at the same rank as a reference and makes certain adjustments based on firm size and the executive's education and working experience. Compensation for other executives will then be certain proportions of the top executive's pay level. For instance, the vice president's salary will be 80

per cent of the CEO's salary, and so on. The compensation figures will then be submitted to the board of directors, which will almost always approve them. Although sometimes the board of directors of a listed firm makes recommendations to give bonuses to executives based on good firm performance, these instances are few and far between. (p. 955)

The problems of institutional rigidity and lack of innovation lead to situations where the pay-for-performance is weak in state controlled firms. Despite this, Kato and Long argue that there are forces for positive change via the ongoing economic reforms, but overall pay-setting arrangements are far from ideal.

Firth et al. (2006, 2007) examined a sample of 549 listed firms in China from 1998 to 2000, with a total of 1647 firm-year observations. They estimate the determinants of the level of pay and, in addition, perform regressions of the change in the logarithm of executive pay on the change in performance. As with other studies of this period they use cash compensation of the three highest paid directors. Two main performance measures are used, a market-based measure (shareholder returns) and an accounting-based measure (return on sales). They find that firms with a dominant SOE shareholder relate their CEO's payment to accounting profit, while those controlled by private blockholders or foreign shareholders are more likely to link executive pay with shareholder returns. Firth et al. (2007) also document a stronger pay–accounting performance linkage in firms with a higher proportion of non-executive directors, and a weaker pay–accounting performance linkage in firms with leadership duality. However, none of these results holds when performance is measured using stock returns.

Conyon and He (2011) investigate a period when market reforms have deepened in China, by using a larger set of 1342 firms from 2001 to 2005 with 5928 firm-year observations. They investigate the pay-for-performance relation controlling for management quality via firm fixed effects, the role of ownership structure, and the effect of independent directors on the main board. They find that executive total pay and incentives are positively correlated to the firm's stock market and accounting performance. They show that the effect is robust to firm fixed effects, but the lag performance structure may be important in isolating a robust relationship. Second, they show that the pay-for-performance relation tends to be weaker in firms that are state controlled. Third, there is some evidence that the pay-for-performance relation is stronger in firms that have a greater fraction of independent outside directors on the main board. In addition, they compare executive compensation in China with that of the United States and find that American executives earn about seventeen times more than their Chinese counterparts. The difference is significantly reduced after controlling for the economic determinants of executive pay. They show the same variables determine pay in each country, particularly firm size and performance.

In a recent study Chen et al. (2010a) investigate the determinants of executive pay in a panel of 502 Chinese firms from 2001 to 2006. They find a positive correlation between executive compensation and return on equity, after controlling for firm fixed effects and other economic determinants. They find that executive pay is positively correlated to firm size with an estimated elasticity of around 10 percent to 15 percent. Their study also finds little relation between internal corporate governance variables, such as board independence, and executive pay. They interpret this as evidence that internal control mechanisms are weak and ineffective at controlling excessive managerial pay demands.

In another study Chen et al. (2010b) investigate the determinants of executive compensation from 1999 to 2009. Their data set includes 33,968 individual directors' remuneration over an eleven-year period. They collect 7,518 firm-year observations, and much of the data is available only since about 2005. In contrast to other studies they show cash compensation for each top-three individual executives separately. They test managerial power and tournament theories of executive compensation. They find support for both theories. To operationalize the concept of 'power' they define managerial structural power by the executive's share ownership and prestige power by the executive's education and document that it is significantly positively related to executive pay. Their measure of political power is whether the executive is a Party Secretary and this is positively but weakly related to executive pay. In terms of tournament theory, they find that the number of organization levels is positively related to executive pay and the relationship is convex. The tournament prize is only weakly related to the number of contestants in the tournament and is negatively related to the interaction term between number of contestants and government intervention. Lastly, they find that firm performance is positively related to the pay gap between contestants. The results support tournament models, but the quantitative effects do not seem to be as pronounced as those found in the prior literature using US and UK data.

Ding et al. (2010) study the effects of the size of the supervisory board and its meeting frequency on executive compensation in China's publicly traded firms. Their sample consists of approximately 1350 listed firms in 2005 and 2006. The authors find that: "before the new Corporate Law became effective, supervisory boards did not affect executive compensation, although their role after that became significant; both supervisory board size and meeting frequency affect total executive compensation, and supervisory board size also influences pay–performance sensitivity."

Wang and Xiao (2011) investigate how potential conflicts of interests between controlling shareholders and minority shareholders could affect executive compensation contracts. They use data on Chinese listed companies from 1999 to 2005. Wang and Xiao define controlling shareholders' tunneling activity as the amount of cash transferred from a listed company to the controlling shareholders as disclosed in the footnote of year-end balances of 'Other Receivables'. It is normalized on total assets of listed companies in the same fiscal year. They find that the average value has fallen from 1.47 percent in 1999 to 0.72 percent in 2005. They show that controlling shareholders' tunneling leads to a lower pay-for-performance sensitivity in the executive compensation contract. The results are consistent with other studies that show there is a link between executive pay and performance. They suggest the results imply that "controlling shareholders who obtain private benefits from listed companies have less incentive to strengthen the relationship between executive pay and firm performance."

One enduring, and fundamental, issue is the quality of Chinese executive compensation data. The pay measure used in extant studies is typically the cash compensation received by the three highest paid executives. Generally, this is the salary and bonus awarded to these three individuals. The primary concern is that reported pay may be systematically biased downwards. There are several reasons for this. First, measurement bias can arise if Chinese executives enjoy considerable non-disclosed perks (medical, social welfare provision, job security etc.). In which case, the relevant economic measure of pay is greater than that reported. Kato and Long (2006) estimate that perks can range from about 15 percent to 32 percent of total executive compensation. In a related study, Adithipyangkul et al. (2010) estimate that the median value of perks (enjoyed by all company employees including management) is about 1.06 million RMB compared to total management compensation of 0.3 million RMB. Second, Chinese executives may enjoy some 'grey' incomes such as bribery and kickbacks. At the macroeconomic level, Transparency International provides a Corruption Perception Index that ranges from 0 to 10, with higher scores meaning less corruption. In 2005, the USA scored 7.6 and China 3.2; the relative global ranks were 17 for the USA and 78 for China, assessed from 158 nations. Third, one may be concerned that accounting standards are lax, or that private political incentives lead to underreporting of executive compensation. For example, in a socialist economy the gap in pay between executives and workers may be a cause for concern. Fourth, from 2006 onwards equity compensation is becoming more important as the CSRC moves reforms forwards. A total pay measure excluding the value of equity compensation will be biased downwards. A significant challenge for future research, as compensation disclosure becomes better in China, is to more accurately measure CEO pay.

3.2   Executive Pay in Hong Kong Firms

Hong Kong is a special administrative region (SAR) of the People's Republic of China (PRC), and is administered under the principle of 'one country, two systems'. The political and economic system in Hong Kong is significantly different from mainland China. It has an independent judiciary and operates under the common law framework. Hong Kong was under British colonial rule from 1841. In January 1997, 156 years of British rule was ended and sovereignty passed to China. Before the 1997 transition, certain rights and safeguards were agreed between China and the UK. It resulted in Hong Kong Basic Law as the constitutional bedrock of the new Hong Kong under PRC rule. According to the agreement, Hong Kong would retain a high degree of autonomy for at least fifty years after the transition.

Corporate securities law and governance arrangements in Hong Kong are different from those in mainland China, including the governance of executive compensation. The Hong Kong Stock Exchange had 1,413 listed companies with a combined market capitalization of US$21 trillion by the end of 2010. A special segment in the Hong Kong Stock Exchange is 'Red Chip stocks'; these are mainland China firms that are incorporated outside mainland China and listed in Hong Kong. There are about 100 Red Chip firms listed on the Hong Kong Stock Exchange.[6] In terms of executive compensation, listed firms in Hong Kong are required to disclose information about salaries, bonuses and equity pay separately for each member of the board of directors and top management. Stock options have been used since 1989, but at that time rules governing their use were vague. Since 2001 stricter rules on options have been in place. For example, firms are

---

[6]   Data is at December 2010. Listed firms on the HK market are available at: http://www.hkex. com.hk/eng/stat/statrpt/mkthl/mkthl201012.htm and Red Chip listings are at http://www.hkex. com.hk/eng/stat/smstat/chidimen/cd_rcmb.htm. (Information retrieved on 2 February 2011.)

precluded from granting 'in-the-money' options, where the market price exceeds the grant price.[7]

In an early study Firth et al. (1999) studied the determinants of executive compensation in Hong Kong. Their sample consists of 351 HK listed firms for the years 1994 and 1995. At that time executive compensation information disclosure was weaker than today. They test the standard agency model and find that firm size is an important driver of compensation – they report a pay–size elasticity of about 30 percent. In addition, they find that there is a positive correlation between executive compensation and accounting performance. However, they find little evidence of a correlation between CEO pay and stock returns. They conclude, therefore, that: "Overall, the results imply agency arguments that advocate pay-for-performance compensation schemes are not major factors in setting top management remuneration in Hong Kong."

Chen et al. (2010c) analyze executive compensation in Hong Kong firms, specifically Red Chip firms, state-controlled Chinese firms that are incorporated outside China and traded on the Hong Kong Stock Exchange. They test whether managerial stock option compensation increases shareholder value in these firms. Their analysis is based on 76 Red Chip firms over the period 1991 to 2005. They find that by 2005 all Red Chip firms had adopted stock option programs, and the popularity of options had increased over time. They find that the granting and exercise of stock options differ significantly between Chinese firms and a control sample set of US firms. Interestingly, they find that economic factors do not explain Chinese firms' stock option grants. Also, they find that stock market reactions to announcements of stock option scheme proposals are insignificant. Overall, the authors find that: "There is no improvement in earnings performance after the stock option grant. We conclude that Chinese firms' stock option compensation does not increase shareholder value."

4   FURTHER EVIDENCE ON CHINESE EXECUTIVE PAY

This section presents further evidence on Chinese executive pay, focusing on three main issues. First, we test the hypothesis that there is a positive relation between Chinese executive pay and firm performance. Second, we test the relation between executive pay and firm revenues (i.e. enterprise size). Third, we test whether the pay-for-performance relation is weaker (or stronger) in state controlled firms. We find that executive pay is positively related to firm stock return as well as return on assets. We find also that executive pay is positively related to firm revenue, and that the elasticity is about 15 percent – consistent with many Western studies, but a little lower. Third, we find that the correlation between pay and performance is weaker in state controlled firms. We interpret this as meaning that the private control of enterprise is better suited to providing incentives for value creation. We think that one policy implication of this finding is the need for further private control of enterprise to promote value creation and growth.

---

[7]   Rules on the issuing of options can be found in Chapter 17 of the Main Board Listing: http://www.hkex.com.hk/eng/rulesreg/listrules/mbrules/vol1_2.htm. (Information retrieved on 2 February 2011.)

4.1   Data

We use executive compensation and governance data supplied by the China Center for Economic Research SinoFin Information Service (CCER/SinoFin). This data source has been used in previous studies (e.g. Conyon and He, 2011, Kato and Long 2006, Chen et al., 2010a). Financial performance and accounting data were matched to the CCER/ SinoFin data using the CSMAR-A financial database. This data source, too, has been used in previous studies (e.g. Chen et al., 2010a).

The original China Center for Economic Research data we use consists of 1381 unique publicly traded firms on the two domestic Chinese exchanges for the years 2001 to 2005. These firms account for about 98 percent of all listed firms. The near universal coverage of firms helps decrease any sample selection biases. Thirty-nine firms were excluded due to missing observations on key variables, or because we required each firm to have at least two years of continuous data. The final sample consists of 1342 unique firms with 5928 firm-year observations from 2001 to 2005. The resulting unbalanced data set has multiple time-series observations per firm. This reflects firms joining or leaving the stock exchanges.[8]

4.2   Descriptive Results

Table 20.1 presents descriptive statistics on executive compensation for China's listed firms by year (Panel A) and broad industrial sector (Panel B). Panel A shows that mean (median) executive compensation over the 2001–2005 sample period is about 152,000 (107,000) renminbi (RMB). Using the official 2005 exchange rate of 1 US\$ = 8.20 RMB, mean (median) executive compensation over the period is approximately \$19,000 (\$13,000) US dollars. However, using the Penn World Table purchasing power parity (PPP) rate of about 2.2 in 2005 then the US dollar amount is about \$69,000 (\$49,000).[9]

Although Chinese executive pay may seem low by US or Western standards, it is high compared to the typical employee wage in China. Annual average employee income in 2005 was about 18,000 RMB, suggesting that the ratio of executive to employee pay was about eight. Annual employee pay (in RMB) was 10,870 in 2001; 12,422 in 2002; 14,040 in 2003; 16,024 in 2004; and 18,415 in 2005 (using information contained in the China Statistical Yearbook).

Table 20.1 also shows that executive pay grew from 2001 to 2005. Mean executive compensation rose from about 105,000 RMB in 2001 to approximately 196,000 RMB in 2004, and then fell to about 154,000 in 2005.[10] To estimate the rate of growth in executive

---

[8]   To be concrete, there are 119 firms with 2 years of data (238 observations), 96 firms with 3 years of data (288 firm-year observations), 233 firms with 4 years of data (932 firm-year observations), and 894 firms with 5 years of data (4,470 firm-year observations). The number of unique firms is therefore 1342 (=119+96+233+894) and the total number of firm-year observations is 5928.

[9]   We discuss the issue of PPP rates in Section 5 below when contrasting China to the USA.

[10]   The full explanation for the decline in 2005 is unclear. One reason may be declining firm performance between 2004 and 2005, since return to shareholders and return on assets also fell over this time period.

Table 20.1   Descriptive statistics: executive compensation

Panel A: Listed firms by year

Year	N	Mean	sd	Lower quartile	Median	Upper quartile
2001	1017	104975	217392	38467	71000	126000
2002	1147	127558	127181	50516	90000	163333
2003	1217	162881	153353	66800	120033	212667
2004	1318	195745	183175	81667	146214	250667
2005	1229	153512	194846	57567	107684	193333
Total	5928	151477	179778	57333	106667	192700

Panel B: Listed firms by industrial sector

Industry	N	Mean	sd	Lower quartile	Median	Upper quartile
Agriculture	143	94667	62669	52400	80000	122533
Communication	49	146733	109876	56000	133333	203333
Construction	105	154867	120206	68825	132717	200000
Finance	23	86030	57475	30000	73333	133200
Information technology	359	214219	217880	100000	160000	251000
Manufacturing	3402	139662	193994	50533	93602	170167
Mining	95	126937	96534	57333	106667	152081
Others	369	153411	120238	66000	123000	200000
Real estate	276	183101	183907	62200	129500	261717
Services	173	208055	199898	83000	149329	273868
Transportation	247	171156	137938	67948	122033	223333
Utilities	251	166132	151276	68155	123333	213333
Wholesale & retail	436	155455	132128	64000	115808	206667
Total	5928	151477	179778	57333	106667	192700

Note: Executive compensation is average executive compensation. It is the sum of three highest paid executive members' total compensation disclosed as a single number divided by three. Executive compensation is calculated as the sum of basic salary, bonus, stipends, and other benefits. Executive compensation is denominated in Chinese RMB.

pay we ran a regression of the logarithm of executive pay on a linear time trend. The results indicate that executive pay has grown by about 10.3 percent per year over the period 2001 to 2005 (β=0.098, t=11.8).[11] Panel B shows the distribution of compensation across broad industry groups, and associated pay levels. Most of the firms are within the manufacturing sector.

Table 20.2 shows the average values of key variables used in the study. Panel A pro-

---

[11]   Calculated as $e^{0.098}-1$.

Table 20.2   *Descriptive statistics: Compensation, ownership and control*

Panel A: Executive compensation and boardroom structure

Year	PAY (RMB, 000s)	CEO_OWN (RMB, 000s)	BOARD_ SIZE	IND_DIR (%)	COMBINE	COMP_COM
2001	104.97	767.30	9.40	5.97	0.12	0.08
2002	127.56	1375.27	9.92	23.65	0.11	0.31
2003	162.88	1979.39	9.89	32.36	0.11	0.42
2004	195.75	3285.02	9.80	33.82	0.11	0.46
2005	153.51	3150.18	9.66	34.34	0.11	0.51
Total	151.48	2187.57	9.74	26.88	0.11	0.37

Panel B: Ownership

Year	STATE	PRIVATE	OTHER	LG1_OWN	LG2_OWN	LG3_OWN
2001	0.82	0.11	0.07	0.44	0.08	0.03
2002	0.78	0.16	0.06	0.44	0.09	0.03
2003	0.74	0.22	0.04	0.43	0.09	0.04
2004	0.70	0.26	0.04	0.42	0.10	0.04
2005	0.71	0.27	0.02	0.41	0.10	0.04
Total	0.74	0.21	0.05	0.43	0.09	0.04

Note: Panel A: PAY: CEO cash pay (RMB 000s); CEO_OWN (RMB 000s): value of CEO shareholdings is the number of shares held by the CEO multiplied by the firms stock price (units are millions); IND_DIR: the fraction of the board comprised of independent directors; BOARD_SIZE: board size is measured as the number of individuals on the main board; COMBINE: leadership structure of the firm is a dummy variable set equal to one if the posts of CEO and chairman are combined, and zero otherwise; COMP_COM: a dummy variable equal to one if the firm has a compensation committee and zero otherwise. Panel B: STATE = 1 if the Chinese state is the ultimate firm owner; PRIVATE = 1 if the ultimate owner is a private institution; OTHER is the residual ownership category; LG1_OWN: the percentage ownership of largest shareholder; LG2_OWN and LG3_OWN are the second and third largest ownership percentages.

vides information on executive compensation, the value of CEO share ownership, and boardroom structures variables, such as the percentage of independent directors on the board. Executive compensation and the value of CEO share ownership are expressed in thousands of RMB. A key point is that the value of CEO share ownership is higher than the level of executive pay. Over the period from 2001 to 2005 the average value of cash compensation is about 151,000 RMB. In contrast, the average value shareholding is approximately 2,177,000 RMB. The notional value of the stock of CEO shareholdings is about fourteen times the value of cash compensation. Since the value of CEO share ownership varies directly with asset prices, this provides an automatic mechanism to motivate CEOs to create firm value. Conyon and He (2011) highlight the importance of equity ownership (compensation).

The governance of China's publicly traded firms has changed over time. In terms of boardroom structure, we find an increased adoption of Western style governance practices. The percentage of independent members on the board has increased from about 6 percent in 2001 to about 34 percent in 2005.[12] The size of the main board of directors is about ten members and relatively constant over time. About 11 percent of firms combine the posts of CEO and chairperson over the sample period. Finally, the proportion of firms that have adopted a compensation committee for setting executive pay increased from about 8 percent in 2001 to approximately 50 percent in 2005. As noted, the raw data show significant changes in the internal control and governance of firms.

Table 20.2 Panel B provides further institutional context to our study. State ownership control has declined from 2001 to 2005. The state was the ultimate owner in about 82 percent of firms in 2001 and only 71 percent in 2005. In contrast, private ownership and control has more than doubled over the same short period. About 27 percent of firms were privately controlled in 2005 compared to 11 percent in 2001. This result shows that the state's ownership control of firms has diminished, as market reforms deepened. The ownership of publicly traded firms is highly concentrated in China. For expositional purposes we present the ownership stakes of the largest three shareholders separately. The largest shareholder owns about 43 percent of the firm's shares, the next largest about 9 percent and the third largest about 4 percent. The situation contrasts markedly with Anglo-Saxon economies.

Figure 20.1 shows the level of executive compensation, by quintiles of firm performance (low performance: 1st quintile, and high performance: 5th quintile). The height of each bar is the average executive compensation in that quintile over the period 2001 to 2005. The figure shows that firms with low stock returns pay their CEOs less than firms with high stock returns. Similarly, the figure indicates that firms with low return on assets pay their executives less than those with high return on assets. The evidence suggests a positive pay-for-performance correlation, but we stress the raw data do not control for other determinants of pay that may confound the pay–performance link. In non-graphed results we also found a positive correlation between the *growth* in executive compensation and firm performance. The growth in executive pay was significantly greater in firms with high stock returns, or high return on assets, compared to low performing firms.

4.3   Econometric Results

The following fixed-effects panel data model is estimated, controlling for firm size, economic and corporate governance variables:

$$\ln(PAY)_{it} = \alpha_i + \beta_1 PERF_{it} + \beta_2 \ln(STATE)_{it} + \beta_3 \ln(PERF*STATE)_{it} + \beta_4 X_{it} + \varepsilon_{it} \tag{20.1}$$

The term $\ln(PAY)_{it}$ is the logarithm of executive cash compensation in firm i at time t. Executive compensation is the aggregated pay of the top three executives, defined as the sum of basic salary, bonus, stipends, and other benefits. We divide this executive pay figure by three, as an estimate of the 'typical' executive's pay.

---

[12]   The significant increase of independent directors on the board is due to the regulation issued by CSRC in August 2001, "Guides to the Establishment of Independent Directors System", which mandate that at least one third of the board members in listed firms should be independent directors.

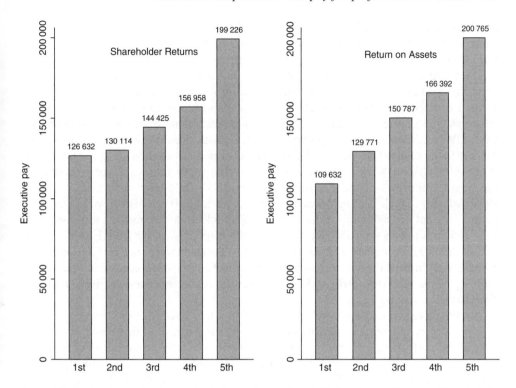

Note: The bar heights are the average level of executive pay in quintile from low performance (1st quintile) to high performance (5th quintile).

Figure 20.1   The level of executive pay and quintiles of firm performance

Two performance measures are used, consistent with the extant literature (Murphy, 1999). First, we use a market-based measure: the firm's annualized stock return over the previous twelve months (SHR) [mean = −0.04]. Second, we use an accounting-based measure of performance: return on assets, defined as net profits divided by the book value of assets (ROA) [mean = 0.10]. We use lagged values of the performance term to mitigate endogeneity issues. We predict that these variables are positive (i.e. $\beta_1 > 0$), consistent with principal–agent theory. The term STATE is a dummy variable equal to one if the Chinese state is the ultimate owner of the firm, and zero otherwise [mean = 0.74]. The term PERF*STATE is an interaction variable. If state controlled firms provide weaker performance incentives then we predict that $\beta_3 < 0$.

A fixed-effects estimator is used to control for heterogeneity in firm and managerial quality (Wooldridge, 2002). These are the α_i terms in equation (20.1). The fixed effects filter out time-invariant factors that may contaminate the pay-for-performance estimates. Cross-section regressions typically omit significant explanatory variables, potentially causing statistical bias in the estimated pay-for-performance relation (Murphy, 1985). For example, if managerial quality is correlated with firm performance and executive pay, then its omission from the pay regression may result in erroneous estimation of the pay–performance relation. Variables such as managerial quality, corporate culture, or the quality of the firm are likely to be especially important factors in the China context. Controlling for fixed effects (i.e. focusing on the within-firm variation) provides a strong test of the correlations between pay, firm performance and the state.

The model contains a set of control variables, X. Their inclusion is motivated by results from the extant executive pay literature. The variable Ln(SALES) is firm size measured as the logarithm of firm sales [mean = 20.3]; we also control for ownership structure. Ownership concentration is measured as the share ownership of the largest shareholder, LG1_OWN (Shivdasani, 1993) [mean = 0.43]. Growth opportunities are defined as the market value of the firm divided by the book value of assets, MKT_BK (Smith and Watts, 1992) [mean = 1.57]. The boardroom governance variables are: the percentage of the board comprised of independent directors, IND_DIR (Hermalin and Weisbach, 1998) [mean = 26.9]. The independent director variable is sourced from the SinoFin dataset. We defined a dummy variable B or H SHARE equal to one if the firm issued any B or H shares [mean = 0.075]. We also defined a dummy variable FOREIGN equal to one if the ultimate owner was foreign [mean = 0.01]. Finally, the regression models contain a set of time dummies to capture year effects and macro-economic shocks. The term ε_{it} is the equation error, which is assumed to be independent and identically distributed.

The empirical results are contained in Table 20.3. Since cross-section regressions may be subject to omitted variable bias, we present panel data firm fixed effects estimates. The performance terms are lagged one period to mitigate endogeneity concerns. Implicitly, we investigate executive rewards this period as a function of firm performance last period. Column 1 shows that there is a positive correlation between pay and performance. We find a statistically significant correlation between pay and shareholder returns (SHR) and pay and return on assets (ROA). The model also shows a positive and significant correlation between executive pay and firm size. The estimated elasticity is approximately 15 percent and is in agreement with estimated pay–size elasticity using Western data (Murphy, 1999). We find that executive pay is lower the higher the ownership of the largest shareholder. Controlling for firm fixed effects, the state has little statistical effect on the level of executive compensation.[13] We find that when the ultimate owner of the firm is a foreign entity then executive pay is higher. However, we find that executive pay is not affected by whether the firm issues B or H type shares. Column 2 presents an expanded model that contains an interaction term between the performance term and the state. Controlling for fixed effects and economic determinants, we find a significantly negative interaction between state and stockholder returns. This implies that the pay-for-performance relation is weaker in state controlled firms. However, the pay-for-performance term overall remains positive. On the other hand, the interaction between the state and return on assets is not significant.

---

[13]   Because firms do not frequently change ownership control from state to private or vice versa, there is little within-firm variation in the variable when using a firm fixed effect. This may explain why the relationship between state and executive compensation is insignificant. In our un-tabulated OLS result, the state variable is significantly negatively related to executive compensation, which suggests executives in state controlled firms on average earn less than their counterparts in private firms.

Table 20.3   *Executive compensation regressions: China 2001 to 2005*

Variables	(1)	(2)
	Ln(PAY)	Ln(PAY)
SHR	0.05*	0.10***
	(1.96)	(2.61)
ROA	0.06*	0.06
	(1.91)	(1.39)
Ln(SALES)	0.14***	0.14***
	(9.92)	(9.85)
STATE	−0.03	−0.04
	(−0.90)	(−1.07)
LG1_OWN	−0.50***	−0.49***
	(−3.33)	(−3.29)
MKT_BK	0.01	0.01
	(1.63)	(1.53)
VOL	−0.02	−0.02
	(−0.87)	(−0.61)
IND_DIR	0.00	0.00
	(1.28)	(1.19)
FOREIGN	0.40***	0.39***
	(2.83)	(2.76)
B or H SHARE	0.14	0.14
	(1.00)	(0.98)
STATE*SHR		−0.07*
		(−1.77)
STATE*ROA		0.01
		(0.10)
Constant	8.59***	8.61***
	(30.16)	(30.21)
Observations	5653	5653
R-squared	0.25	0.25
Number of firms	1342	1342

Note: Variable definitions: the dependent variable ln(PAY) is the log of executive pay. The independent variables are: SHR: annual shareholder returns; ROA: return on assets; ln(SALES): the natural logarithm of firm sales; MKT_BK: market value of the firm divided by the book value of assets; VOL: natural log of the standard deviation of stock returns over the year; STATE: dummy variable equal to one if the firm's ultimate owner is the Chinese state, and zero otherwise; LG1_OWN: percentage share ownership of the largest shareholder; IND_DIR: the fraction of the board comprised of independent directors; FOREIGN: ultimate owner is foreign (mean = 0.1%); B or H SHARE: the firm issues B or H shares (mean = 7.5%). The regressions contain a set of 4 time dummies, from 2002 to 2005, with 2001 as the base year. Coefficients on the industry and time dummies are suppressed for expositional convenience. *** p<0.01, ** p<0.05, * p<0.1. Standard errors are adjusted and clustered on the firm identifier.

Methodologically, it is important to use fixed effects. If unobservable firm heterogeneity is correlated with the observable variables then the estimating equation could be misspecified, leading to omitted-variable bias. It is therefore important to control for such unobserved firm heterogeneities. We performed a Hausman specification test to compare the random effects models to the fixed effects specification. The tests rejected the hypothesis that fixed effects are uncorrelated with the observable determinants. Also, we could not reject the hypothesis that the random effects estimates are inconsistent at the 1 percent level. Therefore, the fixed effects models are the appropriate specification.

5   CONCLUSIONS

This chapter has investigated executive compensation in China. Our goals were to describe executive compensation practices, review the existing literature, and provide some new evidence on the pay-for-performance relation in China. We addressed some important questions. Are Chinese executives paid in the same way as Western executives? Are the drivers of executive pay, such as firm performance and size, as important in socialist China as in the West? How does the Chinese state affect the provision of incentives in Chinese firms? We have reviewed evidence from the recent extant literature. In addition, we have provided some further evidence on the determinants of executive pay from 2001 to 2005.

A number of conclusions can be drawn. First, compared to the United States there is less information available on executive compensation in China. Second, executive compensation is made up mainly of salaries and bonuses. Equity compensation in the form of stock options and restricted stock has only been introduced since 2006. There may be a concern that aspects of pay may be hidden in the form of perks or other forms of social pay. Third, we have reviewed the recent Chinese literature on executive compensation. Our understanding of this literature is that the consensus view is that there is a positive correlation between executive pay and firm performance in China. Studies generally examine the relation between cash compensation and firm performance, because equity compensation (such as stock options) is not present or is difficult to collect.

We have also presented some new empirical results. First, we find that executive cash compensation is positively correlated to stock returns (a market-based measure) and return on assets (an accounting-based measure). Chinese executives, therefore, are rewarded implicitly for performance. Our results are in agreement with existing studies. We have stressed the importance of controlling for firm fixed effects to control for variation in firm and managerial quality. Second, we find that executive pay is positively correlated to firm size and that the estimated elasticity is about 15 percent. Again, this is in agreement with a standard result using Western data: executives at bigger firms earn more. In this sense the Chinese compensation contract shares features with those found in Western firms. Third, we find that institutions matter. The state plays a dominant role in economic activity in China. We find that the state is the ultimate owner of about 70 percent of the public firms on the domestic stock exchanges. Moreover, the largest shareholder on average owns about 40 percent of the firm. The influence of the state is therefore important. Fourth, we find evidence that the pay-for-performance link is weaker in state controlled firms. We interpret this as meaning that the private control of enterprise is better suited to provide incentives for value creation. We think that one policy implication of this finding is the need for further private control of enterprise to promote value creation and growth.

Finally, as noted, China is now the world's second largest economy. Since 1992 its capital markets have grown significantly, both in terms of market valuation, and the number of IPOs and corporate listings. China's macro-economic performance, relative to similar sized countries, is unrivalled. Against this background we think that there have been relatively few executive compensation studies. Such studies are important to better understand executive incentives to promote economic growth.

REFERENCES

Adithipyangkul, Pattarin, Ilan Alon, and Tianyu Zhang. 2010. Executive Perks: Compensation and Corporate Performance in China, *Asia Pacific Journal of Management* (forthcoming).

Allen, Franklin, Jun Qian, and Meijun Qian. 2005. Law, Finance, and Economic Growth in China, *Journal of Financial Economics*, 77 (1): 57–116.

Chen, Jean, Xuguang Liu, and Weian Li. 2010a. The Effect of Insider Control and Global Benchmarks on Chinese Executive Compensation, *Corporate Governance: An International Review*, 18 (2): 107–23.

Chen, Jing, Mahmoud Ezzamel, and Ziming Cai. 2010b. Managerial Power, Tournament Theory and Executive Pay in China, working paper, Managerial Compensation conference, Cardiff (September).

Chen, Zhihong, Yuyan Guan, and Bin Ke. 2010c. Does Managerial Stock Option Compensation Increase Shareholder Value in State-Controlled Chinese Firms Listed in Hong Kong? Working paper, SSRN: http://ssrn.com/abstract=1249526.

Conyon, Martin J. and Lerong He, 2011. Executive Compensation and Corporate Governance in China, *Journal of Corporate Finance*, 17 (4): 1158–75.

Core, John E. and Wayne R. Guay. 1999. The Use of Equity Grants to Manage Optimal Equity Incentive Levels, *Journal of Accounting and Economics*, 28 (2): 151–84.

Core, John E., Wayne R. Guay, and David F. Larcker. 2003. Executive Equity Compensation and Incentives: A survey, *FRBNY Economic Policy Review*, April: 27–44.

Core, John E., Robert W. Holthausen, and David F. Larcker. 1999. Corporate Governance, Chief Executive Officer Compensation, and Firm Performance, *Journal of Financial Economics*, 51 (3): 371–406.

CSRC (China Securities Regulatory Commission). 1998. Guidelines on Contents and Formats of Information Disclosure of Annual Report for Listed companies – 1998 version. China Securities Regulatory Commission.

CSRC. 2000. Guidelines on Contents and Formats of Information Disclosure of Annual Report for Listed companies – 2000 version. China Securities Regulatory Commission.

CSRC. 2002. Code of Corporate Governance for Listed Companies in China. China Securities Regulatory Commission.

CSRC. 2002. Guidelines on Contents and Formats of Information Disclosure of Annual Report for Listed Companies – 2002 version. China Securities Regulatory Commission.

CSRC. 2005a. Regulation for the Stock Options Grants in Public Firms. China Securities Regulatory Commission.

CSRC. 2005b. Guidelines on Contents and Formats of Information Disclosure of Annual Report for Listed companies – 2005 version. China Securities Regulatory Commission.

CSRC. 2007. Guidelines on Contents and Formats of Information Disclosure of Annual Report for Listed Companies – 2007 version. China Securities Regulatory Commission.

Demsetz, Harold and Kenneth Lehn. 1985. The Structure of Corporate-ownership – Causes and Consequences, *Journal of Political Economy*, 93 (6): 1155–77.

Ding, Shujun, Zhenyu Wu, Yuanshun Li, and Chunxin Jia. 2010. Executive Compensation, Supervisory Board, and China's Governance Reform: A Legal Approach Perspective, *Review of Quantitative Finance and Accounting*, 35: 445–71.

Ding, Yuan, Hua Zhang, and Junxi Zhang. 2007. Private vs State Ownership and Earnings Management: Evidence from Chinese Listed Companies, *Corporate Governance: An International Review*, 15 (2): 223–38.

Fama, Eugene F. and Michael C. Jensen. 1983. Separation of Ownership and Control, *Journal of Law and Economics*, 26 (2): 301–25.

Fan, Joseph P. H., T. J. Wong, and Tianyu Zhang. 2007. Politically Connected CEOs, Corporate Governance, and Post-IPO Performance of China's Newly Partially Privatized Firms, *Journal of Financial Economics*, 84 (2): 330–57.

Firth, Michael, Peter M. Fung, and Oliver M. Rui. 2006. Corporate Performance and CEO Compensation in China, *Journal of Corporate Finance*, 12: 693–714.

Firth, Michael, Peter M. Fung, and Oliver M. Rui. 2007. How Ownership and Corporate Governance Influence Chief Executive Pay in China's listed Firms, *Journal of Business Research*, 60 (7): 776–85.

Firth, Michael, Michael Tam, and M. Tang. 1999. The Determinants of Top Management Pay, *Omega*, 27: 617–35.

Hermalin, Benjamin E. and Michael S. Weisbach. 1998. Endogenously Chosen Boards of Directors and Their Monitoring of the CEO, *American Economic Review*, 88 (1): 96–118.

Holmstrom, Bengt. 1979. Moral Hazard and Observability, *Bell Journal of Economics*, 10 (1): 74–91.

Hu, Helen Wei, On Kit Tam, and Monica Guo-Sze Tan. 2010. Internal Governance Mechanisms and Firm Performance in China, *Asia Pacific Journal of Management*, 27: 727–49.

Jensen, Michael C. and William H. Meckling. 1976. Theory of the Firm – Managerial Behavior, Agency Costs and Ownership Structure, *Journal of Financial Economics*, 3 (4): 305–60.

Jensen, Michael C. and Kevin J. Murphy. 1990. Performance Pay and Top-Management Incentives, *The Journal of Political Economy*, 98 (2): 225–64.

Jensen, Michael C. and Jerold B. Warner. 1988. The Distribution of Power Among Corporate Managers, Shareholders, and Directors, *Journal of Financial Economics*, 20 (1–2): 3–24.

Jingu, Takeshi. 2007. Corporate Governance for Listed Companies in China – Recent Moves to Improve the Quality of Listed Companies, *Nomura Capital Market Review*, 10(2): http://ssrn.com/paper=1016912.

Kato, Takao K. and Cheryl X. Long. 2006. Executive Compensation, Firm Performance, and Corporate Governance in China: Evidence from Firms Listed in the Shanghai and Shenzhen Stock Exchanges, *Economic Development and Cultural Change*, 54 (4): 945–83.

La Porta, Rafael, Florencio Lopez-de-Silanes, Andrei Shleifer, and Robert Vishny. 1998. Law and Finance, *Journal of Political Economy*, 106 (6): 1113–55.

La Porta, Rafael, Florencio Lopez-de-Silanes, Andrei Shleifer, and Robert Vishny. 2000. Investor Protection and Corporate Governance, *Journal of Financial Economics*, 58: 3–27.

Mengistae, Taye and Lixin C. Xu. 2004. Agency Theory and Executive Compensation: The Case of Chinese State-Owned Enterprises, *Journal of Labor Economics*, 22 (3): 615–37.

Mirrlees, James A. 1976. Optimal Structure of Incentives and Authority within an Organization, *Bell Journal of Economics*, 7 (1): 105–31.

Murphy, Kevin J. 1985. Corporate Performance and Managerial Remuneration – An Empirical Analysis, *Journal of Accounting and Economics*, 7: 11–42.

Murphy, Kevin J. 1999. Executive Compensation, in *Handbook of Labor Economics*, vol. 3b, Orley Ashenfelter and David Card, eds, North Holland, 2485–563.

Qian, Yingyi. 1995. Reforming Corporate Governance and Finance in China, in *Corporate Governance in Transitional Economies: Insider Control and the Role of Banks*, Masahiko Aoki and Hyung-Ki Kim, eds, The World Bank, 215–52.

Shivdasani, Anil. 1993. Board Composition, Ownership Structure, and Hostile Takeovers, *Journal of Accounting and Economics*, 16: 167–98.

Smith, Clifford W. and Ross L. Watts. 1992. The Investment Opportunity Set and Corporate Financing, Dividend, and Compensation Policies, *Journal of Financial Economics*, 32 (3): 263–92.

Wang, Kun and Xing Xiao. 2011. Controlling Shareholders' Tunneling and Executive Compensation: Evidence from China, *Journal of Accounting and Public Policy*, 30: 89–100.

Wooldridge, Jeffrey. 2002. *Econometric Analysis of Cross Section and Panel Data*. Boston: The MIT Press.

Xu, Liping. 2004. Types of Large Shareholders, Corporate Governance, and Firm Performance: Evidence from China's Listed Companies, Ph.D. thesis, School of Accounting and Finance, The Hong Kong Polytechnic University.

21 Executive compensation in India

Rajesh Chakrabarti, Krishnamurthy Subramanian,
*Pradeep K. Yadav and Yesha Yadav**

1 INTRODUCTION

The issue of executive compensation in corporate India has gained increasingly in significance since the advent of economic liberalization in 1993–94, the subsequent rise of India as a leading center for international investment, and the rapidly increasing domestic equity participation by retail investors in Indian capital markets. Salaries for senior management have grown sharply since 1994, and are sizable in the Indian context, particularly when compared with non-managerial employee salaries. The sharp rise in salary levels, and the wide regulatory latitude afforded to boards to set executive pay after the 1993–94 reforms, have prompted concerns long analyzed in developed markets in relation to the play of incentives governing executive employment contracts, and in particular, the better alignment of pay with performance to reduce "agency costs," and the use and abuse of managerial power to extract rents and thereby disgorge shareholder value. As India seeks to progress the creation of corporate governance systems in avowed alignment with international best practice, it presents an interesting case-study in the context of executive compensation, from an economic as well as a regulatory policy perspective.

From an economic perspective, the agency costs that are of greatest concern in an Indian context are "horizontal" agency costs between controlling (potentially minority) shareholders and other (passively investing) shareholders. These are fundamentally different from the "vertical" agency costs between managers and dispersed shareholders that are widely regarded as a potential explanation for high CEO pay among widely held Anglo-American listed companies. The argument there is that the interests of arm's-length managers do not necessarily conform to what is in the best interest of shareholders; and when managers act in a self-serving manner that is sub-optimal from the perspective of shareholders, shareholder value is destroyed, generating (vertical) agency costs.

However, such sub-optimality can arise also in other ways. In particular, a distinguishing characteristic of the Indian corporate sector is that the control of large Indian listed companies has historically tended to be concentrated in the hands of "promoters" and affiliated companies that are part of business groups, and these controlling groups exercise control rights and cash-flow privileges that are often significantly higher than the cash-flow rights conferred by their share of ownership in the firm, thereby potentially generating a different type of agency cost: that which arises because the interests of this

* The authors thank Chandrasekhar Mangipudi, Rajkamal Vasu, and ZongFei Yang for excellent research assistance. The authors remain responsible for all errors.

controlling group can be at variance with the interests of the other passive shareholders. In fact, the term "promoter" is not commonly used internationally, but is extensively used and widely understood in an Indian corporate context to essentially signify a controlling shareholder group.

These horizontal agency costs can arguably be further exacerbated by the fact that Indian companies have continued to benefit from passive state equity investment notwithstanding liberalization and the changing architecture of company ownership as increasing levels of foreign direct investment gradually alter the allocation of interests and influence. In view of the above, the Indian corporate environment presents an extremely interesting analytical laboratory to examine whether horizontal agency-related misalignments in the interests of controlling and other shareholders lead to higher executive compensation in the same way as vertical agency costs do. This is an important economic focus in this chapter, where we proxy these horizontal agency costs by the proportion of promoters' equity, and whether a firm is part of a closely held business group (like, e.g., Tatas or Reliance) or widely held (like, e.g., Infosys).

From a regulatory perspective, an analysis of Indian executive compensation is interesting for several reasons. First, institutionally, as in other emerging economies, concerns have been raised with respect to inefficiencies in the enforcement of sanctions for corporate misfeasance. Specifically in India, with strong codification of laws but a slow-moving court system, the responsibility for enforcement has come to rest largely with the Securities and Exchange Board of India (SEBI), the equivalent of the US SEC. The SEBI has thus far evidenced an uneven record on the enforcement of securities laws in the Indian context, arguably obscuring an understanding of the compliance profile of Indian companies. Second, it is interesting to observe how the financial crisis has subtly shifted the normative emphasis in the regulatory discourse on executive compensation from a focus on the pay–performance misalignment to one seeking to curb executive appetite for excessive risk-taking in the short-term through reform of the incentive structures underlying executive compensation schemes. Finally, as a member of the G-20 Group of Nations, India faces pressure to ensure broad alignment of its laws with policy reflecting the international consensus on executive compensation for financial firms. A question mark remains as to whether modifications to laws for financial firms are also likely to creep into broader corporate regulation in India to affect the compliance habits of public companies in India more generally.

Despite its importance, there is very limited extant literature focusing on an empirical or regulatory analysis of executive compensation in listed companies in India. In this context, Section 2 of this chapter presents an introductory analysis of the Indian legal and regulatory framework specific to executive compensation. Section 3 provides a descriptive analysis of levels and trends in the fixed and variable components of CEO salaries, and the salaries of executive directors other than CEOs (hereafter "CXOs"). Section 4 presents the results of an introductory empirical investigation into the economic drivers of executive compensation, especially the important issue of horizontal agency costs that is particularly important in India. Finally, Section 5 offers concluding remarks.

2　LEGAL AND REGULATORY FRAMEWORK

2.1　Overview

Regulators in India have, alongside their counterparts in developed and emerging markets, sought to exert renewed focus on the issue of executive compensation in the wake of the financial crisis (Reserve Bank of India (2010)). Attention has arguably been sharpened following well-publicized recent lapses in corporate governance seen at leading Indian enterprises, notably in the case of the accounting fraud perpetrated at Satyam Computer Services, a high-profile IT and outsourcing services firm in India (Chatterjee (2009), Duggal (2010); also see Securities and Exchange Board of India, 2010). Regulatory action in this regard may be situated in the context of a broader consensus reached at the international level on executive compensation regulation, under the auspices of the G-20 and the Financial Stability Board (FSB; formerly the Financial Stability Forum), for example Financial Stability Forum (2009), as well as efforts underway in a number of developed markets to legislatively rein in the perceived excesses of executive compensation in the run-up to the crisis.[1] We set out below a brief introduction to the regulation of executive compensation in India. While this cannot purport to provide a comprehensive analysis of the many particularities of the Indian legal framework for regulating executive compensation, it seeks to highlight the key areas in the regulatory landscape, with the goal of raising issues for further research and reflection going forward.

2.2　From State Control to Liberalization

Historically, executive salaries in India had been low and tightly regulated by government regulations. Legislation had, in the past, set prescriptive caps on salary levels as well as on the composition of pay packages for executives, such that strict limits also existed with respect to the relative percentage of pay that could be given in the form of incentive-related compensation as against base salary. In the early nineties, pursuant to the Companies Act 1988, salary caps had been increased in local currency terms from approximately Rs. 7,500 per month in 1974 (approximately USD 950) to Rs. 15,000 in 1993 (approximately USD 500) per month for managers working in firms with capital of Rs. 150 million (approximately USD 5 million in 1993).[2] Expenditure on perquisites was also restricted to Rs. 135,000 per annum (approximately USD 4,500 in 1993) (see Sen and

---

[1]　For example, Financial Services Authority (FSA) (2009) and the Dodd-Frank Wall Street Reform and Consumer Protection Act (Pub.L. 111-203, H.R. 4173) set out provisions in relation to enhanced disclosure relating to executive compensation schemes at publicly listed firms (e.g. section 955 of the Act now requires disclosure of any hedging arrangements that may have been entered into by the employees and directors of an issuer with respect to the issuer's securities) as well as in relation to allowing shareholders to have a stronger voice on compensation schemes (Section 951 requires non-binding advisory votes of shareholders about executive compensation and golden parachutes). Also see German Federal Financial Supervision Authority (2009).

[2]　Schedule XIII of the Companies Act 1988. The practice in India is to use the nomenclature "lakh" and "crore", particularly in the context of Indian rupees: One "lakh" is Rs. 100,000 and one "crore" is Rs. 10 million. It should be noted that the USD equivalents used here are approximate and based on the exchange rates in effect at that time. The rupee depreciated over that period.

Sarkar (1996), Jaiswall and Firth (2007)). These ceilings were subsequently raised until being virtually eliminated with the advent of capital and financial market liberalization in 1993–94.

The reforms ushered in by the liberalizing movement provided considerable latitude to boards to set the terms of executive contracts. Since the implementation of reforms in 1993–94, salary levels have increased steadily and dramatically. Recent data and more comprehensive analysis to this effect is set out in this chapter; however, as early as 2002, it was noted in a small study of prominent Indian firms that growth in pay packages of managers in the period 1979–2001 was approximately five times that of the growth of employee salaries in these firms. The annual growth rate of managerial remuneration during this period was 20.43 percent (Kakani and Ray (2002)). As variously reported in the literature (Bebchuk and Fried (2004), Gordon (2005)), the sharp, swift rise in salary levels for managers and CEOs were justified, as elsewhere, on competitive pressures necessitating that remuneration levels be sufficient to attract and retain top managerial talent as well as to better align their pay with company performance through increased flexibility in the design of executive compensation packages (e.g. through stock option grants) (Kakani and Ray (2002)).

While pre-1993 ceilings have largely been eliminated, Indian corporate law sets broad limits on the levels of remuneration that may be paid out to executives. Two provisions in the legislation merit particular mention. The Companies Act 1956, by section 198(1), provides that the overall maximum remuneration that may be paid out by a company to its managers is 11 percent of the company's net profits.[3] Section 309(1) of the Companies Act 1956 states that the remuneration payable to both executive and nonexecutive directors must be determined by the board in accordance with the provisions of section 198 either through specific mention in the articles of the company or by ordinary or special resolution, depending on the articles of the company. The Act also limits the compensation that may be payable in cases where a company is loss-making. The 1956 Act stipulated a salary cap of Rs. 40,000 (approximately USD 4,000) to Rs. 87,500 (approximately USD 8,750) for loss-making enterprises, which was subsequently raised to Rs. 200,000 (approximately USD 20,000). As such, although ceilings determining levels of executive compensation have seen considerable relaxation since 1993, some restrictions continue to (very) broadly limit the discretion available to the board in this regard – in contrast to jurisdictions such as the US or the UK, which have not thus far set such restrictions limiting levels of executive pay (Treanor (2011)).

2.3 The Regulatory Framework

In addition to this legislative backdrop, the issue of executive compensation also falls within the regulatory purview of India's corporate governance framework. The regulatory pillars underlying executive compensation in India are Clause 49, which arguably sets the key normative parameters in this area, the Voluntary Guidelines for Corporate Governance issued by the Ministry of Corporate Affairs in 2009, as well as the Reserve

---

[3]   The percentage of net profits under Section 198(1) is computed in the manner laid down in Sections 349, 350 and 351 in the Companies Act 1956.

Bank of India (RBI) Guidelines on Compensation of Whole Time Directors/Chief Executive Officers/Risk takers and Control Function Staff 2010 issued in response to the release of the FSB's Guidelines on Sound Compensation Practices. Each is discussed briefly below.

As India has grown in stature as an international financial center since liberalization, and as an important destination for foreign direct investment, the introduction of robust corporate governance is widely perceived as a necessary complement to pushing India's development forward in this regard. As a practical matter, a number of prominent foreign investors, such as mutual funds, pension or money market funds may be restricted in investing their capital without assurances as to high standards of corporate behavior and transparency in the countries where they invest. Accordingly, success in attracting vigilant and active investors such as the CalPERS (California Public Employees Retirement System), a prominent US pension fund, has been cited as evidence of the significance of corporate governance as a live development issue (TNN, 2004). Moreover, and relatedly, notwithstanding the compliance costs involved, tighter corporate governance regulation has been championed by the industry at large, including its smaller, less capitalized players, keen to attract foreign investment and to themselves assure regulatory signaling desirable to facilitate listing their securities abroad (Black and Khanna (2007), Afsharipour (2010)).

A number of India's largest companies have been active in international capital markets by listing depositary receipts on foreign exchanges.[4] Cross-listing on exchanges in developed markets such as in the US or the UK, often with high regulatory barriers to entry,[5] has necessitated that many of India's leading companies undertake thoroughgoing internal corporate governance review and reform to secure their place on the international scene (Black and Khanna (2007)).[6] Indeed, Black and Khanna noted that the announcement of far-reaching corporate governance reform in 1999 (the introduction of Clause 49, discussed below) increased the stock price of large Indian firms in India by around 4–5 percent over a three day window of time (Black and Khanna (2007)).

The work of high-level committees, chaired by luminaries of Indian business Mangalam Birla (see Report of the Committee Appointed By SEBI on Corporate Governance under the Chairmanship Of Shri Kumar Mangalam Birla (1999)) and Narayana Murthy,[7] laid

---

[4]   For example, Infosys Limited and WIPRO Limited, technology companies that are listed on NASDAQ. Mittal Steel merged with Arcelor in 2006 to form Arcelor Steel which is listed in a number of foreign markets, including the NYSE. Similarly, ICICI Bank ADRs are listed on the NYSE.

[5]   For example, compliance with US GAAP, as well as with the Sarbanes-Oxley Act 2002.

[6]   Also see ENS Economic Bureau (2000). More recently, the National Stock Exchange (NSE) entered into a cross-listing agreement with the Chicago Mercantile Exchange (CME). The agreement should eventually allow Indian investors to trade in US indexes. Under this arrangement, Indian rupee-denominated S&P 500 futures contracts will be listed for trading on the NSE and in return CME will list US dollar-denominated contracts on India's S&P Nifty Index, India's benchmark stock index for large companies. For more detail, see National Stock Exchange and Chicago Mercantile Exchange (2010).

[7]   Report of the SEBI Committee on Corporate Governance, 2003. The Murthy Committee sought to address the perceived deficiencies in Indian corporate governance through the lens of the Enron scandal. As such, its recommendations focused on the role of directorial independence to recommend the exclusion of directors related to owners of a company or key stakeholders. In

the groundwork for sweeping corporate governance reform in India. This reform was introduced in 1999/2000 not through legislation (such as a Companies Act amendment) but under SEBI's regulatory authority. SEBI formalized the recommendations of the BIRLA Committee in 2000 by including these as part of the Listing Agreement's Clause 49. Recommendations of the Murthy Committee were later incorporated in 2006 into Clause 49, ostensibly to apply lessons from the Enron scandal into the Indian corporate governance framework. Prior to these reforms, corporate governance standards in India had widely been perceived as falling well short of international best practice and being of limited and uncompetitive import (Black and Khanna (2007)). Legislative work has also been underway since the implementation of the Murthy reforms to modify company legislation to assure conformity with Clause 49, and moreover to include classificatory provisions more sensitive to the needs of smaller companies. These proposed reforms seek to allow small and medium sized enterprises to benefit from a reduced compliance burden. The Companies Bill 2009 remains under review in the Indian Parliament (Afsharipour (2010)).

Clause 49 seeks to regulate executive pay primarily through annual disclosure in a company's Annual Report. Section IV(E) of Clause 49 mandates that "all elements" of a director's compensation package be disclosed in the Annual Report, to include salary, bonus payments, stock option grants, pension contributions as well as any other benefits (perquisites such as houses, cars etc.). This disclosure requires to be accompanied by information regarding the fixed portion of the compensation package as well as details of performance-linked pay and performance criteria.[8] Details of stock option grants should include information as to whether the options were issued at a discount, and the period through which the options are exercisable.[9] With respect to non-executive directors, a company must disclose any and all pecuniary relationship/transactions between the company and the non-executive directors and details of the criteria applied in determining their compensation levels.[10] As an additional check in this regard, Clause 49 requires companies to assure that the compensation package for non-executive directors, including independent directors, be determined by the board and be subject to a binding vote by shareholders at the annual general meeting.[11]

The Ministry of Corporate Affairs (MCA), India's government ministry charged with company regulation, including with respect to the elaboration of the Companies Bill 2009, promulgated Voluntary Guidelines for Corporate Governance in 2009.[12] The Guidelines are not intended to be binding but instead to have persuasive force and, it has been suggested, to broadly introduce into Indian corporate governance the UK's "comply-or-explain" model (Varottil (2010)). Pursuant to the Guidelines, executive com-

---

addition, the report focused on the role of audit committees, recommending for example that members be educated in matters of finance and that they have appropriate access to company documentation.

  [8]   Clause 49 (IV)(E)(ii)(a) and (b).
  [9]   Clause 49 (IV)(E)(ii)(d).
  [10] Clause 49 (IV)(E)(iii).
  [11] Clause 49 (I)(B).
  [12] Ministry of Corporate Affairs: Government of India, *Corporate Governance Voluntary Guidelines 2009.*

pensation packages should be sufficient to attract talent, but also to assure a close alignment between the pay and performance of the executive. As such, the Guidelines recommend a package that includes a fixed element, together with incentive pay that is clearly linked to long and short term performance benchmarks. In this regard, the Guidelines propose a compensation framework for directors that is substantially comprised of performance-related pay. Finally, the Guidelines also suggest that companies include a remuneration committee in their organizational architecture, which is chiefly staffed by non-executive and independent directors. The Guidelines give the remuneration committee the responsibility for determining and elaborating criteria underlying the company's compensation policy, as well as for designing the pay packages of executive directors and the chairman.[13]

As noted earlier, executive compensation arrangements have come under intense scrutiny for the role played by underlying incentive structures in motivating the reckless and risky market conduct seen leading up to the financial crisis. In their response, the international regulatory community, represented by the G-20 and the FSB (formerly the FSF), issued the FSF's Principles for Sound Compensation Practices in 2009, a statement of a broad, globally agreed consensus on executive compensation supervision and regulation for financial firms (Financial Stability Forum (2009)). While not binding on member states (and others) in the strict sense, the policy positions elaborated under the auspices of the G-20 and FSB are seen to carry considerable normative force (Brummer (2011)). In giving domestic effect to the FSF Principles, the RBI issued a set of Guidelines on Compensation of Whole Time Directors/Chief Executive Officers/Risk Takers and Control Function Staff in 2010, designed to be followed by banks operating in India (Reserve Bank of India (2010)). The RBI Guidelines slightly shift the regulatory emphasis of executive compensation oversight by emphasizing the centrality of risk as a product of ill-designed, and under-supervised executive compensation policy. Whereas Clause 49 and the MCA's Voluntary Guidelines chiefly underscore the role of remuneration policy as a mechanism for better tying pay with short and long-term performance, the normative weight of the RBI's Guidelines rests on the role of remuneration policy as a check against excessive risk taking.

Accordingly, the Guidelines recommend that banks adjust compensation for all types of risk, taking into account long and short-term projections of risk and ensuring alignment of compensation with possible risks (Reserve Bank of India (2010)). It should be noted that, notwithstanding the emphasis on reducing and controlling risk through better design of executive compensation packages, the RBI Guidelines nevertheless underscore tying executive pay closely to performance, for example by rewarding senior management with a higher proportion of incentive-related variable pay designed to contract in cases of poor performance and/or be subject to claw-backs. The Guidelines also recommend that the annual increase in the fixed pay element of executive compensation should not generally be more than between 10 and 15 percent (Reserve Bank of India (2010)).

While the RBI Guidelines echo Clause 49 and the MCA Guidelines in promoting full and detailed disclosure with respect to executive compensation packages and in

---

[13] Ministry of Corporate Affairs: Government of India, *Corporate Governance Voluntary Guidelines 2009*, Section C.

establishing a sound organizational structure to elaborate and give effect to executive compensation policies (Reserve Bank of India (2010)), they have gone further than prior regulatory efforts in some key respects. In particular, the RBI Guidelines include anti-hedging policies to prevent executives from undermining the pay–performance–risk nexus. For example, it is possible for executives to game executive compensation rules where they may stand to benefit financially (e.g. through shorting stock) from falls in the company's stock price, reducing incentives to perform in the better interest of the company. Provisions with respect to hedging have, for example, been included in the Dodd-Frank Act,[14] which requires companies to disclose any hedging arrangements entered into by executives. Executives in firms benefiting from federal support under the Troubled Asset Relief Plan (TARP) have generally not been permitted to enter into hedging arrangements with respect to securities awarded as part of their executive compensation packages.[15]

Nevertheless, given their still short time in operation, the RBI Guidelines require to be tested meaningfully in practice. As such, it remains to be seen how, for example, definitions of hedging may be applied (whether these may be narrowly or more comprehensively construed) (Bebchuk and Fried (2010)), or whether more diligent disclosure of remuneration packages will lead to a greater intensity of shareholder scrutiny of executive pay in financial firms in India.

2.4 Complexities in Indian Corporate Governance

As noted above, corporate governance reform in India has sought to strengthen the reputation of the country's markets and its players and to thus foster investor confidence both domestically and internationally. In this regard, authorities have professed fidelity to international standards in order to cement the credentials of Indian capital markets as comparable and competitive with those in developed and, certainly, other emerging market countries. This being said, corporate governance in India is arguably subject to the play of regulatory particularities that may be said to preclude linear comparisons with other markets and complicate projections as to how corporate governance rules may be applicable in the Indian context. Within the broader contention set out in this chapter, notably with respect to the role played by horizontal as well as vertical agency risk, it is argued that the current legal and regulatory framework neither recognizes this duality of agency risk, nor effectively puts in place an enforcement culture that can control the negative externalities generated. A brief outline of some of these issues is set out below.

2.5 Ownership Structure and Agency Risks

A conventional point of theoretical departure for the analysis of executive compensation regulation lies in the principal–agent relationship and the risks that may be generated in

---

[14] Dodd-Frank Wall Street Reform and Consumer Protection Act (Pub.L. 111-203, H.R. 4173), section 955.

[15] US Department of the Treasury (2010) ("employees should be prohibited from engaging in any hedging, derivative or other transactions that undermine the long-term performance incentives created by a company's compensation structures").

this context. The division between owners and management, traditional at widely held corporations, can give management considerable influence in controlling the daily fortunes of the company, without managers necessarily holding any economic stake in the corporation. Compensation policies thus seek to align the interests of management with those of owners, for example, through the grant of stock options or performance-related bonus payments. To assure managerial performance, and thus mitigate the effects of this vertical agency risk, the work of executives is (in theory) supervised and monitored by the board and more broadly by the company's shareholders (Bebchuk (1999), Bebchuk and Fried (2002)).

While agency risks generated by the division of labor and influence between owners and managers may be said to apply most vividly in the context of widely held companies, where professional managers are engaged by the board to represent the interests of a diverse shareholding, their salience may be more nuanced in the context of closely held corporations. Historically, as discussed in this chapter, companies in India have tended to be family-owned or owned by a small network of affiliated companies. While the Companies Act 1956 does not define "family" ownership, reference is common to companies that are closely held by so-called "promoters" or founders of a company. These founders have traditionally been part of a single family.[16] Arguably, the tighter nexus between owners (promoters) and managers in a closely held company should better align the interests of owners and managers and reduce the incidence of agency risks (Gomez-Mejia et al. (2001)). In such companies, executive pay should, at first glance, be comparatively lower. However, recent studies show otherwise, and have instead reported that executives related to the founding family of a family-owned corporation in India have, on average, appropriated higher levels of pay (Fagernäs (2006), Jaiswall and Firth (2007)).

However, in addition to the vertical agency risks noted, this chapter argues that the Indian corporate environment also gives rise to the play of horizontal agency risks. Briefly, horizontal agency risks refer to the ability of promoter shareholders holding relatively small, non-majority stakes in a company to exert a high valence of influence through their promoter status on other shareholders, and on managers as noted above. In particular, as brought out in greater empirical detail, this chapter presents data to show that the play of horizontal agency risks impacts positively on higher levels of executive pay.

A discussion of the (potentially simultaneous) dual play of both vertical and horizontal agency risks in the Indian corporate context has not yet been undertaken in the literature. This chapter seeks to take the first analytical step to close that gap. Notwithstanding the lack of attention given to this issue, it has nevertheless gained significance in recent years as Indian shareholding patterns evidence progressively greater degrees of diversification, while staying hewn to the cultural and strategic pull of the original promoters of an enterprise. In broad terms, the presence of both vertical and horizontal agency risks raises key regulatory questions. First, as discussed above, Indian law and regulation has sought to

---

[16]   While "promoter" is not a defined term in the Companies Act 1956, it is central to many of its controlling provisions governing issues of corporate control and liability; see for example, section 62 of the Act on civil liability for misstatements.

replicate some of the regulatory levers common to international developed markets to control executive incentives governing pay and performance. Given the duality of agency risks, analysis may be helpful to better determine whether current regulations are appropriate to this specific balance of risks affecting executive compensation in India. Secondly, the dual play of both vertical and horizontal agency risks makes for the possibility that regulation to control one or other risk in the Indian context may be used opportunistically to arbitrage compliance obligations and costs. Thirdly, and related to the above, it is timely to consider the normative implications of how laws and regulation may be better tailored to control the specific legal risks created by this legal environment. Detailed consideration of these issues is beyond the scope of this chapter. However, some brief observations may be made.

From the regulatory perspective, these findings and the traditional ownership structure of Indian companies may be interpreted as presenting a more textured normative starting point for the study of agency risks and executive compensation in India. As discussed above, rules and guidance promulgated under Clause 49 and MCA and RBI Guidelines propose disclosure of executive pay packages to shareholders, as well as the establishment of remuneration committees as setting the essential organizational checks and balances for assuring discipline with respect to executive compensation. Further, more recently, for example in the US and the UK, an executive compensation package is increasingly being brought to a (usually) non-binding but nevertheless influential "say on pay" vote by shareholders at a general meeting. A species of "say on pay" provision is currently included as part of Clause 49 for remuneration packages for non-executive, including independent, directors. While these measures have arguably been introduced in most developed and other markets to deal with vertical agency costs, their implementation in India seeks to remedy incentive asymmetries created by vertical agency risks arising in the context of closely held companies, and where promoter shareholdings appear to give promoters disproportionately high influence on issues of managerial significance.[17]

As discussed, owner-managers exercise powerful influence on corporate decision-making in India. However, corporate governance reform has broadly followed the trends and tenor of developed economies which tend to have companies with a more widely held ownership structure. It is therefore arguable that checks and balances put in place in India that rely on disclosure to shareholders or on their assent and approval may be largely symbolic, where those shareholders comprise promoters or are heavily influenced by the promoter's "moral" sway on the shareholding.

As has been noted in recent studies, owner-managers in India are perceived to exercise considerable "managerial power," with increased benefits and pay for staff generated through close links to the owning family or group. As a result, reliance chiefly on disclosures as a way to discipline managers on executive compensation policy may be of little practical import, where managers are either closely connected/related to company promoters and/or where influence exerted by promoters dictates how these disclosures are received and interpreted. Similarly, organizational structures such as the remuneration committee, although staffed by independent and non-executive directors, may be vulnerable to capture by powerful owner-managers. In this context, members of the remunera-

---

[17]   Clause 49 (I)(B).

tion committee seek to gain stature and institutional approval within the company and thus exercise more relaxed scrutiny than expected in the legislation over pay practices (Bebchuk and Fried (2002), Bebchuk (1999)).

One interesting area for further study may be on say-on-pay. On the one hand, say-on-pay votes may have limited disciplining effect in India where owner-managers exercise a controlling or blocking shareholding, and hold influential, "moral" sway over the company. In such cases, where owner-managers have a controlling shareholding, executive compensation practices are likely to face little shareholder headwind when brought for a vote, binding or otherwise. However, in the context of controlling horizontal agency risks, the say-on-pay tool may exert greater bite. In this scenario, promoters usually hold a relatively small and non-majority shareholding and by numbers alone (except, potentially, in cases where resolutions require supermajority approval), their holdings are not decisive. As a result, say-on-pay can in theory give shareholders an opportunity to make their voice heard on executive compensation policy, despite the influence and sway held by promoters and owner-managers.

Some issues nevertheless remain. First, Indian company law makes provision for the protection of minority shareholders' rights, for example, through sections 397/398 of the Companies Act 1956, allowing minority shareholders to petition the Company Law Board for redress where a company may not be being properly run. Under these sections, the Company Law Board has strong adjudicative and remedial powers to order investigations and redress. Further, minority shareholders can also pursue remedies to wind the company up in the High Court. It is possible that minority shareholders, for example those who are promoter-shareholders, may either use such remedies to challenge say-on-pay votes or potentially use the threat of such votes to exert influence on how a say-on-pay vote should turn out. Additionally, given the horizontal agency costs noted in this chapter and empirically analyzed in the following sections, it is arguable that tools such as non-binding say-on-pay votes may be used by non-promoter shareholders to express broader dissatisfaction with promoter policies, or otherwise to symbolically undermine promoter influence. In such cases, the vote may be interpreted less as a vote on the appropriateness of compensation policies, and potentially more as a form of protest against the disproportionate influence exerted by powerful promoters and owner-managers. To recall however, say-on-pay votes currently play a very limited disciplining vote in executive compensation regulation in India, being applied only in cases of votes brought to determine the pay packages of non-executive directors of a public company.

2.6   Enforcement and Governance Challenges

The Indian corporate governance framework rests largely on the operation of Clause 49, compliance with which is made mandatory on public companies through incorporation in the Listing Agreement used by exchanges. As a first step, companies are required to report their compliance with Clause 49 by way of quarterly reports submitted to the country's exchanges.[18] In addition to self-reporting, studies of the compliance patterns of Indian firms with Clause 49, as suggested by Clause 49's self-reporting mechanism, have

---

[18]   Clause 49 VI(ii).

indicated that the larger companies have demonstrated greater diligence in their compliance with Clause 49. Smaller companies, presumed to face high compliance costs, and likely to be less familiar with international best practice standards, have evidenced a more patchy compliance profile. Public sector firms showed considerable under-compliance (Afsharipour (2010)).

SEBI can theoretically exercise considerable enforcement authority with respect to breaches of Clause 49 provisions. Under the Securities Laws (Amendment) Act 2004,[19] SEBI can impose a range of fines for non-compliance that may be levied on directors as well as on the company and SEBI may, as a nuclear option, order the delisting of a repeatedly recalcitrant company. Notwithstanding its enforcement powers under law, SEBI has only rarely exercised its enforcement authority to either fine or delist companies in frequent breach of Clause 49.[20] Commentators have lamented the lack of disclosure by SEBI of its enforcement actions, such that data to better understand the agency's enforcement culture and practice is very difficult to obtain. Low and non-expert staffing at the SEBI has been raised as an issue significant to possible institutional inertia, as has the matter of agency capture to the powerful family-owned enterprises (Afsharipour (2010)).

Moreover, the effectiveness of private rights of action against firms may be questioned in light of weak enforcement routes available through Indian courts. The World Bank's 2004 Corporate Governance Report noted that proceedings through Indian courts were routinely subject to extremely long delays, often of decades. Efforts to create special commercial tribunals such as the National Company Law Tribunal, to speed up the administration of commercial cases and reduce the burden on courts, have largely floundered.[21] Accordingly, despite the considerable legislative effort expended in enacting executive compensation regulation and corporate governance provisions more generally, moral hazard arising through light enforcement of securities laws and weak investor protection may be seen as allowing executives to more easily appropriate value from their companies, irrespective of performance. Moreover, challenges in enforcement, tight resources at the level of regulators such as SEBI as well as limited training opportunities to develop technical expertise, may result in a laxer standard of oversight over corporate practice, where horizontal and vertical risks may continue unchecked.

2.7 The Developing Role of Institutional Shareholders

The role of institutional shareholders in India remains to be developed. Historically, Indian companies have received investment from the state. The World Bank's 2004 Report noted the high involvement of state pension funds and unit trusts as equity

---

[19]   The Securities Laws (Amendment) Act, 2004, section 11.

[20]   Press Release, SEBI (2007). As noted by Afsharipour, only 20 companies were prosecuted from a possible pool of hundreds of firms in breach. Furthermore, she notes that complaints against the public sector companies in breach were subsequently dropped on account of political pressure. See Afsharipour (2010).

[21]   *Union of India v. R. Gandhi*, May 11, 2010. In this case, the Indian Supreme Court held that certain provisions of the Company (Second Amendment) Act 2002, establishing the National Company Law Tribunal and Appellate Tribunal, suffered from unconstitutional "defects."

contributors to Indian business. However, the Report suggested that many of these early institutional shareholders were passive participants at company general meetings and little involved in enforcing good governance standards, failing to leverage their stature and voting power (World Bank (2004)). The influx of foreign investment in India has resulted in the entry of some powerful institutional shareholders, for example, CalPERS. However, their presence, while growing, remains to be cemented into the corporate landscape. It may be argued that, in addition to cross-listing, the introduction of institutional shareholders which diversifies the traditional shareholding models of Indian corporations, also imports very directly international norms on corporate governance practice. As yet, it remains to be seen whether the greater presence of international and more active domestic institutional shareholders in India is likely to temper the hold of powerful owner-managers in the area of executive compensation, and good corporate governance more broadly.

3   DESCRIPTIVE OVERVIEW OF EXECUTIVE PAY IN INDIA

3.1   Our Data Sources and Sample

As noted above, this chapter seeks to fill an analytical gap in the study of corporate governance in India by studying the probable impact of horizontal agency costs (in addition to the more traditionally examined vertical agency risks) on executive compensation policy in India. In this regard, we have undertaken an empirical study of a sample of Indian public companies to examine the potential correlation between horizontal agency risks and executive compensation policy. Our intention here has not been to present a comprehensive study, but one that raises the essential issue, with a view to substantiating not only the economic costs of these agency risks, but also how regulatory action may most optimally be configured to manage them (as discussed in section 2 of this chapter).

Our data comes from the Prowess database (prowess.cmie.com) maintained by the Centre for Monitoring Indian Economy, Mumbai, India (CMIE), which contains information on firm characteristics for all publicly traded companies. The Prowess database provides information on director compensation and their designations as well as annual financial information for each of the companies. Stock grants and stock options to executives are, however, not reported in this dataset. The compensation figures are reported at the close of the financial year in India which is on March 31st. (For instance, the pay figure reported by the company as on March 31st of year 2004 is taken as the compensation for the year 2004 in our analysis.)

We generate our CEO and CXO compensation data using the universe of all companies listed on the Bombay Stock Exchange (BSE). Our sample spans seven years from 2004 to 2010. We start from 2004 because prior to that year, the compensation details for the board of directors are not available on the Prowess database. We use the fiscal year rather than the calendar year because the compensation details of the board of directors are reported at the end of the fiscal year. We consider firms which satisfy the following criteria:

(a)   We are able to identify someone designated as a CEO or an equivalent designation.[22]
(b)   To be able to compare the CEO's salary vis-à-vis those of the next level of executives, we restrict our attention to those firms where there is at least one executive director other than the CEO. An executive director is identified as a board member for whom the salary component of compensation is non-zero. The non-CEO executive directors constitute the sample of CXOs for our study. Firms for which the salary component of all directors is zero or missing are dropped from the sample.

We convert nominal cash values of CEO and CXO pay as well as firm-level values such as assets, market capitalization and sales to constant 2004 rupees by deflating them using the consumer price index for a year[23] and we convert the currency from rupees to US dollars using an exchange rate of 45 INR/USD.

We focus on total CEO and CXO pay as well as their fixed and variable components. We follow these figures on an annual basis over the sample period. Finally, in order to understand how firm-specific features drive cross-sectional differences in compensation, we track firm characteristics like assets, sales and market capitalization. We also employ the promoters' holding in the firm and a dummy variable to capture whether the firm forms part of an Indian business group or not to factor in the ownership structure. We also record from Prowess the annual closing value of the Indian stock market index Sensex for the respective years. Our variables of interest and their definitions and measurement units are listed in Table 21.1 along with the specific sources of the data.

3.2   Trends of Executive Compensation in India

The descriptive statistics for the variables used in the analysis are provided in Table 21.2. Panel A shows the evolution of our sample of firms and executive directors over the time period 2004–2010. Regarding column 1, we notice that the number of firms for which we have reliable executive compensation data increases consistently over the sample; in fact, on average 8 percent more firms report reliable data on their executive compensation every year during our sample. In relation to column 3, we note that across our sample period, we have information about the compensation provided to the CEO and two other executive directors. Furthermore, the fact that the average number of executive directors per firm is quite stable across the sample period indicates that the increase in the number of executive directors that we track is because of more firms reporting their executive compensation data in later years. The increase is not because we are better able to identify the executive directors in a firm in the later years when compared to the earlier years.

---

[22]   The list of designations which we considered equivalent to the CEO designation in terms of the managerial powers and responsibilities were: CEO & Deputy MD; CEO & Director; CEO & Exec. Director; CEO & Manager; CEO & President; CEO, President & MD; Chairman & CEO; Chairman & Exec. Director; Chairman & Jt. MD; Chairman & MD; Chairman, MD & CEO; Chairperson & MD; Co-Chairman & MD; Deputy Chairman & MD; Director & CEO; Director, CEO & Compliance Officer; Exec. Chairman; Exec.Director & CEO; Exec. Vice Chairman & MD; Jt. MD & CEO; MD & CEO; and Vice Chairman & CEO.
[23]   We obtain the consumer price index from http://labourbureau.nic.in/indtab.html. The index value for a year is that on the 31st March of each year.

Table 21.1 *Variables and descriptions*

Variable	Description
Year	Fiscal year, i.e. year ending 31st March
Industry	Classification of firms into industries as given in Prowess database.
CEO pay	Total remuneration (which includes salary, sitting fees, bonus & commissions, perquisites, retiral benefits, and contribution to PF) of the CEO in a firm in US$ millions. This value is adjusted for inflation using the Consumer Price Index with base year as 2004.
CXO pay	Average of the total remuneration of all executive directors on the board of a firm excluding the CEO in US$ millions. This value is adjusted for inflation using the Consumer Price Index with base year as 2004.
% variable pay	Bonus and commissions as a percentage of total remuneration of a director.
Board size	Total number of directors on the board of a firm in a year.
Assets	Total assets of a company in a year in US$ millions adjusted for inflation using CPI with base year as 2004.
Sales	Total sales of a company in a year in US$ millions adjusted for inflation using CPI with base year as 2004.
Market capitalization	Average market capitalization of a firm over a year in US$ millions adjusted for inflation using CPI with base year as 2004.
Promoters holding	Percentage shares of a firm owned by promoters.
Non-promoter institutional holding	Percentage shares of a firm owned by non-promoter institutions.
Yearly return	Year-on-year stock return of a firm calculated as the percentage change in stock price of a firm from previous fiscal year end to this fiscal year end.
Ownership group	A categorical variable that indicates whether a firm is: (1) owned by Private Foreign Group, (2) Stand-Alone, (3) owned by Foreign Business House, (4) owned by Indian Business House, (5) a Public Sector Unit (Govt. Owned).
Indian Business Group	A dummy that takes a value of one if the ownership group of the firm is an Indian Business House.

Note: This table gives a brief description of the variables used in the study. All the variables are sourced from CMIE's Prowess database.

Panel B describes the distribution of the variables. First, by comparing the maximum values and the 99th percentile values for each of the variables to their respective 75th and 50th percentile values, we note that the distribution of compensation is significantly skewed to the right. This is also noticeable when we compare the mean values to the medians. A manual check on the data showed that the increase from the 99th percentile value to the maximum value is gradual and not sudden. Thus, these values for executive

Table 21.2 Descriptive statistics

Panel A:

Fiscal year	Number of firms	Number of executive directors	Avg. number of executive directors per firm
2004	415	1212	2.92
2005	457	1322	2.89
2006	521	1537	2.95
2007	552	1591	2.88
2008	602	1764	2.93
2009	662	1929	2.91
2010	665	1948	2.93

Panel B:

Variable	Obsns.	Min.	p1	p25	p50	p75	p99	Max.	Mean	Std. Dev.
Real CEO pay	3875	$0.06*10^{-3}$	0.001	0.02	0.04	0.12	1.9	12.7	0.15	0.47
Avg. real CXO pay	3875	$0.07*10^{-3}$	0.001	0.01	0.02	0.06	0.74	6.1	0.07	0.21
CEO var. pay %	3875	0	0	0	0	0	93.5	98.7	10.8	23.8
CXO var. pay %	3875	0	0	0	0	0	84.9	99.9	7.4	18.5
Yearly return	3281	−81.5	−81.5	−24.5	27.1	113.1	716.9	758.3	69	144.3
1 year avg. market cap.	3479	0.06	0.21	2.5	11.0	54.9	6354.4	55462.7	282.6	2006.8
Promoters holding	3656	0	5.3	38.3	50.4	62.4	85.8	97.6	49.8	17.4
Non-promoters institutional holding	3656	0	0	0.04	2.1	12.6	50	88.2	8.1	11.9
Assets	3831	0.12	0.46	7.6	26.3	88.1	3597.4	70698.9	291.8	2636.7
Sales	3831	0	0	5.6	21.6	70.4	1252.6	28516	129	957.2

Note: The table shows the summary statistics for the variables used in our study. The sample covers the time period 2004–10. The number of firms and number of executive directors varied from year to year as described.

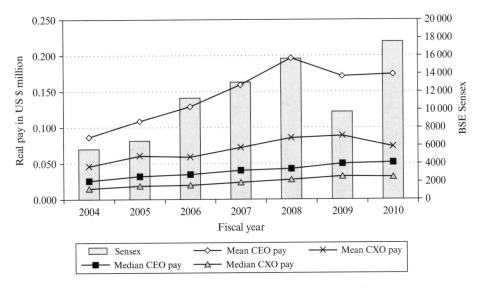

Figure 21.1A   Mean and median pay of CEOs and CXOs across all companies in a year

compensation in our sample of firms are representative of the population of Indian listed firms; they do not constitute outliers in the distribution. Clearly, the distribution of the CEO and CXO pay is highly convex with the largest Indian firms compensating their CEOs at least one order of magnitude more than the other firms. Second, even though we observe this rightward skew in CXO compensation as well, the differences are not as pronounced as that for the CEOs. Third, we notice that the proportion of variable pay to total pay is heavily skewed as well. The proportion of variable pay is significant only for the largest firms. The variable component of compensation is *zero* for the median as well as the 75th percentile firm. In contrast, in the very large firms, more than three quarters of the total executive pay is accounted for by variable components such as "bonus and commissions."

Figure 21.1A provides a visual representation of the annual average executive compensation across all firms in our sample. The rectangular bars in the graph depict the value of the benchmark Bombay Stock Exchange (BSE) index, Sensex, on March 31st of each year. First, we notice that while average CEO pay has closely mirrored the fortunes of the aggregate stock market, median CEO pay does not co-move much with the aggregate stock market. Clearly, this indicates that the sensitivity of CEO pay to stock market movements exists mainly in large firms. However, because CEO compensation in the relatively larger firms varied considerably more with the aggregate stock market (as seen in Figure 21.1B), we find that average CEO compensation exhibited significant co-movement with the aggregate stock market as well. Second, we notice that average CXO compensation varied considerably less with the aggregate stock market when compared to the variation in the average CEO compensation. Third, coinciding with the financial crisis of 2008–09 in the US and Europe, we notice a pronounced dip in average CEO compensation in 2009 when compared to that in 2008. However, coinciding with the financial crisis, we do not see any decline in the median CEO compensation. Together,

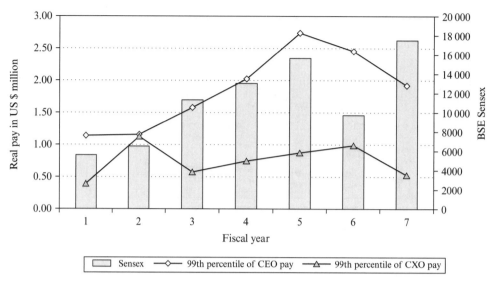

Figure 21.1B   99th percentile of pay of CEO and CXO across all companies in a year

these two facts again imply that the effect of the financial crisis on CEO compensation was restricted primarily to the larger firms; CEO compensation in the smaller firms was largely unaffected by the financial crisis. Since a significant proportion of the revenues of larger Indian firms accrue from their business operations in foreign countries, the financial crisis of 2008 impacted their performance and thereby the compensation that they provide to their CEOs as well; however, this was not, on average, true for smaller firms. Fourth, we notice that this effect of the financial crisis on executive compensation was primarily restricted to CEOs and did not extend to the CXOs. Surprisingly, we also note that the median pay for CXOs has decreased from 2009 to 2010, whereas the median CEO pay has been secularly rising during the time period of our analysis.

Figure 21.2 shows the trend in average CEO pay classified by the nature of the firm's ownership. We notice that while CEO compensation in firms controlled by foreign-owned business houses exhibited a meteoric rise in the years leading up to the financial crisis, it fell dramatically thereafter concurrently with the financial crisis. We do not observe this pattern for any other category of Indian listed firms. Among firms controlled by Indian business houses, we observe a fall in CEO compensation in the year 2009 coinciding with the financial crisis; however, CEO compensation in these firms increased in 2010 to end slightly above the pre-financial-crisis levels. In firms that were controlled by a private foreign entity, CEO pay decreased in 2008, but has increased sharply thereafter. In government controlled as well as in standalone firms, we find that CEO compensation has been increasing in a secular manner, albeit at a considerably slower pace compared to the other categories of firms.

Figure 21.3 shows the variation in mean variable pay for CEOs and CXOs across the years. Variable pay is defined as the ratio of "bonus and commissions" as a percentage of total remuneration. This is potentially an indicator of the fraction of CEO and CXO

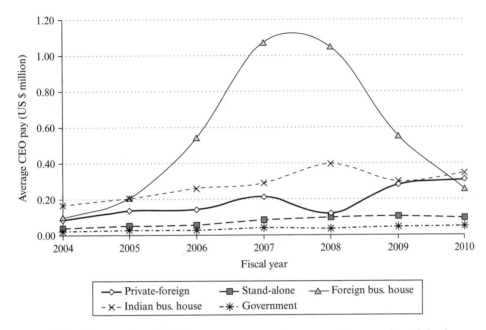

Figure 21.2   Mean value of CEO pay across years by nature of ownership of the firm

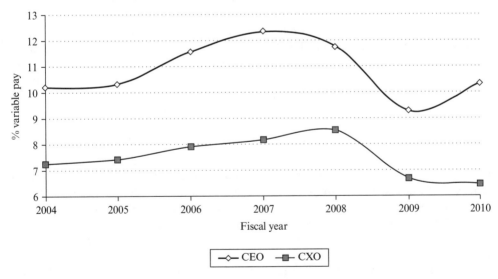

Figure 21.3   Change in mean % of variable pay of CEOs and CXOs with year

pay that is related to performance. For each year, this percentage is averaged across all firms to get the mean variable pay percentage. We observe that consistent with CEO pay being more sensitive to firm performance, the variable component of CEO compensation is considerably more than the variable component of CXO compensation. Though we do not have data pertaining to the amount of stock/stock options granted to the executives

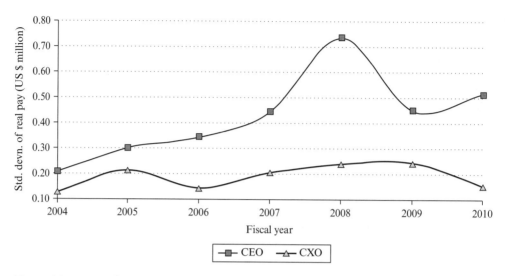

Figure 21.4   Standard deviation of real pay across all companies in a year

in a firm,[24] anecdotal evidence from annual reports suggests that CEO compensation in Indian firms is more closely linked to the firm's stock performance than that of the executives reporting to the CEO. This is consistent with the variable part of total compensation being greater for the CEO than for the CXO.

Also in Figure 21.3, we observe that the variable component of CEO compensation increased till 2007 and then dipped in 2008 and 2009 before increasing again in 2010. In contrast, the variable component of CXO compensation increased every year till 2008, but decreased in 2009 and stayed flat in 2010. Since CEO compensation is linked more closely to a firm's stock performance than that of the CXO in India, the relatively greater sensitivity of CEO variable pay to the financial crisis could have been due to the stock price drops of most firms during that period.

Figure 21.4 shows the cross-sectional dispersion in CEO and CXO compensation for each year during our sample period. For a given year in the sample, the dispersion measure is calculated as the standard deviation of compensation across all companies in that year. We notice that the dispersion in CEO compensation is considerably more than the dispersion in the compensation of other senior executives in the firm. A possible interpretation of this fact is that while firms differentiate a lot between the CEOs based on the extent of their managerial skills, they tend to differentiate less as far as other executives are concerned.

Furthermore, we observe that dispersion in CEO pay increased with the upward movement in the aggregate stock market till 2008. However, dispersion in CEO pay nosedived in 2009 coinciding with the financial crisis and the resultant drop in stock prices across

---

[24]   Stock option based compensation is apparently not as significant in India. Balasubramanian et al. (2009) report on the basis of survey evidence that only 16 percent of firms had some stock option based compensation.

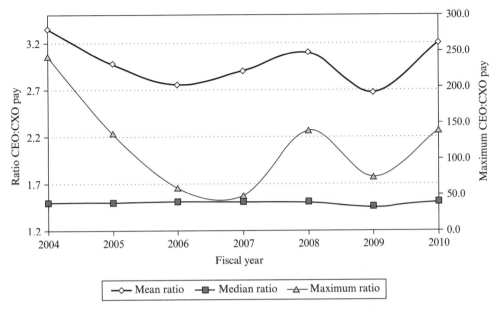

Figure 21.5   Ratio of CEO to CXO pay (mean, median and maximum values of the ratio)

the board. However, such a pattern in the dispersion in CXO compensation is conspicuous by its absence. As mentioned above, CEO compensation in India is more closely linked to the stock market performance of the firm than CXO compensation. Furthermore, consistent with the need to provide more high-powered incentives to CEOs in larger firms, the sensitivity of CEO compensation to stock market performance may have been greater in larger firms. These two facts can together explain why we see the dispersion in CEO pay tracking the fortunes of the aggregate stock market but we do not observe this for CXO compensation.

Figure 21.5 depicts the ratio of CEO pay to CXO pay for each of the years in our sample. This is a measure of the dispersion in pay *within* a firm as opposed to Figure 21.4, which plotted the dispersion in pay across firms. The maximum, median and mean values of this ratio are plotted across all firms for each year. The median ratio of CEO to CXO pay is virtually constant around 1.5, which suggests that in the median Indian listed firm, the CEO is paid 50 percent more than the executives reporting to him/her. In contrast, the mean ratio of CEO to CXO pay varies from 2.7 to 3.3; this variation in within-firm dispersion in executive compensation correlates with the peaks and troughs in the stock market. In particular, such within-firm dispersion in executive compensation is highly volatile for the largest firms. In fact, the maximum ratio of CEO to CXO pay is as high as 250 for some years, which indicates that in some firm-years, the CEOs were compensated orders of magnitude more than the executives reporting to the CEO.

CEOs are arguably expected to possess greater general management skills than CXOs, who may be subject-matter experts without necessarily possessing the general management skills of the CEO. Therefore, Figures 21.4 and 21.5 are consistent with Murphy and

Zabojnik (2004), who argue that CEO pay has risen because of the increasing importance of general managerial skills relative to function-specific/firm-specific abilities.

4   ECONOMIC DRIVERS OF EXECUTIVE COMPENSATION IN INDIA

4.1   Issues Investigated

There is extensive international empirical evidence on the economic drivers of executive compensation (for example, Gabaix and Landier (2008), Frydman and Saks (2010)). Perhaps the most dominant issue in the literature is whether executive compensation schemes are structured to help alleviate agency problems through optimal contracting, or is the high level of CEO compensation the result of powerful managers setting their own pay? A related question is whether the growth in CEO pay is the efficient result of increasing demand for scarce managerial talent (Gabaix and Landier (2008), Tervio 2008), and stricter corporate governance and improved monitoring of CEOs by boards and large shareholders (Hermalin (2005)); or are managers extracting rents, with weak corporate governance and acquiescent boards allowing CEOs to determine their own pay, resulting in inefficiently high levels of compensation (Bebchuk and Fried (2004))?

A comprehensive investigation of the large variety of issues that could be relevant is clearly outside the scope of this chapter. Instead, in this section, we focus on an introductory analysis of two specific economic drivers.

Most importantly, we focus on the distinguishing characteristic of the Indian listed corporate sector, i.e., the extensive existence of *horizontal* agency costs that can arise from the fact that the presence of controlling shareholder groups – in particular, "promoters" and the affiliated business group – potentially leads managers to act on behalf of the controlling family, but not necessarily on behalf of the shareholders. For example, a business group might quash innovation in one firm to protect its obsolete investment in another. As discussed in the introduction, these are different in character from the *vertical* agency costs between managers and dispersed shareholders that are widely accepted as contributing to an upward pressure on CEO pay in Anglo-American companies.[25] Specifically in the Indian context, studies find that owners of business groups expropriate minority shareholders by tunneling resources from firms where they have low cash flow rights to firms where they have high cash flow rights; and such tunneling occurs primarily through the non-operating components of profit (Bertrand et al (2002)). Hence, we use this important feature of corporate India to examine whether the horizontal agency costs stemming from the presence of promoters and business groups leads to higher management compensation in Indian firms.

We also focus on the influence of the size of the firm. Theories of competitive assignment of CEOs to heterogeneous firms predict that the level of pay should increase at the

---

[25]   For example, Morck and Yeung (2003) discuss the horizontal agency costs that arise when a family controls a group of publicly traded and private firms, and provide similar arguments. That said, Indian business and promoter groups are not necessarily family-based.

same rate as the expansion of aggregate firm size (Gabaix and Landier (2008)). In fact, these theories argue that the CEO production function has constant returns to scale, and hence the increase in CEO pay should be proportional to the increase in average firm size in the economy. Accordingly, the six-fold increase in CEO pay between 1980 and 2003 has been attributed to the six-fold increase in market capitalization of large US companies during that period. We specifically investigate this issue for CEO and CXO pay in India.

4.2 Executive Pay in Indian Firms and Firm Size

We proxy firm size using three different measures – market capitalization, assets and sales.[26] In each case, we use logarithms of the variables involved. Following the recent literature on executive compensation (Frydman and Saks (2010)), we decompose the size of a firm into three components: (i) the average size of all the firms in a year, which reflects the size of a typical Indian firm; (ii) the average size of a firm across all years, which reflects firm-specific factors for the specific firm in question; and (iii) the difference of firm size in any particular year from this firm-specific average and the time-varying market average (essentially reflecting short-run fluctuations in firm size that are unrelated or orthogonal to market-wide fluctuations in firm size).

Our dependent variable is $Log(Compensation_{it})$, representing CEO/CXO pay, with the subscript i representing the firm and the subscript t representing the year. The variable S represents firm size. In Table 21.3 columns (1)–(3), we report the results of running the following regression specification using the aforesaid three different proxies for firm size:[27]

$$Log(Compensation_{it}) = \beta_1*Ln(Avg.\ S_{t-1}) + \beta_2*Ln(Avg.\ S_i) + \beta_3*[Ln(S_{i,t-1})$$

$$- Ln(Avg.\ S_{t-1}) - Ln(Avg.\ S_j)] + \varepsilon_{it} \qquad (21.1)$$

Table 21.3 presents the results of this regression for CEO pay. In columns (1)–(3) of Table 21.3, we find that all the three components of size, viz. the idiosyncratic component, firm-specific component and the aggregate market-representative component have a positive effect on the level of CEO pay; these coefficients are statistically highly significant (at the 1 percent level) in all the specifications. Furthermore, the total effect of all the components, as measured by the sum of the coefficients β_1, β_2 and β_3 equals 0.935, 1.339, 1.537. The F-test for the sum of these three coefficients indicates that $\beta_1+\beta_2+\beta_3$ is statistically indistinguishable from one. This indicates that we cannot reject the hypothesis that the CEO production function exhibits constant returns to scale as evidenced for the United States (Gabaix and Landier (2008)).

In columns (4)–(6), we examine the effect of changes in firm size on changes in CEO compensation:

---

[26] Market capitalization or market value of the firm is the sum of the value of debt and the product of the share price and the number of equity shares outstanding.

[27] The presence of the lagged value for firm size as an additional independent variable in (1) ensures that size is not observed after the pay of CEO is determined.

Table 21.3   The effect of firm size on the level of CEO pay

Dependent variable is:	log(CEO Pay$_t$)			Δlog(CEO Pay$_t$)		
Proxy for size is:	Market cap.	Assets	Size	Market cap.	Assets	Size
	(1)	(2)	(3)	(4)	(5)	(6)
Size$_{t-1}$ – Firm avg. –	0.260***	0.276***	0.293***			
Year Avg.$_{t-1}$	(0.035)	(0.066)	(0.106)			
Year avg. of size$_{t-1}$	0.160***	0.457***	0.728***			
	(0.045)	(0.082)	(0.111)			
Avg. firm size	0.515***	0.606***	0.516***			
	(0.019)	(0.027)	(0.025)			
ΔSize$_{t-1}$ – ΔAvg. firm				0.117***	0.202***	0.130***
size$_{t-1}$				(0.033)	(0.057)	(0.044)
ΔAvg. firm size$_{t-1}$				0.050	0.470	0.588
				(0.054)	(0.290)	(0.360)
Constant	−7.545***	−9.845***	−10.477***	0.057***	0.000	−0.002
	(0.342)	(0.508)	(0.597)	(0.017)	(0.046)	(0.048)
Observations	2,395	2,643	2,581	1,621	1,816	1,773
Adj. R^2	0.561	0.521	0.433	0.009	0.008	0.007

Note: This table shows the correlation between the level of a firm's CEO pay in a year and the firm's size in the previous year. Three proxies are used for firm size: natural logarithm of a firm's average market capitalization over a year, natural logarithm of firm's assets, and natural logarithm of firm's sales. In columns (1)–(3) regressions are done in levels while in columns (4)–(6) regressions are done on the changes in the dependent and independent variables. The independent variable 'Year avg. of size' is measured as the mean size of all the firms in a year and the variable 'Avg. firm size' is the average size of a firm across all years where the size is measured as per the definition in each specification. Standard errors reported in parentheses are robust to heteroskedasticity and are clustered by firm. ***, **, and * denote statistical significance at 1%, 5%, and 10% respectively. The time period covered in the regression sample is 2005–2010 in columns (1)–(3) and 2006–2010 in columns (4)–(6).

$$\Delta Log(Compensation_{ist}) = \beta_1 * \Delta Ln(Avg.\ S_{t-1}) + \beta_2 * [\Delta Ln(S_{i,t-1})$$

$$- \Delta Ln(Avg.\ S_{t-1})] + \varepsilon_{it} \tag{21.2}$$

We note that the coefficient estimates for β_2 are positive and statistically significant though they are of a smaller magnitude than the coefficient estimates in columns (1)–(3). However, the coefficient estimate of the changes in average firm size across all Indian firms β_1 is statistically indistinguishable from zero. Thus, we infer that changes in size of a given firm led to changes in CEO compensation in that firm. However, unlike the results found for US firms (Frydman and Saks (2010)), CEO compensation is not affected by changes in the average size of firms in the Indian economy.

Next, we examine whether CXO pay in Indian firms correlates with firm size as well. Table 21.4 presents the results of running the above regressions for CXOs. In columns (1)–(3) of the table, we replicate regression equation (21.1) by replacing the logarithm of CEO pay with the logarithm of CXO pay while in columns (4)–(6), we replicate equation (21.2) using the logarithm of CXO pay. In Table 21.4, we find that firm size is again

Table 21.4   The effect of firm size on the level of CXO pay

Dependent variable is:	log(CXO Pay$_t$)			Δlog(CXO Pay$_t$)		
Proxy for size is:	Market cap.	Assets	Size	Market cap.	Assets	Size
	(1)	(2)	(3)	(4)	(5)	(6)
Size$_{t-1}$ – Firm avg. – Year Avg.$_{t-1}$	0.220***	0.208***	0.278***			
	(0.037)	(0.067)	(0.092)			
Year avg. of size$_{t-1}$	0.170***	0.444***	0.697***			
	(0.042)	(0.077)	(0.101)			
Avg. firm size	0.430***	0.502***	0.430***			
	(0.018)	(0.023)	(0.023)			
ΔSize$_{t-1}$ – ΔAvg. firm size$_{t-1}$				0.071**	0.175***	0.079**
				(0.028)	(0.050)	(0.039)
ΔAvg. firm size$_{t-1}$				0.048	0.951***	0.685**
				(0.045)	(0.212)	(0.323)
Constant	−8.163***	−10.372***	−10.705***	0.054***	−0.078**	−0.019
	(0.333)	(0.484)	(0.528)	(0.014)	(0.033)	(0.043)
Observations	2,395	2,643	2,581	1,621	1,816	1,773
Adj. R^2	0.491	0.446	0.376	0.005	0.016	0.005

Note: This table shows the correlation between the level of a firm's average CXO pay in a year and the firm's size in the previous year. Three proxies are used for firm size: natural logarithm of a firm's average market capitalization over a year, natural logarithm of firm's assets, and natural logarithm of firm's sales. In columns (1)–(3) regressions are done in levels while in columns (4)–(6) regressions are done on the changes in the dependent and independent variables. The independent variable 'Year avg. of size' is measured as the mean size of all the firms in a year and the variable 'Avg. firm size' is the average size of a firm across all years where the size is measured as per the definition in each specification. Standard errors reported in parentheses are robust to heteroskedasticity and are clustered by firm. ***, **, and * denote statistical significance at 1%, 5%, and 10% respectively. The time period covered in the regression sample is 2005–2010 in columns (1)–(3) and 2006–2010 in columns (4)–(6).

strongly positively correlated with CXO compensation. In fact, using the changes on changes specification in columns (4)–(6), we are able to infer that changes in firm size led to changes in CXO compensation as well. However, we note that the coefficient estimates for firm size are almost half in the case of CXO compensation relative to what they were for CEO compensation. Thus, while firm size does affect average CXO compensation, the sensitivity of CXO compensation to firm size is considerably lower than the similar sensitivity of CEO compensation to firm size.

4.3   Executive Pay and Horizontal Agency Costs

We proxy possible horizontal agency costs using two variables: first, the proportion "$\%PromoterHolding_{it}$" that promoters hold in firm i at time t in the firm's equity, hereafter "promoter ownership"; and second, a "dummy" variable "$IndianBusinessGroupDummy_i$" that takes the value of "1" if the firm is owned by a business group, and zero otherwise.

Our objective is to isolate the effect of horizontal agency costs, and therefore we control for the concomitant influence of other confounding factors. First, the literature on executive compensation argues that rent extraction by the CEO and other senior manage-ment in a firm would be more likely in poorly governed firms than in well governed firms (Frydman and Saks (2010)). We therefore attempt to set up controls for the effect of the quality of governance. Since smaller boards may be more effective monitors than larger ones (Yermack (1996)), we employ board size as our first proxy for the quality of govern-ance. Greater block ownership by institutional shareholders has been found to be cor-related with higher intensity of monitoring of the CEO and the senior management (Tirole (2006)). We therefore use the share of non-promoter institutional holdings as our second proxy for the quality of governance. Second, executive pay could be higher simply because the quality of executives hired is better. We control for this using a market-based firm performance proxy: the year-on-year return on stock. This variable also controls for the explicit influence of a firm's stock performance on management compensation. Finally, apart from these, we also include firm size as in equation (21.1) to control for the effect of firm size that we have ourselves documented earlier in the preceding sub-section. We collectively use the symbol "X" for our set of control variables.

As has been argued, the presence of promoters and business groups potentially results in higher horizontal agency costs, and therefore higher compensation of CEOs and CXOs. We accordingly test our hypothesized relation by running the following regres-sion, and look for a significantly positive coefficient for "$\%PromoterHolding_{it}$" and "$IndianBusinessGroupDummy_i$":

$$Log(Compensation_{ist}) = \beta_0 + \beta_1 * \%PromoterHolding_{it}$$

$$+ \beta_2 * IndianBusinessGroup\ Dummy_i + \beta * X + \varepsilon_{it} \qquad (21.3)$$

Columns (1)–(3) of Table 21.5 show the results of running the above regression for CEOs. We find that, consistent with horizontal agency costs being associated with greater CEO compensation, firms that belong to an Indian business house pay their CEOs about 30 percent more relative to other firms. And firms with a higher proportion of promoter holdings pay their CEOs significantly more than other firms. Importantly, when we intro-duce a control for the level of promoters' holdings, the impact of horizontal agency costs is significantly greater when promoters' holdings are minority holdings relative to when they are majority holdings, indicating a greater propensity of promoters to extract agency benefits when they have minority control.

Similarly, columns (1)–(3) of Table 21.6 show the results of running the above regres-sion for CXOs. The results are not only qualitatively identical, but the size and signifi-cance of the coefficients is also quite similar. Once again, firms with a higher proportion of promoter holdings, and firms that belong to an Indian business house, pay their CXOs significantly more relative to other firms; and in particular relative to firms that are not part of business groups. CXO compensation is again about 30 percent greater in Indian firms that are part of business groups, and the horizontal agency costs are again higher when promoters are in minority control.

Next, we classify firms into two categories using the dummy variables 'High promoter holding' and 'Low promoter holding'. The time-invariant variable 'High promoter holding' takes a value of 1 if the promoter holding in a firm in a year is greater than the median promoter holding across all the firms in the year. The time-invariant variable

Table 21.5 The effect of firm size, agency cost and rent extraction proxies on CEO pay

Dependent variable is:	log(CEO Pay$_t$)					
Proxy for size is:	Market cap.	Assets	Sales	Market cap.	Assets	Sales
	(1)	(2)	(3)	(4)	(5)	(6)
Indian Business Group	0.301***	0.221**	0.284***	0.290***	0.210**	0.280***
	(0.083)	(0.094)	(0.098)	(0.082)	(0.093)	(0.098)
Promoters holding$_t$	0.006***	0.009***	0.009***			
	(0.002)	(0.002)	(0.002)			
(Promoters holding$_t$* High promoters holding)				0.010***	0.013***	0.010***
				(0.002)	(0.003)	(0.003)
(promoters holding$_t$* Low promoters holding)				0.015***	0.018***	0.013***
				(0.004)	(0.005)	(0.004)
Board size$_t$	0.026	0.026	0.044**	0.025	0.025	0.044**
	(0.016)	(0.018)	(0.018)	(0.016)	(0.018)	(0.018)
Non-promoter inst. holding$_t$	0.011***	0.025***	0.041***	0.011***	0.025***	0.041***
	(0.004)	(0.004)	(0.004)	(0.004)	(0.004)	(0.004)
Yearly return$_{t-1}$	−0.015	0.016	0.014	−0.017	0.012	0.012
	(0.015)	(0.017)	(0.018)	(0.015)	(0.016)	(0.018)
Size$_{t-1}$ – Firm avg. – Year avg.$_{t-1}$	0.222***	0.239***	0.217**	0.226***	0.233***	0.216**
	(0.037)	(0.077)	(0.108)	(0.037)	(0.076)	(0.108)
Year avg. of size$_{t-1}$	0.166***	0.338***	0.459***	0.155***	0.309***	0.446***
	(0.042)	(0.083)	(0.113)	(0.041)	(0.083)	(0.113)
Avg. firm size	0.429***	0.419***	0.293***	0.432***	0.420***	0.291***
	(0.025)	(0.038)	(0.031)	(0.025)	(0.037)	(0.031)
Constant	−1.261***	−2.926***	−3.321***	−1.432***	−3.018***	−3.362***
	(0.436)	(0.580)	(0.613)	(0.435)	(0.579)	(0.613)
Observations	2,214	2,192	2,147	2,214	2,192	2,147
Adj. R^2	0.579	0.530	0.502	0.582	0.533	0.503

Note: This table shows the correlation between the level of a firm's CEO pay in a year and the firm's size in the previous year, and proxies for agency cost and rent extraction in a firm. Three proxies are used for firm size: 'Market cap.', i.e., the natural logarithm of a firm's average market capitalization over the year; 'Assets', i.e., the natural logarithm of the firm's assets; and 'Sales', i.e., the natural logarithm of the firm's sales. The independent variable 'Avg. firm size' is measured as the mean size of all firms in a year where size is measured as per the definition in each specification, and the variable 'Year avg. of size' is the average size of a firm across all years. The variables 'Indian Business Group' and 'Promoters holding' are used as proxies for agency costs. The variables 'Board size', 'Non-promoter institutional holding', and 'Yearly return' are used as proxies for rent extraction. In columns (4)–(6), the effect of promoters' holding is investigated separately for firms with high and low levels of promoters' holding. The dummy variable 'High Promoters holding' takes a value of 1 if the promoters' holding in the firm in the year is greater than the median promoters' holding across all firms in the year. The variable 'Low promoters holding' is complementary to 'High promoters holding'. Standard errors reported in parentheses are robust to heteroskedasticity and are clustered by firm. ***, **, and * denote statistical significance at 1%, 5%, and 10% respectively. The sample covers the time period 2005–2010.

Table 21.6   The effect of firm size, agency cost and rent extraction proxies on CXO pay

Dependent variable is:	log(CXO Pay$_t$)					
Proxy for size is:	Market cap.	Assets	Sales	Market cap.	Assets	Sales
	(1)	(2)	(3)	(4)	(5)	(6)
Indian Business Group	0.296***	0.231**	0.277***	0.287***	0.223**	0.274***
	(0.080)	(0.092)	(0.095)	(0.080)	(0.092)	(0.095)
Promoters holding$_t$	0.006***	0.009***	0.008***			
	(0.002)	(0.002)	(0.003)			
(Promoters holding$_t$ * High promoters holding)				0.009***	0.012***	0.010***
				(0.002)	(0.003)	(0.003)
(promoters holding$_t$ * Low promoters holding)				0.013***	0.016***	0.012**
				(0.004)	(0.004)	(0.005)
Board size$_t$	0.018	0.021	0.036**	0.017	0.020	0.036**
	(0.015)	(0.017)	(0.017)	(0.015)	(0.017)	(0.017)
Non-promoter inst. holding$_t$	0.003	0.017***	0.030***	0.003	0.017***	0.030***
	(0.004)	(0.004)	(0.004)	(0.004)	(0.004)	(0.004)
Yearly return$_{t-1}$	−0.014	0.008	0.007	−0.016	0.005	0.006
	(0.016)	(0.017)	(0.018)	(0.016)	(0.016)	(0.017)
Size$_{t-1}$ – Firm avg. – Year avg.$_{t-1}$	0.199***	0.163**	0.205**	0.203***	0.158**	0.205**
	(0.037)	(0.076)	(0.095)	(0.037)	(0.075)	(0.094)
Year avg. of size$_{t-1}$	0.173***	0.295***	0.441***	0.165***	0.272***	0.431***
	(0.038)	(0.077)	(0.101)	(0.038)	(0.078)	(0.101)
Avg. firm size	0.381***	0.356***	0.251***	0.383***	0.357***	0.250***
	(0.026)	(0.037)	(0.032)	(0.026)	(0.037)	(0.032)
Constant	−1.687***	−3.303***	−3.473***	−1.818***	−3.374***	−3.504***
	(0.413)	(0.539)	(0.548)	(0.405)	(0.533)	(0.544)
Observations	2,214	2,192	2,147	2,214	2,192	2,147
Adj. R^2	0.508	0.452	0.422	0.510	0.454	0.422

Note: This table shows the correlation between the level of a firm's CXO pay in a year and the firm's size in the previous year, and proxies for agency cost and rent extraction in a firm. Three proxies are used for firm size: 'Market cap.', i.e., the natural logarithm of a firm's average market capitalization over the year; 'Assets', i.e., the natural logarithm of the firm's assets; and 'Sales', i.e., the natural logarithm of the firm's sales. The independent variable 'Avg. firm size' is measured as the mean size of all firms in a year where size is measured as per the definition in each specification, and the variable 'Year avg. of size' is the average size of a firm across all years. The variables 'Indian Business Group' and 'Promoters holding' are used as proxies for agency costs. The variables 'Board size', 'Non-promoter institutional holding', and 'Yearly return' are used as proxies for rent extraction. In columns (4)–(6), the effect of promoters' holding is investigated separately for firms with high and low levels of promoters' holding. The dummy variable 'High Promoters holding' takes a value of 1 if the promoters' holding in the firm in the year is greater than the median promoters' holding across all firms in the year. The variable 'Low promoters holding' is complementary to 'High promoters holding'. Standard errors reported in parentheses are robust to heteroskedasticity and are clustered by firm. ***, **, and * denote statistical significance at 1%, 5%, and 10% respectively. The sample covers the time period 2005–2010.

'Low promoter holding' is complementary to 'High promoter holding'. We repeat the regression represented in equation (21.3) by interacting the promoter holding percentage with these two dummy variables for both CEOs and CXOs. Columns (4)–(6) of Tables 21.5 and 21.6 show the results of this estimation. Both the interaction terms are positive and significant at the 1 percent level in all the three specifications. This implies that the effect of promoter holding is not driven purely by the firms where promoter holding is low, but both by firms where promoter holding is low as well as by firms where promoter holding is high. As regards the magnitude of the effect, the coefficients for the firms where the promoter holding is low are about 20 to 30 percent greater, which is consistent with the intuition of agency costs being greater when promoter holding is lower.

In Tables 21.5 and 21.6, the firm size components still show a positive and significant relationship with the level of CEO pay, though the effect of overall firm size drops considerably, potentially because of the correlation of the size measure with the other explanatory variables. Though not the focus of our analyses, we note that the coefficients on the board size and stock return variables are statistically *not* different from zero, which implies that these variables do not have a statistically significant explanatory power with regard to CEO pay. Similarly, yearly stock return, which is a firm performance measure, also does not have significant explanatory power as well.

5   CONCLUDING REMARKS

We present in this chapter an introductory regulatory and empirical analysis of executive compensation in listed companies in India.

Our descriptive overview of levels and trends leads to several interesting conclusions. First, executive pay in the echelon representing the largest firms is several times greater than in smaller firms. It also includes a much greater component of variable pay, is much more sensitive to stock market movements, and exhibits much greater dispersion both across time and across firms. For this echelon of the largest firms, the features of executive pay are not qualitatively different from those documented for the US by Frydman and Saks (2010). However, for even up to the 75th percentile firm by size, there is little variable component in executive pay. CEO pay is considerably greater than the pay of other executive directors (i.e., CXOs), and the ratio of CEO to CXO pay also displays high dispersion both across time and across firms. CXO pay displays a much lower variable component and much lower sensitivity to stock market movements, and hence a much lower variation across time. The real values of both CEO and CXO compensation have been following a sharply increasing trend in recent years in India.

In the context of economic drivers of executive compensation, we first find that, assuming that the performance sensitivity to talent is constant across firms, CEO pay has constant returns to scale with increasing firm size when using the logarithm of market capitalization as a measure of firm size. The greater the firm size, correspondingly greater is CEO pay. CXO pay also increases with firm size, but less than that of the CEO.

Second, and particularly importantly in the context of India, the potential presence of horizontal agency costs due to the widespread existence of controlling shareholder groups significantly increases executive compensation, both for CEOs and for CXOs. CEO and CXO pay is considerably higher (about 30 percent for both CEOs and CXOs) for firms that are part of business groups, and increases significantly with the proportion of promoters' equity. These results are qualitatively similar to the inferences that currently exist in the literature for the impact of vertical agency costs on executive pay.

Finally, in addition to the implications for assessing the economic costs of shareholder ownership in the Indian context, these findings also have strong implications for the emerging regulation on executive compensation in India. In particular, this chapter has argued that current tools in executive compensation law and policy may not be fully cognizant of the dual play of vertical and horizontal agency costs. As such, normatively, questions must now be asked to better assure that international standards implemented in India are tailored and fit for the specific risks generated, such that disclosure, corporate oversight, and say-on-pay, are meaningful and fulfill the regulatory rationales for which they are intended.

REFERENCES

Afsharipour, Afra, 2010, *The Promise and Challenges of India's Corporate Governance Reforms*, UC Davis Legal Studies Research Paper Series Research Paper No. 223 July, pp. 15–17, 28–9, 31–2.

Balasubramanian, Bala N., Black, Bernard S. and Khanna, Vikramaditya S., 2009, *Firm Level Corporate Governance in Emerging Markets: A Case Study of India*, working paper, at http://ssrn.com/abstract=992529.

Bebchuk, Lucian, 1999, *A Rent-Protection Theory of Corporate Ownership and Control*, NBER Working Paper 7203.

Bebchuk, Lucian and Fried, Jesse, 2002, *Pay Without Performance*, Harvard University Press.

Bebchuk, Lucian and Fried, Jesse, 2004, *Pay Without Performance: The Unfulfilled Promise of Executive Compensation*, Harvard University Press.

Bebchuk, Lucian and Fried, Jesse, 2010, *Paying for Long-Term Performance*, University of Pennsylvania Law Review, 158, pp. 1915–59, pp. 1955–8.

Bertrand, Marianne, Mehta, Paras and Mullainathan, Sendhil, 2002, *Ferreting Out Tunneling: An Application to Indian Business Groups*, The Quarterly Journal of Economics, 117 (1), pp. 121–48.

Black, Bernard S. and Khanna, Vikramaditya S., 2007, *Can Corporate Governance Reforms Increase Firms' Market Value: Evidence from India*, University of Michigan Law School, Olin Working Paper No. 07-002, Oct., available at http://ssrn.com/abstract=914440, pp. 1, 2, 4, 18.

Brummer, Christopher J., 2011, *Soft Law and the Global Financial System: Rule Making in the 21st Century*, Cambridge University Press.

Chatterjee, Sumeet, 2009, *Satyam Scandal Could Be India's Enron*, Reuters, January 7.

Committee Appointed By SEBI on Corporate Governance under the Chairmanship Of Shri Kumar Mangalam Birla, Report 1999.

Dodd-Frank Wall Street Reform and Consumer Protection Act (Pub.L. 111–203, H.R. 4173), Sections 951–955.

Duggal, Arun, 2010, *What Have We Learned in the Year Since Satyam*, Wall Street Journal Feb. 7.

ENS Economic Bureau, 2000, *LSE Signs up with BSE, NSE for Cross-Listing of Shares*, February 25, available online at: http://www.indianexpress.com/Storyold/145859/.

Fagernäs, Sonja, 2006, *How Do Family Ties, Boards And Regulation Affect Pay At The Top? Evidence For Indian CEOs?*, Centre for Business Research, University Of Cambridge Working Paper No. 335, p. 1.

Financial Services Authority (FSA), 2009, *Policy Statement 09/15: Reforming Remuneration Practices in Financial Services*, August.

Financial Stability Board/Financial Stability Forum, 2009, *The Financial Stability Forum's Principles for Sound Compensation Practices*, April.

Frydman, Carola and Saks, Raven E., 2010, *Executive Compensation: A New View from a Long-Term Perspective, 1936–2005*, Review of Financial Studies, pp. 2099–138.

Gabaix, Xavier and Landier, Augustin, 2008, *Why has CEO Pay Increased So Much?*, The Quarterly Journal of Economics, 123 (1), pp. 49–100.

German Federal Financial Supervision Authority (Bundesanstalt für Finanzdienstleistungsaufsicht – BaFin), 2009, Circular (Rundschreiben) No. 22/2009, December.

Gomez-Mejia, Luis R., Nunez-Nickel, Manuel and Gutierrez, Isabel, 2001, *The Role of Family Ties in Agency Contracts*, Academy of Management Journal, 44 (1), pp. 81–95.

Gordon, Jeffrey, 2005, *Executive Compensation: If There's a Problem, What's the Remedy? The Case for Compensation Disclosure and Analysis*, Journal of Corporation Law.

Hermalin, Benjamin E., 2005, *Trends in Corporate Governance*, The Journal of Finance, 60 (5), October, pp. 2351–84.

Jaiswall, Manju and Firth, Michael, 2007, *Top Management Compensation and Firm Performance in the Emerging Markets: Evidence from India*, Indian Institute of Management, Calcutta, Working Paper Series, WPS No. 602/May.

Kakani, Ram K. and Ray, Pranabesh, 2002, *Managerial Remuneration in India: Of Changing Guidelines, Fatter Pay Packets, and Incentives to Performance*, Working Paper 02/03, available at SSRN: http://ssrn.com/abstract=905108, pp. 6–7, 14–17.

Labor Bureau, Government of India, Statistics available online at http://labourbureau.nic.in/indtab.html.

Morck, Randall and Yeung, Bernard, 2003, *Agency Problems in Large Family Business Groups*, Entrepreneurship: Theory and Practice, 27(4), 367–82.

Murphy, Kevin J. and Zábojník, Jan, 2004, *CEO Pay and Appointments: A Market-Based Explanation for Recent Trends*, American Economic Review – Papers and Proceedings, 94, 192–6.

National Stock Exchange and Chicago Mercantile Exchange, 2010, Press Release, *National Stock Exchange of India and CME Group Announce Cross-Listing Relationship*, March 10, available online at: http://www.nseindia.com/content/press/PR_NSE_CME.pdf.

Reserve Bank of India, 2010, *Guidelines on Compensation of Whole Time Directors/Chief Executive Officers/Risk takers and Control Function Staff*, DBOD No. BC./29.67.001/2010-11, July 1, available online at: http://www.rbi.org.in/scripts/bs_viewcontent.aspx?Id=2223.

Securities and Exchange Board of India Committee on Corporate Governance, 2003, Report.

Securities and Exchange Board of India Press Release, 2007, *SEBI Initiates Adjudication Proceedings Against 20 Companies for Non-Compliance of Clause 49 Norms*, Sept. 11, available at http://www.sebi.gov.in/press/2007/2s007257.html.

Securities and Exchange Board of India, 2010, Circular Number: CIR/CFD/DIL/1/2010 (Apr. 5), available at http://www.sebi.gov.in/circulars/2010/cfddilcir01.pdf.

Sen, Anindya and Sarkar, Subrata, 1996, *Age, Experience, Qualification and Remuneration of Managers in some Large Indian Firms*, The Indian Journal of Labour Economics, 39 (1), pp. 111–28.

Tervio, Marko, 2008, *The Difference That CEOs Make: An Assignment Model Approach*, American Economic Review, 98 (3), 642–68.

Tirole, Jean, 2006, *The Theory of Corporate Finance*, Princeton University Press.

TNN, 2004, *India Back on CalPERS' Investment Radar*, the Economic Times, April 20, available online at: http://articles. economictimes .indiatimes.com/2004-04-20/news/27377838_1_local-public -employees-ret irement-and-health-benefits-calpers.

Treanor, Jill, 2011, *Vince Cable Threatens to Get Tough on Executive Pay After 32% Rise*, June 23, available online at: http://www.guardian.co.uk/business/2011/jun/22/vince-cable-executive-pay.

US Department of the Treasury, 2010, *Press Release: Kenneth R. Feinberg, Special Master for TARP Executive Compensation, Written Testimony Before the House Financial Services Committee*, available at http://www.ustreas.gov/press/releases/tg565.htm February 25.

Varottil, Umakanth, 2010, *Voluntary Nature of Corporate Governance Norms*, 9 March, available at http://indiacorplaw.blogspot.com/2010/03/voluntary-nature-of-corporate-governance.html.

World Bank, 2004, *Report on the Observance of Standards and Codes for Corporate Governance in India*, April, available at http://www.worldbank.org/ifa/rosc_cg_ind.pdf

Yermack, David, 1996, *Higher Market Valuation of Companies with a Small Board of Directors*, Journal of Financial Economics, 40 (2), pp. 185–211.

22 The EU and executive pay: managing harmonization risks

Niamh Moloney

1 INTRODUCTION: THE EU CONTEXT

The purpose of this chapter is to place the executive pay debate, and particularly the debate as to whether legal intervention is warranted, in the context of the European Union (EU). Why take a regional approach to executive pay? It might be argued that jurisdictional scope might be better framed in terms of either the domestic or international contexts given the strong local path-dependencies which can influence rule design and the impact of the global competition for executive talent.

Nonetheless, for a number of reasons, the EU's regional experience with executive pay is useful. Given the corporate ownership rift which runs across the EU, the EU provides a useful laboratory for examining how executive pay and executive pay regulation behave in dispersed ownership and in block-holding ownership conditions, and in relation to different agency problems and different managerial incentives. The EU's experience with the harmonization of executive pay rules is relevant to the debate on the dynamics of harmonization and regulatory competition internationally, given current moves, albeit in the financial stability context, to develop an international approach to pay in systemically important financial institutions (Financial Stability Board 2009 a and b and 2010 a and b). The EU's recent reforms to executive pay (European Commission 2009a and 2009b; European Parliament and Council 2010) usefully illustrate the risks which follow legislative intervention. In particular, they highlight the dangers which arise where legislators deviate from a shareholder incentive alignment model as the basis for intervention, and the momentum risks which the financial stability reform agenda can generate for the effective regulation of pay in the corporate sector generally. And the current predominance of board-governance techniques (based on 'comply or explain' enforcement mechanisms) and of disclosure techniques (based on a combination of binding rules and 'comply or explain' mechanisms) as regulatory devices for managing pay risks in the corporate sector across the EU serves as a useful case study for highlighting how these mechanisms operate in practice and how 'law in action' can be best supported.

A brief explanation of the legislative context for this chapter is warranted. A number of harmonizing EU Directives, which are binding on the EU Member States, form part of the EU's regulatory matrix for executive pay in that they are designed to improve corporate disclosure generally and to address management insider dealing risks (European Parliament and Council 2003a, b, and c and European Parliament and Council 2004). The EU pay matrix also contains hybrid measures which 'harden' related soft law measures. From September 2008, for example, publicly-traded firms have been required to include a corporate governance statement in their annual reports, covering whether the firm follows a particular national Corporate Governance Code and whether it complies, or not, with it (European Parliament and Council 2006).

The EU has also adopted an important series of harmonizing Recommendations which focus specifically on pay. These, in effect, form the harmonized EU executive pay 'rule book' for pay in firms other than financial institutions. These measures are not binding and are designed to harness the 'comply or explain' Corporate Governance Codes now common in EU Member States. Binding EU intervention seems, however, likely (European Commission 2010a and 2011). These Recommendations were adopted in two stages. The 2004 Recommendation on Executive Pay (European Commission 2004) and the 2005 Recommendation on the Non-Executive Director (European Commission 2005) were adopted in the wake of the EU's wider policy commitment in 2003 to enhancing corporate governance in the EU (European Commission 2003 and High Level Group 2002). Corporate governance had hitherto not been an EU priority; this new commitment was in part a response to the Enron-era failures in the dispersed-ownership context and the related series of EU scandals in the block-holding context (chief among them the Parmalat scandal (Ferrarini and Giudici 2005)). As noted in sections 2 and 3, this initial association between EU intervention on pay and wider crisis in the financial markets has continued (Ferrarini et al 2010), to problematic effect, with a more intrusive Recommendation being adopted in 2009 (European Commission 2009a).

Finally, binding rules now apply to the pay of senior management in financial institutions under the 2010 Capital Requirements Directive (European Parliament and Council 2010), reflecting an earlier Commission Recommendation on pay in financial institutions (European Commission 2009b).

In terms of scope, this discussion is concerned with board pay rather than with senior management pay, reflecting the focus of EU law and policy on the particular risks which board pay can generate given the close involvement of the board in the pay-setting process. It is also concerned with publicly traded firms, reflecting the strong association in EU law and policy between effective corporate governance and deep and liquid capital markets, and the driving influence of the EU's financial market agenda on corporate law and corporate governance in the EU generally (Moloney 2008). Finally, its focus is on the corporate sector generally, and not on financial institutions, given the particular issues which the association between executive pay, risk management, and systemic stability raises and the different drivers, including the adoption of international standards, for intervention.

The EU's approach to intervention in the executive pay context, at least until the financial crisis, has been based on the assumption that efficient, incentive-based executive pay contracts can support shareholder/manager interest alignment and address agency costs, in both the dispersed and the block-holding contexts, and thereby promote strong capital markets in the EU (Ferrarini and Moloney 2005). Reflecting currently dominant scholarship (Bebchuck and Fried 2004, Cheffins 2009, Bebchuk and Spamann 2010), the EU's original 2004 and 2005 Recommendations are concerned with the risk that a conflicted pay-setting process may lead to the adoption of sub-optimal pay contracts. They are accordingly designed to support optimal 'pay governance' (section 2 below) and do not directly address pay design. The 2004 Recommendation uses disclosure and shareholder voice mechanisms to support the pay-setting process and recommends: disclosure of company pay policy, either in a distinct remuneration report or in the annual report, including extensive disclosure on performance indicators; detailed disclosure concerning individual directors' pay; a shareholders' vote on company pay policy, which can be either binding or advisory; and prior approval of share-based schemes. The role of the board in pay-setting is addressed by the parallel 2005 Recommendation which recommends that: boards should have an 'appropriate balance' of executive and non-executive directors such that no individual or group of individuals can dominate decision-making, and a 'sufficient' number of 'independent' non-executive directors; board committees should be created for issues particularly vulnerable to conflict of interest (including remuneration); and the remuneration committee (its recommended functions are delineated in some detail) should be composed exclusively of non-executive or supervisory directors, a majority of whom should be independent. In 2009, the Commission adopted an updating Recommendation (European Commission 2009a).

Given the difficulties harmonization poses in this area (section 3 below), the Recommendations are based on a voluntary Member State compliance model (by contrast, the bulk of the EU's company law and corporate governance agenda takes the form of mandatory rules which Member States must adopt). The EU has accordingly yet to impose a binding regime on its 27 Member States with respect to executive pay; the Member States remain free to legislate as they wish (apart from in the banking context, in respect of which binding rules apply (European Parliament and Council 2010)). Member States have, however, tended to implement these Recommendations nationally, albeit through market-policed Corporate Governance Codes.

2   PAY, LAW AND CORPORATE GOVERNANCE REGIMES

2.1   Executive Pay and Corporate Governance Regimes

Despite some recent movement towards market finance and greater dispersed ownership (Moloney 2008), the EU remains strongly characterized by bank finance and by block-holding ownership (Enriques and Volpin 2007); predictably, the financial crisis has done little to change this (Committee of European Securities Regulators 2010). The EU is accordingly characterized by a distinction between dispersed ownership (or at least dispersed institutional ownership) in some Member States (notably the UK, Ireland and the Netherlands) and block-holding ownership by controlling shareholders (albeit to differing degrees – there are considerable variations across the Member States with respect to the size of block-holding shareholders) in others (Barca and Becht 2001 and Enriques and Volpin 2007). Germany, Spain, France, and Italy are among the classic block-holding Member States. Concentrations of direct voting power by shareholders are typically intensified into block-holdings and control groups by cross-shareholdings between dominant block-holders, the exercise of control through complex pyramidal ownership structures which allow control to be exercised through cascades of companies, proxy voting by financial institutions connected to the company and voting pacts. This distinction matters in the executive pay context given the different behaviour of executive pay in dispersed-ownership and block-holding ownership settings.

Under the currently pre-eminent analytical model, which has dominated this field since the 1990s following the seminal work of Jensen and Meckling, executive pay in the dispersed-ownership context is a means for addressing the agency costs generated by a misalignment of management and shareholder interests; intervention accordingly should reflect failures which arise in the design of incentive contracts and which lead to misaligned incentives. Healthy, performance-based pay contracts, which link pay to shareholder wealth via performance indicators such as share prices or accounting-based targets, provide a potentially powerful means for attracting, retaining, and motivating board members (and managers) to pursue the shareholders' agenda (Jensen and Murphy 2004). But as is now well known, there is a pathology to executive pay. The design of pay contracts can lead to rents being extracted (Bebchuk and Fried 2004). The very efficiency with which incentive contracts can drive executive behaviour was shown to destructive effect over the Enron era, during which share option pay appears to have created incentives to distort issuer disclosure (Gordon 2002 and Hill 2006). Although the evidence remains contested, the financial crisis also suggests that executive pay structures may have led to excessive risk-taking in financial institutions (Brunnermeier et al 2009, Department of the Treasury 2009, FSA 2009, Walker 2009). Pay contracts can, accordingly, become a source of, rather than a remedy for, agency costs.

In the context of continental European block-holding governance, incentives and conflicts change (Ferrarini and Moloney 2005). In block-holding firms, the agency costs which trouble dispersed owners are reduced as block-holders should wield sufficient power to control management and should suffer less from collective action problems (Garrido and Rojo 2002). The primary agency costs relate instead to the oppression of minority shareholders (including minority block-holders) (Thomsen 2005, Enriques and Volpin 2007). As discussed in section 3 below, it is not necessarily the case that the incentive-based executive pay contract is of no relevance to block-holding governance; it remains an important mechanism for protecting minority shareholders against expropriation (Ferrarini et al 2010). But, in the EU at least, it seems to be the case that the incentive contract has less traction in block-holding governance.

The different role of executive pay in dispersed and block-holding systems, and the related diversity in the risks which it can generate, are reflected in the fragmented picture which executive pay in the EU presents, in terms of pay practices, intensity of legal intervention and market monitoring.

2.2   Executive Pay and Corporate Governance Regimes: Empirical Evidence

Research conducted prior to the EU's major legislative efforts to promote market finance and a single financial market under the 1999 Financial Services Action Plan (European Commission 1999) suggested that monitoring by controlling shareholders had limited the degree of reliance on incentive-based pay contracts in continental Europe (Crespi-Cladera and Gispert-Pellicer 1999 and Brunello et al 2001). Subsequent research (Ferrarini et al 2004 and Ferrarini and Moloney 2005), which examined annual report disclosure by Europe's leading companies in 2001 (based on disclosures by Europe's largest 300 companies in the Eurotop 300 index), similarly found a strong association between equity-based incentive pay and ownership systems. Headline cash and bonus-based pay for chief executives (excluding high-powered incentives in the form of share-based pay), for example, ranged from a high of €1.9 million in France (a block-holding system) to a low of €0.9 million in Finland. A considerable proportion of pay was in the form of variable cash bonuses, ranging from 47 per cent of pay in France to 27 per cent in Finland. But when share-based/long-term incentive pay was factored in, the UK, as its predominant dispersed corporate ownership profile would suggest, displayed the heaviest reliance on incentive pay, with pay representing 78 per cent of total remuneration as compared to 60 per cent in France. Similar trends appeared with respect to share options. In the UK all 68 companies in the Eurotop 300 had established share options pro-grammes. In Spain, by contrast, only 5 of the 18 Spanish companies in the Eurotop 300 had adopted share option plans. Particularly sharp distinctions arose with respect to long-term share-based incentives. While clear evidence emerged from the Eurotop 300 of their use in the UK, reflecting growing institutional investor concern with respect to the effectiveness of share options as alignment devices (Gordon 2009), elsewhere in the EU there was strikingly little evidence of reliance on long-term share-based incentives. This difference in practice across the corporate governance divide was confirmed by a 2003 survey of EU companies which showed that only 28 per cent provided equity based pay (Hewitt 2003). Since then, despite some high-profile instances of Anglo-American style incentive contracts being adopted within block-holding systems, and in some cases gen-erating public outrage and legal challenge (most notably with respect to the compensa-tion payments paid to Mannesmann executives (Milhaupt and Pistor 2008)), a similar trend has followed (Thomas 2008).

While a range of path-dependencies influence executive pay practices, not least among them cultural attitudes, the strength of the association in the EU between block-holding governance and much weaker reliance on equity-based incentive pay can, at least, be related to a substitution of the incentive contract by controlling shareholder monitoring. Equity-based pay is also less likely to be attractive to management where a publicly traded, but closely held, firm has only a small free float and a greater possibility arises of the share price being influenced by noise (Cheffins 2003).

2.3 Legal Intervention and Corporate Governance Regimes

The EU (and the Member States') practice has been to address 'pay governance' or the interlinked mechanisms which support the adoption of efficient incentive contracts by minimizing the opportunities for rent-seeking, namely: board monitoring (particularly by independent directors), disclosure, and shareholder voice. As discussed in section 4 below, EU Member States and the EU have, until very recently, eschewed direct intervention in pay design. Accordingly, and regardless of the prevailing national governance system and the different ways in which board and general meeting governance can operate (Goergen et al 2004, Hopt and Leyens 2004), intervention has generally been designed to support the board in adopting optimal incentive contracts.

The forces which have driven this approach are not entirely clear. Certainly, the influ-ence of the EU on Member States' practices cannot be discounted, even allowing for the EU's adoption of a voluntary compliance model through the use of Recommendations. The EU's approach, in turn, can be related to its wider reliance on a calibrated form of Anglo-American corporate governance in the post-Enron period (High Level Group 2002) and the ready association it has made between corporate governance reform, the regulation of large publicly traded firms, and strengthening the EU's capital market

(European Commission 2003). Public choice dynamics and the considerable opportunities which a focus on the agency costs faced by dispersed owners affords the EU (and in particular, the European Commission – the EU's independent executive and architect of the executive pay agenda) cannot be discounted. Member States have also recently engaged in reforms to Corporate Governance Codes, many of which follow an Anglo-American model, in an attempt to deepen their capital markets (Hansen 2006, Enriques and Volpin 2007, Enriques 2009a, Ferrarini et al 2010), reflecting a range of factors, not least among them the growing influence of international institutional investors across the EU. Nonetheless, even within this more-or-less accepted pay governance model, Member States' legal controls on pay vary. They are typically at their most sophisticated, in terms of managing potential defects in pay-setting which may damage interest alignment, in those Member States where dispersed ownership dominates and where the risks of the incentive contract might be most acute. The EU's initial intervention on pay in 2004–05 provides a useful fulcrum around which to consider how Member States have intervened on pay and the influence of governance regimes.

Prior to the EU's intervention through the 2004 and 2005 Recommendations, and the creation thereby of some incentives for Member States to follow the EU's voluntary rule-book (section 3 below), legal intervention on executive pay was very limited in block-holding regimes (Ferrarini et al 2004). For example, although disclosure is typically regarded as a less interventionist regulatory technique, Member States differed widely in the extent to which they required specific disclosures on pay. With respect to annual report disclosure, the UK, Ireland, the Netherlands, Sweden, France, and Italy all, albeit to varying degrees, required individualized disclosure of executive pay packages. The most rigorous requirements applied in the UK which, since 2002, has required a discrete Directors' Remuneration Report, setting out detailed and individualized disclosure on board pay, including benchmark disclosure (firm performance benchmarked against an index), as well as detailed information on the pay-setting process and on performance indicators, as part of the annual reporting cycle for publicly traded firms. In Ireland, a broadly similar, although not as extensive, regime based on individualized disclosure applied, albeit on a 'comply or explain' basis via the listing system. In France, individualized disclosure of executive pay was required by law in the annual report. In Italy, individualized executive pay awards, specifying particular pay components, were required to be disclosed in the annual report. Similarly in the Netherlands, by law, individualized disclosure, specifying the particular components of pay and explaining performance links, along with a report on pay policy, was required in the annual report. In Sweden, similar binding rules applied as to annual individualized disclosure, but via listing agreements.

While the presence of France and Italy in this group muddies the findings somewhat, the group is dominated by the dispersed-ownership systems of the UK and Ireland and Member States where dispersed ownership is stronger than elsewhere in continental Europe (Sweden and the Netherlands). In the remaining Member States, including the classic block-holding systems of Germany, Austria, and Belgium, mandatory disclosure requirements were generally minimal, with limited and aggregate disclosure of total board pay, often not specifying the different elements of pay, being the norm, reflecting the minimal requirements for annual report disclosure under the EU's harmonized company law regime.

Requirements for a remuneration committee followed a similar pattern. The most demanding requirements, including with respect to the determinants of 'independence', applied in the UK and Ireland, albeit through 'comply or explain' mechanisms via the UK Code on Corporate Governance. A number of Member States, including Spain, Italy and France recommended, however, that remuneration committees be established, although they varied with respect to the extent to which membership was to include independent non-executive directors. In Austria and Germany, however, the position of the remuneration committee was considerably weaker, with neither Member State recommending that a separate remuneration committee be established. While there was therefore some transplantation of the classically Anglo-American remuneration committee device, it was not prevalent across the EU and considerable differences existed with respect to committee membership, reflecting the dominant influence of block-holders. There was some evidence, however, of a movement towards the establishment of remuneration committees among those companies still lacking one, often following media and market pressure (Hewitt 2003).

Direct shareholder voice as a means of managing conflicts in the pay-setting process did not feature strongly across the EU. The UK was most supportive of shareholder voice by imposing, by law, a requirement for a non-binding shareholder vote on the annual Directors' Remuneration Report. No other Member State required a shareholder vote. The UK (and Ireland) also imposed shareholder approval requirements on the adoption of certain option and long-term incentive plans via the listing process. While most of the other Member States also required shareholder approval of option plans, approval was usually linked to shareholder approval of a capital increase, and was not a form of shareholder control over executive pay.

The distinction between dispersed and block-holding systems in terms of the intensity of intervention has persisted as wider legal and market conditions have changed. In 2004 and 2005 the EU's Recommendations on executive pay were adopted. In addition, institutional investors have become more of a force in the EU, market-based finance, at least prior to the crisis, was strengthening, outlier pay packages have generated wider public outrage (Gow 2008), with the €50 million golden parachute paid to departing Porsche CEO Wiedeking in 2009 becoming something of a poster-child for public discontent, and a number of new Corporate Governance Codes, together with reforms to established Codes, came into force across the EU (Moloney 2008 and Ferrarini et al 2010). Nonetheless, the divergences across the Member States remain striking.

Research conducted over 2007–09 on Member States' regulation of pay (Ferrarini et al 2009 and Ferrarini et al 2010) has, reflecting the Commission's somewhat sketchy review of Member State experience with the 2004 and 2005 Recommendations (European Commission 2007), found persistent differences across the Member States with respect to legal intervention on executive pay. With respect to disclosure, for example, most Member States, with the exception of the UK, do not, notwithstanding the 2004 Recommendation, require companies to produce a separate remuneration report, impose standardized format requirements, or require detailed disclosure on pay policy or performance indicators. To the extent these requirements apply, it is typically through non-binding Corporate Governance Codes (which, as outlined in subsection 2.4 below, are not subject to close institutional investor monitoring) and there is considerable divergence in the detail which different Codes require.

The majority of Member States, including block-holding States, have, however, now imposed binding rules requiring companies to provide individualized disclosure on pay, in a striking change from the earlier position. Most notably, Germany, a classic block-holding regime, now requires individualized disclosure, by law, with respect to management and supervisory board pay (although non-compliance is permitted if a 75 per cent majority of the general meeting so resolve (until 2011)). But the standardized and qualitative information on pay policy (including how targets are set) necessary for the market to economize its information costs and to assess the efficiency of pay arrangements without the 'noise' generated by stark pay statistics, has not been supported through a mandatory obligation in most block-holding regimes. The persistence of the influence of block-holding governance can also be seen in the persistence of rules which still require only aggregate disclosure of board pay; in Austria, Belgium, Denmark and Spain, for example, individualized disclosure is not required by law, although it is recommended by the relevant national Corporate Governance Code.

Divergences also persist with respect to board monitoring and the remuneration committee. Most Member States now address the remuneration committee, albeit generally by means of a 'comply or explain' based Corporate Governance Code. Significant differences have, however, arisen with respect to the composition of the committee and, in particular, the extent to which the committee must be composed of independent directors; in a considerable number of Member States, it is neither recommended nor required that independent directors sit on the remuneration committee (Ferrarini et al 2009 and 2010, European Commission 2007). The picture is somewhat muddied by recent reforms in Germany; 2009 legislation has rendered board members personally liable in damages where remuneration does not reflect legal requirements. While this development sits uneasily with the wider evidence which suggests that legal intervention is less intrusive in block-holding regimes, it also serves to reinforce the range of factors, including, in this case, public hostility to perceived Anglo-American pay excesses, which can influence the intensity of intervention on pay.

The evidence on the 'say on pay' is somewhat contrarian. Very few Member States have followed the Commission's 2004 recommendation for a shareholder vote on pay, arguably reflecting the influence of controlling shareholders as well as the more limited role of the general meeting in block-holding governance. But there are signs of change. The Netherlands and Sweden have recently adopted a binding requirement for a pay vote; notably, both of these Member States are associated with market finance. Germany has also introduced a pay vote as part of its wider reforms to executive pay.

The strong stakeholder dynamics often associated with block-holding regimes, and particularly with those regimes based on co-determination (or close involvement by labour) (Hopt and Leyens 2004, Goergen et al 2004, Gelter 2010), can also be seen in recent reforms by some Member States which show some enthusiasm for curbing perceived 'excesses' and so for a move away from the shareholder/manager alignment model which underpins the EU's Recommendations. A number of Codes adopted in traditionally block-holding regimes make general reference to the need for remuneration to be variously 'reasonable' (Denmark) and proportionate to the economic situation of the company (Germany and Austria). The 2009 German reforms similarly require that board remuneration should not exceed 'usual' remuneration levels, with reference to remuneration standards in the relevant industry sector, market standards, and within the firm.

2.4   Market Monitoring and Corporate Governance Regimes

Finally, the influence of governance regimes on pay can also be examined by means of the extent to which firms in practice comply with the requirements of the voluntary Corporate Governance Codes which Member States have generally relied on to implement the EU's Recommendations. As Corporate Governance Codes are the main mechanisms for embedding notionally 'good' practices with respect to pay governance across the EU, an examination of the extent to which firms follow these practices (and so the EU Recommendations) sheds some light on the intensity of market monitoring across different governance regimes. An examination of disclosure practices by firms in the FTSE Eurofirst 300 – Europe's 300 largest companies – as at November 2008 (Ferrarini et al 2009 and 2010) reinforces the persistence of the influence of governance regimes and the weaker influence of market monitoring in block-holding regimes.

With respect to disclosure, firms pay most attention to basic disclosure; the more detailed requirements related to, for example, terms of contracts and qualitative disclosure concerning performance links are not widely followed, suggesting limited market pressure for more sophisticated and comprehensive disclosures. Although more than 90 per cent of the reviewed firms provided some form of remuneration statement, the nature of the disclosure provided varied significantly. Firms in the UK, Ireland and the Netherlands, for example, produce the highest levels of compliance with respect to individualized disclosure (between 90 and 100 per cent – reflecting the mandatory nature of these rules in those Member States), but firms from Belgium (just over 30 per cent), Sweden (20 per cent), Austria (20 per cent), and Greece (5 per cent), where 'comply or explain' Codes dominate, show much lower compliance levels.

These findings are consistent with the influence of block-holding; the outlier Swedish results can be explained by the limited disclosure in Sweden with respect to individual share incentive scheme awards. Compliance with requirements concerning remuneration policy is high in the UK (95 per cent) but lower elsewhere (in the region of 40 per cent in, for example, Italy, Germany, Belgium, Spain, Austria, Denmark and Greece). Similarly, disclosure with respect to performance targets for share-based schemes is provided by some 56 per cent of firms, but the highest level of disclosure is provided by UK and Dutch firms. 70 per cent of firms from the UK, the Netherlands and Sweden provide disclosure on termination payments policy but less than 30 per cent of Italian, Austrian, and Norwegian firms provide this disclosure.

Codes, accordingly, appear to have limited traction in practice. There appears to be a relationship between the level of firm compliance and the dominant governance regime, with block-holding regimes generally slower to provide full disclosure. There also appears to have been little market pressure on firms to enhance disclosure practices.

Whether or not these divergences matter (they may simply appropriately reflect the most efficient means for managing executive pay risks in particular governances regimes) is, of course, another question, discussed further in section 3.

3   HARMONIZATION AND PAY RULES

The EU context provides a useful case study against which to examine the risks of harmonization in this field. The financial crisis has underscored the difficulties which the harmonization of rules governing pay in systemically important financial institutions can raise; the EU's 2010 adoption of binding and prescriptive rules on financial institutions under the EU's new capital requirements regime (European Parliament and Council 2010) has, for example, been associated with an international 'race to the top' and with the EU's concern to control the international reform agenda (Moloney 2010). The EU has, however, been grappling with the complexities of harmonization of executive pay rules for some time.

Certainly, the current EU pay regime is untidy – substantively and conceptually. The EU's 2004 and 2005 Recommendations are based on an Anglo-American model which sits uneasily across a market characterized by dispersed and block-owning governance, by the related different dynamics of board and general meeting governance, and by different pay practices. Member States vary in terms of their adoption of binding or market-discipline-based mechanisms to address weaknesses in pay governance; they also vary very considerably with respect to the intensity with which they approach the regulation of board governance, disclosure, and shareholder voice.

But does it follow that harmonization is appropriate? Considerable caution is called for where Anglo-American reforms are transplanted into a different governance context (Lannoo and Khachaturyan 2004, Enriques and Volpin 2007, Clift 2009). Agency costs and monitoring devices differ as between dispersed and block-holding governance. So does the incidence of riskier high-powered, equity-based incentive contracts. Costly disclosure-based reforms and shareholder-voice reforms may make little sense in an environment dominated by informed block-holders and where related stakeholder dynamics, including those associated with labour co-determination (Hopt and Leyens 2004), can dilute conflicts of interest risk in pay governance. The related risks of harmonization in the corporate governance sphere and in company law have been well documented (Hertig 2005, Enriques and Gatti 2006). So too have the risks to international competitiveness which costly rules can generate (Litvak 2007). More generally, 'one-size-fits-all' regulatory models may be ineffective, as the determinants of good corporate governance vary across firms (Bhagat et al 2007). Similarly, the particular determinants of an effective incentive contract and pay-setting process are likely to differ across firms.

On the other hand, the different techniques for supporting the incentive contract, and particularly disclosure, are relevant in a block-holding context given the risks to minority shareholders which are becoming an increasing concern for EU policy but also continental corporate governance more generally, notably in Italy (Enriques 2009a). In block-holding ownership conditions, different shareholder/manager profiles arise which have varying implications for executive pay and conflict of interest management. Where the shareholder/owner manages the company, there is an alignment of interests, and the need for an incentive contract recedes. Where a professional/outside manager manages for the owner-shareholder, who may also be a director, the owner monitors the manager's performance, reducing the need for an incentive contract. Where ownership is concentrated into blocks, however, and management is carried out by professional/outside managers, monitoring of the same is carried out by the block-holders, but the incentive contract can align managerial interests with those of the firm as a whole. Protections may, however, be needed to prevent collusion between block-holders and management. In particular, where management and block-holders collude on pay-bargaining, a conflict arises between their interests and those of minority shareholders, triggering a potential misalignment of interests, albeit across a different conflict line to the dispersed-ownership conflict line.

Where legal regimes take diverging approaches to executive pay, management may also have incentives, in a competitive seat context (since the seminal European Court of Justice *Centros* decision[1]), to incorporate in EU jurisdictions with opaque approaches to executive pay. Certainly, the playing field between firms in the FTSE Eurofirst 300 is not level, particularly with respect to disclosure. Harmonization also brings advantages for pan-European groups which currently must comply with a range of different regimes.

Harmonization may also prompt better monitoring by shareholders; information costs currently appear high given the lack of standardization across the disclosures of publicly traded companies. Harmonization certainly carries risks, but the benefits of a limited degree of uniformity could be considerable, particularly given what appears to be an entrenched resistance to comprehensive disclosure in this area and quiescent institutional investors. Whether through inertia or because of the influence of block-holders, shareholders do not appear to have pressed for better and standardized disclosure practices across the EU.

In terms of managing the risks of intervention in this area, there are also scale efficiencies in the EU consolidating best practices in this area. EU level law-making may also act as a convenient shield for Member States reluctant to address local vested interests. Careful harmonization may additionally have the benefit of defusing potentially inefficient and populist short-term solutions at Member State level, and, in particular, may dilute the risks of crisis-driven reforms aimed at supporting financial stability being applied to the corporate sector generally (see section 4 below).

But while there may accordingly be an argument for some degree of harmonization, care must be taken with respect to the mechanism employed. There are unresolved tensions between the EU's concern to allow Member States flexibility in how they approach executive pay, and its reliance, accordingly, on Recommendations, and the countervailing need for consistency in best practices, particularly with respect to disclosure. The EU has also hitherto employed a scattergun approach – a wide range of pay governance requirements are recommended. The more effective approach would be to impose a binding harmonized obligation with respect to pay disclosure. Why?

Disclosure has considerable promise as a target for harmonization in the pan-EU context as it does not intervene directly in board or general meeting dynamics. It can promote stronger monitoring by shareholders and, in the block-holding context, act as a deterrent to rent-seeking by block-holders, particularly where they are also managers. Where outside managers are employed, disclosure supports block-holders in monitoring management and provides some protection for minority shareholders against collusion. Applying a uniform disclosure regime may also generate positive externalities with respect to pay governance, although the risk of a pay ratchet also arises. Pan-EU disclo-

---

[1]   Case C-212/97.

sure on executive pay by publicly traded firms currently ranges from boiler-plate statements to detailed, firm-specific discussions of performance sensitivity. Disclosures are scattered across public disclosure documents. Qualitative remuneration policy information is generally poor, limiting the value of individualized disclosure. It is also clear that firms have strong incentives not to disclose voluntarily, based on recent practice by the FTSE Eurofirst 300.

While further attention could be given to the remuneration committee, it remains closely rooted in local governance regimes, particularly with respect to the role of independent directors; neither is the evidence on the correlation between independence and long-term firm performance entirely convincing (Bhagat and Black 1999, Cheffins 2009). The 'say on pay' remains a particularly troublesome device for harmonization given the complexities of national company law and the extent to which the role of the general meeting differs across the Member States. The extent to which the 'say on pay' is effective in enhancing the efficiency of pay practices is also unclear, with the UK evidence equivocal (Gordon 2009).

But the EU has not, thus far, been prepared to adopt a binding disclosure regime. Two Recommendations, which have the distinct feel of war-time intervention, were adopted in 2009 in the teeth of the financial crisis. One of these deals with executive pay in financial institutions (European Commission 2009b). The other (European Commission 2009a) reforms the 2004 and 2005 Recommendations. In addition to adopting highly problematic design recommendations (see section 4), it addresses remuneration policy disclosure, suggesting that the remuneration policy be clear and easily understandable, that an explanation be provided concerning how performance criteria relate to firms' long term interests and with respect to whether those criteria were fulfilled, and that 'sufficient information' be provided concerning termination payments, vesting and other restrictions, and concerning the peer groups on which firm remuneration policy is based. At the very least, the Commission has identified the major weaknesses in current disclosure practice. But whether or not benign effects will follow is very doubtful given the failure to address standardization and enforcement and, in particular, the persistent reliance on a non-binding measure to support good disclosure practices across the Member States.

This failure reflects a general weakness across EU law generally with respect to 'law in action', notwithstanding that it increasingly appears that how laws are enforced is a key determinant of financial development (La Porta et al 2006). In April 2011, however, the Commission's Green Paper on Corporate Governance (European Commission 2011), as part of a general reform of corporate governance practices, noted weakness in the current executive pay framework and concerns related to short-termism and unjustified transfers of value from shareholders. It raised the possibility of a binding legislative regime governing disclosure. While this would represent a welcome development, the Green Paper also raised the possibility of a binding requirement for a shareholder vote on pay policy, which is problematic given the differing functions of the general meeting across the EU.

So what are the lessons for international harmonization? The difficulties faced by the EU in managing block-holder and dispersed-ownership agency conflicts, and given a policy and Treaty-based imperative to promote a single deep and liquid EU capital market, are of a different nature to the competitiveness and regulatory arbitrage questions which arise from the current efforts to seek international convergence on how healthy executive pay practices in financial institutions can be supported through law.

But the EU experience nonetheless underscores the dangers in transplanting law between regimes and the need for any international standardization to be sufficiently flexible to accommodate local conditions. The EU experience also highlights the importance of effective enforcement if standards are to be embedded, particularly given weak market monitoring. There are, however, some heartening signs of an international focus on enforcement. The Financial Stability Board, for example, has been charged with overseeing compliance with its standards on remuneration practices (FSB 2010a and 2010b), while the Basel Committee has similarly produced a supervisory review for standards for compliance with remuneration principles (Basel Committee 2010).

4 THE REGULATION OF PAY, THE FINANCIAL CRISIS AND THE EU: BEYOND SHAREHOLDER INCENTIVE ALIGNMENT?

While the financial crisis has created an EU political and institutional space within which the weaknesses of the current EU executive pay regime can be re-considered, the current context is not helpful for effective reform (Enriques 2009b) and serves as a reminder of the risks attached to legal intervention on pay. The premise of this chapter is that efficient, incentive-based executive pay contracts can provide a powerful means for aligning the interests of shareholders and managers and for addressing agency costs within dispersed and also block-holding firms; legal intervention should accordingly be limited to addressing failures which arise in the process through which the board, acting in the interests of shareholders, sets pay. Further intervention generates the risk that the legislator, whether EU or national, second-guesses the pay-setting process and damages optimal incentive alignment, particularly where pay becomes a vehicle for governmental agendas other than incentive alignment – such as the achievement of wider societal fairness or the quelling of societal anger with respect to the financial crisis. Intervention may also be simply ineffective, at best, and, at worst, generate perverse incentives to structure pay which is less sensitive to interest alignment (Bhagat and Romano 2009).

Executive pay is, of course, an easy target for governments seeking to deflect attention from wider policy and legislative failures and has long been a target for societal anger. But the current period is particularly troublesome in that the dominant shareholder alignment characterization is being recast (Cheffins 2009, Gordon 2009). The recent EU experience suggests that pay reforms designed to address systemic risk in the banking sector, and/or to assuage public anger and meet calls for greater 'fairness', may pull in executive pay generally in their wake – although it is not clear that executive pay governance structures, outside the financial sector, under-performed (or at least more than usual) over the financial crisis (Cheffins 2009).

With respect to financial stability, in the wake of the financial crisis, an association between excessive risk-taking and incentive contracts, both in the EU and elsewhere (Department of the Treasury 2009, European Commission 2009b, High Level Group 2009), combined with the need for regulators to employ a range of tools to address financial stability, has led to the pay-setting process within financial institutions being linked to the bank capital regime; measures controlling bank pay have also been a feature of international bank rescue mechanisms (Ferrarini and Ungureanu 2010). In the EU, recent reforms have created the possibility for capital penalties to be imposed on financial institutions where pay is not appropriately calibrated to the achievement of long-term financial stability (Committee of European Banking Supervisors 2009 and 2010, European Parliament and Council 2010); these measures impose specific requirements on the design of pay.

A linkage between executive pay, crisis in the financial markets, and reform is, of course, not new. Executive pay structures were implicated in the last major crisis to afflict the financial markets, in the shape of the Enron-era financial disclosure scandals, including those associated with Enron, Worldcom, Ahold, Vivendi and Skandia (Hill 2006). The financial stability model for pay intervention also reflects a wider and relatively clear stakeholder interest in financial stability, as well as the interests of government shareholders in state-supported banks. But, and by contrast with the Enron-era reforms, dangers to arise were governmental opportunism or carelessness to lead to this financial-stability-based model leaking into the corporate sector generally (Mülbert 2009).

In some respects, banking sector pay is easier to grapple with than corporate pay generally. The current bank pay reform movement has focused on the management of systemic risk as well as on how government debt- and equity-holders can ensure performance alignment in their interests. In the corporate sector generally, which is not subject to these clear policy drivers, the shareholder alignment/performance-based model remains the clearest and simplest model for assessing executive remuneration. EU company law and corporate governance is generally becoming more concerned with the risk management and systems-and-controls questions most strongly associated with financial institutions (Van der Elst and Van Daelen 2009, Van der Elst 2010). But there is some distance from using company law and corporate governance to drive the adoption of better risk management systems, including with respect to financial reporting, to adopting strict controls on pay which are associated with the particular problems generated by poor risk management in the financial sector. The shareholder alignment model is supported by regulatory intervention with respect to risk management which focuses on, for example, financial reporting and fraud. But it is not supported where pay controls are used to import a risk management model associated with the financial sector. The costs of more direct intervention on pay, given the information asymmetry between government and the corporate sector and the very considerable nuances which pay-setting demands, are considerable. The implicit threat of intervention arising from the financial stability reform agenda should also not be discounted as a brake on excessive and poorly designed pay in the corporate sector.

There is also a strong current public concern that, to be optimal, pay generally should also be 'fair', and widespread public hostility to high levels of pay in financial institutions. The executive remuneration question has accordingly, in some quarters, evolved from a concern as to how to achieve optimal pay structures that reward performance into a concern as to whether pay structures are 'just'. But any imposition of a fairness agenda through law is highly problematic. The shareholder alignment model does lead to the politically unpalatable reality that high or 'excessive' levels of executive pay are not an occasion for intervention – as long as pay is efficiently linked to performance and to shareholder/manager incentive alignment. Prior to the crisis, an alternative critique of executive pay engaged with the social implications of high levels of executive pay and with a fairness agenda (Gordon 2009). High levels of executive pay were criticized for failing to reflect wider stakeholder interests and, in particular, for failing to engage with the social justice implications of stratospheric pay awards (Loewenstein 1996). The financial crisis, however, has seen the wider debate on executive pay become entangled with the notions of fairness, equality, and 'excessive' pay, which, along with systemic risk concerns, are now strongly associated with the 'bankers' pay' debate (Bebchuk and Spamann 2009, Cheffins 2009). Certainly, public opprobrium concerning high levels of executive pay in financial institutions has been intense and the scale of the pay-outs to managers in failed financial institutions, now supported by the taxpayer, would shock the most disinterested observer (Walker 2009).[2]

But however appealing the fairness agenda, it is a troublesome one. Shareholder interest alignment remains a clear and transparent basis for reform which responds to the agency costs experienced by shareholders. Executive pay is not a device for reflecting societal expectations or, as might be the case currently, a desire for retribution. It is (or should be) simply a corporate governance mechanism for driving strong corporate performance in the interests of shareholders and for reducing agency costs. Even assuming 'fairness' could somehow be captured and could displace the primary interests of shareholders, the difficulties in implementing a fairness agenda through regulatory fiat are such as to make the exercise almost pointless. It is very difficult to design an effective incentive contract given the different objectives, even only with respect to interest alignment, that it must serve (Gordon 2009). The design of pay structures, and particularly of equity-based pay, increasingly in the ascendant as a preferred form of pay post-crisis, is notoriously complex, particularly given the risk of rewarding managers for market-wide gains and of complex pay structures being used to hide rent-seeking. Fairness-driven measures would be all the more troublesome, reflecting the difficulties in reflecting wider stakeholder concerns in pay design; whatever its difficulties in practice, the shareholder-interests model has, at least, the merits of relative simplicity (Bhagat and Romano 2009). A fairness-based model would require some form of balancing act between corporate and societal interests as well as some form of monitoring mechanism, beyond the board, to address fairness, through, for example, regulatory proxies in the form of pay limits and design requirements. There is certainly little evidence that intervention in support of 'reasonable' pay works (on the Australian experience, Thomas 2008).

In the EU, the risks arising from this dual recharacterization of pay in terms of risk management and fairness are two-fold: first, that sub-optimal regulatory devices are used to address executive pay (particularly with respect to design); and second, that the EU's traditionally wary approach to harmonization in this area, given the pan-EU governance divide, is trumped by reformist zeal.

With respect to the first, executive pay in non-financial firms appears to have been pulled into the EU's wider financial crisis agenda with the adoption of a 2009 Recommendation on Directors' Remuneration (European Commission 2009a). Reflecting the dangers of momentum and fashion in law-making, the 2009 Recommendation does

---

[2]   The Walker Review noted that the UK taxpayer had provided UK banks with nearly £1.3 trillion in support (equivalent to almost 90 per cent of UK GDP) and that 'political, taxpayer and social tolerance of practices, including unsafe remuneration policies, which led to this calamitous state, is understandably low': at 91.

not address the core enforcement and consistency difficulties generated by the earlier Recommendations, notwithstanding the evidence of poor practice already available to the Commission from its 2007 assessment (European Commission 2007). Instead, the Commission has moved closer to the problematic design sphere and away from the incentive alignment model as the basis for intervention. Noting, albeit without presenting empirical evidence, that remuneration structures had become increasingly complex, too focused on the short term, and leading, in some cases, to 'excessive' remuneration not justified by performance, the Commission adopted a series of voluntary principles concerning the structure of remuneration and imbued with a concern to reduce pay levels, notwithstanding the risks as intervention moves away from remuneration governance, and the strain this approach places on the EU's original incentive alignment model. The recommendation that undefined 'limits' should be placed on variable pay, for example, is troubling given the benefits of incentive alignment; the 2009 German reform, for example, while otherwise an unusually interventionist measure, only raises the possibility of limits on variable pay where the supervisory board deems it necessary in exceptional circumstances. This recommendation is vague, appears to be designed to reflect prevailing public and political opinion and is an undue incursion into corporate autonomy. It may prejudice the remuneration contract as a means for aligning shareholder and managerial interests; it is all the more troubling as the Recommendation has been adopted in the absence of clear and detailed evidence as to how these limits might address specific failures.

The Recommendation's suggestions with respect to the deferral of pay are similarly intrusive. The Recommendation suggests that the 'major part' of variable pay should be deferred for a 'minimum period' of time. It also suggests restrictions on share-based pay, recommending that shares should not vest for at least three years after their award and that share options or similar rights should not be exercisable for three years. The Commission has also suggested that a certain number of shares be retained by directors until the end of their mandate. Restricted shares, particularly those held until a director leaves, could certainly be a very useful mechanism for aligning director interests more effectively with long-term performance (Bhagat and Romano 2009) and are already a feature of some Member States' Corporate Governance Codes. But this restriction appears somewhat arbitrary; three years is not a particularly long horizon in terms of long-term performance. There has been no attempt to explain why this period was chosen or to consider the long-term consequences of these restrictions. This Recommendation represents an unwelcome distraction given the complexities of intervention in this area, the risk of damage to the pay/performance link and the more basic failures which persist with respect to remuneration disclosure and governance.

Given the parallel EU efforts to drive greater institutional investor activism and monitoring (European Commission 2010a), there is also a risk that these recommendations acquire the status of best practice and that it becomes difficult for firms to adopt different practices. An initial 2010 analysis by the Commission of Member State compliance with the Recommendation suggested that only a minority of Member States had required or recommended that firms comply with the provisions with respect to the deferral of variable pay and the vesting of share-based pay (European Commission 2010b); but political pressure from the Commission, combined with the increasing pressure being placed on institutional investors to enhance monitoring, may lead to wider adoption. Ultimately, the 2009 Recommendation suggests a muddle between shareholder and wider (and poorly defined) stakeholder interests. It also fails to get to the heart of the enforcement and consistency difficulties raised by the 2004 and 2005 Recommendations. The braver choice would have been to legislate for binding, core disclosure standards.

The greater danger, however, is that the EU will turn its attention to binding, harmonized rules which may extend beyond disclosure. In its June 2010 Green Paper on corporate governance, the Commission reported its dissatisfaction with compliance with the 2009 Recommendations on pay generally – application was 'neither uniform nor satisfactory' – and suggested that mandatory rules prohibiting share options and golden parachutes, across all firms, might be necessary (European Commission 2010a). However troublesome design rules are, they are all the more so where they are imposed on 27 Member States, across different governance regimes, and following a reform movement which has responded to systemic risks in the banking system. Although design reforms are not proposed in the Commission's 2011 Corporate Governance Green Paper (European Commission 2011), the momentum risks remain significant.

5   CONCLUSION

The EU's experience with executive pay and its regulation reinforces the strength of the link between executive pay and different governance structures – both with respect to pay practices, legal intervention and market monitoring. It highlights accordingly the need to avoid any transplant of Anglo-American governance regimes into systems which are ill-placed to integrate them. But this is not to suggest that the EU should not attempt to harden the currently unsatisfactory regime; minority shareholders are poorly supported by the current EU regime and the possibilities for prejudicial arbitrage are considerable. The challenge for the EU in developing a binding executive pay regime, however, will be to adopt a regime which is sufficiently calibrated to respect the different interests which require protection in dispersed and block-holding governance but which does not import intrusive risk-control-based systems developed for financial institutions in response to the financial crisis.

REFERENCES

Barca, Fabrizio and Becht, Marco (eds). 2001. *The Control of Corporate Europe*, Oxford: Oxford University Press.
Basel Committee of Banking Supervisors. 2010. Compensation Principles and Standards Assessment Methodology.
Bebchuk, Lucien and Fried, Charles. 2004. *Pay Without Performance: The Unfulfilled Promise of Executive Compensation*, Cambridge MA: Harvard University Press.
Bebchuk, Lucien and Spamann, Holger. 2010. Regulating Bankers' Pay, *Georgetown Law Journal*, 98(2): 247–87.
Bhagat, Sanjai and Black, Bernard. 1999. The Uncertain Relationship between Board Composition and Firm Performance, *Business Lawyer*, 54: 921–63.
Bhagat, Sanjai and Romano, Roberta. 2009. Reforming Executive Compensation: Focusing and Committing to the Long-Term. Yale Law & Economics Research Paper No 374. At http://ssrn.com/abstractid=1336978.

Bhagat, Sanjai, Bolton, Brian and Romano, Roberta. 2007. The Promise and Peril of Corporate Governance Indices. European Corporate Governance Institute Law Working Paper No 89/2007. At http://ssrn.com/abstract_id=1019921.

Brunello, Giorgio, Graziano, Clara and Parigi, Bruno. 2001. Executive Compensation and Firm Performance in Italy, *International Journal of Industrial Organization*, 19: 133–61.

Brunnermeier, Markus, Crocket, Andrew, Goodhart, Charles, Persaud, Avanish, and Shin, Hyung Sung. 2009. *The Fundamental Principles of Financial Regulation.* Geneva Reports on the World Economy 11. Centre for Economic Policy Research.

Cheffins, Brian. 2003. Will Executive Pay Globalise Along American Lines, *Corporate Governance*, 11: 8–24.

Cheffins, Brian. 2009. Did Corporate Governance 'Fail' During the 2008 Stock Market Meltdown? The Case of the S&P 500. European Corporate Governance Institute Law Working Paper No 124/2009. Available at http://ssrn.com/abstractid=1396126.

Clift, Ben. 2009. The Second Time as Farce? The EU Takeover Directive, the Clash of Capitalisms, and the Hamstrung Harmonization of European (and French) Corporate Governance, *Journal of Common Market Studies*, 47(1): 55–79.

Committee of European Banking Supervisors. 2009. High Level Principles for Remuneration Policies.

Committee of European Banking Supervisors. 2010. Consultation Paper on Guidelines on Remuneration Policies and Practices. Consultation Paper 42.

Committee of European Securities Regulators. 2010. Annual Report for 2009.

Crespi-Cladera, Rafel and Gispert-Pellicer, Carles. 1999. Board Remuneration, Performance and Corporate Governance in Large Spanish Companies. At http://ssrn.com/abstract=161869.

Department of the Treasury (US). 2009. Financial Regulatory Reform. A New Foundation: Rebuilding Financial Supervision and Regulation.

Enriques, Luca. 2009a. Modernizing Italy's Corporate Governance Institutions: Mission Accomplished? European Corporate Governance Institute Working Paper No 123/2009. At http://ssrn.com/abstract=1400999.

Enriques, Luca. 2009b. Regulators' Response to the Current Crisis and the Upcoming Reregulation of Financial Markets: One Reluctant Regulator's Views, *University of Pennsylvania Law Review*, 30(4): 1147–55.

Enriques, Luca and Gatti, Matteo. 2006. The Uneasy Case for Top-Down Corporate Law Harmonization in the European Union. *University of Pennsylvania Journal of International Economic Law*, 27(4): 939–98.

Enriques, Luca and Volpin, Paolo. 2007. Corporate Governance Reforms in Continental Europe, *Journal of Economic Perspectives*, 21(1): 117–40.

European Commission. 1999. Communication on Implementing the Framework for Financial Markets: Action Plan.

European Commission. 2003. *Modernising Company Law and Enhancing Corporate Governance in the European Union*, COM (2003) 284.

European Commission. 2004. Recommendations on Fostering an Appropriate Regime for the Remuneration of Directors, [2004] OJ L385/55.

European Commission. 2005. Recommendation on the Role of Independent Non-Executive or Supervisory Directors, [2005] OJ L52/51.

European Commission. 2007. Report on the Application by Member States of the EU of the Commission Recommendation on Directors' Remuneration.

European Commission. 2009a. Recommendation Complementing Recommendations 2004/913/EC and 2005/162 (C(2009) 3177).

European Commission. 2009b. Recommendation on Remuneration Policies in the Financial Sector (C(2009) 3159).

European Commission. 2010a. Consultation on Corporate Governance in Financial Institutions and Remuneration Policies.

European Commission. 2010b. Report on the Application of Recommendation 2009/385/EC.

European Commission. 2011. Green Paper. The EU Corporate Governance Framework (COM (2011) 164).

European Parliament and Council. 2003a. Accounts Modernisation Directive 2003/51/EC, [2003] OJ L178/16.

European Parliament and Council. 2003b. Market Abuse Directive 2003/6/EC, [2003] OJ L96/16.

European Parliament and Council. 2003c. Prospectus Directive 2003/71/EC, [2003] OJ L345/64.

European Parliament and Council. 2004. Transparency Directive 2004/109/EC, [2004] OJ L390/38.

European Parliament and Council. 2006. Directive 2006/46/EC, [2006] OJ L224/1.

European Parliament and Council. 2010. Directive 2010/76/EU, [2010] OJ L329/3.

Ferrarini, Guido and Giudici, Paolo. 2005. Financial Scandals and the Role of Private Enforcement: The Parmalat Case. European Corporate Governance Institute Law Working Paper No. 4/2005. Available at http://ssrn.com/abstract=730403.

Ferrarini, Guido and Moloney, Niamh. 2005. Executive Remuneration in the EU: The Context for Reform, *Oxford Review of Economic Policy*, 21: 304–23.

Ferrarini, Guido and Ungureanu, Maria-Cristina. 2010. Executive Pay at Ailing Banks and Beyond: A European Perspective, *Capital Markets Law Journal*, 5(2): 197–217.

Ferrarini, Guido, Moloney, Niamh, and Ungureanu, Maria-Cristina. 2009. Understanding Directors' Pay in Europe: A Comparative and Empirical Analysis. European Corporate Governance Institute Law Working Paper No 126/2009. At http://ssrn.com/abstract=1418463.

Ferrarini, Guido, Moloney, Niamh, and Ungureanu, Maria-Cristina. 2010. Executive Remuneration in Crisis: A Critical Assessment of Reforms in Europe, *Journal of Corporate Law Studies*, 10(1): 73–118.

Ferrarini, Guido, Moloney, Niamh, and Vespro, Cristina. 2004. Executive Pay: Convergence in Law and Practice Across the EU Corporate Governance Faultline, *Journal of Corporate Law Studies*, 4(2): 243–306.

Financial Services Authority. 2009. The Turner Review. A Regulatory Response to the Global Financial Crisis.

Financial Stability Board. 2009a. Principles for Sound Compensation Practices.

Financial Stability Board. 2009b. Principles for Sound Compensations Practices. Implementation Standards.

Financial Stability Board. 2010a. Thematic Review of Compensation. Peer Review Report.

Financial Stability Board. 2010b. Framework for Adherence to International Standards.

Garrido, José and Rojo, Angel. 2002. Institutional Investors and Corporate Governance: Solution or Problem?, in Hopt, Klaus and Wymeersch, Eddy (eds), *Capital Markets and Company Law*, Oxford: Oxford University Press.

Gelter, Martin. 2010. Taming or Protecting the Modern Corporation? Shareholder–Stakeholder Debates in a Comparative Light. European Corporate Governance Institute Law Working Paper No 165/2010. At http://ssrn.com/abstract=1669444.

Goergen, Marc, Manjon Antolin, Miguel C., and Renneboog, Luc. 2004. Recent Developments in German Corporate Governance. European Corporate Governance Institute Finance Working Paper No 41/2004. At http://ssrn.com/abstract=539383.

Gordon, Jeffrey N. 2002. What Enron Means for the Management and Control of the Modern Business Corporation: Some Initial Reflections, *University of Chicago Law Review*, 69: 1233–50.

Gordon, Jeffrey N. 2009. 'Say on Pay': Cautionary Notes on the UK Experience and the Case for Shareholder Opt-in, *Harvard Journal on Legislation*, 46: 323–67.

Gow, David. 2008. European Anger at 'Scourge' of Anglo-American Pay Practices. *The Guardian*, 13 September.

Hansen, Jesper L. 2006. Catching up with the Crowd – But Going Where? The New Codes on Corporate Governance in the Nordic Countries, *International Journal of Disclosure and Governance*, 3(3): 213–33.

Hertig, Gerard. 2005. Ongoing Board Reforms: One Size Fits All and Regulatory Capture, *Oxford Review of Economic Policy*, 21: 269–82.

Hewitt. (2003). Survey Findings: Corporate Governance and Executive Remuneration. A European Perspective.

High Level Group of Company Law Experts. 2002. Final Report.

High Level Group on Financial Supervision in the EU. 2009. Report (de Larosière Report).

Hill, Jennifer. 2006. Regulating Executive Remuneration: International Developments in the Post-Scandal Era, *European Company Law*, 3: 64–74.

Hopt, Klaus and Leyens, Patrick. 2004. Board Models in Europe: Recent Developments of Internal Corporate Governance Structures in Germany, the UK, France and Italy, *European Company and Financial Law Review*, 1(2): 135–68.

Jensen, Michael and Murphy, Kevin. 2004. Remuneration: Where we've been, how we got to here, what are the problems, and how to fix them. European Corporate Governance Institute Finance Working Paper No 44/2004. At http://ssrn.com/abstract=561305.

Lannoo, Karel and Khachaturyan, Arman. 2004. Reform of Corporate Governance in the EU, *European Business Organization Law Review*, 5(1): 37–60.

La Porta, Rafael, Lopez de Silanes, Florencio, and Shleifer, Andrei. 2006. What Works in Securities Laws, *Journal of Finance*, 61: 1–32.

Litvak, K. 2007. Sarbanes-Oxley and the Cross-Listing Premium, *Michigan Law Review*, 105(8): 1857–98.

Loewenstein, Mark. 1996. Reflections of Executive Compensation and a Modest Proposal for (Further) Reform, *Southern Methodist University Law Review*, 50: 201–223.

Milhaupt, Curtis J. and Pistor, Katharina. 2008. *Law and Capitalism: What Corporate Crises Reveal About Legal Systems and Economic Development around the World*, Chicago: University of Chicago Press.

Moloney, Niamh. 2008. *EC Securities Regulation*, 2nd edition, Oxford: Oxford University Press.

Moloney, Niamh. 2010. The EU and the Financial Crisis: 'More Europe' or More Risks, *Common Market Law Review*, 47(5): 1317–18.

Mülbert, Peter O. 2009. Corporate Governance of Banks After the Financial Crisis: Theory, Evidence, Reforms. European Corporate Governance Institute Law Working Paper No 130/2009. At http://ssrn.com/abstract=1448118.

Thomas, Randall S. 2008. International Executive Pay: Current Practices and Future Trends, Vanderbilt Law and Economics Research Paper No 08-26. At http://papers.ssrn.com/abstract=1265122.

Thomsen, Steen. 2005. Conflicts of Interests or Aligned Incentives? Blockholder Ownership, Dividends and Firm Value in the US and the EU, *European Business Organization Law Review*, 6(2): 201–25.

Van der Elst, Christoph. 2010. The Risks of Corporate Legal Principles of Risk Management. European Corporate Governance Institute Law Working Paper No 160/2010. At http://ssrn.com/abstract=1623562.

Van der Elst, Christoph and Van Daelen, Marijn. 2009. Risk Management in European and American Corporate Law. European Corporate Governance Institute Law Working Paper No 122/2009. At http://ssrn.com/abstract=539383.

Walker, Sir David. 2009. A Review of Corporate Governance in UK Banks and other Financial Industry Entities. Final Recommendations.

23 Executive compensation under German corporate law: reasonableness, managerial incentives and sustainability in order to enhance optimal contracting and to limit managerial power*

Brigitte Haar

What do Klaus Esser and Mickey Mouse have in common? This could be the overarching theme when looking at the German corporate law rules of executive remuneration. In the long-lasting *Disney Litigation* the Delaware court finally did not hold the Disney directors liable for damages, even though they had approved a US$140 million compensation package for the number-two executive at Disney, Michael Ovitz, who lacked any managerial experience in a public corporation and whose tenure was considered a failure.[1] According to the Delaware court, the board was protected by the business judgment rule. In the *Mannesmann* case involving a US$17 million bonus payment to the Mannesmann CEO Klaus Esser, the members of the compensation committee of the supervisory board were charged with making illegal payments during the firm's takeover by Britain's Vodafone in 2000 and faced criminal sanctions.[2] Although the latter were based on the *actus reus* of misappropriation, the violation of the German Penal Code required a judicial review of the severance package, which was guided by corporate law standards. Therefore, at the bottom line the court analysis made reference to the appropriateness of the bonus awards under German corporate law, accepting a margin of business judgment as well.

The role of business judgment as a determinant of executive remuneration in judicial review shows the evolution of the underlying corporate law rules because in the *Mannesmann* case a paradigm change was beginning to unfold. With a closer look at the correlation between executive compensation and performance, the role of incentives for management by way of their remuneration started to come into focus (Cheffins 2001). At the same time, the importance of the greed debate is still reflected by the emphasis put on the comparison of Esser's bonuses with other executive bonuses. In order to put this development into a broader perspective, one therefore has to look first at the empirical data on German executive compensation in relation to other countries (see section 1 below). Only then do the change in relevance of this issue today and the legal approaches to solve it as compared with the end of the last century become apparent. It will be interesting to see to what extent economic analysis of corporate governance problems underlies current legislative approaches to problem-solving in the field of executive

---

*   This chapter represents the case law and literature as of 30 June 2011.
[1]   *In re The Walt Disney Company Derivative Litigation* (*Disney I*), 731 A.2d 342, 351 (Del. Ch. 1998); *Disney II*, 825 A.2d 275 (Del. Ch. 2003); *Disney III*, 907 A.2d 693 (Del. Ch. 2005).
[2]   Federal Court of Justice Case No. 3 StR 470/04, BGHSt 50, 331 *Mannesmann*.

compensation. To this end, it is necessary to trace back the former rules on executive compensation and shed light on their doctrinal context in order to evaluate the recent changes (section 2 below). Against this background, the different corporate law rules on executive compensation and their problem-solving capacities can be assessed in relation to characteristic problem areas, such as the question of benchmarks for director compensation (section 3), the regulation of pay components (section 4), and the issue of the say on pay (section 5). This leaves room for an overall evaluation of the latest legislative development of German corporate law in this area and its coherence (section 6).

1   BACKGROUND: EXECUTIVE PAY IN GERMANY AND THE GERMAN CORPORATE GOVERNANCE SYSTEM

1.1   Empirical Evidence on Executive pay in Germany

At the time of the *Mannesmann* case and *Disney* litigation in 2000, the compensation of an average CEO in the United States was 531 times higher than that of an average employee in his or her company. In contrast, in Germany the pay of an average CEO was only 11 times higher. From 1997 to 2005 CEO pay levels have risen significantly in both Germany (8.6 per cent) and the United States (8 per cent) (Geiler and Renneboog 2010). Within Europe in 2005/06 Germany is among the countries where the highest CEO compensation can be found besides France, Switzerland, and the United Kingdom (Tower Perrin 2005/06). At the same time, CEO pay in the US is by far the highest. This huge difference in pay level was particularly clearly highlighted on the occasion of the merger of the German car manufacturer Daimler-Benz and its American rival Chrysler in 1998. Throughout the transaction it became clear that Chrysler's No. 2 executive earned more from salary, bonus and share options than the top ten Daimler-Benz executives combined (Cunningham 1999).

In 2005/06 in the US 95 per cent of this high pay was variable, 30 per cent relying on variable bonuses and the other 65 per cent relying on long-term incentives. In Germany the per centage of variable pay has increased dramatically from 1997 to 2005, starting from 16 per cent variable bonus in 1997 and rising to 70 per cent including 40 per cent variable bonuses and 30 per cent long-term incentive pay (Tower Perrin 2005/06). This changed again in the aftermath of the financial crisis. On average, in 2009 a CEO of a company listed on the German stock index DAX (Deutscher Aktien IndeX) receives 33.2 per cent non-performance-related salary and 44.4 per cent variable bonuses, and 22.4 per cent remuneration that is sensitive to share value (DSW 2010).

Despite these differences with regard to the amount of executive remuneration and its composition there is empirical evidence of similar agency problems underlying executive compensation packages in both corporate governance systems (Elston and Goldberg 2008; Haid and Yurtoglu 2006). Just as shown in studies with respect to the United States, there is some indication that the ability of executives to extract high levels of compensation decreases with a rising degree of ownership concentration. This finding can be taken as evidence of existing agency problems. At the same time it is shown that performance and size are positively related to compensation, just as it has been evidenced with regard to the United States.

1.2   Related Changes in the German Corporate Governance System

Overall the rise of performance-related compensation in German DAX-listed companies is striking and seems to be evidence of existing, possibly increasing agency problems, which are related to the corporate governance system. Therefore the question arises in what way the perception of these agency problems may have changed and how this may be reflected in the rules on executive compensation. Until the hostile takeover of Mannesmann AG by Vodafone in 2000, German companies had been largely protected from hostile takeovers because of the only weakly developed market for corporate control at the time (Beyer and Hassel 2002) and because higher executive compensation resulting from higher performance orientation met with objections from different stakeholders.

Before the amendment of the German Stock Corporation Act in 1998 a stock corporation (AG-Aktiengesellschaft) was not permitted to issue or acquire shares to satisfy option rights exercised by top executives (Kalisch 1998). Instead, performance-related pay in German AGs typically rested on share option plans using convertible and warrant bonds. The latter require a three-quarters majority vote of the company's shareholders (§ 221 of the German Stock Corporation Act [Aktiengesetz, AktG]). The shareholders, however, were afraid of the dilutive effect that such an option plan could have on their equity and were therefore not very much in favor of a high per centage of such components of executive remuneration (Cheffins 2001).

In addition, the German corporate governance system has been bank-based and insider-oriented (Franks and Mayer 2001) and companies have raised most of their external finance from banks. Under this system a company's main bank has long-standing lending relationships with its corporate customers, reaching the status of a "house bank", and may act as monitor providing continuous supervision of the projects it finances. As late as after the Mannesmann takeover German banks started a strategic reorientation from this "house bank" model to investment banking. Since hostile takeovers appeared to be effective control mechanisms and the influence of the capital market started to increase, the German model of corporate governance was beginning to change (Milhaupt and Pistor 2008). Therefore, it goes without saying that banks have always been highly influential stakeholders in German corporations, lending money to them, directly holding equity and often exercising proxy votes that they receive from smaller shareholders (Cheffins 2001). Therefore corporate ownership has been relatively highly concentrated and often characterized by complex cross-holdings and pyramids (La Porta et al. 1998). Other instruments in German corporate law to secure control for insiders who do not necessarily own the majority of voting shares include, among others, shareholder agreements and discriminatory voting rights.

This insider-orientation of the German corporate governance system has been reinforced by legal privileges granted to the employees as another group of stakeholders by way of control rights and seats on the board of directors (Andres et al. 2010). This procedural integration of employee interests illustrates how the German corporate governance system has been geared towards internal compromise instead of relying on the external control by transparent liquid capital markets (Aglietta and Rebérioux 2005). At the same time, it stands to reason that employees are opposed to any performance-related pay that may lead to a divergence of interests between the management and the rank and file employees. In addition, owing to employee representation on German supervisory boards, much emphasis in the debate on executive remuneration is put on income equality (Cheffins 2001). Overall codetermination reflects, among other things, the political priority that is given to distributional concerns in corporate governance in Germany (Clarke 2007).

The integration of such a broad variety of stakeholder interests into the corporation's decision-making process goes hand in hand with a distinct perception of directors' duties and their underlying legal interpretations (Clarke 2007). The orientation towards a wide range of stakeholder interests suggests a broad pursuit of financial interests of the corporation, including creditor interests for example, and a resulting wide interpretation of shareholder value. In fact, the stakeholder model and its underlying concept of legal personhood of the corporation have resulted in a perspective that puts the corporation's self-interest ahead of shareholders or other stakeholders.[3] In light of this corporation-oriented approach, with the organizational framework being its main doctrinal point of reference, it comes as no surprise that, conceptually speaking, German corporate law and the surrounding corporate governance problems have only recently and to a limited extent been analyzed from a principal–agent perspective.[4]

With the Mannesmann takeover and increasing globalization of capital markets the German model had come under attack (Milhaupt and Pistor, 2008). In view of these developments the so-called Baums Report of 2001 recommended nearly 150 proposals and changes to the existing German corporate law in reaction to the pressure of the international financial markets (Baums 2001). Most importantly, this report recommended the development of a corporate governance code incorporating corporate governance best practice. As a result, a follow-up commission drafted the so-called Cromme code as non-binding soft law including the essential statutory regulations for the management and supervision of German listed companies and internationally and nationally recognized standards for good corporate governance (Government Commission of the German Corporate Governance Code).

In order to ensure a regulatory interlocking between the German statutory corporate code and the non-binding German Corporate Governance Code, the Law on Transparency and Disclosure (Transparenz- und Publizitätsgesetz [TransPuG]) of July 26, 2002 (BGBl. 2002 I, p. 2681) included a comply or explain provision, thus relying on the regulatory technique introduced by the Cadbury Code of Best Practice in 1992. Therefore, under § 161 AktG today a company has to provide an explanation of why it has not complied in areas of non-compliance. By adopting this technique, the German legislator makes clear that he is increasingly relying on the pressure of capital markets in his corporate governance model. At the same time this approach seems to be more focused on the resolution of the underlying agency problems than the traditional legal doctrine. It therefore remains to be seen to what extent this development has exerted an influence on the legal treatment of executive remuneration and the ensuing debate and what repercussions the financial crisis may have entailed.

---

[3]   This becomes particularly clear in the analysis of fiduciary duties which shareholders owe towards the corporation (Federal Court of Justice Case No. II ZR 205/94, BGHZ 129, 136).

[4]   Only recent textbooks of German corporate law begin to include this approach (Windbichler, 2009:18); for research see e.g. Ruffner 2000.

2   GERMAN LEGAL DEVELOPMENT IN THE FIELD OF EXECUTIVE COMPENSATION

2.1   Cornerstones laid out in the German Stock Corporation Acts of 1937 and 1965

As early as 1937 the German Stock Corporation Act (Aktiengesetz) included a provision in § 78 para. 1 on executive remuneration stating that the supervisory board had to make sure that the total compensation of the management board of the corporation including salaries, bonuses, stocks, stock options, insurance premiums, and any other benefit of any kind, was reasonable in light of the duties of the respective manager and the overall financial situation of the corporation.[5] This rule was supposed to limit the parties' freedom of contract and it was construed by some contemporary legal scholars from the point of view of the national socialist ideology pervading the German political system at the time. Therefore the requirement of reasonable executive remuneration was seen as an outgrowth of the political ideal to put the public interest before self-interest that was imposed on all parts of the population (Schlegelberger and Quassowski 1939).

The post-war Stock Corporation Act of 1965 adhered in its § 87 para. 1 to the essential criterion of reasonableness as a guideline to limit executive remuneration (Fleischer 2005, Hoffmann-Becking 2005).[6] In essence, this provision has aimed to protect the corporation, the shareholders and the creditors against too high executive remuneration (Fleischer 2005, Hoffmann-Becking 2005) by prescribing the responsibility of the supervisory board members to ensure that the amount of the executive remuneration is proportionate to the respective manager's duties and the company's financial condition. In providing for such a responsibility, the legislator has specified general fiduciary duties in this field that have been dealt with on a similar basis of fiduciary duties to the waste doctrine under US corporate law.

2.2   The Role of the Courts

Under the theory of corporate waste, directors can be held liable for excessive compensation practices in cases of extraordinary disproportionality.[7] Whereas the American courts only set an outer limit to the directors' discretion to make decisions about executive compensation, at first sight it could seem that German judges have played a more important substantive role in determining executive compensation thanks to the explicit standards laid down in § 87 para. 1 AktG. However, in order to capture the true importance of this standard one has to consider potential procedural constraints that may stand in the way of any redress against the members of the supervisory board (Cheffins 2001). First of all, shareholders have only limited enforcement possibilities because in principle it is the

---

[5]   Aktiengesetz of January 30, 1937, Reichsgesetzblatt I, p. 107.
[6]   Aktiengesetz of September 6, 1965, Bundesgesetzblatt I, p. 1089.
[7]   For the first recognition of this doctrine see *Rogers v. Hill*, 289 U.S. 582 (1933); for a dismissal of a waste claim cf. *Brehm v. Eisner*, 746 A.2d 244 (Del. 2000); *In re Walt Disney Co. Derivative Litig.*, 906 A.2d 27, 73–75 (Del. 2006); evidence for a renewed interest in the waste doctrine and its application: *In re Citigroup Inc. S'holder Derivative Litig.*, 964 A.2d 106 (Del. Ch. 2009).

responsibility of the supervisory board to pursue legal claims on behalf of the corporation. The shareholders themselves can only do so under § 147 AktG, if they own ten per cent or more of a stock corporation's equity or shares with a nominal value of one million euros. Second, case law reveals little willingness on the part of the courts to interfere with the business judgment of the supervisory board over what constitutes reasonable executive remuneration, when the Regional Court of Munich concluded in 2007 that despite not being in accordance with common practice executive remuneration can still be considered reasonable.[8]

2.3 The Control and Transparency in the Corporate Field Act of 1998 ("KonTraG")

Therefore the refinement of the general fiduciary duty of the supervisory board with respect to executive remuneration in the Stock Corporation Act of 1965 § 87 para. 1 and the criterion of reasonableness did not by themselves improve the reviewability of executive remuneration and did not ensure that executive compensation was correlated to performance. At the same time, under the German Stock Corporation Act of 1965 incentive-oriented compensation could not easily be included in a managerial contract. One way to implement such an incentive-oriented financial component would have been for the corporation to issue new shares or to repurchase outstanding equity in order to fulfill the obligations under the option plan (Kalisch 1998). In light of the above-mentioned illegality of such a repurchase of stocks, until 1998 German stock corporations had to rely on convertible or warrant bonds each requiring a three-fourths majority vote (§ 221 AktG) in order to implement stock option plans for executives. Therefore it is hardly surprising that, according to a number of studies, company size and ownership concentration rather than performance seemed to have a decisive influence on the level of executive compensation (Haid and Yurtoglu 2006; Prigge 1998).

These restrictions were supposed to be done away with by an amendment of the Stock Corporation Act in 1998, the so-called Control and Transparency in the Corporate Field Act of April 27, 1998 ("KonTraG") that, by and large, aimed to reinforce shareholder rights and improve monitoring by the supervisory boards (Bundesgesetzblatt [BGBl.] 1998 I, p. 786). Under this Act the repurchase of stocks was deregulated. Namely § 71 para.1 no. 8 AktG has now made it possible for the board to be authorized by the shareholder meeting to repurchase stocks without any predetermined objective, as long as the repurchase takes place within a period of eighteen months after the shareholder authorization and the repurchase does not exceed ten per cent of the general stock. Meeting obligations under stock option plans constitutes a permissible objective under § 71 para.1 no. 8 of the revised AktG. As a result, reliance on share option plans in German stock corporations has notably increased following the enactment of the KonTraG in 1998. The per centage of variable pay rose from 19 per cent in 1998 to 70 per cent in 2005 (Tower Perrin 2005/06). This changed, however, in the course of the financial crisis 2009, when a CEO of a DAX-listed company received on average 33.2 per

---

[8] *Landgericht München I*, Case No. 5 HK O 12931/06, reprinted in: *Die Aktiengesellschaft* 2007, p. 458.

cent non-performance-related pay, 44.4 per cent variable bonuses, and 22.4 per cent share-based pay (DSW 2010).

2.4   Legislative Reform in the Aftermath of the Recent Financial Crisis

Against the background of this development the German Parliament (Bundestag) enacted a law on the appropriateness of director compensation ("Gesetz zur Angemessenheit der Vorstandsvergütung" [VorstAG]) on June 18, 2009 that took effect on August 5, 2009 (Bundesgesetzblatt 2009 I, p. 2509). With regard to executive compensation it covers three dimensions of appropriateness: benchmarks, pay structure, and the role of the supervisory board in the pay process, by amending the pertinent provisions of the German Stock Corporation Act.

The point of departure of the legislative debate had been the concern about a "fairness gap" between the directors' pay and that of the rank and file employees (Seibert 2009). In the course of the financial crisis the discussion was then increasingly centering on different aspects. There was a debate as to the extent to which short-term incentive-based compensation had exacerbated the crisis. There was a growing impression that an alignment of shareholder and manager interests could not be easily achieved by way of share-price-based compensation. Instead, it became clear that a general rise in share prices did not necessarily result from good management performance in a specific business, but could just as easily be the product of favorable economic conditions that would – as the case may be – bring about a considerable pay increase for managers and pay them for luck (Bertrand and Mullainathan 2001). At the same time, there was a lot of criticism to the effect that share options could create unfavorable incentives for managers to aim for short-lived increases in share prices and to engage in excessive risk-taking rather than aiming for sustainable growth of the company's business (Congressional Oversight Panel 2009; Seibert 2010). The European Council had already addressed these concerns with regard to the banking sector in mid-October 2008 (Council of the European Union 2008). In its Recommendations 2009 the European Commission had then similarly pointed out that wrong incentive pay had caused the financial crisis and therefore it recommended pursuing a remuneration policy aiming at sustainable long-term business growth (European Commission 2009). The G20 Declaration of the 2008 Washington Summit likewise made reference to the need to review ". . .compensation practices as they relate to incentives for risk taking. . ." (Group of Twenty 2008).

This was the political background against which the German legislator specified the rules and principles for directors' pay in the amendment of the Stock Corporation Act of 2009. The key issues of this amendment are the benchmarks to determine the appropriateness of director compensation (§ 87 para. 1 AktG) and the requirements as to its composition. In addition, the role of the supervisory board is newly defined in the amendment: it is given the authority to reduce the compensation in case of a subsequent deterioration of the condition of the company (§ 87 para. 2 AktG), its members can be held liable in case of illegality of the compensation and the shareholder meeting possibly has a non-binding say on the remuneration system (§ 120 para. 4 AktG).

3   BENCHMARKS FOR DIRECTOR COMPENSATION UNDER § 87 PARA. 1 AKTG OF THE AMENDMENT

3.1   Reasonableness

As mentioned above, even before the amendment of 2009, § 87 para. 1 AktG of 1965 provided for reasonable executive compensation that had to take into account the duties of the respective executive and the overall situation of the company. The initial version of the German Corporate Governance Code of February 26, 2002 already included a further specification of reasonable compensation in its section 4.2.2 by referring to the executive's performance, the success and the future prospects of the company (Regierungskommission Deutscher Corporate Governance Kodex 2002). The amendment of 2009 has now adopted the reference to personal performance as an additional criterion.

Apart from that, the German legislator has refrained from introducing a mandatory upper limit for the highest compensation, thus relying on the fundamental freedom of contract as the basic principle of private law. Therefore, the general rule in § 87 para. 1 AktG serves as a guideline and provides the supervisory board with possible criteria to differentiate among the executives according to the size and the importance of the field of responsibility and according to their position on the board, to distinguish the CEO from the simple board member. As far as the overall situation of the company is concerned, this factor is not limited to the consideration of the financial assets of the company, but also includes the entire financial condition as a whole. Therefore apart from present assets, financial and earning position, future developments and external determinants, such as markets, political and legal environments have to be taken into account (Fleischer 2005).

In the amendment of 2009 the German legislator explicitly refers to the executive's individual performance in § 87 para. 1 AktG in order to determine the reasonableness of his or her compensation, even though it could also be considered under the former versions of this provision. This aspect was, however, not only based on the idea to create incentives. Instead, with regard to the close corporation (Gesellschaft mit beschränkter Haftung–GmbH) the Federal Supreme Civil Court (Bundesgerichtshof) took into account the character, the size, and the potential of the company, the age, education, experience, and skills of the manager as well as the range and the importance of his or her activities (Bundesgerichtshof, Judgment May 14, 1990, Neue Juristische Wochenschrift [NJW] 1990, p. 2625; Hüffer 2007). Ultimately these criteria indicate the factors that are usually relevant for the compensation in the labor markets. This point of reference highlights the significance of reasonableness of compensation under § 87 para. 1 AktG and its conceptual framework: it establishes a link between the compensation agreement between the parties and the market and therefore provides for default rules completing the parties' "optimal contracting" by compensating market weaknesses.

3.2   Standard Practice

In addition to the criterion of reasonableness, § 87 para. 1 AktG provides that executive compensation has to be in line with standard practice. Even though standard practice will not always be distinctively separable from reasonableness, the German legislator made a point of establishing standard practice as an independent criterion that should serve as an upper limit and be disregarded only in very rare cases. That is because the German legislator was afraid of a ratchet effect, if compensation only had to be reasonable with regard to standard practice.[9]

Standard practice has to be evaluated along two dimensions, that is a horizontal dimension according to the market position of the company's business and a vertical dimension according to the internal payment structure of the company. According to the German legislator's understanding the horizontal dimension typically refers to standard practice in terms of industry, business size and country (Deutscher Bundestag, Bundestags-Drucksache 16/13433 of 17.6.2009, p. 10). This seems questionable for several reasons. To begin with, the reason for defining standard practice by country is not clear, even if a board member may have a profitable job offer from abroad or if he or she actually has equivalent job opportunities in the international job market for executives (Seibert 2010). At the same time, the comparison between countries may be difficult because of the differences between the one-tier and two-tier systems. More generally speaking, it is risky to define standard practice according to average compensation for board members because then only average quality will be available. Thinking about basketball, one will never get a Dirk Nowitzki for a salary of five million dollars, even though that is the average salary of all NBA players. Therefore, understanding standard practice by markets may result in a leveling of compensation that is contrary to the essential selection of the best in the companies' global competition for top talent. That is why a horizontal market comparison is only useful to a limited degree, because the qualification needed is difficult to evaluate and to quantify in monetary terms (Suchan and Winter 2009).

The vertical dimension allows for the consideration of the internal payment structure of the company. It is supposed to make sure that a company is following a coherent remuneration policy over all levels throughout the firm. This approach may also lead to certain tensions with the idea of market-based and performance-based compensation as well as with the idea of horizontal market comparison. The legislative history indicates, however, that the legislator is inclined to give priority to the horizontal comparison and to consider the vertical dimension simply as an additional possible criterion (Deutscher Bundestag, Bundestags-Drucksache 16/13433 of 17.6.2009, p. 10). Therefore the vertical comparison seems to imply an "outrage constraint" as an upper limit of executive compensation (Bebchuk and Fried 2004) in case standard practice in related markets is not an appropriate yardstick. In addition, a vertical comparison disregards different degrees of homogeneity of employees in different industries. Wage differentials will play different roles depending on whether a small, innovative firm or a DAX-listed established firm is concerned. In both cases remuneration policy is a part of the company's business strategy that must be responsive to specific circumstances in the industry and cannot be lumped together as part of a mandatory vertical comparison (Suchan and Winter 2009).

At first sight, standard practice overall seems to integrate external markets on the basis

---

[9]   See the amendment that was inserted in the Committee on Legal Affairs of the Deutscher Bundestag during the legislative process, Deutscher Bundestag, Bundestags-Drucksache 16/13433, p. 10.

of a horizontal comparison and internal markets with regard to the vertical payment structure into the evaluation of the executive compensation agreement. That is why specifying standard practice with reference to horizontal and vertical market comparisons may adjust market weaknesses that these agreements may suffer from. At the same time, the outrage constraint that can be defined by reference to the company's vertical payment structure shows a far-reaching mistrust on the part of the legislator towards the contracting parties in that it is considered necessary to introduce such a constraint that limits market influences on the firm. Overall, market delimitations turn out to be impracticable and therefore the criterion of standard practice under the current common understanding does not appear to be very useful. Therefore the supervisory board is well advised to give good reasons for its remuneration decision (Wagner and Wittgens 2009). Especially if the standard remuneration will possibly be exceeded, this has to be well justified and documented on the basis of compensation reports of comparable companies. In addition to this, the supervisory board may decide to rely on an independent compensation advisor, whose independence has to be verified beforehand under Section 4.2.2 para. 3 of the German Corporate Governance Code (Kling 2010). In light of the growing complexity of executive compensation under the amendment of the German Stock Corporation Act of 2009, an increasing involvement of compensation advisors in the remuneration governance of larger German companies can be expected (Fleischer 2010).

4 PAY COMPONENTS

4.1 Sustainable Development under § 87 para. 1 of the Stock Corporation Act

In addition to reasonableness and standard practice as the benchmarks for executive compensation, § 87 para. 1 AktG provides for a sustainable development of the company's business as a guideline for the structure of the executive compensation system. According to the legislative history, executive compensation should therefore aim to create incentives for board members to pursue sustainable profitable performance rather than short-term profits (Deutscher Bundestag, Bundestags-Drucksache 16/13433 of 17 June 2009, p. 10). The significance of this requirement can be best explained against the background of the negative experience with adverse incentives that resulted from well-established stock option schemes. The latter led to managers' view to key dates of their options and to their ensuing short-term orientation towards single parameters for success, such as turnover and the amounts of commissions and total borrowings (Hüffer 2010). This reading of the provision also follows from the wording of § 87 para. 1 AktG that provides that ". . . the compensation structure has to be aimed toward a sustainable development of the company's business . . . [and] *therefore* variable components should have a long-term basis for assessment . . ."

It is, however, complicated to implement such an influence on executive behavior. The first question that arises is at what point in time to evaluate whether a certain behavior can be considered sustainable (Suchan and Winter 2009). If the behavior itself should be geared toward long-term success, the supervisory board would have to check whether the executives' decisions and their implementation are suitable to increase long-term business performance. It stands to reason that the problems of evaluation going hand in hand with this approach can hardly be overcome. On the other hand, the alternative would be to look at the actual success as an indicator of sustainability. In this case, however, compensation would not be based on performance, but rather on success (Suchan and Winter 2009). The latter understanding would require a waiting period until the success becomes clear. This may seem plausible in light of the extension of the blocking period for share options and a more consistent approach to make sure that adverse incentive structures are eliminated.

Despite the desirable relation between sustainability and performance under § 87 para. 1 AktG, parameters have to be found to ensure a workable implementation and therefore to limit the time period to establish and verify sustainability (Suchan and Winter 2009). Otherwise this criterion of executive compensation will not lead to any management motivation. That is why the assessment of performance should be generally based on a period of at least two years, as provided for with regard to variable pay under § 87 para. 1 3rd sent. AktG. It goes without saying, however, that it will not be possible to come up with a one-size-fits-all approach to this question. Different levels of innovation in different industries and the ensuing different length of life-spans of projects will bring about either rather short-term or long-term results. Despite the legal requirement under § 87 para. 1 AktG, the legislator did not want to keep the parties from coming up with different solutions to this problem (Hüffer 2010). In practice, quite a few German DAX-listed companies provide for an obligation on their executives to buy their shares and hold them continuously under share ownership guidelines. Such an obligation may reach an amount as high as 100 per cent of the annual fixed income or 300 per cent of the basic compensation.

Despite the express provision in § 87 para. 1 AktG for a period of at least two years underlying the performance assessment, the amended version of § 193 para. 2 no. 4 AktG now provides for a mandatory four-year exercise period for share options. According to the explanatory memorandum of the amendment of 2009, this period can be taken as a certain guideline for other variable pay components (Deutscher Bundestag, Bundestags-Drucksache 16/12278 of 17 March 2009, p. 5). Therefore, a four-year period would be the rule that the parties can however deviate from. It is in line with the discussion at EU level where a period between three and five years is recommended (European Commission Recommendation of 2009, p. 3). Such a guideline is particularly convincing with regard to pay components that are similar to share options, such as phantom stocks, share appreciation rights and comparable share-based payments. A phantom stock is a promise to pay an employee a bonus that is directly tied to the value of a company's stock, but without actually giving an individual share. Compared to stock options, it has the advantage of not diluting existing shareholders and not lowering the value of new shares that have to be issued to pay the employees.

Accounting problems and confusion on the part of the employees about what exactly they are getting, however, are serious drawbacks and may outweigh any motivational impact. Share appreciation rights similarly provide employees with a cash or stock payment based on the increase in the value of a stated number of shares over a specific period of time. In both cases the right holder receives an award based on the value of the company's stock, so that the vesting period becomes crucial for the eventual benefits flowing from these share-based payments just as is the case with stock options.

4.2 Stock Options

Even though stock options have been highly criticized throughout the recent financial crisis for creating adverse incentives for managers to take excessive risks, they are still common as part of executive compensation. In the interest of long-term behavioral control they are however subject to some restrictions, such as extended holding periods, so that they can now only be cashed in after four years (§ 193 para. 2 no. 4 AktG). In addition, according to a decision of the Federal Civil Court of Justice of 2004, compensation of supervisory board members may not consist of stock options (Bundesgerichtshof, Judgment February 2, 2004, Neue Juristische Wochenschrift [NJW] 2004, p. 1109). The court held that the legislator had not wanted to subject the supervisory board members to the same behavioral control emanating from shareholder value-oriented compensation. Such an alignment of compensation interests of supervisory and management board members would jeopardize the monitoring and supervisory role of the supervisory board. Along similar lines, the German Corporate Governance Code explicitly lists stock options and similar variable payments only for executive board members (Section 4.2.3), but not for supervisory board members (Section 5.4.5). Another constraint imposed on the grant of stock options is provided for by the Corporate Governance Code in its Section 4.2.3 that aims to exclude the retroactive change of performance targets, so that repricing of stock options would be illegal (Ringleb 2010).

In light of the ban on repricing of stock options, there has been a debate about the legislative goal to control management behavior in the interest of the company and to avoid adverse short-term incentives (Baums 1997). This approach was supposed to resolve the underlying principal–agent conflict and the associated monitoring problems. Before the amendment the parties themselves had not been able to come up with a satisfying solution because the stock options provided for in executive compensation agreements did not create the desired incentives. The question to address now is whether the legislator was successful in finding a remedy and in optimizing executive compensation agreements according to the understanding of the optimal contracting hypothesis.

4.3 Incentive Effects

Such a solution rests on the basic assumption that stock options have an actual effect on earnings per share. This legislative point of departure has been subject to a fierce debate spilling over from economics to German legal doctrine. There are indeed some early studies finding a weak correlation between the amount of executive compensation and earnings per share (Abowd 1990; Masson 1971). However, there is hardly any evidence of an immediate effect of stock option pay for CEOs and stock price performance (Murphy 1999). In addition the mere correlation between executive pay and stock price performance does not indicate the direction of this effect (Benz et al. 2002). It could very well be that successful companies simply pay more. Usually, an increase in stock prices is also caused by favourable economic conditions. There has also been evidence that analysts consider the composition of executive pay in their analysis and their investment recommendations and evaluate stock options positively, so that the correlation between stock option pay and stock price performance may be based on a self-fulfilling prophecy.[10] Therefore the empirical basis for an incentive effect of stock options seems to be rather weak.

This is why the question has been raised in the debate about executive compensation in Germany of whose interests are served after all by stock option pay. Stock option programs have undoubtedly turned out to be quite lucrative for executives, but not necessarily for shareholders. In light of the negative effects of incentive pay on risk preferences (Larraza-Kintana et al. 2007) and on strategic risk management (Cheng and Warfield 2005; Heron and Lie 2007) as well as in view of its possible adverse effects on intrinsic motivation (Deci et al. 1999), stock option pay has been increasingly called into question in the German legal debate (Fleischer 2009, Langenbucher 2008). Against this background, the regulation of variable pay in § 87 para. 1 AktG along the lines of a sustainable development of the company has not been sufficiently fleshed out yet in order to actually enhance the alignment of interests between executives and shareholders. In particular, the mandatory extension of the holding periods for stock options to four years in § 193 para. 2 no. 4 AktG does not by itself ensure such an alignment. Instead the length of this period of four years seems to be arbitrary and without empirical basis. Overall this missing foundation seems to confirm the growing opinion in German legal debate that the economists have failed to communicate convincingly their findings and their arguments on how to align shareholder and executive interests in the regulation of executive compensation (Homann and Wolff 2010).

4.4   Additional Component of Pay

Even though § 87 para. 1 sent. 3 AktG explicitly provides for an assessment basis for performance of at least two years, it does not completely exclude short-term performance-related payments. After the amendment of 2009, short-term or reference-date-based payments can still be stipulated, such as an annual bonus. This possibility can be inferred from the non-mandatory character of § 87 para. 1 sent. 3 AktG. That is why it is crucial to look not only at single components, but at the payments structure in its entirety that has to ensure a sustainable business development under § 87 para. 1 AktG.

In light of the legislative aim to prevent adverse incentives and strategic risk taking the amendment is limited to the regulation of variable pay that helps to promote this goal without however imposing a duty on the parties to rely on variable pay and excluding fixed pay. Even though the German Corporate Governance Code recommends executive compensation that is composed of both base salary and variable pay (Section 4.2.3.), the Stock Corporation Act does not include any provision to the effect that such a mix of fixed and variable pay is mandatory (Thüsing 2009).

The question whether a pay component is incentive- and performance-based or not is the most decisive distinguishing feature that separates appreciation awards from termination payments. Both are evaluated under different standards as to their legality. Whereas appreciation awards are ex post premiums to remunerate good performance, termination payments replace the previous compensation, if the executive and the company agree on the termination of the contract (Hüffer 2010). Therefore the latter can be viewed as part

---

[10]   Benz et al. 2002 (p. 116) cite a large-scale survey conducted by Pearl Meyer & Partners.

of an efficient multiperiod incentive contract with the company's objective to keep corporate secrets and avoid negative publicity when an executive leaves (Geiler and Renneboog 2010). As a consequence, the German Corporate Governance Code recommends a cap for any termination payment equalling the compensation for the smaller of the remaining contract period or a period of two years (Section 4.2.3.IV.).[11]

Since appreciation awards do not aim to incentivize executives for the future, but rather reward them for the past, there has been much debate about their legality in light of the public outrage their use has caused in the past, especially on the occasion of the *Mannesmann* case. The latter raised the issue whether the appreciation award of €15 million paid to the Mannesmann CEO Klaus Esser by the compensation board of Mannesmann's supervisory board entailed criminal liability for the members of the compensation board. The Federal Court of Justice considered a bonus payment to be waste that had not been called for in the compensation agreement and served mere reward purposes without any future benefits to the company, so that the responsible members of the supervisory board had breached their fiduciary duties when granting it to Esser (Federal Court of Justice Case No. 3 StR 470/04, BGHSt 50, 331 *Mannesmann*). Along these lines, appreciation awards have been criticized when they cannot be based on the compensation agreement because the initial agreement should deal conclusively with the compensation for any services rendered by the board members (Brauer 2004; Martens 2005).

However, there is no denying the fact that appreciation awards can have important incentive effects, as has been underlined in defense of such payments in German literature. The compensation agreement is, like any other long-term contract, subject to modifications agreed on by the parties (Baums 2006). The company may have an interest to incentivize executives to better performance or to signal contractual fairness to third parties. These considerations can be taken as legitimate reasons for the supervisory board members under the business judgment rule to pay an appreciation award (Spindler 2008).

5 SAY ON PAY

The scope of discretion of the supervisory board under the business judgment rule in compensation decisions raises the question who should set executive compensation in order to ensure an interest alignment between shareholders and managers. The amendment of the German Stock Corporation Act of 2009 provides for an advisory vote of the shareholder meeting on executive remuneration in § 120 para. 4 AktG. Under this provision the shareholder meeting can take a vote to approve the compensation system designed for the management board. The vote does not have any binding effect, however. The underlying rule is based not only on a corresponding recommendation of the European Commission (European Commission 2004, Section 6) but also follows the example of the English Directors' Remuneration Report Regulations (s. 439 Companies Act 2006). The non-binding effect of the vote that is explicitly provided for in § 120 para. 4 sent. 2 AktG raises the question why such a vote may still serve a purpose and what the

---

[11] In German practice the recommendation is widely followed (Lutter 2009).

legislator's objective was. The vote does not discharge the supervisory board from its liability (§ 120 para. 4 sent. 2 AktG).

There is no empirical evidence that the new rules on say on pay have slowed down the further increase of executive pay (Ferri and Maber 2011). In addition, there has been concern that institutional investors and proxy advisory firms will favor "one size fits all" compensation plans in order to keep proxy review costs low, so that it will be unlikely that compensation systems under a mandatory shareholder vote regime will better link pay and performance (Gordon 2009). On the other hand, there is evidence for some effects of a non-binding shareholder vote on compensation systems. There seem to be fewer rewards for failure and overall the assumption advanced earlier in the literature holds that the shareholder say on pay may be suitable to remedy specific abuses and avoid sudden pay boosts at a single company rather than prevent too lucrative compensation agreements altogether (Cheffins and Thomas 2001). These findings may be signs of a greater sensitivity in remuneration matters resulting from a say on pay and would therefore indicate that such a non-binding shareholder vote may be a legal tool to reduce "outrage costs" (Bebchuk et al. 2002).

This is in line with the reach of the German version of the shareholder say on pay. According to § 120 para. 4 AktG it only applies to listed companies which may not require quite as individualized compensation plans as smaller companies and the threat of a "one size fits all" approach will be less severe because smaller firms may differ greatly from the conventional corporate governance framework (Gordon 2009).

Looking at the practical experience in the United Kingdom, say on pay seems to have furthered the dialogue between the board and the institutional investors about remuneration issues (Davies 2008). The link between pay and performance may improve because the responsible board members contact the main shareholders and proxy advisory firms and clarify in advance their expectations about the company's compensation system (Fleischer and Bedkowski 2009). This goal may be furthered by the restraint provided for in § 122 para. 2 AktG. Under this provision shareholders holding 20 per cent of the stock or a proportionate amount of 500,000 euros of share capital can demand that the shareholder vote on executive compensation be put on the agenda and be made public. According to the legislative history, the rules on say on pay therefore do not serve minority protection, but aim to improve communication between the board and the institutional investors with regard to compensation issues (Deutscher Bundestag, Bundestags-Drucks. 16/13433 p. 12).

The ensuing vote, however, only refers to the past, but does not touch on the decision-making power of the supervisory board (Deutscher Bundestag, Bundestags-Drucks. 16/13433, p. 12). This becomes particularly clear in light of the responsibilities of the supervisory board with regard to compensation. Apart from the duty to adopt the compensation decision in plenary, the supervisory board is under a duty to reduce the compensation in case of a deterioration in the financial circumstances of the company that make the compensation seem unjust (§ 87 para. 2 AktG). When mentioning the deterioration of the company, the law exclusively refers to the circumstances of the company and does not offer a possibility to reduce compensation retroactively, if the supervisory board has mistakenly set a too high compensation (Hüffer 2010). A shortcoming on the part of the supervisory board in terms of non-intervention under these circumstances gives rise to liability for damages of its members. Since such a liability does not require a serious deterioration, some criticism as to the practicality of this provision and maybe its coherence in terms of continuity of contract seems to be in order (Martens 2010). This has been criticized even more so with regard to the extension of this duty to pensions during the first three years after retirement, because of the retroactivity of the interference.[12]

In conclusion, by introducing a non-binding shareholder say on pay the German legislator tries to limit outrage costs. This rule is based on the managerial power hypothesis without however discharging the supervisory board from their ultimate responsibility for compensation agreements. The bottom line is that the effect of the say on pay according to the German legislative concept seems to rest on the "Power of the Pen" (Core et al. 2008).

6   ENHANCEMENT OF OPTIMAL CONTRACTING AND RESTRAINING MANAGERIAL POWER IN THE GERMAN REGULATION OF EXECUTIVE PAY

In the aftermath of the *Mannesmann* case German corporate law has undergone substantial changes and has increasingly moved towards a capital market-oriented corporate governance model. This is reflected in the development of the German law of executive compensation that has, more and more, been supporting incentive-based payments until the recent financial crisis and now appears to steer a middle course between an enhancement of optimal contracting between the parties and the attempt to restrain managerial power in the corporation. With regard to the considerable increase of variable pay, which had resulted from the Control and Transparency in the Corporate Field Act of 1998, and its problems with regard to share options throughout the recent financial crisis, in 2009 the German legislator enacted an amendment to the German Stock Corporation Act on the appropriateness of director compensation. By further specifying the crucial benchmarks for a reasonable compensation under § 87 para. 1 AktG, such as individual performance and standard practice, the legislator aims to improve the parties' contracting and to align it with market forces. At the same time, § 87 para. 1 AktG provides for a sustainable development of the company's business as a guideline for the structure of the compensation system, ultimately trying to limit the short-term influence of the market on the compensation agreement and management behavior. This goal becomes particularly clear from the now mandatory four-year exercise period for share options under § 193 para. 2 no. 4 AktG. Since stock option programs may have negative effects on risk preferences and risk management as well as on intrinsically motivated managers, the interest alignment between shareholders and managers on the basis of such programs could be called into question and the extension of the holding period for stock options seems arbitrary and to be lacking any empirical basis. At this point the enhancement of optimal contracting between the parties by the amendment of the Stock Corporation Act is therefore questionable.

---

[12]   Bauer and Arnold (2009), Hoffmann-Becking and Krieger (2009). On the other hand, this provision is not without historical example and possible doctrinal basis in contract law (Thüsing 2009).

As far as further incentive-based components of executive compensation are concerned, the differentiation between appreciation awards and termination payments has turned out to touch on the issue of whether and how they aim to incentivize directors. Termination payments replace the previous compensation and therefore are part and parcel of the compensation agreement. Appreciation awards, however, have to have a contractual basis as well. Otherwise, the award of such bonus payments may be considered to be waste and a breach of fiduciary duty by the responsible supervisory board members who generally enjoy a wide discretion in their decision about such awards. The responsibility of the supervisory board in compensation matters is complemented by the advisory vote of the shareholder meeting on the compensation system under § 120 para. 4 Stock Corporation Act. In light of its non-binding effect, the German legislator seems to rely on the ensuing constraint on the outrage effect emanating from such a say on pay and therefore it shows some distrust towards managerial power at this point. At the same time, it does not take away any of the decision-making power of the supervisory board, which is even under a duty to reduce compensation in the event of a deterioration in the financial circumstances of the company making the compensation seem unjust (§ 87 para. 2 AktG). Again, the legislator fears managerial power which could lead to a misappropriation of corporate assets in the time of crisis. Therefore, all things considered, the German amendment of the Stock Corporation Act on director compensation is marked by the legislator's dilemma whether to enhance optimal contracting as a governance mechanism or to primarily restrain managerial power to extract rents from shareholders.

REFERENCES

Abowd, John, 1990. Does Performance-based Managerial Compensation Affect Corporate Performance? *Industrial and Labor Relations Review*, 43(3): S52–S73.

Aglietta, Michel and Antoine Rebérioux, 2005. Corporate Governance Adrift: A Critique of Shareholder Value, Cheltenham: Edward Elgar Publishing.

Andres, Christian, André Betzer, Marc Goergen and Daniel Metzger, 2010. Corporate Governance Systems, in Corporate Governance: A Synthesis of Theory, Research, and Practice, Kent Baker and Ronald Anderson, eds., Hoboken NJ: Wiley, 37–56.

Bauer, Jobst-Hubertus and Christian Arnold, 2009. Festsetzung und Herabsetzung der Vorstandsvergütung nach dem VorstAG. *Die Aktiengesellschaft*, 717–31.

Baums, Theodor, 1997. Aktienoptionen für Vorstandsmitglieder, in Festschrift für Carsten Peter Claussen, Klaus-Peter Martens, Harm Peter Westermann and Wolfgang Zöllner, eds., Cologne: Carl Heymann, 3–48.

Baums, Theodor, ed., 2001. Bericht der Regierungskommission Corporate Governance; Unternehmensführung – Unternehmenskontrolle – Modernisierung des Aktienrechts, Cologne: Otto Schmidt.

Baums, Theodor, 2006. Anerkennungsprämien für Vorstandsmitglieder, in Festschrift für Ulrich Huber, Theodor Baums and Johannes Wertenbruch, eds., Tübingen: Mohr Siebeck, 657–75.

Bebchuk, Lucian and Jesse Fried, 2004. Pay Without Performance: The Unfulfilled Promise of Executive Compensation, Cambridge, Mass.: Harvard University Press.

Bebchuk, Lucian, Jesse Fried, and David Walker, 2002. Managerial Power and Rent Extraction in the Design of Executive Compensation, *University of Chicago Law Review*, 69: 751–846.

Benz, Matthias, Marcel Kucher, and Alois Stutzer, 2002. Aktienoptionen für Topmanager – Die Möglichkeiten und Grenzen eines Motivationsinstruments, in Managing Motivation; Wie Sie die neue Motivationsforschung für ihr Unternehmen nutzen können, Bruno Frey and Margit Osterloh, eds., Wiesbaden: Gabler, 107–36.

Bertrand, Marianne and Sendhil Mullainathan, 2001. Are CEOs Rewarded for Luck? The Ones Without Principals are, *Quarterly Journal of Economics*, 116: 901–32.

Beyer, Jürgen and Anke Hassel, 2002. The Effects of Convergence: Internationalisation and the Changing Distribution of Net Value Added in Large German Firms, *Economy and Society*, 31: 309–32.

Brauer, Markus, 2004. Die aktienrechtliche Beurteilung von "appreciation awards" zu Gunsten des Vorstands, *Neue Zeitschrift für Gesellschaftsrecht*, 502–9.

Cheffins, Brian, 2001. The Metamorphosis of "Germany Inc.": The Case of Executive Pay, *American Journal of Comparative Law*, 49: 497–539.

Cheffins, Brian and Randall Thomas, 2001. Should Shareholders have Say over Pay: Learning from the US Perspective? *Journal of Corporate Law Studies*, 1: 277–315.

Cheng, Qiang and Terry Warfield, 2005. Equity Incentives and Earnings Management, *The Accounting Review*, 80(2): 441–76.

Clarke, Thomas, 2007. International Corporate Governance: A Comparative Approach, London and New York: Routledge.

Congressional Oversight Panel, January 2009. Special Report on Regulatory Reform, Modernizing the American Regulatory Financial System: Recommendations for Improving Oversight, Protecting Consumers, and Ensuring Stability; Submitted under Section 125(b)(2) of Title I of the Emergency Economic Stabilization Act of 2008, Pub. L. No. 110–343, downloadable under http://cop.senate.gov/documents/cop-012909-report-regulatoryreform.pdf.

Core, John, Wayne Guay and David Larcker, 2008. The Power of the Pen and Executive Compensation, *Journal of Financial Economics*, 88: 1–25.

Council of the European Union, 2008. Presidency Conclusions, Brussels, 15 and 16 October 2008, downloadable under http://www.consilium.europa.eu/uedocs/cms_data/docs/pressdata/en/ec/103441.pdf.

Cunningham, Lawrence, 1999. Commonalties and Prescriptions in the Vertical Dimension of Global Corporate Governance, *Cornell Law Review*, 84: 1133–93.

Davies, Paul, 2008. Gower & Davies: Principles of Modern Company Law, 8th edn, UK: Sweet & Maxwell.

Deci, Edward, Richard Koestner and Richard Ryan, 1999. A Meta-analytic Review of Experiments Examining the Effects of Extrinsic Rewards on Intrinsic Motivation, *Psychological Bulletin*, 125: 627–68.

Deutscher Bundestag, Beschlussempfehlung und Bericht des Rechtsausschusses (6. Ausschuss) a) zu dem Gesetzentwurf der Fraktionen der CDU/CSU und SPD – Drucksache 16/12278 – Entwurf eines Gesetzes zur Angemessenheit der Vorstandsvergütung (VorstAG), Bundestags-Drucksache 16/13433 of 17 June 2009.

Deutscher Bundestag, Gesetzentwurf der Fraktionen der CDU/CSU und SPD, Entwurf eines Gesetzes zur Angemessenheit der Vorstandsvergütung (VorstAG), Bundestags-Drucksache 16/12278 of 17 March 2009.

Deutsche Schutzvereinigung für Wertpapierbesitz e.V. (DSW), 2010. Studie zur Vergütung der Vorstände in den DAX- und MDAX-Unternehmen im Geschäftsjahr 2009.

Elston, Julie Ann and Lawrence Goldberg, 2008. Executive Compensation and Agency Costs in Germany, in Corporate Governance and Corporate Finance: A European perspective, Ruud Frederikslust, James Ang and Sudi Sudarsanam, eds., Oxford and New York: Routledge, 450–66.

European Commission, 2004. Commission Recommendation of 14 December 2004 fostering an appropriate regime for the remuneration of directors of listed companies 2004/913/EC, 2004 O.J. (L 385) 55.

European Commission, 2009. Commission Recommendation K(2009) 3177 complementing Recommendations 2004/913/EC and 2005/162/EC as regards the regime for the remuneration of directors of listed companies, SEC (2009) 580, Brussels, 30 April 2009.

Ferri, Fabrizio and David Maber, 2011. Say on Pay Votes and CEO Compensation: Evidence from the UK (November 24), *Review of Finance*, forthcoming, downloadable under http://ssrn.com/abstract=1420394.

Fleischer, Holger, 2005. Zur Angemessenheit der Vorstandsvergütung im Aktienrecht (Teil I), *Deutsche Zeitschrift für Steuerrecht*, 2005, 1279–83.

Fleischer, Holger, 2009. Das Gesetz zur Angemessenheit der Vorstandsvergütung (VorstAG), *Neue Zeitschrift für Gesellschaftsrecht*, 801–6.

Fleischer, Holger, 2010. Aufsichtsratsverantwortlichkeit für die Vorstandsvergütung und Unabhängigkeit der Vergütungsberater, *Betriebs-Berater*, 67–74.

Fleischer, Holger and Dorothea Bedkowski, 2009. "Say on Pay" im deutschen Aktienrecht: Das neue Vergütungsvotum der Hauptversammlung nach § 120 Abs. 4 AktG, *Die Aktiengesellschaft*, 677–86.

Franks, Julian and Colin Mayer, 2001. Ownership and Control of German Corporations, *Review of Financial Studies*, 14(4): 943–77.

Geiler, Philipp and Luc Renneboog, 2010. Executive Compensation: Incentives and Externalities, in Corporate Governance: A Synthesis of Theory, Research, and Practice, Kent Baker and Ronald Anderson, eds., Hoboken NJ: Wiley, 263–83.

Gordon, Jeffrey, 2009. "Say on Pay": Cautionary Notes on the UK Experience and the Case for Shareholder Opt-in, *Harvard Journal on Legislation*, 46: 323–67

Government Commission of the German Corporate Governance Code. German corporate governance code, downloadable under http://www.corporate-governance-code.de/eng/kodex/index.html.

Group of Twenty, 2008. Declaration Summit on Financial Markets and the World Economy, November 15, downloadable under http://www.g20.org/Documents/g20_summit_declaration.pdf.

Haid, Alfred and Burcin Yurtoglu, 2006. Ownership Structure and Executive Compensation in Germany, Working Paper, available at SSRN: http://ssrn.com/abstract=948926.

Heron, Randall and Erik Lie, 2007. Does Backdating Explain the Stock Price Pattern Around Executive Stock Option Grants? *Journal of Financial Economics*, 83: 271–95.

Hoffmann-Becking, Michael, 2005. Rechtliche Anmerkungen zur Vorstands- und Aufsichtsratsvergütung, *Zeitschrift für das gesamte Handels- und Wirtschaftsrecht*, 169: 155–80.

Hoffmann-Becking, Michael and Gerd Krieger, 2009. Leitfaden zur Anwendung des Gesetzes zur Angemessenheit der Vorstandsvergütung (VorstAG), *Neue Zeitschrift für Gesellschaftsrecht*, Beilage 2009, Heft, 26: 1–12.

Homann, Karl and Birgitta Wolff, 2010. Managerbezüge: Eine wirtschaftsethische Perspektive, *Zeitschrift für Unternehmens- und Gesellschaftsrecht*, 39: 959–79.

Hüffer, Uwe, 2007. Der Vorstand als Leitungsorgan und die Mandats- und Haftungsbeziehungen seiner Mitglieder, in Aktienrecht im Wandel, Band 2, Walter Bayer and Mathias Habersack, eds., Tübingen: Mohr Siebeck, 334–88.

Hüffer, Uwe, 2010. Aktiengesetz: AktG, Kommentar, 9th edition, München: C.H. Beck.

Kalisch, Ingrid, 1998. Stock Options: Will the Upcoming Amendment of the German Stock Corporation Act Facilitate their Introduction by German Stock Corporations, *International Company and Commercial Law Review*, 9: 111–17.

Kling, Michael, 2010. Die Angemessenheit der Vorstandsvergütung gemäß § 87 AktG n.F., *Deutsche Zeitschrift für Wirtschafts- und Insolvenzrecht*, 220–31.

Langenbucher, Katja, 2008. Aktien- und Kapitalmarktrecht, München: C.H. Beck.

La Porta, Rafael, Florencio Lopez-de-Silanes, Andrei Shleifer and Robert Vishny, 1998. Law and Finance, *Journal of Political Economy*, 106: 1113–55.

Larraza-Kintana, Martin, Robert Wiseman, Luis Gomez-Mejia and Theresa Welbourne, 2007. Disentangling Compensation and Employment Risks Using the Behavioral Agency Model, *Strategic Management Journal*, 28: 1001–19.

Lutter, Marcus, 2009. Das Abfindungs-Cap in Ziff. 4.2.3 und 4 des Deutschen Corporate Governance-Kodex, *Betriebs-Berater*, 1874–6.

Martens, Klaus-Peter, 2005. Die Vorstandsvergütung auf dem Prüfstand, *Zeitschrift für das gesamte Handels- und Wirtschaftsrecht*, 169: 124–54.

Martens, Klaus-Peter, 2010. Rechtliche Rahmenbedingungen der Vorstandsvergütung, in Festschrift für Uwe Hüffer, Peter Kindler, Jens Koch, Peter Ulmer and Martin Winter, eds., Munich: C.H. Beck, 647–62.

Masson, Robert, 1971. Executive Motivations, Earnings and Consequent Equity Performance, *Journal of Political Economy*, 79(6): 1278–92.

Milhaupt, Curtis and Katharina Pistor, 2008. Law and Capitalism: What Corporate Crises Reveal about Legal Systems and Economic Development around the World, Chicago: Chicago University Press.

Murphy, Kevin, 1999. Executive Compensation, in Handbook of Labor Economics Vol. 3B, Orley Ashenfelter and David Card, eds., Amsterdam: Elsevier, 2485–563.

Prigge, Stefan, 1998. A Survey of German Corporate Governance, in Comparative Corporate Governance: The State of the Art and Emerging Research, Klaus Hopt et al., eds., Oxford: Oxford University Press, 943–1044.

Regierungskommission Deutscher Corporate Governance Kodex, 2002. Deutscher Corporate Governance Kodex vom 26. Februar 2002 (gültig bis 7. November 2002), downloadable under http://www.corporate-governance-code.de/ger/download/DCG_K_D20020223.pdf.

Ringleb, Henrik-Michael, 2010. 2.Teil. Kommentierung zum Deutschen Corporate Governance Kodex, 4. Vorstand III.–XIII. in Kommentar zum Deutschen Corporate Governance Kodex, Henrik-Michael Ringleb et al., eds., Munich: C.H. Beck.

Ruffner, Markus, 2000. Die ökonomischen Grundlagen eines Rechts der Publikumsgesellschaft Zurich: Schulthess.

Schlegelberger, Franz and Leo Quassowski, 1939. Aktiengesetz: Gesetz über Aktiengesellschaften und Kommanditgesellschaften auf Aktien vom 30. Januar 1937; Kommentar, 3rd ed., Berlin: Vahlen.

Seibert, Ulrich, 2009. Das VorstAG: Regelungen zur Angemessenheit der Vorstandergütung und zum Aufsichtsrat, *Zeitschrift für Wirtschafts- und Bankrecht*, 1489–93.

Seibert, Ulrich, 2010. Die Koalitionsarbeitsgruppe „Managervergütungen": Rechtspolitische Überlegungen zur Beschränkung der Vorstandsvergütung (Ende 2007 bis März 2009), in Festschrift für Uwe Hüffer zum 70. Geburtstag, Peter Kindler, et al., eds., C.H. Beck: München, 955–72.

Spindler, Gerald, 2008. In Münchener Kommentar zum Aktiengesetz, Wulff Goette and Mathias Habersack, eds., 3rd edition, Munich: C.H. Beck, § 87.

Suchan, Stefan and Stefan Winter, 2009. Rechtliche und betriebswirtschaftliche Überlegungen zur Festsetzung angemessener Vorstandsbezüge nach Inkrafttreten des VorstAG, *Der Betrieb*, 2531–9.

Thüsing, Gregor, 2009. Das Gesetz zur Angemessenheit der Vorstandsvergütung, *Die Aktiengesellschaft*, 517–29.

Tower Perrin, 2005/06. Worldwide Total Remuneration Report.

Wagner, Jens and Jonas Wittgens, 2009. Corporate Governance als dauernde Reformanstrengung: Der Entwurf des Gesetzes zur Angemessenheit der Vorstandsvergütung, *Betriebs-Berater*, 906–11.

Windbichler, Christine, 2009. Gesellschaftsrecht, 22nd ed., Munich: C.H. Beck.

24 Director and executive compensation regulations for Italian listed and closed corporations
Carlo Amatucci and Manlio Lubrano di Scorpaniello

1 INTRODUCTION

The aim of this chapter is to examine the regulation of director and executive compensation in Italy in the context of both public listed corporations and unlisted corporations. As will be discussed, a complex array of laws, regulations, corporate governance principles and stock exchange rules affect this issue in Italian corporations.

Many Italian corporate law scholars (Bonafini 2005a; Cappiello 2003; Ferrarini 2005) agree on the importance of performance-based pay as a mechanism to align the interests of corporate directors and managers with those of shareholders, particularly in the case of listed corporations that have a clear separation between ownership and control. The Italian Securities and Exchange Commission ("Consob"), Italy's main corporate regulator, also takes this view.

Yet, the basic concept of interest alignment can itself be problematical. For example, in 2007 Consob noted in a consultation document that "compensation plans could, on the one hand, be considered a potential means of giving top managers excessive compensation, and on the other hand be considered as incentives for managers and directors to make business decisions that are not in the interest of shareholders, or even an incentive to commit fraud and manipulate markets" (Consob 2007). Consob's warning was given added force by the onset the global financial crisis. The Financial Stability Board ("FSB") considered compensation practices at large financial institutions to be a contributing factor to the crisis, stating that "[h]igh short-term profits led to generous bonus payments to employees without adequate regard to the longer-term risks they imposed on their firms. These perverse incentives amplified the excessive risk-taking that severely threatened the global financial system and left firms with fewer resources to absorb losses as risks materialised" (FSB 2009).

It is only in the last decade that issues of excessive pay, and the criteria for director and executive remuneration, have attracted scholarly attention in Italy. However, the global financial crisis has resulted in great public sensitivity to allegations of overpayment and unjustifiably high bonuses awarded to senior executives.

As Consob's 2007 consultation document noted, Italian law concerning director and executive pay is underpinned by two fundamental regulatory principles. These principles are: (1) shareholder voting to approve compensation plans comprising securities, such as stock options; (2) disclosure of adequate corporate information to investors and the market.

This chapter is structured as follows. Section 2 provides an overview of regulation of director and executive compensation in Italy. Section 3 discusses the effect of concentrated ownership, which is the predominant structure of Italian corporations, on the issue of director and executive compensation. Section 4 examines different types of compensation for executive and non-executive directors. Sections 5 and 6 discuss the key regulatory principles discussed in Consob's 2007 consultation document, namely shareholder voting to approve compensation plans and disclosure of adequate information about those plans. Section 7 considers the operation of additional Consob regulatory requirements for listed corporations. Section 8 assesses the operation of the Corporate Governance Code of the Italian Stock Exchange. Finally, sections 9 and 10 deal with the issue of director and executive pay in the specialized contexts of government owned corporations and banks respectively.

2 AN OVERVIEW OF REGULATION OF DIRECTOR AND EXECUTIVE COMPENSATION IN ITALY

The Italian Civil Code, which underwent significant reforms in 2003, provides the basis for regulation of Italian corporations generally, including, in the absence of any special laws, listed corporations.

The Civil Code recognizes three corporate governance systems relating to the board of directors. The first is a two-tier board model, which includes a supervisory board (consiglio di sorveglianza) and a management board. The other two permissible corporate governance structures are the traditional Italian system, comprising a board of directors and a board of auditors (collegio sindacale), and a unitary or one-tier board.

The Civil Code contains relatively few rules about director and executive compensation. Those that exist are mainly found in art. 2389, which sets out four basic rules:

- The remuneration of the board and the executive committee[1] is, unless determined by statute,[2] decided by the general meeting of shareholders for the entire term (maximum of three years) or each year.
- Such pay can consist, partly or wholly, in profit sharing or in stock options.[3]
- The compensation of board members appointed with "special duties" is determined by the board. Although there is no definition in the Civil Code of "special duties", the general consensus is that it refers to additional pay for executive directors.
- The statute can empower the general meeting of shareholders to determine the global amount of board members' compensation.

---

[1] Art. 2389, §I literally states "The remuneration of the board and of the executive committee is determined at the moment of their appointment or by the general meeting". This text was changed in 2003: the previous version said: ". . . . is determined by the statute or by the general meeting". Some commentators (e.g. Mosco 2004, p. 637) consider that this change in wording has resulted in a shift in the power to determine the executive committee's compensation from the general meeting to the board, since the latter appoints executive committee members. However, to date, few have agreed with this interpretation of the statutory amendment (Bonafini 2005a, p. 101; Rainelli 2004, p. 743).

[2] This exception, permitted by art. 2364 n. 3, applies rarely, and almost entirely in smaller corporations.

[3] Defined as "the right to subscribe future stocks at a strike price fixed in advance".

In the case of listed corporations, the primary source of law is art. 114-bis of the Consolidated Act of 1998 ("the Consolidated Act"),[4] in which shareholder voting and disclosure are both central themes. Art. 114-bis modifies the application of art. 2389 of the Civil Code, by granting the general meeting of listed corporations the power to approve all compensation plans, for both executive and non-executive directors. This introduces a more stringent rule for listed corporations than for unlisted corporations, where the Civil Code permits the board to approve compensation arrangements for executive directors (Pollio 2009, p. 130). In addition, art. 114-bis grants Consob substantial powers to regulate specific aspects of compensation plans for listed corporations.

Although art. 114-bis of the Consolidated Act establishes shareholder voting and disclosure as the central regulatory procedures for corporate compensation plans of listed corporations, it is silent regarding the structure and content of such plans. These structural matters are dealt with in the Corporate Governance Code of the Italian Stock Exchange, which is a self-regulatory code for listed corporations.

3   CONCENTRATED OWNERSHIP AND "ARM'S LENGTH" NEGOTIATION BETWEEN DIRECTORS AND CONTROLLING SHAREHOLDERS

As is common in continental Europe, most Italian companies have concentrated ownership, with block holders or controlling shareholders. In theory at least, this scenario minimizes conflicts between directors and shareholders. The relevant parties are assumed to negotiate remuneration plans at "arm's length". The composition and measure of pay reflect, in economic terms, an agreement on the distribution of the annual profits between the shareholders and the board, even though in legal terms the formal decision resides in the general meeting.

Unlike the situation in jurisdictions with dispersed shareholding, controlling shareholders can monitor the corporation's directors on a continuous basis. It is for this reason that the Italian debate has been more focused on the danger of controlling shareholders pursuing their self-interest than the problem of excessive pay for directors and executives (Bonafini 2005b, p. 385).

In practice, boards of Italian unlisted corporations sometimes award executives appointed with "special duties" far higher compensation than other directors. This can occur without previous negotiation with shareholders, or even controlling shareholders, using the board's inherent power in art. 2389 of the Civil Code. More frequently, however, the pay level of the executives is decided by directors who are closely aligned with, and strongly influenced by, the controlling shareholders. This can create a corporate governance "dark zone", whereby the controlling shareholders may pressure the board to pay high executive salaries, at the expense of minority shareholders' expectations as to dividend payments. This problem is exacerbated by the fact that in Italy many executives are also controlling shareholders, either directly, or indirectly through other corporate vehicles.

---

[4]   As amended by l. n. 262/2005, and subsequently modified by d. lgs. n. 303/2006.

Except for banks, which are subject to supervision by the Bank of Italy, pay in unlisted companies is generally determined via free negotiation, mostly at arm's length. It is strongly influenced by tax law,[5] which essentially treats fixed pay as an employee's wages, and grants some conditional exemptions for stock options.

Director and executive remuneration still tend to be regarded as an internal matter rather than a major corporate governance issue, with the quantum and structure of pay mainly determined through face to face negotiations. The primary reason for this is the prevalence of small to medium sized companies with concentrated ownership, and the relatively small number of listed corporations in Italy. There are, for example, fewer than 300 listed corporations out of a total of approximately 50,000 corporations. In listed corporations with dispersed ownership, however, executive compensation is viewed as a key agency-cost control mechanism, and this has given rise to greater complexity and sophistication in pay controls for these corporations (Ferrarini et al 2004).

4   TYPES OF COMPENSATION FOR EXECUTIVE AND NON-EXECUTIVE DIRECTORS

Art. 2389.2 of the Civil Code provides for three different kinds of compensation. The first is fixed pay. The second and third are in the form of variable compensation, through profit sharing and stock options.

Italian law accords corporations considerable flexibility in structuring compensation policies in a way best suited to their needs, for instance, by determining pay entitlements for the entire term of appointment or on a year by year basis. Italian law does not currently include any rules which interfere with the structure of compensation plans. This contrasts with legislation in some other jurisdictions, such as Germany, where a rule concerning the "adequacy" of director pay was introduced in 2009 (Portale 2010, p. 134)

Nonetheless, this structural freedom under Italian law in relation to compensation plans is not unlimited. For example, although profit sharing is explicitly permitted by law, several court decisions have determined that compensation based on a percentage of annual billing is prohibited[6] (Rainelli 2004, p. 740), mainly because it is considered that a compensation system linked to gross billing may encourage excessive managerial risk-taking.

A special regulatory regime applies to stock option plans under art. 2441.8 of the Civil Code. This regime requires that stock option plans must be based upon a special need or interest of the corporation, and must be approved by majority vote of the shareholders in general meeting. Nonetheless, it has been observed (Mosco 2004, p. 640) that art. 2441.5 permits the devolution of many types of capital increase, including the stock option plans, from the general meeting to the board. Where devolution to the board has occurred, it raises the risk of possible conflicts of interest at board level, particularly since the law does not impose any specific directives or behavioral duties on the directors in these circumstances.

---

[5]   See, for example, art. 50, lett. C bis e 51, lett. G and G bis, D.P.R. n. 917/86).
[6]   Trib. Milano, 17/09/1987, in *Giur. comm.*, 1987, II, 797 .

Although stock option plans are impliedly permitted under art. 2389.3, the provision is ambiguous as to the legal validity of some alternative types of performance-based remuneration, such as phantom stock plans, stock grants or stock purchase plans, which are currently of limited relevance to unlisted corporations.

A particular question has been raised about the remuneration of members of the supervisory board (consiglio di sorveglianza) in two-tier boards, which are permitted under the Civil Code. The law contains no specific rules for the compensation of supervisory board members under this model. Such directors perform many duties that, under the traditional Italian "collegio sindacale" model, comprising a board of directors and a board of auditors, would have resided in the shareholders' general meeting and the board of auditors. There has been uncertainty as to whether the compensation of members of the supervisory board is restricted to fixed pay, or may also include variable pay, such as stock options. The prevailing view, which is also held by the Bank of Italy, is that variable pay for supervisory board members is prohibited under Italian law, in the light of their monitoring and oversight duties.

5   SHAREHOLDER VOTING TO APPROVE COMPENSATION PLANS

In the case of public corporations, the first principle articulated in art. 114-bis of the Consolidated Act concerns the need for shareholder voting to approve certain compensation plans of listed corporations. According to art. 114-bis, compensation plans must be approved at the shareholder meeting when these plans involve securities issued to the following specified individuals:

1.   members of the board;
2.   members of the managing board (in a two-tier board system);
3.   employees and consultants not linked to the corporation by a labour contract;
4.   members of the boards and of the managing boards, employees and consultants of controlling and controlled corporations.

There are a number of matters worth noting about the shareholder voting rule in art. 114-bis. First, unlike art. 2389 of the Civil Code, which applies to unlisted corporations, the rule in art. 114-bis of the Consolidated Act makes no distinction between compensation packages to executive and non-executive directors. As noted earlier, art. 2389 of the Civil Code does not require shareholder voting on compensation plans for executive directors, and such plans may therefore be approved by the board, in conjunction with the internal auditors. Art. 114-bis, which applies to listed corporations, however, requires shareholder approval of compensation plans for both executive and non-executive directors.

Second, shareholder approval under art. 114-bis is required for compensation plans involving securities, such as shares, options, bonds, and other negotiable financial instruments.[7] The regulatory net is further extended in this regard by Consob regulations

---

[7]   It should be noted, however, that art. 114-bis of the Consolidated Act refers to all compensa-

requiring shareholder approval for compensation plans that, while not involving a grant of securities *per se*, nonetheless provide cash payments based on variations in the value of securities over a specific time period (so-called "phantom stock"). Regulation of such plans is justified on the basis that they involve similar incentives as compensation plans offering securities.

Third, as noted in 4 above, the rule under art. 114-bis extends to the corporate group context, in that it requires shareholder approval for securities issued by controlling and controlled corporations.

It has been claimed that "shareholder voting requirements imposed by corporate law constitute a potential constraint on executive pay levels" (Thomas 2010, p. 32). Such a requirement also motivates negotiation between management and shareholders on matters that affect "the ownership structure and on the value of the shares" (Santosuosso 2010, p. 370). Yet, the effectiveness of shareholder voting from a corporate governance perspective may differ depending upon whether the corporation's shareholding is dispersed or concentrated. Where shareholding is concentrated, as is the case for the great majority of Italian corporations, a shareholder voting requirement would hardly be expected to deliver significant regulatory benefits, since "dominant shareholders already determine executive pay regardless of whether a shareholder vote is required" (Thomas 2010, p. 32).

6 DISCLOSURE OF COMPENSATION PLANS

Disclosure constitutes the second fundamental principle on which regulation of compensation plans for listed Italian corporations is based. It performs the dual functions of ensuring informed voting by shareholders at company meetings, and providing accurate information regarding compensation plans to the market generally. However, it is worth noting that disclosure is not necessarily an unmitigated benefit. According to some Anglo-American literature, stringent disclosure requirements may sometimes have negative "ratcheting" effects. It has been said, for example, that such regulation may "accelerate increases in executive compensation. The availability of information about what similarly situated competitors are paying their executives will likely alert top managers who are receiving less than their peers" (Thomas 2010, p. 35).

In the context of Italian listed corporations, art. 114-bis, paragraph 1 of §1 of the Consolidated Act provides that, prior to general meeting approval of any compensation plan, the corporation must publicly release a Directors' Report. The report must contain all information about the compensation plans considered necessary to allow shareholders to make a fully informed decision.[8] This form of public disclosure is required when the

---

tion plans based on securities the value of which is determined by the financial market, but not to compensation plans based on corporate performance judged by Ebitda or net income.

[8] The rule provides that promulgation of the Directors' Report containing information about compensation plans should be in accordance with the terms and conditions specified by art. 125-ter, §1 of the Consolidated Act. Relevant information which must be included in the Directors' Report includes the following: (i) reasons for the adoption of the compensation plan; (ii) names of the members of the board of directors (or of the managing board in a two-tier board system), of both

plan is initially approved and at the time of any subsequent modification. Publication of the Directors' Report under this rule must occur a specified number of days prior to the general meeting. Furthermore, Consob is granted additional power to require corporations to disclose more detailed information under art. 114-bis, §3 in relation to costly compensation plans, which are discussed in section 7.

Finally, the Italian Government introduced a new provision into the Consolidated Act in December 2010.[9] This provision, art. 123-ter, implements the recommendation of the EU Commission 2009/385, and requires that a listed corporation publicly release,[10] 21 days prior to the general meeting, a compensation report divided in two sections. The first part of this report explains the corporation's compensation policy and the procedures adopted to implement it. The second part describes particular compensation entitlements, including the termination payments, and explains the rationale of the corporation's compensation policy. Shareholders are required to pass a non-binding resolution with respect to the first section of the report in this regard.

This new provision reflects a fundamental regulatory choice of Italian and EU policymakers. They appear to believe that the most effective means of regulating executive compensation is to increase the quality and quantity of information provided by the corporation to its shareholders. The legislative assumption is that informed shareholders can determine the most reasonable and adequate compensation policy for their particular corporation. Yet, if this is indeed the best regulatory solution, one might question why the legislature has stopped short of requiring a binding shareholder vote.

In relation to unlisted companies, it is fair to say that the Italian Civil Code pays markedly less attention to disclosure of directors' remuneration than many other jurisdictions, such as the United States and some other European countries. There is no obligation for smaller corporations[11] to disclose information in their balance sheet concerning individual directors' compensation. The general law merely requires[12] an additional note to the balance sheet to state the global sum of directors' pay. Any disclosure of additional information is on a voluntary basis only. Even though companies under this regulatory regime are unlisted and generally have highly concentrated ownership, this informational deficit is hard to justify in the light of the emphasis in modern corporate governance on transparency and protection of third party rights. As a policy matter, there would seem little reason to allow compensation policies and practices to be treated as akin to industrial secrets.

---

controlled and controlling corporations, who will benefit from the plan; (iii) categories of corporate employees and consultants, including those of controlling and controlled corporations, who will benefit from the plan; (iv) relevant clauses and preconditions of the compensation plan; (v) the likelihood that the compensation plan could be supported by the Special Fund for worker participation incentives for business organizations, regulated by art. 4, §112, of Law Dec. 24, 2003, n. 350; (vi) criteria determining the price at which directors and managers will subscribe or purchase relevant securities; and (vii) contractual restrictions (e.g., liens, life interest) on the securities, including stock options.

[9]   See d. lgs. N.259/2010.

[10]   Disclosure is required at the corporate headquarters and on the company's internet site.

[11]   I.e., those that fall under specified size restrictions set out in art. 2435-bis. These size restrictions relate, for example, to matters such as billing, assets and number of employees.

[12]   See art. 2427 n.16.

7 CONSOB REGULATION FOR LISTED CORPORATIONS: DISCLOSURE, "COSTLY COMPENSATION PLANS" AND "RELATED PARTY TRANSACTIONS"

Listed corporations are subject to additional requirements concerning compensation plans as a result of regulation by Consob. Art. 78 of Consob Regulation 11971, for example, requires listed corporations to disclose all compensation, regardless of form or title, paid to executive and non-executive board members, members of the audit committee of the corporation or its subsidiaries. Compensation to other managers with strategic responsibilities of the corporation and subsidiaries needs to be disclosed only on an aggregate basis.

Another important provision in Consob Regulation 11971 is art. 84-bis, §1, which confirms art. 114-bis §1 of the Consolidated Act, by requiring directors who reside in Italy to publish a compensation plan report within a specified number of days of a listed corporation's general meeting. This report must be provided to the Stock Exchange (Borsa Italiana S.p.a.), and made publicly available at the corporation's headquarters and on its internet site for the duration of the compensation plan.

Art. 84-bis of Regulation 11971 includes a section dealing with "costly compensation plans". The definition of "costly compensation plans" depends not on the nature of the plans *per se*, but rather on whether particular categories of persons benefit under them. These beneficiaries include, for example, a listed corporation's board members, executives, and managers, who have regular access to privileged information and have power to make decisions influencing the corporation's evolution and future. The existence of a "costly compensation plan" relating to one of the specified categories of beneficiary will require disclosure of more detailed information, including reasons for the adoption of the plan, relevant approval procedures and timetable for the compensation, as well as the technical characteristics of the plan.[13]

Consob rules concerning "related party transactions" may also be relevant to compensation plans of listed companies. In March 2010, Consob approved a regulation[14] which introduced more rigorous rules to ensure the transparency and fairness of related party transactions. The new regulation applies to many situations involving conflicts of interest, including in the area of director and manager compensation (Pollio 2009, p. 128). Nonetheless, there are a number of exceptions to the new rules including, for example, the situation where compensation plans involving stock options have been approved by the general meeting. Justification for exempting listed corporations in these circumstances

---

[13] Specific information to be disclosed in relation to "costly compensation plans"will include, for example:

- the reasons and criteria underlying the relationship between performance-based pay comprising stock options and the other components of overall salary;
- the goals of long-term performance-based compensation plans;
- criteria used to set a time horizon for performance-based compensation;
- the determinants of overall compensation;
- the relationship and ratio between pay and performance;
- the relevance of previous compensation packages to the decision.

[14] See Consob Resolution n. 17221, 12 March 2010.

is based on the fact that there has already been full disclosure and general meeting approval of these plans pursuant to art. 114-bis of the Consolidated Code and art. 84-bis of the Consob Regulation.

8   THE CORPORATE GOVERNANCE CODE OF THE ITALIAN STOCK EXCHANGE

Another element in the regulatory matrix is the Italian Corporate Governance Code. This code, which was first introduced in 1999, applies only to corporations listed on the Italian Stock Exchange. The code sets out a number of corporate governance principles, including art. 7, which deals with remuneration of directors. Like many other international self-regulatory codes, the Italian Corporate Governance Code operates on a "comply or explain" basis only. It nonetheless constitutes the most stringent Italian regulation in this field, by virtue of its adoption of the rigorous requirements of EU Commission Recommendation 2009/385 regarding the structure of director and executive compensation plans in listed corporations.

In March 2010, the Corporate Governance Committee of the Italian Stock Exchange ("Corporate Governance Committee") made significant modifications to art. 7 of the Corporate Governance Code. Listed corporations will be subject to the new regulation from the end of the 2011 accounting period. This revised version of art. 7 contains important guidelines and recommendations relating to the structure of compensation plans.

The Corporate Governance Committee drew up four principles in response to the 2009 EU Commission Recommendation. The first of these principles is that director and executive compensation must be sufficient to attract, retain and motivate people who have the professional skills necessary for the efficient management of the corporation.

According to the second principle, compensation of executive directors and managers with strategic responsibilities should be designed to align their interests with the pursuit of the main objective of increasing shareholder value on a "medium-long term" horizon, and should be based on "effectively achieved corporate results". Concepts such as "medium-long term" and "effectively achieved corporate results" are novel, and of considerable significance, to the regulation of executive pay in Italy. Inclusion of these terms reflects the adaptation of the Italian Corporate Governance Code to the requirements of EU Commission Recommendation 2009/385.

These concepts have also been adopted by other countries and by international institutions, such as the Financial Stability Board ("FSB"), to address the problem of perverse incentives and excessive risk-taking in executive pay, which are often coupled with poor performance. Similarly, the Italian Corporate Governance Code recommends against the adoption of compensation plans that may induce the recipients to favour short-term increases in share price at the expense of medium and long-term firm value. In a Report to the European Parliament[15] on the implementation of its Recommendation 2009/385 by member states, the EU Commission echoed the views of the FSB, by asserting that general consensus now exists that "compensation plans, based on short term corporate

---

[15]   Dated 2 June 2010.

profits, without adequate consideration of the correlated risks, contributed to banks and financial institutions taking on excessive risk".

The Corporate Governance Committee's second principle also states that compensation of non-executive directors should be commensurate with their responsibilities, including their likely participation in one or more committees, and that, in the absence of shareholder approval, their compensation should not comprise stock options.

The Committee's third principle requires the board of directors to establish a Remuneration Committee, composed of non-executive directors, the majority of whom are independent. In addition, at least one member of this committee must have experience in the financial sector and be financially literate. This committee performs a monitoring role, which includes drawing up general remuneration recommendations (Lener 2010, p. 95).

The fourth principle requires the board of directors, at the request of the Remuneration Committee, to establish a general compensation policy with regard to executive directors, directors with special duties, and executives with strategic responsibilities. The board should present a detailed report describing this policy to the general meeting annually.

The Corporate Governance Committee has established a list of criteria relating to the design and composition of director and executive compensation in compliance with EU Commission Recommendation 2009/385. Some of the most significant of these criteria are as follows:

- Fixed and variable components of compensation must be adequately balanced, according to the corporation's strategic objectives and risk management policy, given the business sector in which the corporation operates.
- Maximum limits for the variable component of compensation must be provided.
- The fixed component of compensation should constitute sufficient remuneration, should the director fail to satisfy the preconditions to payment of variable compensation.
- Performance hurdles must be predetermined, measurable and linked to shareholder value in a medium to long-term horizon.
- Payment of a relevant portion of variable compensation should be deferred for an adequate period of time.
- In relation to golden parachutes, payments for termination, or non-renewal of contract cannot exceed a fixed amount of the director's annual pay. Such payments cannot be made where the termination of contract is due to inadequate performance.
- Awards of shares and options must have a vesting period of at least three years.
- Directors must keep a specified proportion of assigned or purchased shares until they leave office.
- As a general principle, remuneration of non-executive directors should not be linked to corporate profits or comprise stock options, unless approved by shareholders.
- The Remuneration Committee must periodically evaluate the adequacy, overall coherence and effectiveness of the implementation of the corporation's compensation policy. The committee must also assess selected performance objectives, and monitor achievement of those objectives.

- Directors may not participate in Remuneration Committee meetings concerning their own pay.

In relation to the EU Commission's recommendations on the subject of appropriate remedies, the Italian Corporate Governance Code does not as yet have any claw-back provision that would permit recovery of variable compensation payments based on incorrect financial information.

9   REGULATION OF DIRECTOR AND EXECUTIVE PAY IN GOVERNMENT-OWNED CORPORATIONS

A number of corporations in Italy are owned, either partly or sometimes wholly, by the State, or by local governments and councils. Some are listed, and, where this is the case, will be subject to the regulatory regime applicable to listed corporations. Most unlisted government-owned corporations, however, are in the public services and utilities sector (including public transport, water, electrical power or gas distribution, and waste collection). Corporations which are only partly government owned and also have private minority or majority shareholders, are commonly referred to as "mixed" corporations.

The legal framework of these unlisted corporations is complicated due to the distinctive separation of the Italian legal system into civil law, which includes corporate law, and administrative law, each of which legal category attracts different rules and different courts. All wholly or partly government-owned corporations are *prima facie* regulated by civil law. Nonetheless, their government ownership and resulting fiscal structure, which involves dependence on public expenditure, also have administrative-law regulatory consequences. Many of these corporations are not profitable for several reasons. The reasons include problems relating to inefficiency due to lack of skills by managers, who are often politically appointed, and to the fact that prices and tariffs for the corporation's services are often fixed below cost by law or decree. Since these corporations are operating at a perpetual loss, they require new injections of equity on an annual basis to continue their operations.

In the case of corporations that are wholly owned by local governments or councils, remuneration levels for managers are no longer left to market mechanisms, but, instead, are subject to strict legislative controls. The regulatory approach is not, however, particularly sophisticated. It is based on a pay ceiling for the chairman and each director, equivalent to a per centage of the annual pay received by the President or the Mayor of the local government which owns the relevant stock. For the purposes of this pay ceiling, the only differentiation made is between the chairman, who may receive up to 70 per cent of the relevant pay benchmark, and all the others directors, who are limited to 60 per cent. Variable pay is only permitted when profits are made, and it is restricted to twice the amount of fixed pay. No distinction is made between directors and executives in this regard.

The policy underlying these rules is clearly to prevent waste of public funds through excessive compensation. Justification for the restrictions is based on the fact that local government is dependent on State funding. However, as with all basic legal rules, incentives, enforcement and consistency are also critical issues. For example, the directors of two corporations may receive the same pay regardless of the fact that one corporation is run efficiently and the other inefficiently. No allowance is made for the particular demands and difficulties of each business. Indeed, low pay may ultimately deter the most skilled applicants from assuming managerial positions, ultimately relegating such corporations to inefficiency and lack of best practice.

In recent times, a temporary salary cap was introduced for a few months for directors and senior managers of state-owned corporations and other public administrations.[16] The pay criterion here was somewhat more generous than in the case of corporations wholly owned by local government or councils discussed above. Under this temporary salary cap, directors and senior managers of state-owned corporations could not be paid more than the President of the Court of Cassation, who receives the highest pay in Public Administration. This form of pay cap, which had many exemptions, was finally repealed. In early 2010, a reform proposal was presented to Parliament to apply the same restriction to all corporations, including listed and closed corporations. The controversial proposal was withdrawn, however, after only a few days, following a storm of criticism.

In Italy, as in many other developed countries, the global financial crisis has necessitated public spending cuts, as a means of curbing growth of the national deficit and averting recession. In response to a request by the European Commission, the Italian Parliament passed legislation in 2010, Law n. 122/2010, which contained a large number of fiscal cuts aimed at saving €25–26 billion in public expenditure over the next three years. Some of the fiscal cuts embedded in this legislation also affect the pay of directors and auditors of wholly government-owned corporations.[17] Article 6.6. of the law, for example, imposes a general 10 per cent reduction of the 2010 annual pay of directors and auditors, commencing from their next appointment and continuing for the duration of that term. The specified 10 per cent reduction affects the entire compensation package, including fixed and variable pay components. Again, no distinction is made in the law between directors and executives.

Another provision of Law n. 122/2010, Art. 33.1, imposes a 10 per cent tax on bonuses and stock options. This tax applies only to amounts that exceed triple the sum of the relevant fixed pay. Somewhat surprisingly, however, the tax seems to apply exclusively to the compensation of financial officers and financial consultants/advisors, and not to that of directors or executives.

10 REGULATION OF DIRECTOR AND EXECUTIVE PAY IN BANKS

In recent times, executive compensation in the banking sector, where high levels of pay are commonplace, has become a sensitive issue. As demonstrated by the global financial crisis, remuneration policies in this field may have international ramifications. Supervision

---

[16] See l. 296/2006, art. 1.725; and l. 244/2007, art. 3.44.
[17] Listed and mixed corporations are, however, exempted from the operation of Law n. 122/2010.

and controls in the banking sector are enforced by the Bank of Italy, which in recent years has engaged in rule setting, modelled on the OECD Principles of Corporate Governance and the Basel Committee on Banking Supervision's paper of February 2006.[18]

In March 2008, the Bank of Italy issued a set of new regulations, "Supervisory Provisions Concerning Banks' Organization and Corporate Governance" ("the 2008 regulations").[19] These regulations, in which the Bank of Italy focuses on compensation systems and their associated problems for the first time, establish two basic principles. The first is that banks can adopt remuneration policies to attract and retain highly skilled top management. This is a clear acknowledgement of the traditional relation between pay and fair and efficient governance. The second principle is that compensation plans must not conflict with the fundamental need for prudent risk management and long-term business strategies. This implicitly recognizes the dangers of short-term incentives in performance-based compensation in the banking sector reflected in the global financial crisis. Thus, performance-based pay must be proportional to the risks assumed by the bank in its business, and avoid short-termism and conflicts of interest.

The operative guidelines in the 2008 regulations are far more detailed than the Civil Code rules, and compliance is compulsory for banks under Italian law. According to the guidelines, each bank must delegate to the general meeting the power to determine annual compensation and remuneration policies regarding directors, auditors, employees and consultants. A bank's compensation choices must be compatible with a fair risk profile, ensure a balance between fixed and variable pay, adopt a long-term perspective, and be related to measurable performances. The general meeting must be informed about effective implementation of company policies in this regard.

Variable pay schemes and bonuses to non-executive directors of banks are permissible only in very limited circumstances. Where a two-tier management structure exists, such payments are absolutely prohibited for members of the supervisory board, to ensure that their monitoring responsibilities are not compromised by conflicts of interest. It is recommended that the boards of larger banks should establish remuneration committees comprising a majority of independent directors.

In October 2009, the Bank of Italy revised the 2008 regulations in accordance with the Implementation Standards of FSB *Principles for Sound Compensation Practices*. These revised guidelines pay particular attention to remuneration problems in a two-tier board structure, which is the preferred governance model of some of Italy's largest banks (Lener 2010, p. 93).

REFERENCES

Bonafini, Anna Laura. 2005a. I Compensi degli Amministratori di Società per Azioni, *Quaderni di Giurisprudenza Commerciale*, Milano: Giuffrè.
Bonafini, Anna Laura. 2005b. Commento all'Art. 2389 – Compensi degli Amministratori, in Piergaetano

---

[18]   "Enhancing corporate governance for banking organizations" (February 2006).
[19]   See Banca d'Italia, Communicato Stampa: Diffuso a Cura Del Servizio Segreteria Particolare, 4 March 2008 (Rome).

Marchetti, Luigi Bianchi, Federico Ghezzi and Mario Notari, *Commentario alla Riforma delle Società, Amministratori*, Milano, Egea: 343–96.

Bonelli, Franco. 1985. Gli Amministratori di Società per Azioni, Milano: Giuffrè.

Bonelli, Franco. 2004. Gli Amministratori di S.P.A. Dopo la Riforma delle Società, Milano: Giuffrè.

Borgioli, Alessandro. 1986. L'Amministrazione Delegata, Firenze: Nardini-Centro Internazionale del Libro.

Cagnasso, Oreste. 1991. L'Amministrazione Collegiale e la Delega, in G.E. Colombo and G.B. Portale, *Trattato delle Societa per Azione, Amministratori-Direttore Generale*, vol. IV, Torino, Utet: 241.

Cappiello, Stefano. 2003. Stock Options e Corporate Governance, *Analisi Giuridica del"Economia* 1/2003: 135–45.

Cappiello, Stefano. 2005. La Remunerazione degli Amministratori. «Incentivi Azionari» e Creazione di Valore, *Quaderni Romani di Diritto Commerciale*, Milano: Giuffrè.

Caselli, Giovanni. 1999. Vicende del Rapporto di Amministrazione, in G.E. Colombo and G. B. Portale, *Trattato delle Societa per Azione, Amministratori-Direttore Generale*, vol. IV, Torino, Utet: 52.

Chiomenti, Filippo. 1988. Compenso degli Amministratori Mediante Partecipazione agli Utili e Clausole di Compenso Mediante Partecipazione al Fatturato, *Rivista del Diritto Commerciale e del Diritto Generale delle Obligazioni* 86: 285–90.

Consob. 2007. Documento di consultazione sulla disciplina attuativa dell'art. 114-bis TUF, February 23.

Ferrarini, Guido. 2005. Grandi Paghe, Piccoli Risultati: «Rendite» dei Managers e Possibili Rimedi (a Proposito di un Libro Recente), *Rivista delle Società* 50(4): 879–90.

Ferrarini, Guido, Niamh Moloney and Cristina Vespro. 2003. Executive Remuneration in the EU: Comparative Law and Practice, European Corporate Governance Institute Law Working Paper No. 09/2003, available at SSRN: http://ssrn.com/abstract=419120.

Ferrarini, Guido A., Niamh Moloney and Cristina Vespro. 2004. Governance Matters: Convergence in Law and Practice Across the EU Executive Pay Faultline, Journal of Corporate Law Studies Vol. 2, 2004, available at SSRN: http://ssrn.com/abstract=498362.

FSB. 2009. Financial Stability Board, FSF *Principles for Sound Compensation Practices*.

Gualtieri, Paolo. 1993. Dirigenti e Capitali d'Impresa, i Piani di "Stock Option", Bologna: Il Mulino.

Jaeger, Pier Giusto. 1980. Determinazione del Compenso dell'Amministratore e Conflitto di Interessi, *Quaderni di Giurisprudenza Commerciale* II: 396.

Jaeger, Pier Giusto. 1987. Ancora sulla Determinazione del Compenso degli Amministratori: Conflitto di Interessi, Commisurazione al "Fatturato", Principio di "Ragionevolezza", *Quaderni di Giurisprudenza Commerciale* II: 797–810.

Lener, Raffaele. 2010. "Speciali Remunerazioni" dei Consiglieri nelle Banche a Governo Dualistico, in Carlo Amatucci, *La Remunerazione degli Amministratori di Società di Capitali, Quaderni di Giurisprudenza Commerciale*, Milano, Giuffrè: 93–106.

Melis, Andrea, Silvia Carta and Silvia Gaia. 2008. Executive Director Remuneration in Blockholder-Dominated Firms: How Do Italian Firms Use Stock Options? Available at SSRN: http://ssrn.com/abstract=1102152.

Mosco, Gian Domenico. 2004. Commento all'Art. 2389, in Giuseppe Niccolini and Alberto Stagno d'Alcontres, Società di capitali – Commentario, Napoli, Jovene: 579.

Pisani Massamormile, Andrea. 2010. Uno Sguardo (Appena un Po' Indiscreto) sui Pagamenti, Diversi da Quelli di cui Parla l'Art. 2389 c.c., dalla S.p.a. in Favore dei Propri Amministratori, in Carlo Amatucci, *La Remunerazione degli Amministratori di Società di Capitali, Quaderni di Giurisprudenza Commerciale*, Milano, Giuffrè: 107.

Pollio, Nicoletta. 2009. La Remunerazione degli Amministratori di Società Quotate: Aspetti Societari e Profili di Trasparenza Informativa nel Nuovo Art. 114-bis t.u.f., *Quaderni di Giurisprudenza Commerciale* 1, I, Giuffrè: 128.

Portale, Giuseppe B. 1987. Compenso Quotativo del Consiglio di Amministrazione e Delibere Assembleari Modificative del Criterio di Remunerazione, *Contratto e Impresa* 3: 796–802.

Portale, Giuseppe B. 2010. Un Nuovo Capitolo del Governo Societario Tedesco: l'Adeguatezza del Compenso dei Vorstandsmitglieder, in Carlo Amatucci, *La Remunerazione degli Amministratori nelle Società di Capitali, Quaderni di Giurisprudenza Commerciale*, Milano, Giuffrè: 133.

Rainelli, Paolo. 2004. Art. 2389, in Gastone Cottino, Guido Bonfante, Paolo Montalenti and Oreste Cagnasso, Il nuovo diritto societario, Bologna-Roma, Zanichelli Editore: 736.

Santosuosso, Daniele U. 2006. Il Principio di Ragionevolezza nella Disciplina della Remunerazione degli Amministratori, in P. Abbadessa and G. B. Portale, *Il Nuovo Diritto delle Società, Liber Amicorum Gian Franco Campobasso, Assemblea-Amministrazione*, vol. 2, Torino, Utet.

Santosuosso, Daniele U. 2010. Conflitti di Interessi nella Remunerazione degli Amministratori, Paper Presented at "Il Diritto Commerciale Europeo di Fronte alla Crisi", Roma, Italia, organized by Orizzonti del Diririto Commerciale, available at: www.orizzontideldirittocommerciale.it.

Thomas, Randall S. 2010. International Executive Pay: Current Practices and Future Trends, in Carlo Amatucci, *La Remunerazione degli Amministratori nelle Società di Capitali, Quaderni di Giurisprudenza Commerciale*, Milano Giuffrè: 1–56.

Tombari, Umberto. 1999. L'Assicurazione della Responsabilità Civile degli Amministratori di Società per Azioni, *Banca Borsa Titoli di Credito* 52(2, I): 180–211.

Weigmann, Roberto. 1991. Compensi Esagerati agli Amministratori di Società a Base Ristretta, *Giurisprudenza Italiana* 1, (2): 793–802.

Index

Abe, N. 385
Abegglen, J. 369
Ablen, D. 221, 345
Aboody, D. 34, 192, 303
Abowd, J. 163, 370, 497
Abramowicz, M. 301
accountancy
  policies 30–34, 53, 77, 223, 351, 423, 424, 496
  scandals 15–17, 18, 28–9, 37–8, 437
Acharya, V. 134
Adam, S. 294
Adams, R. 124
Adithipyangkul, P. 399, 423
Afsharipour, A. 439, 440, 446
agency costs
  EU, harmonization risks, management of 467, 469, 471, 475, 478, 480
  and executive remuneration failures 201
  Germany, corporate law 488, 489
  horizontal, India 435–6, 442, 443–4, 445, 446, 456–7, 459–63
  say on pay and outrage constraint 256–7
agency theory and incentive compensation 101–19
  agency costs 104–5, 107
  agency theory disaggregated 103–10
  board size and composition 108, 113, 114, 116–17, 118
  China, performance-related pay 419
  compensation value and incentive effects 111
  control transfer mechanisms 106
  corporate governance system 106–8, 109–10, 114
  equity incentives 107–8, 112–13
  executive compensation debate 111–18
  fair deal perspective 115
  free-lunch fallacy 116–17
  hedge funds 108–9
  hierarchies perspective 103–6, 107, 111, 112–15
  hostile takeovers 104, 107, 108
  incomplete-contracts theory 106
  institutional investor preferences 242–3
  legal model of the firm 104, 105, 109–10
  management restructuring 107–8
  markets perspective 106–10, 111–12, 115–18

ownership and control, separation of 104–5, 106, 185, 188, 190–91
shareholder involvement 105, 106, 107, 108–9, 113, 114–15, 117–18
staggered boards, decline of 108
stock options in IPO firms 186–7, 188
takeover era and thereafter 103–5
Aghion, P. 106
Aglietta, M. 488
Agrawal, A. 76, 77
AIG 140, 145, 289
Ali, P. 279
Alissa, W. 255
Allen, F. 369, 418
Alpern, R. 22
Amatucci, Carlo 506–20
Amihud, Y. 191
André, P. 335
Andres, C. 488
Andrews, E. 141
Antle, R. 163
Aoki, M. 369, 385
Ariely, D. 203
Armour, J. 108, 261
Armstrong, C. 145, 330, 332, 333
Arnold, C. 501
Arulampalam, W. 294
Athanassiou, P. 296
Australia, executive remuneration practices 341–68
  accountancy problems 351
  ASX (Stock Exchange) listing rules and recommendations 343, 344, 345–6, 357
  board chairman and CEO, separate positions of 355
  board powers 342–3, 345, 346
  clawback provisions 233, 348–9
  conflicts of interest 347, 357, 360–63
  corporate governance 342–6
  Corporate Law Economic Reform Program 221
  Corporations Act 2001 220–21, 227, 342–4, 346, 348, 353
  Corporations Amendment Bill 357
  Corporations (Audit Reform and Corporate Disclosure) Bill (CLERP 9) 346
  disclosure requirements 18, 234, 260, 269, 343–6, 348, 349, 351, 357–8, 363